Points of View
in the Modern History
of Psychology

Points of View
in the Modern History
of Psychology

Edited by

Claude E. Buxton

Department of Psychology
Yale University
New Haven, Connecticut

1985

ACADEMIC PRESS, INC.

(*Harcourt Brace Jovanovich, Publishers*)

Orlando   San Diego   New York   London
Toronto   Montreal   Sydney   Tokyo

Passages from the following are reprinted by permission of the publishers:

Newell, A., Duncker on Thinking, in S. Koch & D. Leary (Eds.), *A Century of Psychology as Science*. Copyright 1985 by McGraw-Hill.
Neisser, U., *Cognitive Psychology*. © 1967 by Prentice-Hall.

ACADEMIC PRESS, INC.
Orlando, Florida 32887

United Kingdom Edition published by
ACADEMIC PRESS INC. (LONDON) LTD.
24–28 Oval Road, London NW1 7DX

LIBRARY OF CONGRESS CATALOGING IN PUBLICATION DATA

Main entry under title:

Points of view in the modern history of psychology.

    Includes indexes.
    1. Psychology—History.   I. Buxton, Claude E.
BF81.P57   1985   150'.9   85-4010
ISBN 0-12-148510-2 (alk. paper)

PRINTED IN THE UNITED STATES OF AMERICA

85 86 87 88   9 8 7 6 5 4 3 2

Contents

7   The Growth of Behaviorism: Controversy and Diversity

Alexandra W. Logue

8   Paradigm Found: A Deconstruction of the History of the Psychoanalytic Movement

Robert S. Steele

9   Paradigm Lost: Psychoanalysis after Freud

Robert S. Steele

14   Retrospect and Prospect: The Era of Viewpoints, Continued

Claude E. Buxton

Contributors

Numbers in parentheses indicate the pages on which the authors' contributions begin.

Mitchell G. Ash (295), Department of History, University of Iowa, Iowa City, Iowa 52242

William Bevan (259), John D. and Catherine T. MacArthur Foundation, Chicago, Illinois 60603

Arthur L. Blumenthal (19, 51), Department of Psychology, University of Massachusetts at Boston, Boston, Massachusetts 02125

Claude E. Buxton (1, 85, 113, 417), Department of Psychology, Yale University, New Haven, Connecticut 06520

Horst U. K. Gundlach (383), Institut für Geschichte der Neueren Psychologie, Universität Passau, Federal Republic of Germany

Rom Harré (383), University Lecturer in Philosophy of Science, Fellow of Linacre College, Oxford University, Oxford OX1 4JJ, England, and Department of Philosophy, State University of New York, Binghamton, New York 13901

Frank S. Kessel (259), Department of Psychology, University of Houston, Houston, Texas 77004

Alexandra W. Logue (141, 169), Department of Psychology, State University of New York, Stony Brook, New York 11794

Alexandre Métraux (383), Institute of Psychology, University of Heidelberg, Federal Republic of Germany

Andrew Ockwell (383), Fellow of Wolfson College, Oxford OX2 6UD, England

Karl H. Pribram (345), Departments of Psychology and Psychiatry and Behavioral Sciences, Stanford University, Stanford, California 94305

Daniel N. Robinson (345), Department of Psychology, Georgetown University, Washington, D. C. 20057

Robert S. Steele (197, 221), Department of Psychology, Wesleyan University, Middletown, Connecticut 06457

Kathleen V. Wilkes (383), St. Hilda's College, Oxford OX4 1DY, England

Preface

There are always some people, and I am one of them, who are curious about why an author takes on the hard labor of producing a book or, in the present era of edited books, why anyone should take on the business of persuading collaborators, editing, indexing, and the rest of it. The matter is rather simple, however, in this case. After teaching the history-and-systems course to psychology undergraduates for several decades, I gave it up because I finally found the available reading material beyond redemption by my lifelong interest in teaching. This gave me both opportunity and cause to analyze my boredom with the course I had just quit teaching. It did not take me long to realize (I suppose I had "known" it earlier) that the traditional books of Heidbreder and Woodworth, and their successors and imitators as well, had a "low ceiling" for contemporary students. The question then became how to provide the intellectual stretch and the interest that were so badly needed.

It was clear enough that new material was needed, but preparing it presented two problems. One, it seemed to me, was that to set out deliberately to write a textbook in this particular case would be knowingly to intend a rehash. When that is realized, it is at once clear that what is needed is to redirect scholarship so that historiography can yield a higher level of understanding of why and how various systems or viewpoints arose. Any textbook writing, to be worthwhile, must be informed by that new scholarship. Edna Heidbreder's *Seven Psychologies* of 1933 and Robert Woodworth's *Contemporary Schools of Psychology* in its editions of 1931, 1948, and 1964 did a great service to several generations of students. However, since about 1965, history has become a resurgent field of study in psychology, and one realization has been that while Heidbreder's and Woodworth's books are a rich source of historical materials, the history in them is, in a way, incidental to their comparative presentation of points of view. Furthermore, as a result of the many recent studies, history can now be the main focus, and the result, as the text shows, is a more advanced and more interesting treatment of psychological points of view.

The second problem in writing history in this area arises from the need for special knowledge, the expert knowledge that enables the historian to appreciate subtleties of the history being written. To be sure, such intimate knowledge of an area *can* blind one to one's preconceptions of it, but it is important to remember that the discipline of historiography emphasizes avoiding that very weakness. With that reassurance, I was persuaded that the most desirable history of systems or points of view would come from people who had considerable experience of the viewpoints about which they wrote, and it was this kind of person who should be invited to participate. (Let it be noted that no known partisans were approached.) I am sure I was convinced of the validity of this approach partly because, in my more impressionable years, I was a student or faculty colleague of some historically great proponents of particular viewpoints, most notably Kurt Lewin, Wolfgang Köhler, Kenneth Spence, and Clark Hull. Each was convinced he was on the right track, each "gave off sparks" intellectually and energized his faculty associates and students into research and theoretical activity, and each acknowledged (if only in private!) the imperfections as well as the prospective perfectibility of the viewpoint for which he stood. They were members of a mighty intellectual tribe, and I still admire their contributions.

Of the mechanics of seeking authors who would agree to my sketchy conceptions of the chapters and accept final responsibility for writing them as they "should" be written, I say nothing further except that I am grateful for their scholarship and for the cooperation that saw the task finally to completion.

1

Of History, and the Nature of This Book

CLAUDE E. BUXTON

INTRODUCTION

In the past, psychology has had its important historians whose names every psychologist knows. Within the last two decades, however, the number of scholars in the field has multiplied rapidly. There are several reasons for this.

The immediate cause relates to the familiarly named "knowledge explosion." Increasing numbers of graduate students and faculty, in academic pursuits reflecting broadened opportunities for scholarship, have shared in the spillover of time, energy, and resources to fields less well studied in the past—in this instance, the history of psychology. As is true in many other flourishing areas of psychology, the study of its history has been marked with significant names such as Brett, Boring, and Murphy, scattered across the twentieth century. Attributes shared by these scholars include an unusually broad personal mastery of diverse subfields of psychology and a long life-span, during which a balanced perspective and a capacity for mature evaluation could accrue.

A number of scholars in this near-heroic mold have since appeared, and in addition more and more people are absorbed in limited, specifically defined historical researches leading to journal publications and

1

presentations of scholarly papers. Such efforts require some degree of specialized competence and frequently result in a book by several authors expert in their respective subfields of the history of psychology. This kind of book, even though it may be an interim phenomenon in the growth of many scholarly fields, constitutes a valuable addition to the tools and scholarly resources used to explore and interpret our history.

It seems to be increasingly true that history is seen as a way to find meaning in the mass of contemporary psychological scholarship. This explanation for the enhanced interest in history is supported by a realization that in psychology, more than in most fields, historical study is relevant to the present. Julian Jaynes (1973) feels rather strongly about this:

> As a laboratory investigation, psychology is only a century old . . . (but) its history . . . is . . . a continuing discussion of the perennial and enduring problems of human and animal nature . . . Current work on the nature-nurture problem, on emotion and intellect, on thought and language, on the problem of consciousness—all are simply the most recent voices in discussions which have been reverberating through history for more than two thousand years . . . It is relevant to present research. (p. *x*)

In psychology, perhaps in contrast to some other scientific fields, it would be only a little unusual, and not at all irrelevant, if an experimentalist studying the fundamental nature of memory should get it into his or her head to reread Ebbinghaus, or if a clinical psychologist should develop a hypothesis from an idea of Freud's to be tested against an alternative interpretation of adolescent behavior. The number of examples is easily multiplied.

Since E. G. Boring (1950, Preface) repeated Ebbinghaus's comment that "psychology has a long past but only a short history," we have often been reminded that our daily scholarly work has many connections, some of them with a past of long ago in psychology. The now familiar comment does not reveal, however, another significant reason that the relation of past to present is so readily demonstrated in psychology: Many of the old problems or questions, some known to date back to the ancient philosophers of Greece, are with us still in the form of "persistent problems," to use the words of Robert MacLeod (1975), or "fundamental issues," as Michael Wertheimer (1972) termed them.

The problem of how people attain knowledge—how they perceive, imagine, think, and remember—was formulated anew in the eighteenth century. One group of philosophers emphasized empiricism, in the sense of accumulating experience as the basis of knowledge. For them, experience was the source of all knowledge and contained its own criteria of truth. No regulation by a higher power or soul was needed (the negative statement was necessary at that time). Other philosophers emphasized rationalism, in two senses. First, as in Aristotle, mental activities implied preexisting mental capacities revealed in experience but not created by it. In the second sense, rationalism maintained that activity was an essential characteristic of mental life, that is, the mind generates its own activity.

This disagreement about the nature of knowing, and of knowledge, is exemplified by studies of what is now called cognitive psychology. Work in such fields actually reflects the ancient philosopher's question about the nature of human beings. One kind of enquiry asks whether people innately have "mental structures" that shape their learning of the grammar of their native language, or whether they acquire that grammar solely by experience (i.e., through environmental determination). Research on this question assumes fuller significance if a scholar understands its historical connections with, for example, early linguistic observations, the origins of behaviorism, studies of cognitive development in young children, and cross-cultural studies. All these studies reveal something about human nature. So, in psychology, past is firmly adjacent to present (cf. Robinson, 1981, pp. 321–322), and study of the past promises a better understanding of the present.

A third reason for the increased interest in psychology's history is found in its many linkages with other exciting and expanding fields of knowledge. As we demonstrate repeatedly in this book, psychology has been both stimulated by, and itself has stimulated, important developments in other fields. In particular, the enormous increase of interest and knowledge in the field of biology, and the challenges and questions posed to all the sciences by philosophy, lead us again and again to consider the origins of psychology as well as its future directions.

As Boring (1950, Preface) anticipated, history can and should be revised when there are new discoveries, second thoughts, or an increased perspective on earlier events. Using the 1950 edition of Boring's *History of Experimental Psychology* as a natural reference point, one might ask: Do fresh minds see our history as such a scholar did? Are there new facts? Where should we revise, extend, or reinterpret psychology's history? Boring's book has been the object of considerable revisionist criticism in recent years, but the best of his critics do not lose sight of the fact that as a work of scholarship, it was an enormous accomplishment. It incorporated so much that was valuable, and, while there were innumerable opportunities for error, to date only one important line of thought has been shown to be wrong (see Chapter 2, this volume). Other errors may appear in the future, but Boring himself cheerfully anticipated this in the preface to his revised edition.

It was inevitable that a Boring, a Heidbreder (1933), a Murphy (Murphy & Kovach, 1972), or a Woodworth (1948) would see history through his or her own unique spectacles. Consequently, it is essential that later scholars review that history in their own way and in their own time to reaffirm or restate it in such respects as they find appropriate.

THREE PHASES IN THE HISTORY OF PSYCHOLOGY

History books in psychology have tended to be very comprehensive, and therefore have loped across the centuries with occasional pauses for closer attention to a facet, a movement, a person, or a theme in thought. Psychology's history is presumably no different from that in other areas; it has been conceived and written by scholars who inevitably mark it with their interests or competence and limit it according to their energy or readiness to write. No one can deny the immense service done by Brett (see Peters, 1912/1965), Boring (1942, 1950), Murphy (1972), or Watson (1978). But in touching upon so much, these histories cannot fully perform another service to scholarship—that of thoroughness—at least not in enough of their pages. As Robert Young (1973) neatly phrases it, "The history of psychology is in a very primitive state and . . . its practitioners have . . . tended to write synoptic surveys—*The History of Psychology from Plato to NATO*" (p. 182). I have tried to subdivide the long history of psychology in a way that permits selection of a meaningful part on which to focus within the scope of one book.

Psychology's "Long Past"

The Ebbinghaus comment cited earlier points to the essentially prescientific era in psychology's history. Here too, as in many instances to come, it must be noted that any particular historical era or reference point, such as a supposed "beginning point" for science, has a hazy, indefinite quality. The chronology is more or less correct, but the exact chronology depends on "what you mean" and often involves overlapping events or developments.

From the time of the ancient philosophers, there has been interest in human nature and human society, and the place of both in the general scheme of nature. In the beginning, there were occasionally ideas that turned out eventually to be at the core of science, but certainly there was then no regularized or accepted science. Review of the ancient questions is not part of our task here, but we may note that the achievements of philosophers, from Plato and Aristotle forward, led in the 17th century to the stirrings of science. Most notably, as a reaction against earlier philosophy, the writings of Francis Bacon launched the empirical movement that was to provide an essential step toward modern science. In this context, again, empiricism holds that the primary data of knowledge come via the senses, rather than by way of innate ideas or powers of reasoning, and that intellectual processes rest upon and must use such experience-based data in formulating all valid propositions about the real world. Rationalism persisted, as mentioned earlier, but after Bacon's formulation it became possible to foresee the shape of a future science of psychology.

Complex and rich though this psychological and philosophical past is, it has been described and analyzed sufficiently well and often that it need not be done again in this book. (Robinson, 1981, makes an important contribution to the intellectual history of psychology in the early periods mentioned here.)

The Present

It is difficult to say just what constitutes the present era in psychology, or even when it began. In contrast with past psychology, the present field is enormously broad and complicated, divided into numerous fields of special interest. To offer a few necessarily imprecise examples: Some of these special-interest fields are known by their methods (psychometrics, experimental this or that, clinical psychology). Others are identified by the subjects of investigation (animals, the abnormal, children, minorities, the military, or the aged). Still others are designated by psychological processes of central interest (learning, sensory processes, adjustment, development, motivation, attitude change, schizophrenia, and myriad others). Altogether, psychology is a rich, provocative, intensely active, sprawling field, as exemplified by the six volumes of *Psychology: A Study of a Science* (Koch, 1959–1963), to which some 85 authors contributed.

Such fractionation of psychology reflects the attempts by scholars to get a grasp of a seemingly amorphous subject matter, or, changing the metaphor, to avoid choking on the mass of it. It is only natural that they should split off those portions of it that seem to them most significant or most interesting. One can plausibly say that there is a human necessity to single out a manageable area of work and study.

The advancement of scholarship in any particular subfield of psychology has led to more or less formal efforts to organize and theorize about knowledge in that area. Thus, in the recent past, psychology has in large measure become a domain, not simply of myriad special interests but, to a considerable degree, of minitheories that organize thought and data in limited fields. Neither the nature of people in general nor the psychology of any subgroup of persons or infrahuman animals has seemed a truly achievable goal of study. Rather, in some narrower area—some aspect of the learning process, say, or speech conceived as a communication process, or attitude change, or schizophrenia—the available knowledge has been used to generate a minitheory that accounts for what is known, in the sense of interpreting, explaining, and summarizing.

Earlier approaches attempted in their way to encompass much (sometimes as much as possible) of all that was known in psychology. That is quite literally impossible at present, and only future scholarship can clarify whether, or to what degree, a unified science in psychology is possible and what should be included in it. Thus, in this work we do not attend very much to the most recent developments in psychology. Rather, we simply assume, in a nontrivial way, that the future will in its turn clarify the past.

The Era of Points of View

Lying unclearly between the ancient past and the complicated present in psychology has been an era notable for certain features that led to the organization of this book. Not so clearly at the beginning of the modern scientific era (that is, at the time of Bacon), by the midnineteenth century when the first psychologists can be identified by that label, psychology had gained a principal origin and a primary guiding influence. For the former, philosophy served, and for the latter, natural science, particularly biology. Psychology was in fact aided fundamentally in its progression toward independence from philosophy by the advent of biological science. In general, this development was more significant for psychology than the admittedly important examples—from physics, say, of investigative method (particularly experimentation), or procedures for formulating concepts, or strategies of theory construction and evaluation.

As often happens, many factors led to diverging points of view in the world of scholarship generally, and in psychology in particular. One factor to be noted here is that in psychology there were as yet both insufficient knowledge and inadequate procedures by which to evaluate and stabilize what knowledge there was—hence the predominance of this or that great and widespread view about whatever problem was prominent, whatever question as yet unclarified. This situation persists even now in many ways—for example, in the diversity of sweeping statements about the nature of growth in infancy and childhood, with all but ungoverned swings of both scientific and public opinion about desirable child-rearing practices.

In the natural sciences there were what Thomas Kuhn (1962/1970) calls "paradigms." By paradigm, Kuhn means a universally recognized achievement of thought that for a time provides model problems and solutions to a community of practitioners in a scientific field. A single example must suffice: A line of thought from Aristotle up to the time of Galileo attributed to its own nature the determination of the way a heavy body swings back and forth on a string or chain until it finally comes to rest. In the fourteenth century this took form as the impetus theory, according to which the continuing motion of a heavy body is due to an internal power implanted in it by the initiator of its motion. Galileo looked at things differently, however. He observed the swinging body and saw a pendulum, a body almost succeeding in repeating the same motion over and over, and he saw other properties as well. From such observations he hit upon a new "way of looking," a new perception, that led him to develop a new dynamics of pendulum movement in which weight and rate of fall were independent, and in which vertical height was related to the terminal velocity of motion down an inclined plane (Kuhn, 1970, pp. 118–119).

Kuhn sees the growth of such paradigms—including their overthrow by other paradigms and the reasons therefore—as a realistic account of the history of science, more accurate than a description of scientific history as a steady and gradual accumulation of knowledge. In adopting a new paradigm, such as the Newtonian laws of motion, scientists looking at the same phenomena were seeing them in a new way. The new perception, encompassing beliefs and attitudes, was the new paradigm.

In Kuhn's view (1970, p. 160), the less developed social and behavioral sciences are not yet in the paradigmatic stage (see also Robert Watson, 1967, 1973). Kuhn's proposals have been attacked by some social scientists, and by sociologists especially, but in one respect they nevertheless afford a relevant and important judgment about psychology. In the early history of recognizable psychology—in, say, the 100 years after 1850— there was no real obstacle to the persistent and idiosyncratic development of a particular way of defining and viewing psychology's problems. Nor was there much of an obstacle to the simultaneous or successive development of largely different, even contrary, views on such matters. Of criticism, argumentation, persuasion, there was of course a great deal, just as, particularly after 1940, there was increasing sophistication about the nature, evaluation, and worth of theory. Yet we shall see that the era from about 1850 to a little after 1950 was essentially one of more or less expansive efforts to develop, exploit, and defend particular broad viewpoints in psychology. The uneven and, in some respects, continuing movement from this phase of psychology's history into the present is paralleled in other disciplines, such as linguistic anthropology (Hymes, 1963).

It is not true, of course, that conflicting points of view never existed in psychology's long past, or in the present. Nor was it ever true that enlistment in the belief system or activities of psychologists who held one point of view or another accounted for an overwhelming proportion of psychologists. In fact, Woodworth (1948, pp. 254–255) notes that a large number of psychologists did not consider themselves adherents of any school. Rather, the schools were merging, he thought, as they should. Mary Henle (1957/1961) criticizes such eclecticism, saying that it tended to achieve a reduction of conflict by glossing over differences and issues that might otherwise provoke new theory and fruitful discovery. Perhaps Woodworth himself changed, for he later indicated that while rapprochement had increased, in his view, "It would be a mistake to overstress the unanimity effect" (Woodworth & Sheehan, 1964, p. 387). (From considerable personal experience with zealots, I strongly support this latter statement.)

It is essential to understand how contemporary psychology not only has links with its ancient past, but often with its troublesome, always provocative period of viewpoint formation. Therefore, a historical reexamination of the topics discussed in the essentially comparative books of the Heidbreder and Woodworth genre now seems indicated. Some sense of this era is conveyed by saying that it is akin to the period (or the conception) of adolescence. There was (is) occasional stress, conflict, unevenness of development, and yet a continual urge to move toward an "improved" state. The points of view of interest here are not, as one author would have it, out of date or old hat. Rather, to a historian's way of thinking, they constitute a complicated and fascinating phase in psychology's development.

THE SHAPING OF VIEWPOINTS

The primary business of historians is not chronology but meaning, a statement that would be gratuitous if directed to a professional historian of, say, eighteenth-century French politics. In psychology, however, it is still a necessary preface to comments on how the authors of a history book, such as this one, may be expected to search for meaningful interpretations of historical "facts." We now suggest a few of the more common lines of interpretive thought.

Selectivity and Antinomy

As the various points of view we discuss were becoming identifiable, they tended to show one particular pattern of development that can now be seen as predictable and therefore of interest to the historian—namely, the "natural" tendency for scholars interested in any aspect of psychology to notice just those facts, make just those observations, and invent just those hypotheses or theories that most readily fitted their field of study. Then, as their understanding increased and they saw connections with other observations, hypotheses, or theories, they expanded or generalized their ideas to incorporate additional data or ideas in the developing scope of their starting viewpoint.

It would be a mistake to derogate this process; it is, in a sense, inevitable. But it thus happened that the Gestalt psychologists exploited an initial breakthrough in the understanding of perception by experimental tests of various expectations about the nature of perceptual processes. In so doing, they developed conceptions of brain function that seemed promising because they fit so well with the popular ideas about perception (Köhler, 1929/1947). In the interests of a broader science of psychology, the Gestalt psychologists began to generalize the founding ideas about perception into fields like learning and memory, or motivation (see Koffka, 1935). It gradually became evident that the Gestalters had an essentially perceptual approach to these topics—that is, they thought about learning and memory from a perceptual point of view. This approach, though stimulating and productive in its way, in time produced not simply difficulties for themselves (as in Koffka's brilliant but vain attempt to cope systematically and logically with the neuro-anatomical requirements of a memory trace), but also difficulties in the form of criticism from psychologists of other persuasions (Hebb, 1949). The natural, or at least usual, selectivity of the scholar helps to shape his or her viewpoint, often for better, perhaps, but sometimes for worse.

That these events were not peculiar to Gestalt psychology is seen in Clark Hull's efforts to formulate theory in his particular version of modern behaviorism (1943, 1951, and especially 1952). After some early prodigious efforts at a formal (and formidable) theory of rote verbal memorization by human subjects, Hull concentrated on the role of learning and motivation in animals. At one point, after intensively exploring these topics and casting his theory in mathematical form, he decided to relate it to the field of perception. The connection was a limited one, hardly recognizable, and appeared in the last version of his system (Hull, 1952, pp. 11–12).

In this statement about afferent stimulus interaction (interacting neural consequences of stimuli), Hull intended to recognize the validity of a basic Gestalt principle of perception. Indeed, he saw his idea as practically identical with Köhler's hypothesis of "dependent part qualities," if the latter were stated in neurological terms rather than in terms of consciousness or experience (Hull, 1942, p. 77, fn. 1). Careful scrutiny of this postulate suggests, however, that it obscures the field of perception rather than uncovering and lawfully describing it. After all, as the scope of a viewpoint—that is, its operative field of study—expands, it is likely to become less and less appropriate the further this type of effort extends. This fact has been noticed or pointed out frequently, and the corrective steps that have subsequently been taken, as one expects or hopes in science, have often been improvements. Unfortunately, they have also, on occasion, looked like "cobbling up" deficiencies merely to maintain the appearance of adequacy in a particular point of view.

But what about antinomies? The word (taken from the writings of Kant) now refers to the tendency of theories and approaches to a problem to contain within them the germ of a contrary interpretation (see Crutchfield & Krech, 1962, p. 11). Many interpretive problems arise in the form of antinomies, as we demonstrate using a single, historically important example: Edward B. Titchener was prominent among those who conceived of psychology as the study of immediate experience (see Chapter 3, this volume). The primary aim of experimental psychology, as he defined it, was analysis of the structure of mind, or isolation of the constituents in a given conscious formation (Titchener, 1898, p. 450). However, in the sentence in which he used those two expressions to define his kind of psychology, he also used a third expression, one that was equally part of the definition. He referred to ravelling out *elemental processes* (his language) from the web of consciousness, a notion that led to troublesome differences of interpretation.

As we shall see, many psychologists in the functionalist line of thought emphasized, in defining their point of view, that consciousness consisted essentially of *processes,* and not of the "structural" elements to which Titchener referred as being the constituents of *states* of consciousness. Because Titchener, in the article just cited, and James Rowland Angell (1907/1948), were given to broad systematic analysis, both saw logical justification for studies of both mental structure (morphology) and function (Titchener called it "physiology") in psychology. In Titchener's view, both morphology and function were to be studied by introspection. According to the functionalists, however, they were to be studied by objective means as well as by introspection. Thus, on the surface there appeared to be much agreement between Titchener and Angell. From the beginning, though, they disagreed about both the meaning and centrality of *process* and how it was to be studied. In using introspective data, both the structuralists and the functionalists left themselves open to challenge by critics.

The Great Men in Psychology's History

It is, of course, a longstanding theory or conception of history that it is shaped by "Great Men," or great innovators—powerfully motivated individuals of particular temper and habits of thought. It is easy, especially if one has been the colleague of a significant scholar, to see how a specific achievement, experiment, book, or theory depends upon the capacity, inclination, even the mood, of a particular person. As Boring (1950/1963) said in the same year that his revised *History of Experimental Psychology* was published, with its great concern for scholar-personalities:

> Although the Great-Man theory cannot be wrong, since it is clear that men die having differed from one another in social effectiveness and therefore in greatness, there has been, nevertheless, for almost a century now, a growing suspicion that the theory asserts very little, since it specifies neither the attributes nor the conditions of greatness. (p. 29)

Boring notes that as the search for causes of human action extended further and further into circumstances external to man, a *naturalistic* view developed alongside the *personalistic* view of greatness.

Watson (1971) firmly discounts the Great Man approach, terming it simplistic, limited in scope, and insufficient in its account of environmental factors that shape the course of history. One might ask whether the Great Man becomes great because of what he is, or whether he is simply the agent of progress rather than its initiator (Boring, 1955/1961, p. 49). It seems clear that the historian must always be alert to the personal characteristics of actors on the stage of history, and yet these must be considered but a part of the interpretation of the story being unfolded. As MacLeod (1970) declares, "The history of ideas is the history of *ideas*, not a history of people . . . If . . . some people are misjudged or forgotten, it is . . . regrettable. Ideas must move on" (p. 208). (It is advisable to emphasize that MacLeod was discussing a *concept* here; he personally was a most caring individual.)

The Zeitgeist

Largely missing from the Great Man view of how viewpoints are shaped is the conception of environmental or cultural circumstances that is more or less explicit in the notion of a *Zeitgeist*, or spirit of the times. History is indeed shaped by the environment that influences people and their ideas—that is, by the ways in which scholars, resources, social settings, and establishments help to forward a particular version of the truth. As a summary or capsule reference, it is sometimes convenient to use such labels as the "Protestant work ethic," or the "atomistic mode of thought" in the science of 19th-century Europe. There is, of course, a danger that such labels may appear to be explanatory even when they are generalized beyond the facts to which they are supposed to refer, as in the vague but somehow attractive expression, "American pioneering character during the period of westward expansion." In a basically em-pirical field such as psychology, it is appropriate to use labels or sum-maries expressing the notion of Zeitgeist only to the extent that the label clearly rests on or summarizes specifiable and potentially testable con-nections with empirical reality. This constraint is especially helpful when the Zeitgeist is viewed as continually changing, and hence elusive (Boring, 1955/1961, 1963).

Both the personal characteristics of scholars and the times (and places, Boring, 1956/1963) in which they work can provide variables that help us to interpret history. These are sometimes mere labels for factors that need, and in fact could be given, more exact and empirically oriented meanings.

ORGANIZERS IN WRITING HISTORY

A number of familiar and different methods have been used to orga-nize the written history of psychology. (The term "organizer" refers here to a device—a set of signposts indicating the plan of what is to be said or learned—that acts as an aid to efficient understanding.) It is wise to keep in mind the view of Gardner Murphy and Joseph Kovach (1972):

> Grouping and organizing [in writing history] is indeed possible . . . The only danger is that the reader will attach too much importance to one rather than another equally legitimate method of organizing. There is some reason to believe that the *best* (but not by any means the *only possible*) take-off point is to ask how psychologists conceived the fundamental task of psychology as a science. (pp. 213–214)

It is not necessary to review all the conceivable organizers one might use in planning this book (the list would include schools, systems, problems, polarities, issues, and so on) because there is clearly no "correct" decision to be made. We need only discuss what might be most helpful to particular authors in presenting the results of a study. If viewpoints are chosen as a useful organizer for the purposes of this book, that choice must be construed pragmatically and in light of how the expression is used here.

Viewpoints is a neutral term that carries less surplus meaning than some others. I do not perceive it as arbitrarily demanding any particular consistency from those who hold one historical viewpoint or another, nor does it require any formal plan of analysis such as the one that several authors in the Koch series (1959–1963) found difficult to follow. Rather, the term lends itself to claims like the following: Viewpoints may differ from one another in the strength or clarity of convictions expressed and may be related to one another as successors or predecessors, or as contrary or overlapping. They may vary along dimensions such as innovativeness or testability, and may of course have such other descriptive features as do concepts-in-general in psychology.

Mechanisms by which viewpoints are modified are an additional aspect of viewpoints themselves (although sometimes they are not, which is also worthy of note). The means by which a point of view is modified must be uncovered and stated, be it protest, experiment, logical analysis, loss of interest, changing external circumstances, or whatever. Incompleteness (that is, open-endedness) is nearly always characteristic of viewpoints. There is thus risk, always, of ambiguity.

In no way can it be claimed that a clear formulation of history, organized according to significant points of view, will be the final word. Changing circumstances and, one must hope, developments in the whole of psychology may lead to still better conceptions of our history. For this book, viewpoints will serve merely as minimum organizers around which to construct a major aspect of that history. The points of view discussed are mainly those most often presented and compared in works such as those by Heidbreder (1933), Woodworth (1948), and their successors. The intention here, however, is to study ways of conceiving of psychology as historical developments, with the fullest consideration possible of when, why, and how they arose, and to what end(s).

It remains to specify just what constitutes a viewpoint, or, as Murphy and Kovach (1972) would have it, how the fundamental task of psychology is to be viewed. Instead of a detailed outline to be checked off in explicating, say, psychoanalytic or cognitive psychology, or in comparing such views, only three general expectations can be established: (1) Viewpoints are characterized by their principal *concepts*—definitions, explanations, extensions, and qualifications; (2) they exhibit, usually

explicitly, a *methodological position*—their view of the nature of science
and where psychology fits; how the laws, concepts, or theories are to be
formed or discovered; the nature and place of mensuration as a proper
concern of psychology; procedures for gathering data; and rules governing the evaluation of evidence or theory; and (3) they contain characteristic substantive *laws and theories, including hypotheses.* The latter take
their meaning partly from the whole viewpoint of which they are a part,
but concepts and methods also help to specify the meaning of laws,
theories, and hypotheses. (We examine variations in the types of law
deemed valid or relevant, and in views about whether, or in what way,
theory is really necessary.)

These three categories of ideas vary in prominence in the several
viewpoints, as the latter also vary in completeness and even, at times, in
recognizability. No order of their presentation can be prescribed, nor
any degree of conformity to format. In patterns differing according to
topic and personal inclination, the authors fill in the essentials as history
is understood for each point of view. They agree in deploring the writing of history as merely a recital of chronological facts, just as they decry
presentism, which means interpreting and evaluating historical events
primarily according to their perceived validity or significance in the
present day (Stocking, 1965). Nevertheless, all will agree that "what
happened at the time" and "how we see it now" are both inevitable and
desirable aspects of any historical interpretation. It should be added that
antiquarianism is not a goal of this book; neither firsts nor founders (see
Stocking, 1965), nor (we may now add, with Boring's encouragement)
forefathers are of primary importance in intellectual history, no matter
how important they are for other purposes.

ON PHILOSOPHY AND BIOLOGY

In this introduction, mention has been made (and is made repeatedly
throughout the book) of the roles of biology and philosophy in the
history of psychology. Yet it also seems important to provide separate
presentations of biology as it is seen to influence the history of psychology, and of philosophy as well. Critics might regard it as something of a
misnomer in this context to refer to a biological point of view in psychology. Indeed, it could be argued that a nonpsychological language and
way of thinking merely afford a kind of translation of psychology's
concepts, methods, and laws rather than a new or different way of
conceiving of the field. If there is a logical problem here, it is bypassed in
the interests of learning how biological thought has contributed to psy-

chology's development; the same approach is taken with regard to philosophy. This sort of problem has little to do with the way scholars think and are productive, but it does bear upon the organization of this book. Much of the thinking of psychologists has its roots in biology and philosophy, and it is therefore of the utmost importance that in studying our history we constantly notice and appreciate the lessons of these neighboring disciplines.

PLAN OF THE BOOK

Fourteen authors have prepared this volume. They write as experts; all have a special interest in and the competence to interpret the topics they have chosen. The intention of such a multi-authored book is by now familiar: It places the specialist's thorough familiarity with a particular, suitably limited subject in the service of the well-informed and judicious recording of history. Cross-references connect comparable or relevant lines of thought in different chapters.

The germs of later viewpoints are always contained somewhere in earlier views (though not in *every* earlier view). Thus, chronology was a partial determiner of the order of Chapters 2 to 11, but simple chronology can be somewhat deceiving. Certain views have originated at several different times, yet have had varying spans of influence. This makes strict adherence to any calendar rather witless, and the order of chapters in some degree arbitrary. Within the approximate period studied, the century after 1850, points of view are seen to have gradually become a more outstanding aspect of the history of psychology. In some cases an approach later waned in interest and perceived worth. None of the points of view we discuss has altogether disappeared from the current scene, however, and all are mature enough so that accounts of their history should achieve a reasonable degree of reliability. Several are still highly visible and, in the tradition revealed in this book, have their current adherents and vocal critics.

Influences upon psychological thought by biology and philosophy, discussed in Chapters 12 and 13, have been more or less continuous throughout the period studied, although it will be seen that the nature or intent of the contributions has altered from time to time. Sheer chronology is less important in such cases than questions about specific contributions and their impact. Accordingly, the authors of these chapters have not prepared systematic coverages of their topics but focus instead on certain problems or historical cases that they deem to be of particular relevance and interest.

Just as this introductory chapter has attempted to make clear the rationale for the book's approach to history, and the reasons for this approach, so the final chapter attempts to pick up the threads of thought as they seem to have been woven into the fabric of this general period in psychology's history. It is our concluding task to assess, as may seem appropriate after the various authors have had their say, how the psychology of the era of viewpoints relates to the present. At that point, keeping in mind Boring's (1950/1963, p. 5) injunction, that a knowledge of history can never be complete and often fails miserably to foretell the future, portents of the future are examined (with suitable restraint).

REFERENCES

Angell, J. R. (1948). The province of functional psychology. In W. Dennis (Ed.), *Readings in the history of psychology* (pp. 439–456). New York: Appleton-Century-Crofts. (Reprinted from *Psychological Review*, 1907, *14*, 61–91)

Boring, E. G. (1942). *Sensation and perception in the history of experimental psychology.* New York: Appleton-Century.

Boring, E. G. (1950). *A history of experimental psychology* (2nd ed.). New York: Appleton-Century-Crofts.

Boring, E. G. (1961). Dual role of the Zeitgeist in scientific creativity. In E. G. Boring, *Psychologist at large.* New York: Basic Books. (Reprinted from *Scientific Monthly*, 1955, *80*, 101–106)

Boring, E. G. (1963). Eponym as placebo. In R. I. Watson & D. T. Campbell (Eds.), *History, psychology, and science: Selected papers by E. G. Boring* (pp. 5–25). New York: Wiley.

Boring, E. G. (1963). Great men and scientific progress. In R. I. Watson & D. T. Campbell (Eds.), *History, psychology, and science: Selected papers by E. G. Boring* (pp. 29–49). New York: Wiley. (Reprinted from *Proceedings, American Philosophical Society*, 1950, *94*, 339–351)

Boring, E. G. (1963). Ortgeister. In R. I. Watson & D. T. Campbell (Eds.), *History, psychology, and science: Selected papers by E. G. Boring* (pp. 332–333). New York: Wiley. (Reprinted from *Contemporary Psychology*, 1956, *1*, 145)

Crutchfield, R. S., & Krech, D. (1962). Some guides to the understanding of the history of psychology. In L. Postman (Ed.), *Psychology in the making* (pp. 3–30). New York: Knopf.

Hebb, D. O. (1949). *The organization of behavior.* New York: Wiley.

Heidbreder, E. (1933). *Seven psychologies.* New York: Appleton-Century.

Henle, M. (1961). Some problems of eclecticism. In M. Henle (Ed.), *Documents of Gestalt psychology* (pp. 76–89). Berkeley: University of California Press. (Reprinted from *Psychological Review*, 1957, *64*, 296–305)

Hilgard, E. R. (in press). *Twentieth century psychology in America: A historical survey.* San Diego, CA: Harcourt Brace Jovanovich.

Hull, C. L. (1942). Conditioning: Outline of a systematic theory of learning. *Yearbook, National Society for the Study of Education*, *41*, 61–95.

Hull, C. L. (1943). *Principles of behavior.* New York: Appleton-Century.

Hull, C. L. (1951). *Essentials of behavior.* New Haven, CT: Yale University Press.

Hull, C. L. (1952). *A behavior system.* New Haven, CT: Yale University Press.

Hymes, D. (1963). Notes toward a history of linguistic anthropology. *Anthropological Linguistics, 5,* 59–103.

Jaynes, J. (1973). Introduction: The study of the history of psychology. In M. Henle, J. Jaynes, & J. J. Sullivan (Eds.), *Historical conceptions of psychology* (pp. ix–xii). New York: Springer.

Koch, S. (Ed.). (1959–1963). *Psychology: A study of science* (6 vols.). New York: McGraw-Hill.

Koffka, K. (1935). *Principles of Gestalt psychology.* New York: Harcourt, Brace.

Köhler, W. (1947). *Gestalt psychology.* New York: Liveright. (Original work published 1929)

Kuhn, T. S. (1970). *The structure of scientific revolutions* (2nd ed.). Chicago: University of Chicago Press. (Original work published 1962)

MacLeod, R. B. (1970). Newtonian and Darwinian conceptions of man, and some alternatives. *Journal of the History of the Behavioral Sciences, 6,* 207–218.

MacLeod, R. B. (1975). *The persistent problems of psychology.* Pittsburgh: Duquesne University Press.

Murphy, G., & Kovach, J. K. (1972). *Historical introduction to modern psychology* (3rd ed.). New York: Harcourt, Brace.

Peters, R. S. (1965). *Brett's history of psychology.* Cambridge, MA: MIT Press. (Original work published 1912)

Robinson, D. N. (1981). *An intellectual history of psychology* (rev. ed.). New York: Macmillan.

Stocking, G. W., Jr. (1965). Editorial. *Journal of the History of the Behavioral Sciences, 1,* 211–218.

Titchener, E. B. (1898). The postulates of a structural psychology. *Philosophical Review, 7,* 449–465.

Watson, R. I. (1967). Psychology: A prescriptive science. *American Psychologist, 22,* 435–443.

Watson, R. I. (1971). Prescriptions as operative in the history of psychology. *Journal of the History of Behavioral Sciences, 7,* 311–322.

Watson, R. I. (1973). Psychology: A prescriptive science. In M. Henle, J. Jaynes, & J. J. Sullivan (Eds.), *Historical conceptions of psychology* (pp. 13–28). New York: Springer.

Watson, R. I. (1978). *The great psychologists* (4th ed.). Philadelphia: Lippincott.

Wertheimer, M. (1972). *Fundamental issues in psychology.* New York: Holt, Rinehart.

Woodworth, R. S. (1948). *Contemporary schools of psychology.* New York: Ronald.

Woodworth, R. S., & Sheehan, M. (1964). *Contemporary schools of psychology* (3rd ed.). New York: Ronald.

Young, R. M. (1973). Evolutionary debate. In M. Henle, J. Jaynes, & J. J. Sullivan (Eds.), *Historical conceptions of psychology* (pp. 180–204). New York: Springer.

2

Wilhelm Wundt: Psychology as the Propaedeutic Science

ARTHUR L. BLUMENTHAL

INTRODUCTION

Over the past century, several forces conspired to blur our knowledge of the work of Wilhelm Wundt, the reputed founder of modern experimental psychology. One broad force was the shift of leadership from German to Anglo-American universities, a shift of focus that hovers over several changes from nineteenth- to twentieth-century intellectual traditions, including the success of the American behaviorist movement in suppressing the earlier German mentalistic psychology. Those changes were brutally punctuated by the horrors of two wars that further divided Anglo-American from German cultural traditions. For two or more generations, emotional polemic interfered with attempts at dispassionate examination of experimental psychology's German roots.

Some German work, of course, survived the transition to the Anglo-American setting, although rather awkwardly. One often-noted example is the emigration of the Gestalt psychologists (see Chapter 11, this volume). But Wundtian psychology was deeply rooted in German idealism, even more than was Gestalt psychology, and thus could not or would not conform to Anglo-American trends with their priority for mechanistic materialism and pragmatism (Blumenthal, 1980). Consider-

POINTS OF VIEW IN THE
MODERN HISTORY OF PSYCHOLOGY

ing that Wundt's work remains one of the largest and more systematic parts of the psychological literature, the blind spots and the caricatures that modern psychologists have developed for Wundtian psychology and its satellites must be regarded as one of the larger lapses in intellectual history.

In the United States, the transplanted Englishman E. B. Titchener was often accepted, mistakenly, as the reflected image of Wundt. Danziger (1979) suggests that Titchener, who ignored key parts of Wundt's work, may have encouraged that misinterpretation. Tweney and Yachanin (1980), however, hold Titchener free of blame for what they see as errors of interpretation by later historians.

Titchener's basic education came from Oxford University and from British empiricism, particularly as represented in the work of J. S. Mill. During 1890 to 1892, however, he was in Leipzig pursuing a doctoral degree in psychology, for no psychology doctorate was offered in England. While in Leipzig, Titchener discovered the positivist movement emanating from Austria through the writings of Ernst Mach and Richard Avenarius. His interest in positivism, along with his classical British education, placed Titchener at odds with Wundt from the beginning.

Wundt consistently contested both classical empiricism and positivism while building his foundations in German cognitive psychology, with emphasis on German idealist philosophers such as Leibniz, Kant, Fichte, Herbart, and Schopenhauer. Just prior to Titchener's arrival in Germany, Wundt published his *System der Philosophie* (1889) in reaction to the positivists and empiricists. That reaction was renewed in his *Sinnliche und übersinnliche Welt* (*The Sensory and Suprasensory Worlds*, 1914).

Titchener's closest friend and colleague in Leipzig was Oswald Külpe, who encouraged Titchener's differences with Wundt. Külpe's understanding of psychology had taken shape earlier from the training he received at Göttingen under G. E. Müller, which placed him on a collision course with Wundt; their disagreements concerning the philosophy of science and the definition of psychology soon surfaced to become one of the most discussed episodes in the early history of the world famous Leipzig laboratory (see Chapter 3, this volume).

Blumenthal (1970) and Danziger (1980b) find that among American scholars, John Dewey, George Herbert Mead, and Charles Hubbard Judd, all at Chicago, were the more accurate American interpreters of Wundt. Because no text on the history of psychology came from Chicago, however, the Titchener-related interpretations predominate in the writings of Titchener's devoted student, E. G. Boring. Unfortunately, Boring's *History of Experimental Psychology* (1950) does not acknowledge

Wundt's classical German philosophical background, nor does it mention Wundt's critiques of empiricism and positivism. It also fails to clarify essential elements of Wundt's thought.

We can be more specific about these matters after an examination of Wundt's psychology. That examination involves the following five parts: first, a description of Wundt's intellectual roots; second, the emergence of his psychological system; third, his position on research methods; fourth, the mature structure of Wundtian theory; and fifth, Wundt's cultural psychology. The chapter concludes with a brief analysis of the decline of Wundtian psychology.

INTELLECTUAL ROOTS

The Social Sciences

A recurrent theme throughout Wundt's work, and the overriding subject of his memoirs of 1920, is the relation of the individual to society. Clearly, this is not merely Wundt's retrospective reflection as he lay on his deathbed, for it is evident in the record of his life's work. Examples begin with his early involvement in German political life, including active membership in a reformist political party and the holding of elective office in the Baden parliament of the 1860s. His role as a social critic expanded during the period of Germany's rapid and unrestrained industrialization and continued through the social and political events surrounding World War I, when the octogenarian Wundt was an active political pamphleteer. (Compare this record to E. G. Boring's, 1950, p. 344, observation that Wundt remained withdrawn from the affairs of the everyday world.)

Social interests also flow through Wundt's academic writings, both early and late in his career. It has been argued that his development of experimental psychology was but one step toward the greater goal of a scientific account of human social evolution (see Ungerer, 1980, for an expanded treatment of this point).

Like other German thinkers of his generation, Wundt saw psychology as straddling the boundary between the physical sciences (*Naturwissenschaften*) and the social sciences (*Geisteswissenschaften*). Like some idealist thinkers, he also viewed psychology as the foundational (propaedeutic) science upon which both the social sciences and the physical sciences ultimately depend (i.e., all sciences derive from subjective mental processes)—hence the subtitle of this chapter.

The Early Career

The formal beginning of Wundt's long academic career came in 1857 at Heidelberg University, where he taught his first courses to small gatherings of students. The subjects covered in that first year were anthropology, ethnography, and physiology (E. Wundt, 1927). Wundt held a degree in medicine from Heidelberg but had rebelled against the tedium of medical practice. In 1857, he was working his way back into academia with dreams of conquering scientific frontiers. Even at that early date he was engaged, albeit informally, in experimental psychology. A laboratory came together in his Heidelberg home through his construction of an apparatus to measure reaction times.

Wundt taught his first course in psychology in 1862. The following year he published the two-volume, 1000-page *Vorlesungen über die Menschen- und Thierseele* (*Lectures on the Human and the Animal Mind*, 1863). In later years, he often recalled the youthful precocity of that massive work with some embarrassment. Nevertheless, that "immature" work is perhaps the best single guide to the breadth and orientation of his later accomplishments, for about half of that first edition of the *Vorlesungen* concerns cultural psychology (*Völkerpsychologie*).

Some thirty years later, a different *Vorlesungen* appeared (Wundt, 1892), which Creighton and Titchener translated immediately, and so it appeared in English the following year. Most of the cultural psychology had been removed from the 1892 *Vorlesungen* and published in separate volumes concerning logic, society, philosophy, ethics, and language.

As the 1860s passed, Wundt was at work on several other texts on perception, physiology, causality, and experimental psychology. In 1873, his last year at Heidelberg, he completed the first edition of the influential *Grundzüge der physiologischen Psychologie* (*Principles of Physiological Psychology*, 1874), which almost immediately aroused worldwide interest and received praise from luminaries in several countries (for example, William James at Harvard, whose review was perhaps the most favorable and the most influential). While experimental psychology was already informally in evidence in 1873, it was scattered across the scientific landscape. Wundt pulled it together for the first time between the covers of this one volume, in which he also called for its recognition as an independent discipline.

Wundt had learned experimental techniques in physiology, having studied with the leading physiologists of the day (e.g., Helmholtz, Du-Bois-Reymond) and had published extensively on that subject before devoting himself to psychology. He witnessed and was inspired by physiology's forward leap from the springboard of these new techniques, e.g., Helmholtz's measurement of the speed of the neural impulse in 1850 (Boring, 1950), and proposed that such techniques might be profitably adapted to the study of mental processes.

It must be emphasized that this synthesis of interests is how the title of his book came to refer to *physiologische Psychologie*. The term did not mean "physiological psychology" in its present sense. Indeed, the whole justification for a separate discipline of psychology, as Wundt argues in his *Grundzüge,* was that it concerned phenomena not within the purview of physiological analysis or physiological theory. In the 1870s, physiological psychology merely meant a form of psychology that used experimental techniques analogous to those of physiology.

Wundtian psychology and Wundtian physiology are separate disciplines running in parallel, often observing the same events but looking at different sides of the coin (e.g., changes in nervous tissue versus changes in perceptions and memories). The two sets of data are different, as are the types of explanation. Although Wundt always held to that methodological and disciplinary dualism, resisting the reduction of psychology to physiology, he dismissed the mind–body dualism of Descartes (Wundt, 1885). Indeed, Cartesian dualism seems to have been largely a dead issue in Wundt's intellectual circles. (Nevertheless, some later historical treatments—particularly standard treatments in American textbooks—managed to portray Wundt as fully committed to Cartesian mind–body dualism.)

In 1874 Wundt went to Zurich as professor of philosophy. There, he first lectured on the psychology of language. In the following year he moved on to Leipzig, then Germany's largest university. The courses he taught at Leipzig expanded quickly into the large variety that he continued to teach throughout his career: logic, psychological interpretation of the cortex, elements of mathematical logic, the psychology of society, the history of philosophy, elements of cultural psychology, epistemology and scientific method, elements of ethics, legal philosophy, and, of course, psychology. Wundt taught these subjects at intervals until his retirement from Leipzig in 1917. Although the range appears great, psychology was the core course, and Wundt construed the other subjects as derived from a foundation of psychological principles. In his later years at Leipzig he added a new subject, a course on Kant's philosophy. His last course, in 1917, was cultural psychology. The semester-by-semester record is contained in Eleanor Wundt's list (1927).

Wundt was most active as an experimentalist during the early period at Heidelberg, where he assembled the private collection of instruments that was later transferred to Leipzig to form the nucleus of the new laboratory there. The latter was, in fact, no larger than his earlier private laboratory at Heidelberg (Bringmann & Ungerer, 1980a,b). During the late 1870s and most of the 1880s, Wundt's Leipzig laboratory claimed a good part of his attention. By the end of that period, however, direction of the laboratory fell to others, though Wundt remained the nominal director and an active observer and commentator on experimental work.

In 1893, when Leipzig opened a much larger psychology laboratory, Wundt was no longer actively participating in experimental work. His withdrawal from the laboratory is attributed to the infirmities of old age (e.g., poor vision, arthritis), but he was also increasingly preoccupied with purely theoretical psychology. Soon after his arrival at Leipzig, a stable structure of theory unfolded, particularly in the second edition of his *Grundzüge* (1874/1880). Much elaboration of the theoretical system was yet to come, such as the extensive treatment of emotion and the more detailed work on language, but the essential Wundtian psychology had been established.

THE EMERGENCE OF WUNDT'S SYSTEM

Evolution and Volition

Darwinian evolutionary theory reverberated through German universities during Wundt's formative years. German philosophy had long featured an evolutionary bias that was revitalized as a result of Darwin's work. Yet the concern with biological evolution that appears in German idealist and romanticist philosophy is colored with the notion of a mind or spirit guiding the evolutionary process. In the words of Goethe, "It is the mind that forms the body" (*Es ist der Geist der sich den Körper baut*).

A key term in this German tradition of thought is *Entwicklung*, which translates as "development," "unfolding," or "evolution." (Like the word *Gestalt*, it resists precise translation.) A "doctrine of evolution" is *Entwicklungslehre*; a "degree of differentiation" is *Entwicklungshöhe*. *Entwicklung* is also a key concept in Wundt's work and is prominent in his writings. He viewed mental processes at all levels as the unfolding of primitive, originally undifferentiated mental events. The following statement (my translation) is the concluding paragraph of the 1892 *Vorlesungen*. It highlights the spirit of his psychology, especially his preference for explanation in terms of development and process, and his opposition to metaphors based on material objects:

> Substance is a surplus metaphysical notion for which psychology has no use. And this accords with the fundamental character of mental life, which I would always have you keep in mind: It does not consist in the connection of unalterable objects and various states. In all its phases it is *process*, an *active* rather than a

passive existence, a development (*Entwicklung*) rather than a fixed state. The understanding of the basic laws of this development is the primary goal of psychology. (p. 495)

From the beginning, Wundt's view of active, unfolding processes always raised the question of the forces that underlie or motivate such processes. In addressing that question, he again relied upon a traditional concept in German philosophy: *Trieb* (impulse, striving, drive, desire, urge), an hypothesized innate characteristic of all living things that distinguishes them from nonliving things. Wundt wrote the following summary on this subject in his *Grundzüge* (1880): "The course of both general and individual development (*Entwicklung*) shows that desires or urges (*Triebe*) are the fundamental psychic phenomena from which all mental development originates" (Vol. 2, p. 455). Anglo-American versions of this motivational approach are discussed in Chapters 4 and 5 of this book.

Because of Wundt's position on "the fundamental psychic phenomena," he named his particular school of thought "voluntarism" (*Voluntarismus*), a term derived from *volition*. It should be noted that he never adopted the title of "structuralism," as many American textbooks imply. Rather, that term was Titchener's, who first adopted it in 1898 when he was at Cornell (Titchener, 1898).

Wundt's interest in the *Trieb* concept is evident in even his earliest scientific work in the 1850s, in which he advocates a view of the living organism as purposive and goal-directed. This argument is found in the introduction to an early monograph on muscular action (Wundt, 1858a), in which he observes that something more than a mechanical model is required for an adequate science of living organisms. He further speculates that some events in living systems will remain inexplicable if we exclude purposiveness. As Diamond (1980) indicates, Wundt was thus out of step with the dominant trend of the day in physiology, which had set aside purposivism and related concepts as unscientific.

One leader of such trends was no less than Wundt's mentor at Heidelberg, Helmholtz. In a simple reaction-time experiment, Wundt (1858b) built on Helmholtz's measurement of nerve transmission time when he computed the time for neural impulses to travel from a sense organ to the central nervous system and then out to the musculature. He then discovered an additional time not accounted for by the input-output transmission. That additional interval (a fraction of a second) must, he argued, reflect certain mental processes, namely those of decision, choice, or volition. Temporal measurements of mental phenomena thus became Wundt's key, at least the first key, to experimental psychology as a science of mental processes. Wundt then began to accumulate his private collection of reaction-time instruments.

Wundt, Herbart, and Reaction Times

The predominant authority on psychology in mid-19th century Germany was Johann Herbart, whose *Lehrbuch zur Psychologie* (*Textbook of Psychology*, 1816) and other voluminous writings continued to influence German academic circles throughout most of Wundt's life. Herbart established the vocabulary of 19th-century German psychology, a vocabulary that Wundt and others continued to use even after they had moved beyond Herbart's theories. In particular, we find in Wundt's writings the prevalence of these Herbartian terms: *assimilation, accommodation, fusion, complication, mental representation* (*Vorstellung*), *apperception, schema,* and *threshold.* (Except for *Vorstellung,* the German equivalents of these terms are either cognates of the English or straightforward translations.) Of course, Herbart did not coin all of these expressions—several are traditional to German mental philosophy—but he did weld them into a system of thought that gave them renewed life in nineteenth-century German philosophy and psychology.

Herbart was best known for his associationistic theories of learning. His associationism, however, differed considerably from Anglo-American theories. For example, he employed the notion of an "apperceptive mass," or mental schema, made up of a constellation of connected elementary mental representations. Whenever learning occurs, new representations were assumed to become associated with an internal apperceptive schema either by a process of assimilation (absorption into the schema) or accommodation (a change in the schema to fit the new mental representation). The strongly mechanistic approach that powered Herbart's description of mental events was an essential point of difference between Herbart and Wundt.

With his new experimental techniques in hand, Wundt proceeded to exploit what he perceived as a weakness at the heart of Herbart's system. He refined the reaction-time experiment to devise what he called the "complication experiment." In Herbart's terminology, *complication* refers to the simultaneous arrival in consciousness of two or more impressions (stimuli), each from a different sensory modality. Herbart theorized that the two stimuli would either become fused into one mental representation or be perceived as two simultaneous events. In Wundt's experiment, subjects attempted to judge the position of a visible moving object at the moment they heard an auditory signal (a bell). Their responses were found to reflect the operation of *attention* in that attention was directed first to the bell and then to the pointer, which by then had moved a short distance.

In fact, simultaneity cannot be perceived. We cannot literally attend to two things at once. Wundt's apparatus allowed him to measure the jump of attention between two events. In the earliest tests, this period was about one eighth of a second, a result that is typical of similar measurements today. This finding suggested to Wundt that some central mental process was necessarily limited to one event at a time—an active central control process of a kind that was missing in Herbart's psychology.

Wundt's complication experiment (Wundt, 1861), with many later variations, became a standard item in his early laboratory work and in his psychology texts. Soon after these early experiments, Franciscus Donders (1868), working in Holland, introduced the technique of factoring out subcomponents of reaction times in a way that would reflect the operation of component mental acts—a technique that became known as "mental chronometry." It involves reaction time procedures designed to infer the durations, and thus the very existence, of central mental processes such as choice, discrimination, attention, and others.

To the extent that Wundt was the founder of experimental psychology, the field was based on a program of mental chronometry research. Wundt developed the program into the first historical instance of institutional research being directed toward a specific psychological question and involving a large number of interlocking studies. It began in the 1860s, well before the 1879 opening of the Leipzig laboratory.

Early mental chronometry research reached its peak in the late 1880s, after the first American to work closely with Wundt, James McKeen Cattell, made significant improvements in the technology of reaction-time measurement. Woodworth (1938) describes in detail the development of the Leipzig mental chronometry research program. As it grew in complexity, controversy and alternate interpretations grew proportionally. Interest fell off by the turn of the century, however, leaving a large literature and many unsettled questions. Perhaps that lapse also reflected the sheer age, by then, of the research program and the attraction of newer research topics. Yet a similar research program has appeared in the second half of the twentieth century among modern cognitive psychologists (see, for example, Posner, 1978).

The Principle of Creative Synthesis

Wundt's early critique of Herbart is actually the torch he carried into intellectual battles throughout his career. Its first formulation is found in his early theoretical essays on perception, *Beiträge zur Theorie der Sinneswahrnehmung* (*Contributions to the Theory of Sensory Perception*, 1862a), in which the individual's image of the world is explained as the product of constructive powers in the central control process. Wundt calls this process "apperception," again adopting a term traditional to German philosophy but employing it differently from Herbart's usage. In contrast to Herbart, Wundt's apperception process has the power of "creative synthesis" (*schöpferische Synthese*), which means it is more organic, active, and goal-directed. Wundt's critiques of Herbart soon met defensive reactions from Herbartian scholars (Drobisch, 1864, is a notable example). We return to this issue in discussing the topic of cultural psychology.

Wundt's most ambitious work during his first decade at Leipzig was his two-volume *Logik* (1880-1883), in which logic, linguistics, and epistemology are derived from psychological processes, particularly those of creative synthesis and apperception. The logical judgments that carry most human thought processes, and that underlie the grammatical forms of utterances, are traced to the operating characteristics of selective attention, which distinguishes a focal awareness from a background. Thus the mental field always has a binary character: first, the part that is focused by the attentional process, and second, its background or context. This is the basis of the binary subject-predicate formations that, according to Wundt, underlie all human thinking and language.

WUNDT ON RESEARCH METHODS

The Confusion over Introspection

An essential methodological distinction made by Wundt is that between the armchair introspection (*innere Wahrnehmung* or "inner perception") of traditional mental philosophers and the newer experimental method (*experimentelle Selbstbeobachtung*). When the term *introspection* later came into vogue under the influence of Titchener, Wundt assigned it the first interpretation (Wundt 1900a). Danziger (1980a) has traced some of the history that led to mistranslations in the English-language literature that describe Wundt as an "introspectionist." Wundt defined *Selbstbeobachtung* as the scientific study of mental processes (perception, memory, emotion, attention, etc.) by means of objective techniques such as reaction-time measurements, counts of word associations, or discriminative responses to stimuli. Wundt constrasted those techniques with, and soundly dismissed, *innere Wahrnehmung* or sometimes *reine* (pure) *Selbstbeobachtung*—subjective descriptions and interpretations of one's private experiences—when used as raw data in psychological experiments.

Wundt (1874, p. 4) argues that experimental psychology necessarily involves the separation of the observer from the thing being observed. (The reaction-time experiment was his first example of this principle). As a result, Wundt's collection of chronoscopes, kymographs, tachistoscopes, and response detectors (such as the voice key) formed the basis of his laboratory. Detailed statements of his opposition to traditional introspection appear in two publications from the 1880s (Wundt, 1883, 1888).

In light of these facts, it is ironic that later historical accounts of Wundt, using out-of-context translations and simple mistranslations, led to his being caricatured as the father of the introspectionist school. To test that interpretation Danziger (1980a) searched through the 180 laboratory reports that appeared in Wundt's journal *Philosophische Studien*, the primary record of research in his Leipzig laboratory from 1883 to 1903. He found only four articles containing introspective reports. D. J. Murray (personal communication, 1981) made a similar survey of the same Wundtian literature. Even using more liberal criteria of what counts as introspection, he found a similar proportion of reports. Present-day journals of experimental psychology probably contain introspective reports in greater proportions.

Wundt was often polemical when addressing the issue of introspection. In one article (Wundt, 1882), he compares introspectionists to the mythical Baron Von Munchhausen, a comic character of German folklore who rescues himself when he is stranded in quicksand by pulling himself up by his own hair. In the following year, Wundt's polemic took its customary technical turn in the first volume of his *Philosophische Studien* (Wundt, 1883). Here the widely acknowledged weaknesses of introspection as a research procedure are laid out in detail. Unfortunately, the word *introspection* was used rather too liberally when translating Wundt into English, thus blurring his position on this point for many English-speaking psychologists.

Another source of historical evidence regarding Wundt's techniques is the eyewitness account. James McKeen Cattell was one of the first workers in the Leipzig laboratory and remained there during Wundt's most active years. In the British journal *Mind* (1886), Cattell describes Wundtian laboratory research and points out that in all of the investigations he witnessed, there was always a researcher, who manipulated an apparatus and recorded measurements, and a separate subject whose responses were usually under the control of some apparatus.

Wundt's writings are filled with conjecture, theorizing, and his own subjective impressions, as are the writings of prominent psychologists of any time or school of thought. We find in him, as in most other scientists, the distinction between discovery procedures and verification procedures. Hypotheses, theoretical discussions, and pedagogical illustrations often derive from casual introspection, discussion, or speculation. However, attempts to verify an hypothesis by means of the experimental method is another matter, one that (according to Wundt) demands control, replicability, measurability, and public observability (see especially Wundt, 1907).

Viewed from the distance of a century, Wundt's experimental program seems to have been caught between two opposing viewpoints: On one side were the philosophical psychologists, including the influential Franz Brentano and Wilhelm Dilthey, who either ignored or ridiculed experimentalism in psychology. It was in this spirit that William James affixed the title "brass instrument psychology" to Wundt's laboratory work. On the other side were Wundt's students, who surpassed even him in their dedication to experimentation, accepting no other form of evidence. The commitment to experimentalism soon became a ritualistic requirement in the training of most American psychologists—a trend that, ironically, met opposition from Wundt, who saw the experimentalist movement as getting out of hand and contributing to a lack of appreciation of the role of theory in science (Wundt, 1913).

One other methodological development particularly troubled Wundt. This was the specialized, or "systematic," introspection movement that appeared around the turn of the century in the work of Titchener, Külpe, and their students. As Titchener (1912) describes it:

> The experimenter of the early nineties [when Titchener was in Leipzig] trusted, first of all, in his instruments: chronoscope and kymograph and tachistoscope were—it is hardly an exaggeration to say—of more importance than the observer . . . Now, twenty years after, we have changed all that. The movement toward qualitative analysis has culminated in what is called, with a certain redundancy of expression, the method of "systematic experimental introspection." (p. 427)

In an earlier critical comment on Titchener's methods, Wundt (1900a) uses the phrase "introspective method" to indicate precisely what he considers to be a *verfehlte Methode*, or "false method" (p. 180). In expressing his exasperation at Titchener's backward step toward introspection, Wundt (1900a) writes: "Introspective method [*introspective Methode*] relies either on arbitrary observations that go astray or on a withdrawal to a lonely sitting room where it becomes lost in self-absorption. *The unreliability of this method is today rather universally recognized*" (p. 180, italics added). He concludes: "Clearly, Titchener has himself come under the influence of the deceptions of this method" (p. 180).

Wundt's (1907) critique of the introspectionism of the Würzburg psychologists led by Külpe is better known, although it is often misdescribed as opposition to the use of experiments in the study of higher mental processes. Rather, it is basically a critique of introspection as a laboratory method.

Naturalistic Observation

Wundt held naturalistic observation to be a necessary supplement to experimentation. He saw it as the most effective method for studying many social and developmental processes. It was, after all, Darwin's method, and it was the classic method of many historians, geologists, anthropologists, biologists, and others. For Wundt, such observation was primarily the systematic study of development, which he often called the method of *Geschichte* (history).

One area of Wundt's work that illustrates this position is that concerning language performance. Early experimental psychologists often studied language by means of word-association experiments and interpreted their findings according to classical associationist principles. The studies of Albert Thumb and Karl Marbe (1901) are the prime example, often cited as an example of early psycholinguistic research. One result of the associationist approach was Marbe's Law: The more frequent an associative response, the faster its reaction time when uttered. Reviewing Thumb and Marbe's investigations, Wundt (1901) saw that the demands placed on subjects in the artificial situation of the word-association experiment produced behavior unrepresentative of natural language usage. As an alternative, he promoted the work of Rudolf Meringer of Vienna, who made detailed recordings of speech errors as they occurred in everyday speech (Meringer & Mayer, 1895). In Wundt's opinion, Meringer reached a number of useful conclusions about natural language performance, especially concerning its complex, rule-governed nature. These outcomes were quite different from those derived from the word association research.

We now turn to Wundt's theory of mental processes, a different issue from that of his methodology, and yet the two have sometimes been confused. The fact that one is a mentalist with regard to psychological theory does not necessarily mean that one is also an armchair introspectionist.

THE STRUCTURE OF WUNDTIAN THEORY

Elementism and Synthesis

Throughout his career, Wundt hammered at the point, quoted previously, that consciousness must be conceived of as a process rather than as a thing with an objectlike character. Further, Wundt suggests that any momentary process of consciousness may be viewed as composed of various constituent processes (*Vorgänge*), although these can never be observed in true isolation from one another. Mental processes always form a complex configuration that loses its identity when we attempt to break it into parts. Component processes might nevertheless be inferred through experimental procedures, as in the mental chronometry program described earlier, or through various other tests such as those used in psychophysics research.

It is important to understand Wundt's argument that basic mental processes cannot be isolated in the way we isolate chemical elements. The latter can be examined and varied separately from the compound in which they are found. In contrast, constituents of mental processes have a fleeting identity or existence and owe their identity to the larger contexts or configurations to which they belong (see Wundt, 1880, Vol. 1, p. 271). At the beginning of the second edition of his *Logik,* Wundt (1893) discusses this point in detail, noting that although elementism allows us to discriminate relatively simple mental impressions, that in itself has no particular significance. Rather, it only points to the obvious fact that we may observe attributes of complex configurations—a fact of everyday experience. A cube of sugar, for instance, is sensed as having the properties of whiteness, sweetness, and hardness. Many theorists, according to Wundt, mistakenly took such facts as meaning that we could enumerate irreducible and independent sensory states—pure sensations (*reine Empfindungen*)—that compose all complex experiences. Such elementalist thinking is found in the Viennese positivism of Ernst Mach. It also enjoys an honored place in British empiricism and was carried forward by Titchener.

Scattered throughout Wundt's works are numerous examples that illustrate the process of mental synthesis, the key principle in his theoretical system. One of those examples is an analogy adapted from its use by British associationist philosophers. The analogy is based on the chemical combination of hydrogen and oxygen to yield water. Water has the quality of wetness, which cannot be derived from qualities found in the isolated elements, oxygen and hydrogen. This emergence of a new quality, says Wundt, is typical of mental phenomena, since emergent qualities are lost when we attempt a separation of mental phenomena into parts. Wundt was not entirely satisfied with this analogy, however, as he shows in the following statement:

> The allusion to chemical synthesis is a conspicuous example of our present subject matter. No one can foresee the attributes of water in those of oxygen and hydrogen, although no one doubts that the one is formed by the other. This example, however, is actually not representative because chemical dynamics possibly, and indeed quite likely, will show how the qualities of the compound are derived from its components. But in my view the psychic synthesis is the opposite; it is possible to know the qualities of the components only as they derive from the resultant according to the general character of psychological laws, and never does the latter (resultant) derive completely, without residue, from the former. (Wundt, 1887, Vol. 2, p. 41)

To be sure, classical associationism of both the British variety (principles of frequency, contiguity, and intensity of mental states) and of the Herbartian variety (principles of assimilation, accommodation, and fusion) is subsumed within Wundt's system. But it is there as a subsidiary principle, overshadowed by the central process of apperception (i.e., attention and mental synthesis).

Later interpreters of Wundt sometimes cite the chemistry analogy in an effort to portray him as a "mental chemist" with a close affinity to the British philosophers (see Boring, 1950, p. 336). That view is occasionally supported by an out-of-context quote as well. Such interpretations arose in the 1930s in the atmosphere of the "newer holism" of Gestalt psychology, and in 1944 this drift of misinterpretation provoked Wundt's son, Max, a philosopher at Tübingen University, to make the following comment:

> One may follow the methodologically obvious principle of advancing from the simple to the complicated, indeed even employing the approach that would construct the mind from primitive mechanical elements (the so-called psychology of mental elements). In this case, however, method and phenomena can become grossly confused . . . Whoever in particular ascribes to my father such a conception could not have read his books. In fact, he had formed his scientific views of mental processes in reaction against a true elementistic psychology, namely against that of Herbart, which was dominant in those days. (Wundt, 1944, p. 15, fn)

To verify this claim, one must see the full and explicit statements on these issues in Wundt's major theoretical works, particularly his *Logik* and his theoretical position papers in the *Philosophische Studien*. English translations are few, imperfect, and incomplete, comprising mostly those introductory writings directed at students or laymen (the *Introduction to Psychology* and the *Outlines of Psychology*). Nevertheless, the "mental chemistry" label caught on, as the following statement illustrates rather explicitly:

> Wundt's psychology is a kind of mental chemistry and was reinforced by the
> contemporaneous development of atomic chemistry and the formulation of Men-
> deleev of the periodic law of the chemical elements . . . only three years before
> Wundt published the first edition of his classical mental chemistry, *Gründzuge der
> physiologischen Psychologie.* (Herrnstein & Boring, 1965, p. 400)

In fact, there is no mention in Wundt's writings of any inspiration for psychology taken from Mendeleev and the periodic law of chemical elements. He does give us, however, numerous arguments against the use of any physical science as a source of models for psychological theory.

The difficulties of translating German into English are rarely examined in superficial historical treatments. For an example, Wundt's word *Gebild* (creation, creature, product, formation, organization, system, structure, image, pattern, form, or figure) was translated in some works as "compound," a choice of terms that no German-English dictionary of today (see, for example, Cassell's, 1962) nor of the nineteenth century (e.g., Adler's 1870) would recommend. While "compound" easily suggests the atomistic chemical model, C. H. Judd (1932), the most prolific and the authorized English-language translator of Wundt (though not an especially capable one), summarizes Wundt's psychology as "functional and synthetic, never atomistic and structural."

In 1894, when Wundt's direct participation in experimental work drew to a close, he summarized the previous 30 years' work in the following way:

> If I were asked what I thought the value for psychology of the experimental
> method was in the past and still is, I would answer that for me it created and
> continues to confirm a wholly new view of the nature and interrelations of mental
> processes. When I first approached psychological problems I shared the general
> prejudice natural to physiologists that the formation of perceptions is merely the
> work of the physiological properties of our sense organs. Then through the
> examination of visual phenomena I learned to conceive of perception as an act of
> creative synthesis. This gradually became my guide, at the hand of which I
> arrived at a psychological understanding of the development of the higher func-
> tions of imagination and intellect. The older psychology gave me no help in this.
> When I then proceeded to investigate the temporal relations in the flow of mental
> events, I gained a new insight into the development of volition . . . an insight
> likewise into the similarity of mental functions which are artificially distinguished
> by abstractions and names—such as "ideas," "feelings," or "will." In a word, I
> glimpsed the indivisibility of mental life, and saw its similarity on all its levels.
> The chronometric investigation of associative processes showed me the relation
> of perceptual processes to memory images. It also taught me to recognize that the
> concept of "reproduced" ideas is one of the many forms of self-deception which
> has become fixed in our language to create a picture of something that does not
> exist in reality. I learned to understand the "idea" as a process which is no less
> changing and transient than a feeling or act of will. As a result of all this I saw that

the old theory of association is no longer tenable, and that it must be replaced by the notion of relational processes among elementary feelings, a view that resulted in giving up the stable linkage and close connection of successive as well as simultaneous associations. (Wundt, 1894, pp. 122–123)

Wundt's many discussions of mental synthesis offer examples that go well beyond the problematic chemical analogy. One frequent example is the musical chord, which is not equal to the sum of its constituent notes. Rather, it is a new experience, an emergent psychological phenomenon (or creative synthesis) with affective and aesthetic qualities that are uniquely psychological. None of these qualities derive from an elementalist analysis.

Wundt's examples of creative synthesis are not limited to perception. The same principle appears in discussions of motor control and movement patterns. We may, for instance, analyze the ballistics of muscle or limb movement. But if we consider the movement of the organism as a whole in some goal-directed activity pattern, that whole movement takes on a quality (a meaning or an identity) that cannot be derived from the component muscle movements.

Some 20 to 30 years after those Wundtian writings, the Gestalt psychologists developed more sophisticated descriptions of emergent qualities in psychological events. But they differed from Wundt, who had argued that these effects are controlled by the central attentional process. As a rule, the Gestaltists do not give much notice to attention. For them, the sources of emergent quality are the self-organizing ("autochthonous") properties of physical systems in general (see Chapter 11, this volume).

Creative synthesis, with its emergent qualities, underlies Wundt's separation of *psychological* causality from *physical* causality, a proposal that clearly caused many positivist thinkers to ostracize him. According to Wundt, there is a psychological form of causality. Thus, the causes of psychological events—perceptions, thoughts, emotions and so on—involve anticipations of the future in the form of expectations, goals, or purposes. Wundt claimed that physical analysis would fail if applied to these psychological causes. He argued that, while we could perform a physicist's analysis of some behavioral act—say, of one person talking to another—by recording the sequence of lung, jaw, tooth, and lip movements, that analysis should not satisfy a psychologist, because it lacks references to the goals and purposes of communication. One could, of course, perform the identical behaviors without actually engaging in linguistic communication. (For complete statements on causality, see Wundt, 1866, 1893; for a further summary of Wundt's approach to causality, see Mischel, 1970.)

The Affective-Motivational Base

According to Wundt, the fundamental processes that drive mental activity are emotion and volition, which are closely interrelated. This belief is again traditional to many German thinkers (especially the Romantics), in whose writings the word *Trieb* occurs frequently. Reimarus (1760) uses that word to describe animal instinct, while Fichte (1817), who had a direct influence on Wundt, gave *Trieb* a more metaphysical meaning as a vitalistic life force. For the Hegelians, it referred to the striving of all living things toward self-actualization. Fortlage (1855), who is occasionally cited by Wundt, describes any momentary motivational impulse (*Trieb*) as some combination of a particular state of pleasure or displeasure, an urge to approach or avoid some state of affairs, a temporal relationship between some future positive and present negative state, and certain movement patterns. He proposes that this combination yields a union of mental and physiological processes at a primitive level of life. Following this line of thought, Wundt also suggests that movement and affect are somehow united in primitive forms of life. Only in more highly evolved organisms, he theorizes, do we find emotional states that have become separated from the original impulsive movement patterns.

In Wundt's system, volition develops from primitive, innate feeling-movements, the expressive gestures—innate facial reactions and body movement patterns—that reflect emotional states. Innate expressive gestures are also for Wundt the basis of the origin of human language and the beginnings of language in the child (Wundt, 1900b, vol. 1).

Throughout Wundt's writings, whether he is describing rapid reactions or slowly developing historical processes, behavior change is not viewed as a combination of originally separate entities but rather as a matter of differentiating primitive global forms. The behavior and experience of the newborn infant are, as Wundt interprets them in the later editions of his *Vorlesungen,* diffuse and undifferentiated. Thus, a baby's reaction to a local tactile stimulus involves movements of its whole body; only later does the infant react by moving the particular limb that is touched. This principle of differentiation set Wundt against many of his associationist and Herbartian colleagues who proposed theories of development that, in contrast to Wundt's are additive (that is, the view that mature behavior derives from originally isolated elemental behaviors).

In Wundtian theory, separate forms of volitional activity emerge from an original and diffuse motivational state (*Trieb*) as an organism matures. He divides these eventually differentiated acts into three types: (a) impulsive acts—primitive innate drive activity; (b) voluntary acts—the simultaneous presence of several motives where one predominates; and (c) selective acts—voluntary acts in which the predominance of one motive is preceded by a conscious act of choice controlled by affective processes. Wundt proposed that human development and evolution both progress through these three stages.

At this point, an additional psychological principle of the greatest importance entered Wundt's thought. Innate reflexes, autonomic nervous system functions, and other automatic responses that we observe in highly evolved organisms are to be conceived as having been primitive voluntary activity (primitive *Trieb* states) earlier in the organism's evolutionary history. Only through a long process of either evolution or automatization did these actions become innate and reflexive.

When conscious and voluntary activities become routine through frequent practice, they require less and less volitional and attentional control. This in turn frees the central attentional processes to move in new directions. When an infant first begins to walk or talk, its whole attention is dominated by that activity. Later, when those behaviors have become highly automatic (nonvoluntary), they occur in a reflexive manner so that the child's attention is freer to focus on other goals or behaviors while it is walking or talking.

Wundt did not suggest, of course, that primitive life began with a voluntary consciousness in the same form as present human consciousness and volition. Rather, primitive consciousness was for him the elementary *Trieb* state—a primitive affective impulse. Mental evolution thus starts with an undifferentiated, global state (the primitive volitional state) that, in the course of evolution, or of an individual's development, subdivides into more specific and automatized forms.

Emotion Theory

The affective–motivational base of Wundtian theory underwent elaboration in the 1890s with his development of a tridimensional theory of emotion. Wundt criticized the popular hedonistic theories of emotion as suffering from the limitation of their unidimensionality (pleasure–displeasure). He compared those theories to trying to describe color experiences in terms of just one dimension (Wundt, 1896) rather than in terms of hue, saturation, and intensity.

Wundt accepted pleasure–displeasure as but one dimension of emotion. He derived another from early notions of activation (arousal) mechanisms in the central nervous system, a dimension that varies from extreme activation (mania, excitement) to extreme deactivation (stupor, sleep, depression). The third dimension, which was already inherent in Wundt's psychological system, is called *Spannung–Lösung* (superficially translated as "strain–relaxation"). A study of these terms and of Wundt's particular use of them clarifies his meaning. *Spannung* is used in its sense of driven, striving, attentional effort, or high self-control. *Lösung* refers to the opposite, a relaxed and inactive attentional state, or low self-control, as in "letting go."

To test these conjectures, experimental studies of emotion unfolded at Leipzig in the work of several of Wundt's students, most notably Alfred Lehman. The program focused on discovering reaction patterns in the viscera (autonomic reactions) and the musculature (facial expressions) that reflect dimensions of emotional experience. The whole conception was just about the opposite of the well-known James–Lange theory of emotion, in which emotional experience is viewed as the result of antecedent autonomic and peripheral bodily events. Wundt (1891) argues that James's description of emotion is illogical, because emotion is first experienced or conceived and only secondarily (and not always) expressed in the autonomic system or musculature.

The Leipzig emotion research program was ambitious for its time, in view of what it demanded in laboratory instrumentation, particularly the measurement of delicate autonomic system reactions. Unfortunately, by most accounts the program was unsuccessful; its findings were never well established. Later, however, Harold Schlosberg (1954) did have success with the quantitative analysis of facial expressions that yielded the three dimensions Wundt proposed (although the time Schlosberg's paper appeared, Wundt's emotion theory seems to have been forgotten). A similar tridimensional system appeared again in factor analyses of measures of social–emotional attitudes in the work of Osgood, Suci, and Tannenbaum (1957). Although he does not specifically mention Wundt's theory, Osgood's (1966) analysis of modern dimensional studies of emotion shows that all work up to that time supports Wundt's first two dimensions, while there is moderate support for the third.

The Superstructure of Principles

Reflecting his philosophy of science, Wundt often said that if psychology were to become science, it could do so only by establishing some general explanatory principles. Though he proposed many minor principles—most dealing with very specific phenomena—the six principles described below were his attempt at more general explanatory principles.

His first principle, that of *creative synthesis,* has already been mentioned (the principle of the central construction of emergent qualities). It first appeared in the *Beiträge* (Wundt, 1862a). By the 1890s it had evolved (or had been differentiated) into six principles, three concerned with processes of immediate conscious experience, and three parallel principles concerned with longer developmental and historical processes. This first principle was then renamed the "principle of creative resultants."

Second was the principle of *psychological relativity,* which describes mental processes as having their existence and identity only as part of larger configurations of experience. Whereas the first principle has to do with emergent qualities in the synthesis of experience, the second refers to the apperceptive (i.e., attentional) analysis of experience, showing that any item of mental analysis has meaning or identity only as it is related to some context. In Wundt's psycholinguistics, for instance, words can have meanings only as a function of their membership in a sentence (either stated or implied), and the uttered sentence is a representation of a larger underlying mental context (*Gesamtvorstellung;* see Wundt, 1900b).

Third was the principle of *psychological contrasts,* an elaboration of the second principle. Simply stated, antithetical experiences intensify each other. After a period of pain, a slight pleasure will loom large; similarly, a sweet substance tastes sweeter if eaten after a sour substance. Examples of opponent process effects are endless. Berlyne (1971) took this principle directly from Wundt and applied it in his analysis of emotional behavior.

The first three principles are the more basic ones, reflecting the most general aspects of mental function. The fourth principle was the first of three developmental principles that parallel the original three but apply to long-term social and developmental processes. It concerns the *heterogeneity of ends.* A change produced by a purposive action is often different from the change intended, and that discrepancy results in further action. Wundt considered this process to be a developmental result of considerable scope, since the changes that occur are often emergent cultural forms or new cultural products.

The fifth (or second developmental) principle was that of *mental growth.* As cultural or mental forms evolve and become progressively differentiated, older and simpler forms evolve into more elaborate forms that must be understood in terms of their relation to the earlier parent forms. A historical case is the evolution of the world's languages, in which family trees of languages are found and may be used to interpret linguistic phenomena as well as cultural history. In the case of individual development, one may cite the unfolding of language in the child.

Child speech, observes Wundt, begins with "holophrases," one-word sentences based on innate global emotional gestures and primitive expressive movements. The acquisition of language then proceeds in accord with the unfolding and differentiation of these original germinal forms. (Around the turn of the century, volumes of data were published in support of this view; see Blumenthal, 1970.)

The sixth and final principle is that of *development toward opposites*. Like the third principle of immediate experience, this one states that the development of attitudes or cultural forms fluctuates between opponent processes. Thus, a period of one type of activity or experience evokes a tendency to seek some opposite form of experience or action. These fluctuations, as Wundt observed, are found not only in the life and experience of the individual, but also in the cyclical patterns of history, in economic cycles, social fads, and so on.

Although the six principles described here emerged gradually and were stated in a variety of ways, they appear throughout Wundt's later work and give it a unifying theme. Let us now return to the theme that Wundt envisaged early in his career and that occupied him so much during his later years—cultural psychology.

CULTURAL PSYCHOLOGY

It is sometimes assumed that Wundt abandoned other interests around the turn of the century and thereafter devoted himself to cultural psychology. In fact, that was not the case. Wundt's student manual, *Grundriss der Psychologie* (*Outlines of Psychology*), was concerned mostly with immediate mental processes. It appeared first in 1896 and went through 14 editions up to 1921. Two of the six editions of his experimentally oriented *Grundzüge* came after the turn of the century, and at the time of his death in 1920 he had completed the first volume of a seventh edition of that work. Although the many volumes of the *Völkerpsychologie*[1] (Wundt's major work on cultural psychology) began to appear only in 1900, his work in that area had been prolific in earlier decades (see, for example, his *Ethik, Logik,* sections of the *Vorlesungen, Grundzüge,* and other monographs and essays). It is clear that experimental, philosophical, and cultural psychology held his attention more or less equally

---

[1] *Völkerpsychologie* is a unique German term, one that has generally been regarded as antiquated in the twentieth century. It has often been mistranslated as "folk psychology." However, the prefix *Völker* carries the meaning of "ethnic" or "cultural." Thus, "ethnology" is *Völkerkunde,* while "ethnography" is *Völkerbeschreibung.*

throughout his career (for further illustration of this point, see Ungerer, 1980).

Wundt's most significant work on language occupies the first of the ten volumes in the *Völkerpsychologie* series, and by all accounts it was the most successful part of that series. (Judd, 1932, found it to be the most significant achievement among all of Wundt's psychological works.) It stimulated the interdisciplinary research then known as *Sprachpsychologie* (now known as psycholinguistics). Wundt's work on language not only had a strong impact on linguistic scholars, but in fact divided them for a while into those who were followers of Wundt and those who were followers of Herbart, or more particularly of the Herbartian linguist, Hermann Paul (see Blumenthal, 1970).

Paul's (1880) approach to language was that of taxonomic analysis, which viewed language as sets of elements compounded into associative chains of words or sounds. All the classic principles of association would thus operate to explain language performance. Because Wundt had a very different understanding of language, he engaged Paul in a running debate on these matters for 40 years (1880–1920).

In Wundt's view, language should be analyzed according to a generative model. That is, linguistic utterances result from a constructive mental process in which a germinal mental impression unfolds, or is differentiated through the process of selective attentional analysis, to yield sentences. The unity of the sentence thus reflects the original unity of the germinal mental impression. For example, if a person's momentary state of mind is a desire for information (e.g., a wish for repetition), then a low-level mental analysis of that germinal mental state might yield only the simple utterance, "Huh?" In contrast, a more detailed analysis and unfolding of the same mental state would yield the more articulate expression, "What did you say?" An underlying mental state may unfold or differentiate to greater or smaller degrees, thus yielding various surface forms of utterances.

To describe the structure of sentences, the primary units in Wundt's linguistics, Wundt invented the tree diagram (*Logik*, 1880–1883). This technique of sentence analysis was later adopted by many linguists. Tree diagrams depict relations among sentence constituents, yet in Wundt's psychological terms, these diagrams also show the subdivisions of mental impressions brought about by selective attentional focusings. The mental impression is first subdivided into two impressions that form the basis of the subject–predicate division of the sentence. Each of these impressions can undergo further binary subdivision to yield other mental constituents underlying the utterance.

In the articulate user of language, much of this mental process has become highly automatic. Yet it is also a remarkably creative process, in that a single mental impression may be developed quickly and efficiently into any number of sentence representations (e.g., "Caesar crossed the Rubicon," "The Rubicon was crossed by Caesar," "When at the Rubicon, Caesar crossed," and so on, to quote Wundt, 1900b). This approach to language is in the spirit of the new linguistics that appeared in the later 20th century (the generative or transformational grammar of Noam Chomsky and his colleagues).

The remaining *Völkerpsychologie* volumes provide comparative studies of other cultural forms such as the arts, religions, mythologies, and legal and moral systems. One book appearing in English a half-century later reflects, in abbreviated form, the approach and content of those *Völkerpsychologie* volumes. It is Heinz Werner's *Comparative Psychology of Mental Development* (1948). Wundt also wrote a one-volume work translated in 1916 by E. Schaub as *Elements of Folk Psychology*. This work is still confused with Wundt's *Völkerpsychologie* series in American writings on the history of psychology. The two works are very different, however. The *Elements* is a popularly written work wholly concerned with a speculative global history and a theory of the evolutionary stages of human culture. It has little in common with the ten-volume *Völkerpsychologie*.

After its completion, the *Völkerpsychologie* series was largely ignored outside of central Europe, with the exception of the influential first volume on language. One reason for this neglect was the rise of modern positivistic sociology in the tradition of Auguste Comte and Emile Durkheim. The contrasts between their views and Wundt's are clear, particularly in view of Wundt's effort to subordinate sociology to psychology. (For more information on the debate between Wundt and Durkheim [and Durkheim's students], see *L'Année Sociologique* from 1896 to 1908.)

Despite such opposition, Wundt gathered a following of *Völkerpsychologie* students (any attempt to describe them all would require a separate chapter). One student in the English-speaking community who supported Wundt's work on language was George Herbert Mead (1904). However, Mead did not receive his Ph.D. from Wundt, unlike Charles Judd (1926), an American who did receive a Wundt Ph.D. and who followed Wundt's *Völkerpsychologie*. One American sociologist with a Wundt Ph.D. was Alexander Goldenweiser, who described Wundt's work in a variety of American publications (e.g., Goldenweiser, 1921, 1948). As a rule, however, there were relatively few students of Wundt's *Völkerpsychologie* in the English-speaking world; most came from central and southern Europe. Among Wundt's German students, Alfred Vierkandt deserves special mention for his works, *Naturvölker und*

Kulturvölker (*Primitive and Civilized Peoples,* 1896) and *Die Stetigkeit im Kulturwandel* (*Continuity in Cultural Change,* 1908), as does the prolific Theophilus Boreas, who became president of the Academy of Science at Athens and professor at Athens after receiving a Ph.D. from Wundt in 1899. In addition to much *Völkerpsychologie* research and many books, Boreas also founded a psychological laboratory at Athens and published a series of experimental investigations (see Boréas, 1940).

THE DECLINE OF WUNDTIAN PSYCHOLOGY

Wundt's influence may have hit its peak early in the twentieth century, judged by the attendance figures for his lectures. An audience of 630 students and visiting scholars attended his afternoon lectures in 1912 (Schlotte, 1956). At that time, Wundt was 80 years of age and losing his eyesight. By the time of World War I, many laboratories of experimental psychology built on the pattern of the one at Leipzig had been established around the world. Yet the enthusiasm with which Wundt's American students carried the Leipzig laboratory techniques and instruments back to their home institutions was about to be replaced by enthusiasm for the behaviorist movement.

Wundt's students played a significant role in determining both the shape and activities of his laboratory. James McKeen Cattell, in particular, is a good example of this influence. His technical contributions, in the form of apparatus design and experiments, made a lasting impression on the Leipzig laboratory and led to a lasting personal relationship between Cattell and the Wundt family (Sokal, 1981). Because that pattern seems to have been repeated with many students from several countries, it can rightly be said that the Leipzig laboratory and the research performed there were the products of many different researchers. According to Cattell's account (in Sokal, 1981), Wundt was pluralistic in encouraging students to follow their own interests. The consequent diversity of the Leipzig work resists easy summarization.

Many of Wundt's students, as is well known, went on to establish their own laboratories. Before Mussolini closed down most academic psychology in Italy in the 1920s, a number of Wundt-inspired laboratories had prospered. One of Wundt's foremost students was Federico Kiesow, based in Turin. Kiesow was long accepted as the Italian interpreter of Wundt's thought, notably defending it against the later criticism of the Gestalt psychologists (Kiesow, 1929).

Wundt was also influential in pre-revolutionary Russia, as evidenced by Nicolai Losskii's *Principles of Voluntaristic Psychology* (1904). The most prominent Russian disciple was Georgi Chelpanov, who wrote several texts in the Wundtian mold. The Moscow Psychological Society made Wundt an honorary member in 1885, and more of Wundt's works were translated into Russian than any other language (16 into Russian, 7 into English). A replica of Wundt's Leipzig laboratory was built in Moscow in 1912, but the Marxist movement and its style of thought were hostile to Wundt because of his criticism of materialistic philosophy. Wundt's influence was thus rapidly diminished in the new Soviet Union. The new regime also dismissed Chelpanov from the directorship of the Moscow Psychological Institute in 1923.

In 1920, the year of Wundt's death, his Japanese students and followers were constructing a replica of the Leipzig laboratory at Tokyo University. It survived World War II, only to be burned in a student riot during the 1960s. In 1932, the centenary of Wundt's birth, the *Indian Journal of Psychology* and some followers of Wundt at Calcutta produced the largest commemorative volume on Wundt printed that year.

In view of such recognition, the precipitous decline of Wundtian psychology between the World Wars was breathtaking. The massive body of Wundtian research and writings all but disappeared in the English-speaking world, apparently confirming Wundt's own principle of the development toward opposites, mentioned earlier in this chapter. However, these events should be placed in the context of the convulsive revolutionary movements of early 20th-century intellect and society. The behaviorist, psychoanalytic, positivist, and Gestalt movements, as well as the Marxian and Nazi political climates, all contributed to Wundt's eclipse, as did the differences in native intellectual orientations that had frequently separated Anglo-American thought from that of central Europe.

For the revolutionary movements in psychology that appeared in the early 20th century, Wundt's name became the symbol of a reputedly antiquated past. It became ritual with behaviorist writers to defame Wundt. Descriptions of his work gradually lapsed into clichés and personal anecdotes. The sheer volume of Wundt's work may also have contributed to its superficial treatment.

One of the last of Wundt's controversial stances in academic matters developed during the second decade of the twentieth century, when a simmering controversy concerning the institutional status of psychology flared up in German universities and engulfed the entire German academic community. (This episode and the evolution of German academic psychology departments are reviewed by Ash, 1980a, 1980b; see also Chapter 13, this volume.) German academic administrations were hesitant to grant psychology a new faculty status separate from philosophy.

In Germany, the "philosophical faculty" was very broadly defined, similar to that of an American college of arts and sciences. (However, the American style of separate departments did not exist.) What triggered the dispute was the assignment of narrowly trained experimental psychologists to certain endowed chairs that had previously been occupied by generations of "rennaissance-style" intellectuals, mostly philosopher–scientists of great professional breadth. The petitions, debates, and pamphlets that arose in this dispute degenerated to levels of personal hostility, and both parties agreed, for the most part, that an immediate divorce was in order. Unfortunately, German university administrations lacked the mechanism (and the economic means) to give psychology full institutional independence. The problem continued to simmer until the reorganization of the German academic community after World War II.

As the recognized founder of the experimental psychology movement, Wundt naturally entered the fray as arbitrator. This effort came in the form of an article titled "Die Psychologie im Kampf ums Dasein" ("Psychology in the Struggle for Existence," 1913), a discussion still worth reading. Wundt found valid points in both the philosophers' and the psychologists' criticisms of each other (see Chapter 13, this volume), yet he argued that from the standpoint of administrative and economic realities, psychology should remain within the philosophical faculty. He criticized experimental psychologists for what he perceived as their growing anti-intellectualism and their belief that they were free of philosophy. At the same time, he criticized philosophers for their failure to recognize the importance of psychology to their own work.

Without certain unifying philosophical studies, Wundt noted, psychology would fragment into unrelated specializations and crafts. Pointing to the United States, he claimed that the field was already heading down the path toward conceptual disintegration, in spite of its separate departmental status and greater financial support.

Shortly after Wundt's death in 1920, Germany faced economic collapse. Universities and scholars were soon bankrupt, and Leipzig University found itself unable to purchase several of Wundt's last works for its own library. Wundt's heirs then put his entire personal library of 15,840 items up for auction. The collection was sold to a Japanese group led by Professor Tanenari Chiba, who took it to a new university in Japan (Tohoku) where it resides today (Miyakawa, 1981). Both Harvard and Yale made attempts to bring the Wundt library to the United States, but Wundt's family was adamant in their refusal to allow any part of the Wundt memorabilia to fall into American hands.

The losses and tragedies that awaited Wundt's successors in Germany during the 1930s and 1940s contributed to the decline of Wundtian psychology, and eventually to a general loss of familiarity with it. Outside of Germany, the subject was quickly put to rest without serious examination, but within the country it did not die immediately in 1920. In Germany in the 1920s and 30s, Wundt's later students (Krueger, Sander, Klemm, Volkelt, Wirth, and several others) renamed themselves "the *Ganzheit* school." (Ganzheit translates approximately as "holistic"). This group continued to be centered at Leipzig University, where they revived Wundt's old journal, renaming it *Neue Psychologische Studien* (publication ceased for good during World War II).

The Ganzheitists broadened Wundt's emphasis on emotion, producing a form of depth psychology though nothing Freudian. Krueger became the new director of the Leipzig Psychological Institute in 1920, but he was perhaps the least loyal of these "neo-Wundtians." Though he had studied with Wundt, he spent more time with Wilhelm Dilthey and Hans Cornelius, from whom he received his degree. In addition, he was to have a negative effect on the Leipzig Institute through his Nazi political affiliation. (Several institute members lost their positions because of their anti-Nazi activity.)

During the night of December 4, 1943, a joint Anglo-American bombing raid hit Leipzig. Thus the first officially sanctioned laboratory of experimental psychology, the center of Wundt's waning influence, was decisively blasted from the face of the earth.

After the war, the new Karl Marx University rose from the ashes to become a shining reflection of the spirit of the new German Democratic Republic. Wundtian psychology may have lingered there, but only as a ghost, a reminder to a few East German scholars of a bygone bourgeois era of idealist theory.

Should we reconsider Wundt today? One requirement of any science, I believe, is that it be historically cumulative. But it cannot meet that requirement if we do not know or do not understand its past. I must again cite the current textbook cant about the nature of Wundt's psychology and the reasons for its decline. That account is a pattern of myths and legends that arose over the course of the present century. Its apparent function is not to illuminate the past but rather to place psychologists of a later generation in the best light.

I can foresee an argument to the effect that Wundtian psychology did not decline, that in fact it continues today. Consider the influential survey of experimental work that inspired a generation or more of psychologists—Woodworth's *Experimental Psychology* (1938), a book that many contemporary psychologists still approach reverentially. Examinations of that book from the view of a quantitative historian show it to be heavily based on research that came from Wundtian theory and from the Leipzig laboratory. The index contains 29 citations to Wundt (only G. E. Müller [Chapter 3, this volume] has more [30]). Other, more frequently cited individuals are Ebbinghaus (27), Köhler (27), Fechner (26), Cattell (26), Judd (24), Dodge (25), Pavlov (22), Thorndike (21), Helmholtz (20), and Titchener (20). If one adds to Wundt's citations those of his students, or perhaps just those who remained conceptually close to him, one might well argue that Woodworth's book is heavily Wundtian in content (though Woodworth surely made no such suggestion). Woodworth's coverage of the Wundtians is exceptionally broad; there are even five index citations to the previously mentioned Theophilus Boreas in faraway Athens.

At present, the traditional view of psychology as the study of mind or mental processes is back in vogue in many laboratories of experimental psychology as the study of cognitive processes and human information processing. Most of the topics in this recent work have antecedents in the earlier Wundtian era. In some cases, the Wundtian work is a source of material contributing directly to more recent interests (see, for example, Blumenthal, 1975, 1977; Martindale, 1981). Such a statement is not the historiographic error of "presentism"—forcing the past into the mold of the present—but rather an adherence to the program of science: to regard data and theory as historically cumulative, a view that perforce should recognize those investigators who were first to make particular discoveries or formulate particular hypotheses. The need for that recognition will become clearer in the next chapter.

The next chapter surveys several psychologists who were contemporaries of Wundt and who worked in his shadow. A description of their work is necessary to any adequate understanding of the Wundtian era.

REFERENCES

Adler, G. (1870). A dictionary of the German and English languages. New York: Appleton.

Ash, M. G. (1980a). Academic politics in the history of science: Experimental psychology in Germany, 1879–1941. *Central European History, 13,* 255–286.

Ash, M. G. (1980b). Wilhelm Wundt and Oswald Külpe on the institutional status of psychology. In W. Bringmann & R. Tweney (Eds.), *Wundt studies.* Toronto: Hogrefe.

Berlyne, D. E. (1971). *Aesthetics and psychobiology.* New York: Appleton-Century-Crofts.

Blumenthal, A. L. (1970). *Language and psychology.* New York: Wiley.

Blumenthal, A. L. (1975). A reappraisal of Wilhelm Wundt. *American Psychologist, 30,* 1081–1088.

Blumenthal, A. L. (1977). *The process of cognition.* Englewood Cliffs, NJ: Prentice–Hall.

Blumenthal, A. L. (1980). Wilhelm Wundt and early American psychology: A clash of cultures. In R. Rieber & K. Salzinger (Eds.), *Psychology: Theoretical–historical perspectives*. New York: Academic Press.

Boréas, T. (1940). *Les quarante années scientifique de Théophile Boréas* (Festschrift). (2 vols.). Athens: Pyros.

Boring, E. G. (1950). *A history of experimental psychology* (2nd ed.). New York: Appleton-Century-Crofts.

Bringmann, W. G., & Ungerer, G. (1980a). The establishment of Wilhelm Wundt's Leipzig laboratory. *Storia e critica della psicologia, 1,* 11–28.

Bringmann, W. G., & Ungerer, G. (1980b). Wilhelm Wundt. In J. Brozek & L. Pongratz (Eds.), *Historiography of modern psychology*. Toronto: Hogrefe.

Cassell's German–English Dictionary. (1965). New York: Funk & Wagnalls.

Cattell, J. M. (1886). The psychological laboratory at Leipzig. *Mind, 13,* 37–51.

Danziger, K. (1979). The positivist repudiation of Wundt. *Journal of the History of the Behavioral Sciences, 15,* 205–230.

Danziger, K. (1980a). The history of introspection reconsidered. *Journal of the History of the Behavioral Sciences, 16,* 241–262.

Danziger, K. (1980b). Wundt and the two traditions of pschology. In R. Rieber (Ed.), *Wilhelm Wundt and the making of a scientific psychology*. New York: Plenum.

Danziger, K. (1980c). Wundt's theory of behavior and volition. In R. Rieber (Ed.), *Wilhelm Wundt and the making of a scientific psychology*. New York: Plenum.

Diamond, S. (1980). Wundt before Leipzig. In R. Rieber (Ed.), *Wilhelm Wundt and the making of a scientific psychology*. New York: Plenum.

Donders, F. C. (1868). Over de snelheid van psychische processen; Onderzoekingen gedaan in het Physiologisch Laboratorium der Utrechtesche Hoogeschool. *Tweede reeks, 2,* 92–120.

Drobisch, M. (1864). Ueber den neuesten Versuch die Psychologie naturwissenschaftlich zu begründen. *Zeitschrift für exacte Philosophie, 4,* 313–348.

Fichte, J. (1817). *Die Thatsachen des Bewusstseyns*. Stuttgart: Cotta.

Fortlage, K. (1855). *System der Psychologie*. Leipzig: Brockhaus.

Goldenweiser, A. (1921). Wilhelm Wundt, 1832–1920. *The Freeman,* 397–398.

Goldenweiser, A. (1948). The psychosociological thought of Wilhelm Wundt. In H. Barnes (Ed.), *An introduction to the history of sociology*. Chicago: University of Chicago Press.

Herbart, J. F. (1816). *Lehrbuch zur Psychologie*. Leipzig: Hartenstein.

Herrnstein, R. J., & Boring, E. G. (1965). *A source book in the history of psychology*. Cambridge, MA: Harvard University Press.

Judd, C. H. (1926). *The psychology of social institutions*. New York: Macmillan.

Judd, C. H. (1932). Autobiography. In C. Murchison (Ed.), *A history of psychology in autobiography* (Vol. 2). Worcester, MA: Clark University Press.

Kiesow, F. (1929). Il principio della sintesi creatrice di G. Wundt e la teoria della forma. *Archivo italiano di Psicologia, 7,* 61–79.

Losskii, N. (1904). *Die Grundlehren der Psychologie vom Standpunkte des Voluntarismus*. (Translated from the Russian by E. Kleuker.) Leipzig: Barth.

Martindale, C. (1981). *Cognition and consciousness*. Glenview, IL: Dorsey.

Mead, G. H. (1904). The relation of psychology and philology. *Psychological Bulletin, 1,* 375–391.

Meringer, R., & Mayer, C. (1895). *Versprechen und Verlesen: Eine psychologisch–linguistische Studie*. Stuttgart: Göschen.

Mischel, T. (1970). Wundt and the conceptual foundations of psychology. *Philosophical and Phenomenological Research, 31,* 1–26.

Miyakawa, T. (1981). The Tohoku University Wundtian collection. *Journal of the History of the Behavioral Sciences, 17,* 299.

Osgood, C. (1966). Dimensionality of the semantic space for communication via facial expressions. *Scandinavian Journal of Psychology, 7,* 1–30.

Osgood, C., Suci, G., & Tannenbaum, P. (1957). *The measurement of meaning.* Urbana: University of Illinois Press.

Paul, H. (1880). *Principien der Sprachgeschichte.* Halle: Niemeyer.

Posner, M. (1978). *Chronometric explorations of mind.* Hillsdale, NJ: Erlbaum.

Reimarus, H. S. (1760). *Allgemeine Betrachtungen über die Triebe der Triere, hauptsächlich über ihre Kunsttriebe.* Hamburg: Bohn.

Schlosberg, H. (1954). Three dimensions of emotion. *Psychological Review, 61,* 81–88.

Schlotte, F. (1956). Beiträge zum Lebensbild Wilhelm Wundts auf seinem Briefwechsel. *Wissenschaftliche Zeitschrift der Karl-Marx-Universität Leipzig, 5,* 333–349.

Sokal, M. (Ed.). (1981). *An education in psychology: James McKeen Cattell's journal and letters from Germany and England, 1880–1888.* Cambridge, MA: MIT Press.

Titchener, E. B. (1898). The postulates of a structural psychology. *Philosophical Review, 7,* 449–465.

Titchener, E. B. (1912). Prolegomena to a study of introspection. *American Journal of Psychology, 23,* 427–448.

Thumb, A., & Marbe, K. (1901). *Experimentelle Untersuchungen über die psychologischen Grundlagen der sprachlichen Analogiebildung.* Leipzig: Engelmann.

Tweney, R., & Yachanin, S. (1980). Titchener's Wundt. In W. Bringmann & R. Tweney (Eds.), *Wundt studies.* Toronto: Hogrefe.

Ungerer, G. A. (1980). Wilhelm Wundt als Psycholog and Politiker. *Psychologische Rundschau, 31,* 99–110.

Vierkandt, A. (1896). *Naturvölker und Kulturvölker.* Leipzig: Duncker & Humboldt.

Vierkandt, A. (1908). *Die Stetigkeit im Kulturwandel.* Leipzig: Duncker & Humboldt.

Werner, H. (1948). *The comparative psychology of mental development.* New York: Science Editions.

Woodworth, R. (1938). *Experimental psychology.* New York: Holt.

Wundt, E. (1927). *Wilhelm Wundts Werke: Ein Verzeichnis seiner sämlichen Schriften.* Munich: Beck.

Wundt, M. (1944). *Die Würzeln der deutschen Philosophie in Stamm und Rasse.* Berlin: Junker, Dunnhaupt.

Wundt, W. (1858a). *Die Lehre von der Muskelbewegung.* Braunschweig: Vieweg.

Wundt, W. (1858b). Ueber den Verlauf ideomuskulärer Zusammenziehungen. *Vortrag auf der 34. Versammlung deutscher Naturforscher und Ärzte,* pp. 200–202.

Wundt, W. (1861). Ueber persönliche Differenz zwischen Gesichts- und Gehörsbeobachtung. *Vortrag auf der 36. Versammlung deutscher Naturforscher und Ärzte,* p. 25.

Wundt, W. (1862a). *Beiträge zur Theorie der Sinneswahrnehmung.* Leipzig: Winter.

Wundt, W. (1863). *Vorlesungen über die Menschen- und Thierseele.* (2 vols.). Leipzig: Voss.

Wundt, W. (1866). *Die physicalischen Axiome und ihre Beziehung zum Causalprinzip.* Erlangen: Enke.

Wundt, W. (1874). *Grundzüge der physiologischen Psychologie* (2nd ed.). Leipzig: Englemann. (2nd ed., 1880)

Wundt, W. (1880–1883). *Logik.* Stuttgart: Enke.

Wundt, W. (1882). Die Aufgaben der experimentellen Psychologie. *Unsere Zeit.* (Reprinted in Wundt, W., *Essays,* 2nd ed., Leipzig: Engelmann, 1906.

Wundt, W. (1883). Ueber psychologische Methoden. *Philosophische Studien, 1,* 1–40.

Wundt, W. (1885). Zur Kritik der Seelenbegriffs. *Philosophische Studien, 2,* 483–494.

Wundt, W. (1886). *Ethik.* Stuttgart: Enke.

Wundt, W. (1887). *Grundzüge der physiologischen Psychologie* (3rd ed.). Leipzig: Englemann.

Wundt, W. (1888). Selbstbeobachtung und innere Wahrnehmung. *Philosophische Studien, 4,* 292–309.

Wundt, W. (1889). *System der Philosophie.* Leipzig: Englemann.

Wundt, W. (1891). Zur Lehre von den Gemüthsbewegen. *Philosophische Studien, 6,* 335–393.

Wundt, W. (1892). *Vorlesungen über die Menschen- und Thierseele* (2nd ed.). Leipzig: Voss.

Wundt, W. (1893). *Logik* (2nd ed.). Stuttgart: Enke.

Wundt, W. (1894). Ueber psychische Causalität und das Princip des psycho-physischen Parallelismus. *Philosophische Studien, 10,* 1–124.

Wundt, W. (1896). *Grundriss der Psychologie.* Leipzig: Englemann.

Wundt, W. (1900a). Bemerkungen zur Theorie der Gefühle. *Philosophische Studien, 15,* 149–182.

Wundt, W. (1900b). *Völkerpsychologie* (Vol. 1). Leipzig: Englemann.

Wundt, W. (1901). Besprechung von A. Thumb und K. Marbe, "Experimentelle Untersuchungen über die psychologischen Grundlagen der sprachlichen Analogiebildungen." *Anzeiger für indogermanische Sprach- und Altertumskunde, 12,* 17–20.

Wundt, W. (1907). Ueber Ausfrageexperimente und über die Methoden zur Psychologie des Denkens. *Psychologische Studien, 2,* 301–390.

Wundt, W. (1913). *Die Psychologie im Kampf ums Dasein.* Leipzig: Englemann.

Wundt, W. (1914). *Sinnliche und übersinnliche Welt.* Leipzig: Kröner.

Wundt, W. (1916). *Elements of folk psychology.* (Translated from the German by E. Schaub.) New York: Macmillan.

Wundt, W. (1920). *Erlebtes und Erkanntes.* Stuttgart: Kröner.

3

Shaping a Tradition: Experimentalism Begins

ARTHUR L. BLUMENTHAL

INTRODUCTION

When people spoke of the "new psychology," as they often did in the last quarter of the nineteenth century, they had experimentalism in mind. The effort in that day to bring psychology into the laboratory was truly new, and it caused academic storms. Those storms arose partly because a different type of individual was now being attracted to the study of psychology, one who found reward and pleasure in the mechanical manipulations and quantitative analyses imposed by laboratory work. This chapter focuses on a representative set of those early experimentalists for what they can teach us about the history of psychology and for the trends they established, trends that continue to this day.

The opening of Wundt's small laboratory in Leipzig, an event celebrated widely a century later, ironically marked the decline of his own activity as an experimenter (see the preceding chapter). His interest in problems of experimental methodology never ceased, however, and he continued to be a thorough summarizer and systematizer of experimental findings for the next 40 years. There were, of course, other founding fathers in Wundt's day who helped shape modern psychology. Many of

51

them are best described as philosophers, if only because they were not direct participants in the new experimentalism. Prominent examples are Franz Brentano, Hermann Lotze, William James, and Wilhelm Dilthey. Among these men, the idea of an experimental psychology was received with varying degrees of skepticism. Dilthey's skepticism was greatest. In the late 1880s he planted seeds of opposition to the new experimental psychology; by the 1930s that opposition nearly overwhelmed the field in Germany (Metzger, 1965).

When the opposing camps of philosophical and experimental psychology came to be sharply defined late in Wundt's career, he was placed in the delicate position of mediator. His credentials for that position were, of course, excellent because he was personally committed to both fields. In the creation of an institutionalized experimental psychology, he had been the strongest force. For 20 years after 1879 he cajoled and persuaded Leipzig officials to support the psychology laboratory, and his influence through students and letters helped to establish other laboratories around the world. It is thus ironic that we should find Wundt early in the twentieth century (as noted in the last chapter) fearing that experimental psychology had gone too far, that it was losing touch with philosophical foundations and with other approaches to knowledge, and that it was exhibiting an intellectually debilitating over-specialization. Some of the experimenters described in this chapter could have provoked such fears.

Several early and influential psychologists followed in the pattern of Wundt's career, if not always his psychology, particularly those who introduced the new psychology to American universities, where it enjoyed its greatest support and approval. The stories of several of those individuals have been told and retold many times. Men like Edward Titchener at Cornell, G. Stanley Hall at Clark, and James McKeen Cattell at Columbia were influential organizers, teachers, writers, and academic politicians, and they remain well known.

There were, however, many other early experimentalists, mostly Germans, who were the yeomen of the field. Throughout lifetimes of laboratory work, they erected the scaffolding of empirical research on which modern scientific psychology arose. This latter group of early psychologists began strictly as experimentalists and remained, for the most part, steadfast in that activity throughout their careers. Their autobiographical statements, where available, reflect a life-long focus on the technical and procedural problems of experimentation. It is they who should be regarded as the true paragons of the new experimental psychology. This chapter examines several of these individuals, not for themselves alone, but also for what they illustrate about the history of modern psychology.

There is no more prominent representative of this group than its founding father, Georg Elias Müller. More than anyone in his time, he set a style that came to dominate twentieth-century experimental psychology. Some historical summaries (especially Boring, 1950) cite Müller as second only to Wundt in terms of influence on the "new" psychology of the late nineteenth century, and yet he has received much less attention than Wundt and others in those histories. Nevertheless, the quality and rigor of Müller's work would be quite acceptable to most investigators in the same areas of research today. That rigor came from his tough-minded scientific attitude, which the humanistically minded William James described as "brutal."

After first examining the career and work of Müller, we turn to several other early experimentalists to give a broader view of the rise of modern psychology. As this chapter shows, it is rather short-sighted to dismiss that early work as mere "old-fashioned introspectionism."

GEORG ELIAS MÜLLER, THE EXPERIMENTER'S EXPERIMENTER

When Wundt published his first psychological experiments in Heidelberg in the 1860s, Müller was a philosophy and history student at Leipzig. At an early age, however, Müller had been inspired by the ideals of rigorous and logical thinking, a disposition that eventually brought about his turn toward a scientific career. Little autobiographical information remains, but a personal letter to Edwin Boring mentions what Müller (1928) felt to be a strong formative experience—namely, his voluntary service in the Prussian infantry in 1870 (the Franco–Prussian war). As he recalled, this experience shook him loose from his "softer" interests and produced a dedication to more exact and rigorous disciplines. After his Prussian military training, Müller returned to the university at Leipzig to study under Moritz Drobisch, the Herbartian scholar. Herbart's mathematical and mechanistic psychology was particularly congenial to Müller. As noted in the previous chapter, Drobisch was then defending Herbart's mental mechanics against Wundt's criticism. According to Wundt, Herbart's system lacked a true central volitional process, which we now call selective attention. Later, Drobisch's defense of Herbart's associationist views was to be carried on by Müller.

Müller went to Göttingen University in the early 1870s, having been sent there by Drobisch to study with Herman Lotze. During this interval (it is not clear exactly when), he was first exposed to the idea of an experimental psychology. That notion seemed a perfect fit to the patterns of thought he had been nurturing. His doctoral dissertation, completed in 1873, reveals an interest that opened the way to experimental work and to a life-long disagreement with Wundt. Its title was *Zur Theorie der sinnlichen Aufmerksamkeit* (An Analysis of Sensory Attention).

Müller's dissertation was inspired by his study of Helmholtz's *Physiological Optics* (1866). He responded to parts of Helmholtz's work by further developing a number of Helmholtz's ideas, a style of scholarship that was to continue in Müller's work for the rest of his life. That style consisted of taking over where earlier investigators had left off, extending their work, and giving it more experimental, quantitative, or logical rigor. He eventually elaborated the works of Gustav Fechner on psychophysics, Hermann Ebbinghaus on memory, James McKeen Cattell on reaction time, Wilhelm Wundt on spatial localization, Hugo Münsterberg on the sensory–motor theory of volition, Ewald Hering on color vision, and Mary Whiton Calkins on paired-associate learning. Reviews of those early works are found in Boring (1950) and Woodworth (1938). This list illustrates the breadth of Müller's involvement, in experimental psychology, as well as the fact that his great productiveness was not always a display of originality.

Returning to Müller's dissertation, we find him arguing against the notion of attention as a distinct or separate mental process that directs other mental processes. Rather, he saw it as a byproduct of more fundamental associationistic processes—a restatement of the earlier Herbartian position. Müller also inclined toward physiological reductionism, suggesting, for instance, that changes in cortical blood supply are an important aspect of attention. Because blood is concentrated in different parts of the brain at different times, he proposed that an experience would be enhanced if it were associated with the particular part of the brain where blood concentration occurs. (A century later, modern brain scan technology demonstrated that indeed there are such circulatory changes). Blood circulation is also the basis for Müller's impulse theory of volition, according to which the increased blood supply in certain brain areas, along with the consequent cortical excitation, leads to an overflow of nervous discharge resulting in what we call voluntary movement.

Müller's career progressed rapidly because of what his students later recalled as an aggressive style, or, as David Katz (1935) describes it, "Müller's unusually acute and independent powers of criticism." In 1877, at the age of 27, Müller took apart with surgical precision the whole of 73-year-old Gustav Fechner's *Elemente der Psycho-physik (Elements of Psychophysics,* 1860) in a long critical review published in book form, *Zur Grundlegung der Psychophysik (On the Basis of Psychophysics,*

1878). A correspondence between Müller and Fechner ensued, ending in acrimonious polemics.

Müller had hoped to exorcise the dualism in Fechner's psychology in order to establish a physiological basis for psychophysics. In particular, he criticized Fechner's use of Weber's law that the increase in any stimulus necessary to make a noticeable difference is a constant proportion of that stimulus. Fechner explained this proportion by assuming that some sensory input is always lost when sensory excitation passes from body to mind, and that the loss is in the same ratio as the proportion of added stimulus. Müller argued that the loss of input occurs only in the physical processes of the nervous system. Weaker stimuli, he thought, use up the more readily oxidized substances in the nerves; thus, if an additional excitation is to be produced, a correspondingly greater stimulus is required. Perhaps even more important than the effects of this proposal on later psychophysics are Müller's elaborations of quantitative and experimental techniques.

Müller's critique elicited Fechner's *Revision der Hauptpunkte der Psychophysik* (*Revision of the main points of psychophysics*, 1882), an event that brought fame to Müller. Shortly thereafter he was made professor at Göttingen, taking over the chair that had been occupied by Lotze. These events might lead to the false impression that Müller was a self-promoting individual. In truth, he was the opposite, being universally remembered as a rather shy and retiring person in personal encounters, though an aggressive critic in academic journals. Moreover, he affected no interest in the honors that came his way. Rather, he appeared to be guided by ideals of high principle, morality, and character. As Katz (1935) puts it, he had a "mania for impartiality."

Müller's personal qualities often impressed his students as much as his teachings, and thus played a certain role in the history of experimental psychology. The student who reported this impression most strongly was Erich Jaensch (1935), who in a politically inspired reminiscence, found a life-directing inspiration in Müller, whom he regarded as a bulwark against liberalism, laxity, and cultural decadence, as well as a positive force for intellectual discipline. (Jaensch also found inspiration in the Nazi movement.) Müller was indeed disciplined, as the sheer volume of his highly technical publications shows. The complete list of his publications appears only in a rarely accessible Dutch journal, the pre-war *Nederlandsche Tijdschrift voor Psychologie* (Van Essen, 1935). Edouard Claparéde (1935), a friend of Müller's, recalls that Müller never allowed himself to retire before midnight or to sleep later than six o'clock. Such heroic dedication played an increasing role in the style and temperament of the emerging experimental psychology, as we see in this chapter.

Müller's personal work ethic partially compensated for the relative lack of support from Göttingen University, where he remained until his retirement in 1921. Göttingen had finally granted him space for experimental work in 1887, but it was not until 1891 that he had received funds for his laboratory, and then only a small token. Modest increases in that support came along in later years. However, stories survive of how laboratory funds often came from Müller's private salary.

The first of Müller's assistants was Friedrich Schumann, beginning in 1881. Müller's choice of Schumann is revealing, because in that same year Schumann received his Ph.D. in physics. He thus represented the type of technical skill and orientation that was compatible with Müller's vision of psychology, and he contributed to Müller's own development as a "physically minded" psychologist.

Müller's Teaching and Research

Müller's greatest interest was probably psychophysics, the area of his first large academic success. For him, it provided the model of what correct psychological science should look like, and it was the basis for his research procedures in other areas. Although his research interests covered many areas, some topics are notably lacking. In particular, he was silent on the topic of emotion, a very large topic in other psychology departments at the turn of the century. Perhaps he could not envision ways of extending psychophysical and quantitative methods to the study of emotion. In summarizing Müller's interests in psychophysics, Katz (1935) writes: "It is possible that he (Müller) was the last lecturer in any German university to deliver a special course of three-hour lectures on psychophysics, and indeed few would have held forth on such a dry subject with so much force and impressiveness" (p. 378).

Müller's work on memory illustrates the style of his accomplishments rather well. Ebbinghaus might also have been a fitting focus for this chapter had he persevered in experimental work after his famous memory studies (Ebbinghaus, 1885), but instead he became an editor and a textbook writer. Müller had no more funds or facilities at Göttingen than were available to Ebbinghaus at Berlin, yet Müller literally took over leadership of the study of memory. It was Müller who established the verbal-learning research tradition.

Ebbinghaus had spelled out certain principles for the use of nonsense syllables as stimuli in memory experiments, but it was Müller who fully elaborated the rules for constructing and using those items. Further, he revealed the weakness in Ebbinghaus's work of having one person act as both experimenter and subject. He then published the studies of recall and recognition that established many of the main issues and variables in the field for years to come—for example, the effects of various types of interference and inhibition, massed versus distributed practice, paired-associate learning paradigms (first suggested by Calkins), the use of reaction times as measures of memory strength, and the effects of variations in the intention to learn. Much of this work appears in early issues of the *Zeitschrift für Psychologie* in the decades around the turn of the century.

Some of Müller's work may have been forgotten, only to be re-created by others years later. For example, he invented a productive technique used in studies of recall: After exposure to a list of items, a subject is given one item from somewhere in the list and asked to recall either the preceding or the following item. Both response accuracy and reaction time were used as memory measures. As any modern memory researcher would expect, Müller discovered a serial position curve and made observations on what we now call short-term memory.

The development or modification of apparatus was always a primary focus of Müller's work. His best known invention is the memory drum, a standard item in laboratories of experimental psychology ever since the 1890s. The horizontal drum, with nonsense syllables or other items on its surface, rotates at controlled speeds behind a screen in which a small opening exposes one item at a time. In paired-associate studies, Müller connected this apparatus to an electrically controlled clock in such a way that the clock started when the first item of a pair appeared. It then ran until the subject named the second item of the pair, which caused a voice key to stop the clock automatically. Reaction times were recorded in milliseconds, as they are today.

Müller's last publication on memory filled three long volumes titled *Zur Analyse der Gedächtnistätigkeit und des Vorstellungsverlaufes* (*Analysis of the Processes of Memory and Mental Representation*, 1911–1913). These volumes summarize much of his earlier work, but they also include something new—a detailed case study of a famous mnemonist (named Rückle) that includes systematic studies of mnemonic techniques. Müller hoped to integrate the feats of mnemonics with what was known about the workings of normal memory.

Although Müller frequently observed the effects of attention on memory performance, he avoided the theoretical commitment to attention that we find in Wundt. Instead, he used various circumlocutions when referring to attention, including "attitude," "determining tendency," and "set." One German word that Müller favored and that carried the sense of these terms was *Anlage*.

Another aspect of Müller's memory research reflected his concern for

Gestalt qualities, even before the turn of the century. He claimed that it is more efficient to learn "wholes" (by reading verbal material from beginning to end without interruption) than parts (by separating material into sections and learning each part before proceeding to the rest). The advantage in "whole" learning is that the learner is aided by the configurational properties (*Gestaltsqualitäten*) of the whole, which helps from the outset to organize and stabilize memory. To be sure, Müller treated all holistic phenomena from the viewpoint of Herbartian mental mechanics. That is, elementary memories or perceptions, as he conceived them, fall into clusters that have configurational properties as byproducts. These he called *Komplexqualitäten*.

Shortly after the turn of the century, a number of Müller's students became interested in these *Komplexqualitäten*, particularly Daniel Katz, Friedrich Schumann, Geza Révêsz, and Edgar Rubin. Rubin (1915) introduced into psychology the much-used notions of figure–ground relations and perceptual contour before he had heard anything of Wertheimer's Gestalt movement. Even earlier Schumann had done extensive work along this line. We will briefly consider his work as an extension of Müller's influence.

Instrumentation

The 1880s and 1890s witnessed a burst of mechanical ingenuity in the development of instrumentation for psychological laboratories—a movement dubbed "brass instrument psychology" by William James. Those instruments, some of which survive today as beautiful museum relics, were created for the precise control of stimuli and the precise measurement of reactions. Schumann, with his special skills, took an active part in the design and construction of many such instruments. As a result, he was offered a position at the well-funded University of Berlin, as assistant to Carl Stumpf. Stumpf had been appointed to replace Ebbinghaus, whom the Berlin authorities considered to be an unproductive scholar. As it turned out, however, introspective analysis (rather than laboratory experimentation) was Stumpf's strength, for he was a student of the phenomenologist Franz Brentano. Stumpf admitted that he had little aptitude for laboratory work; he was fond of recalling that on the one occasion he had attempted to learn laboratory techniques (in a university chemistry course), he came close to burning down the chemistry building (Stumpf, 1930).

It fell to Schumann to carry the spirit of experimentalism from the Göttingen laboratory to Berlin. During his 10 years at Berlin, however, that spirit had an uneasy resting place, for Stumpf became entangled in controversy over experimentation. This conflict grew out of a clash with Wundt. Let us summarize briefly the Stumpf–Wundt debate, which received much attention and impelled William James to support Stumpf:

Objective Versus Subjective Observations

Stumpf was a highly competent musician, and the psychology of music was always his predominant interest. One of Wundt's students, Carl Lorenz (1890), published some experimentally derived data on human abilities to discriminate musical intervals. These relatively minor findings contradicted Stumpf's earlier claims about the same abilities, and he then rebutted Lorenz's work. Wundt took up the gauntlet, and a series of six articles followed in which the larger issues of the validity of experimental psychology became the focus of the argument (Stumpf, 1890, 1891a, 1891b; Wundt, 1891a, 1891b, 1892).

Wundt argued that the most valid observations are those taken from naive subjects under the objective conditions of laboratory experimentation. Stumpf, on the contrary, claimed more validity for his own private observations—those of a trained musical expert. Wundt considered Stumpf's private observations to be illusory. Boring (1950) summarizes the whole episode:

> The clash seems to have arisen because Stumpf leaned heavily upon his own musical sophistication, while Wundt relied on the laboratory results with apparatus and the psychophysical methods. Whatever is obtained under unprejudiced, carefully controlled experimental conditions must be right, Wundt virtually said. If the laboratory yields results that are obviously contrary to musical experience, they must be wrong, was Stumpf's rejoinder. (p. 365)

Both Wundt and Stumpf referred to their "experiments," but when Stumpf used that term he was talking about demonstrations and personal experiences.

Microgenesis of Perceptions

Schumann had arrived in Berlin in the midst of this debate—not an auspicious time to begin developing a rigorous experimentalism. Yet Stumpf supported him, and he continued a line of work that he had begun under Müller at Göttingen comprising a series of studies on time perception and the timing of mental processes. In his last years in Berlin (1900–1904), Schumann published four noteworthy experimental investigations on visual perception that emphasized configurational principles. One goal was to study the microgenesis of perceptions; that is, the emergence over fractions of seconds of perceptual wholes or structures. For example, Schumann demonstrated the perception of a spatial configuration when its separate parts were presented in rapid succession at intensities just below the sensory threshold. He then extended this method to the examination of form qualities in word recognition.

As a theoretician, Schumann was more receptive than Müller to the notion of attention as a central mental process. He used attention to explain configurational phenomena in general, arguing that configurational properties of perceptions are under the control of selective attention. Wolfgang Metzger (1940) summarizes a number of other principles concerning configurational aspects of experience that Schumann established around the turn of the century. Briefly stated, they are: (1) Incomplete figures tend to be perceived as complete, (2) the nearness of components makes for the grouping of visual items into larger perceptions, and (3) ambiguous figures are seen as unambiguous. In later years those principles became part of Gestalt psychology.

In 1904 Schumann left Berlin to wander from university to university until he obtained a professorship at Zurich in 1909. Ebbinghaus, then editor of the *Zeitschrift für Psychologie*, died that same year and left the editorship in Schumann's hands. In the following year, Schumann became professor at Frankfurt, where he welcomed Max Wertheimer as a visitor. Using a bicycle wheel, Schumann constructed the apparatus for Wertheimer's study of apparent motion, generally regarded as the foundational study of the new Gestalt psychology (see Chapter 11, this volume). The rise of the Gestalt movement now brings us back to Müller.

Critique of Gestalt Psychology

By the early 1920s, the Gestalt movement was widely publicized and hailed as a revolt against the older psychology. This development coincided with Müller's retirement from Göttingen in 1921 and was a cause of distress to him. In 1923 he published an aggresssive critique of the Gestaltists titled *Komplextheorie und Gestalttheorie*, in which he finds the Gestalt work to be methodologically wanting and lacking in originality. Wolfgang Köhler replied in a long article in 1925, eliciting a rebuttal from Müller in the following year. As Köhler points out, the new Gestalt movement gave more importance to configurational phenomena than had any previous psychological work.

Two members of the Leipzig school, Frederico Kiesow and Felix Krueger, as well as Karl Bühler at Vienna, Eugenio Rignano at Milan, and Charles Spearman at London, joined the debate on the side of Müller. Apparently this debate did not lose steam until the Gestaltists left Germany in the 1930s for their new home in the United States. Most left the dispute behind, and World War II soon suspended further interchanges. Müller died in 1934.

Müller's Legacy

Müller had a life-long passion for methodological precision, a passion that he transmitted to many of his followers. Indeed, at some points his work gives the impression that apparatus and measurement technique were valued more than theoretical significance, which makes his writings difficult to read. Even so, his work often seems contemporary because it bears resemblance to the experimental psychology of today that bears the title "human information processing." A detailed historical study might trace the threads that causally link Müller's work to specific bodies of subsequent experimental studies, but many modern experimentalists are scarcely aware of him, if at all.

If Müller and his data are now largely forgotten, his character lives on in a highly principled, even obsessive concern for precise methodology that has sometimes limited psychology to topics that can be treated with unassailable precision in the laboratory. Significant theoretical integration did not emerge in Müller's work, though after his retirement he made an attempt at it. The unsuccessful result was a short, 124-page book (Müller, 1924) that was uncharacteristically superficial. We may look to Müller's personal character for explanation; he did not permit himself to have idle thoughts. He stayed away from seminars and discussions because, as Katz (1935) reports, "He hated improvisation in any form" (p. 378). To be a theorist, however, perhaps one must allow for some creative daydreaming and idle improvisation.

Experimental psychology began partly as a reaction against idle and unproductive philosophizing. With Müller, more obviously than with Wundt, it became a form of resistance to philosophizing. Thus Müller, moreso than Wundt, began a trend that grew rapidly in the early 20th century. His failure to theorize (or philosophize), however, is no mark against his accomplishments as an experimentalist. On that score he deserves more attention from historians of psychology than he has received.

THE LEIPZIG EXPERIMENTALISTS

The atmosphere at Leipzig differed from that at Göttingen. Wundt's assistants, especially the later ones, took a more commanding role in directing laboratory work than did Müller's assistants. It is frequently assumed that Wundt's first assistant was James McKeen Cattell (during 1885–1886). However, that position was not clearly defined in those years, and Cattell—who in Sokal's (1981) study is shown to be excessively self-promoting—was largely a self-proclaimed assistant to Wundt. He did not have the responsibilities in the laboratory that were given to the later assistants. Fourteen official assistants, de facto laboratory directors, followed Cattell (see Boring, 1950). All of them were active experimenters, although not all continued with laboratory work. None after Cattell was an American nor took a position in the United States. In the following pages I single out three of these individuals— Külpe, Kirschmann, and Wirth—as informative case studies in the progress of the new psychology.

Oswald Külpe

In 1886 Külpe came to Wundt from Müller's laboratory, where he had spent three semesters working on a doctoral dissertation concerning sensation. After a semester of further research at Leipzig and another semester of writing, Külpe's dissertation was accepted. It was dedicated to Müller, not Wundt, and yet it impressed Wundt so much that he appointed Külpe as his assistant beginning the following year (1888).

As Wundt's assistant, Külpe contributed to the mental chronometry program, then the primary research activity in the Leipzig laboratory. He studied the effects of "sets," or instructions, on reaction times. Toward the end of the 1880s, when Külpe was 26 years of age, Wundt suggested to him that psychology students needed a general introductory text. Külpe eagerly took up the task, putting laboratory work aside to concentrate on writing. Titchener arrived from Oxford in 1890 for a two-year stay at Leipzig, during which he worked closely with Külpe on his book—so closely, in fact, that Titchener felt he should have had part ownership of it (see Boring, 1950).

Külpe's teaching ability elevated him in the recollections of many Leipzig students, but he was also remembered as an enigmatic figure torn between the poles of Müller and Wundt, and thus often shifting his interests among experimental psychology, philosophy, and aesthetics. He is particularly interesting here because he transported the viewpoints of the Göttingen laboratory into the Leipzig laboratory—views that were sometimes antithetical to Wundt's.

One especially strong influence on both Müller and Külpe came from Ernst Mach. A physicist by training, Mach also published on psychological topics (visual perception, time perception, and movement sensation). His *Analyse der Empfindungen* (*Analysis of Sensations*, 1886) inspired a radical empiricism in several psychologists of his generation. Mach argued that all scientific data reduce to elemental sensations, but he differed from Wundt in his denial of any central attentional (or volitional) process. He erased Wundt's distinction between psychological science and the physical sciences, so that psychology and physics merge in his writings. That merger eliminated Wundt's purposivism and central apperception process (the source of "creative syntheses"). Machian empiricism, which locates the control of mental processes in external sensation, has always conflicted with Wundtian idealism, which argues for an a priori or internal central control.

Külpe's *Grundriss der Psychologie* (*Outlines of Psychology*) appeared in 1893. Wundt realized then, to his consternation, just how much Müller's and Mach's views were embedded in Külpe's understanding of psychology. The subject of attention was treated from an associationistic standpoint and made up the shortest section of the book. Volition and consciousness received only five pages of superficial treatment.

It was a dramatic time in the Leipzig laboratory as viewpoints polarized around Wundt and Külpe. Kiesow (1930) gives an eyewitness account of these occurrences. Although the Leipzig students were fond of Külpe personally, they generally regarded his book as an intellectual lapse or youthful extravagance. One strong exception was, of course, Titchener (then at Cornell), who immediately translated Külpe's book into English and then set about writing his own *Outlines* (1896), which went even further in its commitment to Mach.

In late 1893, Külpe left Leipzig for a professorship at Würzburg, and Wundt sat down to write yet another *Outlines* (1896a), this one intended to replace Külpe's book. Wundt also wrote a lengthy statement for his *Philosophische Studien* (1896b), partly in reaction to Külpe. Wundt's *Outline* eventually went through 14 editions, 3 of which were translated into English by an American student, Charles Hubbard Judd. (Külpe never revised his book.) A close friendship between Wundt and Külpe, in the form of a private correspondence, continued despite their theoretical differences. Wundt and Titchener, however, were never so close.

As noted earlier, Külpe was an enigmatic individual. A decade after the clash with Wundt, he abandoned his Machian positivism for the neo-Kantian movement in philosophy. He then wrote the most successful introductory philosophy text of his generation (Lindenfeld, 1978), which went through seven editions and was translated into at least four other languages. We now return to his influence on experimental psychology.

Külpe remained at Würzburg from 1894 to 1909. The movement that grew up around him there (the use of radical introspective techniques to study higher mental processes) is still well known (see Mandler & Mandler, 1964). The viewpoints of the Würzburg psychologists evolved rapidly and soon went beyond the *phenomenalism* of Mach to the *phenomenology* of Brentano and Husserl. The major difference was that Mach's phenomenalism concerned only the analysis of experience into sensations, while phenomenology brought volition (or "intentionality") back into view and included the analysis of purpose as an important part of the introspective act. In 1905, Ach formally titled the Würzburg movement "the systematic introspectionism movement." By contrast, Titchener's version of that movement always remained closer to Machian phenomenalism. In both cases there was a turning away from the strictures of objective experimental technique on which so much of the earlier reaction time research, psychophysics, memory research, and other departments of "brass instrument" psychology had been based.

Lengthy protocols of introspection appeared in the publications coming from Würzburg, as well as Cornell. They later spread to the publications of several other research centers. As the movement progressed during the first decade of the 20th century, however, attention to experimental controls became more and more lax. In 1907 Karl Bühler, a student of Külpe's, developed the *Ausfrage* (interrogation) method. In this procedure, subjects not only gave subjective introspections but also interpretations of those introspections.

The Ausfrage method, as well as the whole movement toward systematic introspection, was criticized in detail by Wundt (1907). In earlier articles (1883, 1888) he had attacked introspection on the grounds that it violates requirements of experimental procedure. The subsequent debate with Stumpf (described earlier) reinforced that position. As noted in the previous chapter, Wundt had also rejected Titchener's initial turn toward introspection (Wundt, 1900).

In the end, Wundt was only part of a large chorus of criticism directed at the systematic introspectionist movement. (This observation contradicts Titchener's, 1912, portrayal of introspection as the pervasive and monumentally successful method of psychology.) Illustrations of the dimensions and early date of that reaction include critiques by Cattell (1904), Thorndike (1905), Judd (1907), Pillsbury (1911), Dunlap (1912), and Dodge (1912). Their remarks were directed mostly against Titchener and James, with some mention of the Würzburg work in later papers. All of the critiques that appeared in American journals are rather short and superficial compared with the critiques in the European literature. Aside from Wundt, other critics included Munsterberg (1900), Ebbinghaus (1902), Michotte (1907), von Aster (1908), Sauze (1911), Gemelli (1911), and Müller (1911-1913).

An especially interesting critique was written by Müller who takes pains to examine variations of the introspective technique to determine how it might be made more valid and reliable. In anticipation of later methodological developments, he analyzes the "demand characteristics" of experiments, particularly in Bühler's *Ausfrage* method and suggests that a subject may subtly respond to the interests or biases of the experimenter.

Under the weight of this criticism, the introspectionism that had blossomed in the hands of Titchener and Külpe at the turn of the century largely faded. Its demise predated the appearance of the famous paper by John B. Watson (1913) that founded the behaviorist movement (see Chapter 6, this volume), a movement that portrayed itself as *the* reaction against the introspectionists. In fact, however, the battle between behaviorism and introspectionism was over before it began. By 1910, Külpe had resigned his position at Würzburg to go to the university in Bonn. His interests were again changing. In the following year he went to the University of Münich, where he died prematurely in 1915. Bühler, his former student and then a colleague at Münich, continued as a prolific theorist, writer, and psycholinguist but never again performed laboratory experiments, introspective or otherwise. At Cornell, Titchener remained isolated; his introspectionist movement held no appeal for other Wundtians teaching in American universities. We now consider a dedicated and strict experimentalist who remained true to the technical training he received in Leipzig.

August Kirschmann

In 1890, Wundt appointed Kirschmann as a second assistant, along with Külpe. Throughout his life, Kirshchmann remained a loyal Wundtian, a loyalty that Wundt repaid well when Kirschmann fell on hard times as a result of World War I (see below).

Unlike Külpe, Kirschmann persevered in a rather narrow focus as an experimentalist. Most of his work involved visual perception, but he was also an effective ambassador for the new psychology. His Ph.D. came from Wundt in 1890, and in 1893 he was recruited by the University of Toronto to develop experimental psychology there.

During the 1880s, the Toronto administration had made a policy decision to give strong support to laboratory science, including psychology. Toronto's philosophy department was particularly interested in Wundt's work, having hired James Mark Baldwin in 1889 primarily on the strength of Baldwin's having spent time with Wundt. But Baldwin was not by temperament an experimentalist, and he managed only to organize a small demonstration laboratory at Toronto before he left for a position at Princeton.

Kirschmann provided a strong contrast with Baldwin, for during his 16 years at Toronto, Kirschmann never let up in a relentless and usually successful campaign to expand the experimental program. Eventually, he met with some disaffection on the part of the parent philosophy department after it had come under the influence of George Brett, whose reaction to the new psychology followed the pattern of James's reactions at Harvard. Just as James had derided what he called "brass instrument" psychology, so Brett derided what he called "shirt sleeves" psychology.

Men like Müller, Wundt, Kirschmann, and many others shared one characteristic that was critically important for the survival of the new psychology: They fought tooth and nail for every inch of space in their universities and for every penny of support for their new science. Thus in the early literature there sometimes appears to be an exaggerated emphasis on material successes, with entire journal articles devoted to the description of laboratory space and instruments.

One tactic that Kirschmann employed was to overspend his equipment budget. In his first year at Toronto, he ordered equipment that cost twice his allotment (Marshall, 1980). After continually pressuring the Ontario Ministry of Education to provide funds for more assistants to help run the growing laboratory, he soon had three full-time assistants. By the year 1900, his laboratory was nearly as large as Wundt's. Its 16 rooms included darkroom facilities, special rooms for acoustic studies and photometry, and a specialized library. Much of the work from his laboratory appeared in the *University of Toronto Studies: Psychological Series* (Volume I covered the years 1898-1900).

Kirschmann's own research was limited principally to studies of visual brightness and color contrast. His teaching and research, however, were widely recognized as unsurpassed for methodological rigor, if not for theoretical significance. It was said that no student at Toronto passed through a course of research without learning to specify measurement procedures and experimental parameters. In a harsh judgment of that work, Titchener later wrote that Kirschmann was "incapable" of ever doing any theoretical psychology (Roback, 1952).

Seldom is the early Toronto work mentioned in textbooks today. One reason may be that the laboratory fell upon hard times (there was a period, after Kirschmann, when Toronto had no psychology program). The decline paralleled Kirschmann's own personal exhaustion. From the day he arrived, he drove himself to his physical limits, so that in 1909 he fell seriously ill and returned to Germany for a slow convalescence. He was still in Germany when World War I began, and under a cloud of hostility toward German nationals, Toronto terminated his professorship. In the years following 1909, the Toronto laboratory languished. During the war and for some years after, it was used as a veterans' rehabilitation center.

In 1915 Wundt located Kirschmann in Germany—unemployed, broken in health, and impoverished. Wundt (1915) wrote to Külpe about this situation, proposing to help Kirschmann by taking him on as a private assistant to be paid from his own (Wundt's) pocket. This he did, eventually arranging for a formal appointment at the Leipzig Institute, where Kirschmann remained in recovered health until his death in 1932. In his later years he resumed his research and in 1930 was honored in a formal celebration at the institute.

We now consider briefly one other Leipzig researcher, a man who served longer than any other as assistant to Wundt (from 1900 to 1917). The fact that he and his voluminous experimental work are so little known today is itself something of historical puzzle.

Wilhelm Wirth

Wirth began his advanced education at Munich in the mid-1890s under Theodore Lipps, a phenomenologist close to Brentano, and the philosopher Hans Cornelius, who was concerned with demonstrating the emotional basis of consciousness. Wirth met Schumann at a psychological congress and became inspired by Schumann's enthusiasm for experimental work. A short time later Wirth sent to Wundt a refutation and correction of Wundt's account of color contrast phenomena. Wundt's response was to invite Wirth to come to Leipzig to complete his dissertation there.

In Leipzig, Wirth confronted the hostile character of Robert Müller, then Wundt's primary assistant. Formerly the ablest student of physiologist Ewald Hering and a recipient of special recognition for an uncommonly high score on a state examination in physiology, Müller had been chosen by Wundt to develop the new Leipzig research program on emotion. It was intended that he would develop physiological measures of the dimensions of emotion.

Unfortunately, Robert Müller turned out to be an arch materialist who worked against the treatment of psychology as an independent science. He apparently took the Leipzig job with the intent of subverting the scientific psychology movement. His effect on the laboratory, however, was not entirely negative. According to Wirth's (1936) autobiography, by challenging the Leipzig students with the claim that psychology should be folded into physiology, Müller provoked them to defend their work in ways they might not otherwise have conceived. In Wirth's case this episode provided a strong stimulus to the experimental work in which he persevered for the rest of his life. In 1900, Robert Müller left Leipzig to take up private medical practice, and Wirth was appointed as his replacement.

One reason that Wirth is not well known in English-speaking academic communities is that his work came late in the Wundtian era, at a time when the home of experimental psychology was shifting from Germany to the United States, where it became more and more isolated and ingrown. Another reason is the difficulty of finding unifying or common themes in Wirth's work; it is not easy to know just what he stood for. Still another reason is that although Wirth was prolific, his writing style was difficult, and none of his work was translated.

One masterful achievement that stands out in Wirth's career is a book in which several years of his experimental studies are summarized. Its title can be translated as *The Experimental Analysis of the Phenomena of Consciousness* (1908). The book follows a long tradition of studying the "cognitive span" (now variously termed "perception span," "attention span," "apprehension span," or "absolute judgment span"). This phenomenon is well known today because of George Miller's (1955) often-cited review, "The Magical Number Seven Plus or Minus Two," although it is not clear how much attention was paid to the same phenomenon in the early days of experimental psychology. So far, Wirth's book remains the longest single work devoted to this topic.

Only Charles Spearman (1927, 1937) has summarized Wirth's work for the English-speaking community. Wirth was especially competent in quantitative and statistical techniques, and he may have lifted the level of research in the Leipzig laboratory a notch or two on that score. His quantitative interests had a strong effect on Spearman, who received his Ph.D. from Wundt in 1904 after working closely with Wirth as a doctoral student. Spearman later became a particularly astute observer of the spread of experimental psychology in the United States, a matter to which we now turn.

AMERICAN VARIATIONS

The 1890s saw an influx of experimental psychology to the United States. In 1892, an especially prominent year in this development, students trained by Wundt were appointed to develop laboratores at several American universities. Hugo Münsterberg, wooed by William

James, came to Harvard in 1892 to build a new laboratory there. At Yale, there was George Trumbull Ladd; he had not been trained by Wundt, but his *Elements of Physiological Psychology* (1887) resembles Wundt's (1874) book of the same name. Ladd's book was revised by Robert S. Woodworth in 1911 and thus influenced Woodworth's highly successful *Experimental Psychology* (1938). Ladd in turn selected Wundt's student Edward W. Scripture to organize a laboratory at Yale in 1892. That same year, Cornell attracted Edward B. Titchener to expand the fledgling laboratory founded a year earlier by Wundt's student, Frank Angell, who went to Stanford to found another laboratory. Finally, Cattell returned from his European wanderings to develop experimental psychology first at the University of Pennsylvania and then at Columbia.

In 1893, the arrival of this new science in America was celebrated at the Chicago World's Fair in a pavilion devoted to the field's apparatus and other accomplishments (see Baldwin, 1894). This display was apparently designed to emphasize practical applications.

As the new psychology spread through American universities, some Europeans who observed and commented on the movement viewed it more as a distortion than a direct transplant (e.g., Wundt, 1913; Spearman, 1930). The reason for such harsh assessments was the American tendency to blur the distinction between science and technology, a difference that was deeply ingrained in German academia. Most of Wundt's American students, fresh from Leipzig, turned to some form of "psychotechnology" soon after their return. We now examine the case of a native German who came to Harvard with the best of credentials as a theoretician, and who quickly conformed to American technological and commerical interests.

Hugo Münsterberg

Of all the new arrivals mentioned earlier, the best known and most profusely cited for his innovative work in 1892 was Münsterberg. When he arrived at Harvard, he was made chairman of the philosophy division, which included psychology, and given a large budget for the development of the psychology laboratory. In 1898 he was elected president of the American Psychological Association.

Münsterberg was one of the first to enthusiastically endorse the James-Lange theory of emotion (i.e., that emotion is the felt reaction of visceral organs). This attitude reflected a move away from his teacher, Wundt. Münsterberg was also caught up in the Machian positivism of the 1880s and 1890s, but he provided an interesting variation on it that earned him a good measure of recognition and respect (most of which faded after the turn of the century).

Münsterberg changed the Machian fundamentals in one significant way: Rather than taking the elementary *sensation* as the fundamental unit of psychology, he proposed using the elementary *action*. An action was conceived as an integrated sensory–motor unit; hence, his psychological system was named *Aktionstheorie*. It could be viewed as a significant step toward behaviorism, even though Münsterberg's works (particularly his more philosophical writings) retained overriding elements of German idealist philosophy. His experimental work consisted mostly of variations and extensions of the Leipzig mental chronometry program, but with more emphasis on the sensory–motor arc than the mental states. Contrary to Wundt, Münsterberg, in his doctoral dissertation, located volition in sensory–motor actions.

The group of people who worked and studied with Münsterberg at Harvard were briefly known as the "objectivist" school, a description that he suggested. Members included Robert Yerkes, Knight Dunlap, Richard Elliot, Edward Tolman, Mary Calkins, and E. B. Holt. All were later well known and influential, and their works contain elements of early behaviorism. As students, of course, they had all listened to Münsterberg's *Aktionstheorie* lectures.

Münsterberg's influence was soon tainted and diminished by the political and social entanglements that gradually eroded his academic life. He had become a much-sought-after consultant to government and business, and was thus widely known socially. This position led, somewhat ironically, to popular caricatures of him as the stereotypical authoritarian Prussian professor. In fact, Münsterberg's involvement in a heavily commercial applied psychology was something of a scandal in the academic community at the turn of the century. His writings in English, unlike those in German, mostly concern forms of applied psychology, including psychotherapy, industrial psychology, legal psychology, and the psychology of the cinematic arts. (The latter work landed him in Hollywood as the guest of early movie stars.)

Münsterberg eventually became a social utopian, offering prescriptions for the perfect society (see Hale, 1980). His protobehaviorist views reappeared in his suggestions that the just society may be attainable through scientific behavior controls, particularly the scientific administration of rewards and punishments. As a result, Münsterberg found himself the subject of cartoons in the popular press, turning fame into embarrassment. He died suddenly in 1916 in the pathos of his desperate public appeals to prevent the war with Germany.

Although he was a prolific writer and played an important role in importing German experimental psychology to Harvard, Münsterberg's productivity as a theoretical and experimental psychologist largely declined after he entered the United States. For a brief time he was the most visible and widely known representative of experimental psychology in American society, but soon thereafter it tried hard to forget him. Nevertheless, he left a strong impression of the new discipline as very much an applied science, albeit a distortion of the psychology of Wundt and Müller. By becoming an applied psychologist, however, Münsterberg seemed to be following another powerful representative of experimental psychology who also emphasized applications—namely, G. Stanley Hall. In 1912, Hall wrote: "We need a psychology that is usable, that is dietetic, efficient for thinking, living and working, and although Wundtian thoughts are now so successfully cultivated in academic gardens, they can never be acclimated here, as they are antipathetic to the American spirit and temper" (p. 414).

Edward Bradford Titchener

We now return to the complex issue of instrospectionism in experimental psychology. As in the case of Müller, we gain some insight into an historical trend by examining the personal and cultural background of a particular individual. In doing so, I do not wish to endorse the "great man" theory of history. However, if there was ever an individual who influenced (indeed, dominated) a moment in intellectual history, it could well be Titchener, who eclipsed even the colorful personality of Münsterberg.

Titchener was not typical of those who founded American experimental psychology in the 1890s. He maintained the image of a 19th-century aristocratic Oxford scholar when others were rapidly moving toward the image of modern twentieth-century man, putting aside 19th-century manners in favor of the styles of technicians and pragmatists. That is, he held to a certain aloofness from the common man, seeing the academic life as a place for men of social breeding. As a result, Titchener remained rather isolated at Cornell, though his theatrical teaching style attracted a great many students.

As with Wundt, Müller, Münsterberg, and others, cultural and personal backgrounds strongly shaped Titchener's intellectual development. Titchener's background in an old English family, combined with his classical Oxford education, reinforced his nineteenth-century attitudes and manners, as well as his commitment to Oxford philosophy. (When he arrived at Cornell, he would not accept a dinner invitation from Cornell's president unless it was hand-delivered by a coachman—a display of Oxford manners, if not Oxford philosophy.) His social frills, his precise and elaborate speech, and his wearing of academic robes had a powerful influence on some (see Boring, 1952), but others viewed him with cool skepticism (see Washburn, 1932).

After 6 years at Oxford, during which the psychological writings of James Mill and John Stuart Mill were his guides, Titchener went to Leipzig (1890–1892) to obtain his Ph.D. in psychology (there was no such degree program in England). Unfortunately, there was no place for him in England after he received the Leipzig degree. We now review some of the differences that developed between Titchener and Wundt.

As noted earlier, an important tenet in Wundt's system was the distinction between physical science and mental science, which Wundt defined wholly in psychological terms: The physical sciences, on the one hand, concern the *contents* of experience, even though these may be at times only the products of our conceptual processes. The mental sciences, on the other hand, concern the *processes* of experience—the operations that create experience (involving such processes as selective attention, creative synthesis, and cognitive spans). Titchener, following Mach, eliminated this distinction and defined psychology as merely another form of examining the contents of experience. Thus Titchener never adopted Wundt's "voluntarism," instead proposing "structuralism" to describe his psychology of mental contents (Titchener, 1898). In the preface to his *Outline* (1896), he notes the strong dependence of his views on British empiricism, particularly that of James Mill (1829) and John Stuart Mill (1865).

Trained introspection

Titchener's use of introspection as an experimental technique began in the late 1890s. He described it as a technique developed mostly in the first decade of the 20th century (Titchener, 1912), although his particular approach followed the prescriptions for introspection laid down much earlier by James Mill. This approach had its greatest impact on American psychologists through Titchener's widely used *Laboratory Manuals* (1901–1905).

With the rapid development of experimental psychology in the United States early in the twentieth century, texts like this were sorely needed for the training of graduate students, and Titchener's were by far the best of their kind for approximately two decades. In an opening chapter of one of his manuals, Titchener developed the notion of trained introspection: In many psychological experiments, subjects should, he thought, be specially trained to observe their sensations and feelings. In addition, reports of experiences were to be carefully controlled and guided by instructions to avoid references to the external world, so as to focus introspections entirely on subjective sensations. Later, historical summaries often attributed Titchener's introspective procedure to his brief contact with Wundt, but careful examination of the Wundtian literature reveals not only no evidence for such an interpretation but also show Wundt's opposition to Titchener's introspectionism. (see Chapter 2, this volume). The proportion of Titchener's *Manuals* that concerns introspection is actually quite small; for the most part, the books present an excellent summary of experimental work—the best work from the late-nineteenth-century laboratories.

As noted earlier, the systematic introspectionist movement in Germany declined almost as rapidly as it appeared. In the United States it met its fate in one dramatic ceremony before the assembled psychologists at the American Psychological Association convention at Yale in 1913. Titchener's strongest devotee (see Boring, 1953) was then John Baird, who had introduced Titchener's introspectionism into the Clark University psychology department. With much advance publicity, Baird had arranged a public demonstration by his best trained introspectors before the entire convention at Yale. However, the spectacle was a dismal failure. Baird's introspectors, seated on stage, were presented with a variety of carefully controlled stimuli and then proceeded to give a dull, meaningless account of simple sensory elements that enlightened no one (see Boring's, 1953, eyewitness assessment).

Titchener's Legacy

Much has been written about Titchener—so much, in fact, that it may have distorted historical interpretation relative to other early psychologists. We are therefore interested in the comments of a careful observer of both Titchener and the American scene in his time, the comments of Leipzig-trained Charles Spearman of London University, who maintained close relations with both American and continental psychologists. In his autobiography Spearman (1930) recorded his reaction to Titchener, along with various remarks on American psychology in general:

> My negative reaction reached its highest intensity to that very remarkable, and, I believe, ill-fated man Titchener. . . . He has been the author and champion of a peculiar method of introspection. . . . Introspection degenerates into a sort of inward staring. . . . The ensuing harm was rendered still worse by his doctrine of "structuralism". . . . But Titchener had such extraordinary abilities and such an impressive personality, that these doctrines of his seem to have blocked the advance of psychology for many years. And even when they themselves eventually collapsed, it was only to give birth to reactionary extravagancies nearly as

> bad. Among these may be counted the initial excesses of Behaviorism, as also a
> part of what passes under the name of the doctrine of Gestalt. . . . I am brought
> back to Wundt with his epoch-making introduction of the experimental method.
> To him and to Galton I certainly own more than to anyone else. (pp. 331–333)

I conclude this review of the American scene with a look at the careers of two purely American experimentalists.

Resolute Experimentalists:
Edward Scripture and Raymond Dodge

Today it is often said that researchers limit their work to narrow specializations as a reaction to the enormous expansion of the field of experimental psychology in the twentieth century. However, studies of history suggest that a narrow research specialization reflects as much the temperament of the scientist as of the historical moment in which he or she works. Scripture and Dodge are good examples of this.

In 1890, the same year that Titchener arrived in Leipzig, Scripture also arrived to earn a Wundt Ph.D. However, the interests of these two men, their styles, even their definitions of psychology, were always different. After he came to Yale in 1892, Scripture competed unsuccessfully for recognition as the foremost representative of experimental psychology in the United States. In that competition, it seems that no one could stand up against the commanding personality of Titchener, nor against the popular press won by Münsterberg.

In personality, Scripture was almost the opposite of Titchener, being a champion of the common man and hoping to make psychology intelligible and available to all. His style was that of a businessman–promoter, his approach one of "boosterism." His two books furnish a strong sample of this spirit (*The New Psychology*, 1895, and *Thinking, Feeling, and Doing*, 1897). They also portray psychology as moving rapidly toward the precision of physics.

To achieve a semblance of such progress in psychology, Scripture's own research necessarily became more and more narrowly focused within his specialty of experimental phonetics; he was soon the authority on the technical aspects of measuring speech sounds. But as he increasingly focused on that problem, he drifted away from mainstream psychology. There is little of theoretical significance there, but one does find a tireless search for quantitative precision in data gathering.

Scripture's great self-confidence was abrasive to many who knew him; accordingly, he attracted few students. Carl Seashore (1930), a graduate student at Yale in the 1890s, remembers him as follows:

> I resented Scripture's frequent reference to the futility of getting psychology from
> books, especially his speaking lightly of Ladd and Sneath, from whom I felt that I

> was getting things far more valuable than this laboratory stuff. I did not see then
> what laboratory experiments were about. We spent a long time on experiments
> which seemed nearer to telegraphy than psychology (p. 247).

Scripture was dismissed from Yale in a storm of controversy in 1903. He then studied medicine in Munich, after which he accepted a professorship in experimental phonetics at the University of Vienna, returning to the U.S. only briefly for a period of private practice as a speech pathologist in New York. His last days were spent in retirement south of London.

The tensions expressed in Seashore's remembrance of Scripture were a symptom of deeper problems at Yale. In turn, Yale's situation was a microcosm of the wider struggle of experimental psychology to establish itself in the 1890s.

The Crisis of Departmental Organization

George Trumbull Ladd, head of the Yale philosophy and psychology department, was a classical nineteenth-century scholar with a broad background in philosophy. He was an ardent admirer of Wundt, and in that spirit he had hired Wundt's student, Scripture, to develop the Yale laboratory. From the beginning, however, tensions flared between the two men. Questions of authority came increasingly to the surface, with Scripture believing that his training in Leipzig granted him authority over all experimental projects. Moreover, Scripture found Ladd to represent a strain of old-fashioned interests and manners that the more rough-hewn Scripture rejected. Ladd, for his part, was markedly authoritarian, argumentative, and obsessively devoted to questions of command hierarchy within the university, placing himself high in that hierarchy by virtue of seniority.

Toward the end of the 1890s, Charles Hubbard Judd, another student of Wundt's also joined the Yale laboratory, further complicating the question of authority over laboratory work. Judd had been the translator of Wundt's *Grundriss der Psychologie* (1896a), which had given him more direct contact with Wundt than any other American (except possibly Cattell). Thus Judd felt himself to be in a privileged position of special competence regarding interpretations of the new laboratory psychology. Still others in the Yale philosophy department resented the experimental laboratory altogether.

Political infighting, intrigues, and harsh gestures boiled over at the turn of the century, involving the Yale administration in prolonged and tedious disputes over the laboratory and its place in the philosophy department (see Mills, 1969). In 1903 Yale's president took strong action and dismissed Scripture, while authority over the laboratory was transferred from Ladd to Judd. Ladd then issued ultimatums that left the university no alternative but to dismiss him as well. Then Judd left, and remaining members of the department were reassigned to other departments. By 1904, Yale's philosophy and psychology department, including the laboratory, was gone. The entire episode was symptomatic of similar controversies taking place in other American (and European) philosophy departments that then housed the rapidly growing experimental psychology.

In summary, Scripture was a man who, at the turn of the century, gave an early indication of the style of 20th-century experimental psychology—of both its agressive temperament and the narrowing of the field to rigorous technical specializations.

Dodge and the Victory of Experimentalism

Raymond Dodge's career reflects a lifetime devotion to experimental science unsurpassed by any of his contemporaries. He was, above all, an apparatus man. In his own words, "Linguistic pursuits, including public speaking, are relatively difficult, while mechanical invention and the manipulation of instruments are pleasant and relatively successful" (Dodge, 1930, p. 99). His scientific effort remained at a high level throughout his career. It was , as he put it, "a persistent effort to record with accuracy the behavior of normal and abnormal human organisms at various levels of neural integration, and to describe and understand that behavior as to its conditions, its variations, and its modification as the various levels interact to produce overt acts" (1930, p. 121). (In that statement we have a foreboding of the writing style that came to dominate psychological journals later in the century, revealing a complete departure from the artful phrases of Titchener and James.)

As an undergraduate at Williams College in the 1890s, Dodge developed an early interest in the new psychology, but because of weaknesses in his undergraduate record, he was denied admission to the experimental psychology programs in several American graduate schools. Thus he ended up at the University of Halle in Germany, studying with the philosopher–psychologist Benno Erdmann and receiving the Ph.D. from Erdmann in 1896.

Erdmann was enthusiastic about the movement toward experimentalism in psychology, and was eager to develop that work at Halle, in spite of limited resources. In Dodge he found the instrument to achieve that end. Although Erdmann was well read in the new psychology, he was not adept at laboratory experimentation. Dodge's native genius for that type of work perfectly complemented Erdmann's more theoretical and verbal talents, for Dodge was especially skillful at improvising apparatus out of whatever materials happened to be available. Indeed, he dazzled Erdmann and the Halle technicians with his ability to solve instrumentation problems.

Erdmann became interested in the psychology of reading, which called for improved tachistoscopes and other instruments for measuring eye movement. Dodge tackled these problems and made them the focus of his work for the rest of his life. Soon his new advances in instrumentation, as well as a book that in translation would be titled *Psychological Investigations of Reading* (Erdmann & Dodge, 1898), secured Dodge's career. The book was the first of several collaborations with Erdmann and others that are now classics in research on the psychology of reading. These investigations worked out the basic principles of eye movement that are still acknowledged today.

Photographic recordings of eye movement by means of a beam of light reflected off the cornea constituted Dodge's most clever technical achievement. It made possible the first accurate measurements of the angular velocities during saccadic and pursuit movements. As his career evolved, the measurement of eye movement became a common tool for Dodge in the study of a variety of psychological problems. He found that subtle changes in eye movement patterns can indicate mental fatigue, alcohol intoxication, changes of phase in manic depressive psychosis, states of schizophrenia, brain tumors, and various sensory–neuromuscular disorders.

From 1897 to 1923, Dodge pursued a productive career in research at Wesleyan University, although his teaching ability was, by his own admission, rather limited. In those years he dreamed of founding a "college of mental engineering"—a dream that never materialized. In 1923 he was called to Yale by its new president, psychologist James Rowland Angell, to help restore the spirit of experimentalism that had been abandoned 20 years earlier because of the Ladd-Scripture controversy.

Dodge's talents blossomed with the opportunities presented by military research during World War I. The depth of his involvement, measured by the sheer number of military projects he undertook, may have been greater than that of any other experimental psychologist during the war, and he received a special commendation from the U.S. Navy for helping to solve many problems of man–machine systems and personnel selection. At the end of his life he speculated, perhaps rather naively, about the application of his experimental achievements in human factors engineering to one further problem—namely, gathering data "as to the fundamental positive conditions of protracted happiness." In Dodge's (1930) view, "Positive scientific data on the real conditions [of happiness] are as inconspicuous as scientific interest in the problem" (p. 120).

If Scripture was a sign of the coming style of twentieth-century experimental psychology, then it surely had arrived in the form of Dodge. Who could be cited as a better model of the enthusiasm for innovations in apparatus and technique, and of the coalescence of scientist and engineer, so characteristic of this field today?

A VIEW FROM THE PRESENT

With the rapid growth of experimentalism at the turn of the century, psychology attracted a new kind of person, one with a set of interests, talents, and temperaments that differed from the characteristics more common to the scholars of the nineteenth century. Those earlier scholars, including Wundt, had venerated philosophical training and the classics. In contrast, those who received the torch of the new psychology and carried it into the 20th century belonged to the new age of method, technique, analysis, and apparatus. Because of these differences, the rise of experimentalism was assured only after a fitful struggle.

Although Wundt, James, Ladd, and Titchener surely differed among themselves, they all honored nineteenth-century traditions and styles. In contrast, Müller, Kirschmann, Scripture, and Dodge are good examples of men who were uncomfortable with those older traditions. Scripture was even contemptuous of "book learning." To him, the path to truth was to be found in the laboratory.

The styles and interests of the newer experimentalists strongly affected the content of the new psychology; problems that did not submit easily to experimental manipulation were often neglected. Topics such as volition, aesthetics, emotion, consciousness, attention, and motivation are difficult to approach in the laboratory, whereas learning, memory, sensation, and perception are more easily operationalized. The very conception of certain psychological processes may have been constrained by available experimental techniques.

Experimental psychologists today stand upon territory hard won by the early pioneers who once struggled against heavy odds. Their tenacious efforts in creating laboratories eventually paid off handsomely in the form of a firmly established discipline, and yet the later generations who so rewarded and elevated experimentalism in psychology were also quick to forget the early experimentalists. The names of Külpe and Titchener are known because of the theoretical implications of their work, or because of their influence as teachers and polemicists. However, the lesser known Müller, Schumann, Kirschmann, Wirth, Scripture, and Dodge were more dedicated experimentalists—all technical virtuosos with effective apparatus and research procedures—and there were many others like them. In many instances, their techniques and findings remain valid by present standards.

The lack of attention to this early work was partly the result of the succession of "revolutionary" movements or redefinitions of psychology (e.g., behaviorism, Gestalt psychology, and cognitive psychology) that often too rashly and quickly dismissed previous work. In one sense, however, experimentalism suffered from its own success: The body of data that it produced has grown so large as to obscure its origins. That is a shame, for the heroic efforts of the early experimentalists gave a sound advantage to the new science in its struggle for life. Unfortunately, those efforts produced data that were sometimes forgotten, only to be reproduced unwittingly years later (see Blumenthal, 1977).

At the turn of the century, the success of the experimentalist movement was, as noted earlier, by no means assured. The Yale collapse involving Ladd and Scripture is a poignant example of that early uncertainty. Another is the unrewarded effort of Kirschmann at Toronto. If Müller had not sacrificed his personal funds at Göttingen, his laboratory probably could not have set such an example of methodological rigor. Wundt had second thoughts and fears about the rapid growth of experimentalism in psychology, but if he had not been a tireless promoter of the Leipzig laboratory, it might have remained the small room of 1879. Similarly, if Titchener had not been a dedicated textbook writer, English-speaking psychologists might have long floundered without an adequate laboratory manual.

After several tumultuous decades, the experimentalist and the applied psychologist, rather than the theoretician, are now atop the status hierarchy in psychology, reversing the hierarchy of the late 19th century. This is particularly true in the United States, where the majority of psychologists reside. Further evidence is the elite Society of Experimental Psychologists and the select Psychonomic Society. Other psychological societies concerned with special subjects such as social psychology or child development typically place a notable emphasis on experimentalism. The American Psychological Association, originally a small and select group of theoreticians, has a huge membership composed mostly of applied psychologists—in one sense a monument to its erratic early president, Hugo Münsterberg.

Because we are far advanced in the program established by the early experimentalists, we can afford to ask whether that program could go too far in overwhelming its old adversary, philosophical and theoretical psychology. Sophisticated courses in methodology are now required of every psychology graduate, but there is no comparable requirement for the theoretical and philosophical foundations of psychology, and few students study the technical aspects of theory construction or theory evaluation (the analysis of explanatory power, generality, parsimony, testability, etc.). Could it be that as methodology has become more and more precise, skills in theorizing have fallen behind? May increasing methodological precision be accompanied by theoretical laxity? Have many experimentalists adopted, at least implicitly, the problematic stance that good science should do without theory and philosophy altogether—a stance that could lead to ideational sterility?

The numerous publications offering new data, the newly founded journals, the maze of methdological techniques taught to graduate students, and the heavy research handbooks all threaten to suffocate the researcher. Sheer data gathering in the manner of Müller, Kirschmann, Wirth, Scripture, and Dodge must at some point become self-defeating. That point is reached when data are piled so high that we can no longer see the work done in an earlier time, so that we unwittingly repeat earlier discoveries and reinvent earlier inventions. If experimentalists continue to cultivate a tradition of ignoring the past, they only weaken their own potential influence on the future, for their present work will surely be buried and lost to future generations.

REFERENCES

Ach, N. (1905). *Ueber die Willenstättigkeit und das Denken.* Göttingen: Vandenhoeck, Ruprecht.

Aster, E. von (1908). Die psychologische Beobachtung und experimentelle Untersuchungen von Denkvorgangen. *Zeitschrift für Psychologie, 49,* 56–107.

Baldwin, J. M. (1894). Psychology past and present. *Psychological Review, 1,* 363–391.

Blumenthal, A. L. (1977). *The process of cognition.* Englewood Cliffs, NJ: Prentice-Hall.

Boring, E. G. (1950). *A history of experimental psychology* (2nd ed.). New York: Appleton-Century-Crofts.

Boring, E. G. (1952). Autobiography. In C. Murchison (Ed.), *A history of psychology in autobiography* (Vol. 4). Worcester, MA: Clark University Press.

Boring, E. G. (1953). A history of introspection. *Psychological Bulletin, 50,* 169–189.

Bühler, K. (1907). Tatsachen und Probleme zu einer Psychologie der Denkvorgänge. *Archiv für die gesamte Psychologie, 9,* 297–369.

Cattell, J. M. (1904). The conceptions and methods of psychology. *Popular Science Monthly, 66,* 176–186.

Claparéde, E. (1935). Georg-Elias Müller. *Archiv für Psychologie, 25,* 110–114.

Dodge, R. (1912). The theory and limitations of introspection. *American Journal of Psychology, 23,* 214–229.

Dodge, R. (1930). Autobiography. In C. Murchison (Ed.), *A history of psychology in autobiography* (Vol. 1). Worcester, MA: Clark University Press.

Dunlap, K. (1912). The case against introspection. *Psychological Review, 19,* 404–413.

Ebbinghaus, H. (1885). *Ueber das Gedächtnis.* Amsterdam: Bonset.

Ebbinghaus, H. (1902). *Grundzüge der Psychologie.* Leipzig: Veit.

Erdmann, B., & Dodge, R. (1898). *Die psychologischen Untersuchungen über das Lesen auf experimentelle Grundlage.* Halle: Niemeyer.

Fechner, G. (1860). *Elemente der Psycho-Physik.* Leipzig: Breitkopf, Härtel.

Fechner, G. (1882). *Revision der Hauptpunkte der Psycho-physik.* Leipzig: Breitkopf, Härtel.

Gemelli, F. (1911). L'introspecione sperimentale nello studio del pensiero e della volontà. *Rivista di Psicologie Applicare, 7,* 289–310.

Hale, M. (1980). *Human science and social order: Hugo Münsterberg and the origins of applied psychology.* Philadelphia: Temple University Press.

Hall, G. S. (1912). *Founders of modern psychology.* New York: Appleton.

Helmholtz, H. von. (1866). *Handbuch der physiologischen Optik.* Leipzig: Voss.

Jaensch, E. R. (1935). Was wird aus dem Werk? Betrachtungen über G. E. Müller. *Zeitschrift für Psychologie, 134,* 191–218.

Judd, C. H. (1907). *Psychology: General introduction.* Boston: Ginn.

Katz, D. (1935). G. E. Müller. *Psychological Bulletin, 32,* 377–380.

Kiesow, F. (1930). Autobiography. In C. Murchison (Ed.), *A history of psychology in autobiography* (Vol. 1). Worcester, MA: Clark University Press.

Köhler, W. (1925). Komplextheorie und Gestalttheorie: Antwort auf G. E. Müller's Schrift gleichen Namens. *Psychologische Forschung, 6,* 358–416.

Külpe, O. (1893). *Grundriss der Psychologie.* Leipzig: Englemann.

Ladd, G. T. (1887). *Elements of physiological psychology.* New York: Scribner's.

Ladd, G. T., & Woodworth, R. (1911). *Elements of physiological psychology* (rev. ed.). New York: Scribner's.

Lindenfeld, D. (1978). Oswald Külpe and the Würzburg school. *Journal of the History of the Behavioral Sciences, 14,* 132–141.

Lorenz, C. (1890). Untersuchungen über die Auffassung von Tondistanzen. *Philosophische Studien, 6,* 26–103.

Mach, E. (1886). *Die Analyse der Empfindungen und das Verhältnis des Physischen zum Psychischen.* Jena: Fischer.

Mandler, G., & Mandler, J. (1964). *Thinking: From association to Gestalt.* New York: Wiley.

Marshall, M. (1980). The influence of Wundt's students in Canada: A Kirschmann. In W. Meischner & A. Metge (Eds.), *Wilhelm Wundt—progressives Erbe, Wissenschaftsentwicklung und Gegenwart.* Leipzig: Karl-Marx-Universität.

Metzger, W. (1940). Friedrich Schumann: Ein Nachruf. *Zeitschrift für Psychologie, 148,* 1–18.

Metzger, W. (1965). The historical background for national trends in psychology: German psychology. *Journal of the History of the Behavioral Sciences, 1,* 109–115.

Michotte, A. (1907). A propos de la méthode d'introspection dans la psychologie expérimentale. *Revue Néoscolastique, 14,* 507–532.

Mill, J. (1829). *Analysis of the phenomena of the human mind.* London: Baldwin, Cradock.

Mill, J. S. (1865). *August Comte and positivism.* London: Routledge.

Miller, G. A. (1955). The magical number seven plus or minus two: Some limits on our capacity for processing information. *Psychological Review, 63,* 81–97.

Mills, E. (1969). *George Trumbull Ladd.* Cleveland: Case-Western Reserve University Press.

Müller, G. E. (1873). *Zur Theorie der sinnlichen Aufmerksamkeit.* Leipzig: Edelmann.

Müller, G. E. (1878). *Zur Grundlegung der Psychophysik.* Berlin: Grieben.

Müller, G. E. (1911–1913). *Zur Analyse der Gedächtnistätigkeit und des Vorstellungsverlaufes.* Leipzig: Barth.

Müller, G. E. (1923). *Komplextheorie und Gestalttheorie: Ein Beitrag zur Wahrnehmungspsychologie.* Göttingen: Vandenhoeck, Ruprecht.

Müller, G. E. (1924). *Abriss der Psychologie.* Göttingen: Vandenhoeck, Ruprecht.

Müller, G. E. (1926). Bemerkung zu W. Köhlers Artikel: "Komplextheorie und Gestalttheorie." *Zeitschrift für Psychologie, 99,* 1–15.

Müller, G. E. (1928). [Letter to E. G. Boring]. E. G. Boring papers, Department of Psychology and Social Relations, Harvard University.

Münsterberg, H. (1900). *Grundzüge der Psychologie.* Leipzig: Barth.

Pillsbury, W. (1911). *The essentials of psychology.* New York: Macmillan.

Roback, A. (1952). *A history of American psychology.* New York: Collier.

Rubin, E. (1915). *Synsoplevede figurer, studier i psykologisk analyse.* Copenhagen: Kristiania, Gyldendal, Nordisk.

Sauze, J. B. (1911). L'école de Wurtzbourg et la méthode d'introspection expérimentale. *Revue de Philosophie, 18,* 225–240.

Schumann, F. (1900–1904). Beiträge zur Analyse der Gesichtswahrnehmungen. *Zeitschrift für Psychologie, 23,* 1–32; *24,* 1–33; *30,* 241–291, 321–339; *36,* 161–185.

Scripture, E. (1895). *Thinking, feeling, doing.* New York: Putmans.

Scripture, E. (1897). *The new psychology.* New York: Scribner's.

Seashore, C. (1930). Autobiography. In C. Murchison (Ed.), *A history of psychology in autobiography* (Vol. 1). Worcester, MA: Clark University Press.

Sokal, M. (Ed.). (1981). *An education in psychology: James McKeen Cattell's journal and letters from Germany and England, 1880–1888.* Cambridge, MA: MIT Press.

Spearman, C. (1927). *The abilities of man.* New York: Macmillan.

Spearman, C. (1930). Autobiography. In C. Murchison (Ed.), *A history of psychology in autobiography* (Vol. 1). Worcester, MA: Clark University Press.

Spearman, C. (1937). *Psychology down the ages.* London: Macmillan.

Stumpf, C. (1890). Ueber Vergleichungen von Tondistanzen. *Zeitschrift für Psychologie, 1,* 419–485.

Stumpf, C. (1981a). Wundt's Antikritik. *Zeitschrift für Psychologie, 2,* 266–293.

Stumpf, C. (1981b). Mein Schlusswort gegen Wundt. *Zeitschrift für Psychologie, 2,* 438–443.

Stumpf, C. (1930). Autobiography. In C. Murchison (Ed.), *A history of psychology in autobiography* (Vol. 1). Worcester, MA: Clark University Press.

Thorndike, E. L. (1905). *The elements of psychology.* New York: Seiter.

Titchener, E. B. (1896). *An outline of psychology.* New York: Macmillan.

Titchener, E. B. (1898). The postulates of a structural psychology. *Philosophical Review, 7,* 449–465.

Titchener, E. B. (1901–1905). *Experimental psychology: A manual of laboratory practice* (4 vols.). New York: Macmillan.

Titchener, E. B. (1912). Prolegomena to a study of introspection. *American Journal of Psychology, 23,* 427–448.

Van Essen, J. (1935). G. E. Müller ter gedachtenis. *Nederlandsche Tijdschrift voor Psychologie, 3,* 48–58.

Washburn, M. F. (1932). Autobiography. In C. Murchison (Ed.), *A history of psychology in autobiography* (Vol. 2). Worcester, MA: Clark University Press.

Watson, J. B. (1913). Psychology as the behaviorist views it. *Psychological Review, 20,* 158–177.

Wirth, W. (1908). *Die experimentelle Analyse der Bewusstseinsphänomene.* Brunswick: Vieweg.

Wirth, W. (1936). Autobiography. In C. Murchison (Ed.), *A history of psychology in autobiography* (Vol. 3). Worcester, MA: Clark University Press.

Woodworth, R. (1938). *Experimental psychology.* New York: Holt.

Wundt, W. (1874). *Grundzüge der physiologischen Psychologie.* Leipzig: Englemann.

Wundt, W. (1883). Ueber psychologischen Methoden. *Philosophische Studien, 1,* 1–40.

Wundt, W. (1888). Selbstbeobachtung und innere Wahrnehmung. *Philosophische Studien, 4,* 292–309.

Wundt, W. (1891a). Ueber Vergleichungen von Tondistanzen. *Philosophische Studien, 6,* 605–640.

Wundt, W. (1891b). Eine Replik C. Stumpfs. *Philosophische Studien, 7,* 298–327.

Wundt, W. (1892). Auch ein Schlusswort. *Philosophische Studien, 7,* 633–636.

Wundt, W. (1896a). *Grundriss der Psychologie.* Leipzig: Englemann.

Wundt, W. (1896b). Ueber die Definition der Psychologie. *Philosophische Studien, 12,* 1–66.

Wundt, W. (1900). Bemerkungen zur Theorie der Gefühle. *Philosophische Studien, 15,* 149–182.

Wundt, W. (1907). Ueber Ausfrageexperimente und über die Methoden zur Psychologie des Denkens. *Psychologische Studien, 2,* 301–390.

Wundt, W. (1913). *Die Psychologie im Kampf ums Dasein.* Leipzig: Englemann.

Wundt, W. (1915). [Letter to Oswald Külpe]. Wundt archives, Karl-Marx-Universität, Leipzig.

4

Early Sources and Basic Conceptions of Functionalism

CLAUDE E. BUXTON

INTRODUCTION

Like many other terms that have been adopted by psychology from mathematics or the sciences, *functionalism* is not a very precise expression. It is now common in many fields of study or expression (e.g., sociology, architecture), but in psychology it was used in the early 1900s as a descriptive label for the point of view of certain psychologists and philosophers at the University of Chicago. The intellectual origins or roots of this viewpoint can be traced to earlier ideas in the United States and western Europe. In this chapter we examine early functionalism or the precursors of functionalism, while the following chapter deals with American functionalism. Each chapter covers a period of approximately a half century, before and after 1890, respectively.

A more informative definition of functionalism is contextual (Hempel, 1966; Mandler & Kessen, 1959): Its meaning is determined by associating it with terms that are already part of our psychological vocabulary. Consider the definition, "Functionalism is, in part, the view that actions are oriented toward goals." Add to that statement several others, some overlapping but different from each other, such as "In the view of functionalists, behavior is adaptive." Taken together, the statements become

85

a contextual definition of functionalism. There is no effort to point to the essence or the inherent meaning of a word thus defined. Rather, there is only a set of ways in which the word is used (Functionalism is the view that . . .) and which thereby constitute its meaning. It can be said that the two main purposes of this chapter and the next are (1) to use historical means to provide contextual meaning for the term *functionalism* and, in the process, (2) to describe the development of functionalism as a way of conceiving of psychology. (The problem of definition is of more concern in Chapter 4 than Chapter 5.) We begin with a brief look at some of the circumstances that produced both the Wundtian and the experimentalist views, as well as the precursors of what would finally come to be the accepted functionalist view.

EARLY PHILOSOPHICAL BACKGROUND OF FUNCTIONALISM

As indicated in Chapter 1, the roots of any point of view in psychology may be traced to ancient times. In this case, we extend those linkages only to the more recent past. During the latter half of the nineteenth century, psychology as we know it began to be identifiable and to flourish. Our next comments are limited, however, to the earliest part of that century.

Empiricist Philosophy

We begin by asking what this expression means. Three basic ideas are: First, like the rationalists, the empiricists were *mentalists;* that is, their philosophy was aimed at understanding the mental life. Second, the furnishings of mind (knowledge) come via the senses; that is, by way of experience. Just how this happens was the prime concern. It was here that empiricists and rationalists parted company. While rationalists argued that knowledge accrued from a reasoned analysis of sense data according to innately given laws of thought, empiricists argued that in the acquisition of knowledge the senses provided the primary data upon which all subsequent intellection must be based. The rationalists conceived of thought as being shaped by general concepts (e.g., quantity, quality, relations, and "modalities") that are not themselves formed in experience and that therefore exist logically prior to experience. The empiricists countered by saying that such categories of concepts and thought were themselves products of experience. The rationalists also claimed that objects are sensed inevitably in time and space (Can one conceive, they asked, of an object *not* located in time—in a present that implies a past and a future—or *not* located in space?), and thus that time and space also exist logically prior to experience. According to the empiricists, however, the learning process begins with undifferentiated initial impressions. Further experience then creates the dimensions of sensing, perceiving, and knowing, with this process resting on the principles of association.

Despite their emphasis on experience, almost all empiricists, including twentieth-century behaviorists (see Chapter 6, this volume), admitted that there are at least some innate (inherited, constitutional) determiners of the way mind develops and functions (the third basic idea of empiricism). Behaviorists like Watson were in fact claiming only that it would not be possible in their lifetime to bring certain supposed expressions of such determiners (instinct, intelligence, etc.) within the bounds of scientific psychology. Of course, if one chose to believe in such ideas outside of the laboratory, that was one's privilege. (This discussion is, of course, linked to the sturdy disagreement between two contesting views of man, with authors like Locke, Hume, and both of the Mills disputing Leibniz and Kant. See Blumenthal, 1977; Harré, Gundlach, Métraux, Ockwell, & Wilkes, Chapter 13, this volume; Robinson, 1981, Chapters 7, 8).

The empiricist view was congenial to and arose within the development of western scientific thought, and thus was involved in the increasing exploration of all realms of nature, including human nature, from the seventeenth century onward. As we trace the growth of functional psychology, with its empiricist philosophical roots, we can expect that views regarding the nature of science and its methods of dealing with evidence will be of central interest. After all, it is method, along with substance, that defines functionalism.

Psychological Philosophers

The empiricist tradition is identified by famous names in pre-nineteenth-century British philosophy, including Locke, Berkeley, Hume, Brown, and Hartley. There was also considerable acceptance of empiricist views in France, with a particular leaning toward materialism and a mechanistic view of human beings (see any general history of psychology or philosophy). The empiricist philosophy experienced notable developments during the 19th century due to the work of James Mill and culminated in the works of his son, John Stuart Mill. The younger Mill interacted intellectually with Alexander Bain, who was to become a major figure in early philosophical psychology. (In the latter expression, as in its coordinate, "psychological philosopher," the second word indicates the primary orientation or commitment, while the first acts as a qualifier.)

For James Mill (1829) the object of philosophical inquiry was the understanding of complex mental phenomena (vol. 1, p. 1). But to examine complexity, the simple had to be premised, and that was the elements of which the complex was formed. Accurate knowledge of the basic elements of mind is indispensable to accurate conceptions of what can be compounded from them. Mill (1829) considers two basic elements: sensations, which are the result of activity in the sensory organs (vol. 1, chap. 1), and ideas, which are initially traces or copies of sensation (vol. 1, chap. 2). Both sensations and ideas can be discriminated from one another by their respective qualities (e.g., the color blue, or the experience of pain). The discrimination of one sensation or idea from another of its kind is based on memory, as shown in Mill's (1829) notion that the familiarity of the horse's neigh made it different from the voice of the ox (vol. 1, p. 45). In addition to sense-based ideas, there are ideas originating in the brain, called thoughts. Conscious states are compounded of present sensations plus ideas of them (and thus, by implication, memories) as well as thoughts.

Given the elements of sensations and ideas, there must be a principle by which their interrelations and development can be established. It is known as *association*. Mill observed that sensations occur in an order determined by objects in nature, and that this order may be either synchronous or successive. According to him, ideas that are copies of sensations "spring up, or exist" in the same order as the original sensations occurred. This notion constituted the general law of the "association of ideas" (Mill, 1829, vol. 1, p. 56). Mill intended this expression to be only a label for the fact that ideas occurred in a certain order, implying no explanation or mechanism. Nevertheless, it has often been termed the "contiguity theory" of association.

The spirit of James Mill's thinking is clear. His analysis of the nature of mind begins with the assumption that, like the material world studied by physicists, the mind is also composed of parts in their lawful interrelations. Clearly, the principles of such interrelations are fundamental in discovering how the mind works—that is, what occurs as a person senses, acts, and thinks, as well as how association (learning, memory) is involved in all of these operations.

Most of the important ideas that the functionalists derived from British empiricism were embodied in the writings of James Mill. As a result, it is almost customary for psychological historians to slight his son, John Stuart, by saying that although the latter made great contributions to social thought (including feminist thought) and political economy, he contributed only one major psychological concept. This is not altogether unfair, and yet it is clear that his ideas were significant in other ways for the beginnings of functionalist thought. Nearly all the essentials are to be found in his *System of Logic* (Mill, 1843/1846, books 3 and 6). There is also useful commentary in his edition of his father's earlier volume (Mill, 1869).

The younger Mill's view of how simple ideas combine into complex ones was distinctive (and thus regarded as his "only" major contribution). Whereas James Mill's associationism was constructed along the lines of thought found in physics, his son, in the same spirit of adherence to the tenets of natural science, believed that associations behaved according to a different model—that of chemistry (Mill, 1843/1846, p. 533). We present two of his concrete examples: Seven prismatic colors may be presented in such rapid succession that white is seen. The seven colors are not actually white, but together they *generate* white. Similarly, a complex idea may be formed by blending together several simple ones (the idea of an orange, the fruit). Although it may appear to be *simple in itself* (on the basis of separate elements such as orange color, shape, odor, etc., not consciously distinguished), it should nevertheless be said to result from or to be *generated* by simple ideas, not *to consist* of them. Such cases, Mill concluded, are examples of mental chemistry.

This difference from James Mill's view of complex mental phenomena exposes an issue persisting to the present day—namely, whether (a) parts of a complex event are simply added together to construct (or explain) a whole or a unity, or (b) the latter is a different order of event requiring a different kind of law or conception for its explanation.

John Stuart Mill exerted additional influence stemming from his conviction that not only was psychology fit to become a science, but science itself was to be understood in a manner conforming to his logic. This belief we may justly call his philosophy of science. For him there was exact science—ideally exact in its knowledge of laws and in predictive power—and toward this status all natural sciences move. There was also the kind of science that drew upon exact laws, insofar as they were available or relevant, to explain empirical laws. The latter were approximate generalizations about specific observed phenomena that varied according to ideally exact or general laws. Such sciences yielded empirical propositions that were true in the main, or statistically true. From these propositions, with allowances for degree of probable inaccuracy, predictions might safely be drawn. In psychology, these predictions concerned conduct.

Empirical laws pertaining to or "averaged across" the conduct of a sample of persons were as defensible scientifically as the laws of, say, tidology, in which complex and partly unknown causal principles yielded statistically sound predictions (empirical laws) about tides at a particular location. However, any interpretation of character (personality) was far more complex and uncertain. Ethology (Mill's science of character) could only be arrived at deductively on the basis of the simple (ideal) laws previously found to explain empirical laws of behavior, and no ideal laws were as yet available in psychology. Thus, sheer complexity precluded direct experimental or observational methods in the study of personality.

The Millean conception of scientific procedure was prominent in the 1940s in the writings of, among others, Clark Hull (see Spence & Bergmann in Spence, 1960). Starting with empirical laws of behavior, Hull sought proof of more general postulates or theoretical laws (akin to Mill's ideally exact laws) that would explain the regularities in observations expressed in those empirical laws.

The younger Mill's view of the nature of science continues to be recognizable in psychology. One of its principal effects was to encourage the search for and the freedom to utilize any investigative methods (introspective or other) that would produce data showing lawful regularities—the sine qua non of empirical science. The result legitimated broadening the scope of scientific inquiry in psychology. (The notion that this kind of empiricist philosophy provided a basis for psychology has been challenged by Harré & Secord, 1972, Chapter 2; its technical shortcomings are discussed by Turner, 1965.)

It is clear that the search by the two Mills for simple elements and their modes of combination was a structural kind of beginning point (see the discussion of Titchener's views in Chapter 3, this volume), but the interests and beliefs of these two philosophers went beyond immediate, subjective experience in minds shaped only slightly by their innate characteristics. The Mills were oriented toward active, thinking people and their developing, largely modifiable nature. In spirit, this approach was a forecast of what was to be called the functionalist point of view, and the empiricist philosophers' influence was never to disappear from it.

BIOLOGY FOR PHILOSOPHERS

The kind of philosophy espoused by the two Mills, together with John Stuart Mill's view of psychology as a science, provided an important source for functionalist psychology, but of equal importance in the mid-

19th century was the growing conviction that biological knowledge must be integrated with philosophical psychology. This need was realized with respect to many relevant concepts and principles, methods of investigation (but not immediately), and the vaguely defined subject of explanations and causes. Evolutionary biology (to be discussed later, this chapter; see also Chapter 12, this volume) was of major importance in the history of psychology. However, its influence became visible after that of neurophysiology and its counterpart, neuroanatomy, and the latter will be discussed first.

It is of historical interest to review some of the knowledge readily available in the years just before Herbert Spencer (1855, 1870–1871) and Alexander Bain (1855, 1859) adopted a biological orientation in their early books on psychology. Following are summary statements about the "new" physical neurophysiology and the corresponding neuroanatomy upon which the emerging psychology drew. The books reviewed for this purpose, all medical textbooks, are Jones Quain's anatomy (1828/ 1849), William Carpenter's human physiology (1842/1843), Johannes Müller's elements of physiology (1834–1840/1839–1842), and Robert Todd and William Bowman's physiological anatomy and physiology (1845–1856). Bain cites these works generously, and Spencer refers to some of them.

Biology as an Example of Science

Certain modes of thought revealed in these books yield some insight into what made biological science interesting to writers of psychology books. For one thing, the conception of science reflected in biology (other than taxonomy) during this era had been taken from the prestigious physical sciences. Experimentation was becoming a valued investigative procedure, and the objectivism it implied was regarded as desirable by increasing numbers of scientists. Both clinical data and comparative studies were acceptable where available, but they too were received in an increasingly objective and critical way. Physiology as the fundamental science of life processes was taken as a conceptual model, and some parts of it were capable of being integrated with an aspiring science of psychology.

Rejection of Vitalism

Equally interesting to psychologically inclined scholars was the controversy about vitalistic explanations or theological final causes in the interpretation of biological functions. Some signs of vitalism linger in the biology books reviewed here, but it can be argued that even Müller, who is often described as a vitalist, combed it out of his scientific explanations and refused to commit himself unambiguously to it.

Philosophical psychologists were much aware of the knotty problems with vitalism: some of them, like the physiologists, preferred materialist reductionism.[1] In the mid-nineteenth century, anatomy found its explanations in the chemistry of tissues and organ systems; in turn, physiology was based on anatomy, as well as chemistry and the physics (e.g., optics, hydraulics, and mechanics) of bodily functions. Meanwhile, psychology was founded on physiology that had progressed far beyond what had been known to David Hartley (1749). The possibility was nowhere envisioned in contemporary medical sources that behavior could provide physically describable basic data for a science. In retrospect, however, we note that Bain used such data to seize an initial lead toward the modern behavioral formulation.

Broadly speaking, a reductionist aspiration lay behind the effort to identify in mentalistic conceptions such as volition or emotion some materialistic (i.e., physiological) foundation. By relating the psychological event to a bodily need or condition, such events could be brought into the realm of scientific explanation. The tension between mentalism and this kind of reductionism has usually been obvious in psychology books since the mid-nineteenth century. However, when psychologists or biologists lapsed into mentalism in using, say, association doctrine to explain how mind develops, the reduction was not always from the mental realm to materialist bodily events. Rather, there was an attempted reduction of observed introspective phenomena to laws describing the order and predictability found in the associative process.

One example makes it clear that Bain genuinely aspired to be a materialist. In order to explain remembering as it is known directly in introspection, he first sought to explain the growth of associations. The revealing sentence in his speculation is: "Whether the growth lies in forming new cells, or in modifying the internal conductibility of the nerve fibres and vesicles, we are unable to say; there is no reason why both effects should not take place" (Bain, 1855, p. 326). Many other examples from Bain could be given, especially in the fields to which neurophysiologists were contributing actively, such as sensory processes or emotion.

---

[1] *Reductionism* is used here to mean the definability of the concepts of one discipline in the terms of another, and the analogous derivability of the laws of one discipline from those of another [Mendelsohn, 1964; Smith, 1973]. "Materialist" signifies that scientific definitions and laws have reference only to events or phenomena of the physical world.

Assimilation of Biology to Psychology

Two tendencies characterized the initial convergence of philosophical psychology and biology. One was that both reductionism and "hard" scientific knowledge were favorably received by Spencer, Bain, and others who hoped to reduce, and in that sense explain, psychology by reference to physiology. Second, the extent to which biology could in fact be assimilated depended, then as now, on the clarity with which psychological problems could be formulated. Just as we now feel intuitively that vision and the other senses are more comprehensible because we understand their physical and biological characteristics, some early writers of psychology also found it easy and natural to see such information as a natural explanatory component of their own views. Extending this kind of thinking into psychophysics, depth perception and reaction time seemed appropriate. Indeed, the dominant cognitive emphasis of British empiricist philosophy at the time was congenial to the experimental findings on perceiving as a mode of knowing. In areas such as emotion or volition, the knowledge of philosophical psychologists was less precise and consequently more difficult to connect with physiology.

BIOLOGICAL ASSOCIATIONISM

Alexander Bain was by academic appointment a professor of English and Logic, but for much of his career he taught moral or mental philosophy, the label for philosophy of a psychological sort. He has been called the first psychologist, although much ink has been wasted in fruitless antiquarian argument over who was actually the first. (See Boring, 1950, Chapter 16; Watson, 1978, p. 218. Hearnshaw, 1964, Chapter 1, also has an instructive treatment of Bain's place in the history of psychology). The priorities may be arguable, but Bain did in fact come to prominence just as the analytic framework of associationist philosophy was being transformed into an identifiable discipline of psychology. His leading position thus makes him a reference figure for the beginning of modern psychology. Bain's volumes on *The Senses and the Intellect* (1855) and *The Emotions and the Will* (1859) were influential for most of a half-century and offer the best introduction to his views.

Consciousness and Behavior

Bain decided that mind was to be defined by means of its operations and appearances—or, more specifically, its capacities or attributes—feeling (comprising sensation and emotion), action, and thought (Bain,

1855, p. 1). These were all aspects of consciousness. However, "the consciousness of an act is manifestly not the act," and "the putting forth of power to execute some work or perform some operation is to us a mark of mind" (Bain, 1855, p. 2). That is, mental life encompasses all of consciousness and more ("more" referring to one's own mental actions observable by one's own consciousness or by others, and to the mental actions observable in others). In the next chapter we see that William James adopted a similar view.

Not only was Bain an introspectionist, but he usually used the language of conscious states. Nevertheless, as Hearnshaw (1964, pp. 10–11) makes clear, Bain's introspectionism was but one aspect of what he called his "natural history" method. Bain regarded the observation of others as indispensable; that is, his aim was to achieve a better (scientific) understanding of the human mind, beginning with his own. Toward this end, inferences or conclusions drawn from the observation of others were viewed as more dependable than purely subjective self-analysis. It is clear that Bain thought of mental events as processes, or ongoing activities, and in this respect he was not very different from Wundt (Blumenthal, 1975; see also Chapter 2, this volume).

Physiology and the Mind

In his preface to *The Senses and the Intellect*, Bain (1855) writes: "Conceiving that the time has now come when many of the striking discoveries of Physiologists relative to the nervous system should find a recognized place in the Science of Mind . . . " (p. v), thus establishing one of the most significant themes in his life's work. Before Bain, there had been a few highly speculative attempts at a neurophysiology of mind, notably that by Hartley (1749) in the preceding century. However, *The Senses and the Intellect* was the first approach based on a close study of the rapidly developing scientific physiology of the 1830s and 1840s. Bain devotes a long chapter and discussions elsewhere to the nervous system but elected to develop his psychology from a very different starting point than that of Mills. He begins, not with the major senses—sight, hearing—as did the empiricist philosophers who believed the senses to be the origin of knowledge and intellect, but rather with spontaneous random activity (attributable to body metabolism, appetite, or instinct) and feelings of movement (the muscle sense).

For Bain, motion was primordial (an innate tendency), antedating peripheral sensory experience. Through association, both movement and the muscle sense entered into and became components of all other sensory activity and experience. For example, sensations associated with eye muscle contractions are never absent from seeing, and sensations of movement or posture maintenance are always functional components of touch. To kinesthesis he gave the full status of the traditional senses, insisting that its mode of operation set it apart from "mere" passive sensing. This conception permitted a more complete interpretation of the association of movements, and of movement trains.

By relating the muscle sense to exercise and pleasure, to the "spontaneous" actions of babies, and to the discrimination of movements, Bain made activity, or behavior, central to psychology. Thereby he also balanced up the traditional associationist view. It had leaned toward the sensory or sensationist side of cognition, but Bain's interest in movement led him to create a sensory–motor associationism. He was not the first to do this (see Young, 1970, pp. 114–120), but he was foremost in connecting mentalistic associationism with behavioral and biological ideas.

Association

The biological bases of behavior (or mind, as he usually wrote) were systematically sought by Bain, thereby showing how James Mill's essentially mentalistic associationism had needed supplementation. Bain recognized that before associations can be established, there must be givens, starting points—something to be associated. Here he reflected the same logic that led Kantians to postulate a priori determiners or conditions of thought. This approach appeared, for example, in his comments on how instinctive (unlearned) cravings such as those for sleep or water are modified by education (i.e., experience).

Bain thought of association and association formation as fundamental life processes. He explicitly developed concepts that would displace the prevailing faculty psychology. The familiar law of contiguity was primary, in his view; it was directly qualified only by the principle of repetition (frequency), which he neglected to elevate to equal status, although he gives it quantitative form on the page containing his definition of contiguity (Bain, 1855, p. 318).

The third principle of association was similarity. Its presumed action during the process of repetition was this: The strengthening of an association by repetition is possible only insofar as a past condition or state is reinstated by a present (similar) one; only in this way can there be *re*association, with consequent strengthening.

A fourth principle, that of compound association (Bain, 1855, p. 544), recognized that associations activated in recall could vary in number. Associations involving emotion and volition might also combine with intellectual ones to enhance or obstruct recall. A subprinciple of obstructive association (interference) as a factor in forgetting was thus implied and made explicit later (1855, pp. 564–565). As a general rule, recall varied according to the number of positive associations involved in it (i.e., those not weakened by interference).

Finally, there was a fifth principle of constructive association. It was suggested, not as a basic law of the associative process, but as a formulation necessary to describe or explain imagination, creativity, and other innovative processes. This principle can now be seen as an effort to remedy the principal weakness of associationism, namely its essentially passive picture of the (active) organism. Bain, however, coupled it with motivational principles that were, for their time, relatively dynamic. He boldly, though not very successfully, analyzes creativity in art and the sciences (Bain, 1855, Book 2, Chapter 4).

Emotion

Bain argued forcefully that emotion involves widespread activity of the nervous system and most of the body. Mind—the human being—was first of all unitary in Bain's view. Thus, emotion was at every moment and in many ways part of an associative organization along with sensory processes, sensation, intellective processes, and volition.

Education (i.e., experience or association) can change emotional expressions. Natural outbursts of emotion have been greatly modified by the conventions of modern civilization. Not usually considered in this context is Bain's (1859) idea that "these changes in the allocation of the members that received the recoil of a state of mental exhilaration have no slight influence in changing the character of the consciousness; for it is not the original stimulus alone, but this, in conjunction with all the reflected waves, that determines the nature of the resulting mental condition" (pp. 14–15). Feedback from actions, then, can also influence consciousness in emotion. However, Bain did not claim, as James (1890/1950, Chapter 25) did later, that this process constituted the experience of emotion.

Volition

Bain's explanation of volition was unconventional. He interpreted it, not as the determination of choice or action by the (free) will or mind, but rather as voluntary action that could be explained in a wholly deterministic manner. His theory assumed that the development of voluntary action rested on spontaneous movements (mentioned earlier) present at or before birth.

From the Utilitarians Bain took his conviction that pleasure and pain are fundamental regulators of human conduct, and this notion he integrated with the association doctrine he inherited from his empiricist predecessors. According to Bain, pleasure and pain consequent upon or accompanying the occurrence of any association between external or internal circumstances and a spontaneous movement would selectively influence the likelihood that the sequence would recur. That is, pleasure and pain would shape the development of tendencies to act in specific rather than random ways under particular circumstances. It was but a short logical step to the view that what might appear to be actions determined by a free will were in fact actions having a greater likelihood of occurring than alternative actions seemingly rejected by the will. (The similarity of this reasoning to the later theories of Edward L. Thorndike is often remarked; Clark Hull and B. F. Skinner both note their debt to Thorndike.)

In this view, pleasure and pain, by influencing the formation of association, were the basic "engine" producing action versus inaction, decision making, and directionality in thought or action. As Bain worked this theory out in several places (most succinctly in *The Emotions and the Will*, 1859, p. 343), it was clearly an associationist theory of motivated action, as well as a highly significant step beyond traditional discussions of volition. Theodore Mischel's (1966) carefully elaborated analysis is essentially the same, as is Robert Young's (1970, p. 155).

Bain's long-lasting influence did not stem from his treatment of philosophical questions. Rather, as noted earlier, it derived from his intriguing attempt to integrate biological principles with associationistic psychology.

EVOLUTIONARY ASSOCIATIONISM

Herbert Spencer's evolutionary doctrine introduced a second extremely important theme of biological thought into associationist psychology. In the little-noticed first edition of his *Principles of Psychology* (1855), Spencer refers to some of the same physiological authorities (e.g., Carpenter) as did Bain. However, Spencer showed a wider (if rather superficial) familiarity with biology and found Jean Lamarck's (1809/1963) writings very persuasive. Although it was not his primary interest, Lamarck is most often remembered for his idea that species evolution is based on the inheritance of acquired characteristics. Such earlier ideas, together with his own speculations, led Spencer to a thoroughly evolutionist version of psychology. It lacked only the mechanism of natural selection that Darwin was to supply and, of course, his wealth of specific evidence.

Aside from its evolutionist orientation, Spencer's book did not present a very original form of association psychology. It was, however, pervaded with the view that people are best understood as creatures in whom the relations (correspondences) between external or outer circumstances and inner or physiological circumstances are mediated. The person is the middle term, so to say. Spencer spoke of this process as adjustment, in its current meaning. It is in adjusting that association becomes essential; associations arise from contiguity, and frequency is the conspicuous modifier of associative fixity.

EVOLUTIONARY THOUGHT

It is often said that psychology was never to be the same after Charles Darwin, and that psychologists over the next century came to regard the doctrine of evolution as of primary importance. While evolutionary thought was highly visible in the writings of the functionalists, for example, this should not suggest that others were not aware of it. We mention only a few aspects of evolutionary doctrine that are significant for functionalist thought (see Buxton, 1984).

It is an oversimplification to say that psychology became Darwinian after the appearance of *The Origin of Species* (1859/1964). Spencer (1855/1870–1872) published a theory of evolution that differed in important ways from Darwin's, and yet in two respects his views appealed more directly to the interests of psychologists. Toward the end of the nineteenth century, one of these two lines of thought turned out to be erroneous, and the other was taken over first by medical writers of psychology and then by other psychologists. Consequently, Spencer's role in this part of our history is largely forgotten. We now undertake a brief reconstruction of this history using selected evolutionary concepts put forward by either Darwin or Spencer, or both. We shall return to Spencer.

Natural Selection

This was the conception that put Darwin's theory of evolution far in advance of previous theories, but it was (and is) extremely controversial because it challenges deeply rooted religious beliefs. With one or two notable exceptions, psychologists of the mid-nineteenth century and later not only seemed uninvolved in that controversy but, admiring and accepting biological science as they did, readily accepted the principle of natural selection, even though few found much use for it in their own work.

Adaptation

This was the key idea in Darwin's theory of selective survival and species formation. Most psychologists accepted it in the same spirit as they did the concept of natural selection, but neither idea seemed to be directly relevant to the traditional study of the normal adult mind. Later in the century, William James would find the concept of adaptation to be fundamental to his explanation of the rise and existence of consciousness, but that question was not focal in the 1860s.

Adjustment

Spencer's use of this term anticipated our present-day usage. It refers to the adaptability of structures and functions to the conditions of an *individual's* life, implying the survival relevance of motivation, learning, maturation, intelligence, and so on for that individual. This process is sometimes termed the analogue of adaptation in species survival, but Spencer and some of those who took the idea from him did not see it as such. Rather, it was considered the same process, oriented to the same end—survival. This perspective becomes clear in the realization that the degree of adaptation in individual organisms capable of it (i.e., the quality of adjustment) is one of the factors determining an individual's chances to survive and reproduce, and thus to function as an agent of species survival. David Sohn (1976, pp. 369–372) argues that those who refer to psychology as Darwinian because of its acceptance of the concept of adaptation are in fact referring to what Spencer called adjustment. Darwin himself, while not denying the survival value of the potential for adaptation by the individual, had little interest in studying the process (Gruber & Barrett, 1974, p. 226), whereas Spencer did.

In Spencer's theory of evolution, the best adjusted organisms were the "fittest to survive" (his expression, not Darwin's), with the advantages accrued through learning being retained via use–inheritance (see below).

In Spencer's extended analyses of adjustment, it becomes clear that he was laboriously working out conceptions of growth and development, as well as their determiners, in the manner later made familiar by developmental psychologists. He credited his understanding of the importance of adjustment to certain embryologists, for it was they who pointed out the regularities of very early growth that suggested to Spencer the lawful orderliness of later maturation and the accompanying learning processes. This line of thought was taken over rather completely by later psychiatric-psychological writers such as Henry Maudsley (1876) and William Carpenter (1874/1891), who were important in the thinking of William James (1890/1950) and James Sully (1884, 1891), among others. Thus Spencer's connection with the developmental idea was overrun and lost.

The revision of this bit of mid-19th-century history in psychology supports Sohn's critical analysis of the way psychologists view adaptation (mentioned earlier), as well as Young's (1965) suggestion that Spencer was more important than Darwin in the early history of modern psychology. In sum, psychology's central concern with individual development has important but usually unacknowledged roots in Spencer's analysis of adjustment as the main factor in evolutionary theory of survival of the fittest.

Inheritance

Analysis of British psychological writings influenced by Darwin or Spencer shows (Buxton, in preparation) that the only aspect of evolutionary theory of immediate interest to psychologists was inheritance (Bain, 1868, 1875; Sully, 1874, 1884; Maudsley, 1876; Carpenter, 1874/1891). Further, my initial scanning of contemporary American authors reveals that there was only one convinced Spencerian, John Fiske (1891). Darwin was more widely known than Spencer, and his views had been acclaimed by Chauncey Wright (1870/1877), William James (1868a, 1868b), and several other notables such as G. Stanley Hall (1904/1920, vol. 2, Chapter 10) and James Mark Baldwin (1902). (Inheritance was not the singularly interesting idea in America that it was in Great Britain.) Competent knowledge of genetics would not become generally available for several decades, but of course there was much practical knowledge of it among plant and animal breeders, parents, medical people, and others. One might therefore conclude that the psychologists need not have waited on Darwin and Spencer to think vigorously along these lines, but the fact is that they did, seizing upon the inheritance of both structure and function as an additional source for explanations of traits, abilities, and actions.

Darwin did not doubt that the capacity for adaptive behavior in a species was a survival mechanism, for he specifically mentioned instinct in *The Origin of Species* (1859/1964, Chapter 7) as a "noncorporeal" but nonetheless heritable factor in selective survival. This was a plausible step toward accepting intellectual powers and moral dispositions as not only evolving generally but taking specific forms such as language, tool use, and social habits (Darwin, 1871/1974, Chapter 21). To account for the inheritance of behavioral tendencies, Darwin sometimes referred to Lamarckian theory. Nevertheless, he remained unswerving in his conviction that "accidental," and not necessarily extreme, variations of structure or function were the primary mechanism in selective survival throughout most of the animal kingdom.

Surprisingly, it was not Darwin's proposals about the importance and nature of inheritance, but rather Spencer's that so attracted psychologists. (This was the previously mentioned line of thought in Spencer that turned out to be erroneous.) He had accepted and extended Lamarck's idea of use–inheritance, as Darwin sometimes also did. According to this theory, certain structures or functions (e.g., the long neck of the giraffe, or the camouflage markings of butterflies) that have survival value may, over many generations, become part of the inheritance of a species. There were many psychological applications of the idea, but in the most interesting case, it was theorized that habits formed repeatedly over many generations might take on the (unlearned) properties of instincts.

As psychologists considered human inheritance, especially family resemblances across generations, this version of Lamarck's doctrine seemed genuinely explanatory to many, including Sully and Carpenter. Bain remained rather skeptical, however and Maudsley was a Spencerian early in his career but later became a Darwinian. George John Romanes (1883/1970, 1888/1889), a Darwin "loyalist," leaned toward use-inheritance for the same applications as did Darwin. His successor and cofounder of the field of comparative psychology, C. Lloyd Morgan (1894/1902), did not like but could not quite rule out the possibility of use–inheritance. He finally invented a strictly biological replacement for it that was so similar to a proposal by two Americans, James Mark Baldwin and Frederick Osborn, that they all agreed that Baldwin (1902) should publish it as a joint affair in an appendix to one of his books. The gradual demise of Spencer's views began with Weismann's (1883/1889) proofs of the impossibility of inheriting acquired characteristics. By century's end, Spencer's views had been largely eclipsed in psychology.

Method

Darwin's naturalistic studies helped to persuade many people of the validity and feasibility of objective observation, and his personal care and integrity in observing and reporting set a high standard for the critical assessment of this kind of information. Not only his theory of evolution, but also his scientific example proved to be a contributing force in the long changeover from traditional introspective psychology to a science utilizing all manner of data. Darwin demonstrated that an objective approach could be taken to the study of problems and organisms outside the scope of a subjective psychology, and he is among those to be credited with the enormous advances of psychology in these respects. Before summarizing the impact of these initial developments on the beginnings of functional psychology, we now turn to some corollary events.

BEYOND DARWIN

Individual Differences

In Darwin's day, his ideas stimulated many scholars to study questions related to his theory. For example, his cousin, Francis Galton, was one of the founders of the field of individual differences in psychology, and contributed basic statistical concepts such as correlation to the analysis of its data. Galton's *Hereditary Genius* (1869) broadened the never-ending debate about the relative contributions of heredity and environment to human talents. In his *Inquiries into Human Faculty and its Development* (1883), Galton lays the foundation for techniques of psychological measurement and the assessment of variations among individuals. This imaginative work was one of the key starting points for the enormously important mental testing tradition in psychology.

Comparative Psychology

We have already mentioned the two key persons in the founding of this field, Romanes and Morgan. It must suffice here to say that while comparative psychology did not become part of the mainstream of psychology for several decades, in the meantime it continued to develop as both a naturalistic and experimental science, with Darwin's theory of evolution as one of its main points of reference.

Evolution and Society

Psychology was indeed never to be the same after Darwin, and the same was true of social thought—not only in Darwin's native England, but also in other countries to which his ideas spread. Only the ideas that are of direct import to the history of functionalist psychology can be mentioned here.

Evolutionary doctrine viewed as a biological science hypothesis is, of course, value-neutral, but its outcomes have inspired optimism, despair, or moral condemnation, depending on the viewer's frame of reference. In truth, Darwin's ideas were used to support widely divergent conceptions of society, but his theory was really contributory and provocative, not determinative. In Britain in 1859, when Darwin published *The Origin of Species,* there had already been long-standing concerns about the nature of society. These concerns had their roots in French social and political thought of the eighteenth century (Bury, 1932/1955). By mid-nineteenth century, two themes had become characteristic: the hope of social progress toward happiness for all, and the theme of the perfectability, or at least improvability, of humans. Darwin himself addressed these concerns, as shown by a sentence near the end of *Origin:* "We may look with some confidence to a secure future of . . . inappreciable length. And as natural selection works solely by and for the good of each being, all corporeal and mental environments will tend to progress towards perfection" (Darwin, 1859/1964, p. 489).

Spencer was not only an evolutionist before *Origin;* he saw very early that evolutionary thought could be applied to man's social existence (Spencer, 1851, chapter 30). To him, as to Walter Bagehot (1869/1948), it appeared that the same principle of selective survival in the animal kingdom could be viewed, in human beings, as competition for resources, power, or other means of survival. In this competition, the strongest or best adapted would succeed and propagate, while the weakest were doomed. Spencer saw social change as inevitable, uncontrollable, and "mechanical," a view later termed "social Darwinism" (Hofstadter, 1959). He personally was optimistic about this process; he felt that progress was inevitable, perfectability assured, and morality and happiness as certain as the evolutionary process was inexorable. Meanwhile, authoritarian and hostile tendencies would be self-destructive and would die out. Although they are not recorded here, there have been some strangely contrary and pessimistic interpretations of social Darwinism.

The relevance of social Darwinism to the history of psychology is less clear than it should be, but two things important for functionalism are discernible. First, social critics had to battle the belief of social Darwinists in the "blind" inevitabilities of social evolution. In both Britain and the United States during the latter nineteenth century, that constraining belief in inevitability was only gradually overcome by the increasing interest in the contributions of experience and learning, and of growth and development, to human conduct. These changing emphases were consistent with evolutionary doctrine but extended far beyond Darwin's declaration of faith in progress quoted earlier. Second, continuing attention to evolutionary concepts ensured the continual enlargement of basic understanding of their significance for people and behavior. The spread of evolutionism was thereby facilitated, and by 1890 it had become one of the foundations of the "new" functional psychology in America (see Chapter 5, this volume).

If there were sufficient space, it would be of interest to review the historical origins of child, or developmental, psychology. Like animal psychology, this field was an important addendum to the definition of psychology. It clearly had specific roots in Spencer's thinking, and, in a general and more often recognized way, in Darwin's as well. However, while developmental psychology throve with a functionalist point of view, it did not shape or develop functionalism itself so much as it shaped the growing inclination to study both intrinsic and acquired traits as determiners of how people interact with their natural and social environments. That inclination was focused on the study of personality.

THE FRENCH CONTRIBUTION

We turn now to the last European precursor of psychological functionalism to be discussed here—the latter-nineteenth-century interest of French psychologists and psychiatrists in personality. The psychiatrists used psychology as a basis for their clinical work; their practical accomplishment was enormous progress in the understanding and care of the mentally ill and the retarded. Some of them had the insight that abnormal or retarded persons could be a source of knowledge for understanding the normal. Thus they helped to expand the basic definition and scope of psychological study. The prevailing view in the developing field of personality was functional in the evolutionary sense that behavior was thought to be the instrument of adaptation by which humans became the "highest" species. In everyday usage, behavior and language are indicators of traits, abilities, or modes of thought that are instrumental (functional) in daily adjustment to the natural and social world. The legacy of Spencer is at least as apparent here as that of Darwin.

From the earliest days of psychiatry, orthodox psychology was deemed inadequate to the task of dealing with the retarded and the psychologically ill. Introspection, the traditional psychological method, seemed incomplete or inappropriate for collecting useful and relevant information from disordered or undeveloped mentalities. In established medical tradition, practitioners did not hesitate to use behavioral and other evidence in diagnosis and therapy. To them it seemed rather pointless to try to deal with mind apart from the rest of a person's characteristics, as introspective psychology seemed to do.

Although there was as much confusion here as elsewhere when psychiatrists strayed into philosophical questions such as the relation of mind to body, they uniformly held the working view that the organism—the person—is unitary, a functional, whole being. The idea was not new, but here it assumed a reality that was not lost upon many later psychiatrists and psychologists. Furthermore, with the example of biological science before them as a consequence of their training, the psychiatrists, like other medical people, were above all classifiers of the phenomena they observed. Like the others, however they found it meaningful or essential to go beyond taxonomy to functions related to or explanatory of diagnosis and etiology. This description applies best to two psychiatrists who were both practitioners and investigators. They are Maudsley (1867) and Griesinger (1845/1867).

Against this background, we may notice that certain French psychiatrists can be described as dynamic personality theorists. Théodule Ribot (1885/1891) may be included here, but he, like Maudsley and Griesinger, was also something of a systematist or taxonomist of mental disorders. His influence on Pierre Janet (1889/1921; 1892/1901) was significant; however, Janet was also the student of Jean-Martin Charcot (1889), a neurologist whose early work on hysteria led him to call it a functional disorder (meaning that it could not be attributed to organic causes and perforce was to be explained by the patient's history and circumstances).

It is Janet, however, who can best serve as our exemplar. In a sense, he made a career in hysteria, a common diagnostic category of the time. To explain somnambulism, catalepsy, anesthesia, and alternating or multiple personality, he developed a rather complete personality theory that incorporated concepts such as ego, the subconscious, and fixed ideas. One example of his thinking is his view that all hysterical disorders involve a constriction of attention that alters memory, language, and motor responses. Amnesia, in Janet's view, was a condition in which transformed or selective memory has become subconscious. In order to become functional, such subconscious memories must consist of associations systematized around a diminished but equally subconscious part of the ego, such as wish or need. Under certain conditions, what was subconscious could affect or become the conscious. Observation, suggestion, and hypnosis were the preferred methods of diagnosis and treatment.

In all of this, Janet was both deterministic and dualistic. That is, as he integrated these conflicting views, brain events were seen to give rise to or determine what he termed "superadded" conscious events. Consciousness was thus epiphenomenal. This conclusion required Janet to make further assumptions about how, in reverse, mind might influence the body, thus creating a cluttered sort of theory. Nevertheless, Janet's writings appealed to William James and others, and significantly shaped their views about the nature of psychology itself. Freud acknowledged that the French psychiatrists had had much to teach him, but Janet later acknowledged that it was Freud who developed and reinforced his dynamic theory of personality far beyond what he had offered (Murphy and Kovach, 1949/1972; Janet, 1919/1924).

SUMMARY

This chapter examined the sources of certain ideas as well as some basic conceptions that were clearly precursors to or early forms of functional psychology. We list the following as an interim record, and in Chapter 5 we attempt a gradual integration of these ideas:

1. In the mid-nineteenth-century background of functionalism, the idea that psychology could be a natural science was developed by John Stuart Mill. That era saw an increasingly clear change from a philosophical psychology that was subjective, analytical, descriptive, and concerned with mental elements and compounds toward a psychology that was an independent, objective discipline concerned with explanation (causation) after the manner of natural science concerned with processes rather than states-composed-of-elements, and with the organism as a whole.

2. Early in this period, the dominant mode of psychological thought was cognitive, as befitted its origins in mental philosophy. The co-eval beginnings of psychology on the continent, especially in Germany (as shown in Chapters 2 and 3, this volume), arose from a different philosophical base and drew upon biological thought somewhat differently but were nevertheless based on experimental work in sensory perception, an aspect of cognition. Increasingly, the philosophers' introspective analyses of affective and volitional matters were transformed into biologically based interpretations of emotion and motivation, and these were added to cognition as components of a broader and more scientific psychology.

3. Associationism had mainly been a framework for guiding description and classification, or analysis. It had been a rather simple "ism" in philosophy and earlier psychology, but it was gradually supplemented

with additional or different concepts pertaining to how associations were formed (laws) and activated (motivational roots). As such factors came to be treated as causal, association entered into widely varying formulations of learning, memory, and development, including that of the self.

4. Physiology strongly influenced the newly forming psychology. Thus the biological realm became even more clearly relevant to psychology than the physical science example.

5. Evolutionary thought produced lasting changes in the purposes and scope of psychology. The clearest immediate effect was to make salient to psychologists the idea of inheritance, but evolutionary concepts eventually drew the attention of psychologists to the fundamental importance of the linkage with biological science. Naturalistic observational methods made their mark as well and helped to legitimize a nonintrospective psychology dealing with the entire range and variety of activity in all behaving organisms. (However, the use of introspection would by no means vanish.)

6. Adaptation became the accepted view of the functioning of the organism, and modifications in structure or activity were thought to persist in any species to the extent that they enhanced the likelihood of survival. More importantly for increasing numbers of psychologists, the theory of evolution suggested that the potential for adjustment—that is, adaptation within a lifetime, or the individual's capacity for learning as well as maturation—was both a survival mechanism and a major dimension for psychological analysis.

7. The fundamental ideas of variability and individual differences were explored. Variations in any biological dimension, and in the mentality of people in particular, began to be important in describing and explaining their characteristics. The heredity-versus-environment issue also began to be noted.

8. Most of the early empiricist philosophers held an additive view of mind. That is, when the various predispositions, elements, and associations are added together, the result *is* mind. Developing alongside this view was the alternative functional conception that mind was more accurately thought of as an activity or process, with all its aspects being interdependent, a unity, a whole that is different from a simply mechanical or additive assemblage of elements.

9. Questions about what was observed (description) in human beings provided the essential starting point for a science. Questions about why—explanations, or causes—were of interest as well. (For the functionally inclined, they were of paramount importance.) In psychology, the question was why any observed features of mind or behavior oc-

curred. Sooner or later, this question turned into one of motivation. Volition or will, defined as part of consciousness early in this period, had little to do with conduct, except by implication. Bain and others sought to remedy this situation with action-oriented theories of volition. These new formulations, starting with the will but turning to hedonic, metabolic, or other mechanisms not very well understood, were used to account for directionality in behavior, even the pursuit of ends. The mediating mechanism was association formation. An explicit theory of motivation thus began to emerge that incorporated individual adaptation and motivated adjustment into an early functionally oriented psychology.

10. Personality was also emerging as a field of study. Certain other major topics, such as animal, child, or abnormal psychology, came in on the tide of evolutionary thought combined with the ever-increasing realization that psychology had the whole of life and activity in its purview.

11. Bain took a significant step when he brought together philosophical associationism and the results of experimental neurophysiology to shape a "new" psychology with most of the features that would later be important in American functionalism. (Compare this psychology with that of Chapters 2 and 3.) He began by defining psychology as the introspective study of consciousness but immediately added that it also involved observing the actions of self and others. This description facilitated the introduction of activity or movement (i.e., behavior) into psychology. What had been the study of mind and consciousness was becoming the study of people and behavior. Although the major credit for incorporating evolutionary thought goes to Spencer rather than Bain, psychology was slowly moving toward the presumption that all of mind and conduct served the functions of adjustment, adaptation, and, ultimately, survival.

12. It may be useful to simplify and generalize the contextual definition(s) of early psychological functionalism. Four propositions serve as a summary definition and carry over to the next chapter: (1) Functionalism is the (empiricist) view that human thought and action are to be understood (explained) by the way a person's experience shapes his or her development; (2) equally, functionalism is the view that people, being in and of the biological world, are to be understood (explained) via evolutionary principles, including inherited potentials for behavior and especially for adjustment; (3) equally again, adaptation in the individual (adjustment) follows empirically derivable (scientific) principles, such as those of association, motivation, intelligence, cognition, and so on. Basic to all three statements is (4) the prior assumption that it is essential to search for and understand processes (i.e., functions). This assumption

does not, of course, deny that it is useful, even essential, to understand states or structures.

ACKNOWLEDGMENT

I greatly appreciate the criticisms of an earlier draft by Daniel N. Robinson.

REFERENCES

Bagehot, W. (1948). *Physics and politics*. New York: Knopf. (Original work published 1869)
Bain, A. (1855). *The senses and the intellect*. London: Parker. (3rd ed., Longmans, Green, 1868)
Bain, A. (1859). *The emotions and the will*. London: Parker. (3rd ed., Longmans, Green, 1875)
Baldwin, J. M. (1902). *Development and evolution*. New York: Macmillan.
Blumenthal, A. L. (1975). A reappraisal of Wilhelm Wundt. *American Psychologist, 30*, 1081–1086.
Blumenthal, A. L. (1977). Wilhelm Wundt and early American psychology: A clash of two cultures. *Annals of the New York Academy of Sciences, 291*, 13–20.
Boring, E. G. (1950). *A history of experimental psychology* (2nd ed.). New York: Appleton-Century-Crofts.
Bury, J. B. (1955). *The idea of progress*. New York: Dover. (Original work published 1932)
Buxton, C. E. (in preparation). How British psychologists took to evolution.
Carpenter, W. B. (1843). *Principles of human physiology*. Philadelphia: Lea & Blanchard. (Original work published, London, 1842)
Charcot, J. M. (1889). *Diseases of the nervous system* (Vol. 3). (T. Savill, trans.). London: New Sydenham Society.
Darwin, C. (1964). *The origin of species*. Cambridge, MA: Harvard University Press. (Original work published 1859)
Darwin, C. (1974). *The descent of man* (2nd ed.). Chicago: Rand McNally. (Original work published 1871)
Fiske, J. (1891). The doctrine of evolution: Its scope and influence. In Brooklyn Ethical Association, *Evolution in science, philosophy, and art*. New York: Appleton.
Galton, F. (1869). *Hereditary genius*. London: Macmillan.
Galton, F. (1883). *Inquiries into human faculty and its development*. London: Macmillan.
Griesinger, W. (1867). *Mental pathology and therapeutics* (2nd ed.). (C. L. Robertson & J. Rutherford, trans.). London: New Sydenham Society. (Original work published 1845)
Gruber, H. E., & Barrett, P. H. (1974). *Darwin on man*. New York: Dutton.
Hall, G. S. (1920). *Adolescence*. New York: Appleton. (Original work published 1904)
Harré, R., & Secord, P. F. (1972). *The explanation of social behaviour*. Oxford: Blackwell.
Hartley, D. (1749). *Observations on man. His frame, his duty and his expectations*. London: Johnson.
Hearnshaw, L. S. (1964). *A short history of British psychology, 1840–1940.* New York: Barnes & Noble.
Hempel, C. G. (1966). *Philosophy of natural science*. Englewood Cliffs, NJ: Prentice-Hall.
Hofstadter, R. (1959). *Social Darwinism in American thought*. New York: Braziller.
James, W. (1868a). [Review of The Variation of Animals and Plants under Domestication]. *Atlantic Monthly, 22*, 122–124.

James, W. (1868b). [Review of The Variation of Animals and Plants under Domestication]. *North American Review, 107,* 362–368.

James, W. (1950). *Principles of psychology.* New York: Dover. (Original work published 1890)

Janet, P. (1901). *The mental state of hystericals* (C. R. Corson, Trans.). New York: Putnam. (Original work published 1892)

Janet, P. (1921). *L'automatisme psychologique* (9th ed.). Paris: Alcan. (Original work published 1889)

Janet, P. (1924). *Principles of psychotherapy* (H. M. and E. R. Yuthrie, Grans.) New York: Macmillan. (Original work probably published 1919)

Lamarck, J. B. (1963). *Zoological philosophy* (H. Elliot, Trans.). New York: Hafner. (Original work published 1809)

Mandler, G., & Kessen, W. (1959). *The language of psychology.* New York: Wiley.

Maudsley, H. (1867). *The physiology and pathology of mind.* London: Macmillan.

Maudsley, H. (1876). *The physiology of mind* (3rd ed.). London: Macmillan.

Mendelsohn, E. (1964). The biological sciences in the nineteenth century: Some problems and sources. *History of Science, 3,* 39–59.

Mill, J. (1829). *Analysis of the phenomena of the human mind* (2 vols.). London: Baldwin, Cradock.

Mill, J. (1869). *Analysis of the phenomena of the human mind* (2 vols.). London: Longmans, Green, Reader, Dyer. (New edition by J. Mill with notes by A. Bain, A. Findlater, and G. Grote)

Mill, J. S. (1846). *System of logic, ratiocinative and inductive.* New York: Harpers. (Original work published 1843)

Mischel, T. (1966). "Emotion" and "motivation" in the development of English psychology: D. Hartley, James Mill, A. Bain. *Journal of the History of the Behavioral Sciences, 2,* 123–144.

Morgan, C. L. (1902). *An introduction to comparative psychology.* New York: Scribner's. (Original work published 1894)

Müller, J. (1839–1842). *Elements of physiology* (W. Baly, Trans.). London: Taylor, Walton. (Original work published 1834–1840)

Murphy, G. & Kovach, J. K. (1972). *Historical introduction to modern psychology* (3rd ed.). New York: Harcourt Brace Jovanovich. (Original work published 1949)

Quain, J. (1849). *Human anatomy* (1st Amer. ed. from 5th London ed.). Philadelphia: Lea, Blanchard. (Original work published 1828)

Ribot, T. A. (1891). *The diseases of personality.* Chicago: Open Court. (Original work published 1885)

Robinson, D. N. (1978). *The mind unfolded.* Washington, DC: University Publications of America.

Robinson, D. N. (1981). *An intellectual history of psychology* (rev. ed.). New York: Macmillan.

Romanes, G. J. (1970). *Mental evolution in animals.* New York: AMS Press. (Original work published 1883)

Romanes, G. J. (1889). *Mental evolution in man.* New York: Appleton. (Original work published 1888)

Smith, R. (1973). The background of physiological psychology in natural philosophy. *History of Science, 11,* 75–123.

Sohn, D. (1976). Two concepts of adaptation: Darwin's and psychology's. *Journal of the History of the Behavioral Sciences, 12,* 367–375.

Spence, K. W. (1960). *Behavior theory and learning.* Englewood Cliffs, NJ: Prentice-Hall.

Spencer, H. (1851). *Social statics.* London: Chapman.

Spencer, H. (1855). *The principles of psychology.* London: Longmans, Green.

Spencer, H. (1871–1873). *The principles of psychology* (2nd ed.). New York: Appleton. (Original work published 1870–1872)

Sully, J. (1874). *Sensation and intuition: Studies in psychology and esthetics.* London: King.

Sully, J. (1884). *Outlines of psychology.* New York: Appleton.

Sully, J. (1891). *The human mind.* New York: Appleton.

Todd, R. B., & Bowman, W. (1845–1856). *Physiological anatomy and physiology of man.* London: Parker.

Turner, M. B. (1965). *Philosophy and the science of behavior.* New York: Appleton-Century-Crofts.

Watson, R. I. (1978). *The great psychologists* (4th ed.). Philadelphia: Lippincott.

Weismann, A. (1889). On heredity. In A. Weismann, *Essays upon heredity.* Oxford: Clarendon. (Original work published 1883)

Wright, C. (1877). The limits of natural selection: The genesis of species. In C. Wright, *Philosophical discussions.* New York: Holt. (Original work published 1870)

Young, R. M. (1970). *Mind, brain and adaptation in the nineteenth* century. Oxford: Clarendon.

Young, R. M. (1965). The development of Herbert Spencer's concept of evolution. *Actes du XIᵉ Congrès Internationale d'Histoire des Sciences.* Warsaw: Ossolineum.

5

American Functionalism

CLAUDE E. BUXTON

INTRODUCTION

In Chapter 4 it was shown that the early concepts and methods of
functional psychology became increasingly clear after the mid-nineteenth century, and at the close of the chapter certain themes in this
predominantly British development were summarized. One might expect that steady progress toward a functionalist science would have
continued after this beginning, but it did not. While scholars like Spencer and Bain clearly anticipated the pattern of functionalism, a general
slowing of progress in psychology and certain aspects of natural science
soon occurred. This development requires more than passing notice
before we discuss American functionalism. (While the intentions of
functionally oriented psychologists included the aspiration to be scientific, it was not true that all psychologists aspiring to be scientists were
functionally oriented; see Chapters 2 and 3, and others in this volume).

OPPOSITION TO EVOLUTION, SCIENCE,
AND PSYCHOLOGY

Prior to the momentous publications of Darwin, the sciences had advanced rapidly on the Continent and in Great Britain. Prominent in this

POINTS OF VIEW IN THE
MODERN HISTORY OF PSYCHOLOGY

advance was the rise of materialist philosophy, and the advance of reductionism. Such ideas shocked and threatened established theological views, and certain philosophical views as well. Philosophical psychologists such as Spencer and Bain, and biologists such as Darwin and Huxley, seemed to be using objective concepts to clarify the nature of life and man. As they groped for causes and explanations, they rejected the subjective and the spiritual, thereby arousing vehement reactions. People of religious dedication made critical, even vituperative, attacks. Many clerics and academic philosophers adoped more firmly the idealist philosophy of Kant, and later Hegel, in an effort to resist the growth of a psychology that combined their twin targets of empiricist philosophy and materialistic science. Roman Catholicism was a related and growing force against empiricism (Hearnshaw, 1964, pp. 123–124), but among the educated it had more specific and limited effects than the pervasive rationalist and idealist philosophy of Kant and his successors. The latter called for an idealism that insisted on realities transcending experience, and thus not of the natural world. These realities might be identified as God, the Absolute, or something else.

One proponent of such views in Britain for many years after about 1836 was William Hamilton. His differences with associationist psychology are made clear in his *Lectures in Metaphysics* (1859). Seen in historical perspective, his arguments are cogent and no doubt gave pause to those who believed that the way was clear for an empiricist science of psychology.

The associationist's problem—which was to explain the nature of mind by showing how experience integrates its separate components and, for some, to enlarge this explanation by drawing on concepts from physiology—was not the basic problem in Hamilton's view. Rather, it was first necessary to describe how underlying, innate mental capacities or powers regulated the manner in which mind could be modified by experience. Mind itself was unitary. Moreover, it was active. Hamilton's main contribution rests on such an assumption: Whereas the associationists depicted memory as the elicitation of parts of experience according to principles such as contiguity or similarity, Hamilton argued that any element of an idea or experience had the capacity to reinstate the entire, unitary memory. This principle, which he called *redintegration* (Hamilton, 1859, lect. 31), embodies a rather holistic concept of mental organization that writers such as William James later deemed important. It was Hamilton who expanded Kant's influence in Britain and who gave an idealist and antiempiricist cast to the philosophy of his day.

Submergence of Hamilton's views after his death in 1865 (Hearnshaw,

1964, p. 122) by no means led to the disappearance of idealist philosophy. Rather, it was combined with theological attacks on what was deemed the antireligious challenge of science, especially evolutionary biology. At Oxford University, in particular, eloquent philosophers taught rationalist and idealist views over several decades. Partly for that reason, Hearnshaw (1964, Chapter 8) notes that progress toward scientific psychology slowed in Great Britain from around 1885 until just before World War II, except in the university centers (e.g., Cambridge, Manchester, and University College London) that were partly or mostly free of the idealist philosophy. Oxford, the citadel of the humanities, did not have a laboratory of experimental psychology until 1936, nor a chair until 1947.

The Oxford movement (or the Anglo-Hegelian philosophy, as it is better named) was influential largely because of two notable professors. T. H. Green at Oxford insisted that mind was not completely described by reference to such "outer-determined" characteristics as sensations and ideas. Rather, "Human action is only explicable by the action of an eternal consciousness, which uses . . . [processes and functions] . . . as its organs and reproduces itself through them" (Green, 1883, p. 86). The ultimate cause of actions was an unknowable Agent or Knower. Green (1874, p. 165) accuses the scientific physiologists of rendering, in a preposterous way—"preposterous" in the old and literal sense of "putting the cart before the horse"—the relation of physiological organization to thought when they inferred that the first had a causal relation to the second.

Green's influence at Oxford and elsewhere was reinforced and extended by Francis Herbert Bradley (1883), who claimed that the laws of association were spurious because they treated of fleeting and perishing moments of consciousness that in fact could never be reproduced. According to Bradley, psychology could not possibly be scientific, because his own close metaphysical study showed that its principles were "dogmatic atomism," and therefore false. Without doubt, these men were opposed to biological science, and scientific psychology, just as they favored free will and theism. They almost certainly helped to cool any ardor for empirical and scientific psychology. It is to Bradley's credit, however, that he remained in close touch with many developments in psychology. He was the author of many critical articles, as well as stimulating explanations of his own views.

This type of antagonism was not all that slowed the growth of psychology in Britain. At science- and mathematics-minded Cambridge University, there was James Ward, a philosopher with strong psychological interests who was convinced that psychology was an entirely subjective and introspective study. In his article in the *Encyclopedia Britannica* (Ward, 1886), he analyzes and criticizes associationist psychology in a manner reflecting the German philosophy to which he was attracted as a young man. (William James was also attracted by Ward's thinking; for years they maintained a congenial correspondence.)

Ward had a mixed influence in Britain. Until he was outvoted by skeptical faculty colleagues, he tried hard to establish a German-type psychophysical laboratory as an example of scientific psychology at Cambridge. At the same time, he espoused an intricate psychological philosophy as far removed from science as that of the Anglo-Hegelians. As Boring (1950, pp. 488–495) recounts, British experimental psychology, eventually had a significant beginning at Cambridge in the first decade of the 20th century.

In many respects, of course, scientific psychology developed little in Britain for most of the last quarter of the nineteenth century and only slowly thereafter. Further reasons for this could be cited, but they would only extend the judgment that the move toward functionalism lost its momentum in these years, and that any further progress would have to occur elsewhere. It did come, in due time, in America.

AMERICAN PSYCHOLOGY BEFORE 1890

The phrase "in due time" symbolizes the rather slow and confusing early development of psychology in the United States. Although historians of the colonial and later eras have explored many facets of our early society, until recently the first American developments in psychology have been of primary interest to only two authors, J. W. Fay (1939) and A. A. Roback (1952). Their accounts, though valuable, are limited; Fay is overly concerned with antiquarian questions, and Roback gives a rather personal and sometimes idiosyncratic view of history. E. R. Hilgard's (1986) work contrasts with these in quality but is largely oriented toward the twentieth century.

Partly as a result of limited exposure to our own history, many American psychologists are somewhat startled to realize that scholars in colonial America coexisted with some of the significant British "ancients" such as Hobbes, Locke, Berkeley, Hume, and Hartley. That no such notable has been acclaimed in the corresponding era of psychological philosophy in America may reflect a real difference in scholarship (or audience), but this matter has not yet been studied thoroughly. Therefore, it hardly seems fitting to declare, as Boring (1950, p. 739) does, that American psychology "started off" with William James. Boring's special interest was experimental psychology, as is evident in the title of his book, and this partly justifies his opinion. However, it also disregards what happened in the 250 years between the landings in Massachusetts and the publication of James's *Principles of Psychology* (1890/1950).

Such "presentist" disregard has meant that two important themes in the history of our psychology have received inadequate attention. One is the presence in America of the philosophical climate that originated in German idealism and increasingly retarded scientific psychology's development in Britain after the mid-19th century. (An important contribution to the background of this problem is Rand Evans's chapter on the origins of American academic psychology in Brožek's [1984] history of psychology in the United States.) The other theme is the epoch-making break with idealism by James and by John Dewey in their American-style pragmatism, and the encouragement it gave to a new American psychology.

Because they did not actively contribute to the development of functionalism, we shall not discuss a dozen or more American psychologists who studied with Wilhelm Wundt and other Germans in the latter 19th century, and who then returned to their own country to found laboratories and other adjuncts of European-style introspectionist psychology. Some important figures are J. McKeen Cattell, G. Stanley Hall, Charles H. Judd, Edward W. Scripture, and Lightner Witmer. Soon after returning home, most of them developed psychological views and engaged in activities alien to the German conception of scientific psychology (Blumenthal, 1977). Except for Edward B. Titchener (Chapter 3, this volume), however, they were little opposed to the growing American functionalism. Indeed, they were basically sympathetic to functionalism, as shown by their interest in the uses of psychology.

Religion and Philosophy

As in Britain in the corresponding years, daily life in the colonies and post-Revolutionary America was dominated to a considerable extent by religious beliefs. Consequently, a theological orientation strongly influenced the philosophy that (here as in Britain) was the source of psychology in its early form. It was in mental philosophy that American empiricists would disagree with the rationalists or idealists, just as the two Mills and Bain disagreed with the sympathizers of Kant, Hamilton, and Hegel. Religious and philosophical questions were widely debated or resolved by doctrine in intellectual circles, particularly in the early New England colleges. Beliefs and attitudes carried across the Atlantic from

British universities, especially Cambridge and one or two Scottish institutions, oriented the intellectual, social, and political life of many generations of Americans. The interplay between Scottish and German philosophies and the Puritan mental and moral philosophy is well portrayed by Robert Rieber (Rieber & Salzinger, 1980) in a chapter on the Americanization of psychology before William James, and in the Evans chapter mentioned earlier (Brožek, 1984).

Some remarkable twists and turns soon developed in psychological thought. For example, ideas about predestination and original sin in Calvinist theology contended with the associationism of John Locke in arguments about child-rearing practices. For a time in the early 19th century, there was a compromise in which Calvinists limited the Lockean *tabula rasa* to the rational (i.e., cognitive) faculties. Natural depravity, which had no place in Locke, was retained alongside Locke's system to explain the nonrational will and the passions (Slater, 1977, Chapter 4). By the mid-nineteeth century, however, the least favored philosophy in the American colleges was British empiricism, for that view tended toward the materialistic and the nontheological. When empiricist (and especially associationist) ideas were presented, the usual professorial intent was to criticize and reject them authoritatively.

Two examples of earlier nineteenth-century American psychology are of interest, and the lesson they teach is remarkably similar to that described in the previous section on British opposition to evolution, science, and psychology. One stalwart was Noah Porter, president of Yale University and a prominent figure in pre-Civil War education. He was eminent in the area of philosophical psychology. There was an idealist coloration to the views he taught in a required senior course in mental philosophy (Porter, 1868). According to him, psychology was a science, but it was a science of the soul, and its materials were derived from consciousness by introspection and reflection. Physiology was useful insofar as it informed on functions and states of the body with which the immaterial soul was associated, but physiological laws were of the material world and not themselves part of psychology.

Even less conducive to scientific investigation was Porter's Aristotelian requirement that psychology was a means of seeking not merely an understanding of the phenomena and conditions of mental life, but the final (transcendental) causes of it. In Porter's theology, these became Final Causes, and all of nature exhibited the designs of a Being who was not of this natural world. One consequence of this approach was Porter's (1868, p. 31) strong reservations about evolution, and though he came to accept it as a scientific hypothesis, he continued to deny that it threatened religious belief. In a little-known lecture series late in his career, he preached ardently in this vein (Porter, 1886). His influence on American psychology, then, was clearly like that of Anglo-Hegelian idealism in Britain.

Somewhat more progressive was the Scottish realism underlying the psychology presented by President James McCosh of Princeton University. He held firmly to the "common-sense" philosophy with its Presbyterian overlay, then nearing the end of a long and gradual course of change following Thomas Reid's representational realism (see Robinson, 1981, pp. 236–244). In Hamilton's version, as noted earlier, the "common-sense" view reflected certain aspects of German idealist philosophy, and McCosh favored such a mixed version. It was his view (McCosh, 1886, pp. 24–26), like Reid's, that what is given to the senses is real (we know the object itself, and do not merely infer its existence), and by that token true. However, he further argues that processes such as perceiving, thinking, or loving are as real to introspection as our knowledge of things or matter. At the same time, knowing and perceiving for McCosh the idealist were phenomena of the mind, not bodily physiology (1886, pp. 7–9, 59). Repeatedly, in the history of psychology, such philosophical dualism has obstructed scientific thinking as it did in McCosh's case. To be fair, McCosh, far more than Porter, was impressed with the scientific validity of evolution. Like Porter, however, he held to his religious beliefs, declaring that evolution as science did not conflict with them (McCosh, 1888).

Physiological Psychology

As in Europe, what looked like a promising beginning in biologically oriented psychology was not generally persuasive in this country. George Trumbull Ladd (1887) followed German psychology (Wilhelm Wundt's in particular) in writing a physiological psychology textbook. Stated briefly, his position was that psychology was the science of the phenomena of human consciousness. *Mind* was a useful term referring to the subject or the self, with its more or less stable identity amid all else that changes in consciousness and in the physical environment. The task of introspection was to define the questions about mind that would be studied by scientific psychology. Physiological psychology could then, as it did for Wundt (see Chapter 2, this volume), provide a useful method by which to illuminate various concepts (Ladd, 1887, p. 4).

Unable to lay metaphysics aside, Ladd (1887, Part 3, Chapter 4) wrote as a practicing dualist. Mind was real and nonmaterial, he said in a detailed argument, and a Real Being was required in order to explain how mind works. Ladd's contemporaries praised his physiological contributions but balked at his traditional psychological philosophy. His professional influence was considerable, and he was personally respected, but his stubborn, even irascible insistence on his kind of philosophizing, combined with his failure to take much notice of evolutionary doctrine, prevented his making a long-lasting mark except in physiological psychology narrowly defined.

Evolution

As noted in Chapter 4, Darwin's views were warmly received by Americans like Chauncey Wright and William James. John Fiske became a disciple of Spencer, probably because both were interested in ethics, but initially Fiske (1879/1885) had written several favorable essays on Darwin's theory. In one important respect, the Americans were like the psychologists in Great Britain, for they did not get caught up in the great debate about the merits of the general theory of evolution, as did their colleagues in biology and palaeontology at Harvard, Yale, and elsewhere (Bowler, 1983; Morse, 1876; Pfeifer, 1965). Furthermore, although several important American sociologists and anthropologists sided with the neo-Lamarckian cohort of biologists, only one psychologist of note, G. Stanley Hall, took that position (see Stocking, 1962). James probably knew Spencer's views better than any other American (not excepting Fiske), having used Spencer's writings in his Harvard teaching for several years after 1879 (see William James papers). Nevertheless, he remained a convinced Darwinian, as is evident in several places in his *Principles* (1890/1950).

Just as there was less attention to Spencer than to Darwin among American psychologists, compared to the British, there was also more frequent and general support for the evolutionary approach. McCosh was an example of this, as was Porter, albeit grudgingly. Boring (1950/1963) conveys this supportive attitude in arguing that American psychology of the later nineteenth century was both functionalist and evolutionary. He contends that both descriptions were apt on the basis of his conviction that trends in psychology could be explained on a "national character" hypothesis. According to the hypothesis American culture was practical, individualistic, and survival-oriented in the social Darwinist sense as a consequence of the frontier and laissez-faire circumstances of the earlier 19th century. Boring thought James Mark Baldwin and G. Stanley Hall were exemplars of these twin beliefs in functionalism and evolutionism. (He also named J. McKeen Cattell, but the evolutionist theme is not as important in Cattell.) While I cannot share Boring's enthusiasm for his simplistic national character explanation, I do agree that there was a considerable readiness for the integration of evolutionism with psychology both before and after 1890.

Until the last part of the nineteenth century, then, the climate in which a scientific psychology might develop in America was little different from that in Great Britain during the late nineteenth and early twentieth centuries. There was to be one highly significant difference here, however, one that freed American psychology to develop as it had nowhere else.

THE TURNING POINT

Both cultural and intellectual forces brought about a change in the philosophy and psychology predominating in this country before 1890. Those forces came to a focus in William James, variously described as our foremost native-born psychologist, founder of the philosophy called Pragmatism, and an extraordinary scholar whose temperament was conducive to a tolerant, unstereotyped, and humane conception of psychology as a science and as a basis for living. As a youth, he was exposed to his father's enthusiasm for and partial disillusionment with Emerson's Transcendentalism and Carlyle's philosophy. Perry (1948, p. 38), however, judges that neither gave James his philosophy, though both gave him precepts and apt quotations. By origin, his psychology was essentially European, though he developed it (together with John Dewey) within a new philosophical framework of a peculiarly American orientation. Combined with a wholehearted adoption of evolutionary thinking, this philosophy encouraged an integration that was decisive for the wide acceptance of functionalist psychology.

Basic Concepts

Although James's ideas and presence were well known by the late 1870s, his *Principles of Psychology* (1890/1950) aroused a storm of both favorable and negative comment. It was the most influential academic work in American psychology for several decades. In articles published over a period of years and assembled as chapters in the book, and in the new chapters written for it, James's viewpoints on certain topics were subject to change. On other matters he was simply inconsistent, which makes a concise presentation of his views difficult. It is regrettable that one cannot easily convey the fascination with which James explored and wrote about every aspect of psychology to which his profound curiosity directed him.

"Psychology is the Science of Mental Life, both of its phenomena and their conditions." So begins the *Principles* (1890/1950). The phenomena comprise subjective or introspectively discovered feelings, cognitions, reasoning processes, and the like. They are obviously influenced by physiological conditions, most notably brain conditions. These, and the person in whom they occur, exist in the objective, or real, world. For James, this conception presented no problem. He passed without difficulty from the introspective realm across the "vague boundary line of the mental" and into the real world by adopting Spencer's view that the essences of mental life and bodily life are the same—namely, the adjustment of inner to outer relations (James, 1890/1950, vol. 1, p. 6). (There is no mention here of his earlier severe criticism of Spencer (James, 1878/ 1920,p. 17) for neglecting the inclination of people to transform their world as part of their adjustment to it.)

In analyzing the process of adjustment, James (1878/1920) saw that *"the pursuance of future ends and the choice of means for their attainment are . . . the mark and criterion of the presence of mentality in a phenomenon"* (p. 8). In this statement one can see both the evolutionist–adaptationist theme in James's thinking, and the pragmatist insight that the meaning of a concept (in this case, mentality) becomes apparent through its correlation with observable events (here, the pursuit of ends, or choice). Both the theme and the insight are extensions of functionalist thinking, as summarized at the end of Chapter 4, this volume. Earlier in that chapter, attention was called to diverse interpretations of the consequences of evolution for social progress. Here it may be added that James (1907/ 1909), ever the optimist about human beings and their future (despite his own neurasthenic tendencies of sometimes disabling intensity), rejected Spencer's social Darwinism on grounds of its "dismaying disconsolateness" (pp. 105–106).

James did not long view his training for his only earned degree, the M.D., as pre-professional. His decision to enter medical school was really an expression of his life-long biological interests. These interests and his medical training made it easy for James to see reflex as a component of action, and his acceptance of Darwin's ideas led him to see instinct as centrally important in man as well as in animals. The concept of instinct had its shortcomings (see below), but in adopting it he was pressing to include within psychology, not only conscious actions, but also those that do not seem to be consciously selected or directed.

James's notion of the unconscious was that it involved simple unawareness. Like Janet's similar notion, it was not at all a major concept of personality, as it was for Freud. However, James's later writings did assign functional characteristics such as a threshold—*margin* was his term—to the subconscious (see his discussion of religious conversion in *Varieties of Religious Experience*, 1912/1961).

James argued that any action that was teleological and adaptive was thus interesting to science (the teleological character of an action referred to its being performed for the sake of its results). This approach implied no philosophical paradox, for James meant that whether the mediating mechanism was innate neural connections (reflex), persisting biological states with feedback (tissue need or emotion), unspecified conditions (instinct), or goal anticipation in a learnable motive (interest), the functional outcome was the same: Present conditions elicit, or come to elicit, actions appropriate to attaining the end. Generally speaking, behavior was purposive.

Extending this line of thought, James (1890/1950) introduced the concept of interest as a selector of thought processes (vol. 1, pp. 139–141), with the notion of survival value adduced as an argument for such a directional component in thought and action. Convinced of the unitariness of all mental and behavioral processes, he argued against consciousness as purely cognitive, instead favoring the view that it always encompassed affective and purposive components as well. As a further expansion of his motivational thought, he treated pleasure and pain much as Spencer and Bain did, while roundly criticizing them in detail (1890/1950, vol. 2, pp. 553–555), and declared that affect has a causal role in adaptive behavior. James's inconsistencies on problems of volition and determinism will be noted later, but it is evident here that the widespread American interest in motivation may reflect the Jamesian revolt against purely cognitive psychology as much as it does Freud's persuasive writings.

James on Method

In Chapter 4, it was said that method is as distinctive a feature of functionalism as its psychological content. For James, this was true, and yet he did not break with the introspective method. Rather, he declared it to be fundamental (1890/1950, vol. 1., p. 185), arguing that from the psychological point of view (1890/1950, vol. 2, pp. 221–222), reporting one's own thoughts and actions was logically the equivalent of reporting external events and objects, including other persons, of which one is aware. Both kinds of report are valid as scientific data, although observations of the self might be less reliable. James recognized that his kind of psychology might find its data anywhere in the human condition, and he did not want to overlook any.

James believed in experimentation but did not practice it much himself. Nevertheless, having read widely in German biological science, especially neurophysiology, he profoundly admired its essential experimentalism as an approach to scientific truth. This was a non-British influence of key importance for James's view of what was possible in psychological science. He was rather put off by the then dominant mode of experimentation in German psychology—that of the technical introspectionists such as Wundt. Indeed, he aimed some colorful criticism at this kind of introspective psychology (1890/1950, vol. 1, pp. 192–193). James's preferred mode of introspection was the phenomenal, or "tell-all," procedure, with nothing being excluded from reports. He was deeply concerned, nevertheless, about the accuracy of introspection (1890/1950, vol. 1, pp. 196–197). Clinical methods seemed useful to James, as did hypnosis in certain circumstances. Generally, his methodological preferences must be termed eclectic, as were those of most functionalists, the result of attitude as much as technique.

The Meaning of Experience

Because James's functionalism originated in his considerations of consciousness, the word "experience' is frequently found in his writing. It might give a better sense of his views to discuss all three of the meanings that James gave to the term, but only the one most relevant to this chapter is presented here. In this meaning, experience of consciousness "is for": It *is for* carrying on *functions* such as sensing, perceiving, thinking, self-awareness, attending, discriminating, forming concepts, reasoning, and so on. All are processes mediating adjustment by or in the individual and thereby, in the long view, adaptation in the interest of species survival. A few examples of the functioning of experience or mind in this context may clarify the conception.

Thinking

The "stream of thought," now often termed "stream of consciousness," was James's reference to one function of conscious thinking. Thought, he suggested, has five dynamic characteristics (the word "dynamic" has connotations here such as changing, motivating, causing, or energy-expending): (1) Thought is personal; every thought is part of a personal consciousness. (2) Thought is constantly in flux, never the same twice or in two successive moments, although the constancy of the object of thought may give us the feeling of the same thought happening twice. (3) Thought is sensibly continuous, so that interruptions by sleep or surgical anesthesia are experienced as just that—interruptions of a basically continuous experience: one life, one experiencing person, persisting through time despite the lack of specific awarenesses during times of lowered or diverted alertness. In one famous example (James, 1890/1950, vol. 1, pp. 238–239), Peter and Paul, waking in the same bed, recognize that they have been asleep, and mentally each instantly reaches back across the interruption to make connection with but one of the two streams of thought broken by sleep. Peter's present at once finds Peter's past, never Paul's. (4) Thinking deals with objects independent of itself. It is cognitive and has the function of knowing. (5) Thought is selective; it welcomes, rejects, chooses, and is directed by interests.

The overarching metaphor here is that many substreams compose the stream of thought. All are interrelated and in continuous flux, always moving to the center of interest and out again, affecting one another, and exhibiting the unity of a complex life process moving toward the ends of its existence. Not a theory, nor a causal explanation of thought, James's description remains ever fresh and rich.

The Self

It is characteristic of James's conception of the unified nature of the functioning person that our second example of what experience "is for" or makes possible—the psychological self—has already been implied in our description of thinking. In the stream of thought, various parts are attended to or noticed, and, as noted earlier, there is always choosing or selection in such noticing, for we have no "organ" capable of taking in all that comes at any moment. One part of the stream of thought constantly has to do with the self and its circumstances. This concept of self is a dynamic notion, for the self is always in flux, orienting and considering from moment to moment, and yet always identifiable as the same.

In James's language, there are several kinds of self: (1) The *empirical* self is what anyone calls *me*, and it is difficult to draw the line between me and what I call mine. In the widest sense, a person's self is the sum total of all he can call *his* (James, 1890/1950, vol. 1, p. 291). Included in the empirical self is a material self. It comprises the body and its attire, creations, and possesions, which are perceived as extensions of the body. (2) A person's *social* self is made up of the recognition he or she gains from others. In an intriguing but controversial statement, James (1890/1950) writes: "A man has as many social selves as there are individuals who recognize him" (p. 294). From these social relations arise, for example, one's feelings about honor, or about which side of the self to show in a particular social setting. (3) Most fundamentally, there is what James called a *spiritual* self, by which he meant "a man's inner or subjective being, his psychic faculties or dispositions . . . the most enduring and intimate part of the self, that which we most verily seem to be" (1890/1950, p. 296). It might be called the self that knows, or the active principle in self.

James found motivational properties in the self. For example, by assuming that self-knowledge and self-preservation are, in their evolutionary origins, fundamental instincts, he was able to impute to people such tendencies as bodily, social, and spiritual self-seeking or self-preservation. Then, as the self or ego changes during long-term development or momentary variations, its motivational patterns also change (1890/1950, vol. 1, pp. 323–324). This instinctivist solution exhibits a now familiar logical problem: If one is to put spiritual self-seeking, for example, on a useful scientific footing, one has to go beyond naming an instinct by the behavior it supposedly explains and try to account independently for its origins. Yet, at a descriptive level not requiring such knowledge of origins, James's treatment of intrapsychic conflict (1890/1950, vol. 1, pp. 309–317) is impressively clear.

James intended these considerations to clear the way for a discussion of pure self, or pure ego, the sense of personal identity that surmounts all thinking about the self. His description of identity requires no concepts beyond those already presented and reminds us that much of his work has survived. In James's treatment of the organization of personality, any complications involving his summary of the self were reduced to the sweeping statement, "Personality implies the incessant presence of two elements, an objective person known by a passing subjective thought and continuing in time" (1890/1950, vol. 1, p. 371). Against James's intent, a dualism lies in the thing (objective person) and the thought about it (subjective entity). Against this background, James presented his widely cited discussions of altered memory and personality states, in which he introduced the cases and personality theories of psychiatrists, and of Janet in particular (see Chapter 4, this volume), to his American audience. In so doing, he established both personality and abnormal psychology as components of a functionalist psychology.

Attention

Following is a final example of the function of consciousness. Attention was important to James for two reasons: (1) Attending, like everything else in consciousness, is a process entailing continual mobility from one state to another, focused only as a momentary arrest of ceaselessly shifting thought. Nothing could be further from the Titchenerian clearness of mental states (Titchener, 1896/1919, p. 53). (2) James's interpretation of attention rested on neural processes, on a rising to prominence and then a subsidence of brain processes corresponding to the flow of thoughts as they come to attention and then move on. The biology may have been sheer speculation, but the interactionist connection was necessary in James's view. In retrospect, we can see this bit of "biologizing" as a vague insight into the likelihood that spontaneous brain processes (cf. Bain, Chapter 4, this volume) play a continual role in the course of attending and other psychological processes. Of his rather detailed and traditional description of kinds of attention and their characteristics we need say nothing here.

From Consciousness to Behavior

Turning from the functions of consciousness, we note other functions, not independent of consciousness but relating it to action or behavior. As was true for Bain and Spencer (Chapter 4, this volume), pleasure and pain were also basic to James's concept of volition and the will, traditionally a subject of introspective study rather than an aspect of motivated action (1890/1950, vol. 2, pp. 549–559). Movement or action, James said, was partly explained by neural connections between tissue conditions or stimuli, on one side, and responses on the other. Reflexive, instinctive, and emotional reactions were regarded as primary, in the sense that "the nerve centers are so organized that certain stimuli pull the trigger of certain explosive parts" (1890/1950, vol. 2, p. 487). On first occurrence, these may be regarded as unforeseen or unintended. However, the secondary or voluntary part of human action is intended, stemming from desires, wishes, or willing, all of which James defines as states of mind, or consciousness. His problem then becomes: How is desire or wish, as (subjective) consciousness, translated into intended actions that are tangible or objective in some sense that consciousness is not?

James as a determinist–scientist wanted to avoid a dualistic view of the behaving organism, so he took it as his scientific obligation to explain, quite literally, how thought becomes action. His solution was straightforward but questionable: In memory there is a store of ideas of various possible movements. These ideas include images of movement, or kinesthetic residuals of previous movements, that constitute the bases of what he calls "ideomotor action." After noting that a choice or decision to make specific motion is partly to be understood as dependent on the strength of conflicting alternatives, James (1890/1950, vol. 2, p. 526) postulates that every conscious representation (kinesthetic image) of a movement is, *in its very nature, impulsive.* He continues: "*Movement is the natural, immediate effect of feeling (thought), irrespective of what the quality of the feeling may be. It is so in reflex action, it is so in emotional expression, it is so in voluntary life"* (1890/1950, vol. 2, p. 527).

James here *presumes* the answer to his question: That is, he posits that conscious desires or wishes are inherently present, as impulses, in images of movements that will achieve the desired ends. This accepted, there is no longer a problem of how (conscious) mind is connected with (active) body in ideomotor action. But what is this kind of image that combines impulse with the potential for energizing nerves? This question spoils James's essentially verbal solution and reinstates the puzzle. His orientation can be applauded, but the dualism he so much wanted to avoid continued to frustrate his scientific aspirations.

Although ideomotor action is the basic type of volitional action, James emphasized from the beginning that a choice—that is, any decision to make any specific motion—may, and probably does, depend on strengths of conflicting alternatives. In his words, "Sometimes an additional conscious element, in the shape of a fiat, mandate, or express consent, has to intervene and precede the movement (1890/1950, vol. 2, p. 522). This fiat seemed to William Woodward (1984) to be one of the main conceptual organizers of James's *Principles,* and he has adduced considerable support for this interpretation.

Emotion

One of James's most original notions was his theory of emotion (see also Chapter 12, this volume). It is not the case, he writes (1890/1950, chap. 25), that perception (as a conscious state) excites emotion (as a conscious state), and that the emotional state of mind then gives rise to its bodily expression. "On the contrary . . . *the bodily changes follow directly the perception of the exciting fact, and . . . our feeling of the same changes as they occur IS the emotion* (1890/1950, p. 449; emphasis in original). James proposed the study of such events as a dynamic alternative to the endless and tedious introspective study of emotions. As a willing empiricist, he sought clinical evidence on whether the disruption of sensory feedback affected the occurrence of emotion. The evidence he found was not convincing, but he did defend his basic proposal (James, 1884). While theories of greater anatomical and physiological validity eventually took over the field of emotion, James's theory has always been cited in textbooks because of its distinctiveness and plausibility. The most sophisticated and complete theory of emotions available at present rests partly on a Jamesian interpretation of the nature of emotion (see Chapter 12, this volume).

THE PHILOSOPHY OF PRAGMATISM AND THE "NEW" AMERICAN PSYCHOLOGY

Along with evolutionary doctrine, Pragmatism was crucial to the successful formulation of a new American psychology. James's inclination toward this view can be discerned in his early papers (1879/1920, 1885/1909), as well as in his later *Pragmatism* (1907/1909; see also Perry, 1948, Chapter 32). He himself thought that the new theory took hold only after he had argued for it in an address (James, 1898/1920) some 20 years after it had been enunciated by his colleague, Charles Peirce (1877–1878). Peirce in turn, as Max Fisch (1954) shows, was developing a specialized version of Bain's theory of belief.

Pragmatism may be called a theory of meaning. As such, it has two related implications. The first arises from the recognition that if a concept cannot be translated into the language of experience or practice, it is meaningless; conversely, the meaning of a concept or a term is what it is connected with or points to in experience or reality, and nothing more. Concepts, words, and other symbols do not incorporate reality into themselves but rather are instrumental in connecting thoughts with other thoughts and realities. Second, Pragmatism implies that ideas or concepts arise in experience, change as experience occurs, and are adapted to that experience. Expressed this way, it is also a theory of how we acquire meanings or knowledge; that is, an epistemology stating that what we know is a function of our experience. Expiricism could have no clearer formulation.

CHICAGO FUNCTIONALISM

The new viewpoint in American psychology was, as indicated earlier, not solely James's invention. In a few years he was joined by John Dewey, who initially had been a convinced Hegelian. Gradually, but only after publishing a number of idealist articles and a stolidly traditional textbook (*Psychology*, 1887), Dewey moved toward the pragmatic camp, becoming friendly with James and naming his own variant of the philosophy Instrumentalism. The label "Chicago functionalism" refers primarily to Dewey's contributions to this viewpoint during his stay at the university (1894–1904), along with those of James Rowland Angell and, later, Harvey Carr. James's full awareness of what was happening at Chicago was shown in his characteristically generous laudatory note on "The Chicago School" (1904).

Dewey's Instrumentalism

We now examine Dewey's philosophy, his most important contribution to functionalism in psychology. Late in his career, Dewey testified that as a student he had found Hegel's philosophy personally satisfying because it gave him an inclusive and self-sufficient view of his world. Nevertheless, he had also felt increasingly that philosophy ought to be more in touch with changing intellectual realities—in short, the real world. His reading of Darwin, as he later described it (Dewey, 1909), provided the necessary challenge, as did James's *Principles* (1890/1950). Dewey (1930, p. 25) praised as revolutionary the introduction of evolutionary biology into psychology in that book.

Dewey saw that choosing a method of inquiry was the key to what philosophy should be. The method he decided to use was a form of empiricism as it is understood in this volume. This method specified that what was to be learned or known came from experience—that is, from observation—and that the study of experience was the proper subject matter of philosophy. It was opposed to rationalism and absolutism, and firmly against any commitment to theological presuppositions. Darwin's naturalistic observational method was clearly its prototype. Somewhat more than James, whose orientation was toward the individual, Dewey tended to think of people in an environment, thus treating them as social beings. Dewey's position is summarized in his *Logic* (1938), in the preface to which he notes its long history of development starting from his *Studies in Logical Theory* (1903). He acknowledge his indebtedness to Charles Peirce, even declaring that Peirce was more of a pragmatist than James (Dewey, 1916).

The formulation of Dewey's *Logic* was a statement of both his behavioral psychology and his conception of the method of inquiry exemplified by this psychology and his philosophy. The functionalist view of an example, problem-solving behavior, in the *Logic* is conveniently summarized by Lewis Hahn (1970, pp. 33–35):

1. The first stage in a complete act of reflective thinking or inquiry is awareness of a problem, an indeterminate situation. In this stage something is wrong. There is a breakdown in habitual responses or modes of action, with ensuing perplexity, disturbance, ambiguity, unclarity, conflict, or questioned belief. The problem makes the situation distinctive and gives direction to the inquiry.
2. The problem is clarified through analysis or observation, and then reformulated or better articulated.

3. In problem clarification, hypotheses are formed and solutions suggested.
4. There may be a deductive elaboration of hypotheses; that is, formal or informal statements of the if–then kind.
5. The process of verification or disconfirmation through observation or experiment is next, and in this manner a search takes place for a resolution, or at least clarification, of the problem.

In sum, an indeterminate situation is made more nearly determinate. (The stages are not necessarily ordered as they are listed here.) Why call this a functional approach? Because it emphasizes that the several and successive thoughts or actions are to be understood (explained) as dependent on (functions of) antecedents in the person and the environment.

The approach described here is at the core of a philosophy rounded out by Dewey's views on the nature of experience as seen in the inquiry orientation: Whereas in the traditional view, experience was primarily an affair of knowledge or cognition, for Dewey it was an interaction between a living organism and its physical and social environment. Whereas the traditionalists regarded experience as a subjective inner affair, separate and distinct from objective reality, Dewey thought of it as pertaining to the objective world, which affects the actions and feelings of people and may in turn be modified through human responses (Hahn, 1970), p. 29). Whereas traditional empiricism regarded "simple" data of experience as a given (see Chapter 1, this volume), Dewey considered such data to be the result of analysis, a "reflective product." In addition, Dewey emphasized that experience comprises relations among particulars that, taken together, provide a context for any experience. James also had a holistic inclination in his view of experience and behavior, and in this sense both he and Dewey agreed with the Gestalt psychologists (see Chapter 11, this volume).

Dewey's psychology

It is usually said that Dewey's (1896) article on the reflex arc was a landmark in the development of functionalist psychology. The article itself has defeated many readers with its turgid prose, a style in sharp contrast with that of James. The study was aimed at psychologists like James Mark Baldwin (1891, p. 60), who, upon introspectively analyzing "reactive consciousness," said that like the reflex arc it had three components: (1) a stimulus—a feeling in consciousness; (2) a central process—

attention, intellection; and (3) an action process—muscular, volitional. For a critical analysis of this view, Dewey borrowed his principal example, the reaction of a child to a candle flame, from James's *Principles*. In physiology, Dewey noted, the sensorimotor apparatus of the reflex arc was both a unit of nerve structure and a type of nerve function. He felt that the "image" of this dual relationship had passed over into psychology to become an organizing principle that held together a multiplicity of facts. It was really atomism, however—the associated elements of introspectionism in a new guise.

Dewey's interpretation can be summarized as follows:

1. He objected to treating the components of experience and action as isolated, static elements that are concatenated by practice. Instead, he considered it essential to think of interrelated components or integral parts of a larger entity—a coordination.
2. Once Dewey made it clear that acts are coordinations, he could bring in the notion of their aims (he did not speak of goals). In doing so, he emphasized that aims are the products of an observer's analysis. The individual observed is simply acting; the person's aims are integrated into the coordination itself.
3. Stimuli or responses stand out for the experiencer, the person behaving, only when they are not yet properly "constituted." At this stage, the candle as stimulus and withdrawal as response stand out because (and to the extent that) they have not yet become part of a smooth integration or coordination. Once they do, they are constituted parts of a smooth integration or coordination, and only their functional role is noteworthy.
4. Consciousness as the experience in which an integration develops is of obvious utility to the organism as a survival mechanism. In this regard, Dewey agreed with James.
5. By dwelling on the integration of aims with the means to their attainment, Dewey was laying the groundwork for a psychology in which motivation received major emphasis.
6. He had no specific theory of learning, since he rejected associationism in its traditional form.
7. Coordinations or actions are brought about by and modify the environment.

The import of such an analysis, like Hahn's (1970) analysis of Dewey's *Logic*, is that individual behavior is adaptive and oriented toward aims related to needs. It consists (descriptively), not of muscle contractions or conscious states, but of units of action defined by the outcomes they achieve for the actor. Like James's views, Dewey's seemed cogent and appealed to many people.[1]

University of Chicago Psychology

With full credit to John Dewey the philosopher arguing for a functionalist psychology, it must be noted that most psychologists associate this approach with the name of James Rowland Angell. His ideas are introduced here in contrast with those of E. B. Titchener (Chapter 3, this volume), who adopted the term *structural* to contrast his kind of psychology with the functional (Titchener, 1898). To explain the contrast, Titchener (1899) states that introspection is properly the observation of an "Is" in a mental structure. This pure phenomenalism could be achieved only by a trained introspector. Untrained introspection (without the phenomenalist attitude) naturally yields an "Is-for" functionally. (This is the Is-for meaning of experience explicated earlier for James.) To this distinction the Chicagoan responded at length (Angell, 1903). Accepting Titchener's distinction at face value, Angell attacked the structural aspect (the "Is") of consciousness for its artificiality: It could be identified only after-the-fact by specialized analysis. Structure is not present, not observed, in consciousness itself. Structural psychology is only descriptive, answering the question, What? about the nature of mind or consciousness. However, the more important questions are how and why mind functions as it does. Angell (1903) also begins to remove metaphysics from psychology. In particular, the question of how mind relates to body increasingly seemed to him, as to Dewey, extraneous or irrelevant to psychology.

Rather surprisingly, Darwin's ideas were not exploited as much by Angell as by other functionalists. For example, Angell (1909) recites many of the implications of evolutionism for psychology but has more to say about animals, instinct, and the role of inheritance than about processes of adjustment or adaptation. Evolutionary ideas were mentioned almost incidentally as Angell wrote his rather traditional introductory textbook in 1904.

In an address shortly after that book was published, Angell (1907) revealed a strikingly clear view in which evolutionary doctrine was now of first importance. In suggesting how functionalism should be viewed,

---

[1] To do justice to Dewey's full scholarly impact, it would be necessary to treat at length his contributions to the field of education. However, while they furthered the use of pragmatic psychology and philosophy, these contributions did not substantially extend or perfect the functionalist point of view in psychology.

Angell provides three complementary statements: (1) He contrasted the concept of function with Titchener's notion of structure, in the manner cited above; (2) he said that the functional psychologist "is wont to take his cue from the basal conception of the evolutionary movement, i.e., that for the most part organic structures and functions possess their present characteristics by virtue of the efficiency with which they fit into the extant conditions of life broadly designated the environment (Angell, 1907, pp. 68–69); and (3) he reaffirmed, as did Dewey, the independence of psychology from metaphysical aspects of philosophy: "The mind–body relation (is) capable of treatment in psychology as a methodological distinction rather than a metaphysically existential one" (1907, p. 83). In Angell's view, the psychologist is free to observe mental events as well as behavioral events, and to speak of them in the language customary for each type of observation. There is no implication that either kind of event is more or less real than other facts in the psychologist's realm.

It should be remembered that in Chicago functionalism as represented by Angell (but not Dewey, not Carr), there was the same reluctance to break with the introspectionist tradition as that found in James. This attitude of Angell's spurred revolt in John B. Watson (Chapter 6, this volume).

Chicago functionalism wound down, it is usually said, with the career of Harvey A. Carr. Carr, who had been a student of the young Angell, took it for granted that scientific methodology in psychology was no longer in dispute. Introspection was to be thought of, he said, as subjective observation, in contrast with objective observation. The processes had the same scientific status, differentiated only in what was cognized (Carr, 1925, p. 7). Subjective observation was simply more difficult and less easily shown to be valid—these were only matters of degree. Carr had prepared the way for this view by noting that the traditional study of consciousness involved a logical fallacy—that of assuming that it was an independent entity. In the past, this assumption had created the insurmountable problem of explaining exactly how mental processes could exert any effect on conduct (compare James on ideomotor action). But Carr (1925) moved straight to the explicit declaration that this was "a metaphysical or philosophical problem that does not belong to the domain of an empirical or natural science" (p. 6). This statement implies what is perhaps the prevailing view at present in the United States: Data from either subjective or objective observation have equal scientific status in principle, though they may differ in reliability (see James on this point), and metaphysical aspects are to be disregarded.

In the opening sentence of his textbook, Carr (1925) declares that psychology is primarily concerned with the study of mental activities. Historically, any author who combined those last two words at once faced a logical difficulty. Thus, Carr took care to say that as he saw it, the term "mental activity" was concerned with the acquisition, fixation, retention, organization, and evaluation of experiences, as well as their subsequent utilization in the guidance of conduct. He then added the notion that the conduct that reflects mental activity so defined is adaptive or adjustive, thus summarizing it all for his psychology.

This theory is perhaps best laid out in Chapter 4, called "Some Principles of Organic Behavior" (Carr, 1925). He begins by explicating the reflex-arc concept in a way that should have pleased Dewey (in just four pages). He then explained the adaptive act in clear evolutionist over prose. The key sentence was, "An adaptive act involves a motivating stimulus, a sensory situation, and a response that alters that situation in a way that satisfies the motivating conditions" (1925, p. 72). Within such a framework, most American psychologists have found their own way to specialized interpretations of a host of topics, including motivation, learning, sensing and perceiving, adjustment, and, with some broadening, personality (Carr, 1935, himself wrote a book on space perception).

There were many other important proponents of functionalism in America, most notably Robert S. Woodworth and J. McKeen Cattell at Columbia University. There were also some notable European psychologists such as Edouard Claparède who were attracted to the ideas of James and Dewey, although their international following was smaller in psychology than it was in philosophy. The basic functionalist position has now been presented, however, and its many variants may be viewed as mainly expansions or applications rather than important revisions of that basic position.

SUMMARY

This review is intended to indicate important points in the present chapter and to link them with the ideas or trends presented in the previous chapter.

1. The development of a functionalist view in British psychology after its early anticipation was impeded by critics of science in general and of biological evolutionism in particular who believed that empirical philosophy and the psychology it engendered were threats to religion or theology. Their resistance, while not effective everywhere, nevertheless hindered the development of a scientific psychology in that country until well after the turn of the 20th century.

2. In their historical developments from colonial days until somewhat after the Civil War, the prevailing American philosophy and theology resembled those of corresponding eras in Great Britain. Wherever this thinking dominated colleges and universities, the challenges of evolutionism often aroused great skepticism, even fierce resistance to science. More specifically, the idea that psychology might be scientific had mixed appeal for important academic philosophers.

3. James's rejection of most of the idealist philosophy permitted him to take a less obstructed road toward a scientific psychology. He had first to work out a philosophy more congenial to science; he called it Pragmatism. Dewey soon came to support this approach decisively. Together, the two scholars created a climate of thought than enhanced their new and distinctive viewpoint about the nature of the psychology to which the philosophy of Pragmatism gave rise.

4. James did not always resolve the inconsistencies in his flood of creative ideas, nor, with his tolerance for ambiguity, did this bother him very much. For example, he felt that concerns about free will and indeterminism belonged in contexts other than psychological science. In those contexts (e.g., religious or philosophical), he could and did believe personally in free will. Indeed all of the Chicago functionalists (the agnostics Dewey and Carr even more than Angell) made a cleaner break than did James with traditional philosophy, especially metaphysics.

5. Most traditional users of introspection (but not Wundt; see Chapter 2, this volume) believed that it would yield a description of mental elements of one kind or another. When combined into an essentially infinite variety of patterns by association, these elements would explain the nature of mind. But to James it appeared that introspection revealed only the endless flow and change in mental life, with directions and rates of change determined by impulsive (i.e., motivational) and affective factors as much as by sheerly cognitive events. James's interpretation and Dewey's reanalysis of the reflex arc did not point toward simple and seemingly mechanical associative chains in conscious experience or behavior, but rather toward continuous, internally organized or patterned "coordinations"—acts oriented toward aims that are adaptively functional.

6. After James, American functionalists increasingly emphasized objective over subjective methods. While they all utilized introspection, only James's lingering attachments to traditional psychology led him to retain interest in (and sometimes be confused about) the related philosophical problems. Dewey shifted rather early to an almost exclusive reliance on behavioral evidence (this as psychologist, not philosopher). Angell, while declaring himself free of metaphysical concerns, had

thought, experimented, and written in a seemingly traditional way. If he is read carefully, however, it is clear that he had converted all this into a functional approach and used behavioral data even more than introspection in his science. Even before Watson published his call for a behaviorist psychology (see Chapter 6, this volume) Angell (1913) gave a speech justifying his extensive use of behavioral data to supplement those from introspection. Carr had become quite matter-of-fact and essentially objective in all aspects of method, but especially so in his predominating experimentalism.

7. A highly significant innovation in Great Britain had been Bain's systematic incorporation of physiological ideas into psychology. For some decades this came to nought, whereas evolutionary biology from its inception had been both interesting and capable of integration with psychology (for reasons we have discussed, this too did not happen easily or all at once). In America, Ladd's introduction of European-style physiological psychology had only a modest impact, because along with it came his idealist philosophy in unregenerate and unassimilable form. James, however, was able to see that human biology and human psychology were so closely related as to be parts of the same larger study. Physiological psychology and, even more, evolutionism, were to be keys to his psychology, sharing importance with his groundbreaking Pragmatism. His convictions were shared by the Chicago group with varying emphases, but always with the same ardor for shaping psychology into a functional discipline.

8. It was not a necessary comment previously, but it should now be recorded that, following the brilliant theoretical imaginings of James, attention to theory gradually declined across the years of Chicago functionalism. By Carr's time, Chicago empiricism primarily required close attention to experimental data that had been specifically collected to test limited hypotheses. Such a decline in the importance of theory presumably is related to increasingly strong positivist views about science and its concepts. This possibility is seen in James (1890/1950, Chapter 7) even before he wrote about Pragmatism. That is, Pragmatism, applied to science, led to concise definition and discouraged empirically unfounded speculation about concepts and hypotheses. Positivism, and the positivist strain in Pragmatism, were in the long run not very different from the behaviorist stress on observables in psychological science. In this respect, it has been argued (e.g., G. Mandler, personal communication, Dec. 1979), the earlier part of the 20th century saw an impoverishment of psychological theory in America. To reestablish theory in a more central role in psychology would require, we can see in retrospect, a reexamination of the nature of our science by latter-day psychologists.

To them, the broad outlines of functionalism were congenial, but the variables to be considered within that framework appeared as various as those of psychoanalysis, Gestalt psychology, cognitive theory, and many other contemporary theories in special fields of interest.

THE VANISHING OF FUNCTIONALISM

Nowadays no one is called a functionalist in psychology, and yet almost every psychologist is one. The label has vanished, but the point of view remains in attitudes and practices. By the 1940s and the end of the visible Chicago group, functionalism had become more of a standard framework for scientific psychology than a banner around which sympathizers had any cause to rally. The empiricist view was accepted by nearly all psychologists, few of whom were bothered by philosophical reservations or questions. The pragmatist conviction about how concepts and experimental variables were to be explicated prevailed almost everywhere.

In retrospect, as Angell and Carr themselves said, functionalism was never a school of psychology, and nowadays the word can be deemphasized because functionalism has become everybody's conception of how to do psychology. This interpretation has also been accepted by historians such as Boring (1950, p. 559) and Heidbreder (1973, pp. 281–282). One can say that the functionalist conception is a prior condition—a framework—for specialized work in most parts of psychology's domain. In this respect it is not in conflict with other modern viewpoints. It is not preemptive of any special field of interest, and it is ingrained in almost all of contemporary psychological scholarship.

ACKNOWLEDGEMENTS

Professor John E. Smith of the Department of Philosophy, Yale University, gave me some very helpful critical comments. I benefited also from the advice of William R. Woodward, James Blight, Eugene Taylor, and Mitchell Katz. I am especially indebted to George Mandler for his spirited commentary on several subtopics.

REFERENCES

Angell, J. R. (1903). The relations of structural and functional psychology to philosophy. *Philosophical Review, 12,* 243–271.
Angell, J. R. (1904). *Psychology.* New York: Holt.

Angell, J. R. (1907). The province of functional psychology. *Psychological Review, 14*, 61–91.

Angell, J. R. (1909). The influence of Darwin on psychology. *Psychological Review, 16*, 152–169.

Angell, J. R. (1913). Behavior as a category of psychology. *Psychological Review, 20*, 255–270.

Baldwin, J. M. (1891). Feeling and will. In J. M. Baldwin, *Handbook of psychology* (Vol. 2). New York: Holt.

Blumenthal, A. M. (1977). Wilhelm Wundt and early American psychology: A clash of two cultures. *Annals of the New York Academy of Sciences, 291*, 13–20.

Boring, E. G. (1950). *A history of experimental psychology* (2nd ed.). New York: Appleton-Century-Crofts.

Boring, E. G. (1963). The influence of evolutionary theory upon American psychological thought. In R. I. Watson & D. T. Campbell (Eds.), *History, psychology, and science*. New York: Wiley (Reprinted from S. Persons, Ed., *Evolutionary thought in America*. New Haven, CT: Yale University Press, 1950).

Bowler, P. J. (1983). *The eclipse of Darwinism*. Baltimore, MD: Johns Hopkins University Press.

Bradley, F. H. (1883). *The principles of logic*. London: Kegan Paul, Trench.

Brožek, J. (Ed.). (1984). *Explorations in the history of psychology in the United States*. Lewisburg, PA: Bucknell University Press.

Carr, H. A. (1925). *Psychology*. New York: Longmans, Green.

Carr, H. A. (1935). *An introduction to space perception*. New York: Longmans, Green.

Dewey, J. (1887). *Psychology*. New York: Harpers.

Dewey, J. (1896). The reflex arc concept in psychology. *Psychological Review, 3*, 357–370.

Dewey, J. (1903). *Studies in logical theory*. Chicago: University of Chicago Press.

Dewey, J. (1916). The pragmatism of Peirce. *Journal of Philosophy, 13*, 709–715.

Dewey, J. (1930). From absolutism to experimentalism. In G. P. Adams & W. P. Montague (Eds.), *Contemporary American philosophy*. New York: Macmillan.

Dewey, J. (1938). *Logic: The theory of inquiry*. New York: Holt.

Fay, J. W. (1939). *American psychology before William James*. New Brunswick, NJ: Rutgers University Press.

Fisch, M. H. (1954). Alexander Bain and the genealogy of pragmatism. *Journal of the History of Ideas, 15*, 413–444.

Fiske, J. (1885). *Darwinism and other essays* (2nd ed.). Boston: Riverside. (Original work published 1879)

Green, T. H. (1874). Introduction. In D. Hume, *A treatise on human nature*. London: Longmans, Green.

Green, T. H. (1883). *Prolegomena to ethics*. Oxford: Clarendon.

Hahn, L. E. (1970). Dewey's philosophy and philosophic method. In J. A. Boydston (Ed.), *Guide to the works of John Dewey*. Carbondale: Southern Illinois University Press.

Hamilton, W. (1859). *Lectures in metaphysics*. Boston: Gould, Lincoln. (Original work published 1858)

Hearnshaw, L. S. (1964). *A short history of British psychology, 1840–1940*. New York: Barnes & Noble.

Heidbreder, E. (1973). In M. Henle, J. Jaynes, & J. J. Sullivan (Eds.), *Historical conceptions of psychology*. New York: Springer.

Hilgard, E. R. (1986). *The making of modern psychology: History of twentieth century psychology in America*. San Diego, CA: Harcourt Brace Jovanovich.

James, W. (1884). What is an emotion? *Mind, 9*, 188–205.

James, W. (1904). The Chicago school. *Psychological Bulletin, 1*, 1–15.

James, W. (1909). On the function of cognition. In W. James, *The meaning of truth*. New York: Longmans, Green. (Reprinted from *Mind*, 1885, *10*, 27–44)

James, W. (1909). *Pragmatism: A new name for some old ways of thinking*. New York: Longmans, Green. (Original work published 1907)

James, W. (1920). Philosophical conceptions and practical results. In W. James, *Collected essays and reviews*. New York: Longmans, Green. (Reprinted from *University of California Chronicle*, 1898, *1*, 288–310)

James, W. (1920). Remarks on Spencer's definition of mind as correspondence. In W. James, *Collected essays and reviews*. New York: Longmans, Green. (Reprinted from *Journal of Speculative Philosophy*, 1878, *12*, 1–18)

James, W. (1920). The sentiment of rationality. In W. James, *Collected essays and reviews*. New York: Longmans, Green. (Reprinted from *Mind*, 1879, *4*, 317–346)

James, W. (1950). *The principles of psychology* (2 vols.). New York: Dover. (Original work published 1890)

James, W. (1961). *The varieties of religious experience*. New York: Collier. (Original work published 1912)

James papers. Harvard University, Houghton Library, File 4575a.

Ladd, G. T. (1887). *Elements of physiological psychology*. New York: Scribner's.

McCosh, J. (1886). *Psychology: the cognitive powers*. New York: Scribner's.

McCosh, J. (1888). *The religious aspect of evolution*. New York: Putnam.

Morse, E. S. (1876). What American zoologists have done for evolution. *Popular Science Monthly*, *10*, 1–16, 181–198.

Peirce, C. S. (1877–1878). How to make our ideas clear. *Popular Science Monthly*, *12*, 286–302.

Perry, R. B. (1948). *The thought and character of William James*. Cambridge, MA: Harvard University Press.

Pfeifer, E. J. (1965). The genesis of American neo-Lamarckism. *Isis*, *56*, 156–167.

Porter, N. (1868). *The elements of intellectual science*. New York: Scribner's.

Porter, N. (1886). *Evolution*. New York: Bridgman.

Rieber, R. W., & Salzinger, K. (Eds.). (1980). *Psychology: Theoretical–historical perspectives*. New York: Academic.

Roback, A. A. (1952). *History of American psychology* (rev. ed.). New York: Macmillan.

Robinson, D. N. (1981). *An intellectual history of psychology* (rev. ed.). New York: Macmillan.

Slater, P. Y. (1977). *Children in the New England mind*. Hamden, CT: Archon.

Stocking, G. W. (1962). Lamarckianism in American social science: 1890–1915. *Journal of the History of Ideas*, *23*, 239–256.

Titchener, E. B. (1898). The postulates of a structural psychology. *Philosophical Review*, *7*, 449–465.

Titchener, E. B. (1899). Structural and functional psychology. *Philosophical Review*, *8*, 290–299.

Titchener, E. B. (1919). *A textbook of psychology*. New York: Macmillan. (Original work published 1896)

Ward, J. (1886). Psychology. *Encyclopaedia Britannica* (Vol. 19, 9th ed.). Boston: Little, Brown.

Woodward, W. R. (1984). William James's psychology of will. In J. Brožek (Ed.), *Explorations in the history of psychology in the United States*. Lewisburg, PA: Bucknell University Press.

6

The Origins of Behaviorism: Antecedents and Proclamation

ALEXANDRA W. LOGUE

INTRODUCTION

In 1913 *Psychological Review* published the following statement:

> Psychology as the behaviorist views it is a purely objective experimental branch of natural science. Its theoretical goal is the prediction and control of behavior. Introspection forms no essential part of its methods, nor is the scientific value of its data dependent upon the readiness with which they lend themselves to interpretation in terms of consciousness. The behaviorist, in his efforts to get a unitary scheme of animal response, recognizes no dividing line between man and brute. (Watson, 1913b, p. 158)

A new discipline, behaviorism, had been proclaimed by John B. Watson, professor of psychology at Johns Hopkins University. Watson's announcement of behaviorism shows that in 1913 behaviorism had several defining features: It was an objective, deterministic, scientific, experimental psychology useful in the study of all species, not just humans, and its only data were those of behavior. In sum, behaviorism sought simple principles that would predict and explain all animal behavior. Behaviorism was to become popular, although it was controversial in Watson's time (see Calkins, 1921; Herrick, 1915; Hunter, 1922; Lovejoy, 1922; Ruckmich, 1916; Thorndike, 1915; Titchener, 1914; Samelson,

POINTS OF VIEW IN THE
MODERN HISTORY OF PSYCHOLOGY

1981), and it remains quite visible and controversial today (see, for example, the journal *Behaviorism*, which began publishing in 1972). Few movements in psychology have displayed such longevity or commanded such attention.

The generally favorable reception that greeted behaviorism in 1913 can be attributed to several developments in the intellectual climate of the late 19th and early 20th centuries. First, the principles of natural selection as detailed by Darwin (1859/1958) had increased the likelihood that different species might be subject to similar psychological principles. This possibility spurred the research of some British psychologists, who showed that objective experiments with animals other than humans could yield lawful, comparative data. During this same period, the Russian reflexologists were also performing experiments with nonhuman animals, although their research was specifically directed at elucidating the principles of classical conditioning. Darwinian theory had additional influence in that it led psychologists to see certain nonhuman behavioral and mental characteristics as having human value. This was especially true of certain functionalists in the United States during the early 1900s. At about the same time that functionalism was becoming popular, two schools of philosophical inquiry—positivism and pragmatism—were impressing on psychologists the value of theory and research that is objective and simple. Thus all the major principles in Watson's behaviorism were known and looked upon favorably by much of the psychological community at the time of Watson's announcement in 1913, but a discipline linking them together was lacking.

This chapter describes these principles or tenets, as well as some specific antecedents of behaviorism. The next chapter traces the success and failures of behavioristic psychology from 1913 until about 1950.

ELEMENTS OF BEHAVIORISM, 1850–1912

Evolutionary Theory

One of the essential tenets of Watson's 1913 behaviorism was that nonhuman and human animals could be studied with the same techniques, and that similar principles could describe the behavior of all species. A half-century earlier, such a concept would have been unacceptable to most psychologists. In psychology as a whole, the significance for human psychology of psychological experimentation with other animals was not specified until the advent of modern evolutionary theory. Prior to the publication of Darwin's *The Origin of Species* in 1859, researchers had no overall scientific model or scheme within which they could place the structure and behavior of a particular species in relation to that of other species. By postulating that all species had evolved through natural selection from some small number of ancestors, Darwin provided such a framework.

The theory of evolution demonstrated to biologists and psychologists the continuity between species. It implied, for example, the relevance of research with nonhumans to understanding humans. In *The Expression of the Emotions in Man and Animals,* Darwin (1872/1965) argued that emotions may have evolved from a simpler, though comparable, form in dogs and other nonhuman species to a more complex form in humans. Darwin's argument legitimized for many psychologists the comparative study of consciousness or behavior, as well as that of bodily structure.

The impact of Darwin's work on the type of research performed with animals other than humans was enormous. Such research was no longer of value only to gain information about the species under study; research questions extremely difficult to investigate with human subjects could be investigated using other species and the results extrapolated to humans. Psychologists, like other scientists, could now work with a simple system in order to further their discipline. Despite the recognition that a continuum between species exists, Darwinian evolutionary theory still had no ready answer for the question of just how close various species are along the evolutionary continuum. Such knowledge might be helpful in predicting the degree of similarity between psychological principles describing those two species. Nevertheless, the widespread acceptance of Darwin's work disposed many psychologists to react favorably to Watson's proposal that the study of humans and other animals merited the same approach.

British Psychology with Nonhuman Subjects

The influence of modern evolutionary theory on studies of animal learning and behavior can be directly observed in the work of the British psychologists. During the latter half of the nineteenth century, these researchers progressed from using an anecdotal to an experimental method. The techniques they developed in order to carry out their experiments, as well as the data they obtained, had a strong impact on psychologists in the United States working with nonhuman species prior to the advent of behaviorism. Since advocacy of the experimental method for studying nonhuman animals was prerequisite to the acceptance of behaviorism—an experimentally oriented science covering all species—the influence of British experimental psychology with nonhumans was important in the success of behaviorism in America.

The initial stage of the British progression from anecdotal to experimental psychology for nonhumans is represented by the work of George John Romanes (1882/1965), who lived and worked during the latter part of the 19th century. Romanes inferred nonhuman animals' subjective states from informal reports of their behavior. The first principle he used in making these inferences was simply that of analogy between the subject and himself. In order to attribute a particular conscious emotion to a subject, Romanes required that the subject first exhibit behavior similar to what Romanes would exhibit if he himself were experiencing that emotion. Second, as proof that the emotion was conscious, Romanes required that the subject exhibit learned adaptations to its environment.

For Romanes, studying psychology was equivalent to studying the mind, and he justified studying the minds of nonhuman animals by appealing to Darwin's theory of evolution. Although Romanes's methods were essentially anecdotal, he did attempt to make his judgments systematically and without bias. Romanes based his comparison of psychological attributes across species on evolutionary theory, but he had no objective means for collecting and interpreting comparative data.

In 1894 Conwy Lloyd Morgan published his now famous canon in which he agreed with Romanes's basic approach to comparative psychology but urged caution in the interpretation of any resulting data. Specifically, Morgan's canon stated that complex mentalistic processes should not be inferred in nonhuman animals when explanations presuming simpler processes are adequate. Morgan realized that one could be certain of consciousness only in oneself. Attributing consciousness to another person or to a member of another species is therefore simply an inference based on observing similar behavior in the subject and oneself (Morgan, 1900, p. 42). According to Morgan, natural selection dictates that psychological processes become more complex the higher one goes on the evolutionary scale. He therefore concluded that parsimonious, simple, and objective explanations of nonhuman animal behavior are preferable whenever possible (Morgan, 1894). Like Romanes, Morgan was basing much of his approach to psychology on Darwinian evolutionary principles.

Experimental psychology with nonhumans could not have developed through theoretical breakthroughs alone. Advances in technique were also necessary. Here, too, the British psychologists working with nonhuman species were pioneers.

One of the first psychologists to perform controlled experiments with animals other than humans was Douglas Spalding (1872), whose main goal was to determine the extent to which certain behaviors were inherited or learned. Spalding's ingenuity made up for his lack of modern technology. As the first step, he deprived newly hatched chicks of vision by placing hoods over their heads. In other work, he prevented them from hearing by placing gum paper over their ears. Some days later he removed the hoods or the paper and observed the chicks' behavior. In this way, Spalding learned that visual or auditory deprivation had little effect on, for example, the chicks' pecking or their responses to either their mother or a hawk. He concluded that virtually all of the behavior exhibited by the chicks was inherited.

A specific technological development that for a time symbolized American psychology with nonhumans was William Stanton Small's maze. He used it in the first study of maze running in white rats (Small, 1901). The pathways in the maze formed a replica of the Hampton Court maze designed for humans (the version for humans is still to be seen at Hampton Court Palace, near London).

Like many modern researchers of nonhuman animal behavior, Small wanted to observe his subjects' behavior in a natural environment where the solution to a problem could be monitored under conditions as well controlled as possible. He recorded the number of wrong turns the rats made and the length of time they took to reach the end of the maze; with practice, decreases occurred in both measures. Small concluded that his subjects profited from their chance experiences, eventually showing a recognition of and discrimination between different paths. He did not think that they learned the maze merely by a process of selecting one successful movement out of many random movements (compare Thorndike, 1898). Small's work combined both technological advancement and theoretical development. The science of psychology of nonhuman animals was well on its way.

Russian Psychology with Nonhuman Subjects

Britain was not the only country whose research in experimental psychology with nonhumans was to affect psychology in the United States, for at about the same time as in Britain, an experimental approach to psychology with nonhumans was also developing in Russia. The origin of this development was rather different from that in Britain; it grew out of physiology, whereas in Britain experimental psychology with nonhumans grew out of the study of animal behavior.

Ivan Michailovich Sechenov is considered to be the founder of Russia's experimental psychology with nonhuman subjects. Sechenov was first trained as an engineer and later as a physiologist. He subsequently traveled outside of Russia between the years 1856 and 1860, studying with both physiologists and psychologists. After returning to Russia, he established several laboratories in which he investigated what is now called the reflex (Sechenov, 1965).

Not surprisingly, Sechenov's beliefs about the reflex reflected his training in both physiology and psychology. He defined the reflex as neural activity and claimed that behavior consists entirely of reflexes, so that by studying reflex actions it should be possible to discover all the principles of psychology. Although he was not able to observe the influence of the brain directly, Sechenov conceived of hypothetical brain mechanisms to explain why a response follows a stimulus in a reflex, and also to explain the differences between involuntary behavior (which he defined as behavior following an unexpected stimulus) and voluntary behavior (that following an expected stimulus). Clearly, however, Sechenov thought that the most useful level for describing psychological activity was that of behavior rather than neural activity. He adhered to his deterministic, stimulus–response explanation of behavior to such an extent that he even believed that thoughts were reflexively caused, and solely by external stimulation (Sechenov, 1863/1965); centrally initiated processes played no part in Sechenov's theories. Determinism—the view that behavior is a function of antecedent causes and nothing more—occurs, of course, in varying forms throughout behavioristic psychology.

Vladimir Mikhailovich Bekhterev and Ivan Petrovich Pavlov built on Sechenov's work around the turn of the century. Bekhterev, trained in physiology like Sechenov, conducted research that was mostly concerned with neurological disorders in humans. He was a strong advocate of objective psychology and was opposed to the use of mentalistic terminology. His book, *General Principles of Human Reflexology* (1917/1933), opens with the following statement: "Reflexology, which is a new doctrine, is the science of human personality studied from the strictly objective, bio-social standpoint" (p. 33). Bekhterev then attempts to explain all of human behavior in terms of conditioned and unconditioned reflexes. He was the first to use the word "reflexology," which is now used often to describe Russian experimental psychology with nonhuman subjects. It is in large part for his primacy in this usage that Bekhterev is remembered (Boring, 1950, pp. 637–638).

Pavlov also began his career as a physiologist, winning the Nobel Prize in 1904 for his research on the reflexes of digestion. Just prior to receiving that award, Pavlov began the work for which he is best known—his work in psychology on classical conditioning. During his experiments on digestion, Pavlov had observed that his subjects, dogs, would begin to salivate (a digestive reflex) even before they had any food in their mouths. In fact, if something that usually elicited salivation (the unconditioned response), such as food (the unconditioned stimulus), were paired with something that usually did not, such as a bell, this formerly neutral stimulus would itself come to elicit salivation (i.e., it would become a conditioned stimulus and elicit the conditioned response).

According to Pavlov, the actual conditioning process took place through an attraction of neural excitation between the cerebral location of the unconditioned stimulus and the cerebral location of the conditioned stimulus whenever both were presented close together in time (Pavlov, 1928/1965). Thus Pavlov was joining two concepts: the Russian concept of the neural basis of reflexes, and that of association by temporal contiguity (a popular explanation of human learning from at least the time of Aristotle). Indeed, the strength of Pavlov's unified formulation was due in large part to his integration of these two powerful concepts, one from the study of physiology and one from the study of human learning.

Until his death in 1936, Pavlov continued his work on classical conditioning. Typically, he worked with only a few subjects in a given experiment, studying each in careful detail. He was vehement about the advantages of his objective approach to psychology. Subjective feelings, he claimed, had no place in his research (Pavlov, 1928/1965). Pavlov distinguished himself by amassing a large and cohesive body of data and theory, with the consequence that his was the most fully developed and systematic, as well as the most thoroughly tested, empirical approach in psychology up to that time.

Because there was little communication between Russian and American psychologists around the turn of the century, Pavlov's approach to psychology went unnoticed in the United States until Yerkes and Morgulis's (1909) description of his work appeared in the *Psychological Bulletin*. This article aroused a great deal of interest among American psychologists, and greater attention was thereafter given to the research of Russian reflexologists.

Functionalism

The major movement in American psychology prior to 1913 that had the most in common with behaviorism, and that was influential in preparing American psychologists for behaviorism, was functionalism (see Chapters 4 and 5, this volume). It is difficult to give a specific definition of functionalism because, as with most broadly based movements, no single description fits the beliefs of all the prominent functionalists. It is clear, however, that they all shared a strong connection with Darwinian evolutionary theory. As a rule, they were concerned with objectively determining how and why an organism behaves as it does in terms of the survival value of the behavior; their interest in describing the behavior itself was thus secondary (Angell, 1907).

The main difference between functionalism and Watson's behaviorism is that many functionalists, including William James and James Rowland Angell (1907), emphasized the study of consciousness (Watson's dissatisfaction with this conception of psychology are discussed in detail by Mackenzie, 1977, pp. 73–84, 87–95). Like the behaviorists, however, some functionalists carried out rigorous experiments with animals and strongly advocated the theory of natural selection and the continuity of the species. While Angell was not himself an experimenter with animals, he was one of the directors of Watson's doctoral dissertation, entitled *Animal Education* (1903). Thus the functionalists directly aided in making experimentation with animals—an essential element of Watson's behaviorism—acceptable in the United States.

Positivism

The French philosopher Auguste Comte was the founder of positivism, a philosophy that emphasizes nonspeculative, objective, and observational data. Clearly, introspection and the study of consciousness (anathemas to Watson) have no place in a behavioristic system of thought. Thus positivism might appear to be an important precursor of behaviorism. However, while it is often said that positivism was a strong movement among natural scientists around 1900, a movement that was supposedly spreading to psychology (see, for example, Boring, 1950, pp. 633–634; Mackenzie, 1976; Marx & Hillix, 1973, chap. 7), the researchers of that time certainly did not stress a link between their changing methodology and the philosophy of positivism.

Although it is true that many psychologists around the turn of the century had extensive philosophical training, and that psychologists saw their task as making psychology more scientific (see, for example, James, 1892/1962, p. 15; Jennings, 1908; Titchener, 1910), whether or not such psychologists also saw themselves as positivists is difficult to determine, because positivism was so rarely discussed. Watson (1913b) could have been taking the side of positivism when he declared, "Those time-honored relics of philosophical speculation [mind–body parallelism and interaction] need trouble the student of behavior as little as they trouble the student of physics" (p. 166), but this is doubtful. Indeed, Rom Harré and his co-authors (Chapter 13, this volume) first accept Sigmund Koch's distinction between classical behaviorism (about 1913–1930) and neobehaviorism (about 1930–1950), and then argue that the effect of positivism on the former was of "negligible significance."

Many psychologists of this time certainly acted like positivists, even if they did not assume the label. More probably, positivism and behaviorism were both symptoms of a growing trend toward objectivity in the sciences. Logical positivism, developed later, clearly had a direct and important influence on psychology and behaviorism (see Harré et al., Chapter 13, this volume). This influence is discussed in the next chapter.

Pragmatism

Pragmatism, which was discussed in detail in the previous chapter, was popular among American psychologists around 1900, and an aid in the acceptance of behaviorism. As an empiricist philosophy, it postulates that knowledge arises only through experience; thus ideas and concepts are assumed to be based on external events. Pragmatism is thus compatible with behaviorism, which also accounts for learning in terms of external events.

Two psychologists gave pragmatism a prominent place in their respective presidential addresses to the American Psychological Association: William James (1905) and James Rowland Angell (1907). In his address, Angell likens pragmatism to functionalism, in that both spring from an interest in the effects of evolution on mental processes. As noted earlier, Angell was one of Watson's thesis advisors and his colleague at the University of Chicago until 1908. Therefore, Watson was surely exposed to pragmatism while at Chicago, although he never mentions it. In any event, pragmatism was very much in evidence in American psychology about the time that behaviorism was being formulated, thus helping to create a favorable climate for Watson's announcement in 1913.

AMERICAN PSYCHOLOGY WITH NONHUMAN SUBJECTS, 1898–1912

Because Watson's own research, and his behaviorism, were strongly tied to experiments with nonhuman animals, behaviorism would never have survived had not American psychologists working with nonhuman subjects been favorably disposed toward it. Actually, their work during the 15 years prior to Watson's proclamation already had most of the significant features of behaviorism (but see Washburn, 1908). At that time American psychology with animals other than humans was experimental, functional, objective, and based on an assumption of the continuity between species. For example, Jacques Loeb (1900, chap. 13), in his attempt to make psychology more objective and scientific, claimed that tropisms (simple reflexes) are the basis of all instinctual behavior for all species. In addition, he defined conscious behavior as simply the ability to learn from experience.

Herbert S. Jennings, a biologist at Johns Hopkins, disputed Loeb's claim that much of the behavior of lower organisms was due to tropisms. He maintained instead that a significant proportion of all behavior was the result of learning (Jennings, 1906, chap. 20). Like Loeb, however, he believed that objective criteria are necessary to identify psychological processes (Jennings, 1908). In addition, he stated that because objective data are sufficient evidence for consciousness in humans, such data should also suffice as evidence for consciousness in nonhumans (Jennings, 1906, chap. 20). In this way Jennings strongly affirmed the continuity of species, with particular reference to psychological processes.

Jennings continued to stress his support of experimental, objective psychology, with nonhuman subjects and by 1910 his theories are almost indistinguishable from those found in Watson's proclamation of behaviorism. Jenning's emphasis at this time was on behavior, not consciousness:

> The living interest of the study of behavior of animals lies in the concrete facts: in what the animals *do.* . . . In recent years a new spirit, a new desire, has permeated biological science in every division,—in brief, the desire *to see the processes of nature occurring,* and to modify and control these processes—not merely to judge what processes *must have* occurred. . . . Contrasted with this is an earlier method of work, which may be expressed as follows: Certain conditions were seen to exist. From this, conclusions were drawn as to what *must have occurred,* in order that these conditions might exist. If we succeeded in imagining a process that would satisfactorily account for what exists,—then that was a sufficient explanation. (Jennings, 1910, pp. 349–350)

Jennings seems to have seen through to the crux of the methodological weakness in psychology that behaviorism had attempted to cure— namely, postulating hypothetical mechanisms that can never be shown to exist. Jennings and Watson both came to focus on the point at which organisms interact with the world; that is, at the level of the organism's behavior. Function, objectivity, positivism, and pragmatism (in the sense of utility) all come into play in Jennings' statement. It is not surprising, then, that several people have described him, and not Watson, as the first behaviorist (Jensen, 1962; Roback, 1923, pp. 39–40).

Edward L. Thorndike's contributions to American psychology with nonhuman subjects include the advancement of functional theory by his formulating the law of effect, and his invention of an ingenious apparatus, the puzzle box, for collecting data on learning. Spalding had published experimental research on animal learning prior to Thorndike (see Spalding, 1872), but the latter's work became much better known. In 1898 Thorndike published the first results of his work involving the puzzle boxes (experimental cages or chambers that could be opened by an animal from the inside). Observations of cats learning to escape from the boxes by pulling a loop led him at first to conclude that the subjects were learning associations between sensations and responses. Thorndike (1911/1965) later supplemented this explanation with his formulation of the law of effect: Responses followed by what Thorndike called "satisfaction" will increase in frequency, and responses followed by discomfort will decrease in frequency. Responses function to obtain pleasure and avoid pain through a process similar to natural selection, except that it occurs during the lifetime of a single organism.

Because he could not actually observe a cat's satisfaction or discomfort, Thorndike was content to infer those feelings through his observations of the cat's behavior. Despite his willingness to infer the unobservable, however, his address to the American Psychological Association in 1913 showed that he too agreed with the growing emphasis that psychologists working with nonhuman subjects were placing on behavior and determinism. In that address, Thorndike voiced the criticism that "our belief that an idea tends to produce the act which it is like, or represents, or 'is an idea of' or 'has as its object,' is kith and kin with our forebears' belief that dressing to look like a bear will give you his strength" (1913, p. 105).

Probably more than any other single American psychologist, Robert M. Yerkes helped to make experiments with nonhuman animals acceptable to psychologists, if only because of the sheer volume of his work and the number of species he studied. He promoted the comparative study of psychological principles by his exemplary experiments with species ranging from amphibians to apes (Yerkes, 1932/1961) and, in 1925 and 1930, by his founding of laboratories for primate research in New Haven and Orange Park, Florida, respectively. These centers were the forerunners of the internationally known Yerkes Regional Primate Research Center of Emory University.

Yerkes' technological innovations also hastened the progress of experimental psychology with nonhumans. For example, in 1908 and 1909 he worked with Watson on improving the testing of color vision in nonhuman animals by setting up experiments using monochromatic light instead of colored papers (Yerkes Papers, 1906–1915). In addition, Yerkes published one of the first experimental studies of maze learning in 1901, the same year as Small. Since his maze was not as complex as Small's, and since Yerkes used turtles instead of rats, the first maze study is usually attributed to Small.

The work of Yerkes, Thorndike, Jennings, and others indicates that, except for reference to the term "consciousness" and other hypothetical cognitive mechanisms, American psychology with nonhumans just prior to and contemporary with Watson's announcement of behaviorism was generally quite compatible with behaviorism.

AMERICAN PSYCHOLOGY WITH HUMAN SUBJECTS, 1912

During the time when psychology with nonhumans was becoming increasingly objective, experimental, deterministic, and concerned with the continuity of the species in the years just prior to Watson's (1913b) article, some of the same trends can be seen in psychological research with humans. In studies of human beings, however, the trend toward what might be called "scientific" psychology was much more uneven.

The irregular progress of objective psychology with humans can easily be seen by looking at the research of those functionalists who worked mainly with human subjects. Of these, the best known is William James. He and other functionalists, such as Cattell, felt strongly that the study of consciousness should be retained as part of psychology; they were specifically interested in studying the evolution and function of consciousness.

This group approved of the examination of consciousness through the main technique employed in psychological research with humans at the time: introspection (Angell, 1907; Cattell, 1896; James, 1895). Despite the fact that there was no way to verify a subject's report of what he or she thought or felt, these psychologists believed that introspection was the only way that consciousness could be studied, and that it was a generally reliable method of research. Objectivity in reporting data was important to them (see, for example, Cattell's studies of reaction time in Poffenberger, 1947), but they were willing to sacrifice some objectivity in order to study consciousness.

Some of the psychologists working with human subjects eventually became sensitive to the kinds of issues that Watson later called to everyone's attention in 1913. For example, just prior to Watson's statement, Angell began to voice severe doubts about the role of consciousness in psychology. In an article in the *Psychological Review* (Angell, 1913) that was originally an address at the APA in December 1912 (before Watson's statement appeared), he claimed that the concept of consciousness is not useful in the study of nonhuman animals. He also expressed his conviction that the term "consciousness" would soon disappear from psychology altogether, and that in its place would be simply "behavior." Despite these beliefs, however, Angell was not yet ready to give up introspection, for he felt that it was a good tool for studying the links between a stimulus and its response. He summarized his article by stating that he favored objective psychology, though not to an extreme (Angell, 1913).

Knight Dunlap, Watson's colleague at Johns Hopkins, was another psychologist who worked with human subjects but whose sympathies prior to 1913 appear to have been basically compatible with behaviorist psychology. In 1912 he published a paper, "The Case Against Introspectionism," in which he disputed the usefulness of experiments designed to observe consciousness through introspection. Dunlap felt that the procedure had been removed too far from contact with objective data, as a result of psychologists using introspection to study "introspected" sensations. Like Angell, he wanted psychology to be more objective, but he was not ready to do away with introspection completely (Dunlap, 1932/1961).

One professor of psychology at the University of Missouri, Max Meyer, was willing to make such a leap. His book (Meyer, 1911), except for its focus on humans and the absence of the term behaviorism, had much in common with Watson's (1913b) statement. Meyer advocated an objective, scientific psychology, arguing that it is impossible to know someone else's thoughts, and that data from introspection therefore cannot be verified and are useless. Instead, he suggested using overt behavior as the sole source of data in psychology.

Nevertheless, most psychologists working with human subjects during this period felt that introspection could yield information obtainable by no other method. Since introspection could only be performed by people, its extensive use highlighted the differences between humans and other species, despite the growing emphasis on and belief in the continuity of psychological processes between species. In addition, since introspective reports were subjective and could not be verified by independent means, introspection also conflicted with the growing scientific, or objective, trends in psychology. Still, the attraction of introspection as a way to obtain data on consciousness that could be obtained in no other way was strong. It would take a major revolution in psychology to break that attraction, a revolution that began in 1913.

THE BEHAVIORIST MANIFESTO, 1913–1914

In 1913 and 1914, Watson published three major works that laid the foundations of the behaviorist position. He introduced behaviorism in the first of these works, "Psychology as the Behaviorist Views It" (1913b), from which the opening paragraph of this chapter was quoted. This paper was very probably the written version of a lecture by the same title given by Watson at Columbia in February, 1913 (see "Dr. Watson to Lecture," 1913), and has been termed the "behaviorist manifesto" (see R. I. Watson, 1968, p. 406; Woodworth & Sheehan, 1964, p. 118). "Image and Affection in Behavior" (Watson, 1913a), which appeared in the *Journal of Philosophy Psychology and Scientific Methods*, elaborated on behaviorism's contention that accepting images and feelings as part of psychology lowers the discipline's standing as a science. In 1914 Watson published a book containing a detailed account of behaviorism: *Behavior: An Introduction to Comparative Psychology*. Together, these publications describe in detail the concept of behaviorism that Watson presented to the world in these early years.

Watson's fundamental principle was that psychology should use only observable behavioral data. Such a belief necessarily implies the scientific uselessness of the concept of consciousness, and Watson was quite specific on this point. Psychology "can dispense with consciousness in a psychological sense. The separate observation of 'states of consciousness' is . . . no more a part of the task of the psychologist than of the physicist. . . . [Consciousness is] the instrument or tool with which all scientists work. Whether or not this tool is properly used at present by scientists is a problem for philosophy and not for psychology" (Watson, 1913b, p. 176). In this passage, Watson does not deny the existence of consciousness; he merely states that, as presently defined, it is not a proper object of scientific psychological study. Similarly, his publications in 1913 and 1914 make clear that he did not deny the existence of thinking, and that he regarded thinking as a form of behavior involving slight movements of the muscles of the larynx or very slight head movements. Watson also maintained that these behaviors, rather than some central process, constitute dreaming.

To the extent that thinking and dreaming can be defined as behavior, it follows that thinking and dreaming can be studied with sufficiently sensitive instruments (Watson, 1914, p. 332). Watson therefore opposed introspection because he thought there were other, more objective ways to study the phenomena of consciousness and thinking. This position is reflected in his remark that "two hundred years from now, unless the introspective method is discarded, psychology will still be divided on the question as to whether auditory sensations have the quality of 'extension' " (Watson, 1913b, p. 164).

Watson was quite aware that by removing consciousness and introspection from psychology, he was freeing its practitioners to develop principles that were valid for other species as well as human beings. Psychology, he thought, had gone through a progression similar to that in evolutionary theory. While human beings were once seen as unique, they were now being viewed as part of the continuum of the animal kingdom (Watson, 1913b). At this point in his career, Watson clearly grouped people together with other animals, convinced that his behaviorism applied equally to any species: "The behavior of man and the behavior of animals must be considered on the same plane," (Watson, 1913b, p. 176).

For Watson, the question of the relative contributions of heredity and environment was not yet a major focus. His publications were directed toward making the point that behavior, not consciousness, should concern psychologists. When he did discuss the heredity–environment issue, however, he was neither an extreme hereditarian nor an extreme environmentalist: "Organisms, man and animal alike, do adjust themselves to their environment by means of hereditary and habit equipments" (1913b, p. 167). He was favorably disposed to Lamarck's evolutionary theory and therefore believed that the effects of environment could be incorporated into the genes and thereby passed on to succeeding generations (Watson, 1914, chap. 5).

At this time, Watson did not focus on the means by which organisms learn. It is clear from what he did say, however, that he presumed the existence of what he called "habit formation." According to Watson, behavior consists of reflexes; when a stimulus elicits a large number of reflexes, associative memory or habit (i.e., learning) can occur. Learning is governed by the principles of frequency and recency: If a given response has occurred in a certain situation more often than any other response, or more recently than any other response, then that response will tend to be the one that recurs (Watson, 1914, chaps. 6, 7). Although Pavlov's work had been introduced to the United States four or five years earlier (Yerkes & Morgulis, 1909), Watson seemed unaware of it in his early writings. In addition, he rejected Thorndike's law of effect as an explanation of learning, going so far as to publish what he thought to be an experimental disproof of the law of effect (Watson, 1917a).

When Watson tried to reshape psychology into the science of behaviorism in 1913–1914, he emphasized deterministic principles. In addition to postulating that consciousness and thinking could be inferred only through behavior, he asserted that these central processes could be initiated only through external stimulation (Watson, 1914, chap. 10). Without this postulate, his behavioral psychology would not have encompassed all system inputs and outputs. Add to this his frequent statements that behavior comprises only instincts and habits, both of which consist of reflexes (Watson, 1913b; Loeb Papers, 1914), and the result is a deterministic system in which only observable stimuli cause observable responses.

Psychology as science—Watson's goal—is based on the assumption that under controlled conditions, certain manipulations will bring about certain results. This assumption, if true, has powerful implications for the ability to control human behavior. In fact, Watson (1913b, p. 158) asserted that behaviorism's "theoretical goal is the prediction and control of behavior." Whenever behavioral prediction is improved in a deterministic psychology, the ability to exercise behavioral control is also improved.

To summarize, Watson's (1913b) definition of behaviorism included an insistence on the use of behavioral data in the belief that this strategy was valid for all species and would point toward the goal of predicting and controlling behavior. He did not commit behaviorism to a particular stand on the heredity–environment issue, not did he tie it to a particular type of learning theory. He outlined the way he thought psychology should be practiced, rather than listing a set of principles designed to explain the behavior of individual organisms—a methodological rather than a content approach. He did, however, discuss heredity and environment, as well as learning theory, in his early behaviorist papers.

One question that is considered in the next chapter is how other psychologists interpreted Watson's writings in forming their own definitions of behaviorism, and how these definitions changed over the years. The remainder of the present chapter is concerned with explaining why Watson's behaviorist publications constituted a quantum leap away from the rest of psychology rather than just part of its ongoing development, and how Watson, specifically, came to make this leap.

WATSON: THE FIRST BEHAVIORIST

Many authors, including Watson himself, have named Watson as the founder of behaviorism (see, for example, Bergmann, 1956; Boring, 1929a; Skinner, 1959; Tolman, 1922; Watson, 1927). There are several justifications for this designation. First, new movements are usually identified by a term, and Watson was the first to use the term behaviorism (Watson, 1913b), as well as the terms behaviorist and behavioristic (see Watson, 1927). The coining of these words alone might provide sufficient cause to consider Watson the first behaviorist, but the reasons go further than that.

There is little doubt that Watson broadcast the message of behaviorism as strongly and widely as anyone could. The opening paragraph of his article in the *Psychological Review* (1913b) sounds like a call to arms. Indeed, many perceived behaviorism as a crusade, with Watson as its leader (see, for example, Berman, 1927; Haggerty, 1916; Herrick, 1915; Hunter, 1922). In the years following 1913, Watson wrote about behaviorism in most of the major psychological journals, including *The Journal of Philosophy Psychology and Scientific Methods, Psychological Review,* and *Psychobiology,* as well as a great many popular magazines (for example, *Cosmopolitan, Harper's Monthly Magazine,* and *Nation;* see Murchison, 1932). Watson and behaviorism were discussed frequently in the *New York Times* and other media (see, for example, "Fifteen Decisive Books in World Thinking," 1923; "Scientists Seek Cure for Childhood's Fears," 1924; "Human Conduct Reduced to a Science," 1925; and "Le Behaviorisme," 1927). Watson even gave radio talks about behavioristic principles (Watson Papers). He maintained that the behaviorist approach was the only sensible one in scientific, as well as private, life. He even published a behaviorist book on child care (Watson, 1928a).

The result of all this activity was that Watson both intrigued and enraged large numbers of researchers and lay people (Boring, 1929b; Burnham, 1968; Woodworth & Sheehan, 1964, p. 118). In many respects, he possessed the characteristics of an agent of a scientific revolution, as described by Boring (1929b); that is, he was young, loud, and extreme. But it is through such people that change occurs, and it is to such people that changes are usually attributed.

Watson was also the first to formulate ideas on behaviorism, beginning in 1903 (Watson, 1928b; see also Carr, 1936; Samelson, 1981). He published these ideas in an article in *The World To-Day* entitled "Studying the Mind of Animals" (1907b), in which he stated:

> Insuperable difficulties confront us if we attempt to get into the mind of the animal and directly see what is going on there. Yet hardly other than those that confront us when we try to figure out the mental state of the man who, after running for six blocks, fails to catch the rear platform of the last down-town express. In the case of the man, however, we feel reasonably sure that we know what he is thinking. True, we can not get into his mind and see for ourselves just what ideas are rising, waxing and waning and rising again: we may be too far away to question him or to hear what he is saying; how then do we come by this proximate knowledge of what he is thinking? By noting carefully what he does! (p. 421)

Thus Watson was not only behaviorism's most vigorous proponent and the originator of the term behaviorism, but also the first to publish explicitly behavioristic theory.

WHY WATSON?

University of Chicago

Watson studied for his Ph.D. and also worked at the University of Chicago between the years 1900 and 1908. During that time he was exposed to a variety of influences from biology and philosophy, as well as psychology. The main area of biology that he studied was neurology. H. H. Donaldson, Watson's neurology professor, was also one of the advisors on his dissertation research, in which Watson attempted to correlate the complexity of behavior with central nervous system medullation in the rat (Watson, 1903). When Watson completed his Ph.D., Donaldson offered him an assistantship. Watson was proud of this offer but passed it up to take a position with Angell instead (Watson, 1936). Still, it was to Donaldson as well as Angell that Watson dedicated his book on *Behavior* (1914).

In retrospect, Watson felt strongly that his behaviorism arose out of his attempt to reformulate psychology so that he could study it in a scientific way that was consistent with his physiological training. He deemed such a reformulation desirable because it "would enable me to mark out an independent field and then work in it without having my conscience prick me all the time because there was something in it that could not be got hold of and studied by methods my brother scientists were using" (Watson, 1926, p. 185). Rather than representing a trend away from physiology (see Chapters 7 and 12, this volume), Watsonian behaviorism was intimately related to it.

The years that Watson spent at Chicago were the years of functionalism's greatest acceptance. Behaviorism is, of course, functional in a general sense, but it focuses particularly on the functional relationships between stimuli and responses (see Fuchs & Kawash, 1974). At Chicago during this period, however, functionalism was specifically linked to the study of consciousness. Consequently, rather than seeing the ties between behaviorism and functionalism, Watson perceived one as a reaction against the other (Watson, 1913b; 1919/1924, p. vii).

Still, Watson felt that he had gained much from Angell, one of his functionalist teachers and his thesis advisor (in addition to Donaldson). He also studied philosophy with John Dewey, another Chicago functionalist, but concerning these courses, Watson (1936) said he "never knew what [Dewey] was talking about then, and, unfortunately for me, I still don't know" (p. 274).

Watson particularly admired two men who worked with nonhuman subjects at Chicago while he was there: Harvey Carr and Jacques Loeb. Carr was a functionalist and a personal friend of Watson's (Watson, 1936), who in fact introduced Carr to work with nonhumans (Carr, 1936). Watson felt that Carr's research was important in helping to found objective psychology (Watson, 1929). Loeb taught Watson in both biology and physiology (see also Chapter 13, this volume). He wanted Watson to do his thesis with him, but Angell and Donaldson advised against it (Watson, 1936). In any event, both Carr and Loeb supported Watson's commitment to research with nonhuman subjects.

Although the Chicago psychology department was populated by functionalists, course materials prepared by more traditional authors were used simply because they were available. For example, Titchener's laboratory manual was used in a course taught by Watson (Bingham, 1952; Carr, 1936). (Watson knew Titchener personally, having first met him about 1909; Larson & Sullivan, 1965.) However, behaviorism conflicted with Titchener's structuralism on two conspicuous counts: It was concerned with function, not structure, and it did not include the study of consciousness (see Watson, 1924/1970, chap. 1). In addition, Watson appears to have had trouble making introspective reports in his laboratory course (Bingham, 1952), and introspection was the structuralists' main research tool for studying consciousness. Therefore, although Watson, like other Chicago functionalists at the time, was aware of structuralism, he agreed with none of it.

Watson's Research at Chicago with Nonhuman Subjects

Watson did a great deal of work at Chicago with several species using a number of objective techniques. This work illustrates his longstanding interest in the behavior of all species. The purpose of his Ph.D. thesis was to show that what Watson called psychical development in rats could be explained by central nervous system medullation. Although Watson used the term psychical development, even at this stage he was careful to define it objectively, as the increasing ability to learn complex tasks (Watson, 1903).

Watson spent the summer of 1904 at Johns Hopkins University learning an operating technique for animals (Watson, 1936). He further broadened his acquaintance with different species in the summer of 1907 by observing the behavior of noddy and sooty terns in the Dry Tortugas

(Watson, 1908a). He also began research on vision in monkeys at Chicago (Watson, 1936). These efforts notwithstanding, the work with nonhuman subjects for which Watson is best known during his years at Chicago was that on sensory deprivation in rats. In these studies he eliminated the rats' senses one by one while assessing their performance in a maze (Watson, 1907a). He found that rats could still learn the maze, and therefore concluded that kinesthetic, intraorganic senses must be used. These studies were not particularly popular with the public, but they were defended in a letter to the editor of *Nation* by James Mark Baldwin (1907).

These sensory deprivation experiments are historically significant not only because they resulted in one of the first public protests over the mistreatment of nonhuman subjects in psychological experiments, but also because they were important for the founding of behaviorism. Indeed, Watson declared them a major impetus to his formulation of behaviorism and to its promotion.

Watson published his sensory deprivation work in 1907, the same year as his *World To-Day* article. The latter contained his first declaration in print of behaviorist principles, and although the article never specifically referred to the sensory deprivation experiments, it was clearly influenced by them. At one point in the article, while discussing what is required of psychologists working with nonhuman subjects, Watson (1907b) noted: "A knowledge of the sensory equipment of the animal—the accuracy, kinds and delicacy of his sensations—is indispensable to further progress in this field" (p. 426). In later years, Watson recalled that increased control in work with nonhuman subjects had permitted the observation of psychological processes in nonhumans without reference to consciousness. It followed that a similar approach could be useful with people (Watson, 1927), and that observing the behavior of any organism, be it a sensation-deprived rat or a human being, could form the basis of a viable objective psychology (Watson, 1909).

While still in graduate school, Watson claimed that he never liked working with human subjects; work with other species made him feel closer to the science of biology that he so admired. It was therefore important to him to demonstrate that human psychology could be investigated using nonhumans (Watson, 1936). He was well read on evolutionary theory (see Yerkes Papers, 1909) and realized that the theory of continuity between species permitted the application to human behavior of principles developed from research with nonhumans (Watson, 1910). In his behaviorist manifesto (1913b), Watson related that he once was embarrassed when people asked him what his work had to do with human beings, but no longer. He had come to understand that the methods he used to study nonhuman subjects could be used to study human subjects as well.

Watson was able to perform his experiments at Chicago only because other psychologists had developed new techniques for working with nonhumans. For example, he used mazes in his thesis research that were modeled after those of Small (1901), and his behavioral techniques were modeled after those of Thorndike (1898), as he acknowledged in his autobiography (Watson, 1936). Despite his rejection of Thorndike's law of effect (Watson, 1917a), Watson maintained that it was Thorndike's work more than anyone else's that had laid the foundations for behaviorism (Watson, 1919/1924, p. viii).

Watson also carried on an extensive correspondence with Yerkes beginning in about 1904 (see Yerkes Papers). They shared a love of experimentation and of studying different species. In 1911 Yerkes and Watson published a monograph entitled "Methods of Studying Vision in Animals." Watson did not discuss much of the research by Small, Thorndike, or Yerkes in his own publications, however. For example, in his *Behaviorism* (1924/1970), he devotes only two lines to Thorndike (p. 206) and nothing at all to Small or Yerkes. Nevertheless, it is clear that Watson knew their work well and was fully aware of the magnitude of their respective contributions.

Oskar Pfungst's (1911/1965) report of the case of Clever Hans in Europe also made an impression on Watson while he was at Chicago. Clever Hans was a horse believed by many to be capable of giving solutions to mathematical problems and of answering other difficult questions by pawing the ground. Hans was shown to be responding to subtle cues from his trainer (Pfungst, 1911/1965). Watson (1908b) reviewed the 1907 German edition of *Clever Hans* that explained the strategy behind the horse's seemingly remarkable feats. He was impressed by this example of how much animal training could accomplish and pointed out that the case of Clever Hans should decrease observers' tendencies to attribute consciousness to animals.

Johns Hopkins

When Watson arrived at Johns Hopkins University as a professor of psychology in 1908, he had been thinking along behaviorist lines for about five years, but his thoughts had not yet crystallized. In a letter to Yerkes in 1909, Watson refers to a book he was writing (possibly his *Behavior*, 1914). The letter expresses Watson's frustration at that time quite vividly:

I am tired of working on that G. D. Book tonight and I proposed to cool off by writing to you. . . . I am terribly at sea as to finding a proper place and scope for psychology. What are our simple presuppositions and what is our scope and what are we good for? . . . . I have come out with this—one chapter will be— Behavior a biological problem—the scientific determination of modes of behavior and the modus operandi of behavior—a part of the problem of natural selection—the second the psychological indications in modes of behavior. My interests are in the first where an objective standards [sic] of discrimination is possible and where interpretation takes the line of the *importance* of *the observed facts*—for the story of selection—facts and interpretation possible without mention of consciousness or deviating from a (wide) biological point of view. What is then left? Am I a physiologist? Or am I just a mongrel? *I don't know how to get on.* (Yerkes Papers, 1909)

Watson did not yet have a name for his movement or a detailed exposition of its principles, although the ideas were there. What he found at Johns Hopkins were a number of colleagues who had behaviorist leanings themselves. It was in this fertile ground that behaviorism was finally to take root.

One of the first people Watson sought out was Herbert Jennings. Watson even went so far as to attend some of Jennings' courses, despite Watson's new status as a full professor. In addition, one of Jennings' biology students, Karl Lashley, worked extensively with Watson after obtaining his Ph.D. Watson later gave credit to Lashley for much of his 1915 APA presidential address on behaviorism (Watson, 1916). He also gave Lashley credit for coining the term "conditioned emotional reflex" (Watson, 1936), which was to become prominent in Watson's later investigation of fear acquisition in young children (Watson & Rayner, 1920).

Two other psychologists at Johns Hopkins during this period were also important to Watson's developing ideas. Yerkes came to the university for a year in 1909, and Watson was finally able to spend some time talking with him face-to-face, as well as to collaborate with him on research involving animal vision (Watson, 1936). Dunlap, who felt that he was the first behaviorist (Dunlap, 1932/1961), was also at Johns Hopkins during this time. Clearly, he and Watson interacted a great deal, for Dunlap was another person whom Watson was to acknowledge as important in the formulation of behaviorism (Watson, 1914, p. vi; 1919/1924, p. ix; 1936).

Two nonpsychologist faculty members at Johns Hopkins, philosopher Arthur Lovejoy and psychiatrist Adolf Meyer, were also helpful to Watson. In a paper in *Science*, Lovejoy (1911) discusses the differences between dualism (the belief in internally as well as externally initiated processes) and mechanism (determinism); it is easy to see why Watson regarded his discussions with Lovejoy as valuable (Watson, 1914, p. vi). Watson respected Meyer a great deal for his psychiatric work and praised him in the same breath with Freud and Jung (Watson, 1912). It was Meyer who later helped Watson start his work with children at Johns Hopkins, and who arranged for his research group to read and comment on chapters of *Psychology from the Standpoint of a Behaviorist* (Watson, 1936). Clearly, in Lovejoy and Meyer Watson had found people peripheral to psychology with nonhuman subjects, yet interesting and sympathetic to his cause.

CONCLUSION

The years between 1900 and 1912 were exciting and stimulating ones for Watson because there were so many first-rate faculty members at Chicago and Johns Hopkins during that time. By 1913, Watson had been exposed to strong influences from neurology, animal behavior, experimental psychology with nonhuman subjects, and functionalism. The focus of such a person very probably would be on the experimental, objective collection of data from human beings as well as other species in order to determine relationships between independent and dependent variables. Although many other psychologists at the time had similar backgrounds, none of them produced anything like Watson's vehement behaviorist proclamation (1913b). What made Watson the one to declare a complete break with the older subjective psychologies?

Without delving too far into Watson's personality, it soon becomes obvious that he was a seeker of attention and publicity. He described himself as combative and rebellious (Watson, 1936); he enjoyed debating (see, for example, Watson & McDougall, 1928). He also admitted pleasure in publicizing his work (Watson, 1917b). Finally, he felt a desperate need for money throughout his career in psychology (Pauly, 1974; Yerkes Papers, 1906–1915), and later in life he admitted that this was a prime reason for his prolific writing in popular journals (Watson, 1936).

Watson was 34 in 1912, and up until then he had enjoyed great success in his career. He had finished his Ph.D. in three years and been appointed to a full professorship 5 years later. A school of psychology all his own would appear to be a logical next step. Clearly, Watson's personality fit the bill for an ideological revolutionary (Boring, 1929b).

By 1914, behaviorism had been proclaimed and its basic principles delineated. What followed was one of the bitterest debates over theory in the history of psychology, as well as an enormous output of experimental research that had far-reaching theoretical and practical implications. The next chapter details these developments.

ACKNOWLEDGEMENTS

I owe many thanks to Sandy Drob, Cedric Larson, Camille W. Logue, Emil Menzel, Telmo Peña, Ian Shrank, and B. F. Skinner for their helpful comments on the material in previous drafts of this chapter and the next. B. F. Skinner also provided unpublished information for Chapter 7.

REFERENCES

Angell, J. R. (1907). The province of functional psychology. *Psychological Review, 14*, 61–91.
Angell, J. R. (1913). Behavior as a category of psychology. *Psychological Review, 20*, 255–270.
Baldwin, J. M. (1907). Professor Watson's experiments on rats defended. *Nation, 84* (2169), pp. 79–80.
Bekhterev, V. M. (1933). *General principles of human reflexology*. London: Jarrolds. (Original work published 1917)
Bergmann, G. (1956). The contribution of John B. Watson. *Psychological Review, 63*, 265–276.
Berman, L. (1927). *The religion called behaviorism*. New York: Boni, Liveright.
Bingham, W. (1952). Autobiography. In H. S. Langfeld, E. G. Boring, H. Werner, & R. M. Yerkes (Eds.), *A history of psychology in autobiography* (Vol. 4). Worcester, MA: Clark University Press.
Boring, E. G. (1929a). *A history of experimental psychology*. New York: Century.
Boring, E. G. (1929b). The psychology of controversy. *Psychological Review, 36*, 97–121.
Boring, E. G. (1950). *A history of experimental psychology* (2nd ed.). New York: Appleton-Century-Crofts.
Burnham, J. C. (1968). On the origins of behaviorism. *Journal of the History of the Behavioral Sciences, 4*, 143–151.
Calkins, M. W. (1921). The truly psychological behaviorism. *Psychological Review, 28*, 1–18.
Carr, H. A. (1936). Autobiography. In C. Murchison (Ed.), *A history of psychology in autobiography* (Vol. 3). London: Oxford University Press.
Cattell, J. M. (1896). Address of the president before the American Psychological Association. *Psychological Review, 3*, 134–148.
Darwin, C. (1958). *The origin of species*. New York: New American Library. (Original work published 1859)
Darwin, C. (1965). *The expression of the emotions in man and animals*. Chicago: University of Chicago Press. (Original work published 1872)
Dr. Watson to lecture. (1913, February 23). *New York Times*, p. 4.
Dunlap, K. (1912). The case against introspection. *Psychological Review, 19*, 404–412.
Dunlap, K. (1961). Autobiography. In C. Murchison (Ed.), *A history of psychology in autobiography* (Vol. 2). New York: Russell, Russell. (Original work published 1932)

Fifteen decisive books in world thinking. (1923, July 1). *New York Times,* p. 8.

Fuchs, A. H., & Kawash, G. F. (1974). Prescriptive dimensions for five schools of psychology. *Journal of the History of the Behavioral Sciences, 10,* 352–366.

Haggerty, M. E. (1916). Reviews and abstracts of literature. *Journal of Philosophy Psychology and Scientific Methods, 13,* 470–472.

Herrick, C. J. (1915). Watson's "Behavior," *Journal of Animal Behavior, 5,* 467–470.

Human Conduct reduced to a science. (1925, August 2). *New York Times,* p. 14.

Hunter, W. S. (1922). An open letter to the anti-behaviorists. *Journal of Philosophy, 19,* 307–308.

James, W. (1895). The knowing of things together. *Psychological Review, 2,* 105–124.

James, W. (1905). The experience of activity. *Psychological Review, 12,* 1–17.

James, W. (1962). *Psychology: Briefer course.* Toronto: Macmillan. (Original work published 1892)

Jennings, H. S. (1906). *Behavior of the lower organisms.* New York: Columbia University Press.

Jennings, H. S. (1908). The interpretation of the behavior of the lower organisms. *Science, 27,* 698–710.

Jennings, H. S. (1910). Diverse ideals and divergent conclusions in the study of behavior in lower organisms. *American Journal of Psychology, 21,* 349–370.

Jensen, D. D. (1962). Foreword. In H. S. Jennings, *Behavior of the lower organisms.* Bloomington: Indiana University Press.

Larson, C. A., & Sullivan, J. J. (1965). Watson's relation to Titchener. *Journal of the History of the Behavioral Sciences, 1,* 338–354.

Le behaviorisme. (1927, September 25). *Paris-Midi,* p. 1.

Loeb Papers, (1914, January 2). Letter from J. B. Watson to J. Loeb. Washington, DC: Library of Congress.

Loeb, J. (1900). *Comparative physiology of the brain and comparative psychology.* New York: Putnam.

Lovejoy, A. O. (1911). The meaning of vitalism. *Science, 33,* 610–614.

Lovejoy, A. O. (1922). The paradox of the thinking behaviorist. *Philosophical Review, 31,* 135–147.

Mackenzie, B. D. (1976). Darwinism and positivism as methodological influences on the development of psychology. *Journal of the History of the Behavioral Sciences, 12,* 330–337.

Mackenzie, B. D. (1977). *Behaviourism and the limits of scientific method.* Atlantic Highlands, NJ: Humanities Press.

Marx, M. H., & Hillix, W. A. (1973). *Systems and theories in psychology.* New York: McGraw-Hill.

Meyer, M. (1911). *The fundamental laws of human behavior.* Boston: Gorham.

Morgan, C. L. (1894). *An introduction to comparative psychology.* London: Scott.

Morgan, C. L. (1900). *Animal behaviour.* London: Arnold.

Murchison, C. (1932). Watson, John Broadus. In C. Murchison (Ed.), *The psychological register* (Vol. 3). Worcester, MA: Clark University Press.

Pauly, P. J. (1974). *Money, morality, and psychology at Johns Hopkins University, 1881–1942.* Unpublished manuscript, Johns Hopkins University.

Pavlov, I. P. (1965). On conditioned reflexes. In R. J. Herrnstein & E. G. Boring (Eds.), *A source book in the history of psychology.* Cambridge, MA: Harvard University Press. (Original work published 1928)

Pfungst, O. (1965). *Clever Hans.* New York: Holt. (Original work published 1911)

Poffenberger, A. T. (Ed.). (1947). *James McKeen Cattell* (Vol. 1). Lancaster, PA: Science.

Roback, A. A. (1923). *Behaviorism and psychology.* Cambridge, MA: University Bookstore.

Romanes, G. J. (1965). On comparative psychology. In R. J. Herrnstein & E. G. Boring (Eds.), *A source book in the history of psychology*. Cambridge, MA: Harvard University Press. (Original work published 1882)

Ruckmich, C. A. (1916). The last decade of psychology in review. *Psychological Bulletin, 13,* 109–120.

Samelson, F. (1981). Struggle for scientific authority: The reception of Watson's behaviorism, 1913–1920. *Journal of the History of the Behavioral Sciences, 17,* 399–425.

Scientists seek cure for childhood's fears. (1924, July 27). *New York Times,* p. 2.

Sechenov, I. M. (1965). On reflexology and psychology. In R. J. Herrnstein & E. G. Boring (Eds.), *A source book in the history of psychology*. Cambridge, MA: Harvard University Press. (Original work published 1863)

Sechenov, I. M. (1965). *Autobiographical notes*. Washington, DC: American Institute of Biological Sciences.

Skinner, B. F. (1959). John Broadus Watson, behaviorist. *Science, 129,* 197–198.

Small, W. S. (1901). Experimental study of the mental processes of the rat. II. *American Journal of Psychology, 12,* 206–239.

Spalding, D. A. (1872). On instinct. *Nature, 6,* 485–486.

Thorndike, E. L. (1898). Animal intelligence: An experimental study of the associative processes in animals. *Psychological Review Monographs, 2* (Whole No. 8).

Thorndike, E. L. (1913). Ideo-motor action. *Psychological Review, 20,* 91–106.

Thorndike, E. L. (1915). Watson's "Behavior." *Journal of Animal Behavior, 5,* 462–467.

Thorndike, E. L. (1965). *Animal intelligence*. New York: Hafner. (Original work published 1911)

Titchener, E. B. (1910). *A text-book of psychology*. New York: Macmillan.

Titchener, E. B. (1914). On "Psychology as the behaviorist views it." *Proceedings of the American Philosophical Society, 53,* 1–17.

Tolman, E. C. (1922). A new formula for behaviorism. *Psychological Review, 29,* 44–53.

Washburn, M. F. (1908). *The animal mind*. New York: Macmillan.

Watson, J. B. (1903). *Animal education*. Chicago: University of Chicago Press.

Watson, J. B. (1907a). Kinaesthetic and organic sensations: Their role in the reactions of the white rat to the maze. *Psychological Monographs, 8* (Whole No. 33).

Watson, J. B. (1907b). Studying the mind of animals. *The World To-Day, 12,* pp. 421–426.

Watson, J. B. (1908a). *The behavior of noddy and sooty terns*. (Carnegie Institution Publication No. *103*(8).) Washington, DC: The Carnegie Institution.

Watson, J. B. (1908b). Literary notices. *Journal of Comparative Neurology and Psychology, 18,* 329–331.

Watson, J. B. (1909). A point of view in comparative psychology. *Psychological Bulletin, 6,* 57–58.

Watson, J. B. (1910). The new science of animal behavior. *Harper's Monthly Magazine, 120,* pp. 346–353.

Watson, J. B. (1912). Content of a course in psychology for medical students. *Journal of the American Medical Association, 58,* 916–918.

Watson, J. B. (1913a). Image and affection in behavior. *The Journal of Philosophy Psychology and Scientific Methods, 10,* 421–428.

Watson, J. B. (1913b). Psychology as the behaviorist views it. *Psychological Review, 20,* 158–177.

Watson, J. B. (1914). *Behavior: An introduction to comparative psychology*. New York: Holt.

Watson, J. B. (1916). The place of the conditioned-reflex in psychology. *Psychological Review, 23,* 89–116.

Watson, J. B. (1917a). The effect of delayed feeding upon learning. *Psychobiology, 1,* 51–59.

Watson, J. B. (1917b). Practical and theoretical problems in instinct and habits. In *Suggestions of modern science concerning education*. New York: Macmillan.

Watson, J. B. (1924). *Psychology from the standpoint of a behaviorist*. Philadelphia: Lippincott. (Original work published 1919)

Watson, J. B. (1926). Behaviorism: A psychology based on reflexes. *Archives of Neurology and Psychiatry, 15*, 185–204.

Watson, J. B. (1927). The origin and growth of behaviorism. *Archiv für Philosophie, 30*, 247–262.

Watson, J. B. (1928a). *Psychological care of infant and child*. New York: Norton.

Watson, J. B. (1928b). What is behaviorism? *The Golden Book Magazine*, pp. 507–515. (Watson Papers, Library of Congress)

Watson, J. B. (1929). Behaviourism. In *The Encyclopaedia Britannica* (Vol. 3, 14th ed.). New York: Encyclopaedia Britannica.

Watson, J. B. (1936). Autobiography. In C. Murchison (Ed.), *A history of psychology in autobiography* (Vol. 3). Worcester, MA: Clark University Press.

Watson, J. B. (1970). *Behaviorism*. New York: Norton. (Original work published 1924)

Watson, J. B., & McDougall, W. (1928). *The battle of behaviorism*. London: Kegan Paul.

Watson, J. B., & Rayner, R. (1920). Conditioned emotional reactions. *Journal of Experimental Psychology, 3*, 1–14.

Watson papers. Washington, DC: Library of Congress.

Watson, R. I. (1968). *The great psychologists: From Aristotle to Freud* (2nd ed.). New York: Lippincott.

Woodworth, R. S., & Sheehan, M. R. (1964). *Contemporary schools of psychology*. New York: Ronald.

Yerkes, R. M. (1901). The formation of habits in the turtle. *Popular Science Monthly, 58*, pp. 519–525.

Yerkes, R. M. (1961). Autobiography. In C. Murchison (Ed.), *A history of psychology in autobiography* (Vol. 2). New York: Russell, Russell. (Original work published 1932)

Yerkes, R. M., & Morgulis, S. (1909). The method of Pawlow in animal psychology. *Psychological Bulletin, 6*, 257–273.

Yerkes, R. M., & Watson, J. B. (1911). Methods of studying vision in animals. *Behavior Monographs, 1*(Serial No. 2). Yerkes papers. New Haven, CT: Yale University Medical Library.

Yerkes papers. (1906–1915). New Haven, CT: Yale University Medical Library.

Yerkes papers. (1908–1909). New Haven, CT: Yale University Medical Library.

Yerkes papers. (1909). New Haven, CT: Yale University Medical Library.

7

The Growth of Behaviorism: Controversy and Diversity

ALEXANDRA W. LOGUE

INTRODUCTION

In 1913 John B. Watson proclaimed the birth of behaviorism, and during the following 2 years he carefully set out its principles. This was only the beginning, however, as the basic principles underlying behaviorism were soon to be modified by the efforts of both its opponents and proponents. One of those contributing to this modification was Watson himself, for he was to change his original statement of behavioristic principles several times prior to his departure from the academic world. This chapter examines the principal criticisms and modifications of behaviorism between 1913 and 1950. It develops an interpretation of behaviorism that emphasizes behaviorism's essential elements and reflects the impact of behaviorism on psychology.

REACTIONS TO WATSONIAN BEHAVIORISM, 1913–1930

During the years between the founding of behaviorism and 1930, many people simply defined behaviorism as whatever Watson said it

POINTS OF VIEW IN THE
MODERN HISTORY OF PSYCHOLOGY

was (see, for example, Berman, 1927; Woodworth, 1931). Discussions of behaviorism occupied countless pages in professional journals as well as the popular press. Watson encouraged this exposure both by deliberately popularizing behaviorism himself and by incorporating into behaviorism controversial—indeed, outrageous—concepts not included in his original manifesto.

Watson's Modifications of Behaviorism

Through 1916, Watson believed strongly that behaviorism could be applied with equal success to humans and nonhumans, and that few differences between species would be important in the study of learning (Watson, 1907, p. 422; 1913, p. 176). In 1917, however, his opinion changed dramatically. No longer did he view psychology as the study of both nonhumans and humans; rather, it was "a division of science which deals with the functions underlying human activity and conduct" (Watson, 1917a, p. 329). He had begun to think that human beings might not have instincts like those of other animals (Watson & Morgan, 1917). He later wrote: "Animal studies have taught us . . . how unsafe it is to generalize on the basis of infra-human animal studies as to what the unlearned equipment of man is" (Watson, 1925, p. 306).

Watson did not disavow Darwin; rather, he believed that evolution had progressed in such a way that generalizations between humans and other animals would be unjustified: "Now, all this has bearing upon the instincts of the 1927 man. Just because he has had an evolutionary history is no proof that he must have instincts like the stock from which he sprang" (Watson, 1927, pp. 228–229). Nevertheless, until recently (Logue, 1978) it was widely believed that without exception, Watson espoused the continuity of species throughout his career (see, for example, Bakan, 1966; Boring, 1963; Herrnstein, 1969; Muckler, 1963; Shimp, 1976; Tilquin, 1942).

When Watson changed his view on the continuity of species, he was also changing his position on the nature–nurture issue. Prior to 1917 his position contained some nativistic elements. Human instincts, he said, "determine in large measure our choice of companions, occupations, and our pleasures" (Watson, 1912b, p. 381). In 1917, however, he (with Morgan) firmly declared that most human behavior may be learned. There were several reasons for this change. First, psychology had increasingly come to emphasize practical applications. Watson himself felt that psychology should be practical (Watson, 1912a, 1917b), and clearly psychology can help people more easily if one believes that people's behavior can be modified. Second, Watson had initially believed (1914, chap. 5) that the environment could affect behavior through the passing on of acquired characteristics through the genes (Lamarckism) as well as through learning, but the developing science of genetics was discrediting Lamarckian evolution in the early 20th century (Stocking, 1968, chap. 8). The learning process was thus the only means by which the environment could affect behavior (see Watson, 1924/1970, Chapter 3). Third, the study of genetics also emphasized the heredity–environment issue, encouraging psychologists to take sides on the issue of behavior being learned versus its being inherited. Given this context, Watson's sudden inclination toward environmentalism is not surprising.

Watson's environmentalist position and his beliefs concerning the continuity of species are undoubtedly linked. He had worked a great deal with nonhuman animals, and it was clear to him that much of their behavior is instinctual (Watson, 1919; Watson & Morgan, 1917). If humans, on the other hand, have few instincts, then studying nonhumans has little relevance to understanding humans. Thus, an environmentalist stance and a belief in substantial evolutionary differences between humans and other species were complementary views for Watson (see Logue, 1978, for further discussion of these issues).

An environmentalist theory of behavior cannot survive unless it specifies exactly how learning occurs. Watson first experimented with conditioned reflexes in 1914 with the help of Lashley (Yerkes Papers, 1915). In 1916 he announced that classical conditioning is responsible for all learning. This assumption meant that in the following year he was able, in theory at least, to explain precisely how humans learn when he claimed (with Morgan) that the majority of human behaviors may be acquired. It is unlikely that Watson would have ventured such a claim without being prepared to give a detailed account of how human learning occurs.

Although Watson initially stated that psychology is independent of morality (Watson, 1917a), in later years he incorporated into his theory of behaviorism many viewpoints that seemed to have little to do with data and much to do with his own ethics. He published much of this material in popular magazines and newspapers. For example, "Urges Rotary Plan to Train Children" (1928) is the title of a *New York Times* article describing Watson's opinions on bringing up children. Apparently, Watson thought that children should be rotated among a different set of adults every three weeks. In this way children could be prevented from knowing who their real parents were, and "objectionable domestic ties" would be avoided. Watson described the home as a "breeder of invalidism and a destroyer of independence and happiness." A year earlier, another *New York Times* article ("For New Marriage Ethics," 1927) had quoted Watson as saying: "The mystery of marriage has been broken down. We must have a new kind of ethics, based on a scientific study of human behavior as a way to more simple marital adjustments."

Watson convinced Rosalie Rayner Watson, his wife and former student, that behaviorism dictated such practices. In "I Am the Mother of a Behaviorist's Sons" (1930), an article in *Parents' Magazine*, she wrote:

> In some respects I bow to the great wisdom in the science of behaviorism, and in others I am rebellious . . . . I secretly wish that on the score of [the children's] affections they will be a little weak when they grow up, that they will have a tear in their eyes for the poetry and drama of life and a throb for romance. . . . I like being merry and gay and having the giggles. The behaviorists think giggling is a sign of maladjustment. (p. 67)

Yet Watson did not necessarily believe in all the unusual practices that his popular articles said were dictated by behavioristic principles; in reality, he wrote provocative articles for the general public partly as a means of earning extra money (Pauly, 1974; Watson, 1936; Yerkes Papers, 1906–1915). Nevertheless, the published statements of Rosalie Watson make it appear that the Watsons truly believed that behaviorism could prescribe how married people should behave and how children should be raised (see Watson's 1928 book on child rearing).

By means of these frequent, outrageous, and controversial interpretations of behaviorism, Watson propelled his views into the limelight more effectively than he could have by propounding only extreme environmentalism. A crowning example of Watson's achievements in this area is the following statement, one of the best known in psychology:

> Give me a dozen healthy infants, well-formed, and my own specified world to bring them up in and I'll guarantee to take any one at random and train him to become any type of specialist I might select—doctor, lawyer, artist, merchant-chief and, yes, even beggarman and thief, regardless of his talents, penchants, tendencies, abilities, vocations, and race of his ancestors. I am going beyond my facts and I admit it, but so have the advocates of the contrary and they have been doing it for many thousands of years. (Watson, 1924/1970, p. 104)

Watson had challenged the psychological community; it did not take them long to respond.

The Recognition of Watsonian Behaviorism

In the 20 years or so following 1913, Watson and behaviorism became extremely well known to both the psychological community and the public. In addition to the support and criticism by scientists (see Samelson, 1981), cries of enthusiastic acceptance and outraged rejection by the public and the press were heard throughout the United States and the world. Between 1925 and 1936, articles about Watson appeared in at least 35 different domestic and foreign newspapers. Watson even appeared in a "Gasoline Alley" cartoon (Watson Papers).

In the scientific arena, between the years of 1920 and 1928, 58 journal articles focused on Watson's work (R. I. Watson, 1976). A conference was held at Oxford University in the fall of 1920 to discuss Watson's claim that thinking consisted simply of "the action of language mechanisms" (*British Journal of Psychology*, 1920). Psychologists disagreed, however, as to how widely behaviorism was accepted among either psychologists or lay people. Opinions ranged from the belief that in the 1920s there were few behaviorists (Hunter, 1922; MacGowan, 1928; Robinson, 1929) to the conclusion that behaviorism in the 1920s was very popular (Boring, 1929; Calkins, 1921; Tolman, 1922). Some commentators, including Watson, took a moderate stance, claiming that behaviorism was very controversial (Winkler & Bromberg, 1939, Chapter 14), or that many, but not all, psychologists advocated it (Watson, 1926, 1929). One fact remains clear, however: Behaviorism was very much on people's minds during these years.

Positive Reactions

Behaviorism was seen by many as a cure-all. For example, one problem that it was supposed to solve was the misbehavior of unruly children. An advertisement for Watson's books on child care (Watson, 1928) and on behaviorism in general (Watson, 1924/1970) in the December 1930 issue of *Parents' Magazine*, stated:

> 50,000 mothers have read John B. Watson's two books. In two years, his PSY-CHOLOGICAL CARE OF INFANT AND CHILD has become recognized as the standard work on child psychology. His BEHAVIORISM, which the *New York Herald Tribune* called "perhaps the most important book ever written," is the psychology of enlightened common sense . . . these two books bring happiness to the families that own them. (p. 67)

In addition, the *New York Times* consulted Watson on such matters as suicide and phobias ("Student Suicides Stir Interest of Scientists," 1927; "Reviews Studies in Human Behavior," 1928).

The J. Walter Thompson Company, an advertising firm that hired Watson in 1920 after he was asked to resign from Johns Hopkins University due to the publicity surrounding his divorce, felt that his skills and knowledge could be of assistance in the field of advertising (Watson, 1936). Certain lawyers (e.g., Malan, 1922) also thought that behaviorism provided new insights in the field of law. George Santayana, a prominent philosopher at Harvard in the first decades of the twentieth century, saw behaviorism as the way to get the most work out of the most people (Santayana, 1922). It is no wonder that behaviorism was even described as a religion (Berman, 1927; Woodworth, 1931). Watson promoted behaviorism as a panacea, and many people were happy to accept it as just that.

In particular, two specific characteristics of Watsonian behaviorism were praised. First, behaviorism emphasized the learning process, and this appealed to those psychologists who felt that previously there had been an overemphasis on the hereditary determinants of behavior (e.g., Bernard, 1924). Second, behaviorism emphasized psychology as a natural science, and most scholars agreed that objectivity in psychology is a good thing (e.g., McDougall, 1926; Titchener, 1914; Tolman, 1922). They did not agree, however, on whether Watson had taken the science of behaviorism too far, as shown in the next section.

Negative Reactions

Many psychologists in the 20 years following Watson's announcement of behaviorism felt that while psychology should be objective, ruling out introspection altogether was too extreme. Such scholars believed that consciousness, objectively defined, was a necessary part of the study of psychology with human subjects, and that consciousness could not be studied through Watson's behavioral methods alone (see, e.g., Baldwin, 1961; de Laguna, 1918; Titchener, 1914). Harvey Carr (1915) specifically criticized Watson's rejection of introspection as arising from an inaccurate perception that the use of introspection in psychology implied that nonhumans must possess human consciousness. Thorndike (1915), by contrast, agreed with Watson that psychology could do without introspection but wanted to know why this point alone was cause for a revolution when much of psychology with human subjects (e.g., Ebbinghaus' work on memory and Cattell's on reaction time) had done very well for many years without the use of introspection (see also Harrell & Harrison, 1938). Apparently, Watson could please no one on this issue.

Determinism was implied, though not directly addressed, by much of Watson's work. All behavior, he believed, is entirely determined by stimuli from the environment or by the genes, and he never mentioned free will. Some people felt intuitively that this removed the essence from life: "The repetitive tom-tom of the Behaviorist drum is insistent that we are wholly and totally the victims of conditions beyond our control from the moment of birth to the moment of extinction. And of course the same applies to before-birth. . . . In the womb the genes in the chromosomes commit their silent crimes upon the personality" (Berman, 1927,

p. 134). At the same time, Thorndike (1915) believed that there was empirical evidence for centrally initiated processes. McDougall's criticism (Watson & McDougall, 1928) of Watson's determinism was likewise couched in scholarly terms; he was concerned about the absence of purpose from Watson's description of behavior.

Finally, although all of psychology can be viewed as a means of predicting and controlling behavior, Titchener's (1914) perception of behaviorism's great potential for behavior control matched his belief that behaviorism would lead to euthenics and eugenics. It is possible that Titchener wished to call attention to this potential in behaviorism because he disagreed with some of its principles (such as its failure to use introspection). However, another factor may have been that behaviorism seemed to work; behaviorists in learning laboratories appeared to have developed the most powerful nonphysiological methods for controlling human behavior up to that time. Titchener himself described behaviorism as a technology with practical goals, rather than a science with no goals other than increasing knowledge. Watson, he thought, could do experiments with nonhumans and later with humans in which he trained his subjects to do what he wanted. This frightened Titchener, as it has since frightened many others. What none of these authors realized was that Watson was not trying to turn human beings into automatons, but rather to provide a scientific description of human beings as they were and always had been.

Some critics of behaviorism were simply opposed to Watson's emphasis on the environment (Jastrow, 1928; Warden, 1928). Most frequently, such criticisms came from lay people who had been reading Watson's publications on child rearing. Between 1913 and 1930, psychologists widely accepted an emphasis on environmental influences and on the study of learning. In fact, one psychologist, Z. Y. Kuo (1929), felt that Watson was not environmentalist enough. Kuo felt that all behavior was determined by external stimulation, thus rendering the learned–inherited distinction meaningless.

All of the foregoing criticisms of behaviorism were objections to what were thought to be its actual theoretical inadequacies, but misinterpretations also abounded. For example, Watson was interpreted as claiming that consciousness did not exist; in fact, he never impugned its existence, only the efficacy of studying it. In essence, he did not believe in using unobservable principles, such as consciousness, to explain what could not otherwise be explained (Watson & McDougall, 1928). According to Watson, any observation that can be made by only one person is not reliable and should not be included in a scientific psychology. While he believed that thoughts and feelings exist, he considered them to be technologically unobservable by another. Thus defined, he felt that thinking and feeling were off limits for a scientific psychology.

Not surprisingly, McDougall (Watson & McDougall, 1928) and Berman (1927) felt that behaviorism neglected feelings in its description of human behavior. They further argued that Watson equated human behavior with that of the so-called lower species, whose acts reputedly had much simpler causes than the acts of humans. For many people, their disagreement with Watson's deemphasis of consciousness and (initial) emphasis on the continuity of the species clouded their reasoned assessment of the rest of his theory (for further discussion of behaviorism's philosophical position, see Chapters 12 and 13, this volume). In addition, disagreements with Watson's behaviorist position led to a proliferation of variants of behaviorism.

Types of Behaviorism

McDougall (1926, pp. 278–279) writes of two types of behaviorism: "strict" (Watsonian) and "purposive." In his view, strict behaviorism incorrectly ignored consciousness and purpose (goal-seeking) in psychology, while purposive behaviorism only ignored the facts of consciousness, and was therefore to be preferred. McDougall believed that a greater emphasis on behavior than that shown by the introspectionists was needed, but not to the exclusion of other types of data.

In his 1928 debate with Watson, McDougall's now expanded list of types of behaviorism blatantly demonstrated his opinion of the discipline (Watson & McDougall, 1928). What McDougall called "true" or "original Watsonian" behaviorism rejects introspection. "Metaphysical behaviorism" considers thoughts and feelings, but only as physical (neurochemical) processes (compare Bergmann's "physicalist behaviorism," 1956). Finally, "sane behaviorism" uses both introspective and observational data. McDougall claimed that he was the originator and chief proponent of sane behaviorism, but careful consideration shows that he was stretching the definition of behaviorism. In the end, objective, verifiable data are its sine qua non.

Calkins (1921) discussed two kinds of behaviorism. She termed the first "radical" or "extreme" behaviorism. Behaviorists of this type either do not discuss consciousness or do not think it exists in either animals or humans. Calkins contrasted this type with what she called "modified behavioristic psychology," which postulates not only that humans as well as other animals possess consciousness, but also that it is possible to study consciousness scientifically, whether directly or indirectly. Lashley (1923) made a similar distinction, naming his two types of behaviorism "extreme" and "methodological." The former refers to behaviorists who do not believe that consciousness exists, while the latter group believe that consciousness exists but cannot be studied scientifically. These categories of behaviorism have persisted until the present, with extreme behaviorism now termed "radical behaviorism" (see, e.g., Marx & Hillix, 1973, Chapter 7; Skinner, 1974, Chapter 1).

The great majority of behaviorists have subscribed to methodological behaviorism. With one possible exception, it would be difficult to identify any radical behaviorists, despite the existence of the term. No behaviorist actually denies the existence of images and feelings; most merely claim that images and feelings are difficult to study (see, e.g., Hunter, 1924; Weiss, 1929). B. F. Skinner (e.g., 1945b) has referred to himself as a radical behaviorist but says he did so because a scientific psychology should be concerned with all events, both public and private, whereas methodological behaviorism is limited to the study of public events. For Skinner, radical behaviorism did not mean denying the *existence* of events that methodological behaviorists describe as "consciousness." Rather, he denied the explanatory value of the fictional term consciousness, preferring to talk about public and private events instead. It is simplest just to remember that no behaviorist has denied the existence of consciousness, and that for all behaviorists anything that can be objectively studied is fair game for scientific research (for additional comments on the reception of radical behaviorism, see Day, 1980, pp. 245–246).

Finally, Roback (1923) presents a chart in which he lists a total of 10 classes and 17 subclasses of behaviorism. These are divided into four general groupings: structural behaviorism (focusing on the mechanics of organisms), functional behaviorism (focusing on the relationship between an organism and its environment), psychobehaviorism (allowing consciousness and introspection a role in psychology along with behaviorism), and nominal behaviorism (encompassing theorists such as McDougall who called themselves behaviorists but whose theories included little of Watson's original behavioristic platform). Roback lists from one to three theorists under each of the 17 subclasses. While this description of behaviorism may not be particularly helpful in understanding the general issues with which behaviorism was concerned at the time, it does point out the intense interest shown in behaviorism during the 1920s, as well as the many factions among those attracted to behaviorism.

FROM THEORY TO EXPERIMENTATION, 1930–1950

The 1930s and 1940s reveal an entirely different focus for behaviorism. Whereas the 1920s were years filled with acrimonious debate about the successes and failures of behaviorism, the following two decades were much quieter (Jones, 1975). Far fewer articles by and on Watson were published during this period (R. I. Watson, 1976). The labeling of people as either behaviorists or antibehaviorists was also much less common. Darwinian evolution and the value of objective, experimental psychology were now advocated in most areas of psychology (Herrnstein, 1969), and these characteristics were no longer a special drawing card for behaviorism. Instead of worrying about whether they really were behaviorists, many researchers devoted their energies to testing and developing theories of learning, particularly with nonhuman subjects. Laboratory and experimental data were the major focus of these efforts, and the research became increasingly quantitative. Once the basic tenets of behaviorism had been accepted, the need for a cohesive behaviorist movement decreased, and disputes were more likely to form around issues of fact than of theory.

Molecular and Molar Interpretations of Behavior

A problem for any science is to decide at what level of data its research and analysis should be conducted—that is, whether to emphasize relatively molecular or relatively molar data (Tolman, 1932). Behaviorism was no exception; although it was agreed that behavior would be the general province of psychology, precisely what consitutes a unit of behavior (for example, one lever press versus a series of lever presses followed by reinforcement) was not clear.

Relative to other approaches, Watson's behaviorism could be classified as molecular because he defined all behavior as consisting of reflexes, and each reflex as consisting of a stimulus and a response (Watson, 1924/1970, Chapter 1). A stimulus would be a relatively specific object or condition, such as a toy or the sensation of falling, and a response would be a relatively specific bit of behavior, such as reaching or crying. Watson was aware of a still more molecular approach, as indicated by his analysis of stimuli and responses into their physiological components, such as the reactions of particular muscles or glands (Watson, 1924/1970, Chapter 4). Nevertheless, he chose to express his laws of learning in terms of the objectively verifiable, less molecular units of behavioral stimuli and responses. At the same time, he believed that with improved research equipment, the reactions of glands and muscles might be more easily observed, at which time he would be open to their use in behavioral psychology (Watson, 1924/1970, Chapter 10).

An entirely different approach was taken by Edward C. Tolman. He like Watson, emphasized observable behavior (Tolman, 1922). However, he felt that Watson had looked so closely at the details of how learning occurs that he had failed to see some interesting and orderly relationships at a more molar level. Tolman proposed that associations could be acquired between sets of stimuli and complex behaviors, not just between specific stimuli and responses (Tolman, 1948), and he typically designed clever experiments to prove his point. For example, after training rats to use a particular path through a maze to food, he then made available several novel paths. Of those, the rats picked the one providing the shortest route to food—something they could do only if they had learned the overall pattern of relationships between the location of food in the maze and the paths in the maze. According to Tolman (1938), the rats showed acquisition of a "cognitive map." Indeed, specific, molecular stimulus–response associations could not explain such a finding. Other types of experiments also demonstrated the inadequacy of molecular explanations of learning. They included studies of latent learning, and of vicarious trial and error learning (Tolman, 1952).

Tolman (1952) attributed much of his molar theorizing to the influence of Gestalt psychology, and he sometimes referred to himself as a field theorist (e.g., Tolman, 1948). He believed that behavior studied at the molar level has emergent properties; that is, properties that do not exist at more molecular levels (Tolman, 1932). Tolman's approach to learning has many contemporary descendants (see, e.g., Evans, 1980; Olton, 1978), a testament to his methodological skill and theoretical acumen.

Clark L. Hull was the best known molar behaviorist during the two decades after 1930. As part of a "hypothetico-deductive" learning theory that he began formulating in 1935 (Hull, 1952), he attempted to define molar behaviors operationally and objectively. For example, Hull (1937) defined "seeking" as "that behavior of organisms in trial-and-error situations which, upon frustration ['the situation is such that the reaction customarily evoked by a stimulus complex cannot take place'], is characterized by varied alternative acts all operative under the influence of a common drive" (p. 15). He also defined the "habit–family hierarchy" as "a number of habitual behavioral sequences having in common the initial stimulus situation and the final reinforcing state of affairs" (1937, p. 16). Behaviors, as he defined them, were the essential hardware of Hull's learning theory.

Hull's software, his system of molar learning, was described by formal mathematical postulates directly subject to experimental test (see Hilgard & Bower, 1975, Chapter 6). At the time, it was the most ambitious and extensive system of its kind. If his system had proved correct, psychologists would have been able to quantitatively predict the behavior of organisms with a precision that until then had only been dreamed of in psychology. Consequently, a vast number of experiments were generated to test particular postulates of Hull's system. For example, between 1944 and 1950, 70 percent of the articles on learning and motivation in the *Journal of Experimental Psychology* and the *Journal of Comparative and Physiological Psychology* cited Hull (Spence, 1952). Unfortunately, like most of the other readily testable mathematical models of learning that have been developed, Hull's postulates also proved to be wanting. Attempts to spell out the system precisely in order to eliminate its inadequacies resulted in a mathematical model of learning so complex that it was unwieldly and in many respects incapable of direct testing.

Hull's system was ultimately abandoned by the mainstream of psychology, but his attempts to create a formal mathematical system have continued to be admired and imitated. His approach has survived, even though his particular system of learning has not. One example of a modern mathematical model of learning that owes much to Hull's hypothetico-deductive approach is that of Rescorla and Wagner (1972). Hull's associates, including notables such as Neal Miller and Kenneth Spence, also extended Hull's influence in animal learning. Among other things, Miller is known for his work on reinforcement theory (e.g., Miller, 1958), and for his comparisons of classical and operant conditioning (e.g., Miller & Banuazizi, 1968). More similar to Hull's approach than was Miller's, Spence's work used formal mathematical postulates. Spence's contribution was extensive and varied, but he is probably best known for his research on discrimination and the perception of relations between stimuli (e.g., Spence, 1936).

Skinner admired and studied the work of both Tolman and Hull early in his career. In the summer of 1931, while doing postdoctoral research at Harvard University, Skinner attended a series of lectures given by Tolman (Skinner, 1979). He first met Hull in 1932. Hull also liked Skinner's work, and a few years later his students began using Skinner's conditioning apparatus, which Hull was the first to call a Skinner box (Skinner, 1979). Skinner (1979, p. 204) later described Hull and Tolman as the two giants in the field of animal learning in the 1930s.

Skinner began to incorporate molar concepts into his own theories during the mid-1930s. In a 1936 letter to Fred Keller, he wrote that his system of psychology now contained two types of behavior: operants and respondents (Skinner, 1979). *Respondents* were simply reflex responses *elicited* by the principles of classical conditioning, while *operants*, upon which Skinner and the majority of his associates and followers were to focus most of their attention in the coming years, were defined as sets of *emitted* responses that had a common effect on the environment. For example, one operant would be the lever press—that is, any and all responses whose consequence was the depression of a lever. Skinner was not interested in the many different ways the lever could be depressed; what concerned him was the molar, functional relationship between lever pressing and reinforcement.

Unlike some other behaviorists, Edwin R. Guthrie advocated no particular units for behavior. Both Guthrie (1935/1952, Chapter 3) and Skinner (1950) felt that the best unit was the one yielding the most orderly quantitative relationships. However, Skinner gravitated toward relatively molar units, while Guthrie was a stimulus–response, associationist theorist. Guthrie rejected Thorndike's law of effect and was thus more inclined to discuss individual reflexes than was Skinner. On the other hand, Guthrie (1935/1952, Chapter 11) criticized Tolman's use of the hypothetical cognitive map in his work as too general and vague to be of much use experimentally.

Respondents and Operants

The distinction between respondents and operants was more than just another way of classifying behavior. It meant that the principles of operant conditioning would now have to be investigated in addition to those for classical conditioning, and Skinner and his colleagues gladly undertook this work. Among the experimental arrangements that Skinner investigated were schedules of reinforcement, punishment, and extinction (for a detailed account of this early work, see Skinner, 1979). This research showed that operant conditioning is characteristic of responses of the skeletal muscle system, while classical conditioning is characteristic of responses of the smooth muscle system. Although the operant–classical conditioning distinction is not as clear-cut today as it once seemed (see Brown & Herrnstein, 1975, chap. 3), it has proved to be an extremely powerful and useful way of categorizing and studying learning.

Skinner began formulating his ideas about two types of learning in 1931 (Skinner, 1979). He first published a description of what he called Type I and Type II conditioning in 1932, along with a description of his initial work on training rats to press a lever. Following several changes in terminology between 1935 and 1937, Skinner settled firmly on the now familiar names of operant and classical conditioning in his book, *Science and Human Behavior* (1953).

Two Polish psychologists, Jerzy Konorski and Stefan Miller, began thinking about a distinction between two types of learning around the same time as Skinner (Konorski, 1974). Together, these two psychologists published a preliminary report of their studies of reward in conditioning a motor response in a dog (Miller & Konorski, 1928/1969). These experiments did not, however, involve waiting for a response by the animal being tested. Rather, leg flexion was initially elicited, either reflexively or manually, by the experimenter. Only later in the experiment, following the contingent reward, did leg flexion occur spontaneously. From 1931 to 1933, Miller and Konorski worked with Pavlov (Konorski, 1974). Soon afterward, they published a monograph on the conditioning of motor responses.

Because all of Konorski and Miller's early work was published in Polish, Skinner was not aware of it (Skinner, 1979). Konorski and Miller did, however, read Skinner's (1935) paper and decided to publish their own version of the Type I–Type II distinction, in English, in 1937 (Konorski, 1974; Konorski & Miller, 1937a, 1937b; Skinner, 1979), accompanied by a reply from Skinner (1937). The first distinction between operant and classical conditioning is usually attributed to Skinner, although Konorski and Miller published the distinction first. This situation is no doubt a result of the fact that Konorski and Miller's initial publications were in Polish, and that Skinner's initial paradigms had all the characteristics of operant conditioning, while Konorski and Miller's did not. In addition, and perhaps more importantly, Skinner has continued to make advances in the area of operant conditioning and has become far better known to American psychologists than Konorski and Miller.

Purpose

A major shortcoming of Watsonian behaviorism was its lack of any explanation of purpose or planning (Herrnstein, 1967). For Watson, purpose was never an issue; he focused simply on explaining how particular stimuli and responses became associated. In contrast, the three major behaviorists who followed Watson between 1930 and 1950—Tolman, Hull, and Skinner—explicitly addressed the problem of purpose.

Tolman's purposive behaviorism was rooted in work by E. B. Holt (Tolman, 1922). Holt's books (*The Freudian Wish and Its Place in Ethics*, 1915, and *Animal Drive and the Learning Process*, 1931) were behavioristic, concerning themselves only with objective, observable data, but they were also concerned with purpose (the "wish"). Holt (1915) described Freudian psychology in behaviorist terms, believing that the unit of study in psychology should be the wish. He then proceeded to define the wish as a course of action: "The spirit of any piece of machinery lies in what it can do, and this specific capacity lies in its plan and structure rather than in the brute matter through which this plan is tangibly realized, so precisely it is with the human spirit and the human body" (Holt, 1915, p. 49).

Tolman (1922) makes it clear that one of the pressing problems of psychology is to explain purpose adequately. He felt that purposiveness should be a characteristic of any molar description of behavior, and that purpose must be defined objectively. In Tolman's (1932) formulation, purpose is demonstrated when a response is "docile" with respect to some end (p. 452). Docility, in turn, is demonstrated when a successful response occurs earlier and earlier in trial-and-error learning (1932, pp. 442–443).

Tolman's (1938) APA presidential address developed this strategy. Here Tolman began to discuss intervening variables in order to describe purpose further. (Marx, 1963, Chapter 1, provides a general discussion of such variables). For example, Tolman trained rats to run down each of two runways for food, with one runway angling slightly to the left of the starting point and the other angling to the right. Each rat was then presented with a choice between the two original runways and a new, third runway inserted between them. The rats tended to pick the new runway. Tolman described them as having acquired a hypothesis (an intervening variable) about the location of food. That hypothesis was simply the vector sum of each rat's past experiences (i.e., the sum of the tendencies to go in various directions as a result of training). Thus, while the rats' purpose appears to be finding the most likely route to the food, Tolman explained their behavior in terms of their past experiences using an intervening variable.

More formally, Tolman (1938) presents a basic equation $B = f(E, I)$ in which B stands for behavior, E for environmental variables, and I for individual variables (heredity and past history). He then describes the variables intervening between the stimuli (E) and the responses (B). The variables E and I can be analyzed into still more intervening variables. Examples for E would be such variables as demand (motivation as influenced by the animal's maintenance schedule), appetite (motivation as influenced by the particular "goal object" available), and hypotheses (as previously defined). Because Tolman considered these intervening, unobservable variables to be abstract constructs and nothing more (see

Marx, 1963, pp. 24–26), and because he defined them operationally, he still considered himself a behaviorist. Using his explanation of purpose, Tolman constructed a complex behavioristic theory of learning.

Hull also made extensive use of intervening variables in order to explain purpose. He presented an early version of such a system in his APA presidential address (Hull, 1937), in which he attempted to explain adaptive, purposive behavior by constructing a formal theory consisting of definitions, postulates, and theorems. Later, Hull (1943) made intervening variables an explicit part of this system. For example, to describe purpose, he used the fractional antedating goal response. He postulated that fractions of a goal response (e.g., some fraction of an eating response) could be elicited by stimuli present in, say, a maze, during the behavioral sequence by which the goal was reached. These fractional responses in turn would produce, for example, kinesthetic stimuli. These, Hull thought, through being paired with successive locomotor responses, selectively direct and guide the organism to the goal. In other words, these fractional response–produced stimuli come to cue the organism for its next step; the organism thus exhibits purpose, undertaking a series of actions that would regularly lead to reinforcement after some repetition (Hull, 1943, Chapter 7). Although Hull was talking about unobservables, he, like Tolman, remained a behaviorist because he defined his intervening variables operationally in terms of observable behavior. Hull did not believe that these intervening variables represented processes that could by themselves initiate behavior.

Measured by staying power, at least, Skinner's attempt to deal with purpose appears to have been the most successful, for it has lasted the longest. From the beginning, Skinner resisted the construction of a formal mathematical system with intervening variables. By defining a response class partly by its effect on the environment (an operant), and by focusing on the reinforcement of prior behavior, he was able to build purpose directly into his description of learning, without the use of special postulates. For example, he would explain the careful uncorking of a wine bottle not as purposive behavior with the intent of executing a plan to obtain some wine, but as behavior that had increased in probability due to the reinforcement of similar behavior in the past.

Skinner rejected criticism that he merely finessed what some psychologists saw as the real problem: trying to explain why people work so hard to obtain what they do not yet have (see Skinner, 1953, pp. 87–90, for more examples and discussion). However Skinner saw his conceptual framework as a simple description of learning that dealt easily with many facets of everyday life as well as with laboratory data. Although Hull and Tolman also described purpose fundamentally in terms of past experience, their special postulates made explanations of behavior complex and unwieldy. These postulates, when properly specific, were also more likely to be disproved. For this reason, Skinner's incorporation of purpose into behaviorism survived while Tolman's and Hull's did not. The lack of purpose in Watsonian behaviorism was not a fatal problem for behaviorism's future.

Operationism

While still in graduate school, Skinner found Bridgman's *The Logic of Modern Physics* (1927) so persuasive (Skinner, 1979, p. 41) that he proceeded to follow Bridgman's lead and defined all his terms operationally (Skinner, 1931), producing one of the first papers so written in psychology. For example, he defined a reflex simply as "an observed correlation of two events, a stimulus and a response" (1931, p. 445). Skinner did not express any of his definitions in the language of hypothetical physiological processes, as had most behaviorists before him (see Watson's and others' descriptions of neural pathways in the reflex), but his analysis did stress function, as had the analyses of previous behaviorist writers.

S. S. Stevens, who was at Harvard while Skinner was a member of the university's prestigious Society of Fellows, published a series of papers on operationism (Stevens, 1935a, 1935b, 1939) in which he defined operationism as the belief that "science . . . is a set of empirical propositions agreed on by members of society. . . . Only those propositions based on operations which are public and repeatable are admitted to the body of science" (1939, p. 227). Stevens and Skinner supported each other in what Skinner (1979, pp. 162–163) saw as the operationist revolution in psychology. Operationism at that time was becoming popular among many branches of the sciences, including psychology. Another movement, logical positivism, similar to operationism, was simultaneously becoming popular in philosophy. In 1934 Skinner felt that there were few theoretical differences between behaviorism, operationism, and logical positivism (Skinner, 1979, p. 161). Although Watson had not defined his terms operationally, by 1940 much of experimental psychology was rigorously operationalist, as were several other sciences. In 1941 Skinner (with W. K. Estes) even attempted to define anxiety operationally for an experiment using rats (Estes & Skinner, 1941).

Skinner defined operationism so as to limit scientific inquiry to the investigation of observations and to the procedures involved in making those observations. Operationism defined in this way is entirely compatible with behaviorism. However, Skinner (1945b) also noted the lack of an established structure for operationist definitions. By 1945, he had lost some of his earlier enthusiasm for operationism. Nevertheless, he thought that a coalition between psychology and operationism might be achieved in the future. Despite Skinner's ambivalence at this point, operationism is now an integral part of much of psychology.

Heredity and Environment

The years between 1930 and 1950 saw more restraint with respect to behaviorists' views on the heredity–environment issue. In the 1920s behaviorists, spurred on by the new emphasis on learning theory, had been strongly environmentalist. In the following two decades, however, few were willing to commit themselves to any particular viewpoint on this ancient problem.

Heredity versus environment was not an important issue in animal learning and was not discussed extensively in print. For example, Hull never raised the heredity–environment issue in his 1943 book except to say that "the environment acts on the organism, and the organism acts on the environment. . . . The terminal phase of any given environmental–organismic interaction depends upon the activity of each" (p. 16). Tolman's 1932 book and 1948 *Psychological Review* paper also did not emphasize the problem either, and Skinner's (1947) paper, "Current Trends in Experimental Psychology," never discussed the extent to which behavior is learned. The amount of space that these researchers devoted in their publications to learning suggests, however, that they all leaned toward environmentalism.

It may be possible to get some idea of how the behaviorist psychologists stood on the heredity–environment issue by examining how many instincts they believed organisms to possess. A short list of specific instincts would imply a belief that little of behavior was inherited, while a longer list would imply the contrary (Herrnstein, 1977). Watson (1924/1970, chap. 5) had the shortest list, for in the latter part of his academic career he believed that only certain neurological reflexes were present at birth, and that these quickly became conditioned. The lists of Tolman (1932), Guthrie (1935/1952), Hull (1943), and Skinner (1938) were somewhat longer, but basically all of the instincts (drives) that these psychologists mentioned were those concerned with the survival of the species. In print, at least, in the two decades between 1930 and 1950 the behaviorists leaned more toward an environmentalist than a hereditarian position (see Herrnstein, 1972, for a detailed discussion of the development of a behavioristic concept of instinct during this and other periods).

THE MATURING OF SKINNERIAN BEHAVIORISM

The year 1953 saw the publication of Skinner's *Science and Human Behavior*. This book was well received and very widely known, in part because it presented a position derived from Skinner's innovative and extensive laboratory work of the preceding 25 years. The principles set out in this book have long served as the basis for most research in operant conditioning. Until this time, research based on Hull's formal system had dominated the journals (Spence, 1952). Although Hull's methods for formulating postulates and theories continued to influence psychology, his theoretical ideas became so particularistic and complex as to be unwieldy and untestable. After Hull's death in 1952, Kenneth Spence, whose work was derived in large part from Hull's, continued to be productive until his death in 1967.

The following sections describe Skinner's lasting contributions arising from his 1953 book.

Consciousness

As far as Skinner was concerned, for an act or thought to be considered unconscious simply meant that relevant behavior was of low probability. Skinner defined all such terms behaviorally; that is, to label an idea unconscious is no different from saying that the idea is not obvious to the person who had it or to anyone else. An unconscious idea is therefore not relevant to a scientific, functional analysis of behavior. In Skinner's view, science can deal only with observables. At the same time, Skinner did not deny the existence of thought. For Skinner, thoughts were private events subject to the same laws as public events, except that they were harder to observe than public ones (see Zuriff, 1979, for further discussion of these points). Skinner advocated refined techniques and equipment to make private events more accessible—an approach similar to Watson's.

Continuity of the Species

Skinner's book showed that he, like most other modern psychologists, believed firmly in Darwinian evolution. One of the best known quotes from Skinner's writings during this period is concerned with the differences among species:

> Pigeon, rat, monkey, which is which? It doesn't matter. Of course, these three species have behavioral repertoires which are as different as their anatomies. But once you have allowed for differences in the ways in which they make contact

with the environment, and in the ways in which they act upon the environment, what remains of their behavior shows astonishingly similar properties. (Skinner, 1956, pp. 230–231)

The first two sentences of this quote seem to indicate that Skinner saw few fundamental differences between species, although he found some fundamental similarities impressive. For example, the properties to which Skinner was referring were the remarkably similar performances of several species on multiple fixed-interval, fixed-ratio schedules of reinforcement. In general, his research with rats and pigeons, from which he made generalizations about human behavior, focused on properties such as these. However, the rest of the quote shows that, in Skinner's opinion, these are simply the most worthwhile aspects of behavior to study in predicting and explaining the behavior of many species, although differences between the behavior of various species do, of course, exist. In *Science and Human Behavior*, Skinner (1953) makes the same point. There, Skinner was careful to say that people are much more complex than other animals but that many of the same psychological principles may be found to apply to humans and other species. Skinner (1953, Chapter 3) advocated studying basic psychological principles in species other than humans because other species are simpler and can be studied under more controlled conditions, not because the behavior of all species is the same.

Learned versus Inherited Behavior

Skinner (1953, chap. 9) never actually stated to what extent he believed that behavior was inherited, and to what extent it was learned. He also did not say how many drives there are. Instead, he talked about how little help such information is to an experimental analysis of behavior. After all, if a behavior is inherited, there is very little that can be done to modify it, and Skinner's concern was not just to predict but also to control behavior. He acknowledged that it may sometimes be helpful to know the extent to which something is learned, because this information can help to indicate the limitations of behavior modification. While he dismissed needs, wants, and hungers as postulated inner causes, he was willing to use hypothetical constructs, such as the hunger drive, if these could assist in the functional analysis of behavior.

The hunger drive construct is useful because it provides a way of summarizing and classifying similar cases. In many instances, however, inner causes are postulated in a way that does not serve this function. For example, the hunger drive is sometimes used as if there were a particular something within the body that *is* hunger and that causes all the effects we see. But since hunger itself is unobservable, postulating its actual existence rather than simply using it to organize data adds nothing to a functional analysis of behavior. Skinner's use of drives was therefore similar in many ways to Hull's and Tolman's use of intervening variables.

Learning Theory

Just prior to the publication of *Science and Human Behavior* (1953), Skinner published an article entitled "Are Theories of Learning Necessary?" (1950) in which he criticized such theories for making reference to hypothetical mechanisms and events. Indeed, explanations of classical conditioning that utilize unobservable, hypothetical neural impulses—such as those by Pavlov and Watson—were unacceptable to Skinner. He defined a learning theory as any description of learning that incorporates these hypothetical mechanisms, including descriptions at other than the behavioral level. By contrast, descriptions of learning that referred only to behavior were not learning *theories* and were therefore preferable. It was within this behavioral context that Skinner (1953) described classical and operant conditioning, referring only to the changes in behavior that occur during conditioning.

By 1953 Skinner was convinced that learning can occur by either operant or classical conditioning, and that some behaviors are more easily acquired by the first, and some by the second type of conditioning. Since classical conditioning occurs with only a small number of unconditioned reflexes, Skinner focused on operant conditioning, which is relevant for a great proportion of our daily behavior. By drawing on the extensive research that he and other operant conditioners had conducted in the preceding quarter of a century, he was able to show how behavior could be modified using the principles found in operant conditioning, including shaping, discrimination, punishment, and avoidance. Most of the learning principles that he set out in 1953 continue to be widely accepted today.

Determinism

Skinner emphasized time and again that he was interested in not only the prediction of behavior but also its control. Skinner's analysis, like Watson's, was based on the assumption that behavior occurs as a result of cause-and-effect relationships; on no other basis could a science be developed. As the functional analysis of behavior progresses and the causes of behavior are better understood—perhaps to be expressed as quantitative laws—behavioral control will become more feasible.

As testament to his beliefs, Skinner devoted many chapters to showing that the experimentally based principles of operant conditioning by which he could control rat behavior were already sufficient to support some alleviation of the ills of society. For example, he discussed how to improve self-control, government, and education. His utopian novel, *Walden Two*, appeared in 1948, and he never lost interest in applying scientific ideas to the design of a culture. Controversy has surrounded these writings, but Skinner did not toss them out as fantasy. Rather, they seemed to him to reflect serious potential for a behavioristic psychology. Clearly, behaviorism since Watson had lost little of its emphasis on determinist explanations, or on using science to help society. The difference was that compared with Watson, Skinner had a great deal more evidence with which to back up his statements.

Skinner: Update

In the years since 1953, Skinner has become one of the best known living psychologists (Dews, 1970; Herrnstein, 1977; Robinson, 1970). He has notably increased behaviorism's reputation beyond that of Watson's day. In large part this increased interest in behaviorism is due to Skinner's forays into areas other than the learning of nonhuman subjects. He and his students developed teaching machines, as well as principles of behavior modification for use in therapy (see Skinner, 1972). In 1958 he was influential in founding the authoritative and active *Journal of the Experimental Analysis of Behavior* (Skinner, personal communication, May 22, 1980). Another foray outside the laboratory related to the birth of Skinner's second child. He built a live-in chamber for her that received coverage in the popular press (see, for example, Skinner, 1945a). Although the chamber was simply a noise-, temperature-, and humidity-controlled crib, some people came to the distressing and erroneous conclusion that its purpose was to allow Skinner to experiment on his daughter as he had on rats (Skinner, 1979). These events, added to Skinner's many theoretical and empirical contributions to psychology, were more than sufficient to make him a household word. He became one of the most significant figures in both the history of behaviorism and of psychology in general.

CONCLUSION

A determination of the principles shared by all of the behaviorists mentioned in this and the preceding chapter results in the following description: All behaviorists emphasize that objective behavioral data are reliable, while data from introspection are not. They are not averse to using hypothetical constructs as a way of grouping together similar cases—for example, by postulating a hunger drive. However, such hypothetical constructs are to be regarded as merely hypothetical, and nothing more. Finally, behaviorists are committed to the scientific and deterministic analysis of behavior. In essence, they are deterministic psychologists who focus on behavioral data and who use hypothetical constructs only to a limited extent.

By examining the differences between behaviorists, it is possible to determine what behaviorism does *not* include. First, it does not always carry with it extreme environmentalism. Watson was originally noncommital on the heredity–environment issue, and only later in his academic career did he become an environmentalist (Logue, 1978). Many behaviorists (e.g., Hull) have not emphasized the heredity–environment argument, and it is only by making inferences from these researchers' statements on the number and types of drives and their focus on learning that we can form an impression about their position on this issue.

Second, behaviorists accept Darwinian evolution, but this does not mean that they equate humans with other species, however much some behaviorists may work with rats and pigeons. In his later years, Watson thought that language made humans so different from rats that it was impossible to generalize from nonhuman data to humans. Skinner was careful to specify that he studied rats and pigeons in order to discover the principles of psychology that would be general across species, but he too was confident that there are many differences between species.

Third, there is no particular learning theory that can be termed behavioristic. Behaviorists have performed experiments using both respondents and operants. Some behaviorists have created theories in which reinforcement is prominent (e.g., Thorndike, Hull, and Skinner), but others have not (e.g., Watson, Guthrie, and Tolman). Behaviorists do tend to construct certain types of learning theories, those which restrict the use of hypothetical constructs, but no specific theory characterizes all behaviorists.

Finally, all behaviorists cannot even be classified as uniformly denying the existence of consciousness. When pressed, virtually all have admitted that thoughts and feelings exist; it is simply difficult to find evidence of such beliefs among behaviorists who in their usual conversation and writing concentrate on overt behavior.

There are still those who identify themselves primarily as behaviorists (e.g., Rachlin, 1980), but they are far fewer than in the 1920s. One of the reasons for this is that there are also fewer psychologists whose work is nonscientific, who employ introspection extensively, and who advocate theories that incorporate centrally initiated causes. There is therefore less need to be identified as a behaviorist in order to be distinguished from the nonbehaviorists (Hunter, 1952). In general, at least in experimental psychology as it is broadly defined, all psychologists tend to be deterministic, using only observable, verifiable behavior as data, and using hypothetical constructs only when necessary. The psychologists most likely to refer to themselves as behaviorists emphasize that their hypothetical constructs are purely hypothetical. For them, such constructs are simply tools to help explain data and construct theories; they do not actually exist somewhere inside the body. However, other psychologists use hypothetical constructs to a much greater extent (see Chapter 10, this volume), and have sometimes attempted to locate these postulated mechanisms inside the nervous system (see Chapter 12, this volume).

Whatever may be the outcome of disagreements between behaviorists and nonbehaviorists, the tenets of behaviorism will probably continue to be characteristic of much of psychology. The future usefulness of the term can therefore be questioned. It appears to identify a certain viewpoint in psychology, a certain way of looking at psychological issues, rather than a specific dogma, and that viewpoint is now widespread. Like one of its forebears, functionalism, it has become a framework within which to construct particular psychological theories encompassing substantive fields of interest, whether cognitive processes, growth and development, personality and social behavior, or whatever. One is thus tempted to abandon the term behaviorism because it no longer distinguishes between either psychologies or psychologists. There are, however, psychologists who still oppose behaviorism, accusing it of slighting introspection or purpose, or of focusing on methodology to the detriment of theory (see, for example, Lieberman, 1979; Mackenzie, 1977; Miller, Galanter, & Pribram, 1960, Chapter 10). As long as these objections exist, the term behaviorism will have more than just a historical place in psychology.

REFERENCES

Bakan, D. (1966). Behaviorism and American urbanization. *Journal of the History of the Behavioral Sciences, 2*, 5–28.

Baldwin, J. M. (1961). Autobiography. In C. Murchison (Ed.), *A history of psychology in autobiography* (Vol. 1). New York: Russell, Russell. (Original work published 1930)

Bergmann, G. (1956). The contribution of John B. Watson. *Psychological Review, 63*, 265–276.

Berman, L. (1927). *The religion called behaviorism.* New York: Boni, Liveright.

Bernard, L. L. (1924). *Instinct.* New York: Holt.

Boring, E. G. (1929). The psychology of controversy. *Psychological Review, 36,* 97–121.

Boring, E. G. (1963). The influence of evolutionary theory upon American psychological thought. In R. I. Watson & D. T. Campbell (Eds.), *History, psychology, and science.* New York: Wiley.

Bridgman, P. W. (1927). *The logic of modern physics.* New York: Macmillan.

British Journal of Psychology. (1920). Vol. 11, pp. 55–104.

Brown, R., & Herrnstein, R. J. (1975). *Psychology.* Boston: Little, Brown.

Calkins, M. W. (1921). The truly psychological behaviorism. *Psychological Review, 28,* 1–18.

Carr, H. (1915). Special reviews. *Psychological Bulletin, 12,* 308-312.

Day, W. F. (1980). The historical antecedents of contemporary behaviorism. In R. W. Rieber & K. Salzinger (Eds.), *Psychology: Theoretical–historical perspectives.* New York: Academic.

de Laguna, G. A. (1918). Dualism in animal psychology. *Journal of Philosophy Psychology and Scientific Methods, 15,* 617–627.

Dews, P. B. (Ed.). (1970). *Festschrift for B. F. Skinner.* New York: Appleton-Century-Crofts.

Estes, W. K., & Skinner, B. F. (1941). Some quantitative properties of anxiety. *Journal of Experimental Psychology, 29,* 390–400.

Evans, G. W. (1980). Environmental cognition. *Psychological Bulletin, 88,* 259–287.

For new marriage ethics. (1927, March 6). *New York Times,* p. 8.

Guthrie, E. R. (1952). *The psychology of learning.* New York: Harper. (Original work published 1935)

Harrell, W., & Harrison, R. (1938). The rise and fall of behaviorism. *Journal of General Psychology, 18,* 367–421.

Herrnstein, R. J. (1967). Introduction. In J. B. Watson, *Behavior, An introduction to comparative psychology.* New York: Holt.

Herrnstein, R. J. (1969). Behaviorism. In D. L. Krantz (Ed.), *Schools of psychology.* New York: Appleton-Century-Crofts.

Herrnstein, R. J. (1972). Nature as nurture: Behaviorism and the instinct doctrine. *Behaviorism, 1,* 23–52.

Herrnstein, R. J. (1977). The evolution of behaviorism. *American Psychologist, 32,* 593–603.

Hilgard, E. R., & Bower, G. H. (1975). *Theories of learning.* Englewood Cliffs, NJ: Prentice-Hall.

Holt, E. B. (1915). *The Freudian wish and its place in ethics.* New York: Holt.

Holt, E. B. (1931). *Animal drive and the learning process.* New York: Holt.

Hull, C. L. (1937). Mind, mechanism and adaptive behavior. *Psychological Review, 44,* 1–32.

Hull, C. L. (1943). *Principles of behavior.* New York: Appleton-Century-Crofts.

Hull, C. L. (1952). Autobiography. In E. G. Boring, H. Werner, H. S. Langfeld, & R. M. Yerkes (Eds.), *A history of psychology in autobiography* (Vol. 4). Worcester, MA: Clark University Press.

Hunter, W. S. (1922). An open letter to the anti-behaviorists. *Journal of Philosophy, 19,* 307–308.

Hunter, W. S. (1924). The problem of consciousness. *Psychological Review, 31,* 1–31.

Hunter, W. S. (1952). Autobiography. In E. G. Boring, H. Werner, H. S. Langfeld, & R. M. Yerkes (Eds.), *A history of psychology in autobiography* (Vol. 4). Worcester, MA: Clark University Press.

Jastrow, J. (1928). Watson's behaviorism. *Saturday Review of Literature, 5,* p. 36.

Jones, M. C. (1975). A 1924 pioneer looks at behavior therapy. *Journal of Behavior Therapy and Experimental Psychiatry, 6,* 181–187.

Konorski, J. (1974). Autobiography. In G. Lindzey (Ed.), *A history of psychology in autobiography* (Vol. 6). Englewood Cliffs, NJ: Prentice-Hall.

Konorski, J., & Miller, S. (1937a). Further remarks on two types of conditioned reflex. *Journal of General Psychology, 17*, 405–407.

Konorski, J., & Miller, S. (1937b). On two types of conditioned reflex. *Journal of General Psychology, 16*, 264–272.

Kuo, Z. Y. (1929). The net result of the anti-heredity movement in psychology. *Psychological Review, 36*, 181–199.

Lashley, K. S. (1923). The behavioristic interpretation of consciousness. *Psychological Review, 30*, 237–272.

Lieberman, D. A. (1979). Behaviorism and the mind: A (limited) call for a return to introspection. *American Psychologist, 34*, 319–333.

Logue, A. W. (1978). Behaviorist John B. Watson and the continuity of the species. *Behaviorism, 6*, 71–79.

Macgowan, K. (1928, October 6). The adventure of the behaviorist. *The New Yorker*, pp. 30–32.

Mackenzie, B. D. (1977). *Behaviourism and the limits of scientific method*. Atlantic Highlands, NJ: Humanities Press.

Malan, G. H. T. (1922). The behavioristic basis of the science of law. *American Bar Association Journal, 8*, 737–741, 762.

Marx, M. H. (1963). *Theories in contemporary psychology*. New York: Macmillan.

Marx, M. H., & Hillix, W. A. (1973). *Systems and theories in psychology*. New York: McGraw-Hill.

McDougall, W. (1926). Men or robots? In C. Murchison (Ed.), *Psychologies of 1925*. Worcester, MA: Clark University Press.

Miller, G. A., Galanter, E., & Pribram, K. H. (1960). *Plans and the structure of behavior*. New York: Holt.

Miller, N. E. (1958). Control stimulation and other new approaches to motivation and reward. *American Psychologist, 13*, 100–108.

Miller, N. E., & Banauzizi, A. (1968). Instrumental learning by curarized rats of a specific visceral response, intestinal or cardiac. *Journal of Comparative and Physiological Psychology, 65*, 1–7.

Miller, S., & Konorski, J. (1969). On a particular form of conditioned reflex. *Journal of the Experimental Analysis of Behavior, 12*, 187–189. (Original work published 1928)

Muckler, F. A. (1963). On the reason of animals: Historical antecedents to the logic of modern behaviorism. *Psychological Reports, 12*, 863–882.

Olton, D. S. (1978). Characteristics of spatial memory. In S. H. Hulse, H. Fowler, & W. K. Honig (Eds.), *Cognitive processes in animal behavior*. Hillsdale, NJ: Erlbaum.

Pauly, P. J. (1974). *Money, morality, and psychology at Johns Hopkins University, 1881–1942*. Unpublished manuscript, Johns Hopkins University.

Rachlin, H. (1980). *Behaviorism in everyday life*. Englewood Cliffs, NJ: Prentice-Hall.

Rescorla, R. A., & Wagner, A. R. (1972). A theory of Pavlovian conditioning: Variations in the effectiveness of reinforcement and nonreinforcement. In A. H. Black & W. K. Prokasy (Eds.), *Classical conditioning II: Current research and theory*. New York: Appleton-Century-Crofts.

Reviews studies in human behavior. (1928, May 24). *New York Times*, p. 35.

Roback, A. A. (1923). *Behaviorism and psychology*. Cambridge, MA: University Bookstore.

Robinson, D. (1970). *The 100 most important people in the world today*. New York: Putnam.

Robinson, E. S. (1929). Behaviorist: L'enfant terrible. *The New Republic, 57*(735), pp. 181–184.

Samelson, F. (1981). Struggle for scientific authority: The reception of Watson's behaviorism, 1913–1920. *Journal of the History of the Behavioral Sciences, 17,* 399–425.

Santayana, G. (1922). Living without thinking. *Forum, 68,* pp. 731–735.

Shimp, C. P. (1976). Organization in memory and behavior. *Journal of the Experimental Analysis of Behavior, 26,* 113–130.

Skinner, B. F. (1931). The concept of the reflex in the description of behavior. *Journal of General Psychology, 5,* 427–458.

Skinner, B. F. (1932). On the rate of formation of a conditioned reflex. *Journal of General Psychology, 7,* 274–286.

Skinner, B. F. (1935). Two types of conditioned reflex and a pseudo-type. *Journal of General Psychology, 12,* 66–77.

Skinner, B. F. (1937). Two types of conditioned reflex: A reply to Konorski and Miller. *Journal of General Psychology, 16,* 272–279.

Skinner, B. F. (1938). *The behavior of organisms.* New York: Appleton-Century-Crofts.

Skinner, B. F. (1945a). Baby in a box. *Ladies' Home Journal, 62,* pp. 30–31, 135–136, 138.

Skinner, B. F. (1945b). The operational analysis of psychological terms. *Psychological Review, 52,* 270–277.

Skinner, B. F. (1947). Experimental psychology. In *Current trends in psychology.* Pittsburgh: University of Pittsburgh Press.

Skinner, B. F. (1948). *Walden two.* Toronto: Macmillan.

Skinner, B. F. (1950). Are theories of learning necessary? *Psychological Review, 57,* 193–216.

Skinner, B. F. (1953). *Science and human behavior.* New York: Free Press.

Skinner, B. F. (1956). A case history in scientific method. *American Psychologist, 11,* 221–233.

Skinner, B. F. (1972). *Cumulative record.* New York: Appleton-Century-Crofts.

Skinner, B. F. (1974). *About behaviorism.* New York: Knopf.

Skinner, B. F. (1979). *The shaping of a behaviorist.* New York: Knopf.

Spence, K. W. (1936). The nature of discrimination learning in animals. *Psychological Review, 43,* 427–449.

Spence, K. W. (1952). Clark Leonard Hull: 1884–1952. *American Journal of Psychology, 65,* 639–646.

Stevens, S. S. (1935a). The operational basis of psychology. *American Journal of Psychology, 47,* 323–330.

Stevens, S. S. (1935b). The operational definition of psychological concepts. *Psychological Review, 42,* 517–527.

Stevens, S. S. (1939). Psychology and the science of science. *Psychological Bulletin, 36,* 221–263.

Stocking, G. W. (1968). *Race, culture, and evolution.* New York: Free Press.

Student suicides stir interest of scientists. (1927, Feb. 20). *New York Times,* p. 5.

Thorndike, E. L. (1915). Watson's "Behavior." *Journal of Animal Behavior, 5,* 462–467.

Tilquin, A. (1942). *Le behaviorisme.* Paris: L'Université de Paris.

Titchener, E. B. (1914). On "Psychology as the behaviorist views it." *Proceedings of the American Philosophical Society, 53,* 1–17.

Tolman, E. C. (1922). A new formula for behaviorism. *Psychological Review, 29,* 44–53.

Tolman, E. C. (1932). *Purposive behavior in animals and men.* New York: Century.

Tolman, E. C. (1938). The determiners of behavior at a choice point. *Psychological Review, 45,* 1–41.

Tolman, E. C. (1948). Cognitive maps in rats and men. *Psychological Review, 55,* 189–208.

Tolman, E. C. (1952). Autobiography. In E. G. Boring, H. Werner, H. S. Langfeld, & R. M.

Yerkes (Eds.), *A history of psychology in autobiography* (Vol. 4). Worcester, MA: Clark University Press.

Urges rotary plan to train children. (1928, March 4). *New York Times,* p. 6.

Warden, C. J. (1928). Books. *Pedagogical Seminary and Journal of Genetic Psychology, 35,* 481–482.

Watson, J. B. (1907). Studying the mind of animals. *The World To-Day, 12,* pp. 421–426.

Watson, J. B. (1912a). Content of a course in psychology for medical students. *Journal of the American Medical Association, 58*(13), 916–918.

Watson, J. B. (1912b). Instinctive activity in animals. *Harper's Monthly Magazine, 124,* pp. 376–382.

Watson, J. B. (1913). Psychology as the behaviorist views it. *Psychological Review, 20,* 158–177.

Watson, J. B. (1914). *Behavior: An introduction to comparative psychology.* New York: Holt.

Watson, J. B. (1916). The place of the conditioned reflex in psychology. *Psychological Review, 23,* 89–116.

Watson, J. B. (1917a). An attempted formulation of the scope of behavior psychology. *Psychological Review, 24,* 329–352.

Watson, J. B. (1917b). Practical and theoretical problems in instinct and habits. In *Suggestions of modern science concerning education.* New York: Macmillan.

Watson, J. B. (1919). A schematic outline of the emotions. *Psychological Review, 26,* 165–196.

Watson, J. B. (1925). What the nursery has to say about instincts. *Pedagogical Seminary, 32,* 293–327.

Watson, J. B. (1926). Memory as the behaviorist views it. *Harper's Monthly Magazine, 153,* pp. 244–250.

Watson, J. B. (1927). The behaviorist looks at instincts. *Harper's Monthly Magazine, 155,* pp. 228–235.

Watson, J. B. (1928). *Psychological care of infant and child.* New York: Norton.

Watson, J. B. (1929). Behaviourism. In *The Encyclopaedia Britannica* (Vol. 3, 14th ed.). New York: Encyclopaedia Britannica.

Watson, J. B. (1936). Autobiography. In C. Murchison (Ed.), *A history of psychology in autobiography* (Vol. 3). Worcester, MA: Clark University Press.

Watson, J. B. (1970). *Behaviorism.* New York: Norton. (Original work published 1924)

Watson, J. B., & McDougall, W. (1928). *The battle of behaviorism.* London: Kegan Paul.

Watson, J. B., & Morgan, J. J. B. (1917). Emotional reactions and psychological experimentation. *American Journal of Psychology, 28,* 163–174.

Watson, R. I. (Ed.). (1976). *Eminent contributors to psychology* (Vol. 2). New York: Springer.

Watson, R. R. (1930, December). I am the mother of a behaviorist's sons. *Parents' Magazine,* pp. 16–18, 67.

Watson Papers. Washington, DC: Library of Congress.

Weiss, A. P. (1929). *A theoretical basis of human behavior.* Columbus, OH: Adams.

Winkler, J. K., & Bromberg, W. (1939). *Mind explorers.* New York: Reynal, Hitchcock.

Woodworth, R. S. (1931). *Contemporary schools of psychology.* New York: Ronald.

Yerkes Papers. (1906–1915). New Haven, CT: Yale University Medical Library.

Yerkes Papers. (1915). New Haven, CT: Yale University Medical Library.

Zuriff, G. E. (1979). Ten inner causes. *Behaviorism, 7,* 1–8.

8

Paradigm Found: A Deconstruction of the History of the Psychoanalytic Movement

ROBERT S. STEELE

INTRODUCTION

Ellenberger's *The Discovery of the Unconscious* (1970) and Sulloway's *Freud, Biologist of the Mind* (1979) are outstanding examples of the many studies exploring the development of psychoanalysis within the intellectual milieu of turn-of-the-century Europe. These works and others have found fault with psychoanalytic versions of the history of psychoanalysis, but there has not been a detailed investigation of why such flawed accounts were written. This is understandable because, although most history comes down to us in textual form, few historical works have used methods of textual criticism to uncover misunderstandings of the past. We use such methods to examine the first historical account of psychoanalysis, Freud's "On the History of the Psycho-Analytic Movement" (1914/1957), showing how it has become the origin of many distortions about the early years of psychoanalysis.

In this first history of his work, Freud was concerned with establishing psychonalysis as a science, and we shall find that several of his historical fictions serve his rhetorical aim of solidifying the psychoana-

POINTS OF VIEW IN THE
MODERN HISTORY OF PSYCHOLOGY

lytic movement. Because Freud's intent was to found a scientific movement, Kuhn's (1970) ideas about paradigms provide a useful heuristic for understanding issues concerning methods, criteria of validity, and analytic practitioners that Freud raises in his essay. Although the notion of paradigm formation is helpful in understanding why Freud addresses certain topics, we show that psychoanalysis confronts Kuhn's theory of the history of science with an anomaly. Kuhn suggests that the difference between the natural and social sciences is that the former are paradigmatic while the latter are preparadigmatic. While Freud was alive, however, psychoanalysis was clearly paradigmatic according to Kuhn's criteria.

Individuals, movements, and nations are all prone to compose histories that highlight their courage, ignore their ignominious deeds, and denigrate their rivals. Psychoanalysis is therefore not aberrant for having fabricated a history of itself that is self-congratulatory and propagandistic. It is ironic, however, because psychoanalysis as a therapy is devoted to helping individuals develop a realistic accounting of their lives; as a hermeneutic perspective, it defines its task as bringing forward the latent, repressed meanings in historical events and people's lives; and as a science, it endeavors to establish a correspondence between its findings and reality. If psychoanalysis is unable to achieve these ends in writing its own history, then one wonders to what extent it can achieve them in its case studies, textual interpretations, or scientific pronouncements.

Psychoanalysis uses the inconsistencies, contradictions, omissions, and fanciful elaborations in a subject's narratives to take his or her history apart. Such deconstructions, by showing how distortions falsify the past, are used to dispel the confusions and illusions created by people when they tell their life stories. It is fitting, then, that we use methods of textual interpretation that are derived in part from psychoanalysis in order to deconstruct Freudian legend.

History and identity are closely intertwined; in formulating a historical account, both individuals and groups make statements about who they are. Constructing the history of a science serves to identify that science as a paradigm, a system of inquiry that has some autonomy from other sciences because it defines its own research questions, prescribes a method for answering those questions, and has agreed-upon criteria for evaluating the answers (Kuhn, 1970). Both the narrative progression and the classificatory structure of Freud's "History" (1914/1957) reveal the author's concerns with founding a paradigm. The essay is divided into three parts: (a) the prehistory of psychoanalysis, in which Freud establishes the independence of his work from that of his teachers and colleagues; (b) the period of discovery, in which Freud presents the essentials of his method and recounts how his first followers came to him; and (c) the founding of the psychoanalytic paradigm, in which Freud establishes the fundamentals of analytic orthodoxy while execrating Alfred Adler and C. G. Jung for their defection from psychoanalysis.

The classificatory system of the essay also serves to define Freud's science, for it addresses the issue of what is and is not psychoanalysis, as well as who practices it and who does not. Freud divides the world into two parts: the critics of and the adherents to psychoanalysis. Critics are united by their denial of the importance of sexuality and its ramifications in psychic life, supporters by their acceptance and use of this fundamental discovery of analysis.

THE PREHISTORY OF PSYCHOANALYSIS

A summary of the first few pages of this essay shows how Freud uses his rules of classification to solve a historical question about the beginnings of psychoanalysis. The question is, who invented psychoanalysis, Josef Breuer or Sigmund Freud? Freud begins his history by correcting his own previous account. He claims that in 1909 he was so carried away by the honor of speaking at an American university that he mistakenly attributed the invention of psychoanalysis to Breuer, declaring that he (Freud) had had "no share in its earliest beginnings" (Freud, 1910/1957, p. 9). However, he says he must now reverse himself and take up this "uninteresting point" which is of "no great importance" because opponents of psychoanalysis were giving the credit for its discovery to Breuer when lauding its accomplishments but blaming Freud for its faults. Issues of priority were very important to Freud, but he did not like to appear vainglorious. Doing battle with opponents allowed him to assert his claims in the name of self-defense, instead of appearing simply to dismiss Breuer's work out of self-interest.

When Freud wrote that critics credit Breuer with inventing psychoanalysis if they found something good in it, he in effect put Breuer and the critics on the same side. This initially minor shift of Breuer from Freud's to the critics' camp was then pushed further by Freud as he recounted his relations with Breuer. When Freud made his initial discoveries about sexuality, Breuer was "the first to show the reaction of distaste and repudiation" with which Freud later became so familiar (1914/1957, p. 12). Breuer had been reclassified. No longer was he the first analyst; he was, according to Freud's history, the first critic.

Throughout his history of psychoanalysis, Freud reclassifies former supporters as critics, and in doing so seriously distorts what happened at the time. The transformation of Breuer from friend into foe is an important psychoanalytic tale that has been repeated many times (see, for example, Erikson, 1954; Freud, 1925/1959; Jones, 1953; Robert, 1966). More realistic reconstructions of Freud's relations with Breuer, which we incorporate here in analyzing Freud's account, can be found in Ellenberger (1970), Sulloway (1979), and Steele (1982).

During the late 1870s, more than 20 years before writing his first psychoanalytic works, Freud met Josef Breuer. Breuer was a prominent Viennese physician and a highly regarded scientific researcher; Freud was finishing his medical studies and working at Ernst Brücke's Institute for Physiology, where he had become an advocate of scientific materialism and physiological explanation. When Freud left the University of Vienna, Breuer took him under his wing, loaned him money, referred patients to him, and voiced approval of his research. For almost 10 years the relationship was close, until the beginning of the 1890s when, at Freud's urging, Breuer collaborated with him in writing *Studies on Hysteria* (Breuer & Freud, 1895/1955, vol. 2). Frictions soon developed. Freud became sensitive about his many debts to Breuer and dissatisfied with Breuer's mild support for his theories about sexuality. It was Freud who wanted to sever the relationship; however, as with so many other lapsed friendships in his life, he blamed the other person for the separation (Steele, 1982).

Besides his financial debt to Breuer, Freud owed him a considerable intellectual debt. It was through Breuer, and specifically Breuer's work with one patient (whose case was later published, again at Freud's urging, as that of Anna O. in *Studies in Hysteria*, 1895/1955) that Freud was convinced that: (1) physical symptoms can have a psychological cause, (2) while in a hypnotic state an individual's resistances to talking about secret problems are reduced, and (3) reliving emotions associated with a trauma helps to relieve its effects. All three insights, in modified form, were to become essentials of psychoanalysis.

Freud (1914/1957) mentions these contributions by Breuer, but he is more intent on explaining what Breuer did *not* see in Anna O.'s case and how this failure on Breuer's part caused him to break off relations with Freud. He and Breuer reportedly differed over the explanation of hysteria—Breuer preferring a physiological explanation, Freud a psychological one—but this was not what led to the breach in their relations. It "had deeper causes, but it came about in such a way that at first I did not understand it; it was only later that I learnt from many clear indications how to interpret it" (Freud, 1914/1957, p. 11). Here we see the quintessential psychoanalytic problem: A situation that is not understood is clarified by interpreting what lies under the surface. Freud's answer is also prototypical: Breuer was blind to the sexual aspects of Anna O.'s neurosis. Both during and after their collaboration, when Freud became increasingly insistent on the sexual nature of neurotic suffering, Breuer reacted defensively by denying the truth of Freud's discovery. Unfortunately, the evidence that Freud presents to support his claim is shaped more by his rhetorical purpose of proving the originality of his sexual theories than by actual events.

About Anna O., Breuer writes: "The element of sexuality was astonishingly undeveloped in her" (Breuer & Freud, 1895/1955, p. 21). Freud uses this statement and the assertion that there was obvious sexual symbolism in many of her symptoms, as well as the observation that Breuer had a strong "rapport" with Anna O., to make a circumstantial case that a transference—a sexual attachment of an analysand to his or her analyst—had developed between patient and doctor. Having presented these hints, which are simply a displacement of emphasis because he cannot really tell what he knows, Freud claims to have "strong reasons for suspecting" that after Anna O. had been cured, Breuer must have discovered the sexual nature of her attachment to him and taken flight. According to Freud (1914/1957), Breuer "never said this to me in so many words," but he had said enough at different times to "justify this reconstruction" (p. 12). Unfortunately, the facts do not justify it.

None of this circumspection would have been necessary if Freud had simply disclosed what Breuer had told him: On the last day of treatment, when Breuer went to see Anna O. she was writhing with abdominal cramps. When asked what was wrong, she replied, "Dr. B.'s child is coming!" (Freud, 1960, p. 413). When Breuer failed to recount this scene as a dénouement to his case study, and when Freud, who told the story in his private correspondence, failed to record it in the history of his relations with Breuer, both men were censoring their work because of a sexual issue. Although Freud held that to be honest and straightforward about sex was essential to the psychoanalyst, he was often quite circumspect in writing about it. In one sense, he was a victim of the very prohibitions he was trying to abolish. As long as things are known in private that cannot be stated in public, there will be distortions in our histories just as there are gaps, and fabrications to bridge those gaps, in individual consciousness when we succumb to intrapsychic censorship by keeping secrets from ourselves.

Freud compensates for leaving out Breuer's story of Dr. B.'s child by reporting a statement that Breuer supposedly made to him about the importance of sexuality in neuroses. Freud says Breuer did not recognize the significance of his own pronouncement at the time and later denied ever having said it. However, combined with a statement by Charcot, it lay dormant in Freud's mind until the substance of the remarks emerged as his own discovery. Breuer had told Freud that in cases of neurotic suffering, "these things are always *secrets d' alcove* [secrets of the marriage-bed]" (Freud, 1914/1957, p. 13). In treating this as a personal communication, and in saying that Breuer denied ever having uttered it, Freud reinforces his previous argument that Breuer could not admit that sexuality was an important factor in neurosis. Nevertheless, Breuer (Breuer & Freud, 1895/1955) writes: "*The great majority of severe neuroses in women have their origin in the marriage bed*" (p. 246, emphasis in original). He also writes that being in love produces reveries charged with emotion, and that sexual orgasm produces both strong affects and a restriction of consciousness. As he sees them, all of these states have aspects in common with the alterations of consciousness associated with hysteria.

Freud could not admit to Breuer's having written about the connection between hysteria and sexuality, because to have done so would have given someone else credit for an essential discovery of psychoanalysis. It also would have violated Freud's criterion of classification; that is, only supporters of psychoanalysis recognize the etiological importance of sexuality. Since Breuer was not an avid supporter of psychoanalysis (although he remained sympathetic to Freud and his work), he must have denied the importance of sexuality in psychopathology, according to Freud's simple scheme. That Breuer's writings contradict Freud's account was of little import to Freud, for he often incorrectly recounted his own findings in the service of his science.

Having made Breuer's work part of the prehistory of psychoanalysis by denying the links established by Breuer between sexuality and neurosis, Freud proceeds to dismiss the considerable impact of Jean-Martin Charcot's influence on his work. Freud writes that Charcot had once said of a woman "sufferer," "In this sort of case it's always a question of the genitals—always, always, always" (Freud, 1914/1957, p. 14), and hints that Charcot, like Breuer, would probably have denied ever having said this. Contradicting Freud's intimation that Charcot failed to fully realize the significance of the connection between sexuality and hysteria, Ellenberger (1970) points out that one of Charcot's assistants had written that hysterical attacks were often reenactments of sexual traumas, and this kind of information was taken for granted by Charcot's group. Thus neither of his two great teachers, Charcot and Breuer, was as blind to the sexual etiology of hysteria as Freud would have us believe.

By dismissing the contributions of Breuer and Charcot to the development of his theory, Freud (1914/1957) established his right to claim as his own discoveries that he regarded as the essentials of psychoanalysis. In his history, he outlines these as the fact of resistance and the theory of repression, the existence of infantile sexuality, and the interpreting of dreams in order to explore the unconscious. Freud treats these as either his own original observations or as his own inductive discoveries, and while he admits that philosophers may have written about some of them (and therefore may claim priority), he swears that he learned of each of them through arduous research. In contrast, Ellenberger (1970) and Sulloway (1979) show in detail that in all his "discoveries," Freud's insights were anticipated not only by philosophers but by other scientific investigators, many of whom Freud had read.

Having spent an entire essay, so far, in claiming credit for all the important psychoanalytic discoveries, Freud next disclaimed responsibility for an error that he had made. After publication of *Studies on Hysteria* (1895/1955), while he was still trying to break away from Breuer, Freud proposed his seduction theory. It held that hysterics and obsessional neurotics had been sexually aroused as children by having their genitals manipulated by an older person, and that as adults their psychoneuroses were delayed and distorted reactions of disgust to their unconscious memories of such events. Freud (1914/1957) explains his creation of the theory: "Influenced by Charcot's view of the traumatic origin of hysteria, one was readily inclined to accept as true and aetiologically significant the statements made by patients in which they ascribed their symptoms to passive sexual experiences in the first years of childhood—to put it bluntly, to seduction" (p. 17).

Bearing this explanation in mind, it is interesting to read Freud's statement that Charcot's theories had led him to believe his patients' stories, for in his first publication on this type of work, he presents "some objections" to Charcot's hereditary theory of hysteria, and in its place proposes his seduction theory, which stresses environmental events (Freud, 1896/1962a, p. 143). In his third paper on seduction, he again presents his work as a correction of Charcot's views, stating that his former teacher would not be likely to accept the primary aetiological significance that he gives to sexual trauma (Freud, 1896/1962c, p. 199). According to Freud the 1896 researcher, it was Charcot's work that was being corrected by the seduction theory; but for Freud the 1914 historian, it was Charcot, along with Freud's patients, who were responsible for his having formulated that theory.

Although Freud does not hold Charcot responsible for the mistake in his retrospective accounts of the seduction theory, he does blame his patients. In three other places he repeats that his patients told him that they had been seduced as children (Freud, 1906/1953, p. 274; 1925/1959,

p. 34; 1933/1964, p. 120). In these passages Freud literally rewrites history by rewriting himself, because in the three 1896 papers in which he set forth the seduction theory, he specifically states that his patients never told him stories of seduction. Indeed, Freud felt that the merit of his new psychoanalytic technique was that it allowed him to piece together from his patients' memory fragments, affective reactions, and fantasies those long-buried incidents of sexual abuse that they could not consciously recall. In all the seduction theory papers, Freud offers as proof against charges that he was taken in by his patients' fantasies, or that his malleable clients simply told him what they knew he wanted to hear, the fact that only under the compulsion of his therapeutic procedure could such histories have been be reconstructed (Freud, 1896/1962a, p. 153; 1896/1962b, pp. 165–166; 1896/1962c, p. 204).

In his last paper on the topic, Freud summarizes his views. He dismisses doubts about the authenticity of the scenes he presents by declaring that before coming to him, his patients knew nothing about such events; indeed, they were indignant when he suggested that such recollections might emerge in treatment. He writes: "Only the strongest compulsion of the treatment can induce them to embark on a reproduction of them." Even when patients had gone through the scenes more than once, "they still attempt to withhold belief from them, by emphasizing the fact that . . . they have no feeling of remembering the scenes." He concludes: "This latter piece of behavior seems to provide conclusive proof" (Freud, 1896/1962c, p. 204). Freud's proof that his patients were not making up their stories was that they denied the reality of the scenes he had reconstructed. Their denials were taken by him as an affirmation of the occurrence of the sexual trauma (and of his construction of it), because denial is a natural defense against reviving a horrid memory. According to Freud's own research reports, then, his patients did not tell him seduction stories. In fact, they would not even assent to his insistence that such events had taken place in their childhoods. Nevertheless, their denials were used as evidence for Freud's theory.[1]

Did Freud the scientist incorrectly report what his patients had said, or did Freud the historian later misrepresent what his patients had told him? Either alternative is troubling: the first because if Freud did not

---

[1] It has become standard practice in psychoanalysis to take someone's denial of the occurrence of an event as confirmation that such things must have happened, and that because they were traumatic they have been disavowed. Yet it is sometimes unwise to accept such evidence, and one is alerted to the pitfalls of this type of empiricism by Freud's actions when he renounced his seduction theory. Instead of criticizing his own work by questioning his logic and his construction and use of such evidence, Freud insisted that he had been led astray by his patients.

accurately report the results of his research, then we are obliged to doubt his veracity in all of his writings; the second because much of Freud's work, and especially his case studies, requires an accurate historical recounting and if he could not get his own findings straight, one wonders how well he could do with another person's life.

It is very likely that Freud's history is incorrect. If the initial product of the psychoanalytic method—and in the earliest seduction theory paper he uses the term psychoanalysis for the first time—were to be found in error because he had mistakenly reconstructed life events that may not have taken place and then insisted on their reality, that discovery would be extremely damaging to the credibility of his subsequent research, which used many of the same methods. Instead, his method was saved at the cost of erring historically—that is, by attributing his error to his having been taken in by his patients' stories, and by not admitting that his analytic method of reconstructing the past had produced these tales.

What was important to Freud in his account of the prehistory of psychoanalysis was conveying the originality and validity of his work, even if this meant denying the influence of his teachers and misrepresenting his scientific findings.

THE PERIOD OF DISCOVERY

The years from about 1897 to 1905 were extremely productive for Freud. As he began to articulate findings and theories that to him were original, he became increasingly concerned with both his claims to priority for these discoveries, and with the reception his ideas received.

In Freud's historical essay, the issue of priorities is addressed when he speaks of his period of "splendid isolation," that time just before the turn of the century when his thought was incubating, he was undergoing his self-analysis, and he was working on *The Interpretation of Dreams* (1900/1953). At this time, he says, his publications could lag behind his thought because there were no claims over " 'priority' to be defended" (Freud, 1914/1957, p. 22). This is another way of saying that he was the only one working on those questions concerning sexuality and neurosis, both of which are at the center of psychoanalysis.

In all his writings, Freud continually dismisses issues of priority as tedious. Jones (1953) also asserts that Freud was never interested in claims about who had the right to a certain scientific discovery. Nevertheless, it is obvious that Freud was obsessed with the issue. We have reviewed his attempts to diminish the role that other people's work played in shaping his thought, and Merton (1976) points out that in

Freud's writings there are more than 150 separate passages in which he expresses concern with priority.

After insisting that for him there were no debates about priority during his period of "splendid isolation," Freud makes a curious error. He writes: *"The Interpretation of Dreams . . .* was finished in all essentials at the beginning of 1896 but was not written out until the summer of 1899" (1914/1957, p. 22). However, as we know from Freud's letters to Wilhelm Fliess, he did not even mention writing such a work until May 1897, and only after that date did he consider many of the important topics raised in the book. Pushing the book's date of creation back in time can be interpreted, of course, as staking an earlier claim on the ideas.

Freud's assertion that priorities were not an issue around 1900 is odd, because the most important fight over priority that Freud ever had was with Wilhelm Fliess, and it had its beginnings at this time. Curiously, there is no reference to Fliess in Freud's history, although he and Fliess were close friends for nearly a decade and conducted an extensive correspondence in which they worked out their scientific theories (Freud, 1954). Fliess, a Berlin physician, had combined his talents as a biologist and mathematician to do pioneering research in the area of biological periodicity. He shared Freud's passion for convincing the world that sexuality lay at the center of human life. Indeed, it was he who formulated some of the ideas on bisexuality and latency that later became fundamentals of psychoanalysis. It was partially his influence that brought Freud to see psychological questions from an evolutionary perspective (Sulloway, 1979). Not surprisingly, the bitter separation between Freud and Fliess at the beginning of the new century was precipitated by Freud's denying Fliess's priority in the discovery of bisexuality, and by his having played a part in Fliess's idea being pirated. By leaving Fliess out of his history and disclaiming any interest in priorities, Freud was free to omit, at least from the public record, an unpleasant affair in his life.

In 1897, a Viennese physician published a book on his investigations of sexual libido. In it he developed his theories of normal and pathological sexuality, talked about the two component instincts of the sexual drive, considered the manifestations of sexuality in childhood (including masturbation and a preferential love for the opposite sex parent), and discussed infantile sexual "perversity." Sigmund Freud read this book, *Untersuchungen über die Libido sexualis*, by Albert Moll (1897). Disturbed by Moll's having anticipated much that he was just now "discovering," especially about repression, Freud (1954, p. 231) wrote to Fliess: "I would not concede priority in the idea to anyone." Moll's book was one of many publications issued around 1900 by neurologists, psychologists, and sexologists that dealt with the normal and abnormal manifestations of sexuality. Therefore, Freud's claim that he had had no need to worry about priorities (1914/1957) is absurd. With no name and no outstanding contributions to his credit, Freud was jealous of every "discovery" he made.

Freud was also concerned with the reception his ideas received. If something can be made true by repetition, then Freud's claim that his work was not reviewed, or that when it was reviewed it was "dismissed with expressions of scornful or pitying superiority," (1914/1957, pp. 22–23) must be true. His complaint about being dismissed is illustrated in his story of the time he addressed a meeting of the Vienna Society for Psychiatry and Neurology. There he read a paper, "The Aetiology of Hysteria" (1896/1962c) the last of his three seduction theory studies. He says in retrospect that he treated his "discoveries as ordinary contributions to science" (1914/1957, p. 21) and claims that he did not expect the reaction of silence and rejection that he received. At the time, however, he had congratulated himself by saying: "I believe that this is an important finding, the discovery of a *caput Nili* [head of the Nile] in neuropathology" (1896/1962c, p. 203)—hardly a modest claim. While the work was indeed criticized at the meeting, within six months Freud himself was full of private criticisms of this very work. This example, then, of the rejection of Freud's discoveries was merely his colleagues' cool response to the seduction theory, a theory that Freud later went to great pains to renounce.

Freud also complains that his work was ignored, claiming that almost no one paid any attention to *The Interpretation of Dreams* (1900/1953). We have already shown how Freud's historical accounts must be read critically, but his tale of the early rejection of his work and the prejudice that his ideas encountered is so well known that it hardly seems possible that it could be untrue. Initial rejection followed by perseverance that leads to triumph is a standard plot, and Freud reconstructed his history along those lines. This tale has in turn been repeated and elaborated by Freud's followers and popularizers (e.g., Eissler, 1951; Jones, 1953; Robert, 1966). Nevertheless, several researchers have concluded that the story is not true. After studying reviews of Freud's work from 1896 to 1907, they agree that his ideas were treated like those of any other investigator. His publications were widely and fairly reviewed; for example, *The Interpretation of Dreams* and its shorter, more popular version, *On Dreams*, were written up in more than 30 publications. Considerable attention was also given to his work on infantile sexuality. There was no blanket rejection of psychoanalysis, because it was not seen as a monolithic theory but rather as a set of interrelated findings, most of which were separately judged (for an extensive consideration of this topic, see Bry & Rifkin, 1962; Decker, 1977; Ellenberger, 1970; Sulloway, 1979.)

Why would Freud bemoan his rejection when an impartial reading of the reviews clearly shows that his work was treated fairly? Steele (1982) lists several reasons: (1) During the early years of his analytic investigations, Freud felt isolated from the scientific community; thus he transformed his sense of being an outcast into a scenario of actually having been rejected by others. (2) From the time of his first work in psychology, he interpreted any questioning of his ideas as rejection of them. (3) He thought he was a genius and knew he had made great discoveries, so when others failed to agree with him he found fault with them, not with himself. (4) He was determined to solidify his followers around him, and stories of the rejection of his revolutionary ideas helped to bond his movement together. At one point he even worked out a formula according to which the rejection of his work was actually a confirmation of it.

An elaboration of this last point shows how Freud used psychoanalysis defensively to rationalize his fantasies, for he claims that psychoanalysis helped him to realize why his ideas had been so widely rejected by critics. According to Freud, his critics, like neurotics in psychoanalytic treatment, were defensively motivated to resist insights into the everyday manifestations of sexuality. Thus they used arguments against psychoanalysis similar to those his patients used. Freud laments that although he could use his position to "pressure" his patients into examining their resistances, he could not do this with his critics. He despairs of ever getting them to examine psychoanalysis "in a cool and scientifically objective spirit" (1914/1957, p. 24). Yet what Freud did was to fantasize rejection from all corners and then attack his "unreasonable" critics (who do not seem to have existed in great numbers) by comparing their criticism to neurotic resistance. In doing so, however, he treated his critics unfairly, for they seem, at least according to several historians, to have reviewed Freud's work in an impartial, objective way.

The most important work to come out of Freud's period of discovery was *The Interpretation of Dreams* (1900/1953). It was the culmination of Freud's efforts to settle on a method of investigation and to define the problems that were to be of interest to psychoanalysis. About dream interpretation, Freud (1914/1957) says that it provided him with a reliable investigative technique and that it became "the shibboleth of psychoanalysis" (p. 57). Here was a method, the practice of which distinguished one group, psychoanalysts, from all others. The method called for dialogue between analyst and analysand, governed by some special considerations. The analysand does most of the talking, and in the case of dreams begins by telling all he or she remembers of a dream. Then, in order to amplify the dream, the analysand systematically associates to each element of it. (This technique of directed association was soon replaced by free association, in which the analysand is not put under the directive to talk systematically about each part of a dream.

The success of this type of analysis depends on the analysand's "noticing and reporting whatever comes into his head and not being misled, for instance, into suppressing an idea because it strikes him as unimportant or irrelevant or because it seems to him meaningless" (Freud, 1900/1953, p. 101). This necessity of the analytic procedure was christened the "fundamental rule of psychoanalysis" in 1912 and was the foundation of Freud's treatment method. Patients, of course, found it difficult to adhere to the rule because when painful, infantile, and consciously inadmissible thoughts and emotions occurred to them, they would resist communicating these to their therapists. This resistance was viewed as a manifestation of repression, and the analyst's job was to interpret the resistance by providing the analysand with insight into it, thereby loosening the internal censorship. As an analyst, one had the duty to listen with evenly suspended attention, not to let one's own resistances distort one's perceptions, and to interpret the analysand's actions in order to provide him or her with insight and the opportunity to express emotions.

Using his patients' associations to dreams and the translation rules provided by his notions of condensation, displacement, the consideration of representability, secondary revision, and symbolism, Freud was able to transform the distorted narratives of manifest dreams into the more coherent and meaningful narratives of interpreted dreams. When a dream, symptom, or faulty action was interpreted, it made more sense; that is, it was brought into connection with the analysand's ongoing life and thereby helped to fill in a history that had been partly lost because defensive reactions had kept emotionally charged experiences dissociated from consciousness.

Freud saw dream interpretation as the "royal road to the unconscious" because it provided a model and a tool for uncovering what had been lost, forgotten, or disavowed in an analysand's life. The interpretation of neurotic symptoms or dreams, he said, always took him into the past as his patients' associations moved backward into childhood. He felt that an essential of psychoanalytic practice was this tracing back of a phenomenon to its origins, and that in repressed infantile wishes, usually having to do with sexuality, were to be found the beginnings of and the motive forces behind both dreams and the symptoms of neurotics (for a thorough critique of Freud's method, and especially his assumption that adult reminiscences are the equivalent of actual childhood events, see Jacobsen & Steele, 1979; Steele, 1982; Steele & Jacobsen, 1978).

Although Kuhn (1970) is not precise about which characteristics are both necessary and sufficient for the establishment of a paradigm, we can see that with the publication of *The Interpretation of Dreams* (1900/ 1953), Freud took a significant step toward founding the science of psychoanalysis. In this text, two essentials of a paradigm are set forth; he both describes his method and shows how it can be used to investigate a set of phenomena such as the psychological processes of the human mind. Three other characteristics that Kuhn sees as important elements of a paradigm were to become part of psychoanalysis by 1914, when Freud published his history (1914/1957). The history itself is one of these elements because it is a progressivist account of Freud's discoveries that makes psychoanalysis appear both revolutionary and scientific. The other two elements—practioners using psychoanalysis, and a statement of criteria for evaluating research—are both discussed in the history. As we have seen, Freud's history is organized around defining what is and is not psychoanalysis. We return to this topic after we consider what caused the number of psychoanalysts to grow so rapidly.

By 1914, Freud was famous, had many followers, and was widely read. Having succeeded in the first half of his history in convincing the reader that psychoanalysis had been completely rejected, he suddenly had to alter the recounting of his fortunes. He accomplishes this with a rhetorical deus ex machina: "In 1907 the situation changed all at once and contrary to all expectations" (Freud, 1914/1957, p. 26); people began to take an interest in psychoanalysis and "even some scientific workers" were ready to acknowledge it.

Actually, however, the situation had not changed. It is only within the context of Freud's history that the rapid spread and acceptance of his ideas could not have been expected. Within a decade after publication of *The Interpretation of Dreams* (1900/1953), the International Psychoanalytic Association had been founded, there were two psychoanalytic journals, and Freud's international reputation had been proven by an invitation to speak at Clark University in America. If it were not still necessary to present evidence showing how the legend of the rejection of psychoanalysis was created by (1) Freud's belief that he alone had made revolutionary discoveries about human sexuality and suffering, (2) his sense that any failure to endorse his ideas totally was to reject them, and (3) his systematic indoctrination of his followers with the feeling that they were rebels with a cause, it would be historically more valuable and far closer to what actually happened to explain why psychoanalysis was so quickly and widely accepted.

The Appeal of Psychoanalysis

To gain acceptance, any paradigm requires researchers; any therapy, patients; any teaching, students; any sect, disciples; and any movement, followers. Psychoanalysis offered its first practitioners something of each of these.

Psychoanalysis as Research

Psychoanalysis provided a scientific framework along with a medical procedure for investigating the mind and psychological illness, thereby combining the possibility of using as subjects for research people who were also paying for treatment. For Freud, this was important. He was never wealthy, and the combination of research and treatment, which he thought essential to psychoanalytic methodology, was also, for him and most of the early associates to whom he made referrals, an economic necessity.

Psychoanalysis as Therapy

Another benefit from becoming an analyst was the opportunity to obtain psychological counseling without initially admitting that one had personal problems. Many of the early analysts, like Freud himself, suffered from mild to severe psychopathological disturbances. Training or self-analysis gave them a professionally sanctioned opportunity to work through their own difficulties.

Psychoanalysis as a Teaching

Psychoanalysis was a school of thought in which students could study under a master. Karl Abraham, one of Freud's most loyal followers, called Freud his teacher. Freud fostered the image of "the professor," and several members of his group came to him by way of lectures he had given at the University of Vienna.

Psychoanalysis as a Sect

Freud also offered a new teaching in the biblical sense. He identified with Moses, most of his close followers were other Jews, and all were imbued with a sense of mission (Klein, 1981). As early as 1910, Alfred Hoche, a psychiatrist and critic of almost all psychiatric treatment, called psychoanalysis "a psychical epidemic." Hoche had observed that devotees of psychoanalysis had much in common with members of religious cults. They were sharply intolerant of other beliefs, held their master in veneration, had a penchant for proselytizing, possessed their own jargon, and had an overly high valuation of their discoveries combined with almost no sense of the history of psychical treatment (Ellenberger, 1970).

Several of Hoche's characterizations apply to Freud himself. In his history, however, Freud dismisses Hoche's charge, saying that the infighting and difficulties at the psychoanalytic conference in Munich in 1913 would have convinced anyone that analysts were not "a fanatical sect blindly submissive to their leader" (1914/1957, p. 45). Nevertheless, the events at Munich, which led in part to Jung's banishment from psychoanalysis, can very easily be interpreted as an attempt by Freud to maintain the purity of his teaching.

Others who were more sympathetic to psychoanalysis than Hoche viewed it as a secular religion. For example, Max Graf, a founding member of the first psychoanalytic group—The Psychological Wednesday Society—but who later left the movement, recalls that in their weekly meetings there was an atmosphere of the founding of a religion: "Freud himself was its new prophet . . . [and his] pupils—all inspired and convinced—were his apostles" (Graf, 1942, p. 471).

Psychoanalysis as a Movement

As a revolutionary movement, psychoanalysis afforded its members several advantages. Most were young physicians beginning their careers in a rigidly hierarchical profession. This new field gave them the opportunity to gain positions of importance and provided them with a vast unexplored area (according to Freud at least) in which to do research. The findings from this work could then be used to challenge the wisdom of their superiors. Freud (1914/1957) alludes to intimidation of his followers that forced them to keep silent about their views for fear of losing their positions. In actuality, however, they were outspoken in their advocacy of psychoanalysis at conferences (Ellenberger, 1970).

Freud sought to inspire his followers by creating a siege mentality among his "soldiers." In letters to Jung, the most important of his lieutenants, Freud on many occasions sounded like a general. He talked of "two warring worlds," traditional psychiatry and psychoanalysis, saying that although he would not see the final victory, he hoped his followers would. In debates, he advised that "attack is the best form of defense," and in order to rouse Jung before the latter presented a paper advocating psychoanalysis at a conference on psychiatry, Freud recalled his own "long years of honourable but painful solitude," his unshakable faith in his findings, and his years of waiting "until a voice from the unknown multitude should answer mine. That voice was yours." He concluded: "Thank you for that, and don't let anything shake your confidence; you will witness our triumph and share in it" (McGuire, 1974, pp. 6, 28, 82). The war that Freud created from his fantasies of rejection was used by him to marshal his forces for the cause.

THE FOUNDING OF THE PSYCHOANALYTIC PARADIGM

Having reviewed the development of his method and the growth of the psychoanalytic movement, and having established the research domain of his science, all within the context of a progressivist history, there is only one element essential to the founding of a paradigm that Freud had not yet addressed in his "History" (1914/1957). This was the definition of criteria by which to evaluate the validity of research. Freud does this in the last section of the essay. The expulsion of Adler and Jung from psychoanalysis, the explanation for which motivated Freud to write his historical account, also forced him to articulate what constitutes proper psychoanalysis.

In Freud's reasons for establishing the International Psychoanalytic Association in 1910 are found the criteria of validity for psychoanalysis. Using a familiar theme, he says that because "official science had pronounced its solemn ban upon psycho-analysis" (Freud, 1914/1957, p. 44), he felt it to be essential that analysts have a system of mutual support in which they could come together and share ideas. Although psychoanalysis, as shown here, was not banned by either "official" or unofficial science, Freud proclaimed that the reigning psychiatric paradigm could not evaluate psychoanalytic research because science had by fiat denied the validity of psychoanalysis. As a result, he felt that an official association was needed to guard the practice of analysis from "abuses." He states: "There should be some headquarters whose business it would be to declare: 'All this nonsense is nothing to do with analysis; this is not psycho-analysis' " (Freud, 1914/1957, p. 43). With the establishment of the association, then, the psychoanalytic paradigm was founded. Not only did it have a method, a research domain, and practitioners, but also a procedure for deciding what was, and was not, genuine analytic work.

The authority for deciding about the legitimacy of someone's particu-

lar practice of psychoanalysis or the validity of a researcher's findings
was to be in the hands of the president of the association. From its
establishment in 1910 until his resignation in 1914, after it was determined that his work no longer conformed to the principles of psychoanalysis, Jung was this person. (Of course, Freud was the actual power
behind the throne.) Freud's push to establish the association and to have
Jung installed as its president led to the first decision about the validity
of someone's research when Adler severed his affiliation with Freud.
Adler, the most prominent of Freud's Viennese followers, had expected
to become president of the association but was not Freud's candidate.
Jung was chosen over Adler for several reasons: Freud liked him better;
he was Swiss, and Freud felt that he would give psychoanalysis an
international look; and he was a Protestant (Adler was a Jew), and as
such his advocacy of psychoanalysis had saved it, in Freud's opinion,
from becoming "a Jewish national affair" (Abraham & Freud, 1965, p.
34).

To compensate him for being passed over, Adler was made president
of the Vienna Society and co-editor of a new journal. According to
Freud, however, he was still dissatisfied and therefore began to ex-
pound his own ideas. Adler resigned as president of the Vienna group
in early 1911 because of what he called "the incompatibility of his scientific attitude with his position in the society" (Nunberg & Federn, 1974,
p. 177). Freud goes to some length to explain Adler's departure and to
dismiss his criticism of psychoanalysis. Freud's response to this first
challenge to psychoanalysis by someone who had used the analytic
method was to deny that Adler had actually used the method. In a
defense filled with *ad hominem* attacks, Freud (1914/1957) claims that
Adler's theories focused on the psychology of the ego because he never
understood what the unconscious was. He says that what Adler claims
to have discovered he, Freud, had discovered long ago, and that Adler
had taken part of psychoanalysis and blown it up into an entire system.
He finds that Adler capitulated to the foes of psychoanalysis by questioning infantile psychosexual determinacy, the most important element
of psychoanalysis and yet the most difficult to accept.

The particular criticism of psychosexual theory that put Adler's work
beyond the pale of the psychoanalytic paradigm, and that was later
repeated by Jung (1913/1961), was that adult neurotics, as part of a
defense against recognizing their current problems, may retreat to memories of their childhood. They infuse these reminiscences retrospectively
with sexual themes in a desperate attempt to relocate the origin of their
problems in the past, with their parents (Ansbacher & Ansbacher, 1964).
This is an important criticism of psychoanalysis and one that Freud

(1909/1955b) had once raised. However, he had dismissed it by asserting that even though adult neurotics remold their childhood histories by infusing them with tales of interpersonal sexual intrigues, his psychoanalytic method led to the discovery of what actually occurs in the sexual lives of children; that is, autoerotic activities and Oedipal conflicts. It is unclear how Freud could be certain that such events constituted infantile and childhood sexual experience when his source for the information was adult reminiscences, but he asserts that "every analysis of a child" serves to verify his findings (1914/1957, p. 65). Yet by 1914 there had been only one major analysis of a child (Freud, 1909/1955a), and this was done by the child's father, who was supervised by Freud. Because an analysis under such circumstances does not conform to any of the methodological criteria of psychoanalysis, its value as evidence is questionable (Steele, 1979).

In response to Adler's questioning of Freud's work, Jung, in his presidential address to the 1911 psychoanalytic congress at Weimar, called for increased loyalty to psychoanalysis. Saying that psychoanalysis must maintain its empiricism and scientific rigor while watching within its ranks for unacceptable deviations from the basic analytic postulates, he concludes: "What fate expects of us is that we faithfully husband the enormous store of knowledge provided by Freud's discoveries and pass it on to our fellow men, rather than pervert it for the gratification of our own ambitions" (Jung, 1911/1950, p. 424). According to Freud, of course, Jung himself soon began to pervert it.

Within a year of the Weimar congress, Freud had taken strong exception to what he felt were Jung's Adler-like revisions of psychoanalytic theory. Like Adler, Jung argued that there was a presexual stage of development and that the sexual activities Freud saw as originating in infancy were actually fantasies retrospectively created by adults (1913/1961). In a vast work on symbolism, Jung (1911-1912, 1956) terms inadequate Freud's method of reductive interpretation, according to which the meaning of a symbol can be found primarily in its sexual referents in the past. Instead, he argues, symbols have a more important prospective significance in that they mediate between conscious and unconscious conflicts by pointing toward a synthesis. By defining libido as life energy, Jung also rejected Freud's view that it was exclusively sexual. Finally, in a paper given at the Munich psychoanalytic congress, he put psychoanalysis on a par with Adler's system by demonstrating that they were two complementary perspectives for investigating psychological phenomena.

At that same congress of 1913, Jung stood for reelection as president of the association. Even without the backing of Freud or his inner circle,

Jung won a majority vote. It is clear that most of the analysts present did not think Jung's work had put him outside psychoanalysis, but their opinion meant very little to Freud, who put such pressure on Jung that he severed all his ties with psychoanalysis within a year.

Psychoanalysis belonged to Freud, and in response to Jung's apostasy he made perfectly clear the sole criterion for evaluating the validity of psychoanalytic research: his own personal judgment. He says he "did not recognize the innovations of the Swiss [Jung] as legitimate continuations and further developments of the psycho-analysis that originated with me" (Freud, 1914/1957, p. 60). Since it was not psychoanalytic, Jung's work must then be opposed to psychoanalysis, according to Freud's black and white distinction. Like the critics of psychoanalysis, and like Adler, Jung had denied the reality of infantile sexuality, and once he did this he was Freud's enemy.

Both Jung and Adler had used the psychoanalytic method. On the basis of what they discovered, they felt justified in putting forward their findings, which initially were reasonable and sympathetic criticisms of their teacher's work. Criticism, however, to Freud meant opposition, and opposition meant that someone had defensive reasons for avoiding the truths of psychoanalysis. Although Freud (1914/1957) tries hard to dismiss Jung's ideas by analyzing and denigrating his character, it is obvious that he failed to understand what Jung had said (Steele, 1982). For example, Freud (1914/1957, p. 58) asserts that in *Wandlungen und Symbole der Libido*, Jung (1911-1912/1956) is arguing for the right of youth to overthrow "hidebound" authority. Because Jung's text disputed Freud's theories about symbolism and sexuality, the latter took it as a direct attack on himself and cast its theme in Oedipal terms; however, that is not what the book is about. It is an explication of the psychological significance of mythological motifs in the hero's journey and an analysis of the symbolism of that mythologem.

On the first page of his "History," Freud (1914/1957) declares that "no one" could know better than he "what should be called psycho-analysis" (p. 7). He used his authority as both the author of a history and the founder of a movement to exile the two most important and original thinkers in his circle, ostensibly because their ideas were unacceptable as psychoanalysis. The difficulties with Adler and Jung led to the founding of "the committee." This was a group composed of Freud and his most loyal followers whose task it was to watch for deviations within their own ranks and within the movement. In a letter to Abraham, a member of the committee, Freud was explicit about what he liked: "The way in which all of you try to show me the value of the work by supplementing and drawing conclusions from it is of course quite marvelous"

(Abraham & Freud, 1965, p. 142). Freud wanted followers, and his treatment of Fliess, Adler, and Jung demonstrates that he was not comfortable with people who claimed an egalitarian relationship by asserting their right to formulate their own ideas.

CONCLUSION

Paradigms are both prescriptive and proscriptive. They define a method and a field of inquiry while also setting limits on how questions are to be answered and establishing criteria by which to judge those answers. All scientific paradigms have the authority to enforce their proscriptions, be it the rule of reason, blind faith in empiricism, or guidelines established by the founders of a research tradition. In declaring his right to define what was psychoanalysis, Freud (1914/1957) established the criterion of validity for analysis. His paradigm was now complete: The method was dialogue, the field of research was the human mind, the acceptability of findings was to be adjudicated by Freud, and whoever accepted the foregoing could call his or her work psychoanalysis.

Those subscribing to Kuhn's model of science agree with him that most human or social sciences are preparadigmatic (Kuhn, 1970; Mujeeb-ur-Rahman, 1977). They assume that with time and the proper effort, these might someday develop into true paradigmatic sciences. By contrast, psychoanalysis is a human science that by 1914, and while Freud was still alive, was fully paradigmatic in the Kuhnian sense. After the appearance of Freud's "On the History of the Psycho-Analytic Movement" (1914/1957), psychoanalysis continued to flourish, and although there were deviations and defections from within the ranks, Freud's creation was kept intact by him and his loyalists until his death in 1939. Freud made new discoveries and modified his theories until the end, but the method, the research area, and the criterion of evaluation never changed. With Freud's death, however, psychoanalysis became postparadigmatic because it no longer had a way to evaluate the validity of research.

We have explored the founding of the psychoanalytic paradigm by showing how in his first extended history Freud retrospectively constructed an account presenting psychoanalysis as his own original and revolutionary discovery that grew into a science despite the prejudices of critics and the defection of former friends and colleagues. If Freud had not been a legend in his own mind and a paradigm in his own time, he probably would not have had so great an impact on twentieth-century thought. However, it is his fame and the grandiose claims that he made about psychoanalysis that have allowed us to deconstruct his legend, for without the publication of his letters and much additional research on the history of psychoanalysis, our only access to its past would have been Freud's historical fictions.

REFERENCES

Abraham, H., & Freud, E. (Eds.). (1965). *A psycho-analytic dialogue: The letters of Sigmund Freud and Karl Abraham, 1907–1926*. New York: Basic Books.

Ansbacher, H., & Ansbacher, R. (Eds.). (1964). *The individual psychology of Alfred Adler: A systematic presentation from his writings*. New York: Harper & Row.

Breuer, J., & Freud, S. (1955). Studies on hysteria. In J. Strachey (Ed.), *The standard edition of the complete psychological works of Sigmund Freud* (Vol. 2). London: Hogarth. (Original work published 1895)

Bry, I., & Rifkin, A. (1962). Freud and the history of ideas: Primary sources, 1886–1910. In J. Masserman (Ed.), *Science and psychoanalysis* (Vol. 5). New York: Grune & Stratton.

Decker, H. (1977). Freud in Germany: Revolution and reaction in science, 1893–1907. *Psychological Issues, 11*(4).

Eissler, K. (1951). An unknown autobiographical letter by Freud and a short commentary. *International Journal of Psycho-Analysis, 32*, 319–324.

Ellenberger, H. (1970). *The discovery of the unconscious*. New York: Basic Books.

Erikson, E. (1954). The dream specimen of psychoanalysis. *Psychoanalytic Psychiatry and Psychology: Clinical and Theoretical Papers, 1*, 131–170.

Freud, E. (Ed.). (1960). *The letters of Sigmund Freud*. New York: Basic Books.

Freud, S. (1953). The interpretation of dreams. In J. Strachey (Ed.), *Standard edition* (Vols. 4, 5). London: Hogarth. (Original work published 1900)

Freud, S. (1953). My views on the part played by sexuality in the aetiology of neurosis. In J. Strachey (Ed.), *Standard edition* (Vol. 7). London: Hogarth. (Original work published 1906)

Freud, S. (1954). *The origins of psycho-analysis: Letters to Wilhelm Fliess, drafts and notes* (M. Bonaparte, A. Freud, & E. Kris, Eds.). New York: Basic Books.

Freud, S. (1955a). Analysis of a phobia in a five-year-old boy. In J. Strachey (Ed.), *Standard edition* (Vol. 10). London: Hogarth. (Original work published 1909)

Freud, S. (1955). Notes upon a case of obsessional neurosis. In J. Strachey (Ed.), *Standard edition* (Vol. 10). London: Hogarth. (Original work published 1909)

Freud, S. (1957). Five lectures on psycho-analysis. In J. Strachey (Ed.), *Standard edition* (Vol. 11). London: Hogarth. (Original work published 1910)

Freud, S. (1957). On the history of the psycho-analytic movement. In J. Strachey (Ed.), *Standard edition* (Vol. 14). London: Hogarth. (Original work published 1914)

Freud, S. (1959). An autobiographical study. In J. Strachey (Ed.), *Standard edition* (Vol. 20). London: Hogarth. (Original work published 1925)

Freud, S. (1962a). Heredity and the aetiology of the neuroses. In J. Strachey (Ed.), *Standard edition* (Vol. 3). London: Hogarth. (Original work published 1896)

Freud, S. (1962b). Further remarks on the neuro-psychoses of defence. In J. Strachey (Ed.), *Standard edition* (Vol. 3). London: Hogarth. (Original work published 1896)

Freud, S. (1962c). The aetiology of hysteria. In J. Strachey (Ed.), *Standard edition* (Vol. 3). London: Hogarth. (Original work published 1896)

Freud, S. (1964). New introductory lectures on psycho-analysis. In J. Strachey (Ed.), *Standard edition* (Vol. 22). London: Hogarth. (Original work published 1933)

Graf, M. (1942). Reminiscences of Professor Sigmund Freud. *Psychoanalytic Quarterly, 11,* 465–476.

Hoche, A. (1910). Eine psychische Epidemie unter Aertzten. *Medizinische Klinik, 4,* 1007–1010.

Jacobsen, P., & Steele, R. (1979). From present to past: Freudian archaeology. *International Review of Psycho-Analysis, 6,* 349–362.

Jones, E. (1953). *The life and work of Sigmund Freud* (Vol. 1). New York: Basic Books.

Jung, C. G. (1950). Annual report by the president of the International Psychoanalytic Association. In H. Read, M. Fordham, & G. Adler (Eds.), *The collected works of C. G. Jung* (Vol. 18). Princeton, NJ: Princeton University Press. (Original work published 1911)

Jung, C. G. (1956). Wandlungen und Symbole der Libido. In H. Read et al. (Eds.), *Collected works* (Vol. 5). Princeton, NJ: Princeton University Press. (Original work published 1911–1912)

Jung, C. G. (1961). The theory of psychoanalysis. In H. Read et al. (Eds.), *Collected works* (Vol. 4). Princeton, NJ: Princeton University Press. (Original work published 1913)

Klein, D. (1981). *Jewish origins of the psychoanalytic movement.* New York: Praeger.

Kuhn, T. (1970). *The structure of scientific revolutions* (2nd ed.). Chicago: University of Chicago Press.

McGuire, W. (Ed.). (1974). *The Freud–Jung letters: The correspondence between Sigmund Freud and C. G. Jung.* Princeton, NJ: Princeton University Press.

Merton, R. (1976). The ambivalence of scientists. In *Sociological ambivalence and other essays.* New York: Free Press.

Mujeeb-ur-Rahman, M. (Ed.). (1977). *The Freudian paradigm.* Chicago: Nelson-Hall.

Moll, A. (1897). *Untersuchungen über die Libido sexualis.* Berlin: Kornfeld.

Nunberg, H., & Federn, E. (Eds.). (1974). *Minutes of the Vienna psychoanalytic society* (Vol. 3). New York: International Universities Press. (Original work published 1910–1911)

Robert, M. (1966). *The psychoanalytic revolution.* New York: Harcourt, Brace, World.

Steele, R. (1979). Psychoanalysis and hermeneutics. *International Review of Psycho-Analysis, 6,* 389–411.

Steele, R. (1982). *Freud and Jung: Conflicts of interpretation.* London: Routledge.

Steele, R., & Jacobsen, P. (1978). From present to past: The development of Freudian theory. *International Review of Psycho-Analysis, 5,* 393–411.

Sulloway, F. (1979). *Freud: Biologist of the mind.* New York: Basic Books.

9

Paradigm Lost: Psychoanalysis after Freud

ROBERT S. STEELE

INTRODUCTION

Freud wrote about a wide range of topics, from the neuronal structure of the brain to the origins of religion, and he speculated on everything from why women invented weaving to why a young boy was afraid of horses. The 23 volumes of the *Standard Edition* of Freud's work provided the impetus for the production of a whole library of books tracing their origin back to him. This collection is too vast to survey here, for it extends from experimental studies on phobic dogs to the interpretation of poetry, painting, and even football. In order to limit and focus this history, we consider the development of four major psychoanalytic perspectives, all of which trace their lineage directly back to Freud. In his texts were found the inspiration, justification, and rationale for such work. We discuss experimental studies, but only as an aspect of ego psychology. We also consider the interpretation of literature, but only as part of our survey of psychoanalytic hermeneutics.

The perspectives, or discourses—for these are more like ways of articulating analytic observations than formal methods or subparadigms—are ego psychology, object–relations theory, hermeneutic psychoanalysis, and feminist psychological analysis. For each of these, we (1) locate

POINTS OF VIEW IN THE
MODERN HISTORY OF PSYCHOLOGY

its historical origins in Freud's thought, (2) trace its development after Freud's death, and (3) discuss the relations of sympathy and antipathy among these descendants of the founder of psychoanalysis.

The unity of the psychoanalytic paradigm dissolved in 1939 when Freud died, but he provided rich soil that has produced a wide variety of thought. While modern psychoanalytic thinkers may not agree on much, and while each discourse has its own technical jargon that insulates it from dialogue with the others (and with nonpsychoanalytic ways of thinking), each perspective has created a theory of human psychology and developed methods for interpreting the psyche.

EGO PSYCHOLOGY

Ego psychology *was* American psychoanalysis from the 1940s to the early 1970s. Its proponents wanted to make Freudian discoveries part of scientific psychology. They did so by translating, simplifying, and operationally defining Freudian notions, by encouraging the experimental investigation of psychoanalytic hypotheses, and by modifying psychoanalytic psychotherapy.

A History of the Ego

While ego psychologists such as Hartmann (1956) and Rapaport (1958/ 1967) trace the origin of their work to Freud's structural theory of the ego (1923), the history of the position and function of the ego in Freud's writings is more complex (Laplanche & Pontalis, 1973).

Freud's first elaborate model of the ego is found in *Studies on Hysteria*. The thesis of this work is: "Hysterics suffer mainly from reminiscences" (Breuer & Freud, 1895/1955, p. 7). That is, their paralyses, coughs, hallucinations and memory loss can be traced back to painful events in their lives that they cannot or do not wish to remember. There are gaps in the patient's memory, and the symptoms of the hysteric are symbolically related to the underlying trauma. Patients are aware of symptoms but cannot rid themselves of them.

Breuer and Freud found that through catharsis—an emotionally vivid recollection of traumatic scenes—patients improved. Taking note of the fact that his patients got better by remembering forgotten fragments of their life stories, Freud conceptualized the ego as a locus of consciousness that resists remembering painful occurrences. The more traumatic a memory, the more completely the ego blocks its recall. In a vivid topographical metaphor, Freud pictures ego–consciousness as a narrow pas-

Models
1) studies in Hysteria
2) Project for a Scientific Model
3) Topographic Model
4) STRUCTURAL Model
Psychology - neurology

9. *Paradigm Lost: Psychoanalysis after Freud*   **223**

sage through which remembrances emerge into awareness one at a time. This defile can be blocked easily by resistance; troublesome scenes and events therefore appear in consciousness in disarray, and memories arrive in bits and pieces. All of this serves the patient's (or the ego's) desire not to remember, for he or she can make nothing of this jumble. It is, Freud says, "the psychotherapist's business to put these together once more into the organization he presumes to have existed" (Breuer & Freud, 1895/1955, p. 291).

After finishing his *Studies on Hysteria,* Freud created another model of the psyche. This one was not closely tied to his empirical observations of how people remember events; rather, it was fashioned after the then popular neurological conceptions of brain functioning. Freud's "Project for a Scientific Psychology" (1895/1966) was his attempt to explain causally the complexities of consciousness, psychical defense, and unconscious mental processes through mechanical, energic speculation on brain functioning (see Chapter 12, this volume).

Freud soon abandoned this model, and although many of the energy concepts that he first introduced in it are incorporated into his later works, he would never again use the elaborate and cumbersome structure of brain mechanisms in an attempt to account for psychological phenomena. In order to create links between psychoanalysis and brain biology, ego psychologists such as Holt (1965) and neuropsychologists like Pribram (Pribram & Gill, 1976) worked to revive and assess Freud's neuronal speculation by comparing it to the findings of later day neuroscientists.

Freud (1900/1953) declared that in constructing a "mental apparatus" to account for dreams and their interpretation, he would "remain upon psychological ground" (p. 536). Thus he was freed from the restrictions of brain anatomy and could henceforth create maps of the mind. His first mental topography was divided into three regions: the unconscious, the preconscious, and the conscious, with boundaries of resistance, or intrapsychic censorship, between them. Consciousness is a function of the ego and is protected from unbridled, infantile emotions, lustful impulses, and painful memories by censorship, a process personified by an agent guarding the passageway between the unconscious and the preconscious, denying unacceptable affects and memories access to awareness. In order to protect the repose of the ego, the censor either blocks or distorts the wishes and desires coming from the unconscious. The psychoanalysis of dreams, neurotic symptoms, and faulty actions is directed at undoing the work of the censor in order to make the latent, wishful impulses behind manifest thoughts and feelings known to the ego, whose perception has been distorted by its own censorship.

In a series of papers written from 1914 to 1917, Freud, while working within the boundaries of this first typography, altered the nature and function of the ego. In the 1900 map, the ego was insulated from the infantile, sexual impulses of the unconscious by a "border guard." It was therefore, within itself, relatively free of conflict. Freud (1914/1957) shows that the ego's sense of self-esteem and feelings of being all-knowing come from an infantile self-love—a narcissistic cathexis of itself as a love object. That the ego loves itself, that *I* may be an object of adoration for *myself*, means that consciousness suffers from many of the same libidinal turmoils as the rest of the mind.

The integrity of the ego was further compromised when Freud demonstrated how it is involved in the creation of its own difficulties. In "Mourning and Melancholia" (1917/1957), Freud demonstrates how the ego models itself on important other people and how, if infantile bonds of love with another person are broken, the ego compensates itself and the unconscious for this loss by imitating the lost object. It is to these innovations that the object–relations theorists trace their work. They have made it their task to explore the interpersonal dynamics of human emotional development. For them, an "object" is the destination of desire. It is usually a person, part of a person, or the image of another, or else aspects of one's own self to which strong emotions are attached

The psyche is not only divided into parts, but the ego itself is split. This discovery, along with Freud's work on the ontogeny and phylogeny of the Oedipus complex, was incorporated into his last and most radical re-visioning of the psyche in *The Ego and the Id* (1923/1961). This is the text to which the ego psychologists trace the origin of their work and the justification of their psychoanalytic investigations. In it, Freud announces that it is time for psychoanalysis to shift its focus from unconscious mental processes to the investigation of those aspects of the ego that are unconscious and a part of its defenses against insight. In this model, the ego (*das Ich*) is one of three regions that constitute the psyche, the others being the id (*das Es,* or the it) and the superego (*das Uber-Ich,* or the "over-I"). The ego itself has three levels of awareness— conscious, preconscious, and unconscious—and its function is to mediate among (a) the lustful, infantile, and unconscious desires of the id, (b) the prohibitions of conscience, which are internalized by the ego when it models itself after the parents and which emanate from the nucleus of their image—the superego—and (c) reality.

In the structural model, the ego becomes the organ of psychic adaptation. It performs its task of mediation through the use of scare tactics. When it senses that the integrity of the organism is threatened by uncontrolled lust from the id, by unreasonable demands from the super-ego, or by threats from reality, it breaks out in anxiety. This reaction is a signal to itself to mobilize its defenses (Freud, 1926/1959a). The ego uses various defense mechanisms, such as denial and repression, to resolve the conflicting demands it makes on itself with those made by the id, the superego, and reality. For Freud, the psyche was a personified battle scene where reason tries to negotiate among the warring forces of self-deception, passion, morality, and necessity.

Toward a General Psychology

Anna Freud's *The Ego and the Mechanisms of Defense* (1936/1946), along with Heinz Hartmann's *Ego Psychology and the Problem of Adaptation* (1939), provide a founding statement of ego psychology. Freud elaborates on how the ego responds to anxiety through defensive maneuvers. In her clear and systematic manner, she simplifies and orders what her father had left in a confused state. She defines and illustrates (using examples drawn from her work with children) some 10 mechanisms of defense, including repression, reaction formation, undoing, and projection. Finally she shows how these are put into operation, the purpose they serve, their symptomatic manifestations, and how they are dealt with in analysis.

From the exploration of how the ego copes in defensive ways, it was only a small step to systematizing psychoanalytic thought about how the ego adapts in general. As Alfred Adler had tried to do 30 years before, Hartmann (1939) riveted analytic interest on the ego and thereby created a revolution in psychoanalysis. Although he is careful to show how all his ideas come from Freud, Hartmann's notion of a "conflict-free ego sphere"—a psychological zone that has consciousness at its center and normally performs functions like perception, speech, learning, and memory in relative freedom from the vicissitudes of instinctual desire—is a significant alteration of Freud's portrait of the beleaguered ego. For Hartmann, the ego is independent of the id and has its own developmental trajectory, a course that is inherently adapted to an "average expectable environment."

Although Hartmann saw that the "primary autonomy" of "ego apparatus," such as perception or memory, could become compromised by neurotic conflict between inner drives and reality, his emphasis was on normal functioning. Because the ego, even in neurotic individuals, retains a sphere of reason that is free from libidinal conflict, Hartmann advocated that a "therapeutic alliance" be formed between analysand and analyst. The analyst teams up with the healthy portions of the analysand's ego in order to work with it in overcoming neurotic suffering.

Erik Erikson's (1968) work on the adaptational crises of the ego during the eight psychosocial stages of development is widely known compared with other ego psychological research. His discoveries, coupled with the aging of America, have led to a growing interest in the investigation of personality change throughout the life cycle.

Works like those of Erikson, which foster closer ties to academic personality research, have been pursued by ego psychology in a general attempt to bring scientific reforms to psychoanalytic observation. Hartmann's "Psychoanalysis as a Scientific Theory" (1959) remains one of the important defenses of the scientific status of psychoanalysis against the attacks of logical positivists. His defense is, however, also a call for reform. He sought in one work after another to make analytic practice more rigorous by systematizing its theoretical structure, by bringing its fundamental assumptions into line with modern scientific knowledge, and by standardizing analytic training. In trying to adapt the European import to American ways, Hartmann provided the conceptual framework needed to bridge the gap between psychoanalysis and experimental psychology. In their comprehensive review of experimental studies that test psychoanalytic hypotheses, Fisher and Greenberg (1977) cite well over a thousand papers. Their conclusion is that while "crucial experiments" allowing one to decide whether a hypothesis is true or false are seemingly impossible to perform in psychoanalysis, the weight of the evidence validates aspects of Freud's hypotheses concerning unconscious mental processes and various character types, while throwing into question his notions about dreams and the effectiveness of psychoanalytic psychotherapy.

Interconnections and Criticisms

Ego psychology and object-relations theory have for the most part complemented each other. Both are concerned primarily with the development and structure of ego, and both are given to abstract metapsychological formulations that often transform the reading of a straightforward case study or debate about a point of theory into an exercise in decoding psychoanalytic jargon. Where ego psychology has put its emphasis on adolescent and adult functioning—addressing itself more to issues of normal and healthy development—object-relations theorists have pursued exhaustive researches into early childhood in their attempts to reconstruct the early emotional traumas of adult neurotics and psychotics. Mahler's research on the infant's symbiosis with and separation from the mother in the formation of its ego is the best example of the blending of these two perspectives (Mahler, Pine, & Bergman, 1975).

Ego psychology has been criticized from both the right and the left. Scientifically oriented critics find fault with its reliance on case studies, with the lack of logical rigor in its theoretical formulations, with its poorly designed experimental work, and with its extrapolations from data to theory (Mujeeb-ur-Rahman, 1977). From the left, and especially from the French school, ego psychology (especially that of Hartmann) has been attacked for betraying Freud's revolutionary insights. As noted in the previous chapter, Freud insisted on the importance of infantile sexuality, the Oedipus complex, and psychological defense. Hartmann's notion of the benign, "average expectable environment" downplays this inherent conflict between cultural prohibitions and instinctual expression, and Erikson (1968) transforms Freud's psychosexual stages into psychosocial ones. These changes reduce the importance of sexual conflict during the child's acculturation, while fostering the view that some course of ideal social development is possible. Lacan (1977) condemns the emphasis on biological and social adaptation as a capitulation to American optimism, which served to mitigate Freud's (1930/1961) pessimism about the compatibility of human nature and civilization.

French psychoanalytic thinkers have also condemned ego psychology's attempts to make psychoanalysis conform more closely to natural scientific practice. They argue that psychoanalysis is about the meanings that people assign (or misassign) to their experience, and that experimental techniques emphasizing the observation and recording of behavioral data miss the point of psychoanalysis altogether. For them, psychoanalysis is an exegetical science in which two people in dialogue with each other attempt to create life-giving meaning out of what has been confused and distorted (Ricoeur, 1970).

OBJECT-RELATIONS THEORY

The unifying theme in this theory, a psychoanalytic perspective indigenous to England and brought to America during the 1960s, is that infants are in close, emotion-filled relationships with their mothers or other primary caretakers. This mundane observation, which is clearly evident if one has ever cared for a newborn, leads to a significant departure from some fundamental Freudian postulates.

Freudian Primaries

Although Freud wrote a great deal about infancy and childhood, it must be kept in mind that he did not observe or interact with children. His psychoanalytic work was done with adults. Using their memories, and guided by psychoanalytic theory, he constructed a speculative account of the earliest years of life (Steele & Jacobsen, 1978). As a father, he spent little time with his children, and his wife forbade his bringing his work into the nursery (Freud, 1954).

For Freud, the infant was a creature constructed through speculation, a nearly self-contained monad seeking immediate instinctual gratification. Driven by the ego or self-preservation instincts (the prime example being hunger), the infant seeks to quell them as quickly as possible. In the case of hunger, the baby does this by eating, or, if food is not available, by hallucinating satisfaction. The mental organization of the newborn-to-3-year-old functions by primary process and is governed by the pleasure principle. Primary process is an energic conceptualization of the mental economy that holds that any energy buildup caused by endogenous excitation will be discharged as quickly as possible. Whether the discharge is directed toward a fantasy object or a real object that can satiate a need, it brings satisfaction.

Freud realized that any youthful organism that sought immediate gratification without regard to reality would perish because of external dangers, its own helplessness, or the inability to differentiate between a hallucinatory satisfaction and a real one. He admits that the pleasure principle and primary process are to some extent fictions but maintains that they are "justified when one considers [that] the infant—provided one includes with it the care it receives from its mother—does almost realize a psychical system of this kind" (Freud, 1911/1958, p. 220). Even though Freud must include here the mother's presence, the attraction to him of the theoretically elegant picture of an instinctually driven organism goaded only by biological necessity led him to insist that the original condition of human existence was self-contained.

Even the sexual instincts are bound to the infant's own body. Freud's (1905/1963) notion of anaclitic object-choice maintains that early manifestations of the sexual instinct are linked or attached to the self-preservative activities of taking nourishment. Sucking not only brings milk, but also pleasure: "The sexual instinct has a sexual object outside the infant's own body in the shape of the mother's breast" (Freud, 1905/1963, p. 222). However, hunger and sex can be separated. When the sexual instinct, or (in the case of sucking) the "oral component" of the sexual instinct, loses its object—the breast of the absent mother—the infant satisfies its sexual desire through its own body, usually by sucking its thumb. Thumb sucking is the prototype for all autoerotic activity, and Freud's (1914/1957) elaborate theory of primary narcissism follows this model: The infant's first love is what brings it sexual pleasure, and that is itself.

Primary process, primary narcissism, the pleasure principle, and auto-eroticism are interlocking concepts that describe the psychic state of the infant. While Freud must continually admit the existence of the mother in the infant's world, he resists seeing babies as anything but solitary pleasure systems.

The first interpersonal relationship Freud grants the child is with the father. The Oedipal period (ages 4–6) marks the child's entry into the human community as he or she experiences the conflicts of loving the opposite-sex parent and competing with the same-sex parent. As late as 1930, Freud wrote: "I cannot think of any need in childhood as strong as the need for a father's protection" (1930/1961, p. 72). One wonders what has happened to a mother's care but realizes that this has been assumed as a given by Freud and later discounted in favor of the fiction of the infant wrapped in its own self.

Why did Freud look past the child's relations to the mother and emphasize relations with the father? Freud (1931/1961) explains: In his psychoanalytic work, his patients projected their fantasies about their fathers onto him, and he therefore failed to see the more primitive attachment to the mother that lay behind these fantasies. Not surprisingly, it was women analysts who elicited mother transference from their women patients, and who thereby discovered the strong emotional relations between infants and their mothers.

Three things central to psychoanalysis, then, kept Freud from seeing the infant's emotional attachment to the mother: (1) his commitment to instinct theory and energy models, (2) his reconstruction of early experience from adult reminiscences, and (3) the fact that his paternal presence evoked memories of fathers, not mothers.

Although there are hints of the importance of the mother–child bond in a few of Freud's earlier works—for example, "Sucking at the mother's breast is the starting-point of the whole sexual life" (1916–1917/1961, 1963, p. 314)—it is only in one of his final works (Freud, 1940/1964) that he suggests the depth and importance of this relationship. Developing a theme that we have already mentioned, Freud says that the infant's first connections are with the mother's breast. Initially, a baby does not distinguish between the breast and its own body, but because the breast is often absent, the baby forms an internal representation of it. When the infant begins to differentiate between the outside and its own being, this internalized representation of the breast becomes incorporated into the baby's psychic structure. This "part-object" is the child's first internal psychic object, and over time it becomes integrated with an image of the entire mother. Another reason that the infant's tie to the mother is so important is that by her care of the baby's body, she brings it pleasure and "becomes its first seducer." Freud (1940/1964) concludes that in her feeding and pleasure-giving relations with the infant "lies the root of a mother's importance, unique, without parallel, established unalterably for a whole lifetime as the first and strongest love-object and as the prototype of all later love-relations—for both sexes" (p. 188). It is at this point that object-relations research begins.

Mother Love

Object-relations researchers made one vital improvement in Freudian methodology: They directly observed infants. These observations led in turn to significant modifications in psychoanalytic theory.

All object-relations theories have in common a recognition of the infant's bond with the mother. There is no single object-relations theory, however, because each theorist writes with his or her own slant and jargon, because psychoanalytic perspectives are traditionally identified with their authors, and because no synthesis has been made of these viewpoints. It is therefore necessary to review separately four of the most influential object-relations theories—those of Melanie Klein, D. W. Winnicott, Michael and Alice Balint, and W. R. D. Fairbairn.

Klein was one of the first to perform child psychoanalysis and to directly observe interactions between mothers and their infants. She began her work in the 1920s under the influence of both Freud's and Abraham's writings on the oral period, the earliest of the psychosexual stages of development. Throughout her work, there is a split between description and theoretical formulations (see, e.g., Klein, 1961). While her theory is orthodox because it is cast in terms of the instinctual satisfaction of bodily needs through erotogenic zones, her observations clearly show the interpersonal complexity of the infant's first years (Bowlby, 1969). This division is nicely illustrated by her declaration that the infant's relations to its "first object, the mother, and towards food are bound up with each other," and by her resultant decision to study "fundamental patterns of attitudes towards food" as "the best approach to the understanding of young infants (Klein, Heimann, Isaacs, & Riviere, 1952, p. 238).

Klein, like Freud, ignores the mother in favor of talking about oral impulses and their history of gratification. In the service of Freud's libidinal theory and following his emphasis on the breast, Klein reduces the mother's function to that of a provider of food and oral gratification through the breast. Klein (1952) writes: "The close bond between a young infant and his mother centers on the relation to her breast" (p. 243). Kleinian discourses are almost always cast in terms of food, orality, and the breast. They speak of the "good" and "bad" breast, and of the infant's oral greed leading to the devouring of the breast–mother, thereby creating feelings of remorse in the baby. Using notions of the symbolic equivalence of the breast with the penis and of the vagina with the mouth, as well as the assumption that the infant is born with phylogenetic memory traces of vital bodily organs, Klein has moved most of Freud's formulations backward in ontogenetic time to the first 18 months of life. The intrapsychic drama that Klein attributes to infants is rich and complex, filled as it is with references to devouring, excreting, torturing, and making reparations to the real mother and father and to their internal psychic representations within the infant. Klein (1937) admits that her work "presents a horrifying, not to say an unbelievable, picture to our minds of the first year of an infant's life" (p. 187). Although Klein has a strong following in England, her theoretical expositions are too fantastic in what they attribute to infants for most psychoanalysts to accept (Munroe, 1955).

On the other hand, Klein's observational reports are part of the foundation of object-relations work. She describes 3-week-old babies interrupting their sucking to play with the mother's breast and stare at her face, and two-month-olds looking at, listening to, and responding to their mothers. Klein (1952) summarizes these observations by saying: "Such behavior implies that gratification is as much related to the object (the mother) which gives the food as to the food itself" (p. 239). Klein's immersion in Freudian libido theory unfortunately led her to write about the food, and not the mother.

Winnicott's work with both adults and children makes two significant and important advances over Klein's. First, he recognizes the mother's existence. He does not try to imagine her from the infant's perspective but simply describes her presence: She exists and continues to exist; she is available to the infant in many ways, including touch, sound, sight, and taste; she provides warmth; and she provides food. Second, Winnicott is explicit about his usage of the term "mother's breast." For him, it is a metonymy standing for the whole technique of mothering.

The first psychoanalytic theorists to postulate a fundamental emotional interrelationship between the child and its mother, and to develop the implications of this relationship for their theories, were Michael and Alice Balint. They reject the orthodox view of the infant as a passive pleasure receiver and, on the basis of their observations, describe what they call "primary object-love" (Balint, 1939/1964). They see the infant as actively seeking out a wide range of behavioral interchanges with the mother, using as their prototype the way in which infants cling to their caretakers even after they have been fed. Balint (1937/1964) explicitly rejects the idea that this attachment is of an anaclitic type, for it is not linked to any of the erotogenic zones and does not grow by association with oral gratification. Primary object-love exists from the beginning in the relations between the infant and its mother.

Over the course of 20 years of psychoanalytic work with adults, Fairbairn formulated the most coherent, concise, and systematic presentation of the object–relations perspective. His work, more than that of any other member of the English school, realizes the radical departure from orthodox psychoanalytic theory that is required when one recognizes the primary bond between child and mother. Fairbairn asserts that for this connection to form, an ego must be present from birth. By contrast, Freud has assumed that the ego developed out of the id's collisions with reality. Fairbairn does not see libido as the energy of sexual drives, but rather as the intentional force of the ego's seeking out the mother (or other significant objects). In Fairbairn's system there is no death instinct or id, so aggression arises in reaction to frustration or deprivation. Because the ego is "object-seeking," the earliest form of anxiety arises out of separation from the mother.

Given these basics, Fairbairn maps the development of the child's psyche. The infant is disappointed at various times either because of the mother's absence, which causes anxiety, or because her ministrations have been unsatisfying. In order to cope with such traumas, and in the natural course of development, the infant internalizes (into its ego) a representation of the mother. Frustration and anxieties in the infant's actual relations with the mother are worked out on this internalized image of her. The strategy used is one of "divide and conquer." The pleasure-giving or exciting aspects of this internal mother-object are split off from its frustrating elements. These two images of the mother are repressed by the original or central ego and become the libidinal and rejecting objects, respectively. What remains of the original internalized object is neither too exciting nor too rejecting; it is an "ideal" object and remains part of the central ego. It is the image of the good mother, who is neither too enticing or too frustrating. Parts of the central ego that are attached to the exciting and rejecting objects are also split off from it and repressed along with their internal objects.

The resulting psychic structure, which is in place by the end of infancy and serves to organize psychological experience throughout life, is quite different from Freud's model of the id, ego, and superego. The central ego is attached to the ideal object, which, together with the other objects in its constellation, forms the ego ideal. The central ego is the seat of consciousness, and the ego ideal is its model of good behavior. The unconscious portion of the central ego channels aggression inward, using it to repress the libidinal ego, which is tied to the exciting object, and the antilibidinal ego, which cathects the rejecting object. In addition, the antilibidinal ego, which is allied with the rejecting object, adopts "an uncompromisingly hostile attitude to the libidinal ego," thereby reinforcing its repression by the central ego (Fairbairn, 1963, p. 224)

In this elaborate model of the psyche, the closest equivalent to the id is the libidinal ego, which is repressed and yet continually seeking gratifying relations with the internal exciting object. The latter is molded after the seductive mother, with internalized representations constellated around the exciting object of other individuals who have thrilled the child, and of people or things in the world that elicit lust. What Freud describes as the superego is, in Fairbairn's system, a complex internal structure composed of the ideal object, the antilibidinal ego (that part of the child that identifies with the hostile mother), and the rejecting object (the internal image of the frustrating and punishing mother).

Fairbairn's revisions of psychoanalytic theory have many implications for the classification and treatment of psychopathologies. These have been spelled out for individual psychotherapy by Fairbairn (1954) and Guntrip (1961), and for family therapy by Dicks (1967). Fairbairn's method of dream interpretation provides a simple contrast of his system with Freud's. For Freud, dreams were the disguised fulfillment of a repressed wish. For Fairbairn (1954), they were "essentially 'shorts' of situations existing in inner reality" (p. 99). That is, one dreams a "moving picture" in which each of the actors represents an element of the psychic structure, and the interactions among the characters represent the interplay of forces between these elements. To illustrate: A woman dreams that her mother is scrubbing a favorite cat. This illustrates the rejecting object's (the mother's) hostility toward the exciting object (the cat). However, because dream images are multiple-layered, the cat might also represent the woman's own libidinal ego and be identified with masturbatory activities through associations of petting and stroking, along with those of cat-pussy-vagina. The dream situation would then be one in which the mother was punishing the daughter for her sexual desire, or in which those aspects of the woman that are identified with her strict mother—the anti-libidinal ego—are punishing the woman herself.

Interconnections and Criticisms

While the typical scientific criticisms of psychoanalytic research can be made of object-relations theory (e.g., it depends too much on single case studies, there is too much extrapolation from observations to theory, and the techniques of research are not standardized), Bowlby's (1969, 1973) rigorous ethological research has demonstrated that the dynamics of the infant's attachment to and separation from the mother can be shown to exist outside the clinical setting. Bowlby's work has also helped to establish connections between object-relations theory and child development studies such as those of Mary Ainsworth (1978).

Within psychoanalysis there is, as was pointed out in the last section, an affinity between American ego psychologists and British object-relations theorists. The work of Heinz Kohut (1971) on "narcissistic personality disturbances," which he thinks are caused by early developmental problems and the failure of an individual's identity to cohere, depends on both object-relations work concerning the splitting of the ego and research in ego psychology.

Like the ego psychologists, the object-relations theorists focus on individual development. As a result, they have not really examined how the institutions of family or mothering influence the patterning and pathologies of child care. By contrast, R. D. Laing's (1969) popular cultural critiques have addressed some of these issues. Using concepts such as the splitting of the ego, he examines how modern child-rearing practices, technology, and urban alienation amplify each other's effects to produce schizoid personalities (i.e., people who are often classified as crazy but whom Laing sees as responding appropriately to an insane world).

The social theory written by psychoanalytically oriented feminists, while critical of object-relations theories for not seeing how child-rearing practices are culturally determined, incorporates the observations of Klein and Fairbairn into its radical critiques of how women as children and as mothers are deformed by the gender arrangements of patriarchy. We consider feminist psychological analysis after first taking up the hermeneutic perspective.

HERMENEUTIC PSYCHOANALYSIS

Hermeneutics is the practice of interpretation, and of reflecting on that practice. Its roots go back to the Greeks, who used interpretation to decipher oracles, and to the gnostics and alchemists, for whose teachings the interpretation of mystical texts was central. Modern hermeneutics had its beginnings in the eighteenth century, when it evolved into a general philological technique for understanding religious and legal texts.

In the late nineteenth century, Wilhelm Dilthey expanded the scope of hermeneutics by making it the method of the *Geisteswissenschaften*, or human sciences. Dilthey observed that while the *Naturwissenschaften* must investigate nature from an objective perspective that distances them from observed phenomena, the humanities have the advantage of being immersed in what they are studying. Historians, literary critics, and psychologists are participant observers and may use their empathetic responses in addition to factual investigation in order to understand events, texts, or people.

There is irony in the fact that psychoanalysis has become one of the most widely practiced forms of hermeneutics in our century, for while Freud paid homage to creative poets and writers as his teachers, and while he practiced the ancient art of dream interpretation and cured souls, he never fully realized the hermeneutic impact of his work. Rather, he insisted that psychoanalysis was a natural science (Steele, 1982). Because Freud did not explicitly reflect upon the hermeneutic nature of his work, one of the tasks of hermeneutic psychoanalysis has been to do this for him by reading and interpreting him. We now return to Freud in order to bring out the hermeneutic nature of his texts, after which we review the post-Freudian growth of hermeneutics and consider its interconnections with other psychoanalytic perspectives.

Freudian Interpretation

Interpretation pervades Freud's work. It is at the center of his presentations of findings, his therapy, his theory building, and his writings about culture.

Early in his investigations, Freud faced a problem. His case histories did not read like psychiatric case studies, but rather "like short stories" (Breuer & Freud, 1895/1955, p. 160). Freud found that because hysterics suffer mainly from (the lack of) reminiscences, his job became one of recovering the lost story of their lives. He did this by letting them talk. When they came upon a point in their histories where they were confused, agitated, or simply could not remember what had happened, he helped them reconstruct these traumatic events by interpreting what they had already told him about their dreams and other symptomatic behaviors. He found that when the gaps in their memories had been filled, and when they responded emotionally to these heretofore unknown frights, they got better.

While patients might complain about physical symptoms, Freud felt that their real problem was one of "knowing, and not knowing" what was troubling them. Under pressure, they could slowly piece together the memory fragments surrounding the appearance of a phobia, an odd physical sensation, or an obsessive conviction. Although they resisted doing this, and suffered greatly as they recalled more and more unpleasant details, once the trauma had been fully explored and brought completely to awareness, they recovered.

It was in case histories that Freud showed how the story of a person's life could be reconstructed. These accounts constituted the evidence in psychoanalysis. For example, when Lucy R. finally agreed with Freud that her hallucinations had been caused by her denial of love for her employer, she said, "Yes, I think that's true." Freud responded, "But if you knew you loved your employer, why didn't you tell me?" Lucy replied, "I didn't know—or rather, I didn't want to know. I wanted to drive it out of my head and not think of it again" (Breuer & Freud, 1895/ 1955, p. 117). Freud's comment on this therapeutic dénouement is that it is difficult to describe "the strange state of mind in which one knows and does not know a thing at the same time. It is clearly impossible to understand it unless one has been in such a state oneself" (1895/1955, p. 117). Here Freud appeals to the empathetic understanding of his readers, to their own participation in the mysterious phenomenon he is trying to explain. At about the same time, Dilthey was making an empathetic understanding of historical figures a necessary condition for understanding our past.

By letting patients have their say, Freud found that they began telling him their dreams and asking him what they meant. His greatest work, *The Interpretation of Dreams* (1900/1953, 1958) is devoted to his method of interpreting his own and his patients' dreams. He first compares this work to translation, in that the analyst helps the analysand transform the language of the unconscious into conscious thought. Psychoanalysis is also compared to solving a rebus, because both involve associating and interpreting fragments and pictures in order to find a latent, hidden, or encoded message. In Chapter 8 we describe the mechanisms of the dream work—condensation, displacement, considerations of representability, secondary revision, and symbolism—that make up Freud's principles of interpretation for translating the distorted, broken, incomplete, and mysterious images of dreams into a coherent narrative that can shed new light on a person's past. For example, the consideration of representability requires that many complex thoughts be captured in a dream image. To make sense of an image, one must translate it into a narrative, just as one does with a rebus.

Toward the end of his *Interpretation,* Freud says that infantile wishes are the motive force for the formation of dreams, but this assertion inverts what he knew through the historical analysis of his patients' dreams and memories. It also covers over his interpretive work. In the dreams of adults, images are present that are associated with childhood. Freud used these and the reminiscences they evoked to create facsimiles of childhood events. Given this retrospective method, infantile experience is a historical (but not an observational) phenomenon.

While Freud was continually recasting his models of the psyche, modifying his instinct theory, and tinkering with metapsychology, the hermeneutic method remained stable throughout his work. At the end of his career, his method was nearly identical to what it had been in 1900. He summarizes:

> We gather the material for our work from a variety of sources—from what is conveyed to us by the information given us by the patient and by his free associations, from what he shows us in his transferences, from what we arrive at by interpreting his dreams, and from what he betrays by his slips or *parapraxes.* All this material helps us to make constructions about what happened to him and has been forgotten, as well as about what is happening in him now without his understanding it. (Freud, 1940/1964, pp. 177-178)

In mid-career, he writes: "In a word, this material (the patient's speech), whether it consists of memories, associations, or dreams, has first to be *interpreted"*(Freud, 1926/1959b, p. 219). This type of interpretive work is conducted within the psychoanalytic session. The session is a dialogue between analyst and analysand:

> The analyst finishes a piece of construction and communicates it to the subject of the analysis so that it may work upon him; he [the analyst] then constructs a further piece out of the fresh material pouring in upon him, deals with it in the same way, and proceeds in this alternating fashion until the end. (Freud, 1937/ 1964, pp. 260-261)

Freud admits that the interpretation of some dreams may not be completed until the end of treatment. He compares his work to assembling a jigsaw puzzle in which the pieces are the memory fragments, dreams, wishes, and symptoms of the analysand. His criterion for the validity of constructions in the analysis is that in the end they all fit together and that there be no pieces missing from the narrative. It is only by completing this *Gestalt* that the analyst is satisfied, for only then can the analysand's doubts about and resistances toward the traumatic past be overcome. When the analysand responds, "Now I feel as though I had known it all the time," the work of interpretation is complete (Freud, 1914/1953, p. 207).

Freud was never satisfied, however, with simply illustrating how to interpret dreams or the stories of his patients. He wanted to build a theory, and to do so he constructed a system of interlocking causal explanations couched in energic terms borrowed from 19th-century physics (Amacher, 1965). Freud's psychical typographies accounted for his findings in the language of cathexes, memory pathways, economic exchanges, and dynamic conflicts. Freud (1905/1960) explains the purpose of such models:

> I am making no attempt to proclaim that the cells and nerve fibres, or the systems of neurons which are taking their place today, are these psychical paths, even though it would have to be possible in some manner which cannot yet be indicated to represent such [psychical] paths by organic elements of the nervous system. (p. 148)

Freud's topographies of the mind were symbolic. They pointed in one direction to an unknown neuronal matrix; in the other they pointed to the mysteries of a person's life. Just a few pages after his naturalistic references to the brain mechanisms underlying psychic representations, he puts the same issue in hermeneutic terms: "The unconscious is something we really do not know, but which we are obliged by compelling inferences to supply" (1905/1960, p. 162). The naturalistic aspects of Freud's work have been developed by the ego psychologists and object–relations theorists, the interpretive side by the hermeneutic psychoanalytic perspective.

In no place is the interpretive strain of psychoanalysis more evident than in Freud's work on culture, where he uses the Oedipal drama as his key to unlocking man's history. Freud introduces this notion in his *Interpretation* (1900/1953) in order to prove the universality of emotional ambivalence toward one's parents. In establishing that a common theme in dreams is falling in love with the mother and hating the father, Freud first announces that in interpreting his own dreams, he has found the emotional remnants of a childhood love for his mother and hatred of his father. (While personal testimony is usually not accepted in science, such personal discovery is essential to both hermeneutics and psychoanalysis, and in the previous chapter we show how closely Freud's own self-analysis was tied to his founding of psychoanalysis.) Freud's next confirmational gambit uses a tactic that became fundamental in his psychoanalytic proofs. Freud (1900/1953) states: "This discovery [of emotional ambivalence toward parents] is confirmed by a legend that has come down to us from classical antiquity" (p. 261) referring, of course, to the play by Sophocles about King Oedipus. Fictions such as the Theban play and Greek mythology are used as proof for the universal nature of the fantasy of incest and murder. Using literary texts to establish the origins of archetypal themes is commonplace in the humanities, but it is highly unusual for a scientist.

After the discovery of Oedipal themes in his own dreams and in those of his adult patients, Freud moved this theme back in time to explain a universal crisis in the development of all children. Having established this ontogeny retrospectively by moving backward from adults' memories to the past of childhood, he took one step further into phylogeny. At the beginning of civilization, he argues, the origins of religion can be found in the totemic practices of primitive tribes, and these totems and taboos have an Oedipal structure. Having thus established through interpretation the crucial significance of children's ambivalent feelings toward parents in the history of both the individual and the species, Freud then appropriates Haeckel's biogenic law ("Ontogeny recapitulates phylogeny") in order to use these points of origin as causes of adult suffering and modern cultural malaise. Thus adult neurosis and religion are viewed as disguised repetitions of individual and cultural conflicts revolving around Oedipal ambivalence (Steele, 1982).

Following Laplanche (1976), one of Freud's most insightful interpreters, we see that Freud's models of the psyche and his historical scenarios create both biological and historical fictions that are used to order human experience. They provide templates for his interpretive work, having themselves been forged from it. Interpretive work always moves in such reflective circles, for, as Dilthey points out, the hermeneut is included within the history he or she is interpreting and trying to imagine.

Interpretive Readings of Freud

Although many have questioned the scientific status of psychoanalysis, critical theorists such as Habermas (1971) and Radnitzsky (1973) argue that Freud's work should provide a paradigm for hermeneutics. This is the case because, as Habermas says, psychoanalysis is one of the few disciplines that incorporates systematic self-reflection into its theory and practice. In textual interpretation, it is the text that provides a check on interpretation: in psychoanalysis, the analysand does so. Furthermore, while a reader may imagine the text to be speaking and hope to engage it in dialogue, in psychoanalysis an ever-deepening dialogue between analyst and analysand is prescribed. Finally, in textual interpretation one must reflect on one's misunderstandings of a book in order to reach a fuller understanding of it; in psychoanalysis, if both analyst and analysand do not systematically reflect on their past confusions, the therapy will grind to a halt.

Nevertheless, psychoanalysis is more than a model of hermeneutics, for Freud's writings themselves are a rich source for interpretation. As we have seen, the scientifically oriented ego psychologists interpret Freud's works in order to ground their research in his words. Their approach has simplified the complexity of Freud's thought in order to test and revise it. The hermeneutic approach is different. Writers in this group celebrate the ambiguity in Freud. They seek to explicate it, follow it, and develop it. The hermeneutic perspective has also treated Freud's texts as he treated his subjects. That is, hermeneuts seek out contradictions in Freud's manifest text and, using interpretive techniques, explicate them by providing a latent context for them that, while not resolving the contradiction, makes it more understandable.

By considering the writings of three psychoanalytic hermeneuts— Paul Ricoeur, Jean Laplanche, and Jacques Lacan—we can see how their work has established an orienting focus for interpretive psychoanalysis. All of these writers are French, and their work has been part of "the return to Freud" in France, a movement that hoped to reinvent Freud by saving him from the natural scientific misinterpretation of his work (Turkle, 1981).

Ricoeur is a phenomenological philosopher whose *Freud and Philosophy* (1970) established connections among psychoanalysis, hermeneutics, and structural linguistics. Ricoeur was mainly concerned with Freud's "semantics of desire," the linkage in Freud's writing between explicating meanings and explaining phenomena in causal, reductive, energic terms. These two styles of exegesis, Ricoeur argues, are necessarily fused in Freud's writings because he is always trying to explain the failure of natural demands to be met within culture. Freud (1930/1961) states that culture requires the renunciation of instinct, and that when an instinctual demand is denied, its force provides an impetus that seeks expression in various substitutes such as dreams, symptoms, and symbols, all of which partially articulate the desire. Only by interpreting these manifestations of instincts as they are represented in speech, behavior, or human artifacts could Freud provide an energic accounting of the dynamics of the psyche. His psychic models in turn provided a coordinating system for his energy metaphors. This system helped him map the various modifications of an impulse as it passes from the unknown and unspeakable realm of the unconscious through the various censorships and pathways to conscious articulation.

Laplanche carried these ideas further. His complex reading of Freud shows how Freud's writings slowly evolved to the point where the death instinct, rejected by most ego psychologists as a piece of mythology, became an essential assumption (Laplanche, 1976). He also shows that no matter how deeply Freud carried an interpretation, there was always something in the analysand's fantasies that could not be said, something covered over with makeshift substitutions. Behind the substitutions was an originary desire to return to a state of quiescence. Such a condition, in which there are no perturbations within the organism, is the insistent goal of the death instinct.

Laplanche and Pontalis's *The Language of Psychoanalysis* (1973) is another work that demonstrates the richness of the hermeneutic approach to psychoanalysis. It is a dictionary (and a history) of Freud's psychoanalytic terms. By tracing the evolution of a concept, Laplanche and Pontalis provide an elaborate, critical interpretation of its meaning.

Lacan was the leader of "Freud's French Revolution", and the history of his expulsion from the International Psychoanalytic Association is a fascinating study in psychoanalytic politics (Turkle, 1981). That drama, in which Heinz Hartmann judged Lacan's practice to be unorthodox, is not discussed here, but we now examine Lacan's three most important reformulations of Freud's ideas: (1) his use of structural linguistics to understand the interplay between the unconscious and the conscious, (2) his classification of experience into three different registers, and (3) his attacks on the ego.

Expanding on Saussure's (1915/1959) theory that there is an arbitrary connection between the signifier (word) and the signified (thing), Lacan (1977) created an elaborate linguistic coordinate system for understanding the transformations of meanings inherent in psychic processes. For Lacan, "the unconscious is structured like a language." That is, the words, symbols, or symptoms that signify desire are continually being substituted for one another as individuals associate to a dream or forgotten memories. This chain of associations forges links between words as one meaning is substituted for another in an attempt to uncover what is not present to the subject's consciousness. That which is "absent" from consciousness is a fundamental desire (a thing or a signified) that can never quite be caught in the net of words that represent it. Unconscious meanings, then, cannot be tied down to any single identity through their conscious formulation, because the psyche is structured like the linguistic sign: The relation of the conscious to the unconscious is inexact, like that of signifier to signified, or of words to things. According to Freud, the unconscious is an *it* (*das Es*, the id), a thing of nature that can never be fully articulated within the sign system of culture—language.

Lacan's (1977) linguistic reinterpretation of Freud led him to modify one of the most fundamental dichotomies in Freud's work, namely the differentiation between the pleasure principle and the reality principle. The pleasure principle refers to fantasy thinking that is free-floating, associative, and instantly gratifying; the reality principle refers to logical thought, articulated in language, that calculates how to get maximum satisfaction with a minimum of pain. The first type of thought is that found in myth, dreams, and hallucinations; the second is characteristic of intentional activities directed toward fulfillment in the real world.

Lacan divides the pleasure principle into two different registers: the imaginary and the symbolic. The imaginary is the realm of the ego and its internalized image. As the infant develops in interaction with others, and especially with the mother, it finds its own needs reflected back to it through the care it receives. In attempting to satisfy itself when its caretakers are absent, the ego seeks fulfillment in fantasy by imagining what the other would do in order to gratify the ego's wants and the desires of the unconscious. The symbolic register overlays the imaginary and is formed during the acquisition of language. Language itself is viewed as superordinate to the individual, subjecting him or her to certain experiences. The most fundamental of these is a splitting of oneself, one's ego, into a subject "I" and an object "me." The "me" is the "I" transformed into an object by being subjected to the wishes of another person or another element of one's own personality. The ego, Lacan (1977) argues, is rarely the "I" it thinks it is, for it is always the object of someone else's care, of the superego's observations, and of the narcissistic redirecting of the id's lustful impulses onto itself.

The reality principle operates successfully when there is correspondence between thought and the world. Freud and other scientists hold that their common goal is the reduction of illusion through the progressive establishment of an identify between man's conception of "the real" and reality itself. Because Lacan distrusts the ego's vanity about its reasons and truths, and because he is critical of the entire positivist tradition, he inverts the reality principle. Instead of reality being the basis for realistic experience, Lacan argues that the real is linked to both the imaginary and the symbolic. Thus it stands for what neither one of them actually is, and yet it is a blend of both that creates something entirely different, a unique register of experience. The real cannot be known (even through psychoanalysis), because it is impossible to articulate one's experience of it in words. Lacan valued mystery, and the real for him takes on mystical significance, for it is at once both obvious and yet difficult to locate.

Interconnections and Criticisms

The hermeneutic perspective is the antithesis of the first two approaches to psychoanalysis that we have considered. The strongest objections to it have come from philosophers of science who believe that psychoanalysis should try to conform to the practices of science (Blight, 1981), and from those who wish to demonstrate that the hermeneutic conception of what constitutes a natural scientific explanation is too simplistic. Such critics argue that while psychoanalysis remains an inadequate science, the rigor of its formulations can nevertheless be judged by the complex explanatory models of modern physics (Grünbaum, 1984). Both of these positions, however, hold psychoanalytic hermeneutics up to a standard that it has rejected. A fundamental requirement of the critics is the scientific demand that explanations be logical and rigorous, and that they demonstrate a correspondence between theoretical statements and observables. Ricoeur (1970) rejects the second point explicitly, claiming that the difference between psychoanalysis and scientific psychology is radical because psychology attempts to establish facts through the systematic, objective observation of behavior—dealing with the manifest by quantifying it. Psychoanalysis, on the other hand, is an exegetical art whose concern is the creation of shared understandings between analyst and analysand through the interpretation of the manifest in order to find what lies behind it.

Lacan's whole style is a rejection of the restrictions of logical rigor. His writing is poetic, associative, enigmatic—and difficult to interpret. Indeed, he announces his intention of confusing the reader in order to immerse him or her in the complexities of language and shake the confidence of the ego, which looks to logic for a guide:

> Writing is distinguished by the prevalence of the *text* in the sense that this factor of discourse will assume in this essay a factor that makes possible the kind of tightening up that I like in order to leave the reader no other way out than the way in, which I prefer to be difficult. In that sense, then, this will not be writing. (Lacan, 1977, p. 146)

With such a style, Lacan will remain an important figure in psychoanalysis, if only because it is difficult to understand him and therefore his work is open to many diverse interpretations.

THE FEMINIST PERSPECTIVE

Because psychoanalysis has mistreated women, and because Freud's writings have been used to justify the physical, mental, and social malpractice that women still face, feminists who have an interest in psychology have been critical of Freud. From a simple review of his speculation about women, it should be obvious why such critiques are essential. However, feminist psychological analysis has gone far beyond simple corrections of Freud to produce a culturally broader and historically richer understanding of sexual assignment and gender arrangements.

Freud on Women

Because more than 60% of Freud's patients were women (Brody, 1973), one would expect to find throughout his work considerations of their psychology. In fact, however, it was only toward the end of his career that he took up the issue of female sexuality (Freud, 1925/1961, 1931/1961, 1933/1964). Written within eight years of each other, the views expressed in these papers are quite similar. They all address the question of how a female infant becomes a girl. The ontogenetic sequence of topics is bisexuality, pre-Oedipal attachment to the mother, the female Oedipus complex, and the post-Oedipal consequences of these experiences.

During the first three years of life, Freud notes only one significant difference between the development of girls and boys: Female infants form a stronger attachment to their mothers. The similarities between the sexes in these early years are accounted for by bisexuality, which Freud assumes to be a human predisposition that is more pronounced in women than in men. By way of explanation, Freud (1931/1961) notes that while a man has only "one leading sexual zone" (the penis), "a woman has two: the vagina, the female organ proper—and the clitoris, which is analogous to the male organ" (p. 228). As a consequence of this anatomical difference, female development after the oral and anal stages (ages 0–3) is divided into two phases and is therefore more complex than the male's. When infant females enter the third stage of psychosexual development (approximately ages 3–4), Freud (1931/1961) writes: "Little girls usually discover for themselves their characteristic phallic activity—masturbation of the clitoris" (p. 232). As a result of active masturbation, it is at the beginning of the phallic phase that "we are now obliged to recognize that the little girl is a little man" (Freud, 1933/1964, p. 118).

Besides finding her clitoris, the little girl makes another fateful discovery. The pleasurable sensual feelings that arise from clitoral manipulation and that aid in the creation of self-love are nearly extinguished and "[h]er self-love is mortified by the comparison [of her clitoris] with the boy's far superior equipment" (Freud, 1933/1964, p. 126). The little boy's seeing the female genitals causes the development of the castration complex in him, because he fears that he too will be punished by the loss of his penis if he continues to masturbate and covet his mother. Similarly, the "castration complex of girls is also started by the sight of the genitals of the other sex" (p. 125). When little girls see the penis, they "at once notice the difference" in size between it and their clitoris, and they realize "its significance too. They feel seriously wronged . . . and fall a victim to 'envy for the penis' " (p. 125). "The discovery," Freud continues, "that she is castrated is a turning-point in a girl's growth," and it leaves "ineradicable traces" on a woman's development and her character (pp. 110, 111). She becomes envious and covetous. She abandons clitoral masturbation and thereby a certain amount of her sexual activity; she becomes passive.

Freud sees three possible lines of development for the girl after she "acknowledges the fact of her castration, and with it, too, the superiority of the male and her own inferiority" (Freud, 1931/1961, p. 229). A woman rebels against this state of affairs in one of the following ways: (a) She becomes revolted by sexuality, (b) she holds on with "defiant self-assertiveness to her threatened masculinity" and "clings to the hope of getting a penis sometime" (p. 229), or (c) by a very circuitous path she may "reach the final normal female attitude, in which she takes her father as her object and so finds her way to the feminine form of the Oedipus complex" (p. 230).

The first line of development leads to sexual dysfunction and neurosis, the second to a "masculinity complex" that often accompanies female homosexuality. The normal line is the one that Freud writes about in detail. Freud says that upon "seeing a male genital," the little girl first thinks her "misfortune peculiar to herself." Only later does she realize that it extends to other children like herself and to certain grown-ups. He concludes: "When she comes to understand the general nature of this characteristic, it follows that femaleness—and with it, of course, her mother—suffers a great depreciation in her eyes" (Freud, 1931/1961, p. 233). In essence, she blames her mother for not giving her a penis. The great pre-Oedipal bond between mother and daughter is thereby broken, and the little girl renounces her infantile love for her mother. Her love turns to hate because she blames her mother for her loss.

The development of penis envy and the castration complex set the stage for the female Oedipus complex. Between the ages of 4 and 6, the girl becomes her mother's rival as she turns to her father in order to get the love and the penis she desires. These psychological changes are accompanied by physiological alterations. The girl's bodily libidinal interest moves from her now-despised clitoris to the "truly feminine vagina" (Freud, 1933/1964, p. 104). Her libidinal aims become passive as she hopes to attract her father's interest. The girl initially turns to the father because of her wish to have a penis; however, the "feminine situation is only established . . . if the wish for a penis is replaced by one for a baby" (Freud, 1933/1964, p. 129).

Unlike the boy whose longing for the mother is denied when he realizes he can be castrated by his father for his lust, there is no great Oedipal crisis for the female. The desire for the penis is slowly transformed into a wish for a baby, along the lines of what Freud (1933/1964) calls "an ancient symbolic equivalence" between the two (p. 128). A female's fulfillment is, in fact, complete and "her happiness is great if later on this wish for a baby finds fulfillment in reality, and quite especially so if the baby is a little boy who brings the longed-for penis with him" (1933/1964, p. 128).

The immediate consequences for the girl of the resolution of the Oedipus complex are not as striking as are those for the boy. The precipitous abandonment of his Oedipal desires brought on by the boy's fear of castration leads to the institution in him of a strong superego. Because the castration complex does not end but sets in motion the female Oedipus complex, the little girl is under no great pressure to give up her rivalry with her mother and love of her father. Freud (1925/1961) says: "Thus the Oedipus complex escapes the fate which it meets with in boys: it may be slowly abandoned or dealt with by repression, or its effects may persist far into women's normal mental life" (p. 257). As a result, the superego in women "is never so inexorable, so impersonal, so independent of its emotional origins as we require it to be in men" (1925/1961, p. 257). In this fact Freud finds justification for the age-old complaints that critics have brought against women: "They show less sense of justice than men" (p. 257), they do not submit as readily to the demands of reality, and their judgments are influenced by their emotions. To these, Freud adds that they do not have the same power as men to sublimate their instincts, and because they have been libidinally exhausted by their childhood disappointments, they show greater psychic rigidity in middle-age (Freud, 1933/1964).

Feminist Psychological Analysis

Given the impact of the women's movement, it is hard to believe that any responsible thinker would propose or defend such misogynous views. The common defense used to save Freud from charges of sexism is that one must view his ideas in the context of his times, and that other psychologists such as Jung (1927/1964), and even female analysts like Deutsch (1925), were saying similar things. However, Freud's ideas on women did not go uncriticized at the time. Before considering some contemporary feminist accounts of childhood, we review these early objections and then summarize later feminist criticisms of psychoanalysis.

Adler was the first to question Freud's nearly exclusive consideration of masculine development and his rather uncritical acceptance of male cultural norms. Adler (1910/1914) proclaims: "The archevil of our culture . . . [is] the excessive pre-eminence of manliness" (p. 88), and in his subsequent work he shows how cultural expectations for female development were crucial in distorting women's characters by encouraging them to be passive, devious, jealous of their rights, and envious of men (Adler, 1982).

Freud did not listen to Adler, and when "the women question" was raised again in the 1920s, Freud's answers were the three papers reviewed earlier. In two of these, he explicitly rejects feminist arguments, asserting that while feminists are "anxious to force us to regard the two sexes as completely equal in position and worth" (Freud, 1925/1961, p. 258), he would not change his views on the inferiority of woman to man. To a call for the equality of women, Freud responded with arguments that provided both a biological and social rationale for their oppression.

Horney (1926/1974) and Jones (1927) both criticize Freud's position, saying that his viewpoint was a symptom of male disparagement of women—belittlement that Freud himself argued was caused by men's denigration of women as castrated beings. Freud (1931/1961) concedes: "It is to be anticipated that men analysts with feminist views, as well as our women analysts, will disagree with what I have said here" (p. 230). However, he then counters their criticism: "It is quite natural that the female sex should refuse to accept a view which appears to contradict their eagerly coveted equality with men" (p. 230). This contradiction is clearly not one of appearance. Freud, as we have shown, stresses the inferiority of women.

In her initial criticism of Freud's position, Horney (1926/1974) makes three critical points: (a) Civilization is male-dominated, and even science is biased by its masculinity; (b) Freud's views on women are precisely the ones he ascribes to little boys; and (c) psychoanalysis, because of its method, cannot produce a true picture of childhood.

The first point is easily made if we review what Freud calls the "masculine ideal," in comparison to which he claimed women fell short. This masculine worldview, identified by men as objective, involves for Freud the detachment of feelings from decision making, the renunciation of fantasy, and an abstract sense of justice. This detachment, which Freud, science, and logical empiricism all require, is identified by both Adler and Horney as part of masculine malaise, and modern feminist philosophers have criticized the male philosophical tradition that puts abstract metaphysical values before human, socioemotional ones (Harding & Hintikka, 1983).

Horney's second criticism took the form of a table. On one side she lists ideas that, according to psychoanalysis, little boys have about little girls. On the other side are the ideas of psychoanalysts about feminine development. For example, the little boy has the "idea that the girl is a castrated, mutilated boy," while the psychoanalyst views the little girl as believing that "she once possessed a penis and lost it by castration" (Horney, 1926/1974, p. 174). The list of comparisons goes on, and there is a remarkable similarity between what boys supposedly believe about girls and what psychoanalysts declare happens in female development. This concurrence in the two lists is rather strange, for Freud usually maintained that children's fantasies were not in accordance with reality, and that adults who persevered in such childhood speculation were neurotic. Either analysts and little boys are right about women, or analysts are projecting onto their female patients' childhoods the remnants of their own boyhood fantasies.

Horney's third point relates to why the latter possibility could be the correct one. Freud's information about childhood came almost exclusively from the reminiscences of adult women, and his job was to construct a scenario that explained their earliest years. Freud seldom hesitated in equating his interpretation of adult memories with actual childhood experience, and so with his women patients he probably failed to see the extent to which their memories of childhood had been retrospectively colored by intervening experiences. They might simply have been projecting back onto their girlhoods many of the complaints they had accumulated after years of oppression. Such retrospective fantasies would have dovetailed with the remnants of Freud's own boyish fantasies, and therefore he would have encouraged them. Freud (1931/1961) admits that his masculinity kept him from seeing the early infantile bond between girls and their mothers, because his paternal presence fostered father transference instead of mother transference. His women patients might then have further acquiesced to his interpretations in an attempt to please a man who was much like their fathers.

Horney and other feminists, including de Beauvoir (1949/1960), continued to criticize Freud's views on women, but it was not until the resurgence of the women's movement in the 1960s and 1970s that several feminist books popularized the criticism of Freud (Firestone, 1970; Friedan, 1965; Greer, 1971). These works, each in its own way, recapitulate both Horney's argument about culture being patriarchical (and therefore valorizing male standards while degrading traditional female ones) and de Beauvoir's point that within a masculine culture, women are cast in the role of the "other" and have attributed to them all that men must deny in themselves.

To such social arguments, these and other feminist critics added an attack on Freud's biological assumptions (Sherfy, 1966). We now summarize these points. Freud (1933/1964) states that science regards the clitoris as an "atrophied" male penis (p. 114) and that the ovum "is immobile and waits passively" for the sperm (p. 115). In fact, neither claim is true. The first could not be the case unless women were descended from bisexual anthropoid creatures, which has never been a commonly held scientific view. The second point is incorrect on two counts. First, by using the immobility of the ovum as an analogy for feminine passivity, Freud commits an error of biological reductionism—namely, assuming that a partial function of the organism explains the whole. Second, he compounds this error by using an inaccurate biological portrait of the active sperm pursuing the passive egg. To begin with, the ovum is not a person; it is an egg, and thus has no "passive" attributes. Even as an egg, however, it is not sessile; rather, it moves down the fallopian tubes and along the lining of the uterus.

Freud, who often argued for more sexual freedom, unfortunately fostered another error—the belief popular since before the turn of the century that in order to develop into "normal" women, little girls had to give up clitoral masturbation. This notion is contradicted by a voluminous amount of women's testimony and sex research.

Using such criticisms as a starting point, modern feminists from several divergent perspectives have constructed a psychological analysis of the development of gender roles. Rich (1977) uses her literary gifts, while Chodorow (1978) relies on object–relations theory, child development studies, and sociological research to argue, along with Dinnerstein (1976), that child-rearing practices in the nuclear family are at the root of many social problems. We now pursue Dinnerstein's presentation, since it includes an interesting mixture of styles and arguments, including those of Rich and Chodorow. *Dinnerstein*

Dinnerstein's thesis is simple: The exclusive or nearly exclusive rearing of children by women, and almost always by their biological mothers, is responsible for much of human malaise. Before pursuing the ramifications of this thesis, we review the evidence for it. That infants in our culture are primarily, if not solely, reared by their mothers is an observation that is well grounded in sociological fact. In exploring the implications of this situation, Dinnerstein uses the work of Freud, de Beauvoir, and Klein as both sources of observations and inspirations for criticism. Both female and male infants develop an early and deep attachment to the mother, since she is both a source of gratification and a reason for pain. Insofar as she feeds, warms, and strokes the infant, she is all-giving. Conversely, when she is absent, or distracted, or when she punishes or makes demands, she is an all-encompassing ogre. The infant's feelings of love for the good mother and its wish to own her exclusively are in powerful conflict with its desires to be rid of the bad mother by destroying, controlling, or eluding her.

Under these conditions, which persist over the first three years of childhood, the psyche is gradually formed. The infant's sense of its self grows in response to the mother. It tries to gain mastery over itself, the mother, and its internal images of her. Psychic mastery over the maternal image is gained by splitting her internal representation into a good object and a bad object. These early, intrapsychic precipitates of infantile experiences with the mother are carried with us into adulthood and provide the core from which both mythological images and fantasies about women are produced. Thus the image of woman remains split: She is a goddess or a whore, an angel or a witch, an inexhaustible source of comfort or a castrating bitch.

At the age Freud associates with the Oedipal crises, Dinnerstein does not see more trouble for the child, but rather deliverance from control by the mother. Until then, the infant's wishes have often been frustrated by the mother, and it has been unable, hard as it has tried, to master her. The introduction of the father into the mother–child dyad offers both boys and girls an emotional refuge from the exclusive tie to the mother.

Most analytic theorists concur that in our culture, the father represents the rule of reason and the world outside the home. He offers to his son a promise of escape from his mother's place to a "man's world." He also offers the little boy a way out of his emotional ambivalence. In reaction to the mother's restrictions, the son projects onto the father his own desires to be free from her and the turbulent emotions she engenders. The mother (and, by generalization, all women) thus becomes associated with powerful and often negative infantile affects. Such emotions remain in the unconscious, but because they represent the ambivalent turmoil of infantile life, they are rejected by the boy. Via projection, he comes to see them in women, but not in himself. He now identifies with the father on whom he models his own ego, through identification. In the name of the father to whom he is heir, and as a way of escaping past imprisonment with his mother, the son erects a persona that denigrates emotion as babyish and sensual gratification as primitive. As a reaction to these, he embraces the necessity to master their remnants not only in himself, but also in others. Mastery over oneself, others, and the world thereby becomes the man's measure of his success.

The father also offers the little girl an ally in her fight to free herself from the mother, but her resolution of infantile ambivalence is not as straightforward as the boy's. The socialization she receives because of her anatomy never allows her to identify totally with the father. His world is held up to her as an ideal to be striven for, but she is never allowed to renounce her primitive identification with her mother. As a girl and as a woman, she is infantilized by her culture. While being denied entrance on an equal basis with men into the wider world of work, she is encouraged by her mother, and by the men around her, to reproduce. Even if she enjoys the role of mother and finds in it a gratifying reproduction of primitive emotions and sensual pleasures, her achievements do not receive the cultural accolades that those of men do. "Women's work" may be celebrated in the anonymous sentiment of Mother's Day cards or in the gratitude of her family, but it hardly ever wins a Nobel Prize.

The asymmetry of the early childhood experiences of boys and girls is maintained by a mutual "neurotic symbiosis" in adult "heterosexual gender arrangements" (Dinnerstein, 1976). Women provide men with a private emotional sanctuary that is free from the coldness, cruelty, and overvaluation of mastery characteristic of the public realm, or the man's world. As wife or lover, she is a man's emotional caretaker, a role that she easily assumes because of her identification with her own mother. In turn, the man expects her to perform this job because his mother did it for him. She is also the man's mirror, reflecting back to him his accomplishments (usually magnified). She assures him of his mastery by her submissiveness and by the vicarious pleasure she takes in his accomplishments (the latter she learned to demonstrate at her father's knee).

Women are, of course, rewarded for some of these sacrifices. For example, they are given immunity from the judgments of mankind's history. Dinnerstein (1976) writes:

> The immunity life offers women is immunity not only from the risks and exertions of history-making, but also from the history-maker's legitimate internal misgivings about the value of what he spends his life doing. The use that both sexes make of this female immunity, their mutual motive in fostering it, is in my view the morbid core of our sexual arrangements. (p. 213)

Unlike Freud, Dinnerstein rejects biological determinism and does not accept culture as it is. Rather, she advocates social change. Beginning with Freud's psychotherapeutic work with women, psychoanalytic and medical treatment in general has long been aimed at adjusting women to their "normal" role as wives and mothers (Ehrenreich & English, 1978). If the trajectory of our culture's history toward the rapacious destruction of nature and the promise of nuclear disaster is to be altered, Dinnerstein feels that the male stance of mastery toward others and nature, and woman's complicity in supporting this posture, must be stopped. She argues that this can be achieved by a combination of personal insight into how each of us participates in maintaining the sexual status quo, along with a commitment to changing cultural gender arrangements.

The most fundamental and radical change we can make, according to Dinnerstein, is to alter our child-rearing practices. She advocates that instead of being single parents, mothers should be joined by fathers in raising children; from birth on, men should be as deeply involved with babies as women are. The equally shared rearing of infants would, of course, prevent both male and female infants from splitting humans into two kinds of people whose anatomical sex is used to characterize the life roles they are expected to play—either as primitive, nurturing, and terrifying emissaries of nature or as masterful, objective, and authoritarian carriers of culture. It would also provide women with an opportunity to enter the public sphere and take on some of the burdens of shaping culture and history. Men would thus have a chance to reexperience the joys of the flesh and become committed to rearing living beings instead of manipulating the dead objects of modern technology.

Interconnections and Criticisms

Dinnerstein's work provides a depth psychology for the growing feminist criticism of the masculine domination of nature through technology (Balbus, 1982). Her work, along with that of Chodorow and Rich, provides a necessary corrective to Freud's near silence on the mother–daughter relationship, and to his uncritical acceptance of the institution of motherhood. These writings also correct an outgrowth of object–relations theory and ego psychological research: Popular psychological advice in the 1950s and 1960s warned women not to be "smothering mothers" to their sons. Daughters were seldom mentioned in these advisories from male authorities, and fathers were held to be only peripherally responsible for rearing their children (Ehrenreich & English, 1978).

Dinnerstein's work does have a flaw that is common to all psychoanalytic accounts of infancy, and in her text it is more pronounced than in most. She allows herself nearly unbridled speculation on the mental life of infants. Unlike Freud, however, Dinnerstein was intimately involved in child-rearing and thus has first-hand observational experience on which to base her formulations.

Another criticism of both Dinnerstein's and Chodorow's work comes from Rich. Both of these authors ignore the fact that throughout history there have been women "who as witches, *femmes seules*, marriage resisters, spinsters, autonomous widows, and/or lesbians—have managed on varying levels *not* to collaborate" in the reproduction of gender arrangements (Rich, 1981, p. 66). Focused as they are on heterosexuality, Dinnerstein and Chodorow do not consider in great detail the alternatives of celibacy, autoeroticism, or lesbianism. But to ignore these possibilities is to deny women anything but heterosexual role models and to foster the oppression of women by a conspiracy of silence that omits women in general, and "deviant" women in particular, from our cultural memory.

The scope of feminist psychological analysis is very broad. It has evolved into far more than close hermeneutic critiques of Freud's work and the writings of other psychoanalysts. Like all good interpretive endeavors, it uses critical reflection on the past to open up possibilities for the present and future. Unlike the works of the hermeneutic psychoanalysts, however, its goal is not solely the liberation of man, but also of woman.

CONCLUSION

We have traced the history of four major psychoanalytic perspectives that evolved from Freud's legacy. We did not become involved in the claims about legitimate descent from Freud that psychoanalytic partisans often use to justify their own work and castigate alternative formulations, but we have shown that each of the perspectives discussed here has its roots in Freud's writings. Two of them, ego psychology and object–relations theory, conceive of themselves as carrying forward Freud's scientific investigations. The other two, hermeneutic psychoanalysis and feminist psychological analysis, see themselves as critical interpretations of Freud that have uncovered much that was long overlooked by the scientific readings of his texts. Hermeneuts and feminists criticize the scientific approaches for their lack of sensitivity to the nuances of Freud, and also for their unexamined commitment to rationalist epistomologies that they fault for many of the same reasons. Scientifically oriented analysts in turn dismiss feminist arguments as politically motivated, but this approach ignores what the feminists and hermeneuts have been arguing for years—that science, and especially social science, is a cultural practice and therefore political. From the conservative epistemological side, all psychoanalytic work, including that of ego psychology, has been attacked because of its lack of rigor in practice and its lack of clarity in formulating rules of evidence.

After Freud's death, the cohesive force that held psychoanalysis together (at times by fiat) was gone, though his name has been invoked as a symbol by his followers and critics alike in order to justify their revisions of his work. Freud left us psychoanalysis, but he did not leave behind a method for arbitrating disputes over theory or practice. While he was alive, he *was* the psychoanalytic paradigm, because he judged the validity of analytic findings; after his death, the paradigm was lost. What stands in his place is a diverse intellectual and social movement guided by four interpretive perspectives, each of which has developed its own history, critical criteria, and social practice. While some mixture of ego psychology and object–relations theory guides the work of most psychoanalysts, psychoanalytically oriented literary and social criticism has come to be dominated by the hermeneutic and feminist perspectives, which are just beginning to inform therapeutic practice in England and America.

REFERENCES

Adler, A. (1914). Trotz und Gehorsam. In A. Adler & C. Furtmuller (Eds.), *Heilen und Bilden.* Munich: Reinhardt, (Original work published 1910)

Adler, A. (1982). *Co-operation between the sexes* (H. Ansbacher & R. Ansbacher, Eds.). New York: Norton.

Ainsworth, M. (1978). *Patterns of attachment: A psychological study of the strange situation.* Hillsdale, NJ: Erlbaum.

Amacher, P. (1965). *Freud's neurological education and its influence on psychoanalytic theory.* New York: International Universities Press.

Balbus, I. (1982). *Marxism and domination.* Princeton, NJ: Princeton University Press.

Balint, A. (1964). Love for the mother and mother love. In M. Balint (Ed.), *Primary love and psycho-analytic technique.* London: Tavistock. (Original work published 1939)

Balint, M. (1964). Early developmental states of the ego: Primary object–love. In M. Balint (Ed.), *Primary love and psycho-analytic technique.* London: Tavistock. (Original work published 1937)

Blight, J. (1981). Must psychoanalysis retreat to hermeneutics? *Psychoanalysis and Contemporary Thought, 4,* 147–205.

Bowlby, J. (1969). *Attachment.* New York: Basic Books.

Bowlby, J. (1973). *Separation.* London: Tavistock.

Breuer, J., & Freud, S. (1955). Studies on hysteria. In J. Strachey (Ed.), *The standard edition of the complete psychological works of Sigmund Freud* (Vol. 2). London: Hogarth. (Original work published 1895).

Brody, B. (1973). Freud's case-load. In H. Ruitenbeek (Ed.), *Freud as we knew him.* Detroit: Wayne State University Press.

Chodorow, N. (1978). *The reproduction of mothering: Psychoanalysis and the sociology of gender.* Berkeley: University of California Press.

Deutsch, H. (1925). The psychology of women in relation to the functions of reproduction. *International Journal of Psycho-Analysis, 6,* 405–418.

de Beauvoir, S. (1960). *The second sex.* London: Jonathan Cape. (Original work published 1949)

Dicks, H. V. (1967). *Marital tensions.* New York: Basic Books.

Dinnerstein, D. (1976). *The mermaid and the minotaur: Sexual arrangements and human malaise.* New York: Harper & Row.

Ehrenreich, B., & English, D. (1978). *For her own good: 150 years of the experts' advice to women.* Garden City, NY: Anchor.

Erikson, E. (1968). *Identity: Youth and crisis.* New York: Norton.

Fairbairn, W. R. D. (1954). *An object–relations theory of personality.* New York: Basic Books.

Fairbairn, W. R. D. (1963). Synopsis of an object–relations theory of personality. *International Journal of Psycho-Analysis, 44,* 224.

Firestone, S. (1970). *The dialectics of sex.* New York: Bantam.

Fisher, S., & Greenberg, R. (1977). *The scientific credibility of Freud's theories and therapy.* New York: Basic Books.

Friedan, B. (1965). *The feminine mystique.* New York: Penguin.

Freud, S. (1946). *The ego and the mechanisms of defence.* New York: International Universities Press. (Original work published 1936)

Freud, S. (1953). Fausse reconnaissance in psycho-analytic treatment. In J. Strachey (Ed.), *Standard edition* (Vol. 13). (Original work published 1914)

Freud, S. (1954). *The origins of psycho-analysis: Letters to Wilhelm Fliess, drafts and notes* (M. Bonaparte, A. Freud, & E. Kris, Eds.). New York: Basic Books.

Freud, S. (1953). Three essays on the theory of sexuality. In J. Strachey (Ed.), *Standard edition* (Vol. 7). London: Hogarth. (Original work published 1905)

Freud, S. (1953). The interpretation of dreams. In J. Strachey (Ed.), *Standard edition* (Vols. 4, 5). London: Hogarth. (Original work published 1900)

Freud, S. (1957). Mourning and melancholia. In J. Strachey (Ed.), *Standard edition* (Vol. 14). London: Hogarth. (Original work published 1917)

Freud, S. (1957). On narcissism: An introduction. In J. Strachey (Ed.), *Standard edition* (Vol. 14). London: Hogarth. (Original work published 1914)

Freud, S. (1958). Formulations on the two principles of mental functioning. In J. Strachey (Ed.), *Standard edition* (Vol. 12). London: Hogarth. (Original work published 1911)

Freud, S. (1959a). Inhibitions, symptoms, and anxiety. In J. Strachey (Ed.), *Standard edition* (Vol. 20). London: Hogarth. (Original work published 1926)

Freud, S. (1959b). The question of lay analysis. In J. Strachey (Ed.), *Standard edition* (Vol. 20). London: Hogarth. (Original work published 1926)

Freud, S. (1960), Jokes and their relation to the unconscious. In J. Strachey (Ed.), *Standard edition* (Vol. 8). London: Hogarth.

Freud, S. (1961). Civilization and its discontents. In J. Strachey (Ed.), *Standard edition* (Vol. 21). London: Hogarth. (Original work published 1930)

Freud, S. (1961). The ego and the id. In J. Strachey (Ed.), Standard edition (Vol. 19). London: Hogarth. (Original work published 1923)

Freud, S. (1961). Female sexuality. In J. Strachey (Ed.), *Standard edition* (Vol. 21). London: Hogarth. (Original work published 1931)

Freud, S. (1961). Some psychical consequences of the anatomical distinction between the sexes. In J. Strachey (Ed.), *Standard edition* (Vol. 19). London: hogarth, (Original work published 1925)

Freud, S. (1961, 1963). Introductory lectures on psycho-analysis. In J. Strachey (Ed.), *Standard edition* (Vols. 15, 16). London: Hogarth. (Original works published 1916, 1917)

Freud, S. (1964). Constructions in analysis. In J. Strachey (Ed.), *Standard edition* (Vol. 23). London: Hogarth. (Original work published 1937)

Freud, S. (1964). Femininity. In J. Strachey (Ed.), *Standard edition* (Vol. 22). London: Hogarth. (Original work published 1933)

Freud, S. (1964). An outline of psycho-analysis. In J. Strachey (Ed.), *Standard edition* (Vol. 23). London: Hogarth. (Original work published 1940)

Freud, S. (1966). Project for a scientific psychology. In J. Strachey (Ed.), *Standard edition* (Vol. 1). London: Hogarth. (Original work published 1895)

Greer, G. (1971). *The female eunuch*. London: Paladin.

Grünbaum, A. (1984). *The foundations of psychoanalysis: A philosophical critique*. Berkeley: University of California Press.

Guntrip, H. (1961). *Personality structure and human interaction*. New York: International Universities Press.

Habermas, J. (1971). *Knowledge and human interests*. Boston: Beacon.

Harding, S., & Hintikka, M. (Ed.). (1983). *Discovering reality: Feminist perspectives on epistemology, metaphysics, methodology, and philosophy of science*. Boston: Reidel.

Hartmann, H. (1939). *Ego psychology and the problem of adaptation* (D. Rapaport, Trans.). New York: International Universities Press.

Hartmann, H. (1956). The development of the ego concept in Freud's work. *International Journal of Psycho-Analysis, 37,* 425–438.

Hartmann, H. (1959). Psychoanalysis as a scientific theory. In S. Hook (Ed.), *Psychoanalysis, scientific method and philosophy*. New York: New York University Press.

Holt, R. (1965). A review of Freud's biological assumptions and their influence on his theories. In N. Greenfield & W. Lewis (Eds.), *Psychoanalysis and current biological thought*. Madison: University of Wisconsin Press.

Horney, K. (1974). The flight from womanhood: the masculinity complex in women as viewed by men and by women. In J. Strouse (Ed.), *Women and analysis*. New York: Grossman. (Original work published 1926)

Jones, E. (1927). The early development of female sexuality. *International Journal of Psycho-Analysis, 8,* 459–472.

Jung, C. G. (1964). Woman in Europe. In R. F. C. Hull (Trans.), *The collected works of C. G. Jung* (Vol. 10). Princeton, NJ: Princeton University Press. (Original work published 1927)

Klein, M. (1937). *The psycho-analysis of children* (2nd ed.). London: Hogarth.

Klein, M. (1961). *Narrative of a child analysis*. New York: Dell.

Klein, M., Heimann, P., Isaacs, S., & Riviere, J. (1952). *Developments in psycho-analysis*. London: Hogarth.

Kohut, H. (1971). *The analysis of the self*. New York: International Universities Press.

Lacan, J. (1977). *Ecrits: A selection* (A. Sheridan, Trans.). New York: Norton.

Laing, R. D. (1969). *Self and others*. New York: Pantheon.

Laplanche, J. (1976). *Life and death in psychoanalysis* (J. Mehlman, Trans.). Baltimore, MD: Johns Hopkins University Press.

Laplanche, J., & Pontalis, J.-B. (1973). *The language of psychoanalysis* (D. Nicholson-Smith, Trans.). New York: Norton.

Mahler, M., Pine, F., & Bergman, A. (1975). *The psychological birth of the human infant*. New York: Basic Books.

Mujeeb-ur-Rahman, M. (Ed.). (1955). *The Freudian paradigm*. Chicago: Nelson-Hall.

Munroe, R. (1955). *Schools of psychoanalytic thought*. New York: Holt.

Pribram, K., & Gill, M. (1976). *Freud's "Project" re-assessed*. New York: Basic Books.

Radnitzky, G. (1973). *Contemporary schools of metascience*. Chicago: Regnery.

Rapaport, D. (1967). A historical survey of psychoanalytic ego psychology. In M. Gill (Ed.). *The collected papers of David Rapaport*. New York: Basic Books. (Original work published 1958)

Rich, A. (1977). *Of woman born: Motherhood as experience and institution*. New York: Bantam.

Rich, A. (1980). Compulsory heterosexuality and lesbian existence. *Signs, 6,* 62–91.

Ricoeur, R. (1970). *Freud and Philosophy: An essay on interpretation* (D. Savage, Trans.). New Haven, CT: Yale University Press.

Saussure, F. de (1959). *Course in general linguistics.* New York: Philosophical Library. (Original work published 1915).

Sherfey, M. (1966). The evolution and nature of female sexuality in relation to psychoanalytic theory. *Journal of the American Psychoanalytic Association, 14,* 28–128.

Steele, R. (1982). *Freud and Jung: Conflicts of interpretation.* London: Routledge.

Steele, R., & Jacobsen, P. (1978). From present to past: The development of Freudian theory. *International Review of Psycho-Analysis, 5,* 393–411.

Turkle, S. (1981). *Psychoanalytic politics: Freud's French Revolution.* Cambridge, MA: MIT Press.

Winnicott, D. (1958). *Collected papers: Through paediatrics to psycho-analysis.* London: Tavistock Publications.

10

Notes toward a History of Cognitive Psychology

FRANK S. KESSEL AND WILLIAM BEVAN

APOLOGIA AND AGENDA

We have concluded that the early 1980s are both the best of times and the worst of times to be writing about the history of cognitive psychology. Since this conclusion has a direct bearing on what and how we have chosen to write, we must amplify. This leads to what we think the agenda should be for a comprehensive history of cognitive psychology and at the same time will explain why the character and cast of this chapter differ somewhat from others in the present volume.

The domain of cognitive psychology lies close to the center of much of disciplinary and institutional psychology over the past 25 years. Indeed, it is not implausible that cognitive psychology stands at the epicenter of change in psychology's recent past. Thus, while no history of cognitive psychology would have been deemed worth contemplating until a decade or so ago, now it seems that such a history both can and should be of value.

Yet the very recency of "the cognitive revolution," to borrow a familiar phrase, creates at least a couple of obvious conundrums of the kind that would have faced someone undertaking to scrutinize, say, the history of psychoanalysis in 1925 or the history of behaviorism in 1940. For example, given the still-evolving character of contemporary cognitive psychology, how can the domain or field of inquiry whose history we seek to write best be defined or mapped out? What if cognitive psychologists themselves are not of one mind in drawing the boundaries of their domain of inquiry, in characterizing and evaluating its cardinal features? Such a less-than-homogeneous (and doubtless healthy) state of affairs is underlined by Neisser's (1976) critique, offered only nine years after his seminal survey (1967), and exposed by the vigorous debate over foundational issues in cognitive science (Haugeland, 1978, 1981; Pylyshyn, 1978, 1980; see also the 10th anniversary issue of *Cognition*, 1981). And what of cognitive science, a phrase and conception that have come into wide currency, and been institutionalized, as we have wrestled with the definitional conundrum? Should cognitive psychology be placed within the scheme of cognitive science? And if so, should the perspective from which our history is written be modified correspondingly?

Attention to the perspective from which history is written highlights the second conundrum created by the recency of the cognitive revolution. Despite our being too close to the domain to discern its defining features with confidence, we have to place around cognitive psychology some kind of frame, however provisional, within which to view its past. In other words, how we choose to characterize latter-day cognitive psychology will surely shape our view of its history; and this amounts to what historians typically strive to circumvent—namely, "presentism." Is presentism avoidable here? If, by the nature of the case, it isn't, then we are obliged to adopt to a minimal degree a suitably self-critical stance.[1]

Against this challenging background, why and how have we chosen to proceed with this chapter? The "why" rests in the fact that cognitive psychology has emerged as a major domain of psychological thought and inquiry in the second half of the 20th century. This emergence from a variety of less and more distant antecedents, in the context of a complex array of intellectual, disciplinary, and cultural forces, will surely be

[1] We offer biographical details in such a spirit: One of us (WB), after an undergraduate psychological education shaped in the Chicago functionalist tradition, began graduate studies at Duke in the early 1940s, a time when the behaviorist tide was at a high point but a place where psychology from its inception represented an alternative tradition. Here he was introduced by Karl Zener and Donald Adams not only to the Berlin Gestaltists, but to Bartlett, Duncker, McDougall, Piaget, and Vygotsky as well. The other (FK), after undergraduate and early postgraduate study in a generalist, British mold, received a Ph.D. from Minnesota in 1969, both a time and a place where "revolution" à la Kuhn, as well as the names of Chomsky and Piaget, were frequently on the lips and the minds of such persons as James Jenkins and John Flavell.

a prime topic of historical scholarship in psychology as the century draws to a close. Indeed, cognitive psychology could well serve as a singularly instructive and illuminating focus for the kind of historical research program that Toulmin (1972) envisages within his analysis of the growth of rational and scientific human understanding. Within Toulmin's framework and in his terms (see his Appendix for a detailed exposition), the following sorts of questions can be posed regarding cognitive psychology as an emerging or evolving disciplinary domain:

1. What are cognitive psychology's explanatory goals, how do they relate to such goals in other areas of psychology, and how have psychology's problematics been influenced by these emerging goals? And if they weren't so affected in other generations, why not?
2. To the degree that cognitive psychology has embodied conceptual variants, what are they, and through which avenues have these intellectual innovations been expressed and taken hold (or, at other times, not taken hold)? What arguments have led to cognitive psychology's being recognized or, earlier, ruled out?
3. In competing (successfully or unsuccessfully) for an established place in psychology, how have cognitive psychology's conceptual variants been responded to and evaluated? Which were the authoritative reference groups that adopted these procedures of intellectual selection?
4. How has the social or cultural context affected the nature and development of cognitive psychology? Has the introduction and evolution of its explanatory concepts depended upon and then influenced related technologies? Are such technologies or techniques, in turn, expressions of philosophical and social presuppositions?
5. How have the collective goals of cognitive psychology influenced or shaped the problem-solving activities of individual psychologists? And how, on the other side of the coin, have different individuals' personal preoccupations and intellectual interests been manifested in their work and lives as cognitive psychologists?

Given such a long-term history agenda, our goal in this chapter is modest. We propose to draft a series of preliminary, programmatic notes on the questions listed here. We make no claim that the notes avoid all or any of the ever-present historiographical pitfalls, nor that they address in critical depth all items on the agenda.[2] But embedded in the questions we have posed and in our notes are interesting and intriguing elements of any comprehensive history of cognitive psychology. In presenting these questions and notes we shall shift, with little explicit marking and in a primarily descriptive way, from "internalist" to "externalist" considerations, and from intellectual to sociological to psychological aspects of cognitive psychology's history.

CONTEMPORARY COGNITIVE PSYCHOLOGY: FORM AND FORMATIVE YEARS

Cognitive Psychology in the 1980s

Cognitive psychology is a broad and diverse domain of enquiry, particularly when it is viewed as embedded in cognitive science. Building on foundations laid in the 1960s, cognitive psychology became institutionalized and grew in size and scope in the 1970s, with one sociological indicator being the establishment of journals—*Cognitive Psychology* in 1970, *Cognition* in 1971, *Memory and Cognition* in 1973, and *Cognitive Science* (with its allied society) in 1977. Furthermore, the lines of communication have been extended beyond scholars in psychology and other disciplines to a broader audience via *New York Times*-style journalism and popular books and articles based on scholarly sources, as well as television interviews with leading scientists in the field (Gleick, 1983; Hunt, 1982; Miller, 1983).

What, then, are the boundary markers of the almost omnipresent cognitive psychology and cognitive science, and what, as a corollary, have been the consequences of the field's emergence and consolidation? One answer to the first question can be found in the "Information for Authors" sections provided by the relevant journals: *Cognitive Psychology* deals with "memory, language processing, perception, problem-solving, and thinking." *Cognitive Science* "publishes articles of any length on such topics as representation of knowledge, language processing, image processing, question-answering, inference, learning, problem-solving, and planning."

So described, cognitive psychology can be thought of as these content areas and roughly synonymous with "the psychology of cognition."

---

[2] Even writing in such an agenda-setting spirit, we have constantly struggled to bracket, phenomenologically if not in print, a variety of qualifications, extensions, and explanations. Since it is not possible to incorporate all such points here, we will be pleased to provide copies of draft footnotes upon request.

Here the field's emergence and consolidation represent a sizable, even exponential, increase in psychological research but with no noteworthy qualitative change. In other words, this growth is but a revival of earlier interests in problem-solving, perception, and the like.

Each journal, however, provides qualifying details that put a different shading on the definitional issue. *Cognitive Psychology* adds, simply but significantly, that the journal emphasizes work on "the organization of human information-processing." *Cognitive Science* reiterates the field's and journal's problem areas in an opening editorial and then notes:

> Recently there has begun to grow a community of people from different disciplines, who find themselves tackling a common set of problems in natural and artificial intelligence. The particular disciplines from which they come are cognitive and social psychology, artificial intelligence, computational linguistics, educational technology, and even epistemology. The work of these researchers is converging toward a coherent point of view that is different from the focus of any of the current journals. This view has recently begun to produce a spate of books and conferences, which are the first trappings of an emerging discipline. This discipline might have been called applied epistemology or intelligence theory, but someone on high declared it should be cognitive science and so it shall . . . I hope the journal will transmit the excitement surrounding the paradigm shift in the study of cognition made possible by the synthesis of artificial intelligence, psychology, and linguistics. (Collins, 1977, p. 1–2)

As described here, cognitive psychology, whether on its own or as one segment of cognitive science, is generally equated with the information-processing metaphor or model, and therefore taken to represent or incorporate a "paradigm shift." As such, it is taken to represent a change in some, if not all, of the presuppositions governing psychology's choice of problem domains, theoretical tools, and research techniques (Lachman, Lachman, & Butterfield, 1979). While in principle such a shift could be narrowly confined to the content areas of cognition, the emergence of cognitive psychology (and cognitive science) has generally been thought of in broader terms bearing on the view of psychology as a whole, on its problematics and conceptual framework(s), to use Toulmin's terms, and on its consequent relations with and explanatory potential for philosophy and other disciplines. Consider these views:

> Just as the physical sciences can be conceived as the study of energy in its many aspects, the behavioral and social sciences can be characterized in terms of their concern with the processing and transformation of information. (Estes, 1975, p. 1)

> I do not think of myself as a cognitive psychologist: I think of myself as one interested in the mechanisms of human information processing . . . I am interested in all of human behavior, whether conscious or subconscious, careful thought and inference or behavior based on intuitions, feelings, and emotions. . . . The scope of information processing psychology, therefore, is all of psychology. (D. A. Norman, personal communication, September 1979)

Cognitive psychology is a theory-rich psychology concerned to a large extent with problems of representation and process. . . . If one surveys theory and practice in psychology today, the conclusion is that cognitive psychology is mainstream psychology. . . . To be interested in human information processing is to be concerned with the flow of information/knowledge within the organism and between it and its environment. . . . The information-processing approach cannot be incorrect or correct. It is a way of looking at the world, a façon de parler, *not* a theory. For most of us it is a synonym for cognitive psychology. (Mandler, 1981, p. 1, 16)

In the early 1940s, when I was a graduate student in psychology at Harvard, there wasn't anything called cognitive science. In those days there wasn't even anything called cognitive psychology. Today, Centers for Cognitive Science are springing up everywhere. Obviously, an important change took place sometime during the 40 years I have been studying psychology. When did it happen? . . . In my own life I can narrow the important period down to the 1950s. In 1951 I published a book, *Language and Communication,* and in the preface I wrote: "The bias is behavioristic—not fanatically behavioristic, but certainly tainted by a preference. There does not seem to be a more scientific kind of bias, or, if there is, it turns out to be behaviorism after all" (p. v). In 1962, only eleven years later, I published another book, *Psychology, the Science of Mental Life,* whose very title (drawn from William James) objected to the definition of psychology as the science of behavior. . . . A new generation of psychologists has now grown up without feeling naughty when they talk about mentalistic concepts like conception, attention, memory, intuition, expectation, planning, intention, will, and so on, all of which had been banned by behaviorists as unscientific. (Miller, 1979, p. 1, 12)

Times have changed. Psychology has become "cognitive" or "mentalistic" (in many quarters) and fascinating discoveries have been made about such familiar philosophical concerns as mental imagery, remembering and language comprehension. Even the brain scientists are beginning to tinker with models that founder on conceptual puzzles . . . Many problems arising in these sciences—problems about concept learning, reasoning, memory, decision—also have an unmistakably philosophical cast. Philosophy of mind has responded to these developments by becoming "naturalized"; it has become a branch of the philosophy of science concerning itself with the conceptual foundations and problems of the sciences of the mind. This has changed the shape and texture of philosophical theories of mind by introducing into the discussions of the traditional issues many of the data and conceptual tools of the new scientific approaches, and raising new issues arising from the puzzles and pitfalls of those approaches. (Dennett, 1978, p. xiii–xiv)

Mr. DeMey . . . explains how the study of computer models of human perception and reasoning throws quite a new light on the philosophy, psychology and sociology of science. . . . The fundamental new development is summed up in the "cognitive" principle, which DeMey states as follows: "Any form of information processing, whether natural or artificial, requires a device that has, in some way or another, an internal model or representation of the environment in which it operates" (p. xv). In the theory of artificial intelligence, this internal model is called a frame, defined as "a collection of questions to be asked about a hypothetical situation; it specifies issues to be raised and methods to be used in dealing with them" (p. 204). In theories of perception, this model generates expectations of what will be seen—not, of course, in complete detail, but within certain general categories derived from previous experience. In scientific epistemology, the frames are the Kuhnian paradigms that delimit the puzzles to be solved by normal science, and act as blinkers against revolutionary theoretical conceptions. Summarized thus, the cognitive view would probably be familiar to most contemporary epistemologists. . . . It seems to me that one can find in the "cognitive" view the main ingredients for a recipe for science, where psychological, philosophical and sociological tastes are intimately combined. (Ziman, 1983, p. 15, 17)

This, then, is the cognitive psychology whose history, or small parts thereof, we are sketching: the cognitive psychology that (1) has, from the 1950s on, with increasing scientific self-confidence and a generally greater conceptual reach, brought the mind back under systematic scrutiny; (2) has, in a liberalized postpositivist climate, and in the company of allied disciplines, begun to re-address perennial philosophical questions about the form and functioning of mental representations and processes; (3) has, to varying degrees of detail and subject to continuing debate, adopted the information-processing metaphor or paradigm in doing so; and (4) would appear to have adopted, as a core thematic commitment (Holton, 1973, 1978), a constructivist conception of active (human) mental functioning.

As a summary of the directions and dimensions of contemporary cognitive psychology, and as a means of moving toward more explicit historical considerations, we can do no better than quote from the work that, probably more than any other, served to focus the field, not least as a text for graduate courses and hence as a socializing influence for a new scientific generation.

As used here, the term "cognition" refers to all the processes by which the sensory input is transformed, reduced, elaborated, stored, recovered, and used. It is concerned with these processes even when they operate in the absence of relevant information, as in images and hallucinations. Such terms as *sensation, perception, imagery, retention, recall, problem-solving,* and *thinking,* among many others, refer to hypothetical stages or aspects of cognition. Given such a sweeping definition, it is apparent that cognition is involved in everything a human being might possibly do; that every psychological phenomenon is a cognitive phenomenon. But although cognitive psychology is concerned with all human activity rather than some of it, the concern is from a particular point of view. . . . The present approach is more closely related to that of Bartlett than of any other contemporary psychologist, while its roots are at least as old as the "act psychology" of the nineteenth century. The central assertion is that seeing, hearing, and remembering are all acts of *construction,* which may make more or less of stimulus information depending on circumstances. . . . A generation ago, a book like this one would have needed at least a chapter of self-defense against the behaviorist position. Today, happily, the climate of opinion has changed, and little or no defense is necessary. . . . The basic reason for studying cognitive processes has become as clear as the reason for studying anything else: because they are there. Our knowledge of the world *must* be somehow developed from the stimulus input. . . . Cognitive processes surely exist, so it can hardly be unscientific to study them. (Neisser, 1967, p. 4, 5, 10)

If Neisser's book was significant in the late 1960s, what were the earlier tributaries contributing to the steady stream of cognitive psychology? Where lay the source(s) of these tributaries, notably in the second half of the 1950s, when by most accounts major intellectual realignments and shifts in the direction of inquiry took place? We consider these questions in the next section.

Cognitive Psychology in 1960

Since the signs of the times around 1960 are numerous and generally known, we will mention only four as a prelude to scrutiny of the preceding period.

1. *Hebb and the American revolution.* In 1960 came Donald Hebb's call for the second stage in "the American revolution." Examining mind, consciousness, hallucination, body image, and the self, and denying that his use of such terms was intended "to annoy the bull-headed behaviorist," Hebb (1960) urges: "Let us press on with the serious, persistent, and if necessary daring, exploration of the thought processes, by all available means. I conclude with Conant's quotation from Bridgman: 'The scientific method, as far as it is a method, is nothing more than doing one's damnedest with one's mind, no holds barred' " (p. 744). For Hebb, such a position was merely an extension of his earlier examination of perception in terms of "cell assemblies" (Hebb, 1949), an effort that represents a significant neuropsychological stream in the emergence of cognitive psychology. Tracing that thread back to Karl Lashley and others and forward through Karl Pribram and others will be a necessary part of any comprehensive historical account. (See Hebb, 1980, for a survey of the evolution of his ideas in the 1940s and 1950s.)

2. *Piaget and cognitive development.* In April 1960, a conference was held under the auspices of the Social Science Research Council's then recently established Committee on Intellective Processes Research. The committee's focus was on "the problems—stretching at least through philosophy, education, psychology, sociology and anthropology—that are presented in the study of children's thinking," while its first sponsored conference was "dominated, as it was explicitly intended to be, by attention to the work of Jean Piaget and his colleagues in Geneva" (Kessen & Kuhlman, 1962). Since this was a moment when the fundamental characteristics of the cognitive developmental terrain were being

identified and mapped out, these papers and their attendant discussions are of more than passing interest. So too are the prescient comments provided by the proceedings' editors:

> One may suggest that Piaget has built a normative theory of cognitive development which borders on classical epistemology: empirical evidence is relevant to it, but not decisive in any prescribable methodological sense. Instead, the observations of children can be seen as illustrations—or more bluntly, as demonstrations—of the appropriateness of his *Erkenntnistheorie*. . . . Piaget has not fallen between two stools in this view, but with remarkable agility, on the far side of both. . . . Unless all signs are amiss, Piaget is the chief bandit in the theft of epistemology from normative philosophical treatment and its transmutation into a psychological specialty. The implications of this transfer are too distant in time and too far from the present course of American Psychology to be readily stated, but the development of a truly empirical approach to the theory of human knowledge will owe an incalculable debt to Piaget. (Kessen & Kuhlman, 1962, p. 168–170)

Thus the conference was a harbinger of and contribution to the subsequent explosion of interest in Piaget, while Flavell's soon-to-follow (1963) book-length exposition served a socializing function for students in developmental psychology, much as Neisser's did for those in experimental psychology.

Although we will have occasion to mention Piaget briefly, we only note here that cognitive development has been a major tributary in the flow of cognitive psychology. As such, it calls for specific historical scrutiny, as does language development (Brown & Bellugi, 1964; Kessel, 1982). We may also note that in U.S. cognitive developmental thought, as in other areas of what was to become cognitive psychology, European expatriates, of whom Heinz Werner and Kurt Lewin are noteworthy exemplars, must be seen as exerting a broadening influence in the decades up to 1960. As part of a significant process of "cultural transfer and adaptation," they kept the cognitive flame alive (Heilbut, 1983; Jackman & Borden, 1983).

3. *Miller, Galanter, and Pribram and the computer model.* It is no coincidence that both Hebb and Simon (in Kessen & Kuhlman, 1962) discuss Miller, Galanter, and Pribram's concurrently published and widely cited work (1960). It was no coincidence for Simon since, as Miller et al. (1960) acknowledge in their preface, they had access to a large mass of material supplied by Simon and his colleagues. Simon observed: "Miller et al. have written about thinking in information-processing terms without using actual computer programs. Their results would seem to indicate that this way of describing cognitive processes, which is independent of the computer, may in itself lead to new and different ways of looking at behavior" (in Kessen & Kuhlman, 1962). Hebb's mention of Miller et al.

is also not coincidental, because their "way of looking at behavior" was consistent with his and the spirit of the revolution he was calling for:

> There may be convergence with the fundamentally important line of analysis developed by Lashley as the problem of serial order, and by Miller et al. in their conception of Plan and Metaplan. This concerns the control of skilled performances extended in time, such as speech, typing, and violin playing. Lashley characteristically posed the problem without attempting theoretical explanation. Miller et al. have now laid down the general lines of explanation, using the computer model. (Hebb, 1960, p. 743)

The computer model and its implications for psychology and psychological theory were indeed at the heart of Miller et al.'s (1960) book and their TOTE unit of analysis, with Simon and his colleagues, Allen Newell and J. C. Shaw, providing much of the immediate conceptual energy. Miller et al. cite "Wiener, Ashby, von Neumann, Minsky, Shannon, MacKay, McCulloch, Chomsky"—all nonpsychologists—as sources of guiding ideas, as well as other "cognitive theorists" such as Frederic Bartlett, Edward Tolman, Wolfgang Köhler, Karl Lashley, Kurt Lewin, and William James. In their engaging and historically valuable Prologue and Epilogue, they explain how and why they found themselves moving in a cognitive direction in the late 1950s, and what the implications were of this move:

> To psychologists who like alternatives to nickel-in-the-slot, stimulus–response conceptions of man, Image has considerable appeal. (It is so reasonable to insert between the stimulus and the response a little wisdom. And there is no particular need to apologize for putting it there, because it has already been there before psychology arrived.) . . . Arrayed against the reflex theorists are the pessimists, who think that living organisms are complicated, devious, poorly designed for research purposes . . . They maintain that the effect an event will have upon behavior depends on *how the event is represented in the organism's picture of itself and its universe* . . . any correlations between stimulation and response must be *mediated by an organized representation of the environment*, a system of concepts and relations within which the organism is located. A human being—and probably other animals as well—builds up *an internal representation, a model of the universe, a schema, a simulacrum, a cognitive map.* . . . We shall simply announce that our theoretical preferences are all on the side of the cognitive theorist. . . . A conviction grew on us that we were developing *a point of view toward large parts of psychology.* We then began to wonder how we might best characterize our position so as to contrast it with others more traditional and more familiar [behaviorism and Wundtian introspectionism]. . . . It suddenly occurred to us that we were subjective behaviorists. When we stopped laughing we began to wonder seriously if that was not exactly the position we had argued ourselves into. At least the name suggested the shocking inconsistency of our position. . . . What matters to us far more than a name, however, is whether or not we have glimpsed an important aspect of human intelligence [emphasis added]. (Miller et al., 1960, p. 2–9, 211–213)

4. *Center for Cognitive Studies and the institutionalization of cognition.* It seems unlikely that George Miller and Jerome Bruner, searching in 1960 for a suitable title for their new collaborative enterprise at Harvard, seriously contemplated "Center for Studies in Subjective Behaviorism." "What's in a name?" is, of course, a nontrivial historical question with sociological and psychological overtones, especially at times of real or perceived competition between conceptual frameworks and of possible "paradigm shifts." This pivotal period in the emergence of cognitive psychology contains signs of such conflict and of how different individuals came to terms with it (by holding to the established view, or at least its terminology, by finding some apparent compromise, or by adopting the novel view). One notable example is the founding of a journal in 1962 whose very title expresses a conception of the relation between one kind of psychology and one kind of linguistics—the *Journal of Verbal Learning and Verbal Behavior*. What makes the story of the founding of this journal instructive, as told by Cofer (1978), is that the behavioristic conception of psycholinguistics cultivated throughout the 1950s was precisely then in the process of being overthrown by another: "As Jenkins has put it, Chomsky 'dynamited the structure at the linguistic end' " (Cofer, 1978; for other examples of such tension, see Anderson & Ausubel, 1965; Harper, Anderson, Christensen, & Hunka, 1964; Hebb, 1960; Stevenson & Berlyne in Kessen & Kuhlman, 1962).

At Harvard, close to where the explosion had been taking place, the new conception of language and of cognition in general was given unambiguous, confident institutional expression. In his personal account of the Center for Cognitive Studies, Miller (1979) confesses: "In 1960 we used 'cognitive' in our name defiantly. Most respectable psychologists at the time still thought cognition was too mentalistic for objective scientists, but we nailed it to the door and defended it until eventually we carried the day. And now there are Cognitive Centers everywhere." For his part, Bruner (1980) records: "What seemed to *us* the center of psychology—the cognitive processes viewed in the broad—was being neglected at Harvard. And it would only grow if connected with other fields concerned with the nature of knowledge—philosophy, linguistics, anthropology." (p. 122)

Whereas the Center's founding can be regarded as serving an important symbolic function, through the 1960s it was a major catalyst in the substantive and social-network development of cognitive psychology, not least because of its mode of operation and the diversity of the scholars who visited. Miller (1979) notes:

> As I look back, I am surprised that so heterogeneous a crowd of people could have collaborated so fruitfully at our busy little Center. . . . Anyone whose ideas

appealed to both of us was invited to join us for a year, and many accepted. . . .
Our focus was on cognitive psychology, of course, but many of our strongest
allies in reforming psychology were not themselves psychologists. (p. 11)

Norman (personal communication, September 1979) also refers to the
Stanford summer workshops in the mid-1950s involving "young, promising mathematical psychologists: . . . almost every major person today
who is labeled to be in the field of information-processing and cognitive
psychology and who is over 35 years old was part of the group that met
at Harvard or Stanford."

Cognitive Psychology in the 1950s

Norman's reference to the Stanford workshops brings us to the 1950s,
particularly the period between 1955 and 1960 when the immediate
foundations of contemporary cognitive psychology were laid.

It is very rare that one can specify the beginnings of a historical movement—
whether in science, politics, economics, or whatever—as precisely as we can
identify the beginnings of modern cognitive psychology. For reasons that are
obscure at present, the various tensions and inadequacies of the first half of the
twentieth century cooperated to produce a new movement in psychology that
first adopted the label of information processing and later became known as
modern cognitive psychology. And it all happened in the five-year period between 1955 and 1960. What is particularly fascinating about that period is that
major changes in attitude, method and approach occurred more or less simultaneously in a number of different fields. These disciplines—including artificial
intelligence, anthropology, cybernetics, communication theory, linguistics and
psychology—had rather tenuous connections with one another at the time . . .
Cognitive science started during that five-year period . . . [a period] marked by
new questions raised, old assumptions abandoned, and new theoretical solutions
proposed. Within psychology, the ferment reached memory, attention, emotion,
perception, personality theory, developmental psychology and many others, and
by the mid-nineteen sixties, the changed approaches to psychology were well-
established. (Mandler, 1981, p. 8–9)

Aware that the details of this period call for at least a chapter of their
own and equally aware of historiographical dangers, we extend our
focus on Miller and Bruner back to the 1950s. With no intention of
endorsing any simplistic Great Man view of history, we do so for two
principal reasons: First, their accounts of the period are the most informative that we have found. Second, and more to the substantive historical
point, we believe that these scholars can be taken to represent cognitive
psychology's two overlapping, yet discernibly different major tributaries, each with different affinities, intellectual styles, and origins, and
each running its own course through to the present.

Acknowledging his debt to Newell and Simon's (1972) "Historical Addendum," Miller (1979) provides a list of noteworthy events in computer theory, psychology, linguistics, and anthropology to underline the significance of 1956 as "a rich year for those of us interested in information-processing theories of the mind." (Newell & Simon, 1972, examine 1954–1958 as "the critical years" in the development of their thinking.) Miller proceeds to identify a particular day—September 11, 1956—when, for him, cognitive science was born; the occasion was the Second MIT Symposium on Information Theory. On the second day of the meeting, "nearly every aspect of what we now call cognitive science was represented" (Miller, 1979), most notably Newell and Simon on "The Logic Theory Machine" and Chomsky on "Three Models of Language."

Three Miller comments on these events provide informative historical comparison points. On the emerging conceptual framework and intellectual connections, he remarks:

> I went away from the Symposium with a strong conviction, more intuitive than rational, that human experimental psychology, theoretical linguistics, and the computer simulation of cognitive processes were all pieces from a larger whole, and that the future would see a progressive elaboration and coordination of their shared concerns. It was that faith, incidentally, that inspired my contributions to the book, *Plans and the Structure of Behavior*. (Miller, 1979, p. 9)

On the appeal of Chomsky's work, says Miller (1979): "Chomsky was the first linguist to make good on the claim [that language had all the formal precision of mathematics]. I think that was what excited all of us. We saw the first substantive results from a new field of mathematical linguistics, and the formalisms Chomsky used were more important to us than they were to Chomsky" (p. 8). And on the Zeitgeist and its roots: "Many of us were riding the same wave, which began with advances during the war: servo theory, information theory, signal-detection theory, computer theory, and computers themselves. We could see the possibilities, and no one had explored them far enough to discover the difficulties" (Miller, 1979, p. 3–4).

It was also in 1956 that *A Study of Thinking* by Bruner, Goodnow, and Austin appeared. In their preface, they declare: "The past few years have witnessed a notable increase in interest in and investigation of the cognitive processes—the means whereby organisms achieve, retain, and transform information." This revival is then attributed to the move away from "the impeccable peripheralism" of stimulus–response learning theories; to the recognition that information theory would have to pay attention to how incoming signals are sorted and organized by mediating cognition; and to the fact that "psychoanalysis and personality theory generally have become increasingly interested in what has come to be called 'ego psychology' " (Bruner et al., 1956). The "new look" in perception, which Bruner and Leo Postman had promulgated in the late 1940s and early 1950s, was thus extended to "a search for links between general laws of perception and cognition on the one side and general laws of personality functioning on the other" (Bruner et al., 1956).

To this general survey, Bruner (1980) adds some instructive detail, suggesting points of contact and divergence between his and Miller's ideas and sources of inspiration. On the emerging conceptual framework and intellectual connections, he writes:

> One of the major effects of this [new look] research . . . was its role in creating and consolidating new intellectual alignments in psychology. Students of personality, of social behavior, of classical perception, of attention met and argued about their work: Tolman and Krech and Brunswik from Berkeley, Fritz Heider from Kansas, Lazarus and Chapanis from Hopkins, George Klein and Gardner Murphy in search of personality correlates, the Gibsons and Julie Hochberg from Cornell, Hans Wallach and Gleitman and Prentice from Swarthmore (representing Gestalt theory), Hilgard from Stanford, etc. (Bruner, 1980, p. 107)

Bruner recounts events subsequent to the publication of *A Study of Thinking* (1956):

> The book done, I packed off to the University of Cambridge for the autumn of 1955–56. . . . That summer, Bartlett and I had been co-hosts at a conference on thinking at Cambridge—with Zangwill, Miller, Oldfield, Pribram, Werner, Mackaye, Gregory, and others interested in problem-solving and thinking. It was one of those occasions of high exchange when many of us were encouraged to find that others shared what were "private" or outlandish ideas. Under Bartlett, British psychology had been steadily becoming more cognitive than its American cousin. . . . It was also the time of my first visit to "le Patron," Piaget, in Geneva. We struck it off very well. . . . He saw *A Study of Thinking* as a blow for the common cause . . . In turn I was becoming much more conversant with and enthusiastic about his latest theoretical writing. (Bruner, 1980, p. 114–115)

Two Streams of Cognitive Psychology

Naturally, a more developed and analytical account of cognitive psychology's (re-)birth in the 1950s will go beyond these personal accounts. For one thing, aside from assisting in the corroboration of factual detail, other individuals—as a function of their own background, interests, and style—will doubtless recall different reactions to different aspects of the intellectual tide of the time. Having said that, we believe a fuller historical narrative will testify that Miller's and Bruner's accounts accurately represent two different and now fast-flowing streams in cognitive psychology. One is characterized more by formalized, mathematically inclined, and explicitly detailed information-processing analyses of cognitive functioning. The other represents a relatively informal use of the information-processing metaphor, one that is found more often in conjunction with ideas drawn from anthropology and sociology. The first stream runs closest to traditional areas and methods of experimental psychology—attention, perception, and memory—while the second blends more readily with developmental, social, and personality psychology.

As a significant corollary, these two streams have different origins. The Miller form of cognitive psychology, as he (1979) and Newell and Simon (1972) point out, has its principal conceptual roots in the general postwar cybernetic revolution, and in ideas that can be safely regarded, in many respects, as genuinely original (even though some traces and resonances can be found in earlier writings). The other form of cognitive psychology can be traced more directly to earlier antecedents within psychology itself. Thus Bruner's undergraduate days at Duke (see Bruner, 1983) saw him introduced to psychology by William McDougall and taking early courses from Donald Adams and Karl Zener, both of whom were "fresh returned from Berlin where they had worked with Köhler, Wertheimer and the budding young Kurt Lewin."

At this point we are ready to move to a still earlier phase of cognitive psychology. Before doing so, however, we must mention one more significant dimension of the historical picture of the 1950s:

> The history of science is, at least in large part, an account of the manner in which the science expresses larger cultural themes. . . . But what remains opaque is the social and cultural background, the historical reasons in the wider sense, for the ferment of the late fifties. What was it about the decades just preceding this period, what was it about the conditions of the times, that provided the context within which the common themes among diverse disciplines could occur? (Mandler, 1981, p. 1, 8–9)

Miller's (1979) suggestion that "without the American reaction to Sputnik [which led to funding for science, engineering, and education on a large scale], everything would have gone much more slowly and uncertainly," and Bruner's related account (1980) of his report to the National Academy of Science on education provide one set of beginning answers to Mandler's question. But here, even more than elsewhere, a long and complex historical agenda awaits a comprehensive history.

SCHEMATIC COGNITIVE PSYCHOLOGY: ANTICIPATIONS AND ANTECEDENTS

Having sketched the outline of cognitive psychology's directly formative years, we turn to the question of whether and how psychologists in the generations prior to World War II anticipated the modern movement's main ideas. Our principal purposes here are to consider in what sense Tolman, Bartlett, and others can be regarded as cognitive psychologists; in so doing, to add some substantive weight to the earlier characterization of cognitive psychology's central thematic commitment as "constructivism"; to explore which and whose notions were accepted, either by their peers or as an agenda for later work, as well as why they were or were not accepted; in so doing, to examine possible connections between those earlier theories and theorists and current thinking; and, finally, in light of our preliminary exploration of such matters, to offer brief observations on how the cognitive wheel seems to be coming full circle.

Running Great Man historiographical risks again, we examine the contributions of particular individuals to schematic cognitive psychology. In representing a significant theoretical point of view, in addressing central conceptual issues, or in illustrating a pertinent pattern of historical events, such individuals must form part of any comprehensive historical account.

Tolman and Cognitive Leadership

Surveying cognitive psychology before 1945, Newell and Simon (1972) note:

> On the American side of the Atlantic Ocean there was a great gap in research on human complex cognitive processes from the time of William James almost down to World War II. Although the gap was not complete, it is fair to say that American cognitive psychology during this period was dominated by behaviorism, the nonsense syllable, and the rat. (p. 874)

They also note that Clark Hull's doctoral thesis on concept formation (1920) was an exception to this trend, but that he soon moved on to problems more compatible with the *Zeitgeist*. Next, they suggest that "of the leading American psychologists of the period, [Edward] Tolman was the farthest from the dominant S-R position (except for those Gestalt psychologists who migrated from Europe). . . . He treated man (and rat) as a goal-seeking, hence decision-making, organism" (Newell & Simon, 1972). Donald Campbell (1979) comments: "Tolman's was the only cognitive learning theory of the 1930s," although he overlooks the fact that others (e.g., Adams, 1929, and Zener, 1937) were casting learning into cognitive terms.

Not that Tolman (1951), writing in ever-engaging prose about "purpose", "insight," "hypotheses," "sign–gestalt expectancies," and actively constructed "cognitive maps", functioned outside the mainstream. As Campbell observes, his laboratories conducted important experiments, his papers appeared in the major journals, and he was elected APA president in 1937. Further, Tolman was "a charismatic leader who attracted, [and was beloved by] the best graduate students" (Campbell, 1979), among the many, Campbell himself, John Garcia, Henry Gleitman, Julian Hochberg, and David Krech (formerly I. Krechevsky). And yet—and here lies the "puzzle" that animates Campbell's (1979) article—"Tolman's students, with rare exceptions, almost completely stopped doing recognizably Tolmanian studies using Tolmanian concepts and terms once they left the University of California at Berkeley." The question thus becomes: "Why were Tolman's students the least loyal when, of all the learning theories of the 1930s, Tolman's can now be seen to have been the best?" (p. 187)

In the context of cognitive psychology's history, this is a significant question, answered by Campbell in terms of Tolman's qualities of intellectual leadership or, more accurately, his failure to exercise leadership of a certain kind.

> For a theory to be thoroughly explored, it may be necessary that its followers have an unreasonable, exaggerated faith in the theory's value. Understatement, modesty, or a nonpartisan objectivity in estimating one's theory's chances of being true may amount to a default on an essential leadership requirement and result in a promising theory failing to be properly explored, elaborated, and disseminated. (Campbell, 1979, p. 188)

As Campbell documents, and as remembered by his fellow graduate students, Tolman's writing and teaching were characterized by precisely these qualities of understatement and modesty (for the larger study of which Campbell's data were a part, see Krantz & Wiggins, 1973). Such qualities were expressed in "playful self-deprecation" of his own theoretical innovations, a happy acceptance of students as "equal-status fellow explorers on the cutting edge of science," and a concomitant granting of autonomy in students' choice of research problems, all of which, in Campbell's view, amounted to "active discouragement of discipleship."

Can we then conclude that the history of cognitive psychology would have been different had Tolman taken himself more seriously, insisted on unswerving loyalty to his theory from "his" graduate students, and thereby created a more self-sustaining cognitive community? Perhaps. But as Campbell's (1974) view of "evolutionary epistemology" and the sociology of science suggest, any such community would still have had to struggle to have its view prevail in a less-than-receptive intellectual climate. Cases of resistance to the Tolman-inspired ideas of individuals such as Krech, as engagingly recounted by Garcia (1976), provide sobering examples of the strength of the opposition in the 1930s and later. Even a coherent, committed group of cognitively oriented "Tolmaniacs" would have had to face the views and assumptions of the dominant, well-entrenched behaviorist band. The fact that the primary scientific agenda, its paradigmatic problems, conceptual possibilities, and research priorities were framed by Tolman no less than by anyone else in terms of learning—rather than perception, problem-solving, language, or thinking—is a significant sign of those times. (There were of course some, such as Zener at Duke in the late 1930s and early 1940s, who consistently cast their teaching and writing in "alternative" terms.)

In assessing Tolman's significance, one would do well to take the broader and long-term view, especially since intellectual influence is given and received in varied forms, not always amounting to direct and immediate leadership and discipleship. These are voices from a later, changing time: Bruner et al.'s (1956) laudatory references to Tolman's metaphor or model of intervening cognitive maps; Miller et al. (1960) paying homage to him among other early cognitive theorists; the recent spate of studies on spatial cognition, some surveyed by Neisser (1976) in a chapter entitled "Cognitive Maps"; and, more notably, Simon's (1947) acknowledgment of James and Tolman as the major sources of the psychological conceptions embedded in his own work, begun in the 1930s, on administrative decision making. Serving as an early intellectual inspiration for a line of thought that culminates in the Nobel Prize would doubtless have struck someone given to "playful self-deprecation" as a pleasing irony. In our judgment, any comprehensive history of cognitive psychology would have to regard Tolman as one of several persons who gave cognitive notions genuine currency in the 1930s and kept such notions alive for later generations.

Bartlett and Schemata

Whereas later generations have made genuine (if general) bows in Tolman's direction, that much homage and more has been paid to Frederic Bartlett. We have already recorded Bruner's appreciation of Bartlett and Neisser's (1967) characterization of cognitive psychology's constructivism as "more closely related to Bartlett than to any other contemporary psychologist." Since the late 1960s, his standing has steadily strengthened, and Neisser's (1976) critique of contemporary cognitive psychology for its lack of ecological validity (see Brunswik, 1944, 1947)—notably but not exclusively in the area of memory—is built upon a Bartlett foundation stone:

> It was from Cambridge that Bartlett launched his quixotic challenge to the memory establishment of the 1920s and the 1930s. He was convinced that his contemporaries understood neither the purpose nor the nature of memory, and that standard laboratory procedures just obscure its real characteristics. His challenge went almost unheard for 40 years . . . but it is unheard no longer. There is suddenly a host of theorists talking about "schemata" (e.g., Rumelhart, 1975; Anderson, 1977) and a host of experimenters studying memory for stories (Bransford & Johnson, 1972; Mandler & Johnson, 1977). In my view this work is somewhat deficient in ecological validity . . . but it is still a great step forward. Perhaps, as someone once said of something, the naturalistic study of memory is an idea whose time has come. (Neisser, 1982, p. 3–4)

The currency of Barlett's ideas and the acknowledgment of his importance are reason enough for paying him extended attention in any historical account; but there is yet another. Thanks largely to his own accounts, modestly and gracefully integrated into his two principal works (Bartlett, 1932; 1958, Chapter 8), and to those of others (Northway, 1940; Zangwill, 1972), the persons and ideas shaping Bartlett's thoughts can be discerned. Thus the future historian will have a special, if not unique, opportunity to trace a rich thread from past to present in the tapestry that is cognitive psychology. We now present the beginning of such an exercise.

The immediate starting point for Bartlett's *Remembering* (1932), announced in the Preface, was "disappointment and a growing dissatisfaction" with memory research that he had been doing for some time since 1913, employing Ebbinghaus's "exact method" of nonsense syllables.

> The upshot was that I determined to try to retain the advantages of an experimental method of approach, with its relatively controlled situations, and also to keep my study as realistic as possible. I therefore built up, or selected, material which I hoped would prove interesting in itself, and could be of the type which every normal individual deals with constantly in his daily activities. (Bartlett, 1932, p. v)

The first chapter is a subtle exposition of this stance vis-à-vis experiment in psychology, an exposition generalizable, as Bartlett fully intended, to all areas of research and timeless enough to carry much meaning today. Succeeding chapters recount how he put that point of view into research practice, with one chapter each on "perceiving" and "imagining," and five—the empirical heart of the work—on "remembering". There follow four more conceptually directed chapters, the core being "A Theory of Remembering," and seven on "Remembering as a Study in Social Psychology."

The theoretical chapters and this latter section show that Bartlett's thinking was animated by far more than a specific dissatisfaction with Ebbinghaus's experimental methods. Such dissatisfaction was, in fact, but one expression of a broader conceptual and philosophical framework that had arisen, in part, from his varied intellectual contacts. Bartlett (1958) later suggested as much in analyzing his own memory research as a case study of "Adventurous Thinking." Notes Zangwill (1972): "No one who had been a pupil of Ward and a disciple of [W. H. R.] Rivers [the anthropologist] could be expected to embrace the Ebbinghaus methods with any enthusiasm. From the beginning, Bartlett was evidently seeking methods more flexible, more life-like and more appropriate to *bring out the characteristics of remembering envisaged as an ongoing individual and social activity"* [emphasis added]. (p. 124) Thus, as Mary Northway (1940) demonstrates, it was from James Ward, the most influential Cambridge teacher in Bartlett's time, that he drew a good deal of his psychology, notably the emphasis on the active, constructive nature of perception and memory so ringingly reinforced by the *Remembering* research.

> The first notion to get rid of is that memory is primarily or literally reduplicative, or reproductive. In a world of constantly changing environment, literal recall is extraordinarily unimportant . . . Condensation, elaboration and invention are common features of ordinary remembering, and these all very often involve the mingling of materials belonging originally to different "schemata." . . . If there be one thing which I have insisted more than another throughout all the discussions of the book, it is that the description of memories as "fixed and lifeless" is merely an unpleasant fiction. (Bartlett, 1932, p. 204–205, 311)

The expression "schema," in its turn, came from Henry Head, with whom Bartlett had established a close personal relationship around the end of World War I, when Head was carrying out his pioneering work on aphasic patients and Bartlett was examining the products of his own quite different array of experiments. Given the opportunity to read and discuss Head's drafts, he came to see "schemata [as] the chief clue to reduce to order what often seemed to me the tangled mass of my own results" (Bartlett, 1958). Schema thus became the core concept in Bartlett's (1932) attempt to account theoretically for the actively organized, constructive character of remembering:

> "Schema" refers to an active organization of past reactions, or of past experiences, which must always be supposed to be operating in any well-adapted organic response . . . All incoming impulses of a certain kind, or mode, go together to build up an acitive, organised setting. . . . There is not the slightest reason, however, to suppose that each set of incoming impulses, each new group of experiences persists as an isolated member of some passive patchwork. (p. 201)

Now, 50 years later, "considerable psychological interest has developed in abstract knowledge structures or *schemata"* (Abelson, 1981), and "schemata are assumed to guide constructive comprehension activities as well as reconstructive processes at the time of remembering" (Bransford, 1979). Have we thus a case of clear continuity, an unbroken line of influence from Bartlett to the present pattern of theory and research? Some of the following observations suggest that, as ever, intellectual life does not unfold quite so simply.

What is beyond question is that for at least 30 years after 1932, Bartlett was barely recognized. In a world of highly energetic memory research, the Ebbinghaus mold—associationist in conception and nonsense-syllabic in experimental form—stringently set the pattern, leaving little space for an alternative approach. Writing relatively recently Zangwill (1972) observed: "By and large, what one may call the verbal learning industry has paid scant attention to this stricture [that the use of artificially simplified material . . . leads to the neglect of important principles of organization over time] and operates for the most part with materials and methods which we students of Bartlett's in the thirties would have regarded as quaintly old-fashioned." (p. 132)

Yet the world was changing as Zangwill spoke, and barely a decade later, the memory mold had been manifestly broken and recast along cognitive constructivist lines (Cofer, 1977; Jenkins, 1974). At least some of the researchers responsible for this revision acknowledge drawing their initial inspiration and some of their orienting assumptions from Bartlett (e.g., Bransford, Barclay, & Franks, 1972; Bransford & Franks, 1971, 1972). Doubtless a full recounting of this period, of when and how particular ideas were expressed and took hold, would reveal a range of relevant circumstances, events, and personages. But we are confident that history will record that after some four decades, Bartlett's general constructivist view of memory and other aspects of cognition was given its due on the American side of the Atlantic.

Is it true that in Great Britain, by contrast, Bartlett was accepted early and widely? At a general professional level he certainly was, having made a "great contribution to the development of experimental psychology in Britain [and] of the work of the Department which he built up and fostered over a period of some 30 years" (Zangwill, 1972), as well as virtually singlehandedly creating the famed Applied Psychology Unit at Cambridge. In theory and research, however, the picture is not unlike that for Tolman. Although Bartlett had a number of students eminent in their own right (notably Donald Broadbent and Brenda Milner), none of them could be said to be true-believing "Bartlettians." Moreover, there are hints that if no loyalist tradition took hold at Cambridge, if a 1930s memory theory now seen by many to have been the best was not widely pursued and promulgated, the reason lies partly in a "default in leadership" that may have had roots similar to Tolman's. This notion is suggested to us by the modest tones of Bartlett's writing and corroborated by Zangwill (1972), whose own memory research diverged early on from Bartlett:

> I was myself an undergraduate in his Department not long after the book appeared and remember vividly the lively discussions it provoked, in which—characteristically—the author was often his own most incisive critic . . . I was—and am—deeply impressed by *Remembering* but, if some of my remarks should strike a critical note, I do not think this would have been taken by my predecessor in office to imply disrespect. It was he, after all, who taught us how to criticize. (p. 123)

Honoring such a spirit we close this section with two brief considerations of Bartlett and schema that indicate how a more complete historical account can be developed, though it may, to some degree, "diminish" Bartlett's standing. First, Paul (1967) reminds us: "The term 'schema' was not new to psychology when Bartlett chose to employ it. Among students of thinking and problem solving it was often used to denote a frame or plan of operation that needs to be filled in (see Woodworth, 1938). Oldfield and Zangwill (1942–1943) and Brain (1950) have discussed the origins and definitions of the schema concept". (p. 220). And Woodworth (1938) is worth noting for more than just his nine index entries for schema. Estes (1981) observes:

> Virtually every modern treatise on memory or cognitive psychology reviews fully the extent to which, prior to about 1960, research and theory on memory was almost wholly dominated by behaviorism, associationism, and the empirical foundations of functional psychology . . . [Yet] the thumbnail sketch of the modern view of memorizing given in the preceding paragraph [in terms of groups or even larger structures, meaningful components and relationships] is in fact a paraphrase, close to a verbatim transcription, of the summary of the memorizing process given in Woodworth. Further, Woodworth indicates that the passage actually was included in precisely that form of the mimeographed edition of the chapters written 25 years before its actual publication. . . . So much for the purportedly revolutionary changes in outlook from the simple connectionist to the cognitive outlook on verbal memory. . . . It seems undeniable that in instance after instance Woodworth's general outlook, orienting ideas, and conceptual framework are scarcely discernibly different from those taken to characterize modern cognitive psychology (p. 329)

A host of intriguing questions and issues spring to mind. For example, where lay the origins of Woodworth's prescient point of view around 1910–1915, when he began writing the book? Having given unequal time to one of Bartlett's co-equals as a schematic cognitive psychologist, we draw this conclusion: The fact that Woodworth, an accepted major figure in U.S. experimental psychology, had minimal impact on the form and course of memory research merely highlights our point that the rich vein of ideas in schematic cognitive psychology remained essentially unmined for decades, not simply because of Tolman's or

Bartlett's default of leadership, or Bartlett's residing across the Atlantic, but more because most other experimental psychologists set their sights, circumscribed by a set of associative and scientistic spectacles, on quite different surface features of the human landscape.

As our second and final consideration of schema, we call attention to the fact that the impetus for the current widespread use of the term and the allied acceptance of the role of knowledge structures in memory and comprehension arises, at least in some measure, elsewhere than in Bartlett. Abelson (1981) points out: "The concept of the schema is not new in psychology, dating back at least to Piaget and Bartlett. What is new is the growing influence on that concept of developments in artificial intelligence." It remains, therefore, for the present theorist and future historian to tease out the different shades of meaning of "schema," "script," "frame," and the like (Schank, 1980), and to trace their intellectual and social genealogies.

Interestingly, Bartlett (1932) confesses: "I strongly dislike the term 'schema.' It is at once too definite and too sketchy." In arguing that "it does not indicate what is very essential to the whole notion, that the organised mass results of past changes of position and posture are actively *doing* something all the time; are, so to speak, carried along with us, complete, though developing," Bartlett (p. 201) gives voice to a reservation that Neisser (personal communication, July 1983) holds about scripts. Cole (1983) expresses a corollary complaint: "The socially constitutive nature of cultural facts has to be built into the theory and at present is not [since] the 'schemata' and 'scripts' of cognitive science are the static imprint left by the event." These words sound a chord inspired by Bartlett and anthropology, and also suggest that the theorist and historian have here before them an intriguing agenda. In actuality, then, Bartlett's stature may be anything but diminished by these sorts of considerations.

Duncker and Gestalt Thinking

While the current wide usage of schema provides the ideal opportunity for scrutinizing how the past is woven into the fabric of current cognitive psychology, other worthwhile cases can be found. At least one is already at hand. Conducting a deft analysis of Karl Duncker's (1935) view of problem solving both in the context of his predecessors and contemporaries, and in light of current information-processing ideas, Newell (1985) seeks to answer the following questions: What have we learned since Duncker? What did he know and what were his scientific tasks? What does cognition now know and where does it stand on

Duncker's tasks? Briefly tracing the outlines of Newell's chapter will enable us not only to learn of Duncker's contributions but to give due (if abbreviated) attention to the Gestaltists and their place in schematic cognitive psychology.

Like that of his mentors Max Wertheimer and Wolfgang Köhler, most of Duncker's research and writing dealt with perception. Also like them, however, he made productive forays into the area of thinking and problem solving. In comparing what Duncker knew with what we now know, Newell (1985) considers a study in which Duncker examines how adults solve a variety of practical and mathematical problems.

As early as 1926, Duncker was writing about the processes of problem-solving; in a 1935 monograph (posthumously published in English 10 years later) he detailed and illustrated via thinking-aloud protocols what Newell considers a "full-bodied model" containing a series of mechanisms and a wide range of general heuristic methods. As an expression of the Gestaltists' core contentions against associationistic psychology, function was his theory's "crucial mediating construct, the central realization that comes to the subject when engaging in thinking" (Newell, 1985). Overall, Newell regards Duncker's process model as "by far the most explicit of his contemporaries (Luchins, Katona, Wertheimer)."

Duncker's scheme is, of course, not without its limitations; its "informality" and its "coarse-grained use" of protocols are underlined when compared with Newell and Simon's (1972) General Problem Solver (GPS). But Newell (1985) is even-handed enough to note: "In terms of general outline, GPS is just an instance of Duncker's scheme." And while the precise theory of functional value embodied in GPS is a definite advance, even this, concedes Newell, "is not all gain . . . A trade-off invariably occurs when attaining added precision in theoretical formulation. We can project from this what a general theory of functions might actually be like, but GPS hardly provides this, nor does other modern work" (p. 404).

In one other respect, however, modern work has, in Newell's view, produced a noteworthy advance over the Gestalt position on problem-solving—namely, in proposing and validating a detailed array of executive search strategies that lie at the heart of the information-processing view of intelligent activity. Yet even here, where varied ways of working forward (e.g., heuristic search) and backward (e.g., means-end analysis) are—contra the Gestaltists—considered symmetrical, Newell (1985) notes: "We must be careful in this claim [because] Duncker genuinely makes room for search in his theory, separating himself thereby from the other Gestaltists."

Newell then considers Duncker's treatment of insight and once again balances the limitations through a careful analysis, leading to the conclusion that Duncker's theoretical agenda was commendably consistent with later cognitive psychology, since he was "attempting to pose the question of what elementary information processes need to exist for the problem solver to reason. He was not saying that some special and unanalyzable process called insight occurred" (Newell, 1985). We might reasonably wonder, then, about the extent of Duncker's influence, both on his contemporaries and succeeding generations. Is Duncker to be regarded as a major figure in the founding of cognitive psychology? And if not, was it only his early death (at age 37) that stood in the way?

The answers to those questions, both largely in the negative, emerge from Newell's discussion of the last part of Duncker's monograph, where the focus is on a particular phenomenon, functional fixity. A string of ironies unwinds here, stretching across and highlighting the distance between the schematic cognitive psychologists and the conceptual and methodological preoccupations of most of their peers. Newell (1985) underscores how a discipline's or subfield's preoccupations and preferences, both theoretical and methodological, can color the intellectual contacts that are (and are not) made within and across scientific generations.

> This is the smallest part of the monograph . . . Yet it had by far the largest impact. Functional fixity generated one of the major streams of research in problem-solving until the shift to information processing. . . . It became included in the problem of set. . . . There followed an enumeration of independent variables that affected the formation of set of one kind or another, with experimental demonstrations of which way the effects went. . . . Little increase occurred in understanding theoretically what processes caused set. This simply reflects the general distance of the forties and fifties from an adequate and accepted model of processing, the area being in no wise special vis-à-vis the larger Zeitgeist of experimental psychology. *This provides a direct explanation of why psychology chose this third part of Duncker, leaving all the rest either unattended or simply grist for overviews or reviews. Duncker's own approach in this third part meshed exactly with the experimental attitudes and capabilities of the times, and his findings were provocative enough to provide issues to pursue* [italics added]. . . . The research simple ceased [in the early sixties], because modern cognitive psychology shifted its concerns to internal memory structure and problem-solving processes [the latter much like the earlier sections of Duncker] . . . [And yet] the modern theory of problem-solving has not made great strides in predicting why problems are difficult. Functional fixity remains an item of our agenda, though there seems no way to predict when it will capture our attention again. (p. 413–416)

Newell provides a fine example of one way to analyze cognitive psychology historically, not least because of the critical yet generous light in which he has cast the past and its possible connections to the present:

> I have found things in Duncker I did not find or understand twenty years ago [when I first encountered his writing]. These seem central to his own research—

therefore not of my own construction—and also consistent with what modern cognitive psychology is trying to do and understand. Could anything more be asked from a modest historical exercise? Yes, perhaps one more thing: That we not forget how far Duncker had come in his understanding. (Newell, 1985, p. 417)

In summary, if Newell is correct and is heeded, the future historian of cognitive psychology might record, first, that the Gestaltists' theory of thinking, at least as expounded by Duncker, eventually came to be assimilated into the cognitive mainstream; and second, that it thereby lived a longer intellectual life than their conceptual accounts of perception which, while better known, seemed to stall just as the cognitive movement was accelerating (Mandler & Mandler, 1964). Whether the future historian will also record cognitive psychology's return to the problems of functional fixity and set, at a higher conceptual level and in a more flexible mode of experimentation than in the past, remains to be seen.

Forgotten Forebears

Since Newell's emphasis on Duncker's importance for the pattern of current cognitive psychology renders valuable service, might not the same sort of attention be profitably paid to other schematic writers and researchers? In this section we offer four capsule commentaries that serve to extend our notes toward the decades immediately adjacent to the turn of the century, and so toward psychology's formal founding.

1. *Selz, Würzburg, and the processes of thought.* Although not directly concerned with Duncker's intellectual forebears, Newell (1985) nevertheless appends this footnote: "The Mandlers (Mandler & Mandler, 1964) . . . treat Otto Selz (1913, 1922) . . . as the repeatedly rediscovered skeleton in cognitive psychology's closet . . . , who understood essential elements of a processing explanation of thinking." It is indeed the case that the Mandlers and a few others (e.g., de Groot, 1964; Humphrey, 1951) have found in Selz admired anticipations of key contemporary notions.

Mandler and Mandler (1964) note that, whereas "Duncker started his analysis . . . within a framework very similar to Selz's," the ground for the latter's theoretical contributions had been laid by "the essentially descriptive work of the Würzburg school." That work, produced principally around the turn of the century by Ach, Külpe, and others, called attention to imageless thought, set, and other phenomena that severely undercut Edward Bradford Titchener's sensationistic and atomistic view of mind.

Selz's primary reaction was against the constellation theory of the associationists . . . However, he also represents the confluence of another point of view insofar as some of his ideas can be traced to the act psychology of Brentano and to Meinong in particular. It seems plausible that one of Selz's main contributions—the notion of *the actively processing mental apparatus* [italics added]—derives from the influence of the German philosophers. (Mandler & Mandler, p, 224)

Since his was "the first voice in the early twentieth century to call for a psychology of thinking that dealt primarily with processes rather than with contents," the Mandlers conclude that "probably the major turning point in the history of thinking came with the work of Otto Selz." They thus record with regret that he "restricted his work in subsequent years, spent in a minor academic position in Mannheim, to a restatement of his position, and much of the psychology of thinking between 1920 and 1950 might have advanced faster had he been given proper recognition" (Mandler & Mandler, 1964).

We find it heartening that Selz's writings were later rediscovered—for example, in Newell, Shaw, and Simon's (1958) initial exposition of an information-processing point of view and in a more recent, extended review by Frijda and de Groot (1981). The field can only benefit from debate on the place and significance of Selz as a schematic cognitive psychologist (Blumenthal, 1983).

2. *Bühler, Würzburg, and psycholinguistics.* In a number of respects, history has taken similar turns in the case of Selz's Würzburg colleague, Karl Bühler. In a series of studies on thinking and memory, Bühler (1907) produced findings extensively cited by Külpe, Selz, and others, developed a related "imageless thought" conception that "presages the concern with the unit of thought that was to reach full flowering in the next decade" (Mandler & Mandler, 1964), engaged Wundt in extended debate over the appropriateness of experimentation in studying higher mental processes, and later criticized Koffka for failing to give Selz due credit in his (Koffka's) theory of thinking (Bühler, 1926). Willem Levelt (1981) notes: "Something . . . which seems to have been completely forgotten about Bühler is the fact that he moved psycholinguistics into the laboratory, something George Miller had to accomplish again half a century later . . . [in 1908 measuring] comprehension latencies for complex sentences" (p. 190).

Bühler's significance for a comprehensive history of cognitive psychology is underscored by the following three considerations: First, he moved from his experimental work to a rich theoretical *oeuvre* on the psychology of language, culminating in the publication of his *Sprachtheorie* in 1934. Second, this work was, for many years, essentially ignored, while Bühler "spent the last 23 years of his life [until his death in

1963] in total oblivion in America" (Levelt, 1981). Third, in the past 15 years, indications of interest and appreciation have begun to appear in mainstream cognitive literature. Blumenthal (1970), for example, provides an informative summary of his intellectual and personal biography. There are also several admiring references to Bühler in a volume reviewing "the current revolution in psycholinguistics and cognitive psychology" (Weimer & Palermo, 1974) and in a cognition text (Bransford, 1979), while a passage from *Sprachtheorie* has even served as the text-to-be-remembered in a knowledge acquisition experiment (Bransford & Nitsch, 1978). Moreover, Toulmin (1972), in a critique of Chomsky, offers Bühler as an example par excellence of a non-empiricist but nevertheless functionalist account of language acquisition. For Bühler, as for Selz, the scales thus show signs of moving toward balance.

3. *Baldwin and cognitive development.* Much the same pattern can be discerned for the ideas of James Mark Baldwin, although his scholarly demise in North America earlier in this century was so precipitous, from a position of such prominence, and in large part for such an intellectually spurious reason that the recent revival of interest in his ideas seems especially just. The details of this process call for careful examination, and Kessen's (1965) perceptive account conveys the historical and substantive gist that we perceive to be significant here: A "friend and warm admirer" of William James, Baldwin was a significant figure in U.S. psychology for 15 to 20 years around the turn of the century. Combining psychological and philosophical concerns in the formulation of a genetic epistemology, he wrote three volumes (1906–1911) of *Thought and Things*. Kessen (1965) writes: "Brilliant and one of the few truly original documents in psychology, crowded with invented words and all the apparatus of a philosophical system, [it] caused a slight flurry among philosophers and was steadfastly and monotonously ignored by psychologists (p. 165).

The reasons for this treatise being ignored by Baldwin's colleages are, according to Kessen, easy to find. "Baldwin allied himself with no school. . . . He wanted to stand between the idealism of the German philosophers and the pragmatism of the Americans. . . . His distaste for the laboratory and his conviction that the ultimate ground on which an understanding of man would arise was an esthetic one made Baldwin's position utterly unassimilable to American psychology in its brawling infancy (Kessen, 1965, p. 165). Added to this was his misfortune in having to resign from academic life because of a personal scandal, whereupon he left the United States in 1909 for Mexico and France. This migration "left him without students and without a platform for the teaching of psychophilosophy. His obituary notices in American journals [in 1934] had the strange tone of describing a man who had been dead in fact for many years" (Kessen, 1965, p. 165).

There have been recent signs of Baldwin's scientific rebirth in North America. Robert Cairn's (1980) review bears the title "Developmental Theory Before Piaget: The Remarkable Contributions of James Mark Baldwin"; John Broughton (1981) provides a valuable summary of Baldwin's theoretical notions, suggesting that "the significance of Baldwin's thought [especially for cognitive developmental psychology] remains unexamined and unappreciated"; and the wide range of papers in a volume edited by Broughton and John Freeman-Moir (1982) provide much grist for the historical mill. For one thing, the specific nature of the intellectual links between Baldwin and Piaget is still subject to discussion, even though the general character of Baldwin's influence has been identified. Be that as it may, the basis and rationale for an important chapter on Baldwin in the history of cognitive (developmental) psychology appear to have been established, though here again it remains to be seen how widespread and influential the present revival will be.

4. *Binet and away-from-associationism.* While Selz, Bühler, and Baldwin are beginning to command cognitive psychology's attention, Alfred Binet remains a long forgotten, or misremembered, forebear. As Kessen (1965) points out: "Binet was concerned with problems of reasoning and intelligence throughout his life, from his early speculative attempts to dissect all cognitive processes into associations to his last and incomplete work on a full system of psychology." Brewer (1974) records that "the first empirical work to support the memory for ideas approach was the early paper of Binet and Henri (1894). . . . This was an extraordinarily thoughtful paper, but due to the associationist–behaviorist trend of memory research, it dropped into obscurity." (p. 275)

Do we stand to gain much from recovering or reconstructing our memory for Binet's ideas? Reeves (1965) answers with a clear affirmative:

> Binet is buried for most people under a distribution of IQs. . . . Never was an author so in need of disinterment. Historians do indeed treat him with respect . . . But Binet remains the man of tests in the textbooks. . . . One can at least start to remove some misconceptions, allow the writer Binet to say something for himself and begin thus to suggest his possible value to us now. For thinking and intelligence were Binet's main concern. He brought to their scrutiny a varied set of skills: training in law, histology and experimentation, wide reading in philosophical as well as physiological psychology, experience in hospitals, schools and society, a sense both of evidence and of daily living, a healthy detestation of narrowly based experimentation, coupled with experience of the power of suggestion, very wide sympathies in the sciences and the arts, and mastery of a lucid

and entertaining style. These were allied with an almost dangerous enterprise in inquiry. One suspects, indeed, that he must at times have been the *enfant terrible* of the august Sorbonne . . . He died, at the height of his powers, in 1911, on the point, it seems, of trying to integrate all he had learnt into a coherent account of thinking. . . . Binet's writing has immense historical worth and, one would like to think, rather more than this, For it reflects, at one extreme, an almost purely mechanical associationism, fathered by forerunners such as Spencer, Mill, and Taine. By the end, simple associationism is completely gone. Instead we find a sketch of thinking, in dynamic terms, as a process remote from a succession of conscious states. Binet treats it as an *a*conscious, because personally involved, activity. Known only as a result of its products, thinking, for him, is in some degree the activity of a whole personality, in which action, feeling and *un*conscious motor attitudes play a vital (though not an exclusive) role. . . . And about the middle of this chronological development from associationism to a view that is very different, we find Binet writing about imageless thought. . . . If simple associationism had to be buried, it is lucky to have been calculated, chess-played and dramatized out in such a richly elegant and entertaining funeral. (p. 185–187, 194)

This engaging example of what Binet's "disinterment" could reveal is sufficient to suggest that he not only has possible value to us now but, in his movement away from associationism toward a view of thinking in dynamic, process terms, might also serve as the prototypical case of schematic cognitive psychology around the turn of the century.

Revisiting Founding Fathers

At the end, then, we are brought back to our beginnings. Having traced some of the threads that run from modern cognitive psychology and cognitive science, through the times of turnabout in the 1950s, to a sample of schematic cognitive psychology in the first half of the 20th century, we are on the threshold of the world of psychology's founding fathers. And on the threshold we must, for lack of space, unfortunately remain. We are convinced, however, that cognitive psychology's 19th-century past is a rich repository of ideas of direct relevance to the present, and specifically that Wilhelm Wundt and William James will come to be properly portrayed as founding cognitive psychologists.

The reasons for this conviction lie in the convergence of contemporary cognitive psychology and the recent resurgence of historical scholarship. In various ways historians have brought to light valuable information for any history of cognitive psychology, as perfectly illustrated by the writings of Arthur Blumenthal (1975, 1979, and Chapter 2, this volume), Kurt Danziger (1979a, 1980a), and others on Wundt. Consistent with the spirit of Reeves's (1965) revival of Binet, they have "removed some misconceptions" about Wundt, "allowed the writer to say something for himself," and begun "to suggest his possible value to us now."

For one thing, they have revealed how, through selective and self-serving interpretation and writing on Titchener's part, several generations of psychologists have had a mistaken understanding of Wundt's views and his visions of psychology. They have also shown (Blumenthal, 1977; Danziger, 1979b) how fundamental philosophical differences and broader social forces were both at work in this process of misrepresentation and misunderstanding. And, of most direct relevance here, they have demonstrated that in his Herbartian, German idealist emphasis on the central apperceptive process as the basis of mental life, in his notion of "creative synthesis" and consequent rejection of elementism, Wundt exemplified and expressed Leibniz's famous rejounder to Locke: *Nihil est in intellectu quod non fuerit in sensu—nisi intellectus ipse* (Nothing is in the intellect that has not been in the senses—except the intellect itself). Emphasizing intellect itself from his early writings onward, Wundt was, in terms of core thematic commitments, a founding cognitive psychologist.

> What makes [his two youthful works works, the *Beitrage* of 1862 and the *Vorlesungen* of 1863] different and identifiably Wundtian is not only their interest in the specifically psychological aspects of problems, but also their emphasis on *the constructive activity of the mind* [italics added]. The latter is expressed in the concept of synthesis which forms the crucial link in his theory of sense perception and of cognition. Already at that time he characterized synthesis as "the creative act in our process of cognition" and as "that which is truly constructive in perception." (Danziger, 1980a, p. 81–82)

If this reappraisal of Wundt signals the prominence of his place in any history of cognitive psychology, it strikes us as equally significant that as cognitive psychology now confronts and debates key issues, historical material is, in many instances, on hand to provide important perspective. As Ericsson and Simon (1980, 1982) and others (e.g., Dennett, 1982) reopen the question of sources of evidence in the study of cognition and their differential value and significance, Danziger (1980b) reconsiders the history of introspection and demonstrates that a variety of positions were taken at the turn of the century on its theory and practice. While Sampson (1981) faults both information processing and Piagetian versions of cognitive psychology for their excessively individualistic orientation, and while Cole (1983) and Toulmin (1978) commend Vygotsky's view of mental life as embedded in social and cultural contexts, Danziger (1980a) and Leary (1979) remind us of Wundt's *Völkerpsychologie*, his emphasis on the historical–cultural character of all higher mental processes, and the consequent distinction, drawn from Dilthey, between *Geistes-* and *Naturwissenschaften*. And as Zajonc (1980) and Lazarus (1982) revive debate over relationships between affect and cognition,

Blumenthal (1975) discusses Wundt's tridimensional theory of feeling and his speculation that affect is the byproduct of apperceptive synthesis.

At this point, and with thoughts that focus naturally on William James, our agenda for a future comprehensive history can be completed thus: to derive substantive value from the scholarly rediscovery of Wundt, to envisage doing the same for James, and, more generally, to extend the encouraging examples of the convergence between cognitive psychology's present and its nineteenth- and twentieth-century past, and thereby to deepen our vision of, and in, psychology's future. In reviving those fundamental issues about the nature and workings of the mind that concerned Wundt, James, Binet, Bartlett, and others, contemporary cognitive psychology would appear to have brought psychology full circle. It remains to be determined whether, and in what ways, this course of conceptual growth has followed a helix, with cognitive psychology now at a higher and more insightful level (Bevan, 1985). We can think of no better overall question to carry forward the quest for a comprehensive history of cognitive psychology.

REFERENCES

Abelson, R. P. (1981). Psychological status of the script concept. *American Psychologist, 36,* 715–729.

Adams, D. K. (1929). Experimental studies of adaptive behavior in cats. *Comparative Psychology Monographs, 6* (Serial No. 27).

Anderson, R. C. (1977). The notion of schemata and the educational enterprise. In R. C. Anderson, R. T. Spiro, & W. E. Montague Eds.), *Schooling and the acquisition of knowledge.* Hillsdale, NJ: Erlbaum.

Anderson, R. C., & Ausubel, D. P. (Eds.). (1965). *Readings in the psychology of cognition.* New York: Holt.

Baldwin, J. M. (1906–1911). *Thought and things: A study of the development and meaning of thought.* New York: Macmillan.

Bartlett, F. C. (1932). *Remembering: A study in experimental and social psychology.* Cambridge: Cambridge University Press.

Bartlett, F. C. (1958). *Thinking: An experimental and social study.* New York: Basic Books.

Bevan, W. (1985). The journey is everything. In S. Hulse (Ed.), *100 years of psychology in America: G. Stanley Hall and the Johns Hopkins tradition.* Baltimore: Johns Hopkins University Press.

Binet, A., & Henri, V. (1894). La mémoire des phrases. *L'Année Psychologique, 1,* 24–59.

Blumenthal, A. L. (1970). *Language and psychology.* New York: Wiley.

Blumenthal, A. L. (1975). A reappraisal of Wilhelm Wundt. *American Psychologist, 30,* 1081–1088.

Blumenthal, A. L. (1977). Wilhelm Wundt and early American psychology: A clash of two cultures. *Annals of the New York Academy of Sciences, 29,* 13–20.

Blumenthal, A. L. (1979). The founding father we never knew: Review of works by Wilhelm Wundt. *Contemporary Psychology, 24,* 547–550.

Blumenthal, A. L. (1983). A rediscovery of the forgotten work of Otto Selz [Review of *Otto Selz: His contribution to psychology*]. *Contemporary Psychology, 28,* 705–707.

Brain, W. R. (1950). The concept of the schema in neurology and psychiatry. In D. Richter (Ed.), *Perspectives in neuropsychiatry.* London: Lewis.

Bransford, J. D. (1979). *Human cognition.* Belmont, CA: Wadsworth.

Bransford, J. D., Barclay, J. R., & Franks, J. J. (1972). Sentence memory: A constructive versus interpretive approach. *Cognitive Psychology, 3,* 193–209.

Bransford, J. D., & Franks, J. J. (1971). The abstraction of linguistic ideas. *Cognitive Psychology, 2,* 331–350.

Bransford, J. D. & Franks, J. J. (1972). The abstraction of linguistic ideas: A review. *Cognition, 1,* 211–249.

Bransford, J. D. & Johnson, M. K. (1972). Contextual prerequisites for understanding. *Journal of Verbal Learning and Verbal Behavior, 11,* 717–726.

Bransford, J. D., & Nitsch, K. E. (1978). Coming to understand things we could not previously understand. In J. F. Kavanaugh & W. Strange (Eds.), *Speech and language in the laboratory, school and clinic.* Cambridge, MA: MIT Press.

Brewer, W. F. (1974). The problem of meaning and interrelations of the higher mental processes. In W. B. Weimer & D. S. Palermo (Eds.), *Cognition and the symbolic processes.* Hillsdale, NJ: Erlbaum.

Broughton, J. M. (1981). The genetic psychology of James Mark Baldwin. *American Psychologist, 36,* 396–407.

Broughton, J. M., & Freeman-Moir, D. J. (1982). *The cognitive developmental psychology of James Mark Baldwin.* Norwood, NJ: Ablex.

Brown, R., & Bellugi, U. (Eds.). (1964). The acquisition of language. *Monographs of the Society for Research in Child Development, 29* (Serial No. 92).

Bruner, J. S. (1980). Intellectual autobiography. In G. Lindzey (Ed.), *History of psychology in autobiography* (Vol. 7). San Francisco: Freeman.

Bruner, J. S. (1983). *In search of mind: Essays in autobiography.* New York: Harper & Row.

Bruner, J. S., Goodnow, J. J., & Austin, G. A. (1956). *A study of thinking.* New York: Wiley

Brunswik, E. (1944). Distal focusing of perception: Size constancy in a representative sample of situations. *Psychological Monographs* (Whole No. 254).

Brunswik, E. (1947). *Systematic and representative design of psychological experiments.* Berkeley: University of California Press.

Bühler, K. (1907). Tatsachen und Problemen zu einer Psychologie der Denkvorgänge: Ueber Gedanken. *Archiv für die gesamte Psychologie, 12,* 1–23.

Bühler, K. (1926). Die "neue Psychologie" Koffkas. *Zeitschrift für Psychologie, 99,* 145–159.

Bühler, K. (1934). *Sprachtheorie.* Jena: Fischer.

Cairns, R. B. (1980). Developmental theory before Piaget: The remarkable contributions of James Mark Baldwin: Reviews of works by Baldwin. *Contemporary Psychology, 25,* 438–440.

Campbell, D. T. (1974). Evolutionary epistemology. In P. A. Schilpp (Ed.), *The philosophy of Karl Popper.* La Salle, IL: Open Court.

Campbell, D. T. (1979). A tribal model of the social system vehicle carrying scientific knowledge. *Knowledge: Creation, Diffusion, Utilization, 1,* 181–201.

Cofer, C. N. (1977). On the constructive theory of memory. In I. C. Uzgiris & F. Weizmann (Eds.), *The structuring of experience.* New York: Plenum.

Cofer, C. N. (1978). Origins of the Journal of Verbal Learning and Verbal Behavior. *Journal of Verbal Learning and Verbal Behavior, 17,* 113–126.

Cole, M. (1983). Society, mind and development. In F. S. Kessel & A. W. Siegel (Eds.), *The child and other cultural inventions*. New York: Praeger.

Collins, A. (1977). Why cognitive science. *Cognitive Science, 1*, 1–2.

Danziger, K. (1979a). The positivist repudiation of Wundt. *Journal of the History of the Behavioral Sciences, 15*, 205–230.

Danziger, K. (1979b). The social origins of modern psychology. In A. R. Buss (Ed.), *Psychology in social context*. New York: Irvington.

Danziger, K. (1980a). Wundt and the two traditions of psychology. In R. W. Rieber (Ed.), *Wilhelm Wundt and the making of a scientific psychology*. New York: Plenum.

Danziger, K. (1980b). The history of introspection reconsidered. *Journal of the History of the Behavioral Sciences, 16*, 241–262.

de Groot, A. D. (1964). *Thought and choice in chess*. The Hague: Mouton.

Dennett, D. C. (1978). *Brainstorms: Philosophical essays on mind and psychology*. Montgomery, VT: Bradford.

Dennett, D. C. (1982). How to study human consciousness empirically, or nothing comes to mind. *Synthese, 53*, 159–180.

Duncker, K. (1926). A qualitative (experimental and theoretical) study of productive thinking (solving of comprehensible problems). *Pedagogical Seminary, 33*, 642–708.

Duncker, K. (1935). *Zur Psychologie des produktiven Denkens*. Berlin: Springer.

Duncker, K. (1945). On problem solving. *Psychological Monographs, 58*, (Whole No. 270).

Ericsson, K. A., & Simon, H. A. (1980). Verbal reports as data. *Psychological Review, 87*, 215–251.

Ericsson, K. A., & Simon, H. A. (1982). Sources of evidence in cognition: A historical overview. In T. V. Merluzzi, C. R. Glass, & M. Genest (Eds.), *Cognitive assessment*. New York: Guildford Press.

Estes, W. K. (1975). The state of the field. In W. K. Estes (Ed.), *Handbook of learning and cognitive processes* (Vol. 1). Hillsdale, NJ: Erlbaum.

Estes, W. K. (1981). The Bible is out [Review of R. S. Woodworth, Experimental psychology]. *Contemporary psychology, 26*, 327–330.

Flavell, J. H. (1963). *The developmental psychology of Jean Piaget*. New York: Van Nostrand.

Frijda, N. H., & de Groot, A. D. (Eds.). (1981). *Otto Selz: His contribution to psychology*. The Hague: Mouton.

Garcia, J. (1976). I. Krechevsky and I. In L. Petrinovich & J. L. McGaugh (Eds.), *Knowing, thinking, and believing: Festschrift for David Krech*. New York: Plenum.

Gleick, J. (1983, August 21). Exploring the labyrinth of the mind. *The New York Times Magazine*, p. 23ff.

Harper, R. J. C., Anderson, C. C., Christensen, C. M., & Hunka, S. M. (Eds.). (1964). *The cognitive processes: Readings*. Englewood Cliffs, NJ: Prentice-Hall.

Haugeland, J. (1978). The nature and plausibility of cognitivism. *The Behavioral and Brain Sciences, 1*, 215–260.

Haugeland, J. (Ed.). (1981). *Mind design: Philosophy, psychology, and artificial intelligence*. Cambridge, MA: MIT Press.

Hebb, D. O. (1949). *The organization of behavior*. New York: Wiley.

Hebb, D. O. (1960). The American revolution. *American Psychologist, 15*, 735–745.

Hebb, D. O. (1980). *Essay on mind*. Hillsdale, NJ: Erlbaum.

Heilbut, A. (1983). *Exiled in paradise: German refugee artists and intellectuals in America*. New York: Viking.

Holton, G. (1973). *Thematic origins of scientific thought*. Cambridge, MA: Harvard University Press.

Holton, G. (1978). *The scientific imagination: Case studies.* Cambridge: Cambridge University Press.

Hull, C. L. (1920). Quantitative aspects of the evolution of concepts. *Psychological Monographs, 28,* (Whole No. 123).

Humphrey, G. (1951). *Thinking.* London: Methuen.

Hunt, M. (1982). *The universe within: A new science explores the human mind.* New York: Simon & Schuster.

Jackman, J. C., & Borden, C. M. (Eds.). (1983). *The muses flee Hitler: Cultural transfer and adaptation, 1930–1945.* Washington, DC: Smithsonian Institute Press.

Jenkins, J. J. (1974). Remember that old theory of memory? Well, forget it! *American Psychologist, 29,* 785–795.

Kessel, F. S. (1982). Developmental psychology and epistemology. *Methodology and Science, 15,* 1–20, 101–130.

Kessen, W. (1965). *The child.* New York: Wiley.

Kessen, W., & Kuhlman, C. (Eds.). (1962). Thought in the young child. *Monographs of the Society for Research in Child Development, 27,* (Serial No. 83).

Krantz, D. L., & Wiggins, L. (1973). Personal and impersonal channels of recruitment in the growth of theory. *Human Development, 16,* 133–156.

Lachman, R., Lachman, J., & Butterfield, E. C. (1979). *Cognitive psychology and information processing.* Hilldsdale, NJ: Erlbaum.

Lazarus, R. S. (1982). Thoughts on the relations between emotion and cognition. *American Psychologist, 37,* 1019–1024.

Leary, D. E. (1979). Wundt and after: Psychology's shifting relations with the natural sciences, social sciences and philosophy. *Journal of the History of the Behavioral Sciences, 15,* 231–241.

Levelt, W. J. M. (1981). Deja vu? *Cognition, 10,* 187–192.

Mandler, G. (1981, August). *What is cognitive Psychology? What isn't?* Paper presented at the meeting of the American Psychological Association, Los Angeles.

Mandler, J. M., & Johnson, N. S. (1977). Remembrance of things parsed: Story structure and recall. *Cognitive Psychology, 9,* 111–151.

Mandler, J. M., & Mandler, G. (1964). *Thinking: From association to Gestalt.* New York: Wiley.

Miller, G. A. (1979). *A very personal history.* Unpublished manuscript, Massachusetts Institute of Technology, Center for Cognitive Science, Cambridge, MA.

Miller, G. A., Galanter, E., & Pribram, K. H. (1960). *Plans and the structure of behavior.* New York: Holt, Rinehart & Winston.

Miller, J. (1983). *States of mind.* New York: Pantheon.

Neisser, U. (1967). *Cognitive psychology.* New York: Appleton-Century-Crofts.

Neisser, U. (1976). *Cognition and reality.* San Francisco: Freeman.

Neisser, U. (1982). *Memory observed: Remembering in natural contexts.* San Francisco: Freeman.

Newell, A. (1985). Duncker on thinking: An inquiry into progress in cognition. In S. Koch & D. Leary (Eds.), *A century of psychology as science.* New York: McGraw-Hill.

Newell, A., Shaw, J. D., & Simon, H. A. (1958). Elements of a theory of human problem solving. *Psychological Review, 65,* 151–166.

Newell, A., & Simon, H. A. (1972). *Human problem solving.* Englewood Cliffs, NJ: Prentice-Hall.

Northway, M. L. (1940). The concept of the "schema." *British Journal of Psychology, 30,* 316–325.

Oldfield, R. C., & Zangwill, O. L. (1942-1943). Head's concept of the schema and its application in contemporary British psychology. *British Journal of Psychology, 32,* 267–286; *33,* 58–64, 113–129, 143–149.

Paul, I. H. (1967). The concept of schema in memory theory. In R. R. Holt (Ed.), *Motives and thought.* New York: International Universities Press.

Pylyshyn, Z. (1978). Computational models and empirical constraints. *The Behavioral and Brain Sciences, 1,* 93–128.

Pylyshyn, Z. (1980). Computation and cognition: Issues in the foundations of cognitive science. *The Behavioral and Brain Sciences, 3,* 111–169.

Reeves, J. W. (1965). *Thinking about thinking.* London: Methuen.

Rumelhart, D. E. (1975). Notes on a schema for stories. In D. G. Bobrow & A. Collins (Eds.), *Representation and understanding.* New York: Academic.

Sampson, E. E. (1981). Cognitive psychology as ideology. *American Psychologist, 36,* 730–743.

Schank, R. C. (1980). What's a schema anyway? [Review of *Paragraph structure inference* and *New directions in discourse processing*]. *Contemporary Psychology, 25,* 814–816.

Selz, O. (1913). *Ueber die Gesetze des geordneten Denkverlaufs.* Stuttgart: Spemann.

Selz, O. (1922). *Zur Psychologie des produktiven Denkens und des Irrtums.* Bonn: Cohen.

Simon, H. A. (1947). *Administrative behavior.* New York: Macmillan.

Tolman, E. C. (1951). *Collected papers in psychology.* Berkeley: University of California Press.

Toulmin, S. (1972). *Human understanding.* New York: Oxford University Press.

Toulmin, S. (1978, Sept. 28). The Mozart of psychology: Review of works by L. S. Vygotsky. *New York Review of Books,* pp. 51–57.

Weimer, W. B., & Palermo, D. S. (Eds.). (1974). *Cognition and the symbolic processes.* Hillsdale, NJ: Erlbaum.

Woodworth, R. S. (1938). *Experimental psychology.* New York: Holt.

Zajonc, R. B. (1980). Feeling and thinking: Preferences need no inferences. *American Psychologist, 35,* 151–175.

Zangwill, O. L. (1972). Remembering revisited. *Quarterly Journal of Experimental Psychology, 24,* 123–138.

Zener, K. (1937). The significance of behavior accompanying conditioned salivary secretion for theories of the conditioned response. *American Journal of Psychology, 50,* 384–403.

Ziman, J. (1983). [Review of *The cognitive paradigm*]. *Society for Social Studies of Science Review, 6,* 15–17.

11

Gestalt Psychology: Origins in Germany and Reception in the United States*

MITCHELL G. ASH

INTRODUCTION

In recent years, scholarship in the history of psychology has taken increasing account of the roles of philosophical presuppositions and social and institutional contexts in the development of psychological thinking (see Ash, 1983; Woodward, 1980; Woodward & Ash, 1982). Gestalt theory was more than a point of view within psychology; it was also a worldview and a philosophy of science (Henle, 1965, 1980; Wertheimer, 1980). The emergence of worldviews in science is seldom a matter of coincidence or personal temperament alone; such views are usually propounded as answers to challenges posed by the social and

* This chapter was supported in part by grant Fr 132/16-1, "Psychology in Exile," of the German Research Council (Werner D. Fröhlich, Project Director, Psychological Institute, University of Mainz). Part Two includes material translated by the author from his article, "Disziplinentwicklung und Wissenschaftstransfer: Deutschsprachige Psychologen in der Emigration," (Berichte zur Wissenschaftsgeschichte, 1984, 7, 207–226, by permission). Quotations from archival sources are given by permission of the holders, here gratefully acknowledged.

cultural environments of their creators. Moreover, the founders of Gestalt theory and many of their students emigrated from Germany, where the theory was first developed, to the United States in the 1920s and 1930s. They were thus required to subject a theoretical approach developed in one sociocultural situation to the demands of another, different situation.

This chapter cannot substitute for a comprehensive history of Gestalt theory. It does not offer a systematic summary of Gestalt psychology, nor does it attempt a final assessment of its contribution.[1] Instead, it presents a preliminary discussion of two historical aspects of Gestalt theory. The first section sets the emergence of Gestalt theory in its institutional and intellectual contexts, emphasizing the complex identity problem of experimental psychology in Germany and concluding with a brief summary of its development and reception in the Weimar period (1920–1933). The second section shows how the reception of Gestalt theory in the United States reflected the significantly different institutional and intellectual situation of experimental psychology in that country. (The work of Kurt Lewin and his students requires and deserves separate treatment and therefore will not be considered here.)

GESTALT THEORY IN GERMANY

The Institutional Background

In the second decade of the twentieth century, experimental psychology in the German-speaking countries had reached a level of organization characteristic of fully developed scientific disciplines. Since Wilhelm Wundt's founding of the first institute for experimental psychology in 1879, a total of 14 laboratories had been established by 1914 (Ash, 1982, p. 26). Four journals reported experimental results, and others published work in applied and pedagogical psychology. Yet the professorships held by the discipline's leaders, Wundt's and Müller's included, were chairs of philosophy. There were historical reasons for this situation. In Germany, psychology had long been viewed as a part of philosophy, and professors of philosophy enjoyed both high social status and a certain amount of practical influence in the training of high school (*Gymnasium*) and university teachers (Ringer, 1969, pp. 110–111). In any case, experimenting psychologists believed that their methods could contribute to the solution of important philosophical problems, especially in the theory of knowledge and logic.

The man who introduced all three founders of Gestalt psychology to experimental research, Carl Stumpf, shared that belief. However,

Stumpf took a different attitude toward the organization and direction of psychological research than did Wundt. When in 1893 the Prussian official in charge of university affairs, Friedrich Althoff, offered Stumpf a professorship of philosophy in Berlin and the opportunity to establish a psychological laboratory comparable in size to Wundt's, along with a higher annual budget and more modern equipment, he refused. He proposed instead to establish a "Psychological Seminar," the more modest budget of which would be used only "to support and extend the lectures by means of exercises and demonstrations." Stumpf believed that "large-scale research in experimental psychology has objective difficulties" and "could not decide to follow the example of Wundt and the Americans in this direction" (quoted in Ash, 1980a, pp. 271–272). This attitude was apparently in line with that of the grey eminence of Berlin philosophy in those years, Wilhelm Dilthey. Dilthey supported Stumpf's appointment from the beginning, in order, as he said in a letter, "to prevent the natural–scientific radicalization of philosophy here" (Schulenburg, 1923, p. 165).

Only a few years later, in response to increased student enrollment in his courses and the appearance of a number of young scholars whom he wished to support, Stumpf altered his position. He renamed his seminar the "Psychological Institute," organized a move to larger quarters, and obtained a series of budget increases to purchase instruments. By 1914 the Berlin institute had become the second largest (physically) and the best supported (financially) in Germany (Ash, 1980a, p. 272). However, Stumpf's basic attitude toward the state of psychological research and the purpose of his institute remained the same. He writes:

> In such a young research tendency [not "science" or "discipline"] with so little developed methodology, so many sources of error, such great difficulties in the exact setting up and carrying out of experiments, it could not be the main goal to produce as many dissertations as possible. Instead, the leading aims must be these two: first, the support of the lectures by means of demonstrations and exercises; second, provision of the necessary aids for the experimental work of the director, the assistants and a few especially advanced workers. (Stumpf, 1910a, p. 203)

Among these "especially advanced workers" were nearly all of the men who later became the founders or leading coworkers of Gestalt psychology: Max Wertheimer, Kurt Koffka, Wolfgang Köhler, Johannes von Allesch, Adhemar Gelb, and Kurt Lewin. Koffka, Köhler, and Lewin received their doctorates for experimental work done in Berlin from 1906 to 1913 under Stumpf's direction. Wertheimer's first teacher was Christian von Ehrenfels in Prague. He spent two years learning experimental technique in the Berlin institute before completing his dissertation under Oswald Külpe in Würzburg in 1904 and returned often to Berlin for research and discussion (Wertheimer, 1980).

Stumpf was not interested in founding a school of psychology. As Lewin (1937) recalls: "Stumpf gave his students an unusual amount of freedom" (p. 193). What Stumpf passed along in his lectures (see Langfeld, 1937) and writings was his general orientation to research, which was characterized by two guiding principles: primary allegiance to the "immediately given," with instruments used only to specify the given more precisely; and the firm conviction that empirical psychology and the theory of knowledge are closely related.

The budget increases that Stumpf obtained for instrument purchases show that he was by no means opposed to the use of precision instruments and careful experimental techniques. Instruction in experimentation was given in Berlin in these years primarily by Friedrich Schumann and Hans Rupp, both of whom had been trained in G. E. Müller's rigorous school (see Chapter 3, this volume). However, Stumpf believed that instruments were useful "only as an introduction and aid to subjective self-observation, which remains decisive as before" (Stumpf, 1906b, p. 25). In 1890 and 1891 he engaged in a bitter polemic with Wundt over some work by one of Wundt's students on an acoustical problem, arguing that if laboratory results contradicted facts known to trained musicians, then something was wrong with the experiment. Friedrich Schumann (1904) supports this view, calling self-observation not a science, but "an art, which can be acquired only by conscientious practice" (p. 34).

Stumpf encouraged his students to acquire a general background in the natural sciences and physiology, for he maintained that only the spirit of modern science, with its "common understanding, division of labor, correction of one by the other and mutual recognition" of results, could lead to genuine progress in philosophy (Stumpf, 1910b, p. 177). Nevertheless, it is clear that for him such knowledge was only part of a more complex whole. Kant's gravest error, Stumpf (1891) writes, was his neglect of psychology:

> The theorist of knowledge cannot ignore the issue of the origin of concepts . . . [However,] the psychologist must at the same time be a theorist of knowledge, not only because judgments of knowledge are a special class of judgment-phenomenon . . . but primarily because he must have clarity about the fundamental basis of all knowledge, as anyone must for whom science is more than artisanry. (p. 508)

In a tribute to Stumpf in honor of his 70th birthday in April 1918, Wertheimer makes it clear that his teacher's views in this regard were also his own:

> As much as you love and support work in specialized science, you have nonetheless taught us to keep our gaze directed to larger questions of principle, to work toward the fruitful cooperation of psychology and the theory of knowledge, with the highest problems of philosophy in view. None of us wishes to be locked up in the workroom of specialized science.[2]

However, when Stumpf's students entered their careers, they discovered that not everyone shared these ideals. Between 1900 and 1914, attacks on "psychologism"—the idea that psychological research could help solve philosophical problems—emerged with mounting intensity. These attacks were often coupled with calls for a return to the metaphysical calling that had distinguished German philosophy in its great days. An underlying motive for such criticisms was the fact that more and more experimenting psychologists were obtaining professorships of philosophy, thanks to the majority support of natural scientists in philosophical (arts and sciences) faculties.

The clearest word in the resulting controversy was spoken by the aged Wundt (1913/1921). In his polemic, "Psychology in the Struggle for Existence," he concluded that no one should be allowed to teach in psychology "who is a mere experimenter and not at the same time a psychologically and philosophically educated man, filled with philosophical interests" (p. 543). This was not only an expression of Wundt's opinion, but also an accurate summary of the appointments policy of German university faculties (for further discussion of this controversy, see Chapter 13, this volume; Ash, 1980b).

The Intellectual Background

As Wundt's statement implies, the institutional threat to experimental psychology was not a matter of academic politics alone. Associationist psychology—or the alliance of that psychology and Newtonian mechanics—had been under attack from both outside and within the community of experimenting psychologists long before Koffka, Köhler, and Wertheimer began their training.

New Philosophies of Mind

Henri Bergson (1889/1961) wrote that experience viewed as a succession of separate, thinglike states is no less an abstraction than time as measured by the hands of a clock. According to Bergson (1889/1961, p. 4), consciousness is a spatiotemporal continuum, "an intimate organization of elements, each of which is representative of the others and neither distinguished from nor isolated by abstracting thought." Because he believed that mathematical science cannot grasp such a continuum,

Bergson declared that consciousness, or "intuition," is the province of metaphysics.

Closer to home for German experimentalists was Dilthey's critique of associationism. For Dilthey, conscious experience is not a collection of simple sensations and their corresponding images, but rather "a structured whole" combining "the intelligence, the life of instinct and feeling, and acts of will." This whole is dynamic, not static, a "living, unitary activity within us" (Dilthey, 1894/1974, pp. 144, 193–194). Dilthey was not opposed to experimental psychology, but he believed that its aims should be subordinated to the development of a typology of "forms of individuality." Only then could psychology become a genuine basis for the human studies, "a tool of the historian, the economist, the political scientist and theologian" (p. 157).

Other thinkers, among them William James, proposed revised concepts of consciousness that they hoped would be compatible with experimental work. Shortly after Bergson's first book appeared in 1889, William James criticized the conception of consciousness as a collection of constant, retrievable ideas. In such thinking, he writes, "the continuous flow of the mental stream is sacrificed, and in its place an atomism, a brickbat plan of construction, is preached, for the existence of which no good introspective grounds can be put forward" (James, 1890/1950, Vol. 1, p. 196). James's critique of atomism and his concept of the "mental stream" often lead to his being mentioned as a forerunner of Gestalt theory. However, James's later treatment of "mental compounds" reveals the limits of his critique of atomism: While the awareness of the alphabet is indeed "something new" compared with 26 awarenesses, each of a separate letter, it is "safer" to treat it as "a twenty-seventh fact, the substance and not the sum of the twenty-six simpler consciousnesses" (James, 1909, p. 188). James's "pluralistic universe" thus remained, in essence, a universe of pluralities, albeit a richer one than before.

Much the same could be said of the descriptive psychology of James's friend, Stumpf. Stumpf distinguished three classes of psychical phenomena, all of which are "immediately given": Appearances, relations, and psychical functions are each described in fine detail (Stumpf, 1906a, pp. 2ff., 5–7; 1906b, pp. 26ff.). The richness of this inventory of consciousness is comparable to that of James and far greater than that of the classical associationists, but Stumpf did not explain whether any of its items had a determinative relation with any other items.

Stumpf's younger colleague, Edmund Husserl, did offer such an explanation. Husserl's view of mind is perhaps best exemplified by his description of what he calls "meaning-giving acts":

> Experienced sensation is besouled [*beseelt*] by a certain act character, a certain grasping [*Auffassen*] or mean-ing [*Meinung*] . . . [T]he content of sensation yields, so to speak, an analogical building material for the content of the object which is presented through it; thus we speak on the one hand of sensed, on the other of perceived colors, extensions, intensities, etc. . . . The evenly distributed coloring of a globe which we see, we have not sensed. (Husserl, 1900–1901, vol. 2, pp. 75–76)

Failure to recognize the psychological primacy of this "mean-ing" experience, and thus of perception over sensation, was, in Husserl's view, the fundamental error in the associationists', and particularly David Hume's, account of consciousness. However, Husserl did not give up elementary sensations. In fact, as the statement just cited shows, he required them as analogical building blocks for perception. When some adherents of the Würzburg school took over Husserl's concept of active mind to explain their experimental results, they went still further. Külpe (1902/1914) summarizes that research: "Modern psychology teaches that sensations are products of scientific analysis . . . We do not discover elementary contents, such as simple colors or brightnesses, tones or noises, elements of any kind in our investigation of what is given in consciousness" (pp. 29–30).

Müller was predictably skeptical about such claims. He argued that the more complex processes the Würzburgers had discovered, such as "determining tendencies," could be assimilated into "pure associationist psychology" (Müller, 1913, pp. 488–489). Other experimenting psychologists were more defensive, for they realized that such criticisms went to the heart of their scientific assumptions. Moreover, research results in other areas had also begun to cast doubt on the workability of those assumptions.

Perceptual Theory and the Problems of Recognition and Form

At the beginning of the twentieth century, the terminology of perceptual theory and research had long been dominated by three overlapping dualisms: peripheral versus central processes, sensation versus intellect, and physiological versus psychological categories. For Hermann von Helmholtz, unquestionably the leading sensory physiologist of his time, these three dualisms were equivalent. Helmoholtz's concept of sensation rested on assumptions drawn from classical mechanics. Vision, for example, resulted from excitations transmitted by nerve fibers from the cones on the retinal surface; each fiber proceeds "through the trunk of the optic nerve to the brain, without touching its neighbors, and there produces its special impression" (Helmholtz, 1868/1971, p. 153; 1856–

1867/1924–1925, vol. 2, pp. 143–146). He acknowledged that the information provided by these excitations is insufficient to account for certain important facts, such as the three-dimensionality of seen objects despite the two-dimensionality of the retinal pattern, and at such points invoked psychological processes such as "unconscious inference." Perception thus became for him the product of a combination of sensory and psychical operations.

By contrast, critics pointed to other phenomena such as color contrast or tonal fusion, which Helmholtz attributed to "illusions of judgment" experienced with the same immediacy as legitimate sensations. In a memorial essay for Helmholtz, Stumpf (1895) wrote that Helmholtz's assumption of the physicists' world instead of the experiencing subject as his point of departure was the fundamental issue dividing the physiology and the psychology of the senses (see also Turner, 1982). Such criticisms did not undermine Helmholtz's authoritative position in the theory of vision, but they enhanced the plausibility of Ewald Hering's alternative view.

Hering's point of departure was the distinction between real and "seen" objects (*Sehdinge*). When we look at a piece of white cardboard from which a zigzag piece has been cut, for example, we see either a hole in the cardboard and a dark place behind it or a black patch in the plane of the cardboard; yet the retinal image is the same for both impressions (Hering, 1879, pp. 569–575). This occurs because "light sensation is not simply a function of the stimulus and the momentary state of the affected neural structures, but also depends on the state of the brain part related to visual activity, in which the optical experiences of one's whole life are contained and in some way organized" (Hering, 1920/1962, pp. 223–224). Hering once likened the relationship between psychological and physiological research to that between teams of tunnel-borers working from opposite sides of a mountain. If the two teams would only cooperate and work according to the same rules, the odds would favor their meeting in the middle.

Hering's metaphor was a more broadly phrased version of the "heuristic principle of research" offered by Ernst Mach as early as 1865:

> Every psychical event corresponds to a physical event and vice versa. Equal psychical processes correspond to equal physical processes, unequal to unequal ones. When a psychical process is analyzed in a purely psychical way into a number of qualities a, b, c, then there corresponds to them just as great a number of physical processes, α, β, γ. To all the details of psychical events correspond details of the physical events. (Mach, 1865/1965, pp. 269–270).

Müller (1896/1897) later summarized Mach's and Hering's formulations in a set of four "psychophysical axioms." Stumpf then pointed to the prospects that such rules for theory construction held for experimenting psychologists. If Müller's axioms proved correct, he wrote, psychology could become "the giver, not the taker discipline" in relation to physiology (Stumpf, 1906a, p. 7). Whether or not they had such ends in view, psychologists soon did productive research on the basis of Hering's "seen objects". In time, this led to the literature on the perceptual constancies (see Boring, 1942, pp. 288ff.). However, some of that literature also pointed up the theoretical difficulties that its findings posed for the still-conventional distinction between peripheral and central processes in perception (see Katz, 1911).

The problematic character of these dualisms was also revealed by the related problems of recognition and form perception. The Danish philosopher and psychologist Harald Höffding (1889/1890) distinguished a new quality located "below" the traditional schema of associationist psychology, "in which a direct differentiation of several elements is not possible for us" (p. 431). This was the "quality of familiarity" characteristic, for example, of situations in which we vaguely recognize that we know a name but cannot place it. The phenomenon appears with the immediacy of a sensation, often without additional reproduction or recall, but does the intellectual work of an idea. Experimental work soon revealed the theoretical and practical relevance of such phenomena. In their research on reading, for example, Benno Erdmann and Raymond Dodge found that up to four or five times more letters could be retained by readers when they were presented as parts of a word or sentence than when they were presented as unrelated jumbles. However, they attributed word recognition to "the repeated perception of gradually more strongly associated complexes of sensations" (Erdmann & Dodge, 1898, p. 149).

Subsequent research questioned this interpretation. Schumann, for example, found that words of up to 25 letters presented with his tachistoscope could be seen clearly and distinctly in all their parts, though the seen word might not be exactly the same as the stimulus word. It seemed difficult to imagine that practice alone could account for such results. Schumann espoused a version of Wundt's assimilation theory: "In the act of recognition the images of former perceptions of the same object are re-excited, fuse with the sensations and give to the perceptual process its quality of familiarity" (Schumann, 1907, p. 170). However, this fusion of sensations and images, aside from being unobserved, did not explain Höffding's finding that recognition could occur without reproduction. Evidently there was some relationship between the organization of stimulus elements and their recognition and retention, but there was little agreement on the nature of that relationship. One researcher reported a total of 14 theories on the subject (Katzaroff, 1911).

The same situation reigned with respect to form perception. Philosophers since Locke and Hume had attributed the perception of form to intellectual or preintellectual, "apperceptive" operations. Mach seemed to be continuing this tradition when he concluded that "all abstractions"—such as the recognition of two differently colored squares as the same shape—must be based on presentations (*Vorstellungen*) of special quality (Mach, 1865/1910). In *The Analysis of Sensations* (1886/1959), however, these became "space sensations." In his well-known example of the square and diamond, he invoked "sensations of direction." Here, where homologous position is not given, additional intellectual effort, such as the direction of attention to particular parts of the figures, is needed to make the affinity of form between them clear. For Mach, such phenomena therefore marked the boundary between sensation and intellect (Mach, 1886/1959, pp. 105ff.; see also Schumann, 1900). When he extended his observation to melody, however, he failed to find a suitable sensation to cover the case (p. 285).

At this point, Christian von Ehrenfels entered the discussion. In a study entitled "On Gestalt Qualities," Ehrenfels (1890/1960) replied to Mach that red patches (simple colored extensions) are immediately recognized as such, even though they have no boundaries or walls from which space sensations might emanate. He then restructured the discussion by taking melody as his paradigm. Noting, as had Mach, that we can recognize two melodies as identical, even when no two notes in them are the same, he labeled what makes this possible—the sameness of relations among tones—the melody's "Gestalt quality." Thus the problem of form perception became intertwined with that of the perception of wholes and parts in general. Psychologically speaking, these Gestalt qualities were evidently neither sensations nor judgments. According to the accepted categories of the day, they were thus neither physical nor psychical. In the discussion that followed, nearly every philosopher and psychologist had something to say about this important issue (for summaries, see Boring, 1950, pp. 441ff.; Hermann, 1976, pp. 578ff.).

Systematic research on Gestalt perception as such began with the work of the so-called Graz school associated with the philosopher Alexius Meinong. Perhaps the best example of this work was Vittorio Benussi's (1904) study of the Muller-Lyer illusion. Benussi asked subjects to concentrate alternately on the whole figure and on one or another of its parts. He found that the analytical attitude reduced but did not eliminate the illusion, while the Gestalt attitude increased it. As Benussi acknowledged, the fact that the illusion was not eliminated even after concentrated attention indicated that central physiological processes were involved. Nevertheless, the effect of the Gestalt attitude was, for him, evidence for the prejudgmental processing (*Bearbeitung*) of sensory material—a process between sensation and intellect—which he called "production" (Benussi, 1904, pp. 308–310). He later found further evidence for this theory in a variety of other phenomena, including reversible and perspective drawings, and illusions of hearing and touch (see, for example, Benussi, 1906, 1911).

Benussi's work with attitudes or cognitive styles, reasonable as it may seem to psychologists today, was nearly totally ignored at the time. The reason was its connection with the model of consciousness offered by his teacher, Meinong, who supported the view of his own teacher, Brentano, that consciousness is intentional (i.e., actively directed at an object), except that Meinong distinguished between the contents of psychical acts and their logical objects. This had the great advantage for philosophy of making it possible to analyze the logic of sentences with fictional objects, such as round squares, at the same level as true sentences (Lindenfeld, 1980). On this view, *Gestalten* need not exist as psychical contents but could be relegated to the realm of "irreal," potentially fictive objects (see Benussi, 1914a). This line of thinking was not destined for wide acceptance among psychologists, concerned as they were to establish the reality and experimental manipulability of such phenomena.

By this time, the Gestalt problem had become "one of the most current issues in psychology," to use the words of Stumpf's student, Adhemar Gelb (1911, p. 1; see also Dunlap, 1912). Thus the intent of Kurt Koffka's dissertation was to determine whether there were acoustical (in this case rhythmic) Gestalten analogous to those in vision (Koffka, 1909). While Koffka's empirical findings were, of course, positive, the theory he offered—a version of Stumpf's attribution of form to a "summation function"—was no better than any of the others in the literature (Koffka, 1909, pp. 104–105; Stumpf, 1906a, pp. 28ff.). By 1914, research such as Karl Bühler's (1913) work on what he called "perceptions of proportion" had clearly established the existence and significance of Gestalten in perception. However, neither psychologists nor philosophers seemed able to integrate these facts into their various categorical frameworks. Like other consistent associationists, Hermann Ebbinghaus preferred simply to accept the existence of form as an ultimate datum alongside sensations, without trying to explain it systematically. Such "honest proverty," he argued, was preferable to "the appearance of wealth" (Ebbinghaus, 1897/1905, p. 462; 1908/1912, p. 67).

The problem of form also exposed weaknesses in the prevailing framework of neurophysiological theory, which rested on the same mechanistic presuppositions that governed Helmholtz's thinking on sensation. Most important was the principle of the isolated conduction of nerve impulses along fixed pathways, a view that was fully compatible with associationist psychology. However, Johannes von Kries (1901) warned that such thinking could not possibly account for even the most common form perceptions, such as the recognition of a horse from different angles as the same animal. The philosopher–psychologist Erich Becher took up this criticism 10 years later, offering psychological evidence for the inadequacy of the conduction model (Becher, 1911).

The challenge to experimenting psychologists at the time was clear. The inadequacy of classical associationism and its concomitant assumptions about science to deal with the complexity of mind seemed established, but no equally comprehensive categorical framework had come along to replace it. To accept the new facts as ultimate data—as Ebbinghaus, Schumann, and others did—and to resolve the problem by quietly reforming or revising associationism, might have been sufficient if experimental psychology had already been established as an institutionally autonomous discipline. In Germany, however, this was not the case. Instead, the new field was only partly insulated from constant and growing criticism. For its critics, the theoretical difficulties sketched here were only further evidence for their denial that experimental psychology could ever provide reliable or philosophically relevant evidence about mental life.

The Emergence of Gestalt Theory

The generation of experimenting psychologists to which the shapers of Gestalt theory belonged thus faced a highly complex orientation problem. Conceptual shifts and research results in both philosophy and psychology led many to suspect that categories taken from mechanistic physics or empiricist philosophy were insufficient to deal with facts about the mind. The response of Wertheimer, Koffka, and Köhler to this situation was a radical reconstruction of psychological thinking intended to satisfy the requirements of both science and philosophy, of method and mind. The reconstruction proceeded in five stages: (1) the laying of the theoretical foundation by Wertheimer; (2) Wertheimer's linking of that foundation with experimental research; (3) the application and further development of the theory by Köhler and Koffka, first to perception and then (4) to behavior in general; and (5) Köhler's extension of the Gestalt principle to the external world and the psychophysical problem.

Each stage was intimately bound up with empirical research, but the implications drawn were conceptual.

Laying the Foundations

Wertheimer first presented the Gestalt orientation in 1912—not, as commonly thought, in his famous paper on apparent motion, but in another article on numbers and number concepts among primitive peoples (1912a). His methodological stance was an extension of phenomenology to ethnology: "It is insufficient to ask what numbers and operations of our mathematics the peoples of other cultures have. The question must be: what units of thought do they have in this field? What tasks for thinking? How does their thinking approach them?" (1912a, p. 323).

Given this approach, it is not surprising that Wertheimer soon discovered number concepts different from those of Western arithmetic. Examples of the difference could be very simple: One horse plus one horse equals two horses; one person plus one person equals two people; but one horse plus one person equals a rider. Such changes of designation indicated for Wertheimer that a new, fundamentally different unit of thought was present. However, the distinction was not always a matter of using different names. A builder goes to find pieces of wood for a house: "One can count them. Or, one can go with an image of a house in one's head and get the pieces of wood that are needed. One has a group image [*Gruppengebilde*] of the posts, which is quite concretely related to the form of the house" (Wertheimer, 1912a, pp. 324–325). Wertheimer claimed that this kind of concrete, functional thinking, characterized by "the preponderance of form," often determines the handling of quantities, not only for so-called primitive cultures, but for "naturally thinking people" in civilized society as well.

Though he was ostensibly writing only about number concepts, which might vary from culture to culture, Wertheimer was already searching for phenomena that could become the basis for general principles of thinking. Immediately after the example just given, he offers this one: "A somewhat blunted triangle is a triangle, not a rectangle or a hexagon, as it would have to be called from a merely mathematical point of view" (1912a, p. 326). There is nothing concretely functional about a figure drawn on a piece of paper, and Wertheimer did not claim that we perceive triangles in this way because we have learned to do so, or because it is somehow in our biological interest. The blunted triangle *is* a triangle—that is, it is immanent in the phenomenon that it is perceived in this way. In such observations Wertheimer went beyond descriptive psychology and expounded a new epistemology that might be called "immanent structuralism." His implicit message was that true philosophy must be based on this conception of experience.

In lectures given in the summer of 1913, Wertheimer made these claims in explicit and general form. One of his listeners summarized their content as follows:

> a. Aside from chaotic, therefore not, or not properly, apprehensible impressions, the contents of our consciousness are mostly not summative, but constitute a particular characteristic "togetherness", that is, a segregated structure, often "comprehended" from an inner center . . . To this the other parts of the structure are related in a hierarchical system. Such structures are to be called "Gestalten" in a precise sense.
>
> b. Almost all impressions are grasped either as chaotic masses—a relatively seldom, extreme case—or as chaotic masses on the way to sharper formation, or as Gestalten. What is finally grasped are "impressions of structure" [*Gebildefassungen*]. To these belong the objects in a broad sense of the word, as well as relational contexts [*Beziehungszusammenhänge*]. They are something specifically different from and more than the summative totality of the individual components. Often the "whole" is grasped even before the individual parts enter consciousness.
>
> c. The epistemological process—knowledge in a precise sense—is very often a process of "centering", of structuring, or of grasping that particular aspect that provides the key to an orderly whole, a unification of the particular individual parts that happen to be present. (Wartensleben, 1914, pp. 1ff.; see also Wertheimer, 1980, p. 14)

Here we have nearly all the fundamental principles of Gestalt theory, presented that the beginning of its development. The most important features of the doctrine at this stage were Wertheimer's use of the term *Gestalt* to refer to both individual objects and organization of objects in the psychological field; his differentiated conception of consciousness, which clearly does not exclude the existence of "elements" but takes them to be unusual, boundary cases; and his use of the term *Gestalt* not only for the objects of consciousness and the system of their relations, but also for the knowledge process thought to underlie their appearance. Wertheimer later applied the metaphor of restructuring, or "recentering" to human problem solving and thinking. The distinction between "natural" and abstract, "arithmetical" thinking thus became a dichotomy between "reproductive" applications of traditional logic and "productive," or genuinely original, dynamic thinking (Wertheimer, 1920/1925; 1945/1957).

The Link to Experimental Research: The Phi Phenomenon

In a paper on apparent motion that is usually cited as the official beginning of Gestalt psychology, Wertheimer (1912b) offers experimental evidence for his new conception. As often noted in the literature on this paper, Wertheimer did not discover apparent motion; the phenomenon had been known and studied since the work of Plateau in the 1820s (O'Neill & Landauer, 1966). What this literature generally ignores, however, is that there was no satisfactory explanation for apparent motion, in part because various theories assigned it a different status. Mach (1886/1959), for example, spoke of "motion sensations," attributing them to eye movements. Karl Marbe (1910) thought fused afterimages were reponsible, while Schumann (1912) referred to "illusions of judgment." The psychophysicist Sigmund Exner had demonstrated as early as 1875 that apparent motion produced negative afterimages in the same way as real motion. He proposed a physiological explanation for such phenomena (Exner, 1875). Wertheimer's careful experimental work in Frankfurt, using Schumann's tachistoscope and having Koffka and Köhler as his principal subjects, successfully refuted the theories of Mach, Marbe, and Schumann while supporting Exner's (see Wertheimer, 1912b, pp. 223ff., 240ff.; see also Seaman, 1984).

Far more significant for the development of Gestalt theory, however, was Wertheimer's discovery of a phenomenon he called "pure *phi*," in which motion was observed without a moving object. For Wertheimer, this was not merely one kind of apparent motion among others, but clearly the essence of motion itself. He drew two implications from this. First, the notion, derived from traditional logic, that a process must necessarily be a process *of* something "is not founded on pure psychological data"; there were, indeed, "pure dynamic phenomena" (Wertheimer, 1912b, p. 246). To explain these—and this was the second point—it would be necessary to break with the conventional dichotomy between sensation and judgment. Here was a phenomenon that appeared, under appropriate conditions, with sensory immediacy and total clarity, but that could not be described as a sum of contents, or as a series of isolated events combined by a process external to them (1912b, pp. 226ff.). Bergson (1903/1946) had made a similar claim about motion in general a decade before. However, he had presented it as evidence of an unbridgeable gap between scientific method and the claims of intuition, while Wertheimer's aim was to show that such a gap need not exist.

Given the nature of the phi phenomenon and his confirmation of Exner's claim that both apparent and real motion were centrally conditioned, it was to be expected that Wertheimer would propose a new physiological model to explain his results. If two neighboring neural points were stimulated within a given time interval, he suggested, "a kind of physiological short circuit, a specific passage of excitation from *a* to *b*" would occur. If process *a* is at its peak when process *b* enters, then a "crossing of excitation" occurs and the phi phenomenon appears. With a succession of exposures under optimal conditions, "a unitary, continuous whole process" would be produced (Wertheimer, 1912b, pp. 246ff.). Going still further, he suggested that there were transverse and total processes that "result as specific wholes from the excitation of individual cells over a larger area." Two connected lines, for example, would then "appear as a *duo in uno,* as a compelling total Gestalt. Not two lines coming from a single point, but an angle is there." Two explain the recognition and reproduction of such objects, "the appearance of previously existing physiological total form . . . would be essential, not the reproduction of specific individual excition" (1912b, p. 92).

For Koffka, at least, this last proved to be the most important part of the paper. He later recalled that he was "enthralled to hear that psychological and physiological events had to be pulled together under the lead of psychological facts."

> To have proved that movement as experience is different from the experience of successive intervening phases meant a good deal at that time. But . . . Wertheimer did very much more: he joined the movement experience, the movement *phi,* to the psychology of pure simultaneity and of pure succession, the first corresponding to form or shape, the second to rhythm, melody, etc. This was the decisive step.[3]

The Reconstruction of Perceptual Theory

While conducting research on hearing with Frankfurt schoolchildren, Köhler found, among other things, that the act of "hearing out" the partial tones in a chord could produce tones that did not exist before (Köhler, 1913, pp. 99ff.). This evidence supported a claim made by Hans Cornelius (1892) against Stumpf 20 years earlier.

In his essay, "On Unnoticed Sensations and Errors of Judgment," Köhler (1913/1971) worked out the implications of this finding, which merged with those of Wertheimer's research. The focus of his criticism was on what he called the "constancy hypothesis" (*Konstanzannahme*), referring to the tendency shared by Helmholtz and Stumpf "to regard perception and sensation as much as possible as unambiguously determined by peripheral stimulation" (1913/1971, pp. 35–36). This assumption had been under attack for a generation; even Stumpf had recently admitted that this "atomism with regard to sensory phenomena" was a hypothesis, not a proven fact (quoted in Köhler, 1913/1971, p. 16). Its value must thus be measured by the coherence it gives to research results, or by its usefulness in experimental practice. Köhler attacked the notion on both grounds. The constancy hypothesis, he claimed, was untenable without assuming entities and acts that could be neither verified nor falsified—hence the "unnoticed sensations" and "errors of judgment" in his title. There were no independent criteria to decide when these auxiliary hypotheses could or should be applied to specific cases. The result was an attitude that stood in the way of research, for "the interests of a conservative system can be overwhelming in the absence of independent criteria" (1913/1971, pp. 26–27).

In essence, Köhler was asking his teacher, Stumpf, his current employer, Schumann, and other experimenting psychologists to take Hering's methodological perspective and their own emphasis on the value of trained observation to their logical conclusions:

> A large and significant part of the properties of perception is neglected, which recedes into the background in those limiting cases achieved by means of [laboratory] isolation, but if often much more important . . . than the usual sensory attributes . . . . This applies particularly to the psychological correlates of stimulus complexity, and specifically to the everyday perception of *things* [italics in original]. (Köhler, 1913/1971, pp. 38–39)

Köhler recommended "tentatively" that the constancy hypothesis "be given up entirely" in favor of the assumption that central factors play "an essential role" in perception; he acknowledged that the theoretical situation would thus become less simple at first, but the result in the end may be "a deeper understanding of the whole field." (Köhler, 1913/1971, p. 39). He took care to assure his readers that he did not intend to deny the correspondence of physiological and psychological processes: "I regard the other variables also as physiological in nature" (1913/1971, p. 24, n. 20). Nevertheless, he did not specify the processes he had in mind. His only reference to Wertheimer's work was a vague allusion to "plausible physiological hypotheses" in a footnote. Koffka was bolder, or less cautious. In a review essay on recent research in perception, he announced that Wertheimer's and Köhler's work had completed a transformation in perceptual theory for which Hering had prepared the way more than 30 years before (Koffka, 1914). Now, in some cases at least, "sensation is understood from the point of view of perception, instead of the other way around" (1914, p. 711).

Koffka explained in more detail what he meant by this declaration in a long polemic against Benussi published the next year (Koffka, 1915). Benussi's theory, he argued, presupposed the constancy hypothesis. Although Benussi claimed to reject that assumption, he referred to "sense impressions that remain constant," on the basis of which "production" processes yield presentations of figures that could be different from one another. But if constant sensory contents cannot be directly observed, yet are objectively necessary, they must be unnoticed. Koffka acknowledged that Benussi's research freed many experiences from their bondage to a stimulus, but by presupposing constant sensory contents upon which these experiences are constructed, the "production" theory merely substituted another form of bondage (Koffka, 1915, pp. 16–17).

Koffka then presented a reconstructed perceptual theory with neither constant sensations nor intervening processes. At the descriptive level, he drew the most radical conclusion from Wertheimer's lectures of 1913: "A pure description of one's experiences cannot be oriented to the concept of sensation; its point of departure is, rather, that of the Gestalt and its properties" (Koffka, 1915, p. 60). By "Gestalt," Koffka clearly meant, as did Wertheimer, not only individual objects (Köhler's "things") but also the changing relations of objects to one another in the psychological field. Taken seriously as a guide to research, such a conception would inevitably result in a significant expansion and complication of the task of description.

The break with the Graz school, and the fundamentally new step described in this critical paper, was Koffka's radical revision of the stimulus concept. The word "stimulus" no longer refers to a pattern of excitations on the retina, but rather to real objects in functional relation to a perceiving and acting organism. Thus "the same object can be for the same organism at one time a 'sensory stimulus' and at another a 'Gestalt stimulus,' depending on the state of the organism." A hungry fish, for example, snaps at a worm; a satiated one leaves it alone (Koffka, 1915, pp. 33–34). Applied to apparent motion, this revised model of experience means that tachistoscopically presented pictures are only stimuli for the movement experience, not the contents on which it is founded. Since the state of the nervous system is related to every act of perception, *the traditional type of psychological analysis is thus ruled out"* (italics in original). In a footnote, Koffka (1915) puts the point still more strongly: "The unambiguous sensation exists only for the psychologist; it is a product of the laboratory" (p. 60, n. 2).

Ironically, Koffka cites a monograph from E. B. Titchener's laboratory in support of this claim (Rahn, 1913), while Külpe had drawn the same conclusion from the Würzburg school's research. In earlier years, Külpe, following the positivist philosopher Richard Avenarius, had substituted the organism, or the "corporeal individual," for the "psychical individual" as the subject of psychology (Danziger, 1979). Later he returned, with Husserl's help, to the primacy of perception, but without giving up the linkage with the organism. Koffka had previously done research on ideation in Külpe's laboratory (Koffka, 1912). He now took over and reworked Külpe's thinking on the basis of Wertheimer's immanent structuralism, making an even more comprehensive addition to that model.

Given this reformulation of the structure of experience, Koffka (1915) claims: "We may in fact place the experiencing of Gestalten squarely beside that of creating Gestalten; to sing or play a melody, dash off a sketch, write, and so forth, are not cases where one sings or plays *tones*, or draws or writes *strokes*. *The motor act is an organized whole process*" (pp. 36–37; italics in the original). After this, the final step to physiology was a foregone conclusion. The physiological correlates of both experience and action are, for Koffka, "not the individual excitation of one brain area plus association, but a whole process with its whole-properties. . . . The entire process is significantly different according to whether we experience Gestalten or sensations" (1915, p. 60).

This conception of experience, particularly the attribution of structure to both perception and action and the emphasis on the functional interaction of organism and environment, was reminiscent of American functionalist psychology (see Chapter 5, this volume). Indeed, Koffka cites John Dewey's *Essays in Experimental Logic* (1916) directly. There was, however, on important difference. for Dewey, the purpose of psychology was "to locate the particular situation in which each structure [of thought and behavior] has its origin" and to trace the "successive modifications through which, in its response to changing media, it has reached its present conformation" (1916, p. 95). Thus, Dewey's view was explicitly evolutionary, developmental, and instrumentalist. For Koffka, however, it was evidently more important to demonstrate the structured character of experience in general than to discover the evolutionary roots of specific structures. His use of the snapping fish as an example of a Gestalt stimulus underscores this point. The central point for Koffka was that "elementary" sensations are neither psychologically, logically, nor historically primary.

The Extension to Behavior and Learning

In his research with anthropoids on the island of Teneriffe, Köhler gathered evidence that seemed to support Koffka's extension of Wertheimer's "knowledge process" from perception and thinking to behavior. Köhler (1917/1973) demonstrates the ability of chimpanzees and other animals to solve problems requiring a grasp of means–ends relationships.

One example, which Köhler regarded as a crucial test, can stand here for many others. To a heavy stone he tied one end of a rope, then wound it around a piece of fruit and laid the rope obliquely to the bars of the apes' enclosure, with the free end extending between them. Some of the animals first pulled in the direction the rope "pointed," but four of them solved the problem by passing the rope hand over hand along the bars sideways until the fruit was in reach "without any hesitation" as soon as they saw the rope (Köhler, 1917/1973, pp. 143ff.; 1925/1959, pp. 177ff.). Thorndike's "trial and error" theory of learning could not account for such achievements, Köhler claimed, because they can occur spontaneously on the first trial, without being the results of either chance or previous training. Hobhouse, too, had noted cases in which animals seemed to find a solution "in a flash," and described them as examples of "perceptual learning" (Hobhouse, 1901/1915). Köhler described the apes' success as "insight"—a spontaneous reorganization of the animals' visual field, in which they grasp the structure of the situation.

Robert Yerkes adduced evidence for insight, or "ideational learning" as he called it, at nearly the same time as Köhler, in experiments done with an orangutan (Yerkes, 1916). However, where Yerkes provided extensive statistical data to support his claim, Köhler relied on careful, detailed descriptions and on films that he made to convince the skeptical. His learning curve was the one described by the animal, when it discovered the solution and rushed to obtain its reward "in one single, smooth motion" (Köhler, 1917/1973, p. 136; 1925/1959, p. 169). It was not his way to put the animals through repeated trials or to gather extensive statistics. He believed that "something is spoiled" in the animals' behavior by frequent repetition (1917/1973, p. 142; 1925/1959, p. 176). Köhler was clearly less interested in deriving measures of learning and problem solving than in discovering paradigmatic instances that reflected such behavior at its best. In this preference for qualitative over quantitative data, he continued the tradition of the Berlin laboratory, while in his extensive observations of chimpanzees' social behavior, he was a forerunner of modern ethology (see Köhler, 1922/1959).

Like Stumpf, Köhler was not opposed to using quantitative methods when needed. In research published in 1915 and 1918, he trained some of his apes to act as "subjects" in cleverly designed analogies to classical psychophysical experiments. The results were clear demonstrations first of color constancy (1915), and then of relational learning in chimpanzees (1918). The later results were the more challenging, especially when he obtained similar results with chickens (Köhler, 1918).

Köhler found that birds trained to peck seeds from the lighter of two grey papers continued to choose the lighter of any presented pair, even when the originally lighter paper appeared as the darker. For him, this was sufficient proof that the relation between the papers had been decisive; he obtained still better results in similar tests with apes, using both achromatic and chromatic colors. Karl Lashley (1912) had earlier found that albino rats could be trained to discriminate the larger of two circles in similar fashion. In essence, Köhler had shown that the relational principle behind all experimentation with difference thresholds also held for infrahuman animals.

Though Köhler preferred to avoid the charge of anthropomorphism by speaking of "structural functions," his findings questioned the exclusive reservation of such functions to animals gifted with language (i.e., human beings). Bühler (1908) described an experience of sudden insight—the so-called "aha" experience—but that was in reference to the sudden comprehension of a sentence. Köhler (1918) argued that functional relations such as "lighter than," once learned, have an independent psychological reality of their own—a system of relations is "reproduced on the basis of its specific structure" (p. 37). His research, along with the observations of biologists that even frogs and lizards react to structured stimuli, showed, in Köhler's opinion, that "only a portion, and hardly the essential portion of the reactions of even the lowest organisms can be understood as mere juxtapositions and successions of absolute stimulus influences in isolation." It followed, then, that models of evolutionary history based on the primacy of sensation were "worthless" (Köhler, 1918, pp. 37–38). It also followed that methodological injunctions such as Lloyd Morgan's "canon" (Morgan, 1894) were not only worthless but positive hindrances to research, as was the constancy hypothesis in perception. Köhler made it clear, however, that he did not wish to reject the idea of evolutionary history, but rather to reconstruct it on a new basis.

The Extension to the External World and the Psychophysical Problem

The nature of the new basis for evolutionary history was already evident, at least implicitly, in Köhler's anthropoid research. In the winter of 1913–1914, he offered a course in Frankfurt called "The Physical Basis of Consciousness," and a number of passages in his monograph on intelligence tests show that he took the word "physical" quite literally. In his critique of Thorndike, for example, he argued that to satisfy a genuine concept of chance, there should be no essential difference whether one is speaking of the motion of molecules in an enclosed chamber of "the so-called chance impulses of a chimpanzee" (Köhler, 1917/1973, p. 152; 1925/1959 p. 187). Darwinists prefer to let the undefined concept of instinct do the work of providing direction and coherence to behavior. Philosophers like Eduard von Hartmann or Henri Bergson, who express dissatisfaction with Darwinian chance, invoke "the unconscious," or the *élan vital*. "But the alternative," Köhler maintained, "is not at all between chance and factors outside of experience. Great parts of physics have nothing to do with chance . . . [A]fter all there are quite other possibilities" (1917/1973, p. 153; 1925/1959, pp. 188–189).

These "possibilities" were actually reducible to one: that there are physical Gestalten, the laws of which correspond to those of behavior and psychological experience. In essence, Köhler's claim in his philosophical masterwork, *Die physischen Gestalten in Ruhe und im stationärem Zustand* (*Physical Gestalten at Rest and in a Stationary State*; 1920/1924), was that what was wrong with experimental psychology was not its allegiance to natural science but the conception of natural science among psychologists. Instead of Newtonian mechanics or Cartesian geometry, he argued, scientific psychologists should model their theorizing on the classical field theory of Faraday and Maxwell. But to sustain this claim, or make it seem plausible, Köhler first had to apply psychological—or rather, psycho-logical—Gestalt categories to field theory. These Köhler called the "Ehrenfels criteria." Physical processes could be called Gestalten, he argued, if they were "suprasummative"—if they had qualities or produced effects not derivable from the qualities and effects of their so-called parts, and if they were transposable—that is, if they retained relations in the same order despite shifts in the parts (Köhler, 1920/1924, pp. 37–38).[5]

Köhler found processes that fulfill these criteria in the field of electrostatics. In an ellipsoidal conductor, for example, the density of charge is greatest at the points of greatest curvature and least at the points of least curvature. The distribution of charge in such a conductor thus has a definite pattern of organization that depends on the shape of the conductor, which Köhler called the system's "topography," but not on the materials of which it is made, or the total quantity of charge involved.

It is impossible to build up such structures piecemeal—for example, by feeding charged particles into one part of the conductor and then another. In such cases the charge immediately redistributes itself over the entire surface (Köhler, 1920/1924, pp. 55ff., esp. p. 58). Such physical systems Köhler called "strong" Gestalten. "Weak" Gestalten, such as a group of isolated conductors connected by fine wires, also fulfill the Ehrenfels criteria but are not immediately dependent on the system's topography. Their specific articulation is not influenced by events in remote parts of the system, but a shift in current input produces changes in the entire structure (1920/1924, pp. 66, 106–109). Since the mathematics of such systems is applicable to a wide variety of other phenomena, Köhler concluded that "temporally constant, continuously extended total entities are present in, it seems, nearly the whole of physics" (1920/ 1924, p. 121).

Köhler (1920/1924) was careful to deny that this claim had anything to do with "the kind of romantic–philosophical inspiration" behind the view that everything is related to everything else (p. 154). Such statements were true in a formal sense, but a system's real degree of independence from or dependence on its surroundings varies with the boundary conditions. It was the task of both physics and psychology to determine these in specific cases. Köhler had just as little use for the idea that only consciousness as a whole is given: "With this kind of reality one really cannot do much." Such "totality" theories miss the important point, namely, "the existence of self-enclosed, finitely extended Gestalten with scientifically determinable, natural laws (1920/1924, pp. 157– 158).

If articulated systems of the kind described here exist in the external world, there is no reason to deny that physiological processes in the brain could have the same characteristics. However, Köhler went much further, postulating an *"objective similarity* between the Gestalt characteristics of psychophysical events and those of the phenomenal field–*not only in general*, in the sense that we are dealing with Gestalten in both cases, *but in the specific character of every Gestalt in each individual case"* (1920/1924, pp. 192–193; italics in original). This was a radical reformulation of G. E. Müller's "psychophysical axioms" on the basis of Wertheimer's immanent structuralism.

However, the postulate of psychophysical isomorphism did not prescribe the precise character of the brain events involved. According to Köhler, there were two possibilities: the "organized whole processes" in specific cortical regions proposed by Wertheimer, and the far more radical option of regarding the entire "somatic field" as one physical system (1920/1924, pp. 176–177). Köhler evidently selected the second possibility for heuristic reasons, in order to have a theoretical framework broad enough to encompass, eventually, not only vision but also the behavior he had observed on Teneriffe. In any case, he made it clear that his choice of the more radical possibility did not preclude returning to the first at a later date.

Köhler's proposal to regard the entire somatic field as one physical system had dramatic consequences. In the case of vision, it meant the elimination of both the retinal image as a fixed, two-dimensional picture and of "local signs" or other retinal elements as cues for depth (Woodward, 1978). For Gestalt theory, the three-dimensional, perceived world is not a construction on the basis of insufficient sensory information; it appears complete as the correlate of process interaction in the three-dimensional optic sector (Koffka, 1935, pp. 59, 115; see also Pastore, 1971, p. 304). A further implication was that there was no projection of simple sensations onto the cortex in the way proposed by Helmholtz. Instead, "the place where a given line of flow will end in the central field is determined in every case by the conditions in the system as a whole" (Köhler, 1920/1924, p. 243). Köhler insisted that such views did not prescribe featureless continuity in the cortex but were perfectly compatible with "rigorous articulation." Nor was it necessary to claim that brain processes must somehow look like perceived objects; they could well be functionally instead of geometrically similar (1920/1924, pp. 194ff.). Wertheimer (1912b, p. 49) makes a similar suggestion.

Köhler tried to show what he meant by functional similarity, and to demonstrate the applicability of his postulate to specific psychological problems in the case of the figure–ground phenomena first reported by Edgar Rubin in 1914 (see also Rubin, 1921). Müller had already suggested in 1896 (pp. 338ff.) that the physiological basis of color vision might best be understood in terms of the reversible chemical reactions described by Walther Nernst. Köhler, who had studied with Nernst in Berlin, knew that such reactions produce electric currents. He now hypothesized that when a small white figure, such as a circle, is exposed on a homogeneous gray background, the result on the retina will be two sets of chemical reactions, with a corresponding "leap" of electrostatic potential along the boundary between the two stimulus regions. If equal amounts of electricity are involved on both sides of the boundary, this quantity will be displaced over a larger area in the region corresponding to the background than in the region corresponding to the disk. It is this difference in current density, functionally reproduced in the cortex, that helps visible things attain "their lively phenomenal existence," for the condition of being set off against surroundings is perhaps the most important requirement for seeing Gestalten of any kind (Köhler, 1920/1924, pp. 26–27, 207).

Köhler then proceeded to raise the discussion to a still higher level. Since all his examples of physical Gestalten had been equilibrium processes, he now claimed that all directed processes governed by the second law of thermodynamics fulfilled the Ehrenfels criteria. Translated into his terms, the second law stated that the amount of energy in a system will be "as small as the Gestalt conditions allow" (Köhler, 1920/1924, pp. 250–251). It followed that psychophysical Gestalt processes in the brain must be directional in the same sense, though admittedly the

Gestalt conditions in this context would be far more complex than those generally holding in physics.

Citing evidence from fluid dynamics adduced by Mach and others, Köhler made the bold suggestion that physical systems tend toward end states characterized by "the simplest and most regular grouping" (1920/1924, p. 256). In such situations a quantitative change such as a decrease in net energy has a qualitative result: a change in the distribution of components in a specific direction. Köhler called this a "tendency to simplest shape," or "the *Prägnanz* of the Gestalt," alluding to a principle enunciated by Wertheimer, albeit rather vaguely, in the discussion of a paper by Benussi at a meeting of the Society for Experimental Psychology (see Benussi, 1914b, p. 149). Here, as so often in the history of science, the logic of discovery was different from the logic of justification. It was almost as though Köhler had undergone immense intellectual effort in order to work out the consequences of this single idea. As he recounted it: "When Wertheimer formulated his principle [of *Prägnanz*] in psychology, I happened to be studying the general characteristics of macroscopic physical states, and thus I could not fail to see that it is the psychological equivalent of Mach's [maximum–minimum] principle in physics" (Köhler, 1938/1976, p. 197).

Summary and Critique

Köhler, Koffka, and Wertheimer belonged to the second generation of experimenting psychologists in Germany. They had seen during their own training that traditional philosophical presuppositions and concepts of science were insufficient guides to psychological reality. However, they all accepted from their teacher, Stumpf, the argument that all philosophy presupposed some conception of mind, and hence some empirically verifiable psychology. Thus, it was logical for them to suppose that a radical revision of psychology would have important philosophical implications. Theirs was a revolt from within; they accepted the institutional situation in which they worked and tried to resolve at the highest possible level the intellectual dilemmas encountered there. Köhler's step to natural philosophy demonstrated most effectively the character of that response.

Köhler's speculations in *Die Physischen Gestalten* (1920/1924), though undeniably brilliant, were open to a variety of criticisms. Some of the more important of these came from Erich Becher within months of the book's publication. Becher (1921) questions Köhler's apparent equation of Gestalten and physical systems. A shadow, for example, is a physical Gestalt, but its parts are not causally coherent, as are the parts of electrical structures. More central was Becher's argument that even if we admit that there are "whole processes" in the brain, we need not believe that they have exactly the same Gestalt characteristics as the experiences with which they are correlated. All that was necessary was a functional relationship in which the cortical processes were sufficiently complex to produce the observed results.

A further problem was the structure of explanation in Köhler's theory. He himself emphasized that his isomorphism held only for the relation between physiological processes and perceived Gestalten. Since the arrangements of incoming light rays on the retina are not physical Gestalten in his sense, seen Gestalten are "not reducible to an image of the physical Gestalten in the environment" (Köhler, 1920/1924, pp. 194–195). The real stimulus objects that had seemed so important to Koffka's conception of experience were thus explicitly excluded. Koffka dealt with this problem later by distinguishing between distal and proximal stimuli (see below). This response may have been satisfactory from the point of view of perceptual theory, if the central question of that field is, "Why do things look as they do" (Koffka, 1935, pp. 76ff.), but the issue of the veridicality of perception was not so easily resolved.

As for the applicability of Köhler's model to research, there were three interrelated problems: anatomy, testability, and reductionism. Köhler (1920/1924, p. 204) conceded that he did not know whether the electrical processes he postulated actually occurred in the optic sector. In any case, it seemed clear that his theory presupposed a less differentiated visual cortex than neuroanatomy had actually discovered. Köhler also admitted that his notion of the difference between "geometrical" and "functional" space in the brain would make it difficult to test deductions from his postulate, even with the appropriate apparatus. This situation led him to adopt the less radical of his two proposed brain theories (see below).

Both of these difficulties were rooted in Köhler's genuine belief in what has since been called "physicalism" as a principle of explanation (Lowry, 1979). A deeper problem with this view was that there are no perfect equilibria in organic life, nor are there states of rest or stationary states. Köhler later dealt with these facts by distinguishing between closed and open systems, a distinction that helped to lay the groundwork for a productive application of physics to biology and that contributed significantly to the development of general systems theory (Köhler, 1924b, 1927/1971; Bertalanffy, 1968).

Gestalt Theory in the Weimar Period

Whatever one might say in criticism of it, Köhler's bold yet measured theoretical stroke offered an intellectually coherent and highly provocative answer to both the philosophical and scientific challenges faced by experimental psychology in Germany. In 1922 Köhler was named to succeed Stumpf as professor of philosophy and director of the Psychological Institute in Berlin, at least partly because of his proven interest in and ability to teach natural philosophy in addition to psychology (Ash, 1982, pp. 507ff). Two years earlier, the institute had been moved to new quarters in a wing of the former Imperial Palace, thereby more than doubling its size and quadrupling its budget (Ash, 1980a, p. 283). In 1916 Wertheimer had come from Frankfurt to Berlin to do acoustical research for the German war effort; in 1919 he resumed teaching and was named associate professor in 1924. In 1921 Kurt Lewin earned the right to teach philosophy and psychology in Berlin and was named associate professor six years later. Under this leadership, housed in one of the largest and best funded psychological laboratories in the world, the "Berlin school" of Gestalt theory became one of the dominant schools of academic psychology in Weimar Germany.

Out of this institutional framework came research of historic significance, some of which is still cited today. Most of this work has been summarized elsewhere; space permits only brief mention of some of the more outstanding contributions. Perhaps the most important of these were the so-called Gestalt laws (or tendencies) formulated by Wertheimer as early as 1913 but not published until 1923. In addition to the law of *Prägnanz*, already mentioned, these included the laws of proximity, closure, and good continuation. Where Müller (1904) had said only that such tendencies made the perception of stimulus complexes easier, Wertheimer maintained that they were determinative for figure (and, by extension, form) perception in general.

In Giessen, where Koffka had been named associate professor and director of the laboratory in 1918, Friedrich Wulf attempted to demonstrate the applicability of the law of *Prägnanz* to memory (see Wulf, 1922). Also in Giessen, Koffka directed a series of studies of apparent motion, most notably Adolph Korte's (1915) attempt to determine quantitative parameters for the phenomenon. The most significant research on movement in Berlin was Karl Duncker's demonstration of induced motion. Under appropriate conditions, subjects who fixated a stationary point while another point in the field was in motion would see the fixated point move, or even think they were moving themselves (Duncker, 1929; see also Koffka, 1935, pp. 284ff.). These findings led to further work on the role of systems of reference in perception, including studies of visual speed and so-called "transposition effects" by J. F. Brown and Hans Wallach (Wallach, 1976). In studies of expression carried out under Wertheimer in Berlin, Rudolph Arnheim (1928) laid the foundation for applications of Gestalt theory to the psychology of art. In work related to that of the Berlin school, Adhemar Gelb and Kurt Goldstein (1920) produced evidence for the plasticity of neural action and the de- and regeneration of perceptual processes in brain-damaged soldiers. As the 1920s progressed, American visitors came to the Berlin institute, and some of them applied Gestalt principles to studies of learning and reasoning (e.g., Maier, 1930, 1931).

The Weimar period saw more than the mere application of an already completed Gestalt theory to research problems. The principles of Gestalt theory evolved as well. Two examples are Köhler's extension of his natural philosophy to biology (mentioned earlier), and of Gestalt theory to the perception of other people. On the latter issue he took the position, similar to that of the phenomenologist Max Scheler (1913/1923), that the givenness of both ourselves and other people in our experience requires no conclusions by analogy or mystical "empathy" feelings, but is as immediate as any perception we have (Köhler, 1929/1971). This position made the development of a social psychology on Gestalt lines at least conceivable.

Also important in this regard was Koffka's effort to present Gestalt principles as adequate foundations for a theory of psychical development. He maintained that the child lives in a perceptual world of its own, from which it gradually emerges during maturation, a process that he regarded as both organic and social in nature. The shape of the process "depends upon the total environment, and above all upon the sociological conditions of this milieu . . .[M]an's entire development, including, of course, his perceptions, is dependent upon society" (Koffka, 1921/1925, pp. 339–340; see also Ash, in press). Koffka's hints about the determining roles of society were taken up enthusiastically in the Soviet Union by the so-called cultural–historical school led by Lev Vygotsky (Scheerer, 1980).

The place of Gestalt theory in the general cultural situation of the Weimar Republic is most evident in the concluding remarks of Wertheimer's 1925 lecture entitled "Gestalt Theory." Though he emphasized the new view's roots in concrete research, he also held out the prospect of a philosophy in which the world is like "a Beethoven symphony, and we would have the possibility of grasping from a part of the whole something of the structural principles of that whole" (Wertheimer, 1925, p. 24; see also Wertheimer, 1922). Many academics in the Weimar period invoked the metaphor of the Beethoven symphony to point up their criticism of the "atomizing" effects of industrial society and political democracy (Ringer, 1969, pp. 396ff.). These writers generally included natural science in their indictment. The Gestalt theorists could join the attacks on atomistic and mechanistic thinking in psychology, but they were able to add that natural–scientific thinking need not possess either characteristic (see Leichtman, 1979).

The reception of that position, and of Gestalt theory in general, was mixed. Psychologists such as Müller and Wundt's successor at Leipzig, Felix Krueger, showed that the Gestalt thinkers had hit an important target by claiming that it had been hit before (Müller, 1923; Krueger, 1924; cf. Köhler, 1925b). Krueger went on to offer an alternative, quite different holistic psychology (*Ganzheitspsychologie*). Taking his cue from Dilthey, he emphasized the role of feeling and will in the structuring of experience (Krueger, 1928/1953).

More significant than these priority disputes, however, were indications that the Gestalt theorists had not fully resolved experimental psychology's intellectual orientation problem. Krueger's reference to the role of feeling and will in the constitution of experience has already been mentioned. The antirationalist thrust of this message fit in well with the increasing criticism of western, rationalist "civilization" and the praise of Germanic *Kultur* among philosophers and conservative intellectuals (Gay, 1968; Laqueur, 1974). A more specific aspect of the so-called Leipzig school critique was that the Gestalt theorists neglected the emergence, or "microgenesis" (*Aktualgenese*), of Gestalten (Sander, 1928). As we have seen, Wertheimer's original conception had provided for this; but it was not a central research issue for the Berlin school. Erich Jaensch reflected another tendency of the times when he rejected Köhler's physicalism as "materialist" in favor of a more biological (i.e., typological or characterological) approach (Jaensch & Grünhut, 1929).

Closer to the heart of the Gestalt theorists' position and concerns were the criticisms of William Stern and Karl Bühler. Stern's critique can be summarized in the slogan, "No Gestalt without a Gestalter." The allusion was to the relative unimportance of the perceiving subject for Gestalt theory. Stern maintained that continuing references to the dependence of perception on the state of the organism at a given time were not sufficient to account for the specifically human aspects of experience—especially for the person's will as giving meaning to his actions—nor could analogies from perception account for the coherence of the human personality over time (Scheerer, 1931; Stern, 1928).

Bühler also focused on a specifically human dimension when he criticized the nearly complete absence of language from the concerns of the

Gestalt theorists (Bühler, 1927). Given Wertheimer's point of departure, the notion of immanent structuralism, this could hardly be otherwise. For Bühler, language constitutes meaning; for the Gestalt theorists, however, language expresses meaning that is already there in appearances. It is difficult, in Bühler's opinion, to see how such a view could lead to an adequate accounting of the roles of symbol and myth as defining constituents of culture.

In the end, the fate of Gestalt theory in Germany was not decided by intellectual considerations. The debate was brought to an abrupt end by the racist politics of the National Socialist regime. Wertheimer, a Jew closely associated with Marxist and socialist philosophers in Frankfurt and a friend of the cosmopolitan humanist Albert Einstein, was, along with Einstein, among the first professors dismissed under the so-called "Law for the Reconstruction of the Civil Service" in April 1933. Wertheimer emigrated to a position at the New School for Social Research before his firing became official (Ash, 1984). Köhler was one of the few German professors to register a public protest against the personnel policies of the "new order." He was not dismissed after this step, but his assistants (Karl Duncker, Otto von Lauenstein, and Hedwig von Restorff) were accused of "communist activites" by students and professors who sought to Nazify the university. After a two-year struggle to maintain his authority in Berlin and to have his assistants reinstated, Köhler finally left for a position at Swarthmore College in the autumn of 1935 (see Ash, 1979, 1985; Geuter, 1984; Henle, 1978).

THE RECEPTION OF GESTALT THEORY IN THE UNITED STATES

The emigration of two of the three founders of Gestalt theory after 1933 posed the problem of transferring their way of seeing and doing psychology across national and cultural boundaries. Fortunately, the ground had been prepared for their coming years before. It thus seems reasonable to divide the history of Gestalt psychology in the United States into three stages that overlap chronologically: the initial reception of the Gestalt theorists and their ideas (1921–1930); the transfer of the Gestalt theorists to the United States (1927–1945); and the integration of ideas and research issues from Gestalt theory into American psychology (since 1935). We now outline each of these stages, placing developments during each period in the context of psychology's situation as a discipline during that time.

The Initial Reception (1921–ca. 1930)

The institutional and intellectual situation of psychology in the United States in the 1920s was quite different from that of psychology in Germany at the turn of the century. Many universities had established independent departments of psychology before World War I; in 1910 there were more psychological laboratories in the United States than there were universities in Germany (Garvey, 1929). Thus the rapid growth of the new field, like that of other disciplines, was aided by the rise of the American university. However, the emphasis that many psychologists placed on the natural–scientific method, or at least the appearance of it, and on the potential social applications of their work (mainly in the schools), favored the discipline's rapid institutionalization (see O'Donnell, 1985).

While they proclaimed the potential applicability of their work, the vast majority of experimenting psychologists remained in academia. Academic psychologists retained both a higher membership status in the American Psychological Association and control of that group's affairs until after World War II (Cattell, 1929; O'Donnell, 1979). Within academic psychology, a form of "establishment" developed, at least with respect to doctoral training. Of the 587 members of the A.P.A. who received their Ph.D. degrees by 1928, 324 (53%) came from only four universities: Columbia, Chicago, Clark, and Harvard. The 10 highest-ranking institutions—including Cornell, Iowa, Johns Hopkins, Pennsylvania, Yale, and Stanford—trained a total of 495 (80%) of all psychologists with Ph.D.s (Fernberger, 1928, p. 420).

Nevertheless, academic psychologists were by no means a unified group. Speaking very broadly, we can say that there were two major lines of division. One ran between the defenders of "pure science," grouped mainly around Titchener, and the advocates of applied psychology. Another line (or lines) of division separated the various schools of psychology, above all separating the emphasis on the contents of consciousness from the various versions of behaviorism (see Chapters 6 and 7, this volume). Other influential approaches included William McDougall's "hormic" psychology and Robert S. Woodworth's "dynamic" psychology.

Even during this period of factional strife, most psychologists attempted, as Woodworth (1931, p. 16) puts it, "to keep in the middle of the road" (see also Woodworth, 1931, Chapter 7). That is, they practiced a rather vaguely defined form of behavioristically flavored functionalism, which allowed them to accumulate data without serious theoretical restrictions. It was this mixture of institutional hierarchy and intellectual flux that the Gestalt theorists encountered as they attempted to make their ideas known in America.

The reception of Gestalt theory began early. In 1921, Koffka and Köhler were approached by American colleagues seeking to renew relations that had been interrupted by World War I. These colleagues were Robert M. Ogden, Dean of the Arts and Sciences College and professor of education at Cornell, who had been a subject in experiments that Koffka had carried out in Würzburg in 1909; Herbert Langfeld, then at Harvard, who had earned his doctorate in Berlin the same year as Koffka; and Robert Yerkes of Yale, who had corresponded with Köhler (from Harvard) about his anthropoid research until America's entry into the war. Köhler and Koffka were soon invited to American universities. Koffka came to Cornell at Ogden's invitation as visiting professor of education in 1924–1925, overlapping for several months with Köhler's stay as visiting professor at Clark University in the spring and summer of 1925 (see also Freeman, 1977; Henle, 1984; Sokal, 1984).[6]

As early as 1922, at Ogden's invitation, Koffka published a full account of the Gestalt theorists' view on perception in the *Psychological Review* (Koffka, 1922). Translations of Koffka's book on development and of Köhler's monograph on anthropoids appeared in 1925 (Koffka, 1921/1925; Köhler, 1925/1959). In the same year, Harry Helson published his Harvard dissertation, "The Psychology of the 'Gestalt,' " in Titchener's *American Journal of Psychology* in four installments (Helson, 1925/1926). The first summary of Gestalt theory for a general readership, Köhler's *Gestalt Psychology* (1929), originally appeared in English four years before its German version. Koffka, whose English was also excellent, quickly accepted invitations to lecture across the country. He and Köhler gave seminars and colloquia at nearly all of the important American research centers, including Harvard, Cornell, Chicago and Berkeley.

On his way to one of these presentations, Koffka wrote to Ogden about the insufficient support for his laboratory in Giessen and mentioned the possibility of taking a position in America[7]. During a second visit to America, while at the University of Wisconsin in 1926–1927, he received offers from both that university and Smith College. The latter offer was arranged by Seth Wakeman, a professor of education at Smith and a student of Ogden's (Henle, 1984; Sokal, 1984). Koffka chose the women's college partly because the cultural atmosphere of a small New England college town attracted him, but mainly because of the unprecedented research opportunity offered by the proposed professorship, which included five years free of teaching duties and a new laboratory built to his specifications, with two assistants of his choice and an operating budget of $6,000. The proferred salary of $9,000 (Sokal, 1984, says it was rumored to be $10,000) made him, according to his own (quite accurate) estimate, "one of the highest paid professors in America"[8].

Koffka thus emigrated to the United States in 1927 mainly for professional reasons, long before such a step became politically necessary. Köhler also received nibbles or offers of professorships from four universities, including Harvard and Yale. Though Köhler apparently weighed seriously the Harvard offer to succeed McDougall, he eventually decided to remain in Berlin (Sokal, 1984). In this way, through the initiative of influential American psychologists, but not least through their own efforts, the Gestalt theorists as well as their ideas became known in America to an extent rivalled at that time by no other approach in German academic psychology.

The American interest was due at least partially to a noticeable shift in the way the Gestalt theorists, especially Koffka, presented their position. This change was already visible in the first papers the Gestalt theorists published in English, in which empirical and methodological issues in perception were emphasized more than questions of worldview (Koffka, 1922; Köhler, 1925a). However, the shift was clearest in the Gestalt theorists' critique of behaviorism. As first presented in English by Koffka (1921/1925, pp. 7ff) this critique consisted of two points. First, Koffka maintained, it makes no practical scientific sense to construct a science of psychology without consciousness, which he called "inner behavior." This could only lead to the reduction of psychology to comparative or animal studies, and eventually to a mere "reactology" of the muscles and glands. Second, it is not only methodologically but also theoretically legitimate to retain consciousness in psychology but also theoretically legitimate to retain consciousness in psychology, for inner and outer behavior are "essentially alike and materially related." According to Koffka (1921/1925, pp. 7ff.), the goal of psychology should be to determine the nature of this relation, not arbitrarily to exclude one side of it.

To these points, Köhler later added a third. As far as the approach to science is concerned, he contended, behaviorism is in principle no different from Titchener's structuralism, which it purports to attack. Both proceed atomistically, breaking down their objects of study, either behavior or conscious experience, into arbitrary parts or pieces and building up a composite whole from these, without first observing whether the pieces are actually present in actual experience or behavior. In any case, the behaviorist draws his observations from the conscious experiences he would otherwise exclude. Analysis is necessary in science, but it is important to select appropriate, natural units from which to begin. "The right psychological formula is therefore: *constellation of stimuli—*

organization—response to the products of organization" (Köhler, 1929, pp. 179–180).

The Gestalt theorists did not reject their philosophical heritage when they criticized behaviorism. In addition to the arguments just summarized, Koffka also took what continues to be the standard humanistic position: "Whatever we are, and of whatever we are proud, our culture, art and religion, would otherwise be incomprehensible" if consciousness were removed from science (Koffka, 1921/1925, p. 17). From the beginning, however, the greatest portion of the Gestalt theorists' critique was focused on the scientific tenability of the behaviorists' position. The Gestalt theorists had responded to the situation in Germany with an approach to science oriented in important ways to the philosophical disciplines. In the United States they faced an already established, aggressively independent psychology, and they presented their argument in ways that would address this audience. There is evidence that this change in the self-presentation of Gestalt theory was deliberate. Koffka (1935, p. 18) says as much:

> When the first attempts were made to introduce Gestalt theory to the American public, that side which would most readily appeal to the type of German mentality which I have tried to sketch [i.e., the idealistic tradition] was kept in the background, and those aspects which had a direct bearing on science were emphasized. Had the procedure been different, we might have incurred the danger of biasing our readers against our ideas.

Despite this self-presentation strategy, the early reception of Gestalt theory in the United States was ambivalent. Psychologists quickly recognized the radical change that the Gestalt theorists wished to carry out, and some reported on it skeptically. Gordon Allport (1923/1924), for example, left it to his readers at the end of his basically sympathetic review to decide whether the Gestalt theorists, "with their assertion of the independence of the whole over against the sum of its parts, are not living in wonderland, where grins exist apart from cats" (p. 360). Other reviewers spoke more sarcastically of "The Phantom of the Gestalt" (Wyatt, 1928), "The Gestalt Enigma" (Lund, 1929), or of "Materializing the Ghost of Köhler's 'Gestalt Psychology' " (Gregg, 1932). However, the Gestalt theorists' critique of behaviorism was favorably received by those who, like Helson and Ogden, sought a scientifically viable alternative to Titchener's sensationist concept of conscious contents without sacrificing consciousness as a subject of psychological research (see Ogden, 1928).

The Transfer Period (1927-1945)

In the transfer phase, marked by the permanent immigration of all three founders of Gestalt theory and many of their students to the United States, the relation between Gestalt theory and American psychology took on two new dimensions. Subtle changes occurred in the presentation, the methodology, and the systematic structure of Gestalt theory, partly as a reflection of intensified interactions with the new environment. Also, the institutional setting of the Gestalt theorists changed in ways that directly affected the future of their theory in its new home.

Perhaps the most important example of increased dialogue between Gestalt theorists and American psychologists was the exchange between Koffka and the neobehaviorist Edward Chace Tolman. Their dialogue began as early as 1913 (Tolman, 1952; see also Tolman, 1926) and intensified in the early 1930s as both set out to develop comprehensive systems of psychology. In a sympathetic review of Tolman's *Purposive Behavior in Animals and Men* (1932), Koffka (1933) noted Tolman's distinction between "molecular" and "molar" behavior, which Tolman employed to distinguish between behavior within the organism and the relations of the organism to the environment, respectively. Koffka remarked that Tolman would have to admit sooner or later that events within the organism, too, are holistically structured. In his reply, Tolman acknowledged that "the evidence is undoubtedly piling up that brain physiology as well as behavior is molaristic or 'gestalt-y' " (Tolman & Horowitz, 1933, p. 464). He was referring here to the work of Lashley, whose findings on the regeneration of learned behavior in rats after the destruction of brain tissue seemed to offer general support to the claims of Gestalt theory (Lashley, 1930). However, Tolman did not concede that the relation between inner and outer behavior must necessarily be isomorphic, as Köhler and Koffka maintained.

This dialogue became one of several influences on the key ideas of Koffka's psychological system: the distinction between the perceiver's geographical and behavioral environment, the additional distinction, derived from the first, between distal and proximal stimuli, and the related differentiation between the phenomenal ego (the perceived self) and the "executive" (the acting organism) (see Koffka, 1935, pp. 27ff., 79–80, 306ff.). James J. Gibson (1971) called the distinction between distal and proximal stimuli Koffka's most significant contribution to perceptual theory.

Of course, there were other sources for these distinctions, one of which was Fritz Heider's "Thing and Medium" (1927). Similar notions were developed by Egon Brunswik (1933) while Koffka was writing. Moreover, the distinction between the geographical and the behavioral or phenomenal environment is implicit in the thinking of the astrophysicist and philosopher Arthur S. Eddington, whom Koffka cited in this connection (Koffka, 1935, p. 28). In his discussion of the executive, he also cited Lewin's notion of the *Motorik*, the tension system of needs within the person (Koffka, 1935, pp. 342ff.). Koffka's reworking of these ideas led to important differentiations in the previously monolithic structure of Gestalt psychology as a system. In carrying through these differentiations, however, Koffka did not alter his basic standpoint.

Köhler was also "Americanized" in specific ways after his permanent move to this country. His dialogue with the American neorealist philosopher Ralph Barton Perry, for example, led to, among other things, his development of a Gestalt theory of value. Taking a functionalist standpoint, Perry (1926) made "interest" the fundamental determiner of value. Köhler responded with the claim that "requiredness" is an inherent feature of many, perhaps most situations. Thus, not the organism's interests alone, but these in tandem with the objective requirements of the given situation, are the criteria that govern choice, including moral choice (Köhler, 1938/1976).

In other respects, however, Köhler's Americanization was more methodological than substantive. He had already begun in Berlin to investigate perceptual phenomena such as successive comparison which, according to his isomorphism postulate, would yield significant clues about brain events (Köhler, 1923; Lauenstein, 1933; Restorff, 1933). When he began work in a modern new laboratory of his own design at Swarthmore College, he attempted for the first time to prove such claims directly, with the help of electroencephalographic measurements (Köhler & Wallach, 1944). This work led to an important debate, discussed below, about the significance of so-called "figural aftereffects" in physiological psychology. Köhler later acknowledged that this field was "primarily an American enterprise," and that "Probably all European psychologists who came to this country learned from their American colleagues to be much stricter about experimental proof than they had been before" (Köhler, 1953/1971, pp. 423, 428). However, it should be remembered that Köhler had already asserted in 1920 that such physiological investigations were both possible in principle and of fundamental importance (Köhler, 1924a, p. 193, n. 1). In the United States he had the technology to carry them out, and he used it.

The most important change in Gestalt psychology during the transfer phase was undoubtedly in the nature of its institutional anchorage. Koffka and Köhler accepted positions at elite colleges, where they could continue their theoretical and experimental work under nearly optimal conditions. In contrast with many of their colleagues at other small colleges, they were largely freed from required lectures and administrative duties. In this respect they may even have enjoyed better working conditions than they had in Germany. Köhler, for example, was able to move into a new laboratory building for biological sciences at Swarthmore, with facilities that were partly of his own design, though it was the middle of the Depression (Blanshard, 1970, pp. 280, 282). With the help of Swarthmore's president, Frank Aydelotte, an experienced fundraiser, he was assured of sufficient support for research assistance and an annual succession of postdoctoral fellows who came to work with him for one or two years. However, the Gestalt theorists paid a high price for such advantages. Neither the colleges nor the New School offered significant opportunities for the training of more than one or two doctoral candidates. The Gestalt theorists were thus unable to ensure the systematic continuation of the research programs they had begun in Berlin, Frankfurt, and Giessen.

This does not mean that the Gestalt theorists had no influence on the development of American psychology. Rather, that infuence ran in ways other than the traditional teacher–student relationship. Among Köhler's postdoctoral fellows and younger colleagues at Swarthmore were Robert MacLeod, Hans Wallach, David Krech, Richard Crutchfield, Richard Held, Ulric Neisser, Edwin Newman, Soloman Asch, Mary Henle, and the editor of this volume, all of whom played influential roles in American psychology. Nearly all have since emphasized the influence of Gestalt theory on their development as psychologists, but only a few became Gestalt psychologists themselves in any strict sense. Instead, Gestalt theory was part of their otherwise eclectic training.

The same is true for Wertheimer's famous seminars at the New School. Even people who worked closely with Wertheimer, such as Asch or Abraham Luchins, received their doctorates elsewhere. Other seminar participants, such as Abraham Maslow, warmly acknowledged Wertheimer's influence on their thinking but trod other paths in the end. There were other centers of sympathy for the Gestalt viewpoint in America at the University of Kansas under the chairmanship of Raymond Holder Wheeler, then later under Ralph White, Martin Scheerer, Fritz Heider, Roger Barker, and Herbert Wright. At Duke University there were Donald Adams and Karl Zener (see Mandler & Mandler, 1969). The Gestalt theorists themselves helped to bring former students and coworkers, such as Rudolf Arnheim, George Katona, Hans Wallach, and Karl Duncker, from Germany to the United States. Nevertheless, the numbers involved were miniscule compared with the number of psychologists trained in courses at even one major American graduate department.

The effects of this situation soon became evident. In the 1930s the discussion of Gestalt theory in the United States came increasingly under the influence of methodological operationalism and neobehaviorist learning theory. In the process, differences of worldview that had already become manifest in the 1920s continued to color the discussion. Now, however, they were exacerbated by disagreements on issues of scientific methodology, or rules for proper theory construction. An example is the critique by the learning theorist, Kenneth W. Spence, of Gestalt theory's interpretation of discrimination learning. As mentioned earlier, Köhler had shown in 1918 that chimpanzees and chickens are capable of choosing the lighter or the darker of two surfaces, even under altered conditions of presentation. Köhler claimed that his work challenged the trial-and-error theory of learning, because the animals could respond relationally to new stimulus situations without retraining. Spence (1937) replied that the Gestalt theorists, "instead . . . of a really systematic investigation, seem to have been satisfied to demonstrate the commonness of response on the basis of relational properties as compared with response to absolute factors. Instances of failure . . . have either been ignored . . . or vaguely accounted for . . . The Gestalt theorists have failed to furnish either a satisfactory explanation of these phenomena or an adequate experimental formulation of the problem" (p. 444). He proposed instead to apply "a sophisticated 'Trial and Error' theory of learning" along lines already developed by his mentor, Hull, for problem boxes and mazes. The aim would be to reinforce the "relative strength of the excitatory tendency of a certain component of the stimulus complex as compared with that of certain other elements until it attains sufficient strength to determine the response" (Spence, 1936, pp. 430, 435).

In order to defend their theory against such an attack, the Gestalt theorists would have profited from the support of advanced students who were thoroughly acquainted with both the theoretical and methodological presuppositions of Gestalt theory, but such support was not forthcoming. Wertheimer wrote an answer to Spence, in which he recognized absolute and relational responses as two possibilities, with the probability of the occurrence of one or the other being related to a third factor, the "behavior attitude." He also noted that Spence's talk of reinforcing stimulus components and elements presupposed the constancy hypothesis. What is learned and transferred, he wrote, is the "direction of relation"; this kind of behaving demands less of the animal than Spence's theory (Wertheimer, 1959, pp. 260, 258, n. 8). Unfortunately,

Wertheimer's reply was never completed; it was published posthumously as a fragment. George Katona and Abraham Luchins both published extensive monographs on organizing and memorizing and on mechanization in problem-solving that were based on Wertheimer's alternative assumptions and can be seen as indirect replies to Spence's criticism (Katona, 1940; Luchins, 1942). Still, this work did not lead to cumulative research that could compete with the mounting stream of work that appeared from the University of Iowa after Spence went there in 1940.

In short, the ambivalent initial reception of the Gestalt theorists' world view in the 1920s, and the fate of both the theory and its founders in the transfer phase, eventually produced a successful but incomplete linkage of Gestalt theory with the disciplinary structure and style of American psychology. The Gestalt theorists were heard with respect, and they were able to continue their research and teaching in America. However, they did not obtain positions from which they could hope to directly shape the theoretical and research orientation of the discipline's establishment.

A Difficult Integration (since 1945)

The effects of this state of affairs became clear even before the deaths of Koffka in 1941 and Wertheimer in 1943. Even in those fields of psychology such as perception, where psychologists recognized the fundamental significance of the issues raised by the Gestalt theorists, they rarely accepted the consequences deduced.

One example is the treatment of the Gestalt approach to the question of memory for form in Woodworth's *Experimental Psychology* (1938). In 1922, as noted earlier, Wulf had presented evidence for the proposition that memory traces tend to organize themselves spontaneously over time in the direction of simpler forms, as prescribed by Wertheimer's "Gestalt laws." This thesis contradicted the view held by Müller and others that learned, schematic reactions were responsible for the simplifications observed. In his summary of the research on the problem up to that time, Woodworth noted that all investigators had found evidence of the tendency noted by Wulf. However, other and sometimes opposite results had also been reported, and there were significant individual differences in subject's responses. Woodworth admitted that none of the experiments had decided between the two theories, and he discussed in detail the methodological problems that stood in the way of such a decision. Some of the results cast doubt upon the idea that redrawn figures are really remembered forms at all. Nevertheless, he concluded that the evidence that spoke for Wulf's thesis was "extremely meager": "Taken as a whole the evidence speaks for the reactive character of learning and reproduction and against the assumption of any positive formative process in retention itself" (Woodworth, 1938, p. 91).

This conclusion did not follow directly from the account that preceded it. Woodworth had let the variety of the findings count against Gestalt theory, but not against the dominant view, a variant of which was also his own. Nonetheless, his opinion remained authoritative for the next generation of work on the topic. The discussion reveals a fundamental difference of opinion about what constitutes scientific proof in psychology. Wulf's and Wertheimer's demands for "good" phenomena could easily be turned around so that all phenomena that do not fit would count against the theory. But accounting for the variance in this way was not the aim of Gestalt theory. That approach sought to isolate the paradigmatic situations that represented the essence of the phenomenon, and to find explanations for these.

A similar pattern recurred in the integration of Gestalt theory into cognitive psychology. According to leaders in the field, such as Jerome Bruner (1980) and Ulric Neisser (personal communication, July 1976), reading Koffka's *Principles* had an influence on their decision to study psychology. However, the "cognitive science" of the 1960s and 1970s, for which those two men and others prepared the way (see Chapter 10, this volume) is based on thinking quite different from Gestalt theory. Proponents of the information-processing approach, and especially references by computer simulators to "bits", often remind the historian of Helmholtz. Leading cognitive psychologists have themselves suggested that their thinking is similar to that of Helmholtz and the Graz school (Neisser, 1976; Rock, 1960). These were, of course, precisely the positions against which the Gestalt theorists originally rebelled. Some of the central problems raised by the Gestalt theorists, such as the role of autochthonous organizing tendencies in perception, were neglected. Recently these issues have been taken up again, with explicit reference to the pioneering achievements of the Gestalt theorists (Kubovy & Pomerantz, 1981). Whether the top-down processing referred to by these writers is what Wertheimer meant when he said that psychology should proceed "from above" is, however, debatable. Most textbook writers in perception provide some space for Wertheimer's Gestalt laws, while some attempt to integrate them with the information-processing approach (Spoehr and Lehmkuehle, 1982). Still others note there is still no adequate theory for many of the phenomena studied by the Gestalt theorists, including apparent motion (Hochberg, 1974; Kaufman, 1974).

The list of such examples could easily be extended to other fields of psychology. Rudolf Arnheim's work in the psychology of art is perhaps the best known example of the contributions of Gestalt theory to fields outside perception (Arnheim, 1954/1974). In social psychology the experiments of Wertheimer's American follower, Solomon Asch, on the effects of group pressure on perception have achieved classical status. However, Asch's attempt systematically to reconstruct the entire field with the aid of Gestalt theory has earned respect, but apparently not a wide following (Asch, 1952). In physiological psychology the work of Köhler, Wallach, and their American-born coworkers on "figural afteref-fects" led to extensive research and discussion. For most participants, however, the discussion ended with the rejection of Köhler's hypotheses about the associated brain events by Lashley, Sperry, and others (e.g., Lashley, Chow & Semmes, 1951). Köhler's methodological and theoretical objections to these refutations and his suggestions for further research were also ignored (Köhler, 1965/1971; see also Henle, 1980). The function of the direct cortical currents discovered by Köhler, however, remains to be explained; and the possibility of holistically operating brain processes continues to be discussed in some quarters. Karl Pribram (1973), for example, believes that Köhler's work can be integrated with his own two-stage "holonomic" model of brain action.

As early as 1950, Edwin Boring tried to formulate a final judgment on the contribution of Gestalt theory. He recognized that the new research issues posed by the Gestalt theorists, taken together, had led to the writing of "a new chapter in psychology." In his view, however, psychology could now proceed without Gestalt theory:

> Gestalt psychology has already passed its peak and is now dying of its own success by being absorbed into what is Psychology [sic!]. If it already seems a little Americanized as compared with what it was in Berlin and Frankfurt, why that is only what should happen to the emigré who has to fit his basic values into a new culture. (Boring 1950, p. 600)

Neither the notion of linear, cumulative progress in science that lies behind this statement, nor Boring's equation of psychology with the discipline established in the United States has been accepted by historians. Perhaps it would be more appropriate to speak of psychology as a discipline fragmented nationally, theoretically, and with respect to its various specialties, in which writers take or leave from Gestalt theory what they will. Gestalt theory as the basis for a reconstruction of psychological science remains the property of a small circle of defenders who continue to influence psychological thinking significantly but from outside its mainstream.

CONCLUSION

This is not the place for a final assessment of Gestalt theory's place in the history of psychology, but this much can be said: The fact that one point of view, emerging in response to the challanges of a particular intellectual and institutional setting, could have a significant impact on theory and research in a very different setting speaks for the international character of psychological science. Indeed, the Gestalt theorists themselves played an important role in the reinternationalization of psychology after World War I. However, the limitations on their impact also point to the limits of the internationalization. The reception of Gestalt theory in the United States was ambivalent from the beginning. Despite Koffka's efforts to present the theory in terms that could be understood and accepted in America, his listeners realized that its presuppositions about psychological reality and science did not conform to their own.

This realization worked against the full institutionalization of Gestalt theory in the United States in the 1930s. As a result, the emigration of the founders of Gestalt theory led to the loss of the theory's unique character as a scientific worldview, and of its institutional identity as a school of thought. The limited nature of the institutionalization that did occur had, in turn, a direct impact on the integration of Gestalt theory into American psychology after 1935. Certainly the Gestalt theorists were not entirely deprived of influence after their immigration; rather, their theory reached new audiences and developed in new ways as a result. But because they did not have positions in which they could train students in greater numbers, their theory became less an active than a passive participant, less a subject than an object of psychology's development. In this case, as in many others—and not only in psychology— it is altogether impossible to separate intellectual from institutional factors in the history of science.

REFERENCE NOTES

1. For brief systematic accounts of Gestalt theory, see Asch, 1968, and Pastore, 1971; the latter treats only the Gestalt theory of perception. For criticism of other systematic and historical accounts, see Pastore, 1974, and Henle, 1980.
2. Feier zu Carl Stumpfs 70. Geburstag, 21. April 1918. Typescript in Max Wertheimer papers, New York Public Library, Box 1.
3. Kurt Koffka, "Beginnings of Gestalt Theory". Lecture delivered 18 April 1931. Kurt Koffka papers, Archives of the History of American Psychology, Akron, Ohio, Box M379, 1–2.
4. Many of Köhler's experiments were borrowed or modified, with acknowledgment,

from L. T. Hobhouse's work with a rhesus monkey, a chimpanzee, and other animals (Hobhouse, 1901/1915; Köhler, 1917/1973, p. 22; 1925/1959, p. 30).

5. Actually, as we have seen, Ehrenfels uses the second criterion, transposability, to prove the existence of the first. Köhler separates the two criteria and gives them equal standing, a step taken earlier by a member of the Graz school, Alois Höfler (1912; see also Hermann, 1976, p. 609; Scheerer, 1931, p. 41).
6. Köhler's invitation was apparently suggested by Langfeld. Cf. Langfeld to Yerkes, 9 June 1924. Robert M. Yerkes papers, Box 48, Folder 935; Department of Manuscripts and Archives, Sterling Memorial Library, Yale University.
7. Koffka to Ogden, 4 July 1925. Robert M. Ogden papers, Box 6; Department of Manuscripts and University Archives, Cornell University Library.
8. Koffka to Wakeman, 10 March 1927. Kurt Koffka correspondence, Smith College Archives, Folder 42. For details of the Smith College offer, see Wakeman to Koffka, 19 March 1927, Koffka correspondence, and William Allen Nielson to Koffka, 18 March 1927, Nielson papers, Smith College Archives.

REFERENCES

Allport, G. (1923/1924). The standpoint of Gestalt psychology. *Psyche, 4,* 354–361.
Arnheim, R. (1928). Experimentelle Untersuchungen zum Ausdrucksproblem. *Psychologische Forschung, 11,* 2–119.
Arnheim, R. (1974). *Art and visual perception: A psychology of the creative eye* (new version). Berkeley: University of California Press. (Original work published 1954)
Asch, S. E. (1952). *Social psychology.* New York: Prentice-Hall.
Asch, S. E. (1968). Gestalt theory. *International encyclopedia of the social sciences.* New York: Macmillan.
Ash, M. G. (1979). The struggle against the Nazis. *American Psychologist, 34,* 363–364.
Ash, M. G. (1980a). Academic politics in the history of science: Experimental psychology in Germany, 1879–1941. *Central European History, 13,* 255–286.
Ash, M. G. (1980b). Wilhelm Wundt and Oswald Külpe on the institutional status of psychology: An academic controversy in historical context. In W. G. Bringmann & R. D. Tweney (Eds.), *Wundt studies.* Toronto: Hogrefe.
Ash, M. G. (1982). *The emergence of Gestalt theory: Experimental psychology in Germany, 1890–1920.* Doctoral dissertation, Harvard University.
Ash, M. G. (1983). The self-presentation of a discipline: History of psychology in the United States between pedagogy and scholarship. In L. Graham et al. (Eds.), *Functions and uses of disciplinary histories: Sociology of the sciences* (Vol. 7). Dordrecht: Riedel.
Ash, M. G. (1984). Max Wertheimer: In memoriam. *History of Psychology Newsletter, 16,* 1–6.
Ash, M. G. (1985). Ein Institut und eine Zeitschrift: Das Psychologische Institut der Universität Berlin und die Zeitschrift 'Psychologische Forschung' vor und nach 1933. In C. F. Graumann (Ed.), *Psychologie im Nationalsozialismus.* Heidelberg: Springer.
Ash, M. G. (in press). The role of developmental concepts in the history of Gestalt theory: The work of Kurt Koffka. In W. G. Bringmann et al. (Eds.), *Contributions to the history of developmental psychology.* The Hague: Mouton.
Becher, E. (1911). *Gehirn und Seele.* Heidelberg: Winter.
Becher, E. (1921). Wolfgang Köhlers physikalische Theorie der physiologischen Vorgänge, die der Gestaltwahrnehmungen zugrunde liegen. *Zeitschrift für Psychologie, 87,* 1–44.
Benussi, V. (1904). Zur Psychologie des Gestalterfassens. In A. Meinong (Ed.), *Untersuchungen zur Gegenstandstheorie und Psychologie.* Leipzig: Barth.

Benussi, V. (1906). Experimentelles über Vorstellungsinadäquatheit.[*Zeitschrift für Psychologie*], 42, 22–55; 45, 188–230.

Benussi, V. (1911). Über die Motive der Scheinkörperlichkeit bei umkehrbaren Zeichnungen. *Archiv für die gesamte Psychologie, 20*, 363–396.

Benussi, V. (1914a). Gesetze der inadäquaten Gestaltauffassung. *Archiv für die gesamte Psychologie, 32*, 396–419.

Benussi, V. (1914b). Kinematische Scheinbewegungen und Auffassungsformung. In F. Schumann (Ed.), *Bericht über den 6. Kongress für experimentelle Psychologie*. Leipzig: Barth.

Bergson, H. (1961). *Essai sur les données immédiates de la conscience* (96th ed.). Paris: Presses Universitaires. (Original work published 1889)

Bergson, H. (1946). Introduction to metaphysics. In *The creative mind* (M. L. Anderson, Trans.). New York: Philosophical Library. (Original work published 1903)

Bertalanffy, L. von. (1968). *General systems theory*. New York: Brazilier.

Blanshard, F. (1970). *Frank Aydelotte of Swarthmore*. Middletown, CT: Wesleyan University Press.

Boring, E. G. (1942). *Sensation and perception in the history of experimental psychology*. New York: Appleton-Century-Crofts.

Boring, E. G. (1950). *A history of experimental psychology* (2nd ed.). New York: Appleton-Century-Crofts.

Bruner, J. (1980). Jerome Bruner. In G. Murphy et al. (Eds.), *A history of psychology in autobiography* (Vol. 7). San Francisco: Freeman.

Brunswik, E. (1933). Die Zugänglichkeit von Gegenständen für die Wahrnehmung. *Archiv für die gesamte Psychologie, 88*, 377–418.

Bühler, K. (1908). Tatsachen und Probleme zu einer Psychologie der Denkvorgänge, II. Über Gedanken. *Archiv für die gesamte Psychologie, 12*, 1–23.

Bühler, K. (1913). *Die Gestaltwahrnehmungen*. Stuttgart: Spemann.

Bühler, K. (1927). *Die Krise der Psychologie*. Jena: Fischer.

Cattell, J. M. (1929). Psychology in America. *Science, 70*, 335–347.

Cornelius, H. (1892). Über Verschmelzung und Analyse. *Vierteljahresschrift für wissenschaftliche Philosophie, 16*, 404–446; 17, 30–75.

Danziger, K. (1979). The positivist repudiation of Wundt. *Journal of the History of the Behavioral Sciences, 15*, 205–230.

Dewey, J. (n.d.). *Essays in experimental logic*. New York: Dover. (Original work published 1916)

Dilthey, W. (1974). Ideen über eine beschreibende und zergliedernde Psychologie. In *Gesammelte Schriften* (Vol. 5). Göttingen: Vandenhoeck & Ruprecht. (Original work published 1894)

Duncker, K. (1929). Über induzierte Bewegung. *Psychologische Forschung, 12*, 180–259.

Dunlap, K. (1912). The nature of perceived relations. *Psychological Review, 19*, 415–446.

Ebbinghaus, H. (1905). *Grundzüge der Psychologie* (Vol. 1, 2nd ed.). Leipzig: Veit. (Original work published 1897)

Ebbinghaus, H. (1912). *Abriss der Psychologie* (4th ed.). Leipzig: Veit. (Original work published 1908)

Ehrenfels, C. von (1960). Über Gestaltqualitäten. In F. Weinhandel (Ed.), *Gestalthaftes Sehen*. Darmstadt: Wissenschaftliche Buchgesellschaft. (Original work published 1890)

Erdmann, B., & Dodge, R. (1898). *Psychologische Untersuchungen über das Lesen auf experimentelle Grundlage*. Halle: Niemeyer.

Exner, S. (1875). Über das Sehen von Bewegungen und die Theorie des zusammengesetzen Auges. *Sitzungsberichte der Wiener Akademie der Wissenschaften, 72*, 156–190.

Fernberger, S. W. (1928). Statistical analysis of the members of the American Psychological Association, Inc. in 1928. *Psychological Review, 35*, 447–465.

Freeman, F. (1977). The beginnings of Gestalt psychology in the United States. *Journal of the History of the Behavioral Sciences, 13*, 352–353.

Garvey, C. R. (1929). List of American psychology laboratories. *Psychological Bulletin, 26*, 652–660.

Gay, P. (1968). *Weimar culture: The outsider as insider.* New York: Harper.

Gelb, A. (1911). Theoretisches über Gestaltqualitäten. *Zeitschrift für Psychologie, 58*, 1–59.

Gelb, A., & Goldstein, K. (1920). *Psychologische Analysen hirnpathologischer Fälle.* Leipzig: Barth.

Geuter, U. (1984). "Gleichschaltung" von oben? Universitätspolitische Strategien und Verhaltensweisen während des Nationalsozialismus. *Psychologische Rundschau, 35*, 198–213.

Gibson, J. J. (1971). The legacies of Koffka's "Principles." *Journal of the History of the Behavioral Sciences, 7*, 3–9.

Gregg, F. M. (1932). Materializing the ghost of Köhler's Gestalt psychology. *Psychological Review, 39*, 257–270.

Heider, F. (1927). Ding und Medium. *Symposion, 1*, 109–157.

Helmholtz, H. von. (1971). Recent progress in the theory of vision. In R. Kahl (Ed.), *The selected writings of Hermann von Helmholtz.* Middletown, CT: Wesleyan University Press. (Original work published 1868)

Helmholtz, H. von. (1924–1925). *Treatise on physiological optics* (J. P. C. Southall, Trans.). New York: Optical Society of America. (Original work published 1856–1867)

Helson, H. (1925–1926). The psychology of Gestalt. *American Journal of Psychology, 36*, 342–370, 494–526; *37*, 25–62, 189–223.

Henle, M. (1965). On Gestalt psychology. In B. Wolman (Ed.), *Scientific psychology: Principles and approaches.* New York: Basic Books.

Henle, M. (Ed.). (1971). *The selected papers of Wolfgang Köhler.* New York: Liveright.

Henle, M. (1978). One man against the Nazis: Wolfgang Köhler. *American Psychologist, 33*, 939–944.

Henle, M. (1980). The influence of Gestalt psychology in America. In R. Rieber & K. Salzinger (Eds.), *Psychology: Theoretical and historical perspectives.* New York: Academic.

Henle, M. (1984). Robert M. Ogden and Gestalt psychology in America. *Journal of the History of the Behavioral Sciences, 20*, 9–19.

Hering, E. (1879). Der Raumsinn und die Bewegung des Auges. In L. Hermann (Ed.), *Handbuch der Physiologie.* Leipzig: Vogel.

Hering, E. (1962). *Outlines of a theory of the light sense* (L. M. Hurwitz & D. Jameson, Trans.). Cambridge, MA: Harvard University. (Original work published 1920)

Hermann, T. (1976). Ganzheitspsychologie und Gestalttheorie. In H. Balmer (Ed.), *Die Psychologie des 20. Jahrhunderts* (Vol. 1). Zurich: Kindler.

Hobhouse, L. T. (1915). *Mind in evolution* (2nd ed.). London: Macmillan. (Original work published 1901)

Hochberg, J. (1974). Organization and the Gestalt tradition. In E. C. Carterette & M. P. Friedman (Eds.), *Handbook of perception* (Vol. 1). New York: Academic.

Höffding, H. (1889/1890). Über Wiedererkennen: Association und psychologische Aktivität. *Vierteljahresschrift für Wissenschaftliche Philosophie, 13*, 420–458; *14*, 27–54, 167–205, 293–316.

Höfler, A. (1912). Gestalt und Beziehung, Gestalt und Anschauung. *Zeitschrift für Psychologie, 60*, 161–228.

Husserl, E. (1900–1901). *Logische Untersuchungen* (2 vols.). Halle: Niemeyer.

Jaensch, E. R., & Grünhut, L. (1929). *Über Gestalttheorie.* Osterwieck: Zickfeldt.

James, W. (1950). *The principles of psychology* (2 vols.). New York: Dover. (Original work published 1890)

James, W. (1909). *A pluralistic universe.* New York: Longmans, Green.

Katona, G. (1940). *Organizing and memorizing: Studies in the psychology of learning and thinking.* New York: Columbia University.

Katz, D. (1911). Die Erscheinungsweisen der Farben und ihre Beeinflussung durch die individuelle Erfahrung. *Zeitschrift für Psychologie,* Ergänzungsband 7.

Katzaroff, W. (1911). Contribution a l'étude de la recognition. *Archiv de Psychologie, 11,* 2–78.

Kaufman, L. (1974). *Sight and mind.* New York: Oxford University Press.

Koffka, K. (1909). Experimentaluntersuchungen zur Lehre vom Rhythmus. *Zeitschrift für Psychologie, 52,* 1–109.

Koffka, K. (1912). *Zur Analyse der Vorstellungen und ihrer Gesetze.* Leipzig: Quelle, Meyer.

Koffka, K. (1914). Psychologie der Wahrnehmung. *Die Geisteswissenschaften, 1,* 711–716, 796–800.

Koffka, K. (1915). Zur Grundlegung der Wahrnehmungspsychologie: Eine Auseinandersetzung mit V. Benussi. *Zeitschrift für Psychologie, 73,* 11–90.

Koffka, K. (1922). Perception: An introduction to the Gestalttheorie. *Psychological Bulletin, 19,* 531–585.

Koffka, K. (1925). *The growth of the mind: An introduction to child psychology* (R. M. Ogden, Trans.). New York: Harcourt, Brace. (Original work published 1921)

Koffka, K. (1933). [Review of *Purposive behavior in animals and men*]. *Psychological Bulletin, 30,* 440–451.

Koffka, K. (1935). *Principles of Gestalt psychology.* New York: Harcourt, Brace.

Köhler, W. (1913). Akustische Untersuchungen III und IV: Vorläufige Mitteilung. *Zeitschrift für Psychologie, 64,* 92–105.

Köhler, W. (1915). Optische Untersuchungen am Schimpansen und am Haushuhn. *Abhandlungen der Königlich Preussischen Akademie der Wissenschaften,* physikalisch-mathematische Klasse, No. 3.

Köhler, W. (1918). Nachweis einfacher Strukturfunktionen beim Schimpansen und beim Haushuhn. *Abhandlungen der Königlich Preussischen Akademie der Wissenschaften,* physikalisch-mathematische Klasse, No. 2.

Köhler, W. (1923). Zur Theorie des Sukzessivvergleichs und der Zeitfehler. *Psychologische Forschung, 4,* 115–175.

Köhler, W. (1924a). *Die physischen Gestalten in Ruhe und im stationären Zustand: Eine naturphilosophische Untersuchung* (2nd ed.). Erlangen: Verlag der Philosophischen Akademie. (Original work published 1920)

Köhler, W. (1924b). Gestaltprobleme und Anfänge einer Gestalttheorie. *Jahresbericht über die gesamte Physiologie und experimentelle Pharmakologie, 3,* 512–539.

Köhler, W. (1925a). An aspect of Gestalt psychology. In C. Murchison (Ed.), *Psychologies of 1925.* Worcester, MA: Clark University Press.

Köhler, W. (1925b). Komplextheorie und Gestalttheorie: Antwort auf G. E. Müllers Schrift gleichen Namens. *Psychologische Forschung, 6,* 358–416.

Köhler, W. (1929). *Gestalt psychology.* New York: Liveright.

Köhler, W. (1959). *The mentality of apes* (E. Winter, Trans.). New York: Vintage. (Original work published 1925)

Köhler, W. (1959). Some contributions to the psychology of chimpanzees. In W. Köhler, *The mentality of apes* (E. Winter, Trans.). New York: Vintage. (Original work published 1922)

Köhler, W. (1971). An old pseudoproblem. In M. Henle (Ed.), *The selected papers of Wolfgang Köhler*. New York: Liveright. (Original work published 1929)

Köhler, W. (1971). On the problem of regulation (M. Henle & E. Goldmeier, Trans.). In M. Henle (Ed.), *Selected papers*. New York: Liveright. (Original work published 1927).

Köhler, W. (1971). On unnoticed sensations and errors of judgment (H. E. Adler, Trans.). In M. Henle (Ed.), *Selected papers*. New York: Liveright. (Original work published 1913)

Köhler, W. (1971). The scientists from Europe and their new environment. In M. Henle (Ed.), *Selected papers*. New York: Liveright. (Original work published 1953)

Köhler, W. (1971). Unsolved problems in the field of figural after-effects. In M. Henle (Ed.), *Selected papers*. New York: Liveright. (Original work published 1965)

Köhler, W. (1973). *Intelligenzprüfungen an Anthropoiden* (3rd ed.). Berlin: Springer. (Original work published 1917)

Köhler, W. (1976). *The place of value in a world of facts*. New York: Liveright. (Original work published 1938)

Köhler, W., & Wallach, H. (1944). Figural after-effects: An investigation of visual processes. *Proceedings of the American Philosophical Society, 88,* 269–357.

Korte, A. (1915). Kinematische Untersuchungen. *Zeitschrift für Psychologie, 72,* 194–296.

Kries, J. von. (1901). *Über die materiellen Grundlagen der Bewusstseinserscheinungen.* Tübingen: Mohr.

Krueger, F. (1924). Wilhelm Wundt als deutscher Denker. In A. Hoffman (Ed.), *Wilhelm Wundt: Eine Würdigung* (2nd ed.). Erfurt: Stenger.

Krueger, F. (1953). Über psychische Ganzheit. In E. Heuss (Ed.), *Zur Philsophie und Psychologie der Ganzheit*. Berlin: Springer. (Original work published 1928)

Kubovy, M., & Pomerantz, J. (1981). *Perceptual organization*. Hillsdale, NJ: Erlbaum.

Külpe, O. (1914). *Die Philosophie der Gegenwart in Deutschland* (6th ed.). Leipzig: Teubner. (Original work published 1902)

Langfeld, H. S. (1937). Stumpf's "Introduction to Psychology." *American Journal of Psychology, 50,* 33–56.

Laqueur, W. (1974). *Weimar: A cultural history*. New York: Putnam.

Lashley, K. S. (1912). Visual discrimination of size and form in the albino rat. *Journal of Animal Behavior, 2,* 310–331.

Lashley, K. S. (1930). Basic neural mechanisms in behavior. *Psychological Review, 37,* 1–24.

Lashley, K. S., Chow, K., & Semmes, J. (1951). An examination of the electrical field theory of cerebral integration. *Psychological Review, 58,* 123–136.

Lauenstein, O. (1933). Ansatz zu einer physiologischen Theorie des Vergleichs und der Zeitfehler. *Psychologische Forschung, 17,* 130–177.

Leichtman, M. J. (1979). Gestalt theory and the revolt against positivism. In A. Buss (Ed.), *Psychology in social context*. New York: Irvington.

Lewin, K. (1937). Carl Stumpf. *Psychological Review, 44,* 189–194.

Lindenfeld, D. (1980). *The transformation of positivism: Alexius Meinong and European thought, 1880–1920*. Berkeley: University of California Press.

Lowry, R. (1979). *The evolution of psychological theory: 1650 to the present*. Chicago: Aldine.

Luchins, A. S. (1942). Mechanization and problem solving: The effect of "Einstellung." *Psychological Monographs, 54,* (Whole No. 248).

Lund, F. (1929). The phantom of the Gestalt. *Journal of General Psychology, 2,* 307–323.

Mach, E. (1910). Bemerkungen zur Lehre von räumlichen Sehen. In *Populär-Wissenschaftliche Vorlesungen* (4th ed.). Leipzig: Barth. (Original work published 1865)

Mach, E. (1959). *The analysis of sensations* (C. W. Williams & S. Waterlow, Trans.). New York: Dover. (Original work published 1886)

Mach, E. (1965). On the effect of the spatial distribution of the light stimuli on the retina. In F. Ratliff (Ed.), *Mach bands: Quantitative studies on neural networks in the retina.* San Francisco: Holden-Day. (Original work published 1865)

Maier, N. R. F. (1930). Reasoning in humans. I. On Direction. *Journal of Comparative Psychology, 10,* 115–143.

Maier, N. R. F. (1931). Reasoning in humans. II. The solution of a problem and its appearance in consciousness. *Journal of Comparative Psychology, 12,* 181–194.

Mandler, G., & Mandler, J. M. (1969). The diaspora of experimental psychology: The Gestaltists and others. In D. Fleming & B. Bailyn (Eds.), *The intellectual migration: Europe and America, 1930-1960.* Cambridge, MA: Harvard University Press.

Marbe, K. (1910). *Theorie der kinematischen Projektionen.* Leipzig: Barth.

Morgan, C. L. (1894). *An Introduction to Comparative Psychology.* London: Scott.

Müller, G. E. (1896/1897). Zur Psychophysik der Gesichtsempfindungen. *Zeitschrift für Psychologie, 10,* 1–82, 321–413; *14,* 1–76, 161–196.

Müller, G. E. (1904). *Die Gesichtspunkte und die Tatsachen der psychophysischen Methodik.* Wiesbaden: Bergmann.

Müller, G. E. (1913). Zur Analyse der Gedächtnistätigkeit und des Vorstellungsverlaufs. *Zeitschrift für Psychologie,* Ergänzungsband 8.

Müller, G. E. (1923). *Komplextheorie und Gestalttheorie: Ein Beitrag zur Wahrnehmungspsychologie.* Göttingen: Vandenhoeck.

Neisser, U. (1976). *Cognition and reality: Principles and implications of cognitive psychology.* San Francisco: Freeman.

O'Donnell, J. M. (1979). The crisis of experimentation in the 1920s: E. G. Boring and his uses of history. *American Psychologist, 34,* 289–295.

O'Donnell, J. M. (1985). *The origins of behaviorism: American psychology, 1870–1920.* New York: New York University Press.

Ogden, R. M. (1928). The Gestalt-hypothesis. *Psychological Review, 35,* 136–141.

O'Neil, W. M., & Landauer, A. A. (1966). The phi-phenomenon: Turning point or rallying point? *Journal of the History of the Behavioral Sciences, 2,* 335–340.

Pastore, N. (1971). *Selective history of theories of visual perception: 1650–1950.* New York: Oxford University Press.

Pastore, N. (1974). Reevaluation of Boring on Kantian influence, nineteenth-century nativism, Gestalt psychology and Helmholtz. *Journal of the History of the Behavioral Sciences, 10,* 375–390.

Perry, R. B. (1926). *General theory of value: Its meaning and basic principles construed in terms of interest.* Cambridge, MA: Harvard University Press.

Pribram, K. (1973). *Languages of the brain: Experimental paradoxes and principles in neuropsychology.* Englewood Cliffs, NJ: Prentice-Hall.

Rahn, C. (1913). The relation of sensation to other categories in contemporary psychology: A study in the psychology of thinking. *Psychological Monographs, 6,* (Whole No. 67).

Restorff, H. van. (1933). Über die Wirkung von Bereichsbildung im Spurenfeld. *Psychologische Forschung, 8,* 299–342.

Ringer, F. K. (1969). *The decline of the German mandarins: The German academic community, 1890–1933.* Cambridge, MA: Harvard University Press.

Rock, I. (1960). The present status of Gestalt psychology. In J. Peatman & E. Hartley (Eds.), *Festschrift for Gardner Murphy.* New York: Harper.

Rubin, E. (1914). Die visuelle Wahrnehmung von Figuren. In F. Schumann (Ed.), *Bericht über den 6. Kongress für experimentelle Psychologie.* Leipzig: Barth.

Rubin, E. (1921). *Visuell wahrgenommene Figuren* (P. Collett, Trans.). Copenhagen: Cyldenalske.

Sander, F. (1928). Experimentelle Ergebnisse der Gestaltpsychologie. In E. Becher (Ed.), *Bericht über den 10. Kongress für experimentelle Psychologie*. Jena: Fischer.

Scheerer, E. (1980). Gestalt psychology in the Soviet Union, I. The Period of Enthusiasm. *Psychological Research, 41*, 113–132.

Scheerer, M. (1931). *Die Lehre von der Gestalt: Ihre Methode und ihr psychologischer Gegenstand*. Berlin: De Gruyter.

Scheler, M. (1923). *Wesen und Formen der Sympathie* (2nd ed.). Bonn: Cohen. (Original work published 1913)

Schulenburg, S. von den (Ed.). (1923). *Briefwechsel zwischen Wilhelm Dilthey und dem Grafen Paul Yorck von Wartenburg, 1877–1897*. Halle: Niemeyer.

Schumann, F. (1900). Beiträge zur Analyse der Gesichtswahrnehmungen. *Zeitschrift für Psychologie, 23*, 1–32; *24*, 1–33.

Schumann, F. (1904). Die Erkennung von Buchstaben und Worten bei momentaner Beleuchtung. In F. Schumann (Ed.), *Bericht über den 1. Kongress für experimentelle Psychologie*. Leipzig: Barth.

Schumann, F. (1907). Zur Psychologie des Lesens. In F. Schumann (Ed.), *Bericht über den 2. Kongress für experimentelle Psychologie*. Leipzig: Barth.

Schumann, F. (1912). Über einige Hauptprobleme der Lehre von den Gesichtswahrnehmungen. In F. Schumann (Ed.), *Bericht über den 5. Kongress für experimentelle Psychologie*. Leipzig: Barth.

Seaman, J. D. (1984). On phi-phenomena. *Journal of the History of the Behavioral Sciences, 20*, 3–8.

Sokal, M. M. (1984). The Gestalt psychologists in behaviorist America. *American Historical Review, 89*, 1240–1263.

Spence, K. W. (1936). The nature of discrimination learning in animals. *Psychological Review, 43*, 427–449.

Spence, K. W. (1937). The differential response in animals to stimuli varying within a single dimension. *Psychological Review, 44*, 430–444.

Spoehr, K. T., & Lemkuehle, S. W. (1982). *Visual information processing*. San Francisco: Freeman.

Stern, W. (1928). Personalistische Psychologie. In E. Saupe (Ed.), *Einführung in die neuere Psychologie*. Osterwieck: Zickfeldt.

Stumpf, C. (1883–1890). *Tonpsychologie* (2 vols.). Leipzig: Hirzel.

Stumpf, C. (1891). Psychologie und Erkenntnistheorie. *Abhandlungen der Königlich Bayrischen Akademie der Wissenschaften, 19*, 467–516.

Stumpf, C. (1895). Hermann von Helmholtz and the new psychology. *Psychological Review, 2*, 1–12.

Stumpf, C. (1906a). Erscheinungen und psychische Funktionen. *Abhandlungen der Königlich Preussischen Akademie der Wissenschaften*, No. 1.

Stumpf, C. (1906b) Zur Einteilung der Wissenschaften. *Abhanglungen der Königlich Preussischen Akademie der Wissenschaften*, No. 5.

Stumpf, C. (1910a). Das Psychologische Institut. In M. Lenz (Ed.), *Geschichte der Königlichen Friedrich-Wilhelm-Universität zu Berlin* (Vol. 3). Halle: Verlag des Waisenhauses.

Stumpf, C. (1910b). *Philosophische Reden und Vorträge*. Leipzig: Barth.

Tolman, E. C. (1926). A behavioristic theory of ideas. *Psychological Review, 33*, 352–369.

Tolman, E. C. (1932). *Purposive behavior in animals and men*. New York: Appleton-Century-Crofts.

Tolman, E. C. (1952). Edward C. Tolman. In E. G. Boring, H. S. Langfeld, H. Werner, & R. Yerkes (Eds.), *A history of psychology in autobiography*. Worcester, MA: Clark University Press.

Tolman, E. C., & Horowitz, J. (1933). A reply to Mr. Koffka. *Psychological Bulletin, 30,* 459–465.

Turner, R. S. (1982). Helmholtz, sensory physiology and the disciplinary development of German psychology. In W. Woodward & M. Ash (Eds.), *The problematic science: Psychology in nineteenth-century thought.* New York: Praeger.

Wallach, H. (1976). *On perception.* New York: Quadrangle.

Wartensleben, G. von (1914). *Die christliche Persönlichkeit im Idealbild: Eine Beschreibung sub specie psychologica.* Kempten: Kosel.

Wertheimer, M. (1912a). Über das Denken der Naturvölker, I. Zahlen und Zahlgebilde. *Zeitschrift für Psychologie, 60,* 321–378.

Wertheimer, M. (1912b). Experimentelle Studien über das Sehen von Bewegungen. *Zeitschrift für Psychologie, 61,* 161–265.

Wertheimer, M. (1922). Untersuchungen zur Lehre von der Gestalt, I. *Psychologische Forschung, 1,* 47–58.

Wertheimer, M. (1923). Untersuchungen zur Lehre von der Gestalt, II. *Psychologische Forschung, 4,* 301–350.

Wertheimer, M. (1925). Über Schlussprozesse im Productiven Denken. In *Drei Handlungen zur Gestalttheorie.* Erlangen: Verlag der Philosophischen Akademie. (Original work published 1920)

Wertheimer, M. (1925). *Über Gestalttheorie.* Erlangen: Verlag der Philosophischen Akademie.

Wertheimer, M. (1957). *Productive thinking* (rev. ed.). (M. Wertheimer, Ed.). New York: Harper. (Original work published 1945)

Wertheimer, M. (1959). On discrimination experiments. I. *Psychological Review, 66,* 252–266.

Wertheimer, M. (1980). Max Wertheimer: Gestalt prophet. *Gestalt Theory, 2,* 3–17.

Woodward, W. R. (1978). From association to Gestalt: The fate of Hermann Lotze's theory of spatial perception, 1846–1920. *Isis, 69,* 572–582.

Woodward, W. R. (1980). Toward a critical historiography of psychology. In J. Brozek & L. Pongratz (Eds.), *Historiography of modern psychology.* Toronto: Hogrefe.

Woodward, W. R. & Ash, M. G. (Eds.). (1982). *The problematic science: Psychology in nineteenth-century thought.* New York: Praeger.

Woodworth, R. S. (1931). *Contemporary schools of psychology.* New York: Rondald Press.

Woodworth, R. S. (1938). *Experimental psychology.* New York: Macmillan.

Wulf, F. (1922). Über die Veränderung von Vorstellungen. Gedächtnis und Gestalt. *Psychologische Forschung, 1,* 333–373.

Yerkes, R. M. (1916). The mental life of monkeys and apes. *Behavior Monographs,* 3:1. Cambridge & Boston: Holt.

12

Biological Contributions to the Development of Psychology

KARL H. PRIBRAM AND DANIEL N. ROBINSON

INTRODUCTION

This chapter concerns several important influences that biology has had on the development of psychology as a science. Specifically, we attempt to account for an apparent paradox: In the nineteenth century, rapid advances were made in relating biology in general and brain function in particular to the phenomena of mind. Throughout much of the first half of the twentieth century, however, these same relationships were all but ignored and the foundations for a scientific psychology were sought in the environment.

The biological aspects of psychology, perhaps more than other special branches of the discipline, resist historical compression. Psychobiology, as we shall call the subject,[1] is deeply rooted in both philosophy and

---

[1] There is still no universally accepted criterion for distinguishing among the terms physiological psychology, psychobiology, neuropsychology, and biopsychology. A growing convention would reserve the term neuropsychology to theory about the human nervous system based on research involving complex cognitive processes, often in settings in which clinical findings are directly relevant. Physiological psychology strikes many as too restricted, for much current work falls under headings such as biophysics, computer science, or microanatomy that are synonymous with physiology. Thus, psychobiology is used here to refer to the broadest range of correlative studies in which biobehavioral investigations are undertaken and referenced to phenomenal experience.

biological science and was the subject of speculative and experimental psychology 2 centuries before Wundt christened the Leipzig laboratory (1874). Thus, while it is generally agreed that instrumental conditioning received its first great impetus from the work of Bechterev (1911) and Thorndike (1943, 1965) and classical conditioning from that of Pavlov (1927), it would be hazardous to date psychobiology from these beginnings. The subject's history (see Robinson, 1981) could plausibly commence in Greece with Aristotle's *Historia Animalium* or *De Anima*, would surely include the works of Democritus, Leucippus, and Epicurus, and then proceed to a host of figures from Galen in the second century to Descartes in the seventeenth.

There has been one or another form of biologically rooted psychology for as long as there has been serious psychological discourse. No narrow range of time can be taken as introducing its modern expression. Owing to its dependence on the biological sciences, it has tended to spurt ahead with many of biology's significant advances, but the history of the specialty has been something of an ensemble of variations on a more or less constant theme. That theme, of course, is the uniqueness of the human mind as an expression of the uniqueness of the brain, which is itself a metaphysical rather than a scientific view: "In the middle ages thinkers were trying to discover proofs for the existence of God. Today we seem to look for proof for the existence of man" (Heschel, 1965, p. 26).

With these qualifications noted, it is still necessary to begin somewhere. The chapter will be developed according to the following outline: First we describe at some length the most influential nineteenth-century neurobiological contributions to psychology and trace their development to the present. We then examine the emergence of a twentieth-century psychology that eschews the brain in favor of evolution, forfeiting the already maturing psychobiology bequeathed by the nineteenth century. We pause to assay possible reasons why nineteenth- and twentieth-century psychologies are so different from each other, and we conclude by noting that toward the end of the twentieth century some rapprochment between nineteenth- and twentieth-century biological influences has appeared in the form of a prosperous cognitive neuropsychology again prepared to wrestle with the problem of relating mind to brain.

Taking the uniqueness of humans as the theme against which controversy and experiment alike were, in a deep sense, ultimately projected during these two centuries, it becomes easier to distinguish genuine fathers of our ideas from godfathers, grandfathers, and mere custodians. We begin with Franz Joseph Gall and the problem of localizing functions in the brain.

BRAIN SYSTEMS AS ORGANS OF MIND

Alexander Bain (1861) observed that "phrenology is no longer a subject of party heat or violent altercation. Men can support or impugn it with the composure becoming a purely scientific controversy" (p. 14). So many accounts of phrenology—the first discipline to study brain as the organ of the mind—are mere caricatures, and so few of Gall's voluminous contributions have been available, that the modern student may still be confused as to just what this "purely scientific controversy" was all about. It involved at once a thesis, a method, and a set of implications. The thesis was expressed most economically by Gall himself (1822–1825/1835, vol. 1):

> If . . . man has faculties which essentially distinguish him from the animal, and which give to him the peculiar character of humanity, he also offers in his brain . . . parts which animals have not; and the difference of effects is thus found to be explained by the difference of causes. (p. 103)

Certainly these are not the words of some misguided popularizer (though popular they may have become) to be relegated to the dusty attic of history. Rather, they evoke the timeless issue of just what it is that gives rise to our humanity. Their contemporary ring is reflected in passages culled from today's concern with this very issue:

> To begin with, let us assume that it makes sense to say, as we normally do, that each person knows his or her language—that you and I know English, for example—that this knowledge is in part shared among us and represented somehow in our minds, ultimately in our brains, in structures that we can hope to characterize abstractly, and in principle quite concretely, in terms of physical mechanisms. When I use terms such as "mind," "mental representation," "mental computation," and the like, I am keeping to the level of abstract characterization of the properties of certain physical mechanisms, as yet almost entirely unknown. There is no further ontological import to such references to mind or mental representations and acts. In the same way, a theory of human vision might be formulated abstractly in terms of certain modes of representation (say, images or stick-figure principles) that determine the nature of such representations and rules, and so on. In the latter case the inquiry belongs to the study of mind in the terminology that I will adopt, though it need in no sense imply the existence of entities removed from the physical world. (Chomsky, 1980, p. 5)

Gall was thus not the last, nor of course the first, to advance the bold scientific claim that the brain is responsible for humanity. Julien de la Meetrie says as much as *L'homme Machine* (1748), and Pierre Gassendi (1644/1962) challenged Descartes' dualism on the same grounds in the seventeenth century. But Gall was the first to present such a thesis with an immense background of data drawn from anatomy, pathology, and clinical neurology. Indeed, when compared with this background, his much (and properly) maligned "bumpology" is seen to form but a small part of his overall program addressing the relationship between faculties of mind and anatomically separated portions of the brain. In defense of his thesis, Gall undertook brilliant and numerous studies not only of the cadaverous adult human brain and cranium, but of fetal brains, the brains of a wide variety of species, and brains and crania representative of a broad range of developmental stages. Thus his contributions to comparative and ontogenetic neuroanatomy were as great as those he made to psychology: "If, at some future day, naturalists should become better acquainted with the structure of the brains of animals, they may perhaps find in the brain the surest principle for the division into genera" (Gall, 1822–1825/1835, vol. 2, p. 113).

For his data, Gall relied on a combination of clinical, naturalistic, and post mortem observations. He never tired of examining the heads of prominent men of his own time, often going out of his way to meet someone whose achievements aroused interest in his skull! What was controversial about Gall's methods was not only what seemed to be their vulnerability to observational bias, but also their aloofness toward an experimental approach that was already becoming "official." Even more than this, Gall's methods were identified with a thesis as objectionable to the scientific community as it was to the still-dominant religious traditions jealously guarded by watchful clerics. Learning from his own observations that no two brains are identical, and that great individual differences are apparent even at the fetal stage of development, Gall insisted that no degree of environmental homogeneity would eradicate the innately established differences among humans, or for that matter among all animals of any degree of complexity. Coming on the heels of the 18th-century Enlightenment's vaunted egalitarianism, this was a thesis bound to excite enmity. Moreover, by insisting that each fundamental faculty (aptitude), intellectual or moral, is conditioned by a specific "organ" of the brain, Gall seemed to be rupturing the integrity of the ineffable self whose oneness was its signal feature.

By what mechanism might the faculties be coordinated and integrated into the self that is phenomenally experienced? Actually, it was mainly because of the potential dismemberment of the self that Pierre Flourens undertook to refute Gall's theory experimentally. The modern habit of crediting Flourens with toppling phrenology fails to convey the fact that in the Gall-Flourens dispute it was Gall, not Flourens, who upheld a rigorously scientific and antimetaphysical perspective. Flourens, proceeding from the premise that the self is indivisible, insisted that the cerebrum functions as a whole. So wed was Flourens to this metaphysical position that Gall was led to protest in desperation:

It is in vain, that we demonstrate to the adversaries of the plurality of organs, that, from the lowest species . . . up to man, the cerebrum becomes more and more complicated. . . . Obstinately bent on explaining the simplicity of the *moi*, they see in all these incontestable facts nothing but a diminution of the simple cerebral mass. (Gall, 1822–1825/1835, vol. 6, p. 87)

Even a brief account of Gall's neuropsychology must make mention of his bumpology. It is important to appreciate that Gall did not claim that the cranial surface perfectly registers the morphological nuances of the cerebral mantle. In fact, it was Gall's own research that proved a less-than-perfect match. Nor did he claim that some specific region of the brain controlled intellect: "There are . . . as many different kinds of intellect as there are distinct qualities and faculties. . . . [A]n organ of intellect or understanding, is as entirely inadmissable, as an organ of instinct" (Gall, 1822–1825/1835, vol. 6, pp. 265–266). Accordingly, his theory was not, and could not be, overturned by any experiment purporting to find the survival of global functions following the ablation of specific structures. General problem-solving, for example, involves any number of more basic propensities, according to Gall, and will not be eradicated by the destruction of this or that small area of brain. In an almost ironic manner, therefore, Gall's system of phrenology is as much a "mass action" system as that proposed by Flourens and later by Lashley, but for fundamentally different reasons. Gall would defend a principle of mass action not in terms of most of the brain being devoted to a given faculty, but rather in terms of a given function arising from a multiplicity of faculties, each one of which depends on a specific organ of the brain.

This is not the occasion for either elegy or eulogy where Gall and his thesis are concerned. It is enough to note that he put the problem of the localization of function on the map of neuropsychology and cast it as a scientific problem to be settled by observation and experiment, a problem requiring careful study of the psychology of lower and developing organisms. Additionally, he did much to promote *characterology*—the study of personality—as a proper subject for a scientific psychology, or *bio*psychology.

Gall was one of the major pre-Darwin architects of the naturalistic and evolutionary perspective that would come to dominate psychology by the end of the nineteenth century. He rebuked those "who still love to believe that animals are only machines, automatons" (Gall, 1822–1825/ 1835, vol. 6, p. 118). Indeed, "the real detractors of the human species are those who think they must deny the intelligence of animals to maintain the dignity of man" (vol. 1, p. 94). Perhaps the Darwinian perspective is most clearly given in Gall's defense of his theory against no less a critic than Napoleon. On inquiring into the nature of Gall's science, Napoleon had been told that Gall "attributes to certain bumps [on the skull], [those] dispositions and crimes which [I, Napoleon, believe to be] not in the nature [of man] but [to] arise [solely] from the conventional arrangements of society" (vol. 6, p. 243). To this, Gall replies:

> In regard to my doctrines, the ideas and prejudices of Napoleon differ in no respect from those of the vulgar. What would become of the bump for thieving, if there were no property? Of that of ambition, if there were no society? What would become of the eye if there were no light?—but light exists . . . In the same way, property and society exist in nature . . . [N]either Napoleon nor his advisers has penetrated sufficiently far into the nature of things, to perceive that the organization of man and animals, is calculated for and adapted to the existences of the external world. (vol. 6, p. 243)

As with any major successful theory, there is danger that popular distortions and misunderstandings may develop, that sublime work and thought may spawn ridiculous consequences. This was the fate of Gall's contributions when they were popularized as the cult of phrenology. Soon, people were feeling each other's skulls in order to gauge their characters. In reaction to this vulgarization continued careful scientific work in the same tradition as that pioneered by Gall disavowed "localization," even when such localization of function was in fact found. Thus, Flourens has come down to us as an antilocalizationist, when in fact his major experimental contribution was to separate motor control from intellectual (problem-solving) abilities.

Specifically, Flourens showed that cerebellar resections impair motor functions, leaving problem-solving ability otherwise intact, while cerebral resections fail to interfere universally with motor function but leave the animal stupid: "The ablation of the cerebrum which abolishes intelligence has absolutely no effect on the control of reflexes and movements. The ablation of the cerebellum which abolishes all regularity of movements, does not in the least affect intelligence. This opposition [of effect] is remarkable" (Flourens, 1858, pp. 48–49).

BRAIN, REFLEX, AND WILL

By the end of the eighteenth century, the time of Gall's earliest contributions to psychobiology, a number of scientists had already made seminal contributions to an understanding of neural functions. Of all the mechanisms examined, the one that would come to serve psychology most significantly was the reflex. It was implicit in the mechanistic part of Descartes' philosophy, and although there was then no firm scientific support for the view, the possibility of a materialistic monism was envisioned. Descartes declared against this possibility, proclaiming instead his famous dualism based on *cogito ergo sum*. But nineteenth-century psychology, rooted in empiricism rather than in rationalism, was not to be convinced so easily.

The earliest truly systematic investigations into the organization of spinal reflexes were completed by Robert Whytt and appeared in the edition of his works published by his son in 1768. By studying the involuntary movements of decapitated frogs, Whytt clearly established that mechanical stimulation of the nerves was the causal antecedent of these movments. Comparing the time course of paralyses induced by vascular ligatures with those resulting from a sectioning of the nerves, he showed unequivocally that paralysis is not a correlate of reduced blood flow but a consequence of denervation. Further, he left no room for doubt regarding the power of the nerves to overcome "acts of will." In the natural state, "VOLUNTARY contraction is owing to the stronger action of the nervous influence upon any muscle, excited by the power of the will . . . In proportion as the *stimulus* is more or less gentle, so (*ceteris paribus*) is the contraction of the muscle to which it is applied (Whytt, 1768, pp. 9–10).

Georg Prochaska, a German physician, was perhaps the first to use the term "reflex" (or *reflexion*) in the modern psychological sense. His research was a conscious extension of Whytt's efforts though, like Whytt, Prochaska had no idea of the means by which nervous "power" is translated into muscular contractions:

> The reflexion of sensorial into motor impressions, which takes place in the sensorium commune, is not performed according to mere physical laws, where the angle of reflexion is equal to the angle of incidence, and where the reaction is equal to the action; but that reflexion follows according to certain laws, writ, as it were, by nature on the medullary pulp of the sensorium, which laws we are able to know from their effects only, and in nowise to find out by our reason. The general law, however, by which the sensorium commune reflects sensorial into motor impressions, is the preservation of the individual; so that certain motor impressions follow certain external impressions calculated to injure our body, and give rise to movements having this object, namely, that the annoying cause be averted and removed from our body; and *vice versa*, internal or motor impressions follow external or sensorial impressions beneficial to us, giving rise to motions tending to the end that the agreeable condition shall be maintained. . . . [T]his reflexion may take place, either with consciousness or without consciousness. (Prochaska, 1784/1851, pp. 431–432)

Prochaska's "general law" is an early formulation of the law of effect, couched in the language of sensory–motor integration. It was not until early in the nineteenth century, however, that Charles Bell (1811) discovered the anatomical basis of the reflex—that is, the division of sensory and motor functions of the spinal cord, a discovery later made independently by François Magendie (1822) and now generally known as the Bell–Magendie law. As the eighteenth century ended, Luigi Galvani published his observations of the electrical foundations of neuromuscular processes (1644/1954), finally providing an explanation of the power involved in translating sensations into movements. Galvani's work was controversial and did not succeed in narrowing the range of theoretical possibilities. Indeed, it was not until the middle of the 19th century that talk of "aethers" and "dephlogisticated air" gave way to the language of electrophysiology in discussions of neural mechanisms.

Between 1850 and 1880, largely through the achievements of Hermann von Helmholtz (1856–1869/1924) and Emile du Bois-Reymond (1848–1884), the electrical theory became official. Du Bois-Reymond advanced a polarization theory of neural excitation conceptually akin to late twentieth-century findings on graded potential changes (see Pribram, 1960, 1971; Schmitt, Dev, & Smith, 1976), especially as these occur in axonless "local circuit neurons" of the brain (Rakic, 1976). Thus, in the century beginning with the research of Whytt (circa. 1750) and culminating in Helmholtz's studies of neural propagation in the 1850s, the anatomy, gross physiology, and theoretical significance of the reflex were uncovered. The foundations for a mechanistic, materialistic integration of the human being had been laid.

Initial attempts at stimulation of neural tissue culminated in the mapping of the motor cortex of the brains of wounded soldiers during the Franco-Prussian war by Gustav Fritsch and Edward Hitzig (1870/1969). These investigators also carried out careful experiments that located the parts of the dog's cortex responsive to electrical stimulation:

> The starting point of the present investigations [was] observations one of us had the opportunity to make on human subjects, which concerned the first movements of voluntary muscles produced and observed after direct stimulation of the central organs.
>
> In the first *experiments* the animals (dogs) were not narcotized, but later the skull was trephined under narcosis, on an as far as possible plane area. The whole half of the calvarium, or only the part of it covering the anterior lobe of the brain, was then removed by means of cutting bone with forceps with rounded tips.
>
> Part of the convexity of the cerebrum in the dog is of motor character (this expression is used in Schiff's sense) and another part of the non-motor character.
>
> Generally speaking, the motor part is situated more in the anterior and the non-motor part in the posterior regions. Electrical stimulation of the motor part can produce combined muscle contractions in the contralateral half of the body.
>
> If very weak currents are used, these muscular contractions can be localized to certain narrowly defined groups of muscles.
>
> Using very weak currents, the possibility of exciting a well-defined group of muscles is limited to very small spots which may be called centres for the sake of brevity. A very slight shift in the position of the electrode still causes movement

in the same extremity, but if initially the stimulus caused extention, for example, now, after the change of position, flexure or rotation would be evoked. (Fritsch & Hitzig, 1870/1969, pp. 353–355)

In both the laboratory and the clinic, these observations were extended over the next century. Careful mappings showed that the arrangement of cortical "centers" reflects the arrangement of the body musculature (but with distortions such that muscles serving finer and more complex operations are represented in a proportionally larger area). This arrangement—a "homunculus" when the human cortex is involved—accounted for the observation of Hughlings Jackson (1873) that grand mal epileptic seizures progressed predictably from one muscle group to an adjacent one. The thesis that the brain is a representational system was thus further established.

The great respect that neurologists and neurophysiologists attained for functions of the cerebral cortex in the nineteenth century made them suspect that these motor regions of the cerebral mantle were in fact the seat of the will (i.e., of volitional action). But it was not until the mid-twentieth century that experimental tests of this possibility proved feasible. By then it was possible to record electrical activity of the brain and relate it to behavior. Changes were shown to occur in recordings from the motor cortex not only when movement occurred, but also prior to those movements, and even in their absence when patients simply willed an act but did not express their will (Kornhuber, 1974).

Meanwhile, indications of a number of mechanistic and materialistic theories began to surface in the second half of the nineteenth century, although it would remain for Bechterev and Pavlov to contribute the necessary experimental procedures and findings to flesh out such theories. For example, Alexander Bain (discussed at length in Chapter 4, this volume), published two important volumes devoted to a biologically based psychology—*The Senses and the Intellect* (1855) and *The Emotions and the Will* (1859)—both of which remained authoritative in the English-speaking world for some thirty years.

The process of association was the linchpin of Bain's psychology, a process governed by Bain's version of Hume's laws of continuity, repetition, and resemblance. Since the time of Hume, British empiricist psychologists had generally defended the associational theory of ideas, as can be seen in the psychological essays of Thomas Brown, James Mill, and John Stuart Mill (one of Bain's close friends). By both diffusion and invention, the continental world of science had arrived at much the same place under the influence of Charles Bonnet, Johann Herbart, and others. The fact that David Hartley (1749/1970) had been obliged to rely on Newtonian "vibratiuncles," whereas Bain could speak in the more modern idiom of "nerve currents" should not be overestimated, however, for Bain avoided an uncritical materialism and reductionism such as that of August Comte, who would have all mental phenomena finally absorbed by the science of physiology. Instead, Bain took a dualistic position, and if he had any doubts, Mill's *A System of Logic* (1843/1874) would have removed them.[2] Compte's kind of radical reductionism was, at best, a metaphysical position, and at worst mere sloganeering. Bain (1861) puts it well in his book on character:

> It is not only incompetent, but wholly unphilosophical even in attempt, to resolve mind into brain, nerve and muscle; the things are radically distinct in their nature, as heat is different from gravity, or light from solidity; the true aim of the inquirer is to find the laws of their relationship. (p. 17)

Bain's assessment of phrenology was grounded in the judgment that Gall had been on the right track but had gone beyond the facts and rushed too quickly into the outer reaches of theory. What he found most commendable in Gall's efforts was just this habit of the inquirer: the search for lawful dependencies between psychological phenomena and brain processes. He also wished that the phrenologists had given more weight to the causal agencies of education and society, but Gall was actually less fatalistic than one would gather from Bain's critique. In any case, Bain's system of physiological psychology was entirely sensitive to the effect of environmental nuances, appreciating that the brain, too, was a malleable organ shaped by a history of sensations and nurtured by exercise, nutrition, and both formal and general education.

Herbert Spencer also sanctioned the biological approach to psychological issues in his *Principles of Psychology* (1855/1897), and men such as Théodule Ribot in France, Wilhelm Griesinger in Germany, and Henry Maudsley in England were now bringing psychopathology under the same explanatory scheme. Thus, the historical and conceptual lines from Whytt through Bain and his contemporaries and then to Pavlov were remarkably direct. A materialistic reflexology, a mechanistic monism, could perhaps account for the integrative function of the nervous system—the transmutation of sensations into action. But around each corner, and after each experimental result had been interpreted, the question of man's consciousness of this integrative activity, his awareness of awareness, remained to be answered.

---

[2] It is in Book 6, Chapter 4, sections 1 and 2, that Mill demonstrates the survival of a science of mind, no matter what the relationship between neural and mental events may prove to be. It may be noted that, in his preface to the 8th edition of *A System of Logic* (1874), Mill acknowledges several debts to Bain's *Logic* (1870). On the whole, Mill's expectations regarding a thoroughly biological science of the mind were tolerant but lacking in conviction.

BRAIN AND CONSCIOUSNESS

Turning to the world of the senses, we again find at the center the issue of the uniqueness of man with his subjective consciousness. Once again the approach is neurophysiological, but this time it is framed in an elegant and sophisticated psychophysics based on correlations between physics and reports of experience. One has merely to list names to call up the image of prodigious progress in this field of inquiry; for example, Johannes Müller, Ernst Weber, Gustav Fechner, Charles Sherrington, Hermann von Helmholtz, Ewald Hering, and Ernst Mach. To Müller (1833–1840/1852) we owe the notion that sensations are kept separated in neural processing, while to Weber (1851) and Fechner (1859) we owe the foundations of psychophysics and their famous law that the felt intensity of a stimulation is a logarithmic function of the physical intensity of the stimulus. Sherrington's work on the visual mechanism is less well known than his studies on the interactions among spinal reflexes, but in *The Integrative Action of the Nervous System* (1911/1947) he reviews his experiments on sensual fusion as examples of interactions among sensory events that, to some extent, parallel those of reflex events.

In his monumental *Sensations of Tone* (1863/1954) and the *Treatise on Physiological Optics* (1856–1869/1924), Helmholtz brought sensory psychophysics and physiology to a peak still unsurpassed in sophistication, thoroughness, soundness, and comprehensiveness. Modifications in detail, however, have engaged scientists since Hering's *Outlines of a Theory of the Light Sense* (1905/1964) challenged Helmholtz's trichromatic color theory with a four-color opponens–process mechanism. As DeValois has since shown, using microelectrode recordings from cells in the visual pathways (DeValois, 1960; DeValois & Jacobs, 1968), both Helmholtz and Hering were correct—Helmholtz at the initial processing level, Hering at somewhat later stages.

In his five editions of *The Analysis of Sensations*(1886/1959), Mach brings to bear his own and some earlier work on broader issues, as the title of one of his chapters indicates ("The Influence of the preceding Investigations on our Conception of Physics"—see also Ratliff, 1965). This joining of experimental results with the larger intellectual scene laid the foundation for logical positivism. It was then reflected back into psychology via the philosophers of the Vienna Circle as operational behaviorism, a scientific discipline firmly rooted in objective observations. It thus became possible for scientific psychology to attempt to banish introspective analysis to philosophy (for another view of this issue, see Chapter 13, this volume). The issue is once again one of mind and brain, and of pitting consciousness against behavior. As Mach (1886/1959) states:

We may thus establish a guiding principle for the investigation of the sensations. This may be termed the *principle of the complete parallelism of the psychical and physical*. According to our fundamental conception, which recognizes no gulf between the two provinces (the psychical and the physical), this principle is almost a matter of course; but we may also enunciate it, as I did years ago, without the help of this fundamental conception, as a heuristic principle of research.

The principle of which I am here making use goes further than the widespread general belief that a physical entity corresponds to every psychical entity and *vice versa*; it is much more specialized. . . . At the same time the view here advocated is different from Fechner's conception of the physical and psychical as two different aspects of one and the same reality . . . . When I see a green leaf (an event which is conditioned by certain brain-processes) the leaf is of course different in its form and color from the forms, colors, etc., which I discover in investigating a brain, although all forms, colors, etc., are of like nature in themselves, being in themselves neither psychical nor physical. The leaf which I see, considered as dependent on the brain-process, is something psychical, while this brain-process itself represents, in the connection of *its* elements, something physical. And the principle of parallelism holds good for the dependence of the former immediately given group of elements on the latter group, which is only ascertained by means of a physical investigation which may be extremely complicated.

This principle has, moreover, always been more or less consciously, more or less consistently, followed.

For example, when Helmholtz assumes for every tone-sensation a special nerve-fibre (with its appurtenant nerve-process), when he resolves clangs, or compound sounds, into tone-sensations, when he reduces the affinity of compound tones to the presence of like tone-sensations (and nerve-processes), we have in this method of procedure a practical illustration of our principle. (pp. 60–65)

The orientation of the nineteenth-century experimentalists was primarily biological, and it has been twentieth-century biologically oriented investigators such as Keffer Hartline, George von Bekesy, and Russel DeValois who have carried on this tradition. Hartline and Bekesy showed that Mach's differential equations accounting for perceptual contrast were a function of lateral inhibition in vision, audition, and somesthesis (see Ratliff, 1965). DeValois (1960) relates Hering's four primary opponens–process color theory to electrical recordings from cells in the lateral geniculate nucleus, the half-way station between retina and cortex in the visual system, thus relegating Helmholtz's trichromatic mechanism to the retinal receptors. The issue of Mach's mind-brain parallelism versus Fechner's multiple-aspect monism was left for the Vienna Circle to resolve, which they did in favor of Fechner (see Feigl, 1960). Not until the end of the twentieth century did Mach's dualism see a revival by one of his Vienna students, the philosopher Karl Popper, working with the neurophysiologist John Eccles (1976). This time, however, the dualism became a trialism involving the "mind world" of cultural artifact that can mediate interaction. In this way interaction, rather than parallelity, became the theme.

BRAIN AND FEELINGS

Brain processes do not operate in isolation from the rest of the organism. In today's computer language, the brain is a "central processing unit" ("CPU") connected to a set of "peripherals" that include input from receptors and output to effectors. Effectors are muscles and glands, and the muscles can be further classified as those moving the organism in its environment (usually striped muscles) and those involved in regulating the internal organs (viscera) of the body (usually smooth muscles). The receptors are of three kinds: (1) those excited by energies originating at a distance, which constitute our sense organs; (2) skin and muscle receptors, which signal what is happening at or near the body surface; and (3) receptors, which derive their input from inside the body—from the viscera, from chemical secretions circulating in the blood stream, and from various interactions among these sources of internal stimulation which, as we shall see, are the basis of our feelings.

The *Milieu Intérieur* and *la Vie Végétative*

Claude Bernard in the 1830s and 1840s performed a series of experiments showing that the brain is critically involved in the regulation of interactions among sources of internal stimulation: the milieu interieur. Previously, feelings had been attributed to the circulation of humors, or chemicals secreted by various visceral organs. In his *Leçons sur la physiologie et la pathologie du systeme nerveux* (1858), Bernard, a physiologist working with the body's metabolic functions and seeking to bring the experimental method into the teaching of medicine, reviews the work of François Magendie. It was the Magendie who distinguished sensory from motor functions of peripheral nerves by sectioning their dorsal and ventral roots as they connect with the spinal cord. On the basis of his own experiments, Bernard further distinguishes the *nerf grand sympathique*—the sympathetic nervous system—from both the sensory and motor systems. He goes on to discuss his famous "picure" experiments, in which he sectioned, or injured by a needle point, various structures in the cervical spinal cord and brain stem. These experiments showed that the sympathetic (and parasympathetic), autonomic, vegetative functions of the organism were under control of the central nervous system:

> The section of the spinal cord between the cervical and the brachial plexus does not simply produce this appearance of organic movements. One must ask, in

addition, whether this section produces only an excitation of the neural and motor systems in "une vie animale" but does not also produce the inverse in "la vie végétative." In actuality, one finds, after this operation, a diminution in the abdominal circulation and the energy of the functions of the abdominal organs becomes corroded; there is a diminution in the blood pressure, the urinary output and in secretory activities.

This operation modifies profoundly certain chemical and organic phenomena to such a point that, when that animal is also starved for several hours one finds his liver completely emptied of sugar, but filled, however, with glycogen.

It is good to note that it is not necessary to section the entire spinal cord: one can limit the cut somewhat to a fairly large prick: the effects are of the same nature. (Bernard, 1858, vol. 1, pp. 379–380)

The distinction that Bernard makes between *une vie animale* and *la vie végétative* has persisted in French physiology and psychology. Animal life is animated; that is, characterized by movement-in-the-world, whereas vegetative functions tend toward the maintenance of a *milieu intérieur,* or internal environment. Animation is oriented outward, vegetative processes are inwardly directed. In Bernard's view, man's vegetative life had to be thoroughly understood before his uniqueness in disease or in health could be assessed.

Bernard's pioneering work was carried forward by the Viennese scientists Johann Karplus and Alois Kreidl (1909), who applied their findings more directly to the human condition. They demonstrated hypothalamic as well as lower brain stem controls over vegetative functions, as well as distinguishing further between sympathetic and parasympathetic portions of the vegetative system and its central controls. They also emphasized the reciprocal catabolic–anabolic nature (metabolic use, metabolic buildup) of the functions of these systems. Together with the Viennese medical community, they applied their findings to psychopathology through a classification of the normally balanced psychic functions dependent on autonomic reactivity.

In the English-speaking community, the peripheral autonomic system was carefully charted by Langley (1900), who is responsible for naming it:

The sympathetic system, as we have seen, supplies nerve fibres to certain structures in all parts of the body. In some parts of the body these structures receive nerve fibres from other sources than the sympathetic. It is, in consequence, convenient to have some term to include the whole nervous supply. The words "organic," "vegetative," "ganglionic," and "involuntary" have all been used, but they have also been used in senses other than we require. The term "visceral nervous system" has been employed by Gaskell and others, including myself. The word "visceral," however, is obviously inapplicable to some of the structures brought under it, such as the nerve fibres which run to the skin. I propose, then, following a suggestion of Professor Jebb, to use the word "autonomic," including under that term the contractile cells, unstriated muscle, cardiac muscle, and gland cells of the body, together with the nerve cells and fibres in connection with them. (pp. 659–660)

The controls of the central brain stem (including hypothalamus) over the autonomic nervous system were studied by Walter Cannon (1929). Cannon enlarged on Bernard's conception of the maintenance of the *milieu intérieur* by developing the concept of homeostasis. In the hands of his student and colleague, Norbert Wiener (1948), homeostasis was given engineering precision by treating it as the mechanism of an error-correcting negative feedback, the basis of cybernetics (i.e., the theory of control systems).

Cannon also addressed the psychological import of his physiological work. Carl Lange (1885/1887) of Copenhagen had taken variations of vegetative functions of the organism to be the basis of emotion defined as the maintenance of stability or its disruption, and William James further developed Lange's ideas into an influential theory: Emotions were felt whenever bodily, and especially visceral, activity was initiated by a sensory input. Testing this idea, Cannon showed that cutting the nervous innervation to and from the viscera does not alter emotional reactivity, whereas electrical excitation of the hypothalamus does. Brain processes, not vegetative functions, are therefore responsible for emotional experience and expression:

> Since visceral processes are fortunately not a considerable source of sensation, since even extreme disturbances in them yield no noteworthy emotional experience, we can further understand now why these disturbances cannot serve as a means for discriminating between such pronounced emotions as fear and rage, why chilliness, asphyxia, hyperglycemia and fever, though attended by these disturbances are not attended by emotion, and also why total exclusion of visceral factors from emotional expression makes no difference in emotional behavior. It is because the returns from the thoracic and abdominal "sounding board," to use James' words, are very faint indeed, that they play such a minor role in the affective complex. The processes going on in the thoracic and abdominal organs in consequence of sympathetic activity are truly remarkable and various; their value to the organism is not to add richness and flavor to experience, but rather to adapt the internal economy so that in spite of shifts of outer circumstance the even tenor of the inner life will not be profoundly disturbed. (Cannon, 1929, p. 358)

We note, however, that the part of the brain that Cannon found to be involved in emotion was, after all, the same part that Karplus and Kreidl (1909) and others had found to control vegetative functions. Of course, William James had never suggested that the peripheral visceral mechanism per se was working in isolation. Rather, he had made it clear that a report to the brain of visceral activity was critical:

> If the neural process underlying emotional consciousness be what I have now
> sought to prove it, the physiology of the brain becomes a simpler matter than has
> been hitherto supposed. Supposing the cortex to contain parts, liable to be excited
> by changes in each special sense-organ, in each portion of the skin, in each
> muscle, each joint, and each viscus, and to contain absolutely nothing else, we
> still have a scheme capable of representing the process of the emotions. An object
> falls on a sense-organ, affects a cortical part, and is perceived; or else the latter,
> excited inwardly, gives rise to an idea of the same object. Quick as a flash, the
> reflex currents pass down through their preordained channels, alter the condition
> of muscle, skin, and viscus; and these alterations, perceived, like the original
> object, in as many portions of the cortex, combine with it in consciousness and
> transform it from an object-simply-apprehended into an object-emotionally-felt.
> No new principles have to be invoked, nothing postulated beyond the ordinary
> reflex circuits, and the local centres admitted in one shape or another by all to
> exist. (James, 1890/1950, vol. 2, pp. 472–474)

Thus the James–Lange theory continued to dominate conceptualizations of the biology of emotions well into the middle of the 20th century.

La vie animale

At this point, new data enlarged the scope of theorizing. Lindsley (1951), working with Magoun and Moruzzi, had shown that destruction of the reticular formation in the core of the brain stem left the organism with only vegetative functions. On the basis of this observation, he proposed that the reticular system produced an activation of the brain, a proposal confirmed by evidence that electrical stimulation of the reticular formation led to a desynchronization of the brain electroencephalogram (EEG). Such desynchronization ordinarily accompanies alertness. These results led Lindsley to an activation theory of emotion in which *une vie animale* (animated, activated movement-in-the-world) rather than *une vie végétative* plays the central role. The following quotation defines emotion for Lindsley:

> As far as it may be considered a theory, the conception to be described here may
> be labeled an "activation theory." It is based largely upon recent findings con-
> cerning the electroencephalogram and particularly the interaction of the cerebral
> cortex and subcortical structures. The activation theory is not solely an explana-
> tory concept for emotional behavior but relates also to the phenomena of sleep–
> wakefulness, to EEG manifestations of cortical activity, and to certain types of
> abnormal behavior revealed in neurologic and psychiatric syndromes.
>
> The theory rests mainly upon the following points, which are supported by
> experimental evidence:

1. The electroencephalogram in emotion presents an "activation pattern," characterized by reduction or abolition of synchronized (alpha) rhythms and the induction of low-amplitude fast activity.
2. The activation pattern in the EEG can be reproduced by electrical

stimulation of the brain-stem reticular formation extended forward into the basal diencephalon through which its influence projects to the thalamus and cortex.

3. Destruction of the basal diencephalon, i.e., the rostral end of the brain-stem activating mechanism, abolishes activation of the EEG and permits restoration of synchronized rhythmic discharges in thalamus and cortex.

4. The behavioral picture associated with point 3 is the antithesis of emotional excitement or arousal, namely, apathy, lethargy, somnolence, catalepsy, hypokinesis, etc.

5. The mechanism of the basal diencephalon and lower brain-stem reticular formation, which discharges to motor outflows and causes the objective features of emotional expression, is either identical with or overlaps the EEG activating mechanism, described under point 2, which arouses the cortex. (Lindsley, 1951, pp. 504–505)

As a counterpoint to Lindsley, let us note that common observation, as well as introspection, caution that something may be missing when emotion is considered simply in terms of activation. For example, weeping is not just more laughing, and fear is not just more love, although there is some truth to the notion of quantitative continuity in these processes. The suggestion thus arises that activation theory, while part of the story, is not in itself the whole story.

Emotion and Motivation

At about the time that Lindsley was developing his activation theory, a group of investigators in John Fulton's laboratory at Yale were demonstrating that both the limbic forebrain and the cerebral cortex were capable of regulating vegetative functions (see Pribram, 1961). These results shifted the locus of control from the brain stem (including hypothalamus) to the forebrain. Following James W. Papez (1937), Paul MacLean (1949) focused on the limbic systems (a ring of forebrain structures at the internal border—the limbus—of the cerebral hemispheres) and their connections with the hypothalamus as a "visceral brain" responsible for vegetatively based emotions. The Papez–MacLean theory thus followed the Bernard–James–Cannon tradition by bringing in ever higher order brain circuitry of control over vegetative functions. The trend, then, was increasingly centralistic and less peripheralistic.

Further experimental observations made possible a more comprehensive theory of feelings (see Pribram, 1984, and Young, 1943/1973) that included the humoral, visceral, and activation themes. This theory distinguishes emotion based on *une vie végétative* (visceroautonomic) and motivation based on *une vie animale* (activating) influences. It derived from a host of research results obtained and reviewed by Pribram (1981).

William James was in part vindicated by Pribram's comprehensive view. What it added was that a brain representation based in part on humoral and vegetative activity, rather than the humoral and vegetative activity per se, must be involved for emotion and motivation to be manifest. Pribram's theory also takes activation into account but differs from Lindsley's in that emotion, as in the classical theories, is conceived to be vegetatively based, while activation, (*une vie animale*) relates to motivation to action (or as James put it, "to enter into *practical* relations with the environment"). In keeping with Lindsley's views, however, since both emotions and motivations can be felt (i.e., experienced), it becomes important to identify feelings as encompassing both motivations and emotions. Feelings of zest for work, love for another person, and so on are as frequently experienced as are those of rapture in listening to music or falling in love. Thus, an overall theory of feelings rooted in neurohumors came to encompass an activation, *vie animale* theory of motivated actions *and* an arousal, *vie végétative* theory of emotional passions.

Finally, the work of Paul Ekman (1973) and Sylvan Tomkins (1962) on the expression of emotions elaborated a direction of research begun by Charles Darwin (1859/1964). In this tradition the variety and subtlety of feelings is delineated, a subtlety in humans that can have no other origin than the participation of the cerebral cortex. Neurophysiological studies have shown that the brain cortex participates in the regulation of visceroautonomic activities (Bucy & Pribram, 1942; Kaada, Pribram & Epstein, 1949; Wall & Pribram, 1950), and that decortication decidedly impoverishes expressions of appetites (e.g., hunger) and passions (e.g., sexual responsivity) in rats, cats, and rabbits (D. Oakley, 1981). Once again, William James's view is in large part corroborated. This time, it is his suggestion that emotions and motivations share in neural systems involved in other aspects of experience and behavior. The road from experiments on the regulation of vegetative functions to those producing some understanding of the feelings of humans took a little over a century. Not a bad yield in such difficult terrain.

BRAIN MODELS OF MIND

Toward the end of the nineteenth century, the popular fad for phrenology gradually faded, and attempts at the localization of function became respectable once more. A series of experimental results and sophisticated models sought to relate brain organization to relevant psychological processes. David Ferrier, Edward Schäfer, and Victor Horsley in Britain, and Friedrich Goltz and Hermann Munk in Germany, resected certain portions of animal brains and observed the effects on behavior. Their publications soon became common knowledge among biomedical scientists.

Models based on these data did not simply equate a brain locus with a psychological faculty; this particular error would once more appear in later popularizations. Rather, the argument followed the lines set forth by Gall: Mental phenomena (psychological processes) depend on the brain, much as respiration depends on the lungs.[3] Of course, no physiologist equates respiration with pulmonary anatomy, or even with pulmonary physiology. The function of respiration depends as well on red blood corpuscles, the hemoglobin they contain, and respiratory enzymes that facilitate the exchange of oxygen and CO_2 across membranes. Similarly, no physiologist, then or now, would identify a psychological process with a brain locus or even the functions of that locus.

It is true that the occipital lobes of the primate brain are centrally involved in visual processing (just as the lungs are centrally involved in respiration), and that other parts of the brain are only tangentially involved (just as the pancreas is only tangentially involved in respiration). However, this fact does not locate the psychological "in" the physiological process. Rather, it identifies and separates the structures involved in a process and specifies their function in the total system. Thus Paul Broca (1861) showed that language is ordinarily dependent on the left, not the right, cerebral hemisphere, and Carl Wernicke (1874) established that a relatively restricted region of the hemisphere is involved. In another classical study, Freud (1953) warns against the popular phrenological error of identifying locus and process. He presents a sophisticated model that accounts for the evidence of language impairment (aphasia) by lesions of the brain.

Freud (1895/1950) also undertook a much more ambitious task that he variously called a "Project for a Scientific Psychology" or a "Psychology for Neurologists." It was meant to be as complete and detailed a statement of the relationship between normal and abnormal mental processes and their brain substrates as evidence at the turn of the century would allow. Freud did not publish his model, but his teacher, Meynert (1890), and his colleague, Exner (1894), did publish models that were similar, if not as brilliantly conceived (see Pribram & Gill, 1976).

---

[3] Gall never tired of distinguishing between a cause and a condition. For him, brain physiology did not cause mind but served as its necessary condition.

These models are remarkably similar to those developed in later years. For example, the regulation of emotional and motivational activity is attributed to physiological drive stimuli impinging on core brain receptors. Such regulation is abetted by neurosecretions (from "key" neurons, in Freud's project) stated to be akin to adrenalin. Memory storage is due to the development of facilitated pathways in the brain through a lowering of synaptic resistance by use (Freud's law of association by contiguity). The cerebral cortex is identified as necessary for self-reflective consciousness in a manner not very different from that proposed by Lawrence Weiskrantz and Elizabeth Warrington (see Weiskrantz, Warrington, Sanders, & Marshall, 1974) on the basis of their "blind-sight" findings on patients with occipital cortex removals, or the proposals of Benjamin Libet (1966) based on his electrical stimulations of the postcentral cortex of man. Patients with blind-sight can identify the location and form of large objects in the part of the field (contralateral of the lesion) that by ordinary test (perimetry) and verbal report of their introspection is totally inaccessible to consciousness. They say they cannot see, that they are totally blind and guessing, even though their performance is 80–90% correct. The Freud-Exner and the Weiskrantz–Warrington theories, a data-filled century apart, are quite similar in essence.

Perhaps even more remarkable is the detailing in Freud's project of the cortical mechanism involved in conscious perception. Freud distinguishes the quantitative, intensive properties of sensory inputs from the qualitative properties that beget consciousness. These qualitative properties are a function of the patterns of periodicity of receptor discharge— that is, patterns reflecting the physical patterns of energy to which the receptors are sensitive. Goldscheider (1906) developed a similar model in some detail:

> The simplest conditions are found in the case of association within the same sensory domain, e.g., the visual domain. Let there be a simple visual object, e.g., a circular line.
>
> Hereby a certain number of ganglion cells of the visual center are excited from the periphery simultaneously or in immediate succession. From each one of these cells the excitation will propagate in the various directions which are indicated by the anatomical conduction pathways emanating from the cell. Each one of these receptive elements of the sensory domain (ganglion cells) can thus be considered as a center which radiates the excitations arriving from the periphery in the various directions like a bundle of force lines. The great majority will lose themselves without effect in the chaos of the fiber network, perhaps only stimulating it trophically. *Only where the force lines meet will they produce a special effect,* namely, as was elaborated above, *produce those unstable chemical agents.* The locations at *which the force lines meet are to be viewed as the resultants of the pulses of different intensities some of which may have originated simultaneously and some in short temporal sequence.*

These locations will form a connected system of lines which can be viewed as a spatially connected bundle. I will call it a *node line* or a *force line* resultant. (p. 146)

The works of Fergus Campbell and John Robson (1968) and of DeValois, Albrecht, & Thorell (1978), to name a few of many contributors, have established that cells in the visual cortex are indeed "tuned" to frequencies (the inverse of period), but that these frequencies are patterns over space rather than (or in addition to) over time. (Physicists know such spatial patterns, when they are described as waves, by the term "wave numbers.") These findings have been augmented by the work of Georg von Bekesy (1957) in audition and somesthesis, and by Nicholas Bernstein (1967), M. T. Turvey (1977), and Pribram A. R. Sharafat and Beekman (1984) in the area of motor functions. Collectively, this work stands in remarkable agreement with David Hartley's theory of neural resonances, and with more refined versions of this theory promulgated in the latter half of the nineteenth century.

A further problem faced in Freud's project is that such resonance is reinforced in some instances yet fails to reach threshold in others. This problem is addressed by the proposal that the sensory input must be matched to a preexisting pattern in order to attain threshold. Once again, twentieth-century psychologists with a biological orientation (e.g., Bruner, 1958; Jasper, 1958; Sokolov, 1960) have developed similar models on the basis of their experiments. Finally, Freud notes that such a patterned lowering of threshold involves reflex circuitry—feedback, in today's terminology—a proposal that has been endorsed by twentieth-century theorists such as MacKay (1966), Teuber (1960), and Holst and Mittelstaedt (1950), and confirmed experimentally (see Spinelli & Pribram, 1966; Lassonde, Ptito, & Pribram, 1981).

Freud's model is, of course, not unique in its prescience. Whether one is reading Schäfer's *Textbook of Physiology* (1898–1900) or Alfred Binet's philosophical treatise on *Mind and the Brain* (1907), the impression remains that the end of the nineteenth century was not very different from the end of the twentieth century in its treatment of the relationship between mind and brain. Mind is dependent on the intricacies of sensory, motor, and brain processing.

These models were, of course, made possible by the accumulation of evidence, the greatest amount of which accrued from shrewd clinical observation coupled with post-mortem pathoanatomical dissections of the brains of persons who had shown a psychological disturbance. These clinical data were supplemented by experimental neurosurgery on animals, where brain extirpations could be carefully controlled. In the hands of David Ferrier (1878), Edward Schäfer (1898–1900), Friedrick Goltz (1892), and Hermann Munk (1881), these attempts at experimental verification of clinical observations reached only a modest state of sophistication, for the experimenters lacked precise quantitative behavioral measures of performance. Thus only obvious changes were observed.

In the clinic and laboratory, knowledge gained about brain–mind relationships during the 19th century was prodigious, and the resulting models sophisticated. Humans were found to be unique in brain and therefore in mind. We must ask, then, why so promising a line of investigation nearly came to a halt during the early decades of our own century. When the body of twentieth-century experimental psychology is reviewed, a very different impression of the human place in the world is obtained. Such a review and some reasons for this difference make up the following section.

COUNTERPOINT: A BRAINLESS AND MINDLESS EVOLUTIONARY PSYCHOLOGY

Psychology, seen solely as the science of behavior (rather than brain function), becomes a platitude toward the middle of the twentieth century. There were, of course, a few throwbacks to the 19th-century notion of psychology as the science of mind (e.g., Miller, 1962), but contrary to their predecessors, they did not reflect a neurobiologically rooted conception of mind. Rather, these writers and their brethren heralded the triumphs of a roguish, adolescent independence from mother philosophy, aunt education, and whatever other family ties might still bind. The stated aim was to mathematize, to develop laws in the image of the mechanistic physics of Newton.

What led to this turn of events? Why, a century after Wundt's achievement of a broad, experimentally based biological and social psychology, did psychological inquiry suddenly espouse only the environmental and social branches and deny its neurobiological roots?

> The behaviorist asks: Why don't we make what we can *observe* the real field of psychology? Let us limit ourselves to things that can be observed, and formulate laws concerning only those things. Now, what can we observe? We can observe *behavior—what the organism does or says*. And let us point out at once: that *saying* is doing—that is, *behaving*. Speaking overtly or to ourselves (thinking) is just as objective a type of behavior as baseball.
>
> The rule, or measuring rod, which the behaviorist puts in front of him always is: Can I describe this bit of behavior I see in terms of "stimulus and response"? By stimulus we mean any object in the general environment or any change in the tissues themselves due to the physiological condition of the animal, such as the change we get when we keep an animal from sex activity, when we keep it from feeding, when we keep it from building a nest. By response we mean anything

the animal does—such as turning toward or away from a light, jumping at a sound, and more highly organized activities such as building a skyscraper, drawing plans, having babies, writing books, and the like. (Watson, 1925/1959, pp. 6–7)

The behaviorist approach initiated by Watson was continued by Clark Hull (1951), Kenneth Spence (1960), and Edward Tolman (1932). In their hands, functional relationships between stimuli and the organism's response were mapped mathematically. Physiological variables were not measured directly but inferred to intervene between stimulus and response. Watson had been interested in physiological measurement—behavior for him meant movement; now, though, at best, physiological constructs replaced physiological observations.

The trend toward environmentalism was taken to its logical conclusion by B. F. Skinner. Behavior became the environmental consequence of the movement, the action that produced a paper record that "could be taken home at night and studied." Environmental consequences, not the physiology of man, became the substance and tool of the behaviorist.

These steps toward environmentalism were embodied in the view of methodological behaviorism (i.e., behavior is indeed a potent measure of man). In testing this potency, it is not altogether surprising that the measure for a while became its own end. Of more importance historically is the shift from physiology to environment. Watson's initial proposal was that peripheral physiological recordings of patterns of muscle contraction would reflect the ongoing *neural* patterns that are coordinate with psychological processes. Skinner took exception to this:

> The important advance . . . that is made by turning to the nervous system as a controlling entity has unfortunately had a similar effect [similar to that of resorting to mental explanations] in discouraging a direct descriptive attack upon behavior. The change is an advance because the new entity beyond behavior to which appeal is made has a definite physical status of its own and is susceptible to scientific investigation. Its chief function with regard to a science of behavior, however, is again to divert attention away from behavior as a subject matter . . . .
> (I am not attempting to discount the importance of a science of neurology but am referring simply to the primitive use of the nervous system as an explanatory principle in avoiding a direct description of behavior.) (Skinner, 1938, p. 4)

Thus peripheral physiological measures gradually gave way to recording the behaviors of the entire organism, which entailed a subtle shift from behavior as movement to behavior as the environmental consequence of that movement. Skinner could thus declare that behavior is the cumulative record of lever depressions. While Watson's psychology (1925/1959) was still physiologically rooted, his message was that behavior should take its own measure, fly free, and leave mind behind in the home nest of philosophy. In the hands of Hull (1951), Spence (1960), Tolman (1932), and Skinner (1938), behavioral science did just that, and successfully—so successfully, in fact, that the question can now be raised as to just what might be the relationship of a science of behavior to a psychology conceived as the study of the psyche (i.e., mental processes; see, e.g., Pribram, 1979).

Focus on the technical excellence of method thus contributed to the growing pains of a psychology that was the successful young offspring of the nineteenth century. Technical achievement can also account for much that has happened during the twentieth century to loosen psychology from its earlier roots in mind and brain. But technical achievement had to operate in a context, and the question arises as to just what context, aside from the very general technical thrust of this century, operated to disengage psychology from its neuobiological moorings.

An answer to this question comes from the fact that in addition to encouraging a brain-based psychology, the 19th century spawned the theory of biological evolution (see Chapter 4, this volume). In a deep sense, Darwinian evolution is as much an environmentalist as a biological theory, something clearly recognized by scholars such as Julian Huxley (1942/1974) and anticipated by Spencer (1852). Though environmentalist, the theory differed[4] from Lamarckian conceptions in that Darwin (1859/1964) suggested a more acceptable process by which adaptation to the environment could occur: The apparent relatedness among the diverse creatures of the earth could be explained on the basis of biological variation coupled with a principle of selection. Selection, the Darwinists noted, is due to environmental contingencies, both physical (Huxley) and social (Spencer).

Nineteenth-century biological psychology had failed to provide any overarching theoretical frame for understanding psychological problems. True, the brain had become identified as the anatomical basis of mental life, but the actual processes and mechanisms, while modeled in general, remained for another age to discover. By contrast, Darwin's biological principles of evolution did provide a universally applicable mechanism by which large parts of the psychological as well as the biological order might be explained.

An illustration of this shift from biological brain mechanisms to evolu-

---

[4] Darwin himself never fully acceded to his own innovation, for he became increasingly Lamarckian the more he thought about the human species. But it was his development of the principles of selection that captured the imagination of many and continues to dominate not only biology and psychology but social and physical (including chemical) theory as well (see, e.g., McGuinness, 1986).

tion as a means of explanation is seen in what happened to Freud after he attempted his comprehensive neuropsychological project. In the project iself, when he was unable to specify a brain mechanism because of a paucity of facts, Freud resorted to a "Darwinian explanation" that he felt must suffice until a mechanistic explanation became available (Pribram & Gill, 1976). Sulloway (1979) carefully documents the argument that Freud's later writings leaned heavily on Darwinism—so heavily, indeed, that Sulloway calls Freud a "biologist of the mind." But as Freud said so often, this resort to Darwinism and his repeated disavowals of mechanism were not disavowals in principle, but only for the interim— the time was not yet ripe for mechanistic explanations (see Pribram & Gill, 1976, pp. 162–168).

More important, the theory of evolution displaced the individual organism, including human individuals, from the center of scientific concern and replaced it with the species en masse. Psychological individuality, like biological individuality, was simply one of the entries in the large table of natural variations from which the pressures of the environment would select winners and losers. Skinner (1971) called for a society in which the freedom and dignity of man were recognized as anachronistic feelings of no utility in the process of survival, but the argument was not convincing to many who also sought to go *Beyond the Punitive Society* (Wheeler, 1973).

In a more subtle way, evolutionary theory emphasized function to so great an extent as to reduce in importance a historical subject of psychophysiological interest—namely, the structure of mental processes such as ideas and their putative sensory foundation. Even instincts (those behaviors shared by species as diverse as birds and bees and humans) became suspect, as Frank Beach notes in "The Descent of Instinct" (1955). Evolutionary theory, with its utilitarian slant, tended to direct the energies of psychological inquiry toward hedonistic variables and their effects on "representative" organisms. To read Darwin is to anticipate Skinner, but not Pavlov. It is to anticipate both comparative and genetic psychology, but not physiological psychology as it would emerge in the twentieth century. This is not to say that there was anything in evolutionary theory that was hostile to such developments, only that the theory was largely indifferent to them. In fact, this indifference was quietly shared even by those working within the framework of physiological psychology, a framework that could not easily assimilate the Darwinian perspective, although paying homage to it.

During the long session of Darwinized psychology, it was often the biologists, neurophysiologists, and neurosurgeons (e.g., Sherrington, Sperry, Eccles, Penfield, and Pribram) who preserved psychology as the study of (brain-related) mind. It is in this latter sense that contemporary psychobiology is descended from Gall and not Darwin, and this is also one of the reasons behind that odd historical tendency that finds the neuropsychological perspective waning when the behaviorist one waxes.

Is it any wonder, then, that the Zeitgeist of twentieth-century psychology, when at all determined by biology, was the Zeitgeist of evolution, not of the brain? For example, the influential ethological studies of animal behavior offered an understanding of human psychology that studies of brain and behavior never seemed to attain. The significant words in the previous sentence are "seemed" and "influential." The point is not whether more understanding might actually have been achieved by the brain–behavior studies. They simply did not attain status as readily, if at all, as the often more remote (e.g., birds versus people) studies in ethology.

This complex point can be illustrated further in the difference between Nobel prizes awarded in the brain–mind and the evolutionary–psychology areas. When Egas Moniz received the prize in 1949, it was in part for intervening in brain tissue (frontal leukotomy) in order to influence the deranged minds of humans. The data base upon which this intervention was inaugurated consisted of two chimpanzees and half a dozen monkeys rather poorly observed, with few control procedures. Still, the human patients were obviously changed by the surgical intervention, so that a definite relationship between brain and mental processes could be clearly discerned from the results. What was missing were the details: clear descriptions and conceptualizations of the mental processes to be influenced, a clear understanding of the functions of the part of the brain being invaded, and an established relationship between these two sets of details.

In contrast, when Konrad Lorenz, Niko Tinbergen, and Ernst von Frisch received their prize in 1973—also in the category of physiology and medicine—a detailed body of data concerning animal behavior had been initiated and developed, as had a body of observational evidence on human behavior. What was completely lacking was evidence of a necessary relationship between the behaviors of birds and bees and those of man. When similarities were observed, were they only analogous, or did they entail some deeper homology? The overriding acceptance of the theory of evolution made such questions seem unnecessary. One has only to think back to another age, one concerned with the uniqueness of human mental and spiritual capacities, to see the sharp contrast between it and the faith of the twentieth century in an evolutionary behavioral science. Some current studies in human ethology (e.g., Eibl-Eibesfeldt, 1979; Reynolds, 1981) bring the techniques of ethology to bear on anthropological observations. They are a recognition of the failures as well as the successes of earlier work and thus address this fundamental issue.

Ethological investigations are only one instance of the influence of nineteenth-century evolutionary doctrine on twentieth-century psychology. Another is seen in Skinner's operant behaviorism (1969), where environmental contingencies, appropriately scheduled, control the behavior of organisms. (The behaviors themselves are biologically diverse initially.) Shaping procedures select by rewarding certain behaviors (an environmental procedure), thus ensuring their recurrence at the expense of others. The behaviors that fit the contingencies survive—a clear instance of survival of the fittest.

Within the regnant spirit of Darwinian evolution, the principles of operant reinforcement were derived from the study of rats and pigeons. In turn, these same principles were brought to bear ipso facto to explain the origin and evolution of language. The success of Chomsky's famous critique (1972) was perhaps due not so much to his detailed analysis of whether a limited aspect of linguistic behavior might be subject to the rules of operant conditioning as to his questioning the legitimacy of wholesaling the then unexamined Darwinian assumptions underlying the operant framework. Skinner (1974) addresses this issue himself, clearly stating his indebtedness to the doctrine of evolution. Only later, however, was it shown that, when applied to man, operant behaviorism must at a minimum take cognizance of man's unique capacities of cognition (Bandura, 1969).

The apparent success of behaviorism, apart from its broad (if not deep) database, should be understood in terms of its ability to retain the Darwinian message while liberating psychology from the hereditarianism that the twentieth-century intellectual community found so objectionable. The post-Watsonian behaviorists (Hull, Skinner, Spence) supplied an experimental psychology devoted to organismic adaptations—a psychology able to assess the manner in which environmental variations come to sample the behavioral potentialities of a species; a psychology (apparently) able to disregard nativistic theories of individual differences by (allegedly) showing them to be grounded in the purely historical details of an organism's development; and a psychology able to get along quite well without aid from the biologist, the clinical neurologist, or the philosopher of science. What was promised was an objective science of behavior based on controlled observation and measurement of the environmental determinants of conduct. "Mentalism" was put on notice, and psychobiology was taken to be virtually beside the point. On the behavioristic account, it made no more sense to look inside the organism for the neural correlates of behavior than to look inside for its mental causes.

CODA: BRAIN AS MACHINERY OF MIND

Had behaviorism offered no more than rhetoric and promises, it surely would not have captured so large a share of modern psychology and held it for decades. But it also offered data, mountains of it. The separation between Thorndike's "puzzle box" and today's computerized operant laboratory is about eight decades. In that time, behavioristic psychology revolutionized techniques, not only in experimental psychology but also in pharmacology, education, psychotherapy, rehabilitation, and other areas. Skinner's pioneering studies of partial reinforcement deepened our understanding of how certain forms of behavior become persistent, and studies of avoidance conditioning clarified the principles governing fear-induced behavior. The behavioristic epoch in modern psychology transformed our perspective and introduced changes in the discipline that will survive long after behaviorism itself, as an *ism*, is merely a historical entry.

The question raised and left unanswered by the plethora of behavioral data was what relevance they might have to the persistent problems of psychology—problems such as the organization of memory or the use of representations in thought, attention, and the deployment of skills. It remained for those working in the latter part of the century to address the problems of psychology with the behaviorists' tools. By 1960 many psychologists, now turned "radical" (Skinner, 1969) or "subjective" (Miller, Galanter, & Pribram, 1960) behaviorists, attended once again to these persistent problems. The latter group now sought to gather data related to the organization of experiential determinants of behavior, under the umbrella of "cognitive science," and to impose the same rigor on them that behaviorism had demanded in the treatment of a far narrower class of phenomena. The problems themselves were those which had been identified earlier as the essence of mind.

In the transition from the old to the new, a certain innocence was lost. The modern cognitive sciences did not adopt the nineteenth century model of the actual biological brain. Instead, they turned to mechanical "brains"—to computers, TV scanners, and other hardware—for their inspiration (see Pribram, 1980). This decision was dictated in large measure by the precise knowledge that can be attained with these engineered devices. The strategy here is based on the thesis that we are concerned with processes, not mechanisms, and that the former can be understood according to certain "design features" that are utterly indifferent to the composition of the actual parts. We understand radar, for example, by understanding the terms—the transfer functions—embodied in the radar equation. Thus we can specify the performance of a given radar system without ever inquiring into its location or its material composition.

In the new technology we have a positive reason for the cognitive sciences to turn away from the biological brain. A negative reason is that the immense accumulation of neurophysiological information compiled during psychology's behavioristic hiatus proved to be inaccessible to those who had not participated directly. Neurobiology, after all, had not stood still waiting to be rediscovered by psychology. Indeed the new neurobiology had remained somewhat aloof as psychology celebrated its utterly independent status. There were, of course, occasional forays into psychological territories: the work of David Hubel and Torsten Wiesel on "feature" selection by neurons in the visual cortex (Hubel & Wiesel, 1959); the discovery that the nondominant hemisphere is specialized for nonlinguistic functions (reviewed in Mountcastle, 1962); and the finding that aspects of mind can be split if the functions of the cerebral hemispheres are separated by severing the corpus callosum (Sperry, 1974). For the most part, however, studies of brain function failed in any immediate sense to suggest answers to the more complex questions again arising within psychology—questions regarding the origins of conscious awareness, memory and retrieval, symbolic coding, relationships between language and thought, and principles of cognitive development.

In *The Self and Its Brain* (Popper & Eccles, 1977), a celebrated philosopher of science and a Nobel laureate in neurophysiology teamed up to address this issue by suggesting, as had Franz Brentano (1874/1924-1925), Freud's illustrious professor of philosophy, that self-consciousness (in contrast with consciousness) is a uniquely human attribute. When it comes to mechanism, however, Popper and Eccles have little to say, even about animal consciousness. Near the end of *The Self and Its Brain*, Popper confides:

> I think that with respect to consciousness, we have to assume that animal consciousness has developed out of non-consciousness—we don't know more about it. At some stage this incredible invention was made. . . . But in saying this I know very well that I am saying very little . . . It is not an explanation, and it must not be taken as an explanation. (p. 560)

It was just this sort of reasoned frustration that turned psychology away from both the biological sciences and philosophy and toward the reassurances of behaviorism. Yet despite these very real differences, in the years since 1960 there occurred, by virtue of the cognitive "revolution" in psychology, a serious resumption of investigations of the brain as the organ of cognition, and therefore of mind.

It is not accidental that, of all specialists within modern psychology, it is the psychobiologist who has the most regular contact with issues ordinarily taken to be philosophical. In view of the historical contacts between philosophy and those branches of biological science devoted to neurology and neurophysiology, such contact is to be expected. In our own century alone, this connection has been amply illustrated in the works of such scientific luminaries as Pavlov, Sherrington, Penfield, Sperry, and Eccles. Each of these men (all but Penfield recipients of the Nobel Prize), first distinguished himself by making fundamental contributions to what we now call the "neural sciences." But each also reserved significant space in his published works to address the larger philosophical, metaphysical, and psychological implications of his scientific discoveries.

Meanwhile, methodological and radical behaviorism developed something of a philosophy of science, an ontology, even something of a system of social ethics. Understood in these terms, behaviorism found much to reprove in both the distant and more recent history of neuropsychology, for in the latter discipline there has been a willingness, even a felt necessity, to accept verbal reports of subjectively experienced cognitive, ideational, conscious, affective, volitional, and motivational aspects of human psychology (see Pribram, 1962, 1971) as determiners of behavior. Radical behaviorism took an ontological stand against a causal role for any subjectively labeled central states or representations in the organization of behavior. It insisted that if they exist at all, it is only as physically specifiable neural or endocrine states, or as epiphenomena of observable behavior.

The issue is important and can perhaps be brought into focus by the following analogy: By observing the properties of hydrogen and oxygen atoms, physicists find lawful relations among interactions, as when two hydrogen atoms combine with one oxygen atom in a certain way to make up a molecule of H_2O. However, H_2O has peculiar properties not shared by either element while separate. For example, it liquifies at ordinary earth temperatures and solidifies when the temperature drops just a bit. And when it solidifies, it floats on its liquid base, something most other compounds don't do. The following issues may be raised by the scientists who made these observations: Some want to label the H_2O combination "water" because common language calls it that, but others state that such labeling is unscientific. The question is then raised as to whether or not water as such is in any way causally related to hydrogen and oxygen. Certainly the H_2O formula places constraints on the distribution of hydrogen and oxygen, and on the uses to which these elements can be put. But water also makes life as we know it possible. The chemical and biological consequences of combining hydrogen and oxygen are far-reaching, but are they therefore any less scientific? In studying the effects of combining elements, is the "downward causation" of their distribution to be ignored? Are chemists and biologists "soft" in their approach to science when they discuss the properties of water?

If we substitute the brain, or more accurately, the body (organism) for hydrogen and the environment for oxygen, behaviorally effective interactions (i.e., combinations) produce a new level of organization. Now the question is whether or not it is acceptable to label some of the combinations vision, others attention, others love, and still others dignity and freedom, just as H_2O is labeled water. Could there be a "causal" relationship between freedom and the distribution of brains and organisms in the world? What might be wrong with a psychology that affirms that freedom makes spiritual life possible, just as the wetness of water makes biological life possible? These were questions addressed by scientists such as Sherrington (1955), Sperry (1976), Penfield (1975), Pribram (1970; 1985) and Eccles (1976) in response to earlier, more classically behavioristic stances such as Gilbert Ryle's "ghost-in-the-machine" (1949).

Radical behaviorism attempted to model itself on Newtonian mechanics. A search had been instituted for lawful relationships between the antecedents (causes) and consequences (effects) in behavior.[5] In this way, behaviorism was a kind of functionalism (see Chapter 6, this volume). By contrast, early 19th-century psychology had been structural in its biological orientation (i.e., it was interested in principles of organization). It was a discipline seeking to define the organizational properties, the faculties of mind, and their biological underpinnings. When, toward the end of the century, the winds of change began to blow, new insights were derived during the development of functionalism. Some were embodied in Freud's psychoanalytic metapsychology, others in Helmholtz's and Mach's physicalistic sensory psychology, and still

---

[5] At the end of the twentieth century, as at the beginning of the nineteenth, the issue of cause versus condition has been raised. When we speak of conditions, we are more apt to use the term reason than cause, but this is not universally the case. Aristotle's distinction between "proximate efficient" and "final" causes is relevant here. Are conditions final causes in the sense that they determine the constraints toward which systems tend? Biologists such as Waddington (1957) suggest that evolutionary doctrine describes such constraints.

others in the development of approaches to problems of psychological assessment, as in Binet's (1907) measures of mental ages.

While a functionalist behaviorism (and its European counter trend, a functional phenomenology) came to hold sway in early and mid-twentieth-century psychology, a new structuralism developed in anthropology and linguistics. All but unknown among psychologists, this structuralism searched not so much for anatomical organs of mental faculties as for the structures of process. "Structure" in this new sense meant stable organizations, identifiable orders in ongoing functional relationships. This time, change came from an unreconstructed functional behaviorism and a functional phenomenology (see, for example, Miller, et al., 1960; Merleau-Ponty, 1963).

At the time (i.e., in the mid-twentieth century) when these developments were taking place in the body of experimental psychology, a growing conservatism characterized physiological psychology. The trend in this subdiscipline was toward a reductionism that if continued, would have seen physiological psychology absorbed by neurophysiology, at the expense of physiological psychology as a psychological discipline (Pribram, 1970). Simultaneously, however, there transpired a courtship of what was previously a branch of physiological psychology, namely neuropsychology, by cognitively oriented psychologists, and this courtship produced a number of results that led in the opposite direction. Not the least of these was the reanimation of psychobiology by such issues and phenomena as attention, problem-solving, complex perceptions, and the contextual determinants of information processing, artificial intelligence, and the like.

Perhaps the most telling change in this nonbehavioristic direction occurred when neuropsychologists faced the clinic and its concomitant facts of human brain function and the correlated phenomena of psychological disturbance and debility. Clinical neuropsychology blossomed in its relationship with the cognitive resurgence to the point that a separate division of "clinical neuropsychology" was established within the American Psychological Association. It has always been the clinical residual of complexities and exceptions that has steered a neurobiologically rooted psychology away from the easy reductionism and metaphysical certainty that often captured other branches of the discipline.

In the latter decades of the twentieth century, biological influences in psychology have indeed reached a frontier. This frontier was established by contributions of the 19th century showing that the mind of man is rooted in a unique brain and, equally, by later contributions viewing behavior universally as a measure of, and often a substitute for, universal mind. The challenge was (and is) to resolve evolutionary radical behaviorism with a brain-structured, human-centered mentalism. When and if such a resolution occurs, we may see strides in understanding the spirit of mankind that will rival the technical advances of the twentieth century.

REFERENCES

Bain, A. (1855). *The senses and the intellect*. London: Parker.
Bain, A. (1859). *The emotions and the will*. London: Parker.
Bain, A. (1861). *On the study of character, including an estimate of phrenology*. London: Parker.
Bain, A. (1870). *Logic* (2 vols.). London: Longmans, Green.
Bandura, A. (1969). *Principles of behavior modification*. New York: Holt.
Beach, F. (1955). The descent of instinct. *Psychological Review, 62,* 401–410.
Bechterev, W. von (1911) *Die Funktionen der Nervencentra*. Berlin: Fischer.
Bekesy, G. von. (1957). Neural volleys and the similarity between some sensations produced by tones and by skin vibrations. *Journal of the Acoustical Society of America, 29,* 1059–1069.
Bell, C. (1811). *Idea of a new anatomy of the brain, submitted for the observations of his friends.* London: Strahan, Preston.
Bernard, C. (1858). *Leçons sur la physiologie et la pathologie du systeme nerveaux.* Paris: Balliere, Fils.
Bernstein, N. (1967). *The co-ordination and regulation of movements.* New York: Pergamon.
Binet, A. (1907). *Mind and brain.* London: Kegan Paul.
Brentano, F. (1924–1925). *Psychologie vom empirischen Standpunkt* (3rd ed.). Leipzig: Duncker, Humblot. (Original work published 1874)
Broca, P. (1861). Remarques sur le siège de la faculté du langage articule, suivies d'une observation d'aphasie (perte de la parole). *Bulletins de la Société Anatomique de Paris, 36,* 330–357.
Bruner, J. S. (1958) Neural mechanisms of perception. In *Brain and human behavior.* Association for Research in Nervous & Mental Disease. Bruner, J. S. (1973). *Beyond the information given—studies in the psychology of knowing.* New York: Norton.
Bucy, P. C., & Pribram, K. H. (1942). Localized sweating as part of a localized convulsive seizure. *Archives of Neurology and Psychiatry, 50,* 456–461.
Campbell, F. W., & Robson, J. G. (1968). Application of Fourier analysis to the visibility of gratings. *Journal of Physiology, 197,* 551–566.
Cannon, W. B. (1929). *Bodily changes in pain, hunger, fear and rage.* New York: Appleton-Century-Crofts.
Chomsky, N. (1972). *Language and mind.* New York: Harcourt Brace Jovanovich.
Chomsky, N. (1980). *Rules and representations.* New York: Columbia University Press.
Darwin, C. (1964). *On the origin of species.* Cambridge, MA: Harvard University Press. (Original work published 1859)
DeValois, R. L. (1960). Color vision mechanisms in monkey. Journal of General Physiology, 43, *115–128.*
DeValois, R. L., Albrecht, D. G., & Thorell, L. G. (1978). Cortical cells: Bar and edge detectors, or spatial frequency filters? In S. J. Cool & E. L. Smith (Eds.), *Frontiers in visual science.* New York: Springer.
DeValois, R. L., & DeValois, K. K. (1980). Spatial vision. *Annual Review of Psychology, 31,* 309–341.

DeValois, R. L., & Jacobs, G. H. (1968). Primate color vision. *Science, 162,* 533–540.

du Bois-Reymond, E. (1848–1884). *Untersuchungen über tierische Elektricität* (30 vols.). Berlin: Reimer.

Eccles, J. C. (1976). Brain and free will. In G. G. Globus, G. Maxwell, & I. Savodnik (Eds.), *Consciousness and the brain: A scientific and philosophical inquiry.* New York: Plenum.

Eibl-Eibesfeldt, I. (1979). Human ethology: Concepts and implications for the sciences of man. *The Behavioral and Brain Sciences, 2,* 1–57.

Ekman, P. (Ed.). (1973). *Darwin and facial expressions.* New York: Academic.

Exner, S. (1894). *Entwurf zu einer physiologischen Erklärung der psychischen Erscheinungen.* Vienna: Deuticke.

Fechner, G. T. (1859). *Ueber ein wichtiges psychophysiches Gesetz und dessen Beziehung zur Schätzung der Sterngrossen.* Leipzig: Hirzel.

Feigel, H. (1960). Mind–body, not a pseudoproblem. In S. Hook (Ed.), *Dimensions of mind.* New York: Collier.

Ferrier, D, (1878). The localisation of cerebral disease. In *Gulstonian lectures of the Royal College of Physicians.* London: Smith Elder.

Flourens, P. (1858). *La vie et de l'intelligence.* Paris: Garnier Fieres.

Freud, S. (1950). Project for a scientific psychology. In J. Strachey (Ed.), *Standard edition of the complete psychological works of Sigmund Freud.* New York: Norton. (Original work published 1895)

Freud, S. (1953). *On aphasia.* New York: International Universities Press.

Fritsch, G., & Hitzig, E. (1969). On the electrical excitability of the cerebrum (D. Harris, Trans.). In K. H. Pribram (Ed.), *Brain and behavior* (Vol. 2). Baltimore, MD: Penguin. (Original work published 1870)

Gall, F. J. (1835). *On the functions of the brain and each of its parts, with observations on the possibilities of determining the instincts, propensities, talents, and on the moral and intellectual dispositions of men and animals by the configuration of the brain and head* (6 vols.). Boston: Marsh, Copen, Lyon. (Original work published 1822–1825)

Galvani, L. (1954). *Commentary on the effects of electricity on muscular motion* (M. G. Foley, Ed. and Trans.). Norwalk, CT: Burndy. (Original work published 1644)

Gassendi, P. (1962). *Recherches metaphysiques* (B. Rochot, Ed.). Paris: Vrin. (Original work published 1644)

Goldscheider, A. (1906). Ueber die materiellen Veränderungen bei der Assoziations-bildung. *Neurologisches Zentralblatt, 25,* 146.

Goltz, F. (1892). Der Hund ohne Grosshirn. *Archiv. für Physiologie, 51,* 570–614.

Hartley, D. (1970). Observations on man. In R. Brown (Ed.), *Between Hume and Mill: An anthology of British philosophy.* New York: Random House. (Original work published 1749)

Helmholtz, H. von. (1924). *Treatise on physiological optics* (J. P. C. Southall, Ed. and Trans.). (3rd ed.). New York: Optical Society of America. (Original work published 1856–1869)

Helmholtz, H. von. (1954). *On the sensations of tone* (A. J. Ellis, Trans.). (4th ed.). New York: Dover. (Original work published 1863)

Hering, E. (1964). *Outlines of a theory of the light sense* (L. M. Hurvich & D. Jameson, Eds. and Trans.). Cambridge, MA: Harvard University Press. (Original work published 1905)

Heschel, A. J. (1965). *Who is man?* Stanford, CA: Stanford University Press.

Holst, E. von, & Mittelstaedt, H. (1950). Das Reafferenzprinzip. *Naturwissenschaften, 37,* 464–476.

Horsley, V., & Schäfer, E. A. (1888). A record of experiments upon the functions of the cerebral cortex. Royal Society, *Philosophical Transactions, 170B,* 1–45.

Hubel, D. H., & Wiesel, T. N. (1959). Receptive fields of single neurons in the cat's striate cortex. *Journal of Physiology, 148,* 574–591.

Hull, C. L. (1951). *Essentials of behavior.* New Haven, CT: Yale University Press.

Huxley, J. (1974). *Evolution: The modern synthesis* (3rd ed.). Winchester, MA: Allen, Unwin. (Original work published 1942)

Jackson, J. H. (1873). *Clinical and physiological researches on the nervous system.* London: Churchill.

James, W. (1950). *Principles of psychology.* New York: Dover. (Original work published 1890)

Jasper, H. H. (Ed.). (1958). *Reticular formations of the brain.* Boston: Little, Brown.

Kaada, B. R., Pribram, K. H., & Epstein, J. A. (1949) Respiratory and vascular responses in monkeys from temporal pole, insula, orbital surface and cingulate gyrus. *Journal of Neurophysiology, 12,* 347–356.

Karplus, J. P., & Kreidl, A. (1909). Gehirn und Sympathicus. *Archiv für Physiologiques Pflügers, 129,* 138–144.

Kornhuber, H. H. (1974). Cerebral cortex, cerebellum, and basal ganglia: An introduction to their functions. In F. O. Schmitt & F. G. Worden (Eds.), *The neurosciences* (Vol. 3). Cambridge, MA: MIT Press.

Lange, C. (1887). *Ueber Gemütsbewegungen* (H. Kurella, Trans.). Leipzig: Thomas. (Original work published 1885)

Langley, J. N. (1900). The sympathetic and other related systems of nerves. In E. A. Schäfer (Ed.), *Textbook of physiology* (Vol. 2). Edinburgh: Young.

Lassonde, M., Ptito, M., & Pribram, K. H. (1981). Intracerebral influences on the microstructure of receptive fields of cat visual cortex. *Experimental Brain Research, 43,* 131–144.

Libet, B. (1966). Brain stimulation and conscious experience. In J. C. Eccles (Ed.), *Brain and conscious experience.* New York: Springer.

Lindsley, D. B. (1951). Emotion. In S. S. Stevens (Ed.), *Handbook of experimental psychology* New York: Wiley.

Mach, E. (1959). *The analysis of sensations* (S. Waterlow, Trans.). New York: Dover. (Original work published 1886)

MacKay, D. M. (1966). Cerebral organization and the conscious control of action. In J. C. Eccles (Ed.), *Brain and conscious experience.* New York: Springer.

MacLean, P. D. (1949). Psychosomatic disease and the "visceral brain": Recent developments bearing on the Papez theory of emotion. *Psychosomatic Medicine, 11,* 338–353.

Magendie, F. (1822). Experiences sur les fonctions des racines des nerfs rachidiens. *Journale Physiologie et Experimentale Pathologie, 2,* 276–279.

McGuinness, D. (Ed.). (1986) *Evolution as a transdisciplinary paradigm.* New York: Paragon House.

Merleau-Ponty, M. (1963). *The structure of behavior.* Boston: Beacon.

Mettrie, J. de la. (1748). *L'homme machine.* Leyde: Luzac Fils.

Meynert, T. (1890). *Klinische Vorlesungen über Psychiatrie,* Vienna: Braunmuller.

Mill, J. S. (1874). *A system of logic ratiocinative and inductive, being a connected view of the principles of evidence, and the methods of scientific investigation* (8th ed.). New York: Harper. (Original work published 1843)

Miller, G. A. (1962). *Psychology: The science of mental life.* New York: Harper. Miller, G. A., Galanter, E., & Pribram, K. H. (1960). *Plans and the structure of behavior.* New York: Holt.

Mountcastle, V. B. (Ed.). (1962). *Interhemispheric relations and cerebral dominance.* Baltimore, MD: Johns Hopkins Press.

Müller, J. (1852). *Elements of human physiology* (W. Baley, Trans.). New York: Leavitt. (Original work published 1833–1840)

Munk, H. (1881). *Ueber die Functionen der Grosshirnrinde.* Berlin: Verlag.

Papez, J. W. (1937). A proposed mechanism of emotion. *Archives of Neurology and Psychiatry, 38,* 725–743.

Pavlov, I. P. (1927). *Conditioned reflexes: An investigation of the physiological activity of the cerebral cortex* (G. V. Anrep, Trans.). London: Oxford University Press.

Penfield, W. (1975). *Mystery of the mind.* Princeton, NJ: Princeton University Press.

Popper, K. R., & Eccles, J. C. (1977). *The self and its brain.* New York: Springer.

Pribram, K. H. (1960). A review of theory in physiological psychology. *Annual Review of Psychology, 11,* 1–40.

Pribram, K. H. (1961). Limbic system. In D. E. Sheer (Ed.), *Electrical stimulation of the brain.* Austin: University of Texas Press.

Pribram, K. H. (1962). Interrelations of psychology and the neurological disciplines. In S. Koch (Ed.), *Psychology: A study of a science.* New York: McGraw-Hill.

Pribram, K. H. (1967). The new neurology and the biology of emotion. *American Psychologist, 22,* 830–838.

Pribram, K. H. (1970). The biology of mind: Neurobehavioral foundations. In A. R. Gilgen (Ed.), *Scientific psychology: Some perspectives.* New York: Academic.

Pribram, K. H. (1971). *Languages of the brain.* Englewood Cliffs, NJ: Prentice-Hall.

Pribram, K. H. (1979). Behaviorism, phenomenology and holism in psychology. *Journal of Social and Biological Structures, 2,* 65–72.

Pribram, K. H. (1980). The role of analogy in transcending limits in the brain sciences. *Daedalus, 109,* 19–38.

Pribram, K. H. (1981). Emotions. In S. B. Filskov & T. J. Boll (Eds.). *Handbook of clinical neuropsychology.* New York: Wiley.

Pribram, K. H. (1984) Emotion: A neurobehavioral analysis. In K. R. Scherer & P. Ekman (Eds.), *Approaches to emotion.* Hillsdale, NJ: Erlbaum.

Pribram, K. H. (1985) A scientist's approach to the mind/brain issue. *Krisis* (Journal of the International Circle for Research in Philosophy, Houston, Texas), 14–31.

Pribram, K. H., & Gill, M. M. (1976). *Freud's "Project" re-assessed.* New York: Basic Books.

Pribram, K. H., Sharafat, A. & Beekman, G. J. (1985) Frequency encoding in motor systems. In H. T. A. Whiting (Ed.), *Human motor actions—Bernstein reassessed.* North-Holland: Elsevier, 121–156.

Prochaska, G. (1851). *A dissertation on the functions of the nervous system* (T. Laycock, Trans.). London: Sydenham Society. (Original work published 1784)

Rakic, P. (1976). *Local circuit neurons.* Cambridge, MA: MIT Press.

Ratliff, F. (1965). *Mach bands: Quantitative studies in neural networks in the retina.* San Francisco: Holden-Day.

Reynolds, P. C. (1981). *On the evolution of human behavior.* Berkeley: University of California Press.

Robinson, D. N. (1979). *Systems of modern psychology: A critical sketch.* New York: Columbia University Press.

Robinson, D. N. (1981). *An intellectual history of psychology* (rev. ed.). New York: Macmillan.

Ryle, G. (1949). *The concept of mind.* New York: Barnes, Noble.

Schäfer, E. A. (1898–1900). *Textbook of physiology* (2 vols.). Edinburgh: Young.

Schmitt, F. O., Dev, P., & Smith, B. H. (1976). Electronic processing of information by brain cells. *Science, 193,* 114–120.

Sharafat, A. R. (1981). *Sensorimotor information processing.* Unpublished doctoral dissertation, Stanford University.

Sherrington, C. (1947). *The integrative action of the nervous system.* New Haven, CT: Yale University Press. (Original work published 1911)

Sherrington, C. (1955). *Man on his nature.* Garden City, NY: Doubleday.

Skinner, B. F. (1938). *The behavior of organisms.* New York: Appleton-Century-Crofts.

Skinner, B. F. (1969). *Contingencies of reinforcement: A theoretical analysis.* Englewood Cliffs, NJ: Prentice-Hall.

Skinner, B. F. (1971). *Beyond freedom and dignity.* New York: Knopf.

Skinner, B. F. (1974). *About behaviorism.* New York: Vintage.

Sokolov, E. N. (1960). Neuronal models and the orienting reflex. In M. A. B. Brazier (Ed.), *The central nervous system and behavior.* New York: Josiah Macy, Jr., Foundation.

Spence, K. W. (1960). *Behavior theory and learning.* Englewood Cliffs, NJ: Prentice-Hall.

Spencer, H. (1852, March 20). The development hypothesis. *Leader,*

Spencer, H. (1897). *Principles of psychology* (4th ed.). New York: Appleton-Century-Crofts. (Original work published 1855)

Sperry, R. W. (1974). Lateral specialization in the surgically separated hemispheres. In F. O. Schmitt & F. G. Worden (Eds.), *The Neurosciences: Third study program.* Cambridge, MA: MIT Press.

Sperry, R. W. (1976). Mental phenomena as causal determinants in brain function. In G. G. Globus, G. Maxwell, & I. Savodnick (Eds.), *Consciousness and the brain.* New York: Plenum.

Spinelli, D. N., & Pribram, K. H. (1966). Changes in visual recovery functions produced by temporal lobe stimulations in monkeys. *Electroencephalography and Clinical Neurophysiology, 20,* 44–49.

Sulloway, F. J. (1979). *Freud: Biologist of the mind.* New York: Basic Books.

Teuber, H. L. (1960). Perception. In J. Field, H. W. Magoun, & V. E. Hall (Eds.), *Handbook of physiology and neurophysiology.* Washington, DC: American Physiological Society.

Thorndike, E. L. (1943) *Man and his works.* Cambridge, MA: Harvard University Press.

Thorndike, E. L. (1965). *Animal intelligence: Experimental studies.* New York: Hafner.

Tolman, E. C. (1932). *Purposive behavior in animals and men.* New York: Century.

Tomkins, S. S. (1962). *Affect, imagery, consciousness.* New York: Springer.

Turvey, M. T. (1977). Preliminaries to a theory of action with reference to vision. In R. Shaw & J. Bransford (Eds.), *Perceiving, acting, and knowing.* Hillsdale, NJ: Erlbaum.

Waddington, C. H. (1957). *The strategy of the genes.* London: Allen & Unwin.

Wall, P. D., & Pribram, K. H. (1950). Trigeminal neurotomy and blood pressure responses from stimulation of lateral central cortex of Macaca Mulatta. *Journal of Neurophysiology, 13,* 409–412.

Watson, J. B. (1959). *Behaviorism.* Chicago: University of Chicago Press. (Original work published 1925)

Weber, E. H. (1851). *Annotations anatomicae et physiologicae: Programmata collecta.* Leipzig: Köhler.

Weiskrantz, L., Warrington, E. K., Sanders, M. D., & Marshall, J. (1974). Visual capacity in the hemianopic field following a restricted occipital ablation *Brain, 97,* 709–728.

Wernicke, C. (1874). *Der aphasische Symptomencomplex.* Breslau: Cohn, Weigert.

Wheeler, H. (Ed.). (1973). *Beyond the punitive society—operant conditioning: Social and political aspects.* San Francisco: Freeman.

Whytt, R. (1768). *The works of Robert Whytt, M.D.* Edinburgh: Balfour, Auld, Smellie.

Wiener, N. (1948). *Cybernetics, or control and communication in the animal and the machine.* New York: Wiley.

Wundt, W. (1874). *Grundzüge der Physiologischen Psychologie.* Leipzig: Engelman.

Young, P. T. (1973). *Emotion in man and animal* (2nd ed.). Huntington, NY: Krieger. (Original work published 1943)

13

Antagonism and Interaction:
The Relations of Philosophy
to Psychology

ROM HARRÉ, HORST U. K. GUNDLACH, ALEXANDRE MÉTRAUX,
ANDREW OCKWELL, AND KATHERINE V. WILKES

INTRODUCTION

A history of the recent interaction between philosophy and psychology requires not only a critical history of psychology but of much of
philosophy as well. Rather than attempt so comprehensive a task, we
illustrate some important moments of interaction through five case histories.

PHILOSOPHY DISOWNS PSYCHOLOGY

It is not uncommon for psychologists of different persuasions to share
a belief about the origin of an independent science of psychology. On
the assumption that philosophy is the mother of all sciences, it is
thought that, in long historical battles, science after science liberated
itself from the custody of philosophers, and that psychology won this
inevitable struggle rather late in the second half of the nineteenth century.

383

POINTS OF VIEW IN THE
MODERN HISTORY OF PSYCHOLOGY

It is doubtful that either the general idea that the sciences were born of philosophy, or the more specific notion that psychology so arose, corresponds to actual processes. There is no doubt that after the introduction of Aristotle's *De Anima* into the university curriculum at the end of the Middle Ages, psychology was considered part of philosophy, and hence fell within the domain of the philosophy faculties. However, modern psychology regards itself as a science apart from philosophy. Institutional ties to philosophy faculties, if they still exist, are considered relics from the past. The question we examine here is whether or not this state of affairs is really the outcome of a struggle for independence.

In nineteenth-century Germany, Kant's verdict against rational psychology had been widely accepted. Under the influence of physiology, empirical psychology was becoming experimental and quantitative. At this point the stage seemed set for psychology in Germany to break the chains tying it to philosophy and to establish itself as an independent discipline. Instead, events took a different turn. Some philosophers tried to ban the pursuit of the nascent science entirely. Then, as if to ridicule the notion of psychology as a new science attempting to emancipate itself as a whole from metaphysics, the philosophers tried to oust only part of it.

We briefly call attention to the dubiousness of present beliefs about the separation of psychology from philosophy by means of a single important example. This prototype case is furnished by the public actions (and the less public interactions) of two persons: Wilhelm Wundt and Wilhelm Windelband. The events we describe took place in a dynamic historical climate; the mid-nineteenth century was a time of rapid economic development and social change. Psychology, armed with its methods of experimentation and techniques of measurement, was expanding into many new fields. For philosophy, by contrast, it was a time of revived interest in metaphysical matters.

On several occasions Windelband deplored the fact that after the post-Hegelian period, around 1850, German academic philosophy seemed to dissolve into the fields of psychology and the history of philosophy. Wundt and Windelband, respectively, happened to be the most influential figures in these areas. Though their renown rests largely on their contributions to these fields, it is essential to remember that both were active in the discussion of philosophy proper. Wundt not only lectured on philosophical topics but also published under such titles as *Logik*, *System der Philosophie*, and *Einführung in die Philosophie* (see References, Chapter 2, this volume). For his part, Windelband lectured on psychology at regular intervals, though he never published much on it. In German, Swiss, and Austrian universities during the period, philosophers were supposed to teach psychology, and psychologists as a rule had chairs of philosophy—though even to talk in this way is to imply a division that belongs to later days.

Wundt, who had a full medical training, was called to the chair of inductive philosophy at the Federal Institute of Technology in Zurich in 1874. The standards prevailing in this institution were at least as high as those of any university. In his inaugural lecture, Wundt (1874) makes several programmatic points:

1. Nowadays, the special sciences give rise to philosophical questions; philosophy is thus the science of sciences.
2. Philosophy must maintain good relations with the special sciences, thereby having access to basic empirical material, and so being in a position to make a general synthesis out of specialized knowledge.
3. As all experience is at first inner experience, there is no absolute validity in the dichotomy of inner and outer experience.

This line of reasoning, giving much weight to epistemological considerations, led to a particular role for psychology: It had the vocation to mediate between the natural and the cultural sciences. In addition, it should be emphasized that in no way did Wundt subscribe to the doctrine that laws established by empirical psychology should serve as building blocks for epistemology and the rest of philosophy.

In 1875 Wundt was appointed to the chair of philosophy at the University of Leipzig. Here he created his Institute for Experimental Psychology and elaborated his *Völkerpsychologie* (1900), as well as his philosophical views (see Chapter 2, this volume). Some central interests of the *Völkerpsychologie* are language, custom, myth and religion, law, and art. The themes of the Zurich lecture also appear in his Leipzig inaugural lecture (Wundt, 1876). Here Wundt further explicates his perception of the relation between philosophy and the sciences. Though its history and the nature of its problems link psychology closely to philosophy, natural science and psychology as empirical sciences are opposed to philosophy as a normative and formal science. Nevertheless, the materials to which the norms of philosophy can be applied must be furnished by the empirical sciences.

We now examine in more detail the views of our other protagonist, Windelband. He began his career as a student of medicine and natural sciences but quickly turned to philosophy.

At the time of Wundt's arrival in Leipzig, Windelband was teaching there in the traditional post of *Privatdozent* (unpaid lecturer), a position he had gained with his *Habilitationsschrift* (postdoctoral dissertation),

"On the Certainty of Knowledge" (1873). In this study he welcomes the new science of psychophysics as showing the empirical way to findings that correspond remarkably well to Kant's teachings. Though Windelband's epistemology at this stage was a unique mixture of psychological, logical, and metaphysical doctrines, it is evident that he was not propagating *psychologism*, the claim that other disciplines (here philosophy) basically rise from psychological foundations.

Windelband was soon called from Leipzig to Zurich to take the chair of inductive philosophy that Wundt had occupied in 1874–1875. As the topic for his inaugural lecture (1876), he chose the current state of psychological research—no doubt with his predecessor in mind. In the lecture he argues that cooperation between philosophy and the empirical sciences is indispensable. Using a familiar cliché, he points out that psychology, the youngest daughter of philosophy, mother of all sciences, has been struggling to leave the parental home for about 100 years. Now, he declares, this struggle for independence has been won. There must be institutional separation through the establishment of university chairs for psychology. Windelband put forward this demand even though he was not actively working in psychology. It was later called "the declaration of the coming-of-age of psychology" by one of Windelband's biographers (Ruge, 1971, p. 47). One elegant way of resisting the psychologism that Windelband feared is, of course, to turn psychology out of philosophy altogether.

For the next phase in the argument we must return to Wundt. In an essay on philosophy and science, Wundt (1885) takes up ideas from his Zurich speech of some years earlier. He too called philosophy the "mother science," with a specific line of argument in mind. In Wundt's view, philosophy had played the mother role only in antiquity. In his day, there was the philosophy of philosophers and the philosophy of scientists, each working in different specialties. Thus it was misleading to claim that the former had priority over the latter. Wundt used the thesis that philosophy is mother to the sciences not so much as a historical proposition as an appeal for closer ties and cooperation between the empirical sciences and philosophy, especially metaphysics, which was defined as the science of principles, or of basic concepts and laws. To clinch his point, he goes on to posit that there should be no such thing as a history of philosophy per se, but only a history of philosophy and the sciences, and of their interaction.

Nonetheless, in the *Festschrift* for Kuno Fischer (Windelband, 1904b), it was Wundt who wrote the first chapter. Right at the beginning he acknowledges that psychology was in a much debated position and that at least three points of view were to be found: Psychology was (1) one of the natural sciences; (2) a general, all-embracing *Geisteswissenschaft* (cultural science), with philosophy as one of its many special sciences; or (3) a part of philosophy. Apart from saying that it should be the major task of psychology to make peace between philosophy and the special sciences, Wundt did not expose his own position on this question.

Wundt never persuaded Windelband to accept his interactive view of the relation between philosphy and psychology. Over the years, Windelband's publications emphasized that psychology was completely independent of philosophy, that it had become a natural science with its methodology, and that it was still far from possessing any well-defined concepts. His remarks about experimental psychology became more and more hostile (see Windelband, 1894, pp. 23ff.; 1904a, p. 6; 1904b, pp. 169, 179; 1909, pp. 89ff.; 1911a, p. 363; 1913, p. 21.)

Windelband was not the only philosopher who thought that all or part of psychology was becoming a nuisance. In 1913 a number of philosophers in university posts considered the time ripe to launch a large-scale attack that would evict (experimental) psychology from their departments. A bitter dispute about the succession to Hermann Cohen's chair at Marburg provided the occasion for six of the most eminent German-speaking philosophers to send a circular to all the departments of philosophy in Austria, Germany, and Switzerland. The six were Rudolph Eucken, Edmund Husserl, Paul Natorp, Heinrich Rickert, Alois Riehl, and Wilhelm Windelband. Recipients were asked to sign a "Declaration Against the Occupation of Philosophical Chairs with Representatives of Experimental Psychology" (see Erklärung, 1913). In all, 107 signatures were gathered. The declaration and the signatures were sent to all ministries of cultural affairs in the countries concerned and then published in most of the German-language philosophical journals.

Even before all the signatures had been received, Wundt took the offensive. In a pamphlet *Psychology's Struggle for Survival*, Wundt (1913) criticizes both the declaration and its initiators, specifically Windelband, by quoting obliquely and without attribution Windelband's (1909) attack on the pretensions of psychophysics.

> For a good while in Germany circumstances were nearly of that kind that one's capability for occupying a philosophical chair was considered proven as soon as he had mastered the task of tapping methodically on electric buttons and of showing in extensive, well-organized data columns and series of experiments that to some people ideas come quicker than to others. (p. 92)

If the concern for the future of psychology expressed in the Declaration comes from people of such conviction, Wundt concludes, then it can hardly be more than pretense.

The Declaration of the Six stirred up heated discussion about the nature and justification of connections between psychology and philosophy. To be sure, a good number of arguments concerned merely institutional and organizational questions, having little bearing on deeper questions about intellectual and methodological relations between the two disciplines. One is tempted to analyze such an affair in detail, but only two points are called to attention here: First, it was not the youngster, psychology, that was struggling for independence from a reluctant mother; on the contrary, we see a large number of philosophers plainly trying to get rid of (experimental) psychology. (So much for the reputed chains of [professional] metaphysics.) Second, in furthering the Declaration, Windelband took a stand that did not square with the opinion he had expressed in 1876. At that time he had declared psychology to be an independent science. Now, in 1913, it was experimental psychology alone that was to be separated from philosophy. Thus, for Windelband and others, the business of philosophy was not the discovery of facts, but rather the formulation and examination of values and norms—in logic as well as in ethics and aesthetics. To be of other than merely theoretical interest, however, these values and norms need a realm of reference. Psychology's business, by contrast, consisted of finding classes and categories of things and events that make up consciousness, and of investigating how these actually interact.

By inspecting one particular case, we have demonstrated the mythological character of the notion that psychology had to liberate itself from philosophy's rule before it could become a "real" science. If nothing else, the Declaration of the Six, backed by no less than 107 philosophy teachers, makes such a view absurd.

PHILOSOPHICAL INFLUENCES ON PSYCHOLOGY: THE CASE OF BEHAVIORISM, 1913–1950

Behaviorism was first propounded systematically in an article written with great verve and confidence by John B. Watson in 1913. The term "behaviorism" itself refers to both a program of research and a collection of theories and empirical findings. As a movement in psychology, it came to be widely and enthusiastically accepted, though it was lacking in empirical support (see Chapter 6, this volume). This situation suggests that there was an intellectual climate favorable to behaviorism, enabling it to capture the imagination of contemporary scholars in the absence of compelling empirical evidence. This section examines that intellectual climate, particularly the role played by the philosophical doctrine of positivism. We first describe in outline form both positivism and behaviorism in their philosophical aspects. We then consider the influence of positivism and other intellectual traditions on those aspects. This material necessarily overlaps with that of Chapters 6 and 7, but the claims of the philosophical doctrine are the focus of interest here.

The term positivism is an ambiguous one that can be used in several different ways. In one usage it refers to the application of methods of the natural sciences to social phenomena. This interpretation relates to early use of the term by Auguste Comte. Another usage is that in the philosophy of science, where positivism is contrasted with the position known as realism. Where a realist asserts that a scientific theory is a statement about actual entities or processes in the world, a positivist holds that theories are summary statements about observables. This position is sometimes known as instrumentalism, since it implies that theories do not have truth value but rather are instruments for predicting or manipulating the world, with their effectiveness assessed by reference to their utility. Positivism also refers to the movement in philosophy known as logical positivism (or logical empiricism) that was preeminent during the 1920s and 1930s in much of the Western intellectual world. This movement help up a certain interpretation of science (broadly speaking, a positivist one) as the paradigm for all knowledge. In doing so, it accepted only certain categories of statements as meaningful. These were analytic statements (definitions and tautologies), together with statements about the world, the truth of which could be determined by observation. In other words, a statement (other than an analytic truth) was considered to be meaningful only if it was verifiable.

If the verification principle were imported into psychology, or any other discipline, it would lead to a positivist interpretation of theories. Theoretical terms would be permissible only if they could be exhaustively specified by means of observation statements. In fact, a notion closely associated with that of the verification principle, that of the *operational definition*, did have considerable impact on much research in psychology.

Another background influence was the American philosophical movement called pragmatism (see Chapter 5, this volume). It flourished in the United States during the later nineteenth and early twentieth centuries and was propounded in rather different forms by Charles Peirce, William James, and John Dewey. At the heart of pragmatist thought was a principle very similar to both the verification principle and the notion of operational definition. Peirce formulated this maxim as follows: "Consider what effects, that might conceivably have practical bearings, we conceive the object of our conception to have. Then, our conception of these effects is the whole of our conception of the object (quoted in Ayer, 1968). It seems clear that pragmatism was America's native-born positivism. Later, we consider whether it did in fact have any significant influence on the conception or development of behaviorism.

Sigmund Koch (1982) divides the behaviorism of the first half of the twentieth century into two phases. The first, extending from 1913 to about 1930, he refers to as classical behaviorism; the second, neobehaviorism, lasted from about 1930 to about 1950. This distinction is particularly useful for our purposes, since it turns out that the influence of positivism on the two phases was quite different, perhaps because of their different philosophical antecedents.

Classical behaviorism was polemical, with its advocates engaged in argument with introspectionist and functional psychologists. It was also programmatic, in that much of its writing was devoted to showing how phenomena previously thought to require introspective study (such as thoughts, images, or emotions) could be described in the language of stimulus and response. A very important—indeed, central—emphasis was placed on the need for objectivity in research methods.

Neobehaviorism was an attempt to translate the classical behaviorist program into rigorous and comprehensive theories. The dominant figure of this time was Clark Hull, whose work we discuss later. Briefly stated, his was an attempt to formulate an all-encompassing theory of learned performance, a theory grounded in a small set of postulates from which predictions about behavior could be deduced. Other important figures in Hull's time were E. C. Tolman and E. R. Guthrie. Both attempted to develop comprehensive theories of behavior.

The most prominent neobehaviorist of later decades, B. F. Skinner, concentrated on investigating a form of conditioning distinct from that studied by Pavlov. Pavlovian, or *respondent*, conditioning is the process whereby a response normally associated with a particular stimulus comes to be given to a second stimulus by virtue of the pairing of two stimuli. However, the form of conditioning of particular interest to Skinner was instrumental, or *operant*, conditioning (see Chapter 7, this volume). Operant learning is said to occur when particular responses are emitted more frequently if followed by a reinforcing stimulus, or *reinforcer*.

The remainder of this section is divided into two parts. In the first we examine the intellectual background of the emergence of classical behaviorism. In the second we show the importance of the positivist influence on neobehaviorism.

The Intellectual Background of Classical Behaviorism

In his book on the development of psychology, George Miller (1962) identifies four intellectual traditions contributing to the emergence of experimental psychology: positivism, materialism, empiricism, and evolutionism. This analysis provides a useful starting point, and although his use of each of these categories requires some modification, Miller's treatment provides the basis of this section.

Experimental psychology was born in the later nineteenth century. The official founding date is 1879, when the first psychological laboratory was established in Leipzig by Wundt. It was during this time, argues Miller, that European thought was dominated by positivism. In the broad sense used by Miller, we may certainly accept that behaviorism (and indeed, the whole of experimental psychology) was positivist. But as noted earlier, positivism also refers to a particular claim on the nature of the language of natural science. While this effect is rather uninteresting, there is a good, prima facie case for positivist influence of the sort that is of some interest.

In the late 19th century, Ernst Mach and others argued powerfully for a "sensationalist" interpretation of science. That is, science was to be no more than an attempt to redescribe sensory experience economically. Consequently, scientists were expected to be highly suspicious of theoretical ideas such as "force" or "absolute space," because these were not presented in sensory experience. In particular, Mach criticized traditional scientific mechanics for going beyond experience to speak of "electrical fluid" or "atoms" when it should speak only of the motions of observable bodies. To believe that a theory was more than a mathematical model, and that its concepts referred to real objects and processes in a real world, independent of men, was to venture from science into metaphysical speculation. According to Machian positivism, science expresses its conclusions not as causal links describing real (but unobservable) influences, but rather as functional relationships between variables describing experienceable properties of observable things (Passmore, 1966).

Following Miller's lead, the second tradition of importance during the nineteenth century was materialism, the belief that the world can be understood as consisting solely of matter and the exchange of energy. The explanation of all phenomena was assumed to reside in the laws of physics and chemistry. A materialist approach to psychology tends to focus on the physiology and anatomy of the nervous system. For example, one particular line of physiological research, the work of the Russian physiologists Sechenov, Bekhterev, and Pavlov, was of great importance to the development of psychology. In its most extreme form, of course, materialism becomes a reductionist metaphysics that denies the existence of mental phenomena.

Empiricism, the third tradition of interest here, is the doctrine that all true knowledge derives from the senses (see Chapter 1, this volume). Miller believed that empiricism played its most important role in the early stages of scientific psychology. This role was a dual one, providing "both a *method* to increase knowledge and a *theory* about the growth of the mind" (Miller, 1962, pp. 26–27). This form of empiricism was also associationist, and hence presaged a central doctrine of later behaviorism—namely, the various laws of learning. The British empiricist philosophers formulated laws of association to account for the relationships between ideas (see Chapter 4, this volume), and the close relation between associationism and positivism determined much of the shape of the behaviorism to come.

The associationist law of contiguity, which states that the associations most easily formed are those between experiences occurring close together, can be viewed as a cousin to the positivist principle that excludes causality from science in favor of mere regularity. The contiguity principle has survived as one of the basic principles of conditioning, and indeed as the central principle of a major learning theory—that of E. R. Guthrie—though his associations were not between simple ideas in the basic empiricist sense. The regularity theory of causality is also still with us, assumed in much naive experimental methodology.

Empiricism thus involved not only a theory of science, but also a theory of meaning. In modern phraseology, the true meaning of an idea, according to empiricist doctrine, was found in the associated sensory impressions (see the discussion of James's pragmatism and Dewey's instrumentalism in Chapter 5, this volume).

The fourth influence noted by Miller is evolutionism. However, the type to which he refers is very much within the Comtean tradition. Comte argued that civilization evolves through three stages, each having a characteristic form of enquiry: theological, metaphysical, and positivistic. In the theological stage, phenomena are explained by the actions of spirits. In the metaphysical stage, "essences" or "powers" or "faculties" are sought. In the third, positive stage, explanation is seen to reside in the relations between phenomena. Thus, evolutionism is not only a theory of science, but also of society. According to Miller (1962): "It is not surprising, therefore, that Comte's followers were among the first to support Darwin's theory of biological evolution when it appeared in 1859. They, with Herbert Spencer and Thomas Huxley, grafted Darwin's theory on to the positive philosophy" (p. 26).

These, then, are the four traditions of 19th-century thought most relevant to the emergence of scientific psychology, and among them we may assess the significance of positivism. As stated earlier, there is indeed a prima facie case for significant positivist influence in the background of behaviorism. We note that the positivist writings of Mach and others were widely known. Additionally, in the United States the dominant school of philosophy became pragmatism, with Watson himself being educated in one of its centers. Not one, then, but two strands of positivist thinking were in a position to influence the shape of the emerging behaviorist viewpoint in psychology. Were they, in fact, significant in the conception of behaviorism? To answer this question, we must examine Watson's own writings to see whether he acknowledges the influence of positivist philosophy, whether his programmatic statements are consistent with positivist thinking, and, most importantly, whether the behaviorism he advocated conforms to a positivist ideal.

On the question of Watson's pronouncements about his own philosophy, the answer is clear. In an autobiographical statement (Watson, 1936), he states that he had a number of philosophy courses but "never knew what Dewey was talking about" (p. 274). Furthermore, Cohen's (1971) biography of Watson reveals no pragmatist or any other positivist influence. While Watson's own writings are remarkably free of philosophical justifications, it is certain that he considered the objectivity of findings to be a central feature of behaviorism. According to Mackenzie (1977), this indicates that behaviorism was, even at this stage, positivist. To make such a claim, however, is to trade upon the broad and uninteresting sense of positivism as no more than the application of natural science methods to social phenomena (whatever these methods were supposed to be). Such an interpretation does not distinguish positivism from realism.

When we examine Watson's writing more carefully, we see that his primary research program was within the field of biology. He is popularly thought (among psychologists) to have been reacting against the introspective method of Wundt and Titchener, which is true. However, he was also reacting against the kind of psychology in which he had been trained—namely, functionalism—and this reaction was influential among psychologists.

In the words of James R. Angell, one of Watson's dissertation supervisors, functionalism treated consciousness "as an organic function whose intrinsic occupation consists in furthering the adaptive responses of the organism to its life conditions" (Angell, 1904). Some psychologists used detailed observations of animal behavior as a basis for speculating about the mental life of animals, thereby implicitly assuming analogous modes of thinking in animals and man. This work resulted in interpretations of animal behavior which, to modern readers, seem rather fanciful. For example: "The pausing of the rat when the door unexpectedly failed to open might seem to imply reflection, but this is not so in any strict usage of the term 'reflect.' That the rat *feels* 'why' and 'what' is certain, that she thinks 'why' and 'what' is both doubtful and unnecessary" (Small, 1901, quoted in Cohen, 1971).

Though it is not certain that it was to Small that he was reacting, Watson (1913) argues that this sort of speculation is irrelevant and unnecessary. In his view, one can assume the presence or absence of consciousness anywhere in the phylogenetic scale without affecting problems of behavior by one jot, and without influencing in any way the mode of experimental attack used on them. Watson was thus aligning psychology with the empiricist biology of Darwin, but without making any explicit commitment to positivism. Of the traditions in the background of behaviorism, positivism was of negligible significance. Classical behaviorism was shaped by an empiricist emphasis on objectivity within a functionalist psychology that owed much to Darwin, together with the successful physiological psychology of Pavlov and Bekhterev.

Positivist Influences on Neobehaviorism

While there was apparently good reason for believing that positivist ideas significantly influenced classical behaviorism, in fact they did not. The case of neobehaviorism is quite different, however, because here the influence of positivism cannot be doubted. Koch describes it as follows: "The transition from classical to neo-behaviorism was influenced by importation of a set of prescriptions (e.g., the analyses of logical positivism) concerning the nature of sound scientific theory" (Koch, 1982, p. 934).

Hull devotes the first 15 pages of his *Principles of Behavior* (1943) to describing his conception of scientific method. For him, science is a hypothetico-deductive enterprise, with the heart of a theory being a set of postulates from which statements can be rigorously deduced. These statements are intended to be predictions (hypotheses) about behavior that can be tested experimentally. When there is a discrepancy between a theoretical prediction and an empirical result, an adjustment of the theory is necessary. Hull explains that a scientific theory, in its deductive nature, "closely resembles mathematics" and adopts an explicitly geometrical terminology.

That what Hull produced resembled, structurally, an idealized positivist theory can hardly be doubted. But within the definition of positivism adopted in this chapter, we must question the status of the theoretical terms used by him. That is, we must decide whether they function as convenient fictions—intervening variables merely summarizing data—or whether they refer to real entities or processes that should be viewed as hypothetical constructs. This method of making the distinction between positivism and realism is due to MacCorquodale and Meehl (1948). When we apply this distinction to behaviorist theory, we have, in effect, a touchstone for psychological positivism: Any theory employing only intervening variables conforms to the positivist pattern because it really does not amount to anything beyond a condensed statement of what has been observed; when hypothetical constructs are involved, however, we know that real entities or processes are held to be their referents, and therefore we are dealing with a theory that conforms to the realist conception of science.

MacCorquodale and Meehl (1948) regard the work of Skinner and Tolman as "almost wholly free of hypothetical constructs." Hull's position is more complex, and they find in his system examples of both intervening variables (e.g., "habit strength") and hypothetical constructs (e.g., "r_g" and "s_d").

Skinner exemplifies most clearly the importance of positivist philosophy to neobehaviorism. His is an uncompromisingly pure behaviorism, attempting to predict behavior from knowledge of the organism's history of reinforcement and current cues, and to control behavior by manipulating contingencies of reinforcement. Yet much of his writing is devoted to applying his brand of behaviorism to human affairs and is clearly speculative. When, for example, he attempts to extend the compass of "the experimental analysis of behavior" (he disdains the term "psychology") to embrace such central human notions as freedom and dignity (Skinner, 1972), he is, in fact, extrapolating far beyond a narrow empirical base. Furthermore, he has been criticized for using material derived from studies of adult animals to explore issues that might more appropriately be dealt with by other sorts of comparisons.

It is ironic that one who so forcefully emphasizes the importance of observation should allow himself to be drawn so far from what his own experiments warrant, but in so doing he demonstrates his faith in a particular methodology and a particular philosophy of science. Skinner (1954) explicitly acknowledges his intellectual debt to positivist writers:

> To me behaviorism is a special case of philosophy of science which first takes shape in the writings of Ernst Mach, Henri Poincaré and Percy Bridgman . . . Behaviorism is a formulation which makes possible an effective experimental approach to human behavior. It is a working hypothesis about the nature of a subject matter. It may need to be clarified, but it does not need to be argued. I

have no doubt of the eventual triumph of the position—not that it will eventually
be proved right, but that it will prove the most direct route to the successful
science of man. (p. 12).

As a statement about the importance of positivism to the development
of neobehaviorism, this excerpt needs no further comment. Though
positivism as an explicit philosophy of science was not among the influences contributing to the origins of behaviorism, its significance for behaviorism's later development now seems undeniable.

The Misunderstanding of Operationalism

There are various residual traces of influences exerted on psychology
by philosophy in the positivist period. One of the more curious leftovers
involved the borrowing, and misunderstanding, of the operationalist
theory of meaning proposed by the physicist, P. W. Bridgman (1929).
The idea of defining scientific concepts in terms of experimental operations goes back to the mid-19th century. At that time, an operationalist
theory of meaning was developed for chemistry but gained few serious
adherents. Bridgman revived the idea in the hope of devising a theory of
meaning for scientific concepts that would prevent, for all future time,
the kind of chaos that ensued when physicists were forced by the advent
of relativity theory to make radical changes in the meaning of basic
concepts such as spatial and temporal intervals. He proposed that the
meaning of scientific concepts be tied to measuring operations and not,
as had been traditional, to the real properties of supposedly real things.
He believed that while the latter were historically determined by the
state of currently accepted theory, the former, as measuring operations,
were independent of changes in our conception of nature.

For example, Bridgman suggested that temporal concepts be understood as no more than the sets of operations required to measure temporal intervals. On this view, Newtonian time and relativistic time were to
be distinct, noncompeting concepts, because they were defined by distinctly different operations of measurement. To operationalize a concept
was not to propose an empirical test for whether that concept should be
applied, but rather to *reduce it to* precisely that test.

Bridgman's theory has been severely criticized. The major difficulty
arises from the fact that there are often several ways of measuring the
same physical property. If each is taken to define an independent empirical concept, the essential unity of science is dissolved and the similarity
of mathematical measures of the same property becomes an inexplicable
coincidence. Like its predecessor in chemistry, Bridgman's operational-

ism is an interesting historical curiosity (Benjamin, 1955), but psychologists continue to talk of operationalizing concepts. It seems clear from context that all they mean by this phrase is finding an empirical test to determine whether a concept is to be applied—for example, whether the strength of an indicated state can be measured. Finding an empirical test does not explicate the meaning of a psychological concept; rather it presupposes it.

In the next section we examine a case of intellectual traffic in the contrary direction as we discuss Piaget's attempt to found a philosophy on psychology.

PSYCHOLOGICAL INFLUENCES ON PHILOSOPHY: THE CASE OF GENETIC EPISTEMOLOGY

Piaget's reputation as an innovative developmental psychologist is firmly established, but throughout his work he aimed at building a new philosophy. In the thousands of pages he wrote, he rarely missed an occasion to demarcate polemically his own ideas from those commonly held in traditional philosophy, yet he failed to acknowledge that he owed much to it. This two-way traffic within Piaget's ideas is untypical of the ways in which philosophy and psychology have interacted during the past few decades, for one of the best documented characteristics of psychology has been its reluctance to address philosophic issues, or even to propose conceptual systems to supplant those offered by philosophy.

In this section we try to substantiate the following theses:

1. Piaget wished to construct a new, better philosophy.

2. He neglected the consequences of the separation of philosophy and psychology into ways of treating distinctive kinds of problems, a separation that was eventually accomplished after the violent debates of the nineteenth century.

3. Though his work appeared to be an amalgam of philosophical and psychological ideas, the central philosophical tenets were independent of psychology and represent a variation of ideas set forth around the turn of the century by thinkers such as Henry Poincaré and James Mark Baldwin.

4. Ironically, Piaget's work could serve as strong evidence that the reasons for separating philosophy and psychology were valid.

Thus, in order to understand the special but ambiguous role that philosophy plays in Piaget's work, one must distinguish between his overt rejection of philosophical ideas and the constant but hidden influence of such ideas on his own theory.

Piaget's conception of what he would call traditional philosophy crystallized in his well-known essay, *Sagesse (Wisdom) et illusions de la philosophie* (1965). Here, a line is drawn between two incompatible cognitive attitudes and their practical results: philosophical wisdom and experimentally validated knowledge. Philosophers, he points out, at best present coherent yet unprovable sets of ideas that may serve as general frames of orientation in everyday life but do not contribute to the progress of science. These ideas are not empirically testable, as they are presented in philosophy.

This view bears some resemblance to the evolutionary account of Auguste Comte. Indeed, Piaget (1967, p. 43) reveals a kind of scientism that permits only empirically testable systems of ideas to be regarded as knowledge. It also illustrates the use of a rhetorical device that gives the appearance of scientific and nonspeculative validity to the way he approaches precisely those questions that philosophers have tried in vain to answer. In reality, though, the scientistic presentation of Piaget's leading ideas must not be taken too seriously. It wrongly suggests that Piaget's research was essentially psychological merely because it was carried out within the domain of empirical and experimental confirmation of hypotheses about reasoning and cognition. It also implies that there is no longer any need to distinguish between theoretical and metatheoretical discourse, because it suffices to construct a single scientific discourse that solves its own foundational problems. Finally, his scientistic presentation reinforces the belief that Piaget's *épistémologie génétique*, the quintessence of his theory, is rooted in a higher level of sophistication than philosophy—that is, in some very general but essentially scientific view of human thought, and ultimately in biological phenomena.

To justify this analysis, we turn now to demonstrating the extent to which the hidden influences of philosophy on Piaget's point of view can still be detected despite his choice of scientistic language. First, however, the term *épistémologie génétique* requires some clarification. Its English translation, genetic epistemology, is perfectly suited to render its Piagetian meaning. But this conceals the fact that *épistémologie génétique* also refers to that discipline which, in English, is called "theory of science" or "philosophy of science" in a narrow sense. Most dictionaries (e.g., Foulquie, 1962; Lalande 1956) point out that, despite identical etymology, *épistémologie* must be distinguished from "epistemology" and that gnoseological considerations (i.e., themes and questions pertaining to the theory of knowledge) must be excluded from *épistémologie*. These belong instead to the *théorie de la connaissance* (knowledge), which includes, or may include, the theory of perception, of concept formation, and the like (Pasquinelli, 1974).

Thus Piaget is a notable exception among French-speaking authors because he uses *épistémologie* in its English sense. By adding the adjective *génétique* (with its obvious psychobiological connotations) to the noun *épistémologie*, he deliberately opposed French philosophy or theory of science. That is, in qualifying *épistémologie* as *génétique*, he shifted from a rigorous and narrow conception of the theory of science to a standpoint heavily inspired, as he admitted, by Baldwin's early psychological and genetic reinterpretation of logic. One of the immediate consequences of this shift was to induce French-speaking philosophers either to ignore Piaget's new approach or, as in Merleau-Ponty's case (1964), to discuss critically only those aspects which directly refer to the cognitive and moral development of children.

Yet the question remains whether the combination of the two terms in Piaget's favorite label really designates the synthesis of two disciplines (philosophy of science and psychology) that he intended to achieve, or whether they remain an unassimilated mixture of disparate elements? This question can be examined by analyzing one of Piaget's many attempts at synthesis. In a bulky chapter dealing with the methodological requirements of any analysis in the theory of science, Piaget (1967) gives three necessary conditions for adequacy:

1. The validity of principles, concepts, and methods of scientific research cannot be determined without looking at how they are applied in the sciences (p. 62).
2. Formal validity does not depend on intuition (or any other kind of psychologically describable process by which an argument may be felt to be right) but must be assessed by purely logical techniques such as axiomatization or the use of truth-tables (pp. 62–63).
3. The theory of science has to address, in addition to problems of validity, questions concerning the epistemic subject (the knowing person) who uses formal logic, makes judgments, perceives things, elaborates constructs, designs measuring instruments, and so on (pp. 63–64).

Formal validity, like any purely normative or standard-setting feature of discourse, especially the rules of logic, can be tested only by deduction (p. 63). However, the truth of propositions concerning the knowing person—for instance, the age at which someone can use a rule of logic—has to be treated by means of the standard scientific procedures at hand, mainly by psychological observation and experimentation (compare Piaget, 1967, p. 64, with Piaget, 1950, pp. 6–7). Under these conditions, Piaget thought, three ways to pursue the theory of science were available: (1) The method of direct analysis, which investigates the conditions of scientific knowledge in given historical circumstances—for instance, the problem of causality in modern physics, caused by the breakdown of determinism in quantum mechanics (Piaget, 1967, pp. 66–78); (2) the method of formal analysis, which determines the general and formal conditions of cognitive processes (1967, pp. 79–105)—for instance, the role of the prohibition of contradiction in defining entailment; and (3) the genetic method, which focuses on the phylogenetic and ontogenetic development of cognitive processes and combines the results of developmental analysis with the results of formal analysis of these processes. The third method is the main tool of genetic epistemology (Piaget, 1967, pp. 66, 105–127).

This list of methods makes it evident that the genetic analysis of cognitive processes was unable, by itself, to develop criteria that would permit one to decide questions in the theory of science. For instance, it seems obvious that the genetic method could not tell us which form of scientific explanation is valid, which concept of causality ought to be adopted in psychology or physics, or which trend in the theory of science (realism or positivism) is better justified. Nevertheless, the genetic method may yield results indicating that there are in fact convergences between a specific conception of scientific thinking (such as the use of mathematics in physics) and the highest stage of cognitive development (conceived by Piaget to be that of formal operations). Thus, an inquiry into the concepts of causality from Newton to Hertz and Mach (see Piaget & Garcia, 1974) may show which cognitive operations on what level of mental development correspond to those concepts. However, it cannot justify the use of any of these notions of causality.

Piaget did not restrict his epistemological analysis to the empirical study of scientific thinking. Rather, in explicating factual convergences between cognitive operations and corresponding conceptions of scientific thinking, he assimilated a philosophical standpoint that seems to come closest to his own psychological theory. This is the view that theories are arbitrary constructions built for cognitive convenience, and that laws of nature are the conventions governing the use of more or less convenient scientific languages.

All of the empirical data derived from Piaget's genetic approach suggest that the constructivism of Pierre Duhem (1954) and the conventionalism of Poincaré (1958, Chap. 11) correspond best to the structure of cognitive operations performed on what Piaget asserted to be the highest level of ontogenetic cognitive development. It is this kind of correspondence that points to the hidden influence of the traditional French philosophy of science on Piaget's genetic epistemology. In turn, the culturally specific philosophical standpoint of the early twentieth century French philosophy of science is supported by post hoc psychological evidence obtained from French-speaking children of upper-middle-class Switzerland. That standpoint served French philosophy of science as a theoretical guideline in formation of the genetic epistemology producing such psychological evidence.

The label "genetic epistemology" thus designates not a new philosophy, but rather a historical position in the philosophy of science to which an original and highly instructive psychological counterpart was added. In spite of Piaget's claims, psychologists were right in studying only his theory of cognitive development in children, without engaging in philosophical debates. So too were the philosophers who hesitated to occupy themselves with a theory that, upon close scrutiny, rehearsed a well-known philosophical doctrine psychologically dressed up, but one that cannot be justified on psychological grounds.

In the mind–body problem we now see a different kind of interaction between philosophy and psychology.

EIGHTY YEARS OF THE MIND–BODY PROBLEM

It is clear, of course, that the question of how mind and body are related presupposes a previous recognition of some distinction between the two; only from the standpoint of some kind of dualism has the problem any meaning (Taylor, 1904).

We begin by examining Jacques Loeb's treatment of the mind–body problem at the turn of the century. We then jump to a discussion of what we take to be the most interesting approaches to the issue, including the work of the neuropsychologist, A. R. Luria (1973). In this way, using comparisons across a 60- to 80-year span, the historically central issues of the mind–body debate should stand out in clearer form. The reason for beginning at the turn of the century and not earlier is that between 1890 and 1910, philosophers and psychologists alike were starting to discuss the differences between their respective disciplines. Psychology was becoming conscious of its independence from philosophy (Ladd, 1894), while psychologists were reflecting upon their relationship with the physiologists (Fullerton, 1896). This is important for a discussion of the mind–body problem because, as we shall argue, it cannot be seen for what it is—nor, importantly, for what it is not—except with an understanding of the different attitudes that philosophy and the sciences bring to the question. It will emerge that the mind–body problem is relatively tractable for the scientists. For the philosophers, however, something genuinely problematic may remain.

Loeb's "Real" Physiological Process

Loeb was convinced that the red herrings of philosophers confused the scent for researchers into brain physiology:

> The physiology of the brain has been rendered unnecessarily difficult through the fact that metaphysicians have at all times concerned themselves with the interpretation of brain functions and have introduced such metaphysical conceptions as soul, consciousnes, will, etc. One part of the work of physiologists must consist in the substitution of real physiological processes for these inadequate conceptions. (Loeb, 1901, p. v)

What Loeb, a physiologist, regarded as a "real physiological process" we should perhaps prefer to call a real *psychological* process, because he claimed that all conscious or psychic phenomena determined by memory conformed to the (surely) psychological notion of associative memory (Loeb, 1901, p. 12). Nevertheless, his reasons for calling associative memory a physiological process quickly become clear when we note that it was viewed as a "physical mechanism which must be just as definite as, for example, the dioptrical apparatus of our eye" (Loeb, 1901, p. 251).

According to Loeb, all reflex or instinctual behavior can be explained as a simple stimulus–response reaction (e.g., the patellar reflex, or the eye-blink when an object approaches the eye). Associative memory is only a little more complicated: When, on some occasions in the past, stimuli $s, s', s'' \ldots$ have evoked responses $e, e', e'' \ldots$, then on a subsequent occasion the single stimulus s can alone evoke (any of) the set of responses $e, e', e'' \ldots$. In other words, the responses associated with s in the past can be produced when stimulus s is present. Just which stimuli and which responses do or do not get associated in this way depends upon the "conductivity of the protoplasm." Thus the great question for physiology, and the research program by means of which the psychic phenomena of the metaphysicians will eventually be hunted down to their protoplasmic earth, is: "Which peculiarities of the colloidal substances can make the phenomena of associative memory possible?" (Loeb, 1912, p. 75).

Loeb was well aware that the goal he suggested would only be attained, if at all, in the distant future. His own preliminary empirical research was designed to show how simple (or relatively simple) reflexes and instinctual behavior could be explained in purely physical terms, thereby bypassing the need to appeal to anything like an "animal will" or a postulate of "consciousness in the spinal cord." The extrapolation of this program to the sophisticated activities of human beings was admittedly speculative, but he was prepared to sketch some ideas by means of which the problem might one day be solved. One example is his theory of conscious volition. He suggested that associative memory might be operating to produce the final complex of sensations *before* the bodily movements yielding those sensations could take place. Thereby, one could say, the person, or agent, might have a conception of the goal before it was reached (Loeb, 1901, pp. 291ff.). The implausibility of such rather obscure speculations is not important here. The central and vital claim was that the difference between what metaphysicians called "animal will" (which Loeb claimed could be explained in physical terms), and human willing and consciousness was one of degree and not kind. Thus human experience and behavior could, in principle, be explained in the same way.

Assessment of Loeb's Position

Modern scientists and philosophers can find much in Loeb's thesis to indict in terms of muddle or question-begging. As far as the mind–body problem is concerned, for example, it is notable that he relied often upon the very dualistic terminology that a physicalist theory of this kind would need to eliminate. This is, of course, inevitable, given that Loeb's program had as yet hardly started. What is more serious is that he often stated his goals in terms that either committed him to a form of dualism or, at best, left open the possibility of dualism. He frequently wrote, for example, that physicochemical conditions would one day be discovered to "cause," to "lie at the foundations of," or "to give rise to" sensations. If this causing or underpinning is thought to be a physical–physical relation, then a central question about the mind–body relation has been begged: In what sense are sensations physical phenomena? If, however, the relation is seen not as physical–physical but as physical-*psychological*, the possibility of dualism is either left untouched or else Loeb has committed himself to dualist interactions or epiphenomenalism. Other examples of blithe carelessness with prickly mental concepts abound.

Loeb saw nothing odd in moving from discussing image as a psychic phenomenon to thinking of it as something that may be found "not only on the retina but also on the cortex" (Loeb, 1912, p. 79). Nor is it just contemporary philosophers, trained by decades of discussing the Identity Theory, who would find totally unconvincing the use of such sledgehammer tactics on the problem of identifying the mental with the physical. Loeb's thesis would not have converted many philosophers and psychologists of his own time, either. Fullerton (1896), for example, remarks of the physiologist: "He has no right to speak of sensations, of feelings, of ideas: they are not in his world. The functioning of a brain, as he is concerned with it, results in motions immediate or remote, not in feelings or thoughts".

Nevertheless, Loeb was more right than he was wrong. It can even be argued that his general approach to the mind–body question, after 70 or 80 years in which the varied concerns of philosophers, psychologists, and physiologists have been emerging more clearly, is the prevailing attitude today.

Clearly, much scientific research into the structure and functioning of the brain has been unnecessarily fogged by the "conceptions of meta-physicians," as evidenced by the very terms that Loeb picks out for his harshest condemnation—"will" and "consciousness." Psychologists of the present virtually never talk of the will, or of willing, not because there is a genuine phenomenon with which they cannot cope, but be-cause they no longer think that these terms denote any entity or process that merits scientific explanation. As for consciousness, Turner (1971) correctly observes: "Doubtless a major difficulty in writing about con-sciousness and awareness . . . is that no one is able precisely to define what it is that either he would affirm or he would deny." Similarly, Sperry (1969) writes that "most behavioral scientists today, brain re-searchers in particular, have little use for consciousness" (p. 532). Surely, Loeb's approach to notions such as these is the right one: Set aside research into consciousness or the will per se, and instead treat of the incredibly heterogeneous phenomena such as seeing, hearing, feel-ing pain, problem-solving, or acting that tend to be called "conscious" or "willed" behaviors.

It may seem at first that Loeb's general approach becomes more diffi-cult to defend when we consider such mental items as sensations, im-ages, and thoughts. It is here that we meet his high-handed neglect of the question concerning what sorts of things mental phenomena might be—whether or not, for example, they are things that could be identi-fied with or reduced to physical phenomena. This neglect is illustrated by Loeb's unargued assumption that once physiologists discover the conditions under which sensations, images, thoughts, and so on arise, the mind–body dichotomy will disappear. To many contemporary phi-losophers it will seem that it is precisely here that the issue arises in its sharpest form, for what the Loeb program might succeed in showing, once carried through, is that whenever physicochemical conditions of type C are present, then mental phenomena of kind K occur (We ignore for now the likely possibility that this chemicomental relation might be many-to-one or even many-to-many, as well as one-to-one.) What has to be done, though, if dualism is to be avoided, is to provide a further argument to the effect that the conditions *C are* the *K* phenomena. Unfortunately, no scientific evidence can establish that the relationship between the mental and the physical is one of identity rather than constant conjunction.

It can be argued, of course, that as far as scientists are concerned, the identity thesis misses the point. To see this, we need to reflect again upon the various concerns of philosophers, psychologists, and physiologists, particularly neurophysiologists. Clearly, the concern of psychologists is with the explanation of behavior. They are trying to account for the most pervasive and fundamental capacities of human beings in a systematic and law-governed manner. Physiologists, by contrast, want to explain the workings of the brain and central nervous system. For such enterprises no ontology—that is, no theory of proper categories of reality—is given in advance. We do not determine a priori anything about the "real" psychological or neurophysiological entities, events, states, or processes. Rather, the ontologies that the psychologist and the neurophysiologist eventually adopt in the course of their investigations will be those that prove most convenient and fruitful for their respective theoretical and explanatory purposes.

There are a number of ways that such ontologies may partition both the psychological and the neural flux. We have already suggested that Loeb was right to distrust the metaphysicians' concepts of will and consciousness, but this general idea should be taken further. There is no reason why psychologists or physiologists should take as "given" any of the mental phenomena that are, as part of what Wilfred Sellars calls the "manifest image" (roughly, the worldview of the layman), picked out by the conceptual apparatus of ordinary language. The "scientific image" (the picture given by scientific theories) requires that scientific concepts earn their place in the conceptual apparatus of the discipline. Hence, no ordinary language terms, such as "memory," have an automatic right to such a place.

It goes without saying, of course, that many familiar terms do crop up in psychology. We find, for example, psychologists talking of memory, perception, learning, problem-solving, motivation, and so forth. The way psychologists use these concepts may agree with the way they are used in everyday contexts. Usually, however, terms are adapted for the purposes of science—for example, they are given a precise definition (compare the psychologist's and the everyday concept of "emotion") so they are no longer synonymous with their ordinary language counter-parts. It is equally obvious that many unfamiliar and technical terms appear in psychology, especially at its more theoretical levels (e.g., information retrieval, simultaneous synthesis), that serve to identify theoretically postulated functions or processes. Conversely, many of the favored terms of the manifest image of our mental life do not appear. For example, the concept of a sensation, a term that purports to identify something introspectable, will scarcely be useful in an examination of perception that seeks to explain how people can see. It is thus doubtful that those most recalcitrant candidates for identification with the physical—that is, the reified mental items of ordinary language, such as sensation—will even be recognized by psychological theory.

When the Mind–Body Problem is a Problem (and when not)

We can now see more clearly why it was important to take up our tale at the beginning of the twentieth century, and not sooner. The inability of Loeb's program to distinguish correlation from identity was shown to be irrelevant once it was pointed out that the ontology and conceptual framework of the psychologist are bound to be different from those of the everyday speaker, or of the philosopher. But this in turn could not be understood before psychology had achieved independence from philosophy. While the two were still confused—philosophy was defined by John Stuart Mill as "the scientific study of man"—the model of mind given by prevailing philosophical theories was the model of mind that also dominated most scientific research.

The dominant philosophical model was one of atomic associationism: The mind was seen as an inner theater, and upon its stage moved discrete atomic entities (e.g., ideas, impressions, sense-data, images). The interrelations of these actors were governed by various laws of association, and scholars were left to argue endlessly and inconclusively about the number and nature of these laws. Philosophy had thus inherited from the Cartesians and the British empiricists a particular model of the mind, carrying with it a specific ontology (ideas, impressions, and principles of association). This model was imposed upon psychology in the belief that the latter was merely a branch of philosophy. Only as psychology came to distinguish itself sharply from philosophy could it start to challenge the assumption that the ontology of philosophers was somehow given or determined by the nature of things. It is in the work of Loeb that we see an effective beginning of this challenge.

Returning to the specific issue of the mind–body relation, we can push this general point much further. Once it is agreed that the ontology, and hence the conceptual framework of the scientist, is not the business of the philosopher, we can see that the decision by psychologists and physiologists to confront the mind–body problem at all depends almost entirely on whether or not they choose to acknowledge it. If one is a psychologist committed to establishing the unity of mind and body, then one sees theory construction as governed by not one but two main constraints: The theory must be constructed not only with the aim of explaining human behavior economically, systematically, and comprehensively; it must also be couched in terms that refer to entities, states, and processes that are amenable to analysis and explanation by neurophysiology.

It is perhaps easier to see the lure of this approach from the neurophysiologist's point of view. His task cannot be merely to chart the activities of neurons and the conditions of such activity. Rather, to discover how the brain works means to discover precisely how it is organized to work as it does. "Scientific attempts to understand a given system . . . face a twofold problem. The first is to conceptualize the task of the system; to decide in what terms to write its job-description. The second is to frame and test theories of how it does the job" (Mackay, 1978). In other words, the neurophysiologist is trying to explain how the brain does what it does, and the job description ("what it does") will be that given by the best psychological and neuropsychological theories. Hence, even if psychology can proceed without troubling with the problem of whether the brain can actually perform the functions that it postulates, neurophysiology has to know from the start exactly what it is trying to explain. Thus the very enterprise of neurophysiology presupposes the viability of physicalism.

To see the two sciences in this light means that the mind–body problem becomes, for them, totally irrelevant. It is boring for psychologists to be told that sensations cannot be identified with brain processes if they do not acknowledge sensations at all. Any postulated entity that, upon examination, emerges as problematic for microreduction provides good reason to rethink one's ontology; as the mind-body split is neared, it is evaded. Furthermore, the very dichotomy of mental–physical loses its sharpness. Since the category of psychological terms includes all and only the terms used in a psychological theory, and since the theory can and does postulate functions that brain structures are expected to perform, there will be a large overlap between psychological and neurophysiological terms. Indeed, the area of overlap is the thriving "hyphenated" discipline of neuropsychology (see Chapter 12, this volume).

Luria's Neurophysiological Approach

The best evidence for the validity of the neo-Loebian approach—that which we have described as blithely rejecting the existence of a mind–body split—is that whereas Loeb explicitly argues for the substitution of scientific concepts for the "inadequate" conceptions of metaphysicians, contemporary psychologists, neuropsychologists, and neurophysiologists tend to make the substitution implicitly. They rarely comment on that aspect of what they are doing, which argues for more strenous research in the philosophy of the brain-and-behavior sciences to make what has been implicit more explicit. A clear example is taken from the well-known work of the late A. R. Luria (1973). Luria was a neuropsychologist, studying the way the brain is organized to exhibit such psychological abilities as perception, hearing, writing and reading, speaking, moving, and remembering. He used ordinary, everyday psychological terms such as *see, hear, touch,* and *speak,* but he also used psychological terminology of a more technical and theoretical kind: "synthesis and coding of stimuli," "simultaneous synthesis," inhibitability of audio–verbal traces," "the action-acceptor function," and "multidimensional matrices for memory." Lastly, he used terms that are clearly neurophysiological, at both the molar level (e.g., *frontal lobes, the primary visual cortex, the angular gyrus*) and the more micro level (e.g., *cells of associative layer II, the optic nerve, superior longitudinal arcuate fasciculus*).

In Luria's work, the mind–body split has ceased to play a role. The explanation of how people can recognize a face, for example—a clearly psychological, indeed, mental phenomenon—proceeds by analyzing the various functions performed by gross cerebral masses. For instance, the primary visual cortex splits up the incoming stimuli into discrete raw data of moving edges, color contrasts, convex edges, and the like. Secondary visual areas synthesize and code the segregated stimuli into ordered gestalts. Other areas set the gestalts into the spatiotemporal array, and so forth. To these gross cerebral masses are ascribed functions that it would be pointless and perverse to classify as either mental or physical. These functions are of the kind postulated by a psychological or neuropsychological theory, and complex brain masses are thought to fulfill them. How the primary visual cortex, for example, fulfills its assigned functions can in turn be explained by a more micro analysis of the functions and structures of cell groups—and so on until we reach the very micro level of what individual cells do or refrain from doing.

In all this we find Luria using terms like "sensation" and "image" solely for heuristic purposes. For example, he reports that stimulation of certain cells within the primary visual cortex yields a simple hallucination of spots, flashes, or flames. The question that is philosophically tempting to ask is whether Luria is identifying X's hallucinations at time t with the stimulation of X's cells at t, or whether he is saying, as a dualist interactionist, that stimulation causes hallucinatory images. By now the irrelevance of such questions is clear; Luria is simply explaining how certain kinds of misperceiving can occur. That this occasion of misperceiving amounts to something the layman calls a "hallucination" is of no interest except for purposes of exposition.

Misperception of the type in question requires, among other things, the stimulation of certain cells. When this and much else has happened, the patient sees, or seems to see, something that is not there. But the sensation, or the hallucination, is not an element in Luria's formal ontology. Although he explains the hallucination, in the sense that he offers an account of a certain kind of misperception, he does not need or want to claim (or refuse to claim) that hallucinations are identical with brain processes.

Philosophy's Problem

If scientists, then, do not have a mind–body problem—unless they create one for themselves by the injudicious adoption of a recalcitrant and outmoded ontology—where does the difficulty lie? This appears to be a purely philosophical question, for one proper function of the philosophy of mind is to examine the ordinary language ontology and conceptual framework. It is this ordinary language framework that also purports to describe and explain human experience and behavior. However, the main explanatory concerns of this kind of discourse are with specific, individual human actions. It does not try to make generalizations about basic and pervasive human capacities. What is more, we need it to fulfill roles that science is not asked to play: to exhort, praise, blame, warn, suggest, criticize, threaten, and so on. To do all this, the everyday conceptual framework must describe the flux of the mental in terms very unlike those required by a scientific psychology.

The dichotomy between mind and body was given to us by Descartes. It began as an epistemological problem that illegitimately grew into an ontological one. To say that the problem, when examined, simply dissolves may have all the advantages of theft over honest toil, but sometimes honest toil is honestly misplaced. The relation between physiology and psychology is not made problematic by any deep philosophical problem.

AFTER THE SECOND WORLD WAR: THE FRUITS
OF INFORMED INTERACTION

Following World War II there was a marked increase in the influence of philosophy on psychology. In many fields philosophers and philosophically minded psychologists began to look deeply into the assumptions behind particular styles of psychological enquiry, to unearth their philosophical foundations and their "political" connotations. The latter was a new and increasingly important feature of the discussion of psychology.

The Deductive–Nomological Doctrine of Explanation

In the period we are discussing, the most important issues were concerned with the philosophy of explanation. The theory of explanation, particularly that associated with logical empiricism, has exerted an enormous (if indirect) influence on modern psychology.

The basic idea was this: A discourse was deemed explanatory if it conformed to a certain ideal logical structure, the deductive–nomological (D–N) layout. Facts were explained by being deduced from laws and the particular conditions of their production. In the simplest version of this theory, the "covering-law" doctrine, an event could be explained when the premises had been reduced to a description of the production conditions and a single law linking those conditions with the effect. Eschewing refinements, the D–N doctrine amounted to the dogma that an explanation was a deductively ordered set of sentences, at least some of which were general, and among the logical consequences of which was a description of whatever event or type of event was to be explained. Since this account is identical with that we would give of the conditions for making a prediction, an important consequence of the D–N theory was that to predict meant to explain, and vice versa.

Because the ability to predict is part of the ability to control, acceptance of the D–N theory raises the possibility of a political interpretation of psychology. Much of the political criticism of psychology, particularly since World War II, reflects this possibility. That is, it is based on the idea that the philosophy of science summed up in the D–N theory of explanation is part of the apparatus by which human aspirations to *self-*control are suppressed (Habermas, 1968).

During this period some philosophers began to contrast explanation as prediction with explanation as understanding. Since understanding links naturally with a contemplative attitude toward the world of men and their actions, this view of explanation has been thought to have political connotations contrary to those of the D–N theory. For example, a psychology based on explanation as understanding has been linked with the idea of a program for the enhancement of human autonomy (see Shotter, 1975, for a short history of the interactions between theories of science, and of the political implications of related psychological research programs).

Historians and philosophers of science have been severe in their criticism of the D–N conception of scientific explanation, even considered in a purely academic context. Indeed, it can be shown to be seriously misleading in a number of ways. One is that is is associated with a particularly unsatisfactory theory of causation—David Hume's regularity theory. According to the Humean view, the empirical content of a causal law reduces to no more than the observed regular concomitance between types of independent events. The idea of causation as active production is supposedly thereby eliminated from a "scientific" view of the worlds of man and nature. It is easy to see how D–N dogma and the Humean analysis of cause are linked: If to explain a phenomenon is merely to be able to predict it, we need to know only the conditions that are antecedent to it in order to satisfy the demands of a causal explanation. We do not need to know *how* an effect is produced.

How could such an implausible cluster of doctrines have come to be accepted, particularly by psychologists? The explanation, as we argued in the second case study of this chapter, is to be found in the confluence of several originally independent developments: the influence of pragmatist philosophy, the modeling of psychological processes on the lines of Pavlovian materialism, and the reinforcement of the reductivist trends set off by that simplistic caricature of scientific method, logical empiricism. In the 1940s and 1950s, psychology was thus deprived of that stream of continuous criticism of its foundations that should have been emanating from the philosophy of science. Add to this the needs of nations at war for large numbers of trained soldiers, and it is clear why testing and training became the central preoccupation of many psychologists.

The first major challenge to orthodoxy of which we are aware is to be found in the seminal paper by McCorquodale and Meehl (1948), who argue for a distinction between intervening variables and hypothetical constructs. The former are merely technical devices such as mathematical equations, logical ciphers that enable one to set up some sort of deductive system. The latter are descriptive terms for possible states, structures and mechanisms that might be productive of observable phenomena. With the help of specific examples, McCorquodale and Meehl show that science could not advance in its understanding of a field if it confined itself to the use of only intervening variables. Unfortunately, these authors had no clear idea how hypothetical constructs were to be created, nor in what way their plausibility could be ensured. These qualities had to await later developments in the philosophy of explanation.

Some criterion for assessing the plausibility of hypothetical constructs was required to judge psychological theories in actual use. Festinger's theory of cognitive dissonance was by no means positivistic, since it involved a hypothetical construct, an alleged component in a causal mechanism—namely, cognitive dissonance. But the use of this concept was not assessed by reference to any supervening theory of existential plausibility. Was the model for the alleged state of cognitive dissonance the feelings of an individual, and the process of resolution some analogue of fleeing from aversive stimuli? Or was the model that of logical contradiction and the resolution thought to derive from socially based demands for displays of rationality? It was impossible to decide. In later uses of hypothetical constructs, the issue of the existential plausibility of the states and processes to which they purported to refer became a central topic of concern. Quite independently of any developments within psychology in the 1950s, philosophers were developing theories of psychological explanation based on the ideas of motive (Peters, 1958) and intention (Anscombe, 1957).

Philosophers on Rule-Following

A second line of philosophical influence on psychology also began at this time. The suggestion had been made in the early 1950s that most kinds of human behavior that ought to be of interest to psychologists were the result of rule following. The idea was very widely canvassed, and influential works were published by Winch (1958) and Miller, Galanter, and Pribram (1960). Philosophical analysis of the concept of a rule goes back to the later works of Wittgenstein (1953, 1956), who insisted that rule-following practices were almost ubiquitous in human social activities. He seems to have thought that rule-following could not be grounded in anything other than a natural tendency among human beings to create order in this way. For some time, discussion of rules and rule-following was confined largely to philosophers, but it began to appear in psychological explanations in the early 1960s. With the rise of transformational grammar, the rule-following idea was fully developed as a psychological concept (see Leiber, 1975). In transformational grammar, rules played a central role in, for instance, the distinction between competence theories (representations of the corpus of rules necessary for adequate action) and performance theories (causal explanations of the production of action on particular occasions). There was no suggestion in any of these theories that correct performance resulted from the conscious following of rules.

In the latter 1960s the idea that men and women were agents following rules began to appear in social psychology. It seemed a particularly appropriate notion where culturally based patterns of action were being studied. Anthropologists had long used somewhat similar notions to understand regularities in the behavior of people in alien societies. In the study of everyday life, social psychologists found a natural field of application for the rule-following model (Collett, 1977; Mischel, 1974). In this 30-year development we can see the direct influence of a philosophical thesis on actual psychological research.

REFERENCES

Angell, J. R. (1904). *Psychology: An introductory study of the structure of human consciousness.* New York: Holt.

Anscombe, G. E. M. (1957). *Intention.* Ithaca, NY: Cornell University Press.

Ayer, A. J. (1968). *The origins of pragmatism.* London: Macmillan.

Benjamin, A. C. (1955). *Operationism.* Springfield, IL: Thomas.

Bridgman, P. W. (1929). *The logic of modern physics.* New York: Macmillan.

Cohen, D. (1971). *J. B. Watson: A biography.* London: Routledge.

Collett, P. (1977). *Social rules and social behaviour.* Oxford: Blackwell.

Duhem, P. (1954). *The aim and structure of physical theory* (P. P. Weiner, Trans.). Princeton, NJ: Princeton University Press.

Erklärung. (1913). Declaration against the occupation of philosophical chairs with representatives of experimental psychology. *Logos, 4,* 115–116.

Foulquie, P. (1962). Epistémologie. *Dictionnaire de la langue philosophie.* Paris: Presses Universitaires de France.

Fullerton, G. W. (1896). Psychology and physiology. *Psychological Review, 3,* 1–20.

Habermas, J. (1968). *Knowledge and human interests.* Boston: Beacon.

Hull, C. L. (1943). *Principles of behavior.* New York: Appleton-Century-Crofts.

Koch, S. (1982). Behaviorism. *Encyclopedia Brittanica* (Vol. 2). New York: Encyclopedia Brittanica.

Ladd, G. T. (1894). President's address. *Psychological Review, 1,* 1–21.

Lalande, A. (1956). Epistémologie. In *Vocabulaire de la philosophie* (7th ed.). Paris: Presses Universitaires.

Leiber, J. (1975). *Noam Chomsky.* New York: St. Martin's Press.

Loeb, J. (1901). *Comparative physiology of the brain.* London: Murray.

Loeb, J. (1912). *The mechanistic conception of life.* Chicago: University of Chicago Press.

Luria, A. R. (1973). *The working brain.* London: Allen Lane.

MacCorquodale, K., & Meehl, P. E. (1948). On a distinction between hypothetical constructs and intervening variables. *Psychological Review, 55,* 95–107.

MacKay, D. M. (1978). The dynamics of perception. In P. A. Buser & A. Bougeul-Buser (Eds.), *Cerebral correlates of conscious experience.* Amsterdam: Elsevier.

Mackenzie, B. M. (1977). *Behaviourism and the limits of scientific method.* London: Routledge.

Merleau-Ponty, M. (1964). *The primacy of perception.* Chicago: Northwestern University Press.

Miller, G. A. (1962). *Psychology: The science of mental life.* New York: Harper.

Miller, G. A., Galanter, E., & Pribram, K. H. (1960). *Plans and the structure of behavior.* New York: Holt.

Mischel, T. (1974). *Understanding other persons.* Oxford: Blackwell.

Pasquinelli, A. (1974). *Nuovi principi di epistemologia* (2nd ed.). Milan: Feltrinella.

Passmore, J. (1966). *A hundred years of philosophy* (2nd ed.). London: Penquin.

Peters, R. S. (1958). *The concept of motivation.* London: Routledge.

Piaget, J. (1950). *Introduction à l'épistémologie génétique.* Paris: Presses Universitaires.

Piaget, J. (1965). *Sagesse et illusions de la philosophie.* Paris: Presses Universitaires.

Piaget, J. (1967). Nature et methodes de l'épistémologie. In J. Piaget (Ed.), *Logique et connaissance scientifique.* Paris: Gallimard.

Piaget, J., & Garcia, H. (1974). *Understanding causality* (D. Miles & M. Miles, Trans.). New York: Norton.

Poincaré, H. (1958). *The value of science.* New York: Dover.

Ruge, A. (1971). *Wilhelm Windelband.* Leipzig: Barth.

Shotter, J. (1975). *Images of man in psychological research.* London: Methuen.

Skinner, B. F. (1954). Autobiographical sketch. In G. Lindzey (Ed.), *History of psychology in autobiography* (Vol. 4). New York: Appleton-Century-Crofts.

Skinner, B. F. (1972). *Beyond freedom and dignity.* New York: Bantam.

Sperry, R. W. (1969). A modified concept of consciousness. *Psychological Review, 76,* 532–536.

Taylor, A. E. (1904). Mind and body in recent philosophy. *Mind, 13,* 476–508.

Turner, M. B. (1971). *Realism and the explanation of behavior.* New York: Appleton-Century-Crofts.

Watson, J. B. (1913). Psychology as the behaviorist views it. *Psychological Review, 20,* 158–177.

Watson, J. B. (1936). Autobiographical sketch. In C. Murchison (Ed.), *History of psychology in autobiography* (Vol. 3). Worcester, MA: Clark University Press.

Winch, P. (1958). *The idea of a social science.* London: Routledge.

Windelband, W. (1873). *Ueber die Gewissheit der Erkenntnis.* Berlin: Henschel.

Windelband, W. (1876). *Ueber den gegenwärtigen der psychologischen Forschung.* Leipzig: Breitkopf.

Windelband, W. (1894). *Geschichte und Naturwissenschaft.* Strassburg: Heitz.

Windelband, W. (1904a). Nach hundert Jahren. *Kantstudien, 9,* 1–16.

Windelband, W. (1904b). Logik. In W. Windelband (Ed.), *Die philosophie im Beginn des zwanzigsten Jahrhunderts: Festschrift fur Kuno Fischer* (Vol. 1). Heidelberg: Winter.

Windelband, W. (1909). *Die philosophie im deutschen Geistesleben des XIX. Jahrhunderts.* Tubingen: Mohr.

Windelband, W. (1911). Die philosophischen Richtungen der Gegenwart. In E. von Aster (Ed.), *Grosse Denker* (Vol. 2). Leipzig: Quelle, Meyer.

Windelband, W. (1913). The principles of logic. In A. Ruge et al. (Eds.), *Logic.* London: Macmillan. (Original work published 1912)

Wittgenstein, L. (1953). *Philosophical investigations* (G. E. M. Anscombe, Trans.). Oxford: Blackwell.

Wittgenstein, L. (1956). *Remarks on the foundations of mathematics* (G. E. M. Anscombe, Trans.). Oxford: Blackwell.

Wundt, W. (1874). *Ueber die Aufgabe der Philosophie in der Gegenwart.* Leipzig: Englemann.
Wundt, W. (1876). *Ueber den Einfluss der Philosophie auf die Erfahrungswissenschaft.* Leipzig: Englemann.
Wundt, W. (1885). Philosophie und Wissenschaft. In *Essays.* Leipzig: Englemann.
Wundt, W. (1900). *Volkerpsychologie.* Leipzig: Englemann.
Wundt, W. (1904). Psychologie. In W. Windelband (Ed.), *Die Philosophie im Beginn des zwanzigsten Jahrhunderts: Festschrift fur Kuno Fischer* (Vol. 1). Heidelberg: Winter.
Wundt, W. (1913). *Die Psychologie im Kampf ums Dasein.* Leipzig: Kroner.

14

Retrospect and Prospect: The Era of Viewpoints, Continued

CLAUDE E. BUXTON

INTRODUCTION

It is time now to give this book some sense of conclusion. It began on the theme that there have been strikingly diverse conceptions of the science of psychology since the mid-nineteenth century, and it offered historical discussions of a number of them. Just as the period of differing points of view has only gradually and unevenly moved toward the contemporary discipline of psychology, so there is no reason to expect that some resounding general conclusion will bring the era, or our book, to a tidy end. Although an understanding of the roots of psychology may, and often does, aid in appreciating its contemporary subtleties and cross-currents, that has not been our primary goal. We have sought, rather, to analyze the thoughts of many authors in their persistent concern with how best to understand mental and behavioral events as seen from several disciplinary standpoints. Such an aim is more likely to lead to continuing inquiry than to neat closure.

Approaches to History

It may be useful to rephrase this kind of interest in psychology's history. In the decades between about 1890 and 1930, even more than in

POINTS OF VIEW IN THE
MODERN HISTORY OF PSYCHOLOGY

the years before and after, the formulation and exploitation of particular points of view was a consuming activity of many (but by no means all) western psychologists, and it was often highly partisan. From an intellectual point of view, that span of some 40 years in psychology can only be termed, to use a well-worn metaphor, a turbulent and churning sea of ideas. Advances or changes in those ideas have been likened to the leading edge of waves surging up a beach, with innumerable local variations wherever obstacles or cross-currents are encountered. Just as the mass of the incoming tide moves successive and uneven wave fronts further and further up the beach, so the irregular leading edges of psychology were part of an almost relentless general advance of the field.

What many scholars (e.g., William Woodward, 1980) have called the *internalist* history of psychology is, for purposes of this chapter, the study of any particular point of view in order to discover when its ideas began to develop, where it got its convictions about methods of investigation, what the course of its development was, and the causal influences within that area of interest. While such study helps explain why certain intellectual wave fronts have preceded others or fallen back within the general pattern of movement, it is apparent in most of our chapters that internalist history is not completely satisfying. To be sure, it is the immediate, obvious, and usual kind of study to answer many important questions about psychology's beginnings and development, but some consideration reveals that externalist history (*contextualist* is a better term) is also important to a satisfying understanding—more difficult to write though it may be.

The Place of Context in Psychology's History

The study of our history had a rebirth of interest in about 1965, and has since grown steadily and begun to find its bearings. A genuine intellectual history is now beginning to emerge, one in which factors both internal and external to the field of psychology are used to explain how it has changed over the years. The value of this approach is indirectly but forcefully implied by several contemporary writers. Robert Young, an American-born English historian of science, became interested in the role that psychology played in the debate in nineteenth-century Great Britain about the human place in nature. He writes:

It is becoming increasingly clear that the psychological and social convictions of Spencer and Wallace and—to a lesser extent—Darwin provided powerful constraints on the acceptability of particular versions, not only of evolutionary social theory but also, of the supposedly straightforward biological theory. So-called "non-scientific" factors have often been seen as contextual; we are beginning to see that they are constitutive; and in the present case there is considerable evidence that they were *determinant* of the biological theories themselves. Consequently, it is becoming evident that "internalist" history of science cannot succeed in deepening our understanding of nineteenth-century biological theory if these issues are ignored. (Young, 1968)

In a similar vein, Frank Turner, an American historian who has studied the relations between science and society (especially its religion) in the same country and period, writes: "Scientists in their capacity as observers and interpreters of physical nature still remain part of the larger social order, and between them and it there exists a dialectical relationship of mutual influence and interaction" (Turner, 1980).

Richard Littman (1979) also expresses a lively interest in the social and intellectual origins of experimental psychology as part of its contextual history. He shows that the variation among academic systems in England, France, and Germany was clearly reflected in the different ways in which psychology arose and developed within their respective national boundaries. Littman is also interested in stereotypical personality styles, public attitudes, economic conditions, and other factors that determine the nature of general intellectual life, as well as academic systems, but we cannot pursue those concerns here.

Granting the desirability of both the internalist and the contextual treatment of the history of psychological viewpoints, we now confront the question of how to achieve both. Their combination and integration in the mind of a single author is clearly a goal of perfection at present, and the plan of this book has therefore pursued a middle-ground policy. It may be called practical, interim, and structural: practical because it can be pursued now by invited scholars of high talent; interim because as our history is more broadly and deeply developed, the desired integration will presumably be found in the same scholars who develop it; and structural because, although contextual discussions are found in parts of every chapter, the plan of the book calls for two complete chapters (12 and 13) to describe two of the most intimate contexts of psychology's history—the biological and the philosophical. Even so, a reader may be justified in feeling that context has not been emphasized enough. We turn now to some summary ideas in the contextual history of psychology, although it would be enormously presumptuous to imply that in a few additional pages we can do more than suggest an orientation to the study of such influences.

Themes Related to Psychology's History

In the nineteenth century and earlier, most of the context of our history is to be found in three sources, each with a prevailing theme. First in time, and frequently (but not always) in importance, were philosophical views and arguments. These were mentioned in Chapters 1, 4, and 13. A second kind of context was provided by biological science in two lines of influence—the physiological (mainly neurophysiological) and the evolutionary. Chapter 12 is, of course, witness to the compelling influences of biology on psychology's history, as are Chapters 2 and 3. Chapters 4 and 5 suggest its bearing on the very definition of early scientific psychology, while the sometimes strained relations of psychoanalysis and biology are apparent in Chapters 8 and 9. The third context, not discussed much previously but not to be overlooked, comprises the powerful influences of religion and theology. Of all the social and cultural influences we might touch on here, these are discussed (rather briefly) now because they tended especially to be directive in mental philosophy as it pertained to human nature, and in biology they underlay the resistance to evolutionary doctrine. We do not include political, economic, and other contexts.

THE PHILOSOPHICAL CONTEXT

Philosophy has always had many facets, of course, but the one most important to the history of psychology was usually called moral or mental philosophy. Confronting mental philosophy has always been a major question: What is the nature of human beings, and how are we to understand their conduct under the varying circumstances of life? Phrased in this way, the psychological import of these questions is very clear. Indeed, several aspects of the questions gradually and unevenly evolved into scientific versions and the resultant efforts of psychologists to answer them by scientific means. (Among our contributors, the two biologically oriented authors of Chapter 12 are the most insistent on confronting the questions about human nature.)

Whatever the particular form of mental philosophy drawn up in the 19th or earlier centuries, it posed the epistemological question of how a person can *know* anything. It thereby foretold the methodological questions of the earliest modern psychologists, some of whom held quite different philosophical convictions. To study "how a person knows anything," scholars devised procedures such as introspection, mensuration, observation, experimentation, and even planned interviews. This was a double-faceted strategy, to be sure, because there was an equivalent personal question for a Wundt, a Bain, or a Freud: Each was a *person* asking how he could know *any*thing. That devising special methods did not even begin to avoid metaphysical concerns is clear. One has only to ask the seemingly straightforward question—"Should data from intro-spection (*a* method of knowing something) have the same status in scientific psychology as "objective" data?"—to see that the answer turns on a question of ontology, the kind of metaphysical query asking, "What exists, what is real?" For over a century, sophisticated psycholo-gists have felt justified in defining their field to exclude such metaphysi-cal puzzles.

If mind is equated with consciousness, if mind *exists* as consciousness, then introspection may seem to be the only fundamental way to learn anything about mind. As Kurt Danziger (1980, pp. 242–244) argues, this conclusion was characteristic of nineteenth-century English and Scottish philosophers and some of their intellectual sympathizers in America. (His exemplars include both of the Mills, Spencer, James, and Titchener, but not Bain; see Chapters 3, 4, and 5, this volume). In contrast, among philosophers who followed Leibniz—among them Kant, Hegel, Her-bart, Hamilton when he differed with Scottish tradition, and Wundt in particular—mind was fundamentally *not* to be equated with conscious-ness. Thus evidence about mental events could not be taken from intro-spection of the characteristic British–American sort, with its problems of bias and unreliability. Rather, a particular form of self-observation—or self-perception, as Wundt called it (Danziger, 1980, pp. 244–245; Chap-ter 2, this volume)—lending itself to employment in experimentation was deemed the only defensible source of scientific data. The "objective experience" of the Gestalt psychologists (Köhler, 1929/1947, p. 20) is a similar conception (see Chapter 11, this volume).

We turn now to the two epistemological lines of thought mentioned in earlier chapters, with their corresponding theories of human nature.

Empiricism

The question, What is human nature? can be reduced to the query, What is the nature of people's minds? One answer reaching back into the earliest record is that *experience* makes people into who they will become, trains them, shapes their character and conduct. Such a view considers the person to be an essentially passive–receptive creature, played upon by all manner of influences in the environment.

In making explicit this conception of how experience works its effects, the empiricist philosophers of Great Britain and France, in particular, thought about the nature of the person in a way that was parallel to the thinking of Isaac Newton. They believed that, like all of nature, people's minds could be analyzed into "atomic" or "elemental" structures and their functional interrelations. Mental nature was thought to be composed of elements such as sensations and ideas, and these were believed to be combined by associations (logically speaking, these were another kind of mental element, a memory element, but they were not usually so named.) From these arose more complex mental events such as concepts, generalizations, and so on as experience had its effects. This much of the theory reflected a structural view of mind (see Chapters 3, 10, and 12, this volume).

Although the empiricist position, especially in its extreme form, assigned to experience the primary role in determining human nature and actions, it could not avoid recognizing that there are aspects of experience not originating in experience itself. For example, the qualities of sensation and their quantitative attributes are obviously dependent on the innate characteristics of sensory systems. Feeling and emotion, unlike sensations from exteroceptors, could not be attributed primarily to sensory structures or their functioning, yet these correlates of internal bodily events are inseparably part of experiencing. The sheer neuroanatomical potential for forming associations, as well as the existence of the requisite bodily apparatus for action and for the production of feelings of movement, strain, and posture, were all obviously related to experience and conduct, and so could not be blithely disregarded by the mental philosopher. In truth, no important empiricist philosopher did so disregard them in principle, although, to be sure, some psychologists (e.g., Watson, Skinner) have been so intent on developing their own ideas that they seem to have largely passed over or taken for granted the person who, as a biological creature, feels and desires (see Chapter 7, this volume).

An important variant on empiricism was the positivism of Auguste Comte and John Stuart Mill (see Chapter 13, this volume). In Comte's three-stage theory of the evolution of society and knowledge (1830–1842/1905), the third and final stage is called the positive or scientific, and here science takes as its positive task the prediction of phenomena so that they can be utilized (Comte's was a social positivism, aimed at promoting a more just social organization). Comte's most widely influential doctrine held that the only valid epistemology was the scientific. That is, the ways in which scientists clarified or purified their observations and conclusions, using rules of procedure and rules for the evaluation of evidence, were the only dependable ways of deriving knowledge from the senses. (As many do not realize, Comte also argued that the purely rational aspects of science were the truly important ones, and thus the experimental and evidential aspects were merely preparation for the formulation of laws constituting the true form of the most highly evolved knowledge.)

Although he agreed with Comte's conviction that the scientific approach was essential in developing socially useful knowledge, John Stuart Mill (1843/1846) differed with some of Comte's particular views. For instance, he rejected the claim that scientific laws, once formulated, provide an unchanging basis for reasoning from such principles, insisting instead that any scientific formulation was subject to further study and emendation. He also rejected Comte's claim that psychology was forever barred from becoming a science because it must be based on introspective observation and that this was impossible because, in observing its own affairs, mind must inevitably distort what is observed by reason of its awareness of self-observing. While this assessment is basically true, Mill, true to his strong belief that wherever there is regularity in observations there is empirical lawfulness, was willing to accept introspection along with other types of observation as quite suitable for making psychological science. For him, types of observation varied only in the clarity or confidence (we might say reliability) with which a possible law might be discerned.

One of the most interesting, not to say dominating, developments in recent empiricist psychology, with roots going back a century or more, was the "new" cognitive psychology. Since its appearance, we have had a near epidemic of cognitive approaches in nearly all applied and scientific fields. As a result, when Kessel and Bevan (Chapter 10) began to write the history of this movement, they learned that agreement on a working definition of the popular cognitive point of view was not easy to find. Some "in-college" members define it by pointing in good positivist fashion to what its researchers do and study. It then comes out that cognitive psychology is highly theoretical, focusing on mental processes such as attention, perception, memory, imagery, thinking, and decision making (the list is *very* long) with the aid of information theory, the latest in statistical design and data analysis, computer models, and sophisticated computerized laboratory experimentation. I once asked one of my colleagues, a fast starter in that field, "Just what *is* this cognitive psychology you are touting with such enthusiasm?" His answer (simplified for me I am sure) was, "It's what used to called human experimental psychology, *up-dated*." By this definition, or by the later definitions ferreted out by Kessel and Bevan, the field is replete with assumptions, theories, and experimental demonstrations that further delineate human nature in the empiricist tradition.

The spirit of positivism, together with many of its specific conceptions, was to provide the basis for an indigenous American pragmatic philosophy (see Chapters 5, 6, and 13, this volume). This was the "enabling legislation" permitting the transition from idealist philosophical psychology to the experimentalism that was the initial goal of scientific psychologists in America. Positivism, with all its constraints on and impoverishment of scientific thought (to which its excesses led in such movements as operationism), has nevertheless been an important force in the history of psychology (for Skinner's reactions to operationism, see Chapter 7, this volume). The contributions of Ernst Mach to the growth of positivism and of science are discussed in Chapter 13, where it is shown that, contrary to common belief, positivism had little impact on classical behaviorism but much influence on neobehaviorism.

As Robinson (1981, pp. 202, 314) points out, there is no logically required connection between empiricism and materialism as philosophical positions. Still, it was increasingly true in the nineteenth century and into the twentieth that the two were partly or wholly combined in the individual views of many psychologists (see Chapter 13, this volume). We turn now to the epistemological view that in its purest form utterly rejected most of what the empiricists did and believed.

Rationalism

We begin by noting again that if the question, What is human nature? reduces to, What is the nature of people's minds? there is an answer different from the empiricist one and yet, like it, reaching back into the earliest record. In the rationalist view, people are understood to be and become what they are mentally because, while they experience themselves and the world and are changed thereby, their sensing, perceiving, and reacting are shaped by inherent, or, to use the Kantian phrase, *a priori* characteristics (see Chapter 1).

From ancient theological times it has been believed that the soul was the repository of God-given ideas and ideals of conduct. While such views were being elaborated, criticized, and revised in western cultures during the 18th and 19th centuries, they evolved into the often-held postulate that mind, and above all rationality, or *reason*, was the primary shaper of individual development and temporal life. As pointed out in Chapter 4, this is the argument that no person, not even an infant, can have an experience that is not shaped or regulated, a priori, by innate characteristics of the sensory, neurophysiological, or motor systems. Reason, the distinguishing mark of humanness, makes use of experiences shaped by the innate capabilities of mind to form and develop mind. Thus, the standard answer of rationalists to the epistemological question, How does the mind know anything? is: "By reasoning." Furthermore, reason was central to the rationalist conception of mind as active, in contrast with the empiricist view of mind as essentially passive, receptive, and molded by experience. The rationalist answer was different from the empiricist's and often in opposition to it, but as noted earlier, it was often combined with parts of the empiricist answer in the views of individual mental philosophers.

One particular tenet of rationalism surfaced early above the theological seas in which it was evolving. This was the doctrine of innate ideas, or principles, in its many forms. Descartes had declared that three classes of ideas were to be found in people's minds. The first arose from experience, the second were constructed by the mind's own activity, and the third originated in God's creation of the mind itself. These latter are the *innate* ideas, so named because they are not derivable from experience. Ideas of God, or mind, or matter, Descartes argued, contain no purely sensory material; they are not images, nor are they memories or copies of sensory experience. Further, they imply in different ways the idea of infinity, which includes the possibility of infinite variations in which mind or matter may be found. The very idea of infinite variations transcends what experience may supply, and that fact also points to innate or inherent characteristics of mind.

Descarte's vision of God-given ideas, not explicable from experience and hence innate, was challenged from his earliest statement of it. Critics noted that from such a negative argument—that empiricism could not, for example, explain the existence of the idea of matter—it was logically impossible to conclude in the positive sense, as Descartes did, that the idea of matter is innate, for there always remained the possibility of non-a priori explanations not yet found. The progress of science, of course, has been a continual illustration of that possibility. Nevertheless, the Cartesian side of the argument has long persisted, often taking the form of claims for the existence of innate features of mind such as concepts of logic and mathematics, or even the claimed existence of innate or absolute moral principles, at which no one could arrive by sheer sensory experience.

The connection of this kind of thinking with psychology may not be entirely evident at first. However, as our earlier discussion of rationalism showed, logically a priori attributes of mind seemed to many to point to the reality of innate features or determiners of mind and conduct. This particular implication of idealist philosophy has seemed essential to many points of view in the history of psychology, including to a greater or lesser degree Gestalt theory (Chapter 11, this volume), developmental cognition theory (Chapter 10), Wundt and other experimentalists of his time (Chapters 2, 3), the Freudians and other psychoanalytic theorists (Chapters 8, 9), the ethologists (Chapter 12), and even functionalists such as James, despite his occasional fulminations against Kant (Chapter 5). Innateness of some features of mind or conduct is accepted in almost all points of view. While the roots of this idea in idealistic philosophy are often unrealized, implicit, or obscure, they may of course be found in other sources, especially biology.

Because the familiar nature–nurture version of the innateness issue has come to be viewed as open to empirical investigation, this strain of thought in idealist philosophy has all but departed from its origins and become a modern scientific topic. Behaviorists (see Chapter 7) and non-behaviorists alike agree to the propriety of the nature–nurture question's being rendered as follows: What proportion of the variance in whatever aspect of mind or conduct is at issue can be attributed to nature or heredity, on the one hand, and on the other to nurture or environment? A reconsidered (some might say unrecognizable) rationalist doctrine of innate ideas has thus been put in harness with a tempered empiricist doctrine that experience is a main (but not the only) determiner of human nature and actions. Research on specific related issues remains lively and frequently controversial.

In the philosophies of Kant, Hegel, and others following the rationalist line in the nineteenth and twentieth centuries, there was another notable idea that seemed to clash with but was increasingly assimilated by empiricist views. This was the conception of mind, self, ego, or person as a *unity*. Clustered around this central idea were many related ideas:

1. Talk about the unity of a self or person was a way of expressing the interrelatedness of all aspects of mind and functioning; a change in any one aspect implied change in others, or in the whole, and vice versa.
2. This interdependence justified calling this approach a dynamic view of mind and action. In our contemporary language, mind had the property of dynamic organization (a term made salient by the Gestalt psychologists; see Chapter 11), this to be contrasted with a passive–reactive, mechanistic view.
3. Associationism was an insufficient or incorrect view of how the mind or ego came to be, given the logically prior existence of organizational principles (i.e., dimensions or categories that modulate the effects of experience). This position was taken by many important psychologists who were not labeled rationalists, such as Wundt (Chapter 2), James (Chapter 5), Freud and the neo-Freudians (Chapters 8, 9), Piaget (Chapter 10), and Köhler (Chapter 11).

It is hoped that this brief summary of the vast philosophical context within which modern psychology has arisen will serve to remind the reader that psychological viewpoints have always had their philosophical roots, whether admitted, slurred over, or denied, and that these often have been constitutive, to repeat Young's interpretive word in the introduction to this chapter. Searching for philosophical connections is essential to the historical analysis of any point of view, for in those connections lies a significant part of their meaning.

THE BIOLOGICAL CONTEXT

In this book it has been implied or said in many places that not just biology but natural science in general has made up a significant part of the context in which psychology has developed. A little further comment may now extend that claim. As Baumer (1977, p. 306) observes, in the 19th century the word science, though still a somewhat protean term, began to approach its modern meaning. It came to refer to the kind of knowledge associated primarily with the natural sciences, especially physics. In this meaning, science was widely assumed to provide the only true, reliable knowledge. Disciplines such as theology, politics, history, psychology, and the like were credible only to the extent that they could assimilate, or at least approximate, the methods and aims of the physical sciences, and yet, as is well known, a high value has been placed on that credibility. (To the last, as noted in Chapter 9, Sigmund Freud insisted that psychoanalysis was a natural science.)

As science became better defined, a line began to appear between it and philosophy. The line soon became a rift, then a chasm. In one of his *Popular Lectures on Scientific Subjects* (1862/1873), Hermann von Helmholtz blames the developing split between science and philosophy on the excesses of Hegelian philosophy:

> The philosophers accused the scientific men of narrowness; the scientific men retorted that the philosophers were crazy. And so it came about that men of science began to lay some stress on the banishment of all philosophic influences from their work; while some of them, including men of the greatest acuteness, went so far as to condemn philosophy altogether, not merely as useless, but as mischievous dreaming.

These sentences were quoted by Baumer (1977, p. 307), and to them we may well add one more from the original source (Helmholtz, 1862/1873, p. 9): "In proportion as the experimental investigation of facts has recovered its importance in the moral [mental] sciences, the opposition between them and the physical sciences has become less and less marked." That is, as the Hegelian influence was put aside, subjects such as psychology took on the characteristics of a proper natural science. We have seen that the experimentalists of early modern psychology, as Blumenthal shows, were indebted to the example of the natural sciences (Chapters 2, 3). More illustrations are to be found in Littman (1979), chap. 2).

The far-seeing French medical investigator, Claude Bernard, in his *Introduction to the Study of Experimental Medicine* (1865/1927), clarifies the distinction between philosophy and science:

> The metaphysician, the scholastic, and the experimenter all work with an *a priori* idea. The difference is that the scholastic [metaphysician] imposes his idea as an absolute truth which he has found, and from which he then deduces consequences by logic alone. The more modest experimenter, on the other hand, states an idea as a question, as an interpretative, more or less probable anticipation of nature, from which he logically decides consequences which, moment by moment he confronts with reality by means of experiment. He advances, thus, from partial to more general truths, but without ever daring to assert that he has grasped the absolute truth. (p. 27)

He continues: "The experimental method is the scientific method which proclaims the freedom of mind and thought. It not only shakes off the philosophical and theological yoke; it does not even accept any personal scientific authority" (1865/1927, p. 43).

Perhaps we can see more clearly how science replaced the aspects of idealist philosophy to which it objected as neurophysiology becomes the focus of our comments. First, and most important, what can be termed observationalism gained priority over supernatural and mystical explanations. The famous Declaration of 1847 by four students and colleagues of the physiologist Johannes Müller (including Helmholtz, Carl Ludwig, Emil du Bois-Reymond, and Ernst Brücke) signaled the closing of an era when vitalism could be used to explain biological phenomena (see Boring, 1950, p. 708; Mendelsohn, 1964, pp. 44–48). This approach was at once applied to the study of human phenomena in particular.

A second "front" against idealism took the form of reductionism. The best known example is that of the materialist or physical physiology that developed before and at the mid-nineteenth century. It sought to explain biological phenomena by reducing them to known chemical or physical principles (see Carpenter, 1842/1843; Müller, 1833–1840/1838–1842). Physiology thus entered a new era of broad advances in which it gained acceptance by many kinds of scientist, including would-be psychological scientists. These advances continue, with one of their most visible off-shoots early in the twentieth century being the "field theory" of brain processes in Gestalt psychology (Chapter 11, this volume). The broader history of these developments, including the theory of brain functioning, is recorded in Chapter 12.

Continuing from ancient history, a problem for psychologists attempting to create a science has been what to say, think, or do about the relation of mind to body. No group has been more exercised about this over the years than the physiological psychologists (see Chapter 12). While it has often been declared an issue for philosophers of science rather than psychologists, in this book it happens, with no editorial connivance, that our philosophers do choose to address this question (Chapter 13). After a close encounter with it, they suggest that physiologists and psychologists do *not* have a mind–body problem; that is, it lies outside the scope of their scholarship unless they inadvertently create a problem by assumptions they make. Philosophers, however, *must* consider the matter, for it is a self-assigned function of the philosophers of mind that they are to examine its language and conceptual framework.

Frequent passages in this book, and a major theme of Chapter 12, attest to the relevant context provided for psychology by evolutionary biology, specifically the theory of evolution. While general development of the theory has never been psychology's business, it has been psychology's concern to find the points at which psychological understanding is increased by evolutionary concepts or reasoning, or when it is buttressed by linking psychology's data with those related to evolutionary doctrine. (Chapters 6 and 7 show how this attitude draws animal research within the purview of psychology.) As shown in Chapters 4 and 5, evolution was only selectively or even reluctantly accepted in psychology, and yet in America it became a sufficient force to produce the paradoxical fact that as evolutionary thought swept into psychology, the physiological approach was largely shunted aside (Chapter 12). Only later did clinical neuropsychology once again begin to redress the balance with evolutionary thinking in psychology.

In our earlier summary-comments on the philosophical context of the history of psychology, it was emphasized that these influences were not usually in the background; rather, they were constitutive. We can now add that there are increasing numbers of examples in which a contextual statement originating in biology (e.g., about sex–hormone balance during pre-adolescent and adolescent development) serves as part of our understanding of some kind of behavior (e.g., social). Such statements thereby become *functionally psychological* in their meaning, despite the biological language in which they are couched. Thus, biological context can clearly be partly constitutive of psychological theory or explanation. I see no reason to doubt that in the foreseeable future biology will be at least as influential as in the present, and this is as likely to be true for practical developments in psychology as for its scientific growth.

THE THEOLOGICAL AND RELIGIOUS CONTEXT

To some, it may seem like going far afield to examine such cultural features for their impact on developments in psychology, but even a short study of modern intellectual histories such as Maurice Mandelbaum's *History, Man and Reason* (1971), or Franklin Baumer's *Modern European Thought* (1977) causes one to look seriously for specific theological and religious influences.

The principal theology of interest here was Christian. In the view widely prevailing before Darwin, human beings were created according to God's design. Their origins and nature were believed to be charted in biblical sources taken literally. Assuming that the ultimate cause and judgment of a person's conduct were to be found in supernatural wish or judgment, it was natural for the theologian to be concerned with the "ought" as well as the "is"—with ethics and morality as well as, or more important than, transient conduct. Whether scientists, including psychologists, were religious believers or agnostics (and they were strongly divided on that point), the questions toward which their science was directed in the nineteenth and earlier centuries had to reflect at any relevant point its possible meaning for the Christian image of the person. Even the psychologists who wished to address topics that they regarded as essential to understanding Christian personhood were frowned upon and sometimes hindered if their ideas seemed to threaten the theologically accepted view of human nature.

Controversy about this point began even before the 1830s—when the "new" historical criticism began to make literal interpretations of some parts of the Bible seem nonsense—and was later exacerbated in western Europe and America by evolutionary ideas. Darwinism had direct effects on theological doctrines about the nature and origin of human beings, and indirect effects through the numerous writers who generalized the evolutionary approach to ethics and to the evolution of society or culture, producing social Darwinism (see Chapter 5, this volume). In consequence, these two broad influences—historical biblical scholarship and evolutionism—gradually convinced English liberal theologians, as well as German romantic and idealist philosophers, that religious belief must surely arise from an inborn and natural human capacity for religious feeling, something different from knowledge but coexisting with it.

The distinctive outcome for such theologians and philosophers (we do not examine their reasoning) was that the object of their (innate) religious feeling became the totality of nature, of which people are a part. Thus, in the latter nineteenth century, among educated people a widely accepted "natural theology" offered an accommodation of the advances of biblical scholarship and of Darwinism. Liberal thinking could thereby accept, as did William Paley at the beginning of the nineteenth century, that all the evidences of the earth's origin and the development of everything in it and on it bear witness to the creative power of God. For those not moved to accept this view, there was a kind of truce or stand-off position: Science and religion were distinct, independent, coexisting intellectual systems, each of them absolute in its own domain, and neither conflicting with the other. For psychologists, whether believers or nonbelievers, and whether personally involved or not, theological and religious disputation was a fact of life in their intellectual world during the second half of the nineteenth century and beyond.

The advances of science, as well as historical religious scholarship, continued to be provocative. No disagreement was greater or longer than that concerning the will. A will free to determine whether a person would act in a certain way, in accord with moral principles resting on theological or religious doctrine, had long seemed to many an essential part of the psychological truth about human beings. Free will was, as well, essential to a Christian theology in which a person who opted for evil or sinful ways could choose to ask to be saved by the grace of God and restored to better ways. (Reverend Billy Graham exhorts his listeners to "*decide* for Christ.") But the will so defined could never be identified, except by individual introspection on familiar impressions or feelings that seemed to reflect free choice. It was therefore deemed incapable of scientific conceptualization or study. Nevertheless, in the nineteenth century even more conspicuously than later, there was enormous social concern about personal responsibility as it entered into morality. The will was central to such discussions, and thus was bound to be of great importance in psychological thinking. Three notable treatments of it are those by Wundt (Chapter 2), Bain (Chapter 4), and James (Chapter 5). Lorraine Daston's (1978, 1982) discussions of the problem are most illuminating.

A variety of earlier comments make it reasonable to speculate that the development of modern scientific psychology, with its seemingly auspicious beginnings in the work of Fechner, Wundt, Spencer, Bain, and Darwin in the third quarter of the 19th century, was thereafter retarded by both its inability to avoid theologically or religiously entangling topics and the hostility of professors, the clergy, and other intellectuals whose orthodox theological and philosophical views were threatened by the new discipline. As Littman (1979) shows, that orthodoxy included, at the universities in Glasgow and Oxford and in other prominent places, the Hegelian philosophy imported from Germany, with its antipsychological and prospiritualist slants. The fact that negative reactions to scientific psychology were partly a spin-off from widespread reaction against evolution does not invalidate our speculation. More than any other developing discipline, psychology's perceived central concern with things of the mind and spirit impinged on the beliefs and standards of many vocations and professions, and of the public as well.

In retrospect, psychology has progressed only as rapidly as it has broken away from theological or religious involvements and become indifferent to them; or made peace with them by joining forces in research, as has happened in some places; or overcome them (rarely if ever) by strength of argument or evidence. Psychology is still a potentially threatening discipline, and yet this fact is all too often unrecognized by its most ardent proponents.

PERSPECTIVE ON POINTS OF VIEW

In our introductory chapter, presentism was decried because it invited a misinterpretation or unwarranted selection of historical facts according to whether they agreed with contemporary beliefs or values. As those familiar with Herbert Butterfield's *Whig Interpretation of History* (1931) sometimes remind us, the winners in politics or wars like to write the history thereof. That is, the history tends to agree, sometimes in wondrous ways, with the way the winners or survivors themselves think it turned out. There are few examples of this as clear or poignant as Freud's own history of psychoanalysis (Chapter 8). Similarly, Boring's histories were unabashedly presentist. As he explains:

> I have written [The *History of Experimental Psychology*, 1929/1950] and this book [*Sensation and Perception in the History of Experimental Psychology* 1942] solely to show how psychology came to be as it is now. If any event important in the past has no demonstrable direct effect upon the present, then it should be omitted from a book that tries to recreate the past merely to explain the present. (Boring, 1942, pp. viii–ix)

The validity of this effort, of course, depends partly on how accurately Boring perceived the present. His view remained the same when he later wrote: "There is . . . a good reason for knowing the history of science. One finds he needs to know about the past, not in order to predict the future, but in order to understand the present" (Boring,

1963, pp. 88–89). Some critics of Boring's histories have attempted to correct this implied selective emphasis on certain historical facts, but they should not presume that Boring was unaware of what he termed "an historian's history" (1942, p. viii), the orthodox kind of history he consciously chose not to write.

Nevertheless, as noted in our introductory chapter, there is always a valid question about any piece of historiography, including that meeting the best scholarly standards: Does it, or how does it, help us to understand present affairs? This question is thought by many to point toward a potential reward for the labors of writing good history. Having seen how various points of view developed, with some gradually disappearing while others remain highly visible, we now ask the fundamental question: What of the impact of those viewpoints on a present and future psychology?

The beginning of an answer is that points of view in psychology may very well turn out to be not only characteristic of an era rather arbitrarily designated as lying between an ancient past and a complex present (see Chapter 1), but also an episodic kind of occurrence that will continue as long as we aspire to a better and more complete science (hence the title of this chapter).

Points of View in the Natural Sciences

We are accustomed to comparing our science with the history of the more mature sciences of physics and biology. I suggest that it is presentist to say that the history of these older sciences shows a reduction in the frequency of differences among views about the nature of phenomena as the corpus of facts and laws (in either science) is enlarged and as the sophistication of methods and logical procedures is increased. The belief that that is the historical way of science is allied with another firmly held belief, namely that the business and virtue of science is to give us an ever more orderly understanding of the phenomena of nature. We feel assured by such orderliness and are uncomfortable with seemingly maverick data, or with any point of view not consistent with the prevailing view on any scientific subject. This hardly makes science different from nonscience. It seems to me, however, that the charge of presentism relates to the stereotyped view that the central function of science is to produce data that will "correct" differences in interpretation and thereby stabilize the accepted view of the phenomena.

On the contrary, many advances in science actually spring from the criticisms or hypotheses of someone who "thinks otherwise," who sees phenomena serendipitously or systematically in some way that would make a difference if it survived experimental or observational test. I submit that logically, seeing or thinking otherwise is in some degree a *point of view* defining what might be true, for whatever reasons, and usually suggesting how it might be studied.

Differences in point of view in the natural sciences may seem to us psychologists to be less confusing than in the social sciences or history because in practice they are not allowed to get very far from available evidence and method. It was not many centuries ago, however, that with a poorer data-base there was enormous disagreement about whether the earth did indeed travel around the sun. In a longer view of the history of science, then, differing points of view about natural phenomena, in their time, are actually the *dis*orderly, the continually upsetting, the invigorating and never-to-be-extinguished energizer of explorations, hypotheses, and tests. Only in some *very* relative sense does the body of scientific knowledge become stabilized. In sum, it is only a comfortable presentist view that stability is what science seeks to provide, and does.

While the content of points of view in science seem to have changed continually over time, their number seems to have changed relatively little. This statement implies a distinction between two aspects of a point of view, a distinction not previously put forward here: its substantive *content*, or what it says, and its *orientation*, within which that content is developed and interpreted. It is content that reflects the gradual process by which science has made available in any particular field a continually enlarging number of facts or laws and, as well, improved methods by which to test new and different ideas. It is in proposals about content that points of view in the natural sciences most often seem to have the character of hypotheses on their way to the laboratory, and their existence is still significant. In contrast, a full-fledged shift in orientation, a "paradigm shift," is as rare historically as it ever was. To me, this interpretation seems to offer a lesson to historians of psychology.

And in Psychology

Each of the points of view discussed in this book rests not only on a selected set of ideas or concepts, but on limited or specialized conceptions of method as well. The range of methods is enormous, from Titchener's "tell-all" kind of introspection to Skinner's automated recording of pigeon pecks. It is also characteristic of these points of view that they were or are rendered with a large and active component of imagination or speculation. Yet in all cases the acceptance or influence of a point of view was determined partly by the range and clarity of its connections with observational and experimental reality, and therein lies the similarity of psychology to the natural sciences. Keeping in mind the historical record of viewpoints in those sciences, I suggest that a realistic perspective on points of view in psychology includes not only their great stimulus value while their scientific content and philosophical sophistication were developing in the past, but also their probable persistence as points of departure, energizers, and organizers of future scholarship resting on increasingly substantial scientific content.

While one might hope the century-long drift away from philosophical content might be redirected, it seems probable that, as in the natural sciences, psychology's momentum will continue toward the relegation of philosophy to an advisory function. Theology and religion no longer help directly to shape psychology, but as influences on people and society they have become sources of relevant variables in investigations and applications of personality and social psychology. In the end it seems rather commonplace to suggest that biology will probably continue not only to provide the context within which psychological thought develops, but also, where appropriate, to be constitutive of and integrated with such thought.

REFERENCES

Baumer, F. L. (1977). *Modern European thought*. New York: Macmillan.

Bernard, C. (1927). *An introduction to the study of experimental medicine*. New York: Macmillan. (Original work published 1865)

Boring, E. G. (1942). *Sensation and perception in the history of experimental psychology*. New York: Appleton-Century-Crofts.

Boring, E. G. (1950). *A history of experimental psychology* (2nd ed.). New York: Appleton-Century-Crofts. (Original work published 1929)

Boring, E. G. (1963). *History, psychology, and science* (R. I. Watson & D. T. Campbell, Eds.). New York: Wiley.

Butterfield, H. (1931). *The Whig interpretation of history*. London: Bell.

Carpenter, W. B. (1843). *Principles of human physiology*. Philadelphia: Lea, Blanchard. (Original work published 1842)

Comte, A. (1905). *The fundamental principles of positive philosophy* (P. Descourse & H. G. Jones, Trans.). London: Watts. (Original work published 1830–1842)

Danziger, K. (1980). The history of introspection reconsidered. *Journal of the History of the Behavioral Sciences, 16,* 241–262.

Daston, L. J. (1978). British responses to psycho-physiology, 1860–1900. *Isis, 69,* 192–208.

Daston, L. J. (1982). The theory of will versus the science of mind. In W. R. Woodward & M. G. Ash (Eds.), *The problematic science: Psychology in nineteenth-century thought*. New York: Praeger.

Helmholtz, H. von. (1873). *Popular lectures on scientific subjects*. London: Longmans, Green. (Original work published 1862)

Köhler, W. (1947). *Gestalt psychology*. New York: Liveright. (Original work published 1929)

Littman, R. A. (1979). Social and intellectual origins of experimental psychology. In E. Hearst (Ed.), *The first century of experimental psychology*. Hillsdale, NJ: Erlbaum.

Mandelbaum, M. (1971). *History, man and reason.* Baltimore, MD: Johns Hopkins University Press.

Mendelsohn, E. (1964). The biological sciences in the nineteenth century: Some problems and sources. *History of Science, 3*, 39–59.

Mill, J. S. (1846). *A system of logic, ratiocinative and inductive.* New York: Harper. (Original work published 1843)

Müller, J. (1838–1842). *Elements of physiology* (W. Baly, Trans.). London: Taylor-Walton. (Original work published 1833–1840)

Robinson, D. N. (1981). *An intellectual history of psychology* (rev. ed.). New York: Macmillan.

Turner, F. M. (1980). Public science in Britain, 1880–1919. *Isis, 71*, 589–608.

Woodward, W. R. (1980). Toward a critical historiography of psychology. In J. Brožek & L. J. Pongratz (Eds.), *Historiography of modern psychology*. Toronto: Hogrefe.

Young, R. M. (1968). "Non-scientific" factors in the Darwinian debate. *Actes, XIIe Congrès International d'Histoire des Sciences, 4*, 221–226.

Author Index

Numbers in italics refer to the pages on which the complete references are cited.

A

Abelson, R. P., 278, 281, *290*
Abraham, H., 214, 217, *219*
Ach, N., 64, *80*
Adams, D. K., 274, *290*
Adler, A., 247, *254*
Adler, G., 34, *47*
Ainsworth, M., 234, *254*
Albrecht, D. G., 365, *377*
Allport, G., 328, *337*
Amacher, P., 238, *254*
Anderson, C. C., 269, *292*
Anderson, R. C., 269, 277, *290*
Angell, J. R., 10, *16*, 133, 134, 137, *138*, *139*, 148, 149, 152, 153, *164*, 393, *413*
Ansbacher, H., 214, *219*
Ansbacher, R., 214, *219*
Anscombe, G. E. M., 412, *413*
Arnheim, R., 322, 335, *337*
Asch, S. E., 335, *337*
Ash, M. G., 44, *47*, 295, 296, 297, 299, 321, 324, *337*
Aster, E. v., 64, *80*
Austin, G. A., 272, 276, *291*
Ausubel, D. P., 269, *290*
Ayer, A. J., 390, *413*

B

Bagehot, W., 103, *109*
Bain, A., 91, 92, 93, 94, 95, 96, 100, *109*, 347, 353, 354, *377*

Bakan, D., 170, *192*
Balbus, I., 252, *254*
Baldwin, J. M., 69, *80*, 100, 101, *109*, 131, *139*, 160, *164*, 174, *192*, *290*
Balint, M., 232, *254*
Banauzizi, A., 180, *194*
Bandura, A., 371, *377*
Barclay, J. R., 279, *291*
Barrett, P. H., 99, *109*
Bartlett, F. C., 276, 277, 278, 281, *290*
Baumer, F. L., 427, 430, *435*
Beach, F., 369, *377*
Becher, E., 306, 319, *337*
Bechterev, W. von, 346, *377*
Beekman, G. J., 365, *380*
Bekesy, G. von, 365, *377*
Bekhterev, V. M., 146, *164*
Bell, C., 351, *377*
Bellugi, U., 267, *291*
Benjamin, A. C., 396, *413*
Benussi, V., 304, 305, 319, *337*, *338*
Bergman, A., 227, *256*
Bergmann, G., 157, *164*, 176, *192*
Bergson, H., 299, 309, *338*
Berlyne, D. E., 39, *47*
Berman, L., 157, *164*, 170, 174, 176, *193*
Bernard, C., 357, 358, *377*, 428, *435*
Bernard, L. L., 174, *193*
Bernstein, N., 365, *377*
Bertalanffy, L. von, 320, *338*
Bevan, W., *290*
Binet, A., 287, *290*, 365, 376, *377*
Bingham, W., 159, *164*

437

Subject Index